JONATHAN EDWARDS

JONATHAN EDWARDS

WRITINGS FROM
THE GREAT AWAKENING

Philip F. Gura, *editor*

THE LIBRARY OF AMERICA

The paper used in this publication meets the
minimum requirements of the American National Standard for
Information Sciences—Permanence of Paper for Printed
Library Materials, ANSI Z39.48—1984.

Distributed to the trade in the United States
by Penguin Group (USA) Inc.
and in Canada by Penguin Books Canada Ltd.

Library of Congress Control Number: 2013930951
ISBN 978–1–59853–254–8

First Printing
The Library of America—245

Manufactured in the United States of America

Jonathan Edwards: Writings from the Great Awakening
is published with support from

THE ANDREW W. MELLON FOUNDATION

Contents

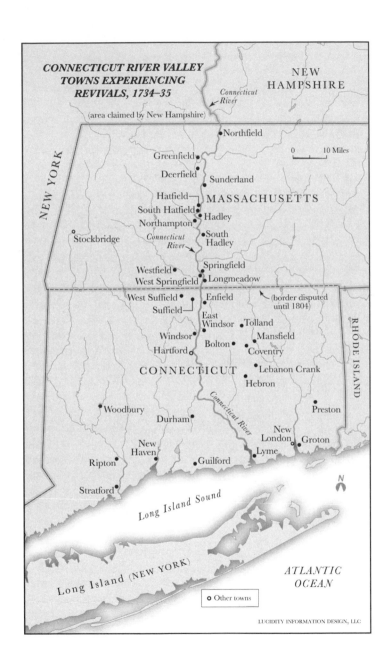

CONNECTICUT RIVER VALLEY
TOWNS EXPERIENCING
REVIVALS, 1734–35

NEW
HAMPSHIRE

*Connecticut
River*

(area claimed by New Hampshire)

Northfield

NEW YORK

Greenfield

Deerfield

Sunderland

Hatfield

MASSACHUSETTS

South Hatfield

Northampton

Hadley

*Connecticut
River*

South
Hadley

Stockbridge

Westfield

Springfield

West Springfield

Longmeadow

West Suffield

Enfield

(border disputed
until 1804)

Suffield

East
Windsor

Tolland

RHODE ISLAND

Windsor

Mansfield

Bolton

Coventry

Hartford

Lebanon Crank

CONNECTICUT

Hebron

Connecticut River

Woodbury

Durham

Preston

New
Haven

New
London

Groton

Ripton

Guilford

Lyme

Stratford

Long Island Sound

0   10 Miles

N

Long Island (NEW YORK)

ATLANTIC
OCEAN

o Other towns

LUCIDITY INFORMATION DESIGN, LLC

A Faithful

NARRATIVE

OF THE

Surprising Work of GOD

IN THE

CONVERSION

OF

Many HUNDRED SOULS in *Northampton*, and the Neighbouring Towns and Villages of the County of *Hampshire*, in the Province of the *Massachusetts-Bay* in *New-England*.

In a LETTER to the Reverend Dr. BENJAMIN COLMAN, of *Boston*.

Written by the Rev^d Mr. EDWARDS, Minister of *Northampton*, Nov. 6. 1736.

Published with a Large PREFACE by the Rev. Dr. WATTS and Dr. GUYSE of *London*:

To which a Shorter is added by Some of the Reverend Ministers of *BOSTON*.

Together with an ATTESTATION from Some of the Reverend *Ministers* of *Hampshire*.

The THIRD EDITION.

BOSTON: *N. E.* Printed & Sold by S. KNEELAND T. GREEN, over against the Prison in Queen-street. 1738.

THE PREFACE

THE friendly Correspondence, which we maintain with our Brethren of *New England*, gives us now and then the Pleasure of hearing some remarkable Instances of divine Grace in the Conversion of Sinners, and some eminent Examples of Piety in that *American* Part of the World. But never did we hear or read, since the first Ages of Christianity, any Event of this Kind so surprizing as the present Narrative hath set before us. The Revd and worthy Dr. *Colman* of *Boston* had given us some short Intimations of it in his Letters; and upon our Request of a more large and particular Account, Mr. *Edwards*, the happy and successful Minister of *Northampton*, which was one of the chief Scenes of these Wonders, drew up this History in an Epistle to Dr. *Colman*.

There were some useful Sermons of the Venerable and Aged Mr. *William Williams* publish'd lately in *New-England*, which were Preached in that Part of the Country during this Season of the glorious Work of God in the Conversion of Men; to which Dr. *Colman* subjoin'd a most judicious and accurate Abridgement of this Epistle: And a little after, he sent the Original to our Hands, to be communicated to the World under our Care here in *London*.

We are abundantly satisfy'd of the Truth of this Narrative, not only from the pious Character of the Writer, but from the concurrent Testimony of many other Persons in *New England; for this Thing was not done in a Corner*. There is a Spot of Ground, as we are here inform'd, wherein there are twelve or fourteen Towns and Villages, chiefly situate in the *County* of *Hampshire* near the Banks of the River of *Connecticut*, within the Compass of Thirty Miles, wherein it pleased God two Years ago to display his free and sovereign Mercy in the Conversion of a great Multitude of Souls in a short Space of Time, turning them from a formal, cold and careless Profession of Christianity to the lively Exercise of every Christian Grace, and the powerful Practice of our holy Religion. The great God has seem'd to act over again the Miracle of *Gideon's* Fleece, which was plentifully water'd with the Dew of Heaven, while the rest

3

of the Earth round about it was dry, and had no such remarkable Blessing.

There has been a great and just Complaint for many Years among the Ministers and Churches in *Old England*, and in *New*, (except about the Time of the late Earthquake there) that the Work of Conversion goes on very slowly, that the Spirit of God in his saving Influences is much withdrawn from the Ministrations of his Word, and there are few that rcccive the Report of the Gospel, with any eminent Success upon their Hearts. But as the Gospel is the same divine Instrument of Grace still, as ever it was in the Days of the Apostles, so our ascended Saviour now and then takes a special Occasion to manifest the Divinity of this Gospel by a plentiful Effusion of his Spirit where it is preached: then Sinners are turned into Saints in Numbers, and there is a new Face of Things spread over a Town or Country: *The Wilderness and the solitary Places are glad, the Desert rejoyces and blossoms as the Rose*; and surely concerning this Instance we may add, that *they have seen the Glory of the Lord there, and the Excellency of our God*, they have *seen the Out goings of God our King in his Sanctuary.*

Certainly it becomes us, who profess the Religion of *Christ*, to take Notice of such astonishing Exercises of his Power and Mercy, and give him the Glory which is due, when he begins to accomplish any of his Promises concerning the latter Days: and it gives us further Encouragement to pray, and wait, and hope for the like Display of his Power in the midst of us. *The Hand of God is not shorten'd that it cannot save*, but we have Reason to fear that *our Iniquities*, our Coldness in Religion, and the general Carnality of our Spirits, have raised a Wall of Seperation between God and us: And we may add, the Pride and perverse Humour of Infidelity, Degeneracy and Apostacy from the Christian Faith, which have of late Years broken out amongst us, seem to have provoked the Spirit of *Christ* to absent himself much from our Nation. "Return, O Lord, and visit thy Churches, and revive thine own Work in the midst of us."

From such blessed Instances of the Success of the Gospel, as appear in this Narrative, we may learn much of the Way of the Spirit of God in his Dealing with the Souls of Men, in order to Convince Sinners, and restore them to his Favour and his Image by *Jesus Christ*, his Son. We acknowledge that some particular Appearances in the Work of Conversion among Men may be occasion'd by the Ministry which they sit under, whether it be of a more or less Evangelical Strain, whether it be more severe and affrighting, or more gentle and Persuasive. But wheresoever God works with Power for Salvation upon the Minds of Men, there will be some Discoveries of a Sense of Sin, of the Danger of the Wrath of God, of the All-sufficiency of his Son *Jesus*, to relieve us under all our Spiritual Wants and Distresses, and a hearty Consent of Soul to receive him in the various Offices of Grace, wherein he is set forth in the holy Scriptures. And if our Readers had Opportunity (as we have had) to peruse several of the Sermons which were Preached during this glorious Season, we should find that it is the common plain *Protestant* Doctrine of the Reformation, without stretching towards the *Antinomians* on the one Side, or the *Arminians* on the other, that the Spirit of God has been pleased to honour with such illustrious Success.

We are taught also by this happy Event how easy it will be for our blessed Lord to make a full Accomplishment of all his Predictions concerning his Kingdom, and to spread his Dominion from Sea to Sea, thro' all the Nations of the Earth. We see how easy it is for him with one Turn of his Hand, with one Word of his Mouth, to awaken whole Countries of stupid and sleeping Sinners, and kindle divine Life in their Souls. The heavenly Influence shall run from door to door, filling the Hearts and Lips of every Inhabitant with importunate Inquiries, *What shall we do to be saved*? And *how shall we escape the Wrath to come*? And the Name of *Christ* the Saviour shall diffuse it self like a rich and viral Perfume to Multitudes that were ready to sink and perish under the painful Sense of their own Guilt and Danger. Salvation shall spread thro' all the Tribes and Ranks of Mankind, as the Lightning from Heaven in a few Moments would communicate a living Flame thro' ten thousand Lamps or Torches placed in a proper Situation and Neighbourhood. Thus *a Nation shall be born in a Day* when our Redeemer pleases, and his faithful and obedient Subjects shall become as numerous as the Spires of Grass in a Meadow newly mown, and refresh'd with the Showers of Heaven. But the Pleasure of this agreeable Hint bears the Mind away from our Theme.

Let us return to the present Narrative. 'Tis worthy of our Observation, that this great and surprizing Work does not seem to have taken its Rise from any sudden and distressing Calamity or publick Terror that might universally impress the Minds of a People: Here was no Storm, no Earthquake, no Inundation of Water, no Desolation by Fire, no Pestilence or any other sweeping Distemper, nor any cruel Invasion by their *Indian* Neighbours, that might force the Inhabitants into a serious Thoughtfulness, and a religious Temper by the Fears of approaching Death and Judgment. Such Scenes as these have sometimes been made happily effectual to awaken *Sinners* in *Zion*, and the formal Professor and the *Hypocrite* have been terrify'd with the Thoughts of divine Wrath breaking in upon them, *Who shall dwell with everlasting Burnings*? But in the present Case the immediate Hand of God in the Work of his Spirit appears much more evident, because there is no such awful and threat'ning Providence attending it.

It is worthy also of our further Notice, that when many profane Sinners, and formal Professors of Religion have been affrighted out of their present Carelesness and Stupidity by some astonishing Terrors approaching them, those religious Appearances have not been so durable, nor the real Change of Heart so thoroughly effected: Many of these sort of sudden Converts have dropt their religious Concerns in a great Measure when their Fears of the threat'ning Calamity are vanish'd. But it is a blessed Confirmation of the Truth of this present Work of Grace, that the Persons who were divinely wrought upon in this Season continue still to profess serious Religion, and to practice it without returning to their former Follies.

It may not be amiss in this Place to take Notice, that a very surprizing and threat'ning Providence has this last Year attended the People of *Northampton*, among whom this Work of divine Grace was so remarkable: Which Providence at first might have been construed by the unthinking World to be a signal Token of God's Displeasure against that Town, or a Judgment from Heaven upon the People; but soon afterwards, like *Paul*'s shaking the Viper off from his Hand, it discovered the astonishing Care and Goodness of God express'd towards a Place where such a Multitude of his young Converts were assembled: Nor can we give a better Account of it than in the Language of this very Gentleman, the Revd Mr. *Edwards*, Minister of that Town, who wrote the following Letter, which was publish'd in *New-England*.

Northampton, March 19th. 1737.

WE in this Town, were the last Lord's Day the Spectators, *and many of us the* Subjects, *of one of the most amazing Instances of divine Preservation, that perhaps was ever known in the Land: Our Meeting-House is old and decay'd, so that we have been for some time building a new one, which is yet unfinish'd: It has been observed of late, that the House that we have hitherto met in has gradually spread at bottom, the Cells and Walls giving way, especially in the Foreside, by reason of the Weight of Timber at top, pressing on the Braces that are inserted into the Posts and Beams of the House. It has so done more than ordinarily this Spring; which seems to have been occasion'd by the heaving of the Ground by the extream Frosts of the Winter past, and its now settling again on that side which is next the Sun, by the Thaws of the Spring: By this means the under-pinning has been considerably disorder'd, which People were not sensible of, till the ends of the Joysts which bore up the front Gallery, by the Walls giving way, were drawn off from the Girts on which they rested; so that in the midst of the publick Exercise in the Forenoon, soon after the beginning of Sermon, the whole Gallery full of People, with all the Seats and Timber suddenly and without any Warning sunk, and fell down, with most amazing noise upon the Heads of those that sat under, to the astonishment of the Congregation, the House being fill'd with dolorous Shrieking and Crying; and nothing else was expected than to find many People dead, and dashed to pieces.*

The Gallery in falling seem'd to break and sink first in the middle; so that those who were upon it were thrown together in heaps before the front Door: But the whole was so sudden, that many of them that fell knew nothing in the time of it what it was that had befallen them; and others in the Congregation knew not what it was that had happen'd with so great a Noise; many thought it had been an amazing Clap of Thunder: The falling Gallery seem'd to be broken all to pieces before it got down; so that some that fell with it, as well as those that were under, were buried in the Ruins, and were found press'd under heavy Loads of Timber, and could do nothing to help themselves.

But so mysteriously and wonderfully did it come to pass, that every Life was preserved; and tho' many were greatly bruised, and their Flesh torn, yet there is not, as I can understand, one Bone broke, or so much as put out of Joint among them all: Some that were thought to be almost dead at first, are greatly recover'd; and but one young Woman seems yet to remain in dangerous Circumstances, by an inward Hurt in her Breast: but of late there appears more Hope of her Recovery.

There is none can give any Account, or conceive by what Means it should come to pass, that Peoples Lives and Limbs should be thus preserv'd, when so great a Multitude were thus imminently exposed: It looked as tho' it was impossible it should be otherwise, than that great Numbers should instantly be crushed to death or dashed in pieces: It seems unreasonable to ascribe it to any thing else, but the Care of Providence in disposing the Motions of every Stick of Timber, & the precise Place of Safety where every one should sit & fall, when none were in any Capacity to take care for their own Preservation. The Preservation seems to be most wonderful, with Respect to the Women and Children that were in the middle Alley, under the Gallery, where it came down first, and with greatest Force, and where was nothing to break the Force of the falling Weight.

Such an Event may be a sufficient Argument of a Divine Providence over the Lives of Men. We thought ourselves called to set apart a Day to be spent in the solemn Worship of God, to humble ourselves under such a Rebuke of God upon us in the Time of publick Service in God's House by so dangerous and surprizing an Accident; and to praise his Name for so wonderful, and as it were Miraculous a Preservation; and the last Wednesday was kept by us to that End: And a Mercy in which the Hand of God is so remarkably evident, may be well worthy to affect the Hearts of all that hear it.

Thus far the Letter.

But it is time to conclude our *Preface*. If there should be any thing found in this Narrative of the surprizing Conversion of such Numbers of Souls, where the Sentiments or the Style of the Relater, or his Inferences from Matters of Fact, do not appear so agreeable to every Reader, we hope it will have no unhappy influence to discourage the Belief of this glorious Event. We must allow every Writer his own Way; and must allow him to chuse what particular Instances he would select, from the numerous Cases which came before him. And tho' he might have chosen others perhaps, of more significancy in the eye of the World, then the *Woman* and the *Child*, whose Experiences he relates at large; yet 'tis evident he chose that of the *Woman*, because she was dead, and she is thereby uncapable of knowing any Honours or Reproaches on this Account. And as for the *Child*, those who were present, and saw and heard such a remarkable and lasting Change, on one so very young, must necessarily receive a stronger Impression from it, and a more agreeable Surprize than the meer Narration of it can communicate to others at a distance. Childrens Language always loses its striking Beauties at second-hand.

Upon the whole, we declare our Opinion, that this Account of such an extraordinary and illustrious Appearance of divine Grace in the Conversion of Sinners, is very like by the Blessing of God to have a happy Effect, towards the Honour and Enlargement of the Kingdom of *Christ*.

May the worthy Writer of this Epistle, and all those his Revd Brethren in the Ministry, who have been honour'd in this excellent & important Service, go on to see their Labours crown'd with daily and persevering Success! May the numerous Subjects of this surprizing Work hold fast what they have received, and increase in every Christian Grace and Blessing! May a plentiful Effusion of the blessed Spirit, also, descend on the *British* Isles, and all their *American* Plantations, to renew the Face of Religion there! And we intreat our Readers in both *Englands*, to join with us in our hearty Addresses to the Throne of Grace, that this wonderful Discovery of the hand of God in saving Sinners, may incourage our Faith and Hope of the Accomplishment of all his Words of Grace, which are written in the Old Testament and in the New, concerning the large Extent of this Salvation in the Latter Days of the World. *Come Lord Jesus, come quickly*, and spread thy Dominion thro' all the Ends of the Earth, *Amen*.

London, October 12. 1737.   *ISAAC WATTS.*
                                                         JOHN GUYSE.

PREFACE

WHEN the Disciples of our glorious Lord were filled with Sorrow upon the heavy Tidings of his Departure from them, He chear'd their drooping Spirits with that good Word, John 16. 7. *Nevertheless, I tell you the Truth; it is expedient for you that I go away: For if I go not away, the Comforter will not come unto you; but if I depart, I will send him unto you.* And after his Ascension, he fulfill'd this great and precious Promise by the extraordinary Effusion of his Spirit, under whose Conduct and Influence, the *Apostles went forth, and preached every where, the Lord working with them*: so that when we read the *Acts of the Apostles*, we must say; *Not by Might, nor by Power, but by the Spirit of the Lord of Hosts.* And tho', soon after the first Days of Christianity, there was a dreadful Apostacy, yet God did not wholly take his Spirit from his People; but rais'd up faithful Witnesses to testify against the Heresies and Corruptions of the Times wherein they lived. And since Antichrist *that wicked One has been reveal'd*, our Lord, according to his Word, has been gradually *consuming him with the Spirit of his Mouth*, in the Reformation.

Nor have we in these remote Corners of the Earth, where Satan had his Seat from Time immemorial, been left without a Witness of the divine Power and Grace. Very remarkable was the Work of God's Spirit stirring up our Fore Fathers to leave a pleasant Land, and transport themselves over a vast Ocean into this then howling Wilderness; that they might enjoy Communion with Christ in the Purity of his Ordinances, and leave their Children in the quiet Possession of the Blessings of his Kingdom. And God was eminently present with them by his Word & Spirit.

Yea, we need look no higher than our own Times, to find abundant Occasion to celebrate the wonderful Works of God. Thus when God arose and shook the Earth,* his *loud Call* to us in that amazing Providence was follow'd, so far as Man can judge, with the *still Voice* of his Spirit, in which He was present to awaken many and bring them to say trembling, *What must we do to be saved*? Yea, as we hope, to turn not a few from Sin to

---

* *October* 29. Anno, 1727.

God in a thorough Conversion. But when the Bitterness of Death was past, much the greater Part of those whom God's Terrors affrighted, gave sad Occasion to remember those Words, Psalm 78. 34.—36 *When he slew them, then they sought him: and they returned and enquired early after God. And they remembered that God was their Rock, and the high God their Redeemer. Nevertheless, they did flatter him with their Mouths, and they lied unto him with their Tongues.* And there has since been great Reason to complain of our speedy Return to our former Sins, notwithstanding some Hopes given of a more general Reformation. Yea when more lately, it pleased God to visit many of our *Towns* with a *very mortal Distemper*, to that Time in a Manner unknown; whereby great Numbers of our hopeful Children and Youth have been cut off, many very suddenly, and with Circumstances exceedingly distressing and awful: Yet alass! We have not generally seen, nor duly considered God's Hand stretched out against us; but have given him Reason to complain, as of his ancient People, *Why should ye be Stricken any more, ye will revolt more and more.* And accordingly His Anger is not turned away; but his Hand is stretched out still. A plain Proof of this awful Truth, that the most awakening Dispensations can no farther humble and do us good, than as it pleaseth God to accompany them with his Spirit, and so command his Blessing upon them. But when the Almighty will work by such Means, or without them, who can hinder him? He acts with sovereign Liberty and irresistible Power. John 3. 8. *The Wind bloweth where it listeth, and thou hearest the Sound thereof, but canst not tell whence it cometh, and whither it goeth: so is every one that is born of the Spirit.* Such was his wonderful Work at *Northampton, and the neighbouring Towns in the County of Hampshire,* and some other Places. The Holy Spirit was in a plentiful and extraordinary Manner pour'd out on Persons of every Age and Condition, without such remarkable Providences going before to awaken them; as the *Dew falls in the Night,* and yet the Effects appear'd as the *Light which goeth forth.* So that we might well admiring say, *What has God wrought!* Great was the Number of them who publish'd the Wonders of the Divine Power & Grace; declaring with Humility, what God had done for their Souls. And others who went among them, acknowleg'd that the Work exceeded the Fame of it.

Now the Psalmist observes that *God has made his wonderful Works to be remembred*. We therefore apprehend that our Reverend Brother has done well to record and publish this surprizing Work of God; and the Fidelity of his Account would not have been at all doubted of by us, tho' there had not been the concurrent Testimony of Others to it. It is also a Pleasure to us to hear what Acceptance the following Narrative has found in the other *England*, where it has had two Impressions already, and been honour'd with a recommendatory Preface, by two Divines of eminent Note in *London*, viz. the Rev. Dr. *Watts*, and Dr. *Guyse*: after whom it may seem Presumption in us to attempt any Thing of this Kind. But it having been tho't proper to Reprint this *Letter* here, and disperse it among our People; We Thankfully embrace this Opportunity to praise the most High, for the exceeding Riches of his Grace, and earnestly to recommend this *Epistle* to the diligent Reading and attentive Consideration of all into whose Hands these shall come. *He that hath an Ear, let him hear what the Spirit saith unto the Churches.* And indeed the particular and distinct *Account* which the *Author* has given of God's Dealings with the Souls of Men, at this remarkable Season, in the variety of Cases then set before him, and many of his Observations thereupon, we apprehend are written with that Judgment and Skill in divine Things, as declare him to be a Scribe well instructed unto the Kingdom of Heaven; and we judge may be very useful to Ministers in leading weary Souls to Christ for Rest, and for the Direction & Encouragement of all under the like Operations of the Holy Spirit.—Yea, as the Author observes, *"There is no one Thing I know of, that God has made such a Means of promoting his Work among us as the News of others Conversion"*—; We hope that the further Spreading of this Narrative may, by the Divine Blessing, still promote the Conversion of Souls, and quicken God's Children to labour after the clearer Evidences of their Adoption and to bring forth Fruits meet for Repentance. And as this wonderful Work may be consider'd as an Earnest of what God will do towards the Close of the Gospel Day, it affords great Encouragement to our Faith and Prayer in pleading those Promises which relate to the glorious Extent and Flourishing of the Kingdom of Christ upon Earth, and have not yet had their full and final Accomplishment. And surely the very threatning Degeneracy of our Times calls aloud to us all, to be earnest in Prayer for this most needed Blessing, the plentiful Effusion of the Spirit of Truth and Holiness. Nor ought the Sense of our own Unworthiness discourage us, when we go to our heavenly Father in the Name of his dear Son, who has purchas'd and receiv'd this great Gift for his People, and says to us, Luke 11. 9—13, *Ask and it shall be given you—If ye then, being Evil, know how to give good Gifts unto your Children, how much more shall your heavenly Father give the holy Spirit to them that ask him.*

But we must draw to a Close. May the worthy Author be restored to Health, and long continued to be a rich Blessing to his People! May he still see the Pleasure of the Lord prospering in his Hand; and in particular, may the Spirit of Grace accompany this pious Endeavour to spread the Savour of the Knowlege of Christ, for the everlasting Advantage of many! May it please God to revive his Work throughout this Land; and may all the Ends of the Earth see his Salvation!

	Joseph Sewall
Boston, Novemb. 4th. 1738.	Thomas Prince
	John Webb
	William Cooper

P.S. Since the writing this Preface, One of us has receiv'd a Letter from a Reverend and very worthy Minister in *Glasgow*, in which is the following Passage;

"The Friends of serious Religion here were much refreshed with a printed Account of the extraordinary Success of the Gospel, of late, in some Parts of *New England.* If you can favour me with more particular Accounts of those joyful Events, when you have Opportunity of writing to me, it will much oblige me."

TO THE REVEREND
BENJAMIN COLMAN, D. D.
PASTOR OF A CHURCH IN *BOSTON*.

Westfield, Octob. 11 1738.

SIR,

In your Letter of *August* 19 you inform us, that the Rev. Dr. *Watts* and Dr. *Guyse* desire that some other *Ministers*, who were Eye and Ear *Witnesses* to some of those numerous *Conversions* in the other Towns about *Northampton*, would Attest unto what the Rev. Mr. *Edwards* has written of them.

We take this Opportunity to assure you, that the *Account* Mr. *Edwards* has given in his *Narrative* of our several *Towns* or *Parishes* is true; and that *much more* of the like Nature might have been *added* with Respect to some of them.

We are, Reverend Sir, Your *Brethren* and Servants

> *William Williams*, Pastor of *Hatfield*.
> *Ebenezer Devotion*——of *Suffield*.
> *Stephen Williams*——of *Long Meadow*.
> *Peter Raynolds*——of *Enfield*.
> *Nehemiah Bull*——of *Westfield*.
> *Samuel Hopkins*——of *W. Springfield*.

A Faithful Narrative
of the Surprizing Work of God

IN THE CONVERSION OF MANY
HUNDRED SOULS IN
NORTHAMPTON, OF NEW-ENGLAND, &C.

In a LETTER to the Revd. Dr. COLMAN of *Boston*, &c.

Reverend and Honoured Sir,

Having seen your *Letter* to my honoured Uncle *Williams* of *Hatfield* of *July* 20, wherein you inform him of the *Notice* that has been taken of the late *wonderful Work of God*, in this, and some other Towns in this *County*; by the Rev. Dr. *Watts* and Dr. *Guyse* of *London*, and the Congregation to which the last of these preached on a monthly Day of solemn Prayer; as also, of your desire to be more perfectly acquainted with it, by some of us on the spot: and having been since informed by my Uncle *Williams*, that you desire me to undertake it; I would now do it, in as *just and faithful a Manner* as in me lies.

The People of the *County*, in general, I suppose, are as *sober*, and *orderly*, and good sort of People, as in any Part of *New-England*; and I believe they have been preserved the freest by far, of any Part of the Country, from *Error*, and variety of *Sects* and Opinions. Our being so far *within* the Land, at a distance from *Sea-ports*, and in a Corner of the Country, has doubtless been one *Reason* why we have not been so much corrupted with *Vice*, as most other Parts. But without question, the *Religion*, and good Order of the *County*, and their Purity in *Doctrine*, has, under God, been very much owing to the great Abilities, and eminent Piety, of my venerable and honoured Grandfather *Stoddard*. I suppose we have been the freest of any Part of the Land from unhappy *Divisions*, and *Quarrels* in our ecclesiastical and religious Affairs, till the late lamentable *Springfield Contention.**

We being much separated from other Parts of the Province, and having comparatively but little Intercourse with them, have from the beginning, till now, always managed our ecclesiastical Affairs within our selves: 'tis the way in which the County, from its Infancy, has gone on, by the practical Agreement of all, and the way in which our Peace and good Order has hitherto been maintained.

The Town of *Northampton* is of about 82 *Years* standing, and has now about 200 *Families*; which mostly dwell more *compactly* together than any Town of such a Bigness in these Parts of the Country; which probably has been an Occasion that both our *Corruptions*, and *Reformations* have been, from time to time, the more *swiftly* propagated, from one to another, through the Town. Take the *Town* in general, and so far as I can judge, they are as *Rational* and *Understanding* a People as most I have been acquainted with: Many of them have been *noted* for Religion, and particularly, have been remarkable for their distinct *Knowledge* in things that relate to *Heart* Religion, and Christian *Experience*, and their great *Regards* thereto.

I am the *third Minister* that has been settled in the Town: the Rev. Mr. *Eleazer Mather*, who was the *first*, was ordained in *July*, 1661. He was one whose Heart was *much* in his Work, abundant in *Labours* for the good of precious Souls; he had the high Esteem and great Love of his People, and was blessed with no small *Success*. The Rev. Mr. *Stoddard*, who succeeded him, came first to the Town the *November* after his Death, but was not ordained till *September* 11. 1672, and died *Feb.* 11. 1728/9. So that he continued in the Work of the Ministry here, from his first coming to Town, near 60 Years. And as he was eminent and *renowned* for his Gifts and Grace; so he was blessed, from the beginning, with *extraordinary Success* in his Ministry, in the Conversion of many Souls. He had *five Harvests*, as he

*The *Springfield* Contention relates to the Settlement of a Minister there, which occasion'd too warm Debates between some, both Pastors and People, that were for it, and others that were against it, on account of their different Apprehensions about his Principles, and about some Steps that were taken to procure his Ordination.

called them: The *first* was about 57 Years ago; the *second* about 53 Years; the *third* about 40; the *fourth* about 24; the *fifth* and last about 18 Years ago. *Some* of these Times were much more remarkable than others, and the ingathering of Souls more plentiful. Those that were about 53, and 40, and 24 Years ago, were much greater than either the *first* or the *last*: but in *each* of them, I have heard my *Grandfather* say, the *bigger* Part of the *young* People in the Town, seemed to be mainly concerned for their eternal Salvation.

After the *last* of these came a far more degenerate time, (at least among the young People) I suppose, than ever before. Mr. *Stoddard*, indeed, had the Comfort before he died, of seeing a time where there were no small Appearances of a divine Work amongst some, and a considerable *Ingathering* of Souls, even after I was settled with him in the *Ministry*, which was about *two* Years before his Death; and I have reason to *bless* God for the great Advantage I had by it. In these *two* Years there were near *twenty* that Mr. *Stoddard* hoped to be savingly converted; but there was nothing of any *General Awakening*. The greater Part seemed to be at that time very insensible of the things of Religion, and engaged in other Cares and Pursuits. Just after my Grandfather's Death, it seemed to be a time of extraordinary *Dulness* in Religion: *Licentiousness* for some Years greatly prevailed among the *Youth* of the Town; they were many of them very much addicted to *Night-walking*, and frequenting the *Tavern*, and *leud* Practices, wherein some, by their Example exceedingly corrupted others. It was their Manner very frequently to get together, in Conventions of both *Sexes*, for Mirth and Jollity, which they called *Frolicks*; and they would often spend the greater part of the *Night* in them, without regard to any *Order* in the Families they belonged to: and indeed *Family-Government* did too much fail in the Town. It was become very customary with many of our young People, to be *Indecent* in their Carriage at *Meeting*, which doubtless, would not have prevailed to such a degree, had it not been that my *Grandfather*, through his *great Age*, (tho' he retained his *Powers* surprizingly to the *last*) was not so able to *Observe* them. There had also long prevailed in the Town, a Spirit of Contention between *two Parties*, into which they had for many Years been *divided*, by which, was maintain'd a *Jealousy* one of the other, and they were prepared to *oppose* one another in all publick Affairs.

But in *two* or *three* Years after Mr. *Stoddard*'s Death, there began to be a sensible Amendment of these Evils; the *young People* shew'd more of a Disposition to hearken to Counsel, and by degrees left off their *Frolicking*, and grew observably more *Decent* in their Attendance on the publick Worship, and there were more that manifested a *Religious Concern* than there used to be.

At the latter end of the Year 1733, there appeared a very unusual flexibleness, and yielding to Advice, in our young People. It had been too long their manner to make the *Evening after the Sabbath*,* and after our publick *Lecture*, to be especially the Times of their *Mirth*, and Company keeping. But a *Sermon* was now preached on the Sabbath before the *Lecture*, to shew the *Evil Tendency* of the Practice, and to persuade them to reform it; and it was urged on *Heads* of *Families*, that it should be a thing *agreed* upon among them to govern their Families, and keep their Children at home, at these times; and withal it was more *privately* moved, that they should meet together, the next Day, in their several Neighbourhoods, to know each other's Minds: which was accordingly done, and the *Motion* complied with throughout the Town. But *Parents* found little, or no occasion for the exercise of Government in the Case: the *young People* declared themselves *convinced* by what they had heard from the *Pulpit*, and were willing of themselves to comply with the Counsel that had been given: and it was *immediately*, and, I suppose, almost *universally* complied with; and there was a thorough *Reformation* of these Disorders thenceforward, which has continued ever since.

Presently after this, there began to appear a *remarkable Religious Concern* at a little *Village*, belonging to the Congregation, call'd *Pascommuck*, where a few Families were settled, at about *three Miles* distance from the main Body of the Town. At this place, a number of Persons seemed to be savingly wrought upon. In the *April* following, *Anno* 1734, there happen'd a

---

*It must be noted, that it has never been our Manner, to observe the *Evening* that *follows* the Sabbath; but that which *precedes* it, as part of holy Time.

very *sudden and awful Death of a young Man*, in the Bloom of his Youth; who being violently seized with a *Pleurisy*, and taken immediately very *delirious*, died in about *two Days*; which (together with what was preached publickly on that Occasion) much *affected* many young People. This was followed with another Death of a young married *Woman*, who had been considerably *exercised* in Mind, about the Salvation of her *Soul*, before she was ill, and was in great *Distress*, in the beginning of her Illness; but seemed to have *satisfying Evidences* of God's saving *Mercy* to her, before her Death; so that she died very full of *Comfort*, in a most earnest and moving Manner *warning*, and counselling others. This seem'd much to *contribute* to the solemnizing of the Spirits of many young Persons: and there began evidently to appear more of a *Religious Concern* on People's Minds.

In the *Fall* of the Year, I proposed it to the *young People*, that they should agree among themselves to spend the *Evenings after Lectures* in *social* Religion, and to that end divide themselves into several Companies to meet in various parts of the Town; which was accordingly done, and those *Meetings* have been since continued, and the *Example* imitated by *elder* People. This was follow'd with the Death of an *elderly* Person, which was attended with many *unusual* Circumstances, by which many were much moved and affected.

About this time, began the great *Noise* that was in this Part of the Country, about *Arminianism*, which seemed to appear with a very *threatning* Aspect upon the Interest of Religion here. The Friends of vital Piety trembled for fear of the Issue; but it seemed, contrary to their Fear, strongly to be *over-ruled* for the promoting of Religion. Many who looked on themselves as in a *Christless* Condition, seemed to be awaken'd by it, with fear that God was about to withdraw from the Land, and that we should be given up to *Heterodoxy*, and corrupt Principles; and that then their *Opportunity* for obtaining Salvation would be past; and many who were brought a little to *doubt* about the *Truth* of the *Doctrines* they had hitherto been taught, seem'd to have a kind of a trembling *Fear* with their Doubts, lest they should be led into *By-paths*, to their eternal undoing: And they seem'd with much Concern and Engagedness of Mind, to enquire what was indeed the Way in which they must come to be accepted with God. There were then some things said *publickly* on that Occasion, concerning *Justification by Faith alone.*

Altho' great *Fault* was found with *meddling* with the *Controversy* in the Pulpit, by such a Person, and at that time, and tho' it was ridiculed by many *elsewhere*; yet it proved a Word spoken in season here; and was most evidently attended with a very remarkable *Blessing* of Heaven to the Souls of the People in this Town. They received thence a general satisfaction with respect to the main thing in question, which they had been in trembling doubts and concern about; and their Minds were engag'd the more earnestly to seek that they might come to be accepted of God, and saved in the Way of the Gospel, which had been made evident to them to be the true and only Way. And *then* it was, in the latter part of *December, that the Spirit of God* began extraordinarily to set in, and *wonderfully* to work amongst us; and there were, very *suddenly*, one after another, five or six Persons, who were to all appearance savingly converted, and some of them wrought upon in a very remarkable manner.

Particularly, I was surprized with the relation of a *young Woman*, who had been one of the greatest Company-Keepers in the whole Town: When she came to me, I had never heard that she was become in any wise serious, but by the Conversation I then had with her, it appeared to me, that what she gave an account of, was a glorious Work of God's infinite Power and sovereign Grace; and that God had given her a *new* Heart, truly broken and sanctified. I could not then doubt of it, and have seen much in my Acquaintance with her since to confirm it.

Tho' the Work was *glorious*, yet I was filled with concern about the *Effect* it might have upon others: I was ready to conclude (tho' too rashly) that some would be *harden'd* by it, in carelessness and looseness of Life; and would take occasion from it to open their Mouths, in *Reproaches* of Religion. But the *Event* was the *Reverse*, to a wonderful degree; God made it, I suppose, the *greatest occasion of awakening* to others, of any thing that ever came to pass in the Town. I have had abundant Opportunity to know the Effect it had, by my private Conversation with many. The news of it seemed to be almost like a *flash of Lightning*, upon the Hearts of young People, all over the Town, and upon many others. Those Persons amongst us, who used to be *farthest* from seriousness, and that I most feared would make an ill Improvement of it, seemed greatly to be *awakened* with it; many went to talk with her, concerning what she had met with; and what appeared in her seemed to be to the Satisfaction of all that did so.

Presently upon this, a great and earnest Concern about the great things of Religion, and the eternal World, became *universal* in all parts of the Town, and among Persons of all Degrees, and all Ages; the Noise amongst the *Dry Bones* waxed louder and louder: All other talk but about spiritual and eternal things, was soon thrown by; all the Conversation in all Companies, and upon all occasions, was upon these things only, unless so much as was necessary for People, carrying on their ordinary secular Business. Other Discourse than of the things of Religion, would scarcely be tolerated in any Company. The Minds of People were wonderfully taken off from the *World*, it was treated amongst us as a thing of very little Consequence: They seem'd to follow their worldly Business, more as a part of their Duty, than from any Disposition they had to it; the *Temptation* now seemed to lie on that hand, to *neglect* worldly Affairs too much, and to spend too much Time in the immediate Exercise of Religion: Which Thing was exceedingly misrepresented by Reports that were spread in distant Parts of the Land, as tho' the People here had wholly thrown by all worldly Business, and betook themselves entirely to Reading, and Praying, and such like religious Exercises.

But altho' People did not ordinarily neglect their worldly Business; yet there then was the Reverse of what commonly is: *Religion* was with all sorts the great Concern, and the *World* was a thing only by the Bye. The only Thing in their view was to get the Kingdom of Heaven, and every one appeared pressing into it: The Engagedness of their Hearts in this great Concern cou'd not *be hid*, it appear'd in their very *Countenances*. It then was a dreadful Thing amongst us to lie out of Christ, in danger every day of dropping into Hell; and what Persons minds were intent upon was to *escape for their Lives*, and to *fly from the Wrath to come*. All would eagerly lay hold of Opportunities for their Souls; and were wont very often to meet together in private Houses for religious Purposes: And such Meetings when appointed were wont greatly to be thronged.

There was scarcely a single Person in the Town, either old or young, that was left unconcerned about the great Things of the eternal World. Those that were wont to be the vainest, and loosest, and those that had been most disposed to think, and speak slightly of vital and experimental Religion, were now generally subject to great awakenings. And the Work of *Conversion* was carried on in a most *astonishing* manner, and increased more and more; Souls did as it were come by Flocks to Jesus Christ. From Day to Day, for many Months together, might be seen evident Instances of Sinners brought *out of Darkness into marvellous Light*, and delivered *out of an horrible Pit, and from the miry Clay, and set upon a Rock*, with a *new Song of Praise to God in their mouths*.

This Work of God, as it was carried on, and the Number of true Saints multiplied, soon made a glorious Alteration in the Town; so that in the Spring and Summer following, *Anno* 1735, the Town seemed to be full of the Presence of God: It never was so full of *Love*, nor so full of *Joy*, and yet so full of Distress, as it was then. There were remarkable Tokens of God's Presence in almost every House. It was a time of Joy in *Families* on the account of Salvation's being brought unto them; *Parents* rejoicing over their Children as new born, and *Husbands* over their Wives, and *Wives* over their Husbands. *The goings of God* were then *seen in his Sanctuary*, God's *Day* was *a delight*, and his *Tabernacles* were *amiable*. Our publick *Assemblies* were then beautiful; the Congregation was *alive* in God's Service, every one earnestly intent on the Publick Worship, every *Hearer* eager to drink in the words of the *Minister* as they came from his Mouth; the Assembly in general were from time to time, *in Tears* while the Word was preached; *some* weeping with Sorrow and Distress, *others* with Joy and Love, *others* with Pity and Concern for the Souls of their Neighbours.

Our publick *Praises* were then greatly enliven'd; God was then served in our *Psalmody*, in some measure, in the *Beauty of Holiness*. It has been observable, that there has been scarce *any part* of Divine Worship, wherein good Men amongst us have had *Grace so drawn forth*, and their Hearts *so lifted up* in the Ways of God, as *in singing* his Praises: Our Congregation excell'd all that ever I knew in the *external* Part of the Duty before, generally carrying regularly, and well, *three Parts of Musick*, and the *Women* a Part by themselves: But now they were evidently wont to sing with *unusual Elevation* of Heart and Voice, which made the Duty pleasant indeed.

In all *Companies* on *other* Days, on whatever *Occasions* Persons met together, *Christ* was to be heard of and seen in the midst of them. Our *young People*, when they met, were wont to spend the Time in talking of the *Excellency* and dying *Love* of *JESUS CHRIST*, the Gloriousness of the way of *Salvation*, the wonderful, free, and sovereign *Grace* of God, his glorious Work in the *Conversion* of a Soul, the *Truth* and Certainty of the great Things of God's Word, the Sweetness of the Views of his *Perfections, &c.* And even at *Weddings*, which formerly were meerly occasions of Mirth and Jollity, there was now no discourse of any thing but the things of Religion, and no appearance of any, but *spiritual Mirth*.

Those amongst us that had been *formerly converted*, were greatly enliven'd and renew'd with fresh and extraordinary Incomes of the Spirit of God; tho' some much more than others, *according to the measure of the Gift of Christ*: Many that before had laboured under *Difficulties* about their own State, had now their *Doubts* removed by more satisfying Experience, and more clear Discoveries of God's Love.

When this Work of God first appeared, and was so extraordinarily carried on amongst *us* in the Winter, *others* round about us, seemed not to know *what* to make of it; and there were many that scoffed at and ridiculed it; and some compared what we called Conversion, to certain *Distempers*. But it was very observable of many, that occasionally came amongst us from abroad, with disregardful Hearts, that what they *saw* here *cured* them of such a Temper of Mind: *Strangers* were generally surprized to find Things so much *beyond* what they had heard, and were wont to tell others that the State of the Town could not be conceiv'd of by those that had not seen it. The Notice that was taken of it by the People, that came to Town on occasion of the *Court*, that sat here in the beginning of *March*, was very observable. And those that came from the Neighbourhood to our publick *Lectures*, were for the most part remarkably affected. Many that came to Town, on one occasion or other, had their Consciences smitten, and awaken'd, and went home with wounded Hearts, and with those Impressions that never wore off till they had hopefully a saving Issue; and those that before had serious Thoughts, had their Awakenings and Convictions greatly increased. And there were many Instances of Persons that came from abroad, on Visits, or on Business, that had not been long here before to all Appearance they were savingly wrought upon, and partook of that Shower of divine Blessing that God rained down here, and went home Rejoycing; 'till at length the *same Work* began evidently to appear and prevail in several other Towns in the *County*.

In the Month of *March*, the People in *South-Hadley* began to be seized with deep Concern about the Things of Religion; which very soon became universal: And the Work of God has been very wonderful *there*; not much, if any thing, short of what it has been here, in proportion to the bigness of the Place. About the same Time, it began to break forth in the West part of *Suffield*, (where it has also been very great,) and it soon spread into all parts of the Town. It next appear'd at *Sunderland*, and soon overspread the Town; and I believe was, for a Season, not less remarkable than it was here. About the same time, it began to appear in a part of *Deerfield*, called *Green-River*, and afterwards fill'd the Town, and there has been a *glorious* Work there: It began also to be manifest, in the South part of *Hatfield*, in a place called the *Hill*, and after that the *whole Town*, in the second Week in *April*, seemed to be seized, as it were at once, with Concern about the Things of Religion; and the Work of God has been *great* there. There has been also a very general Awakening at *West Springfield*, and *Long-Meadow*; and in *Enfield*, there was for a time no small Concern amongst some that before had been very loose Persons. About the same time that this appear'd at *Enfield*, the Rev. Mr. *Bull* of *Westfield* informed me, that there had been a great Alteration there, and that more had been done in *one Week* there than in *seven Years* before. Something of this Work likewise appeared in the first Precinct in *Springfield*, principally in the *North* and *South* Extremes of the *Parish*. And in *Hadley* old Town, there gradually appear'd so much of a Work of God on Souls, as at another time would have been thought worthy of much Notice. For a *short* time there was also a very great and general Concern, of the like nature, at *Northfield*. And wherever this Concern appeared, it seemed not to be *in vain*: But in every Place God brought saving Blessings with him, and *his* Word attended with his *Spirit* (as we have all reason to think) return'd *not void*. It might well be said at that time in all Parts of the County, *Who are these that fly as a Cloud, and as Doves to their Windows?*

As what *other* Towns heard of and found in this, was a great means of awakening *them*; so *our* hearing of such a swift, and extraordinary Propagation, and Extent of this Work, did doubtless for a time serve to uphold the Work amongst us. The continual News kept alive the talk of Religion, and did greatly quicken and rejoice the Hearts of God's People, and much awaken'd those that looked on themselves as still *left behind*, and made them the more earnest that they also might *share* in the great Blessing that others had obtain'd.

This remarkable *pouring out of the Spirit of God*, which thus extended from one end to the other of this *County*, was not confin'd to it, but many Places in *Connecticut*, have partook in the same Mercy: As for instance, the *first Parish in Windsor*, under the pastoral Care of the Rev. Mr. *Marsh* was thus blest about the same time, as we in *Northampton*, while we had *no Knowledge* of each other's Circumstances: There has been a very great Ingathering of Souls to *Christ* in that Place, and something Considerable of the same Work began afterwards, in *East Windsor*, my honoured *Father*'s Parish, which has *in times past*, been a Place favoured with Mercies of this nature, *above any* on this western side of *New-England*, excepting *Northampton*; there having been *four or five* Seasons of the *pouring out of the Spirit* to the *general* awakening of the People there, since my *Father*'s Settlement amongst them.

There was also the *last* Spring and Summer a wonderful Work of God carried on at *Coventry* under the Ministry of the Rev. Mr. *Meacham*: I had opportunity to converse with some of *Coventry* People, who gave me a very remarkable Account of the surprizing *Change* that appear'd in the most rude and vicious Persons there. The like was also very great at the same time in a Part of *Lebanon*, called the *Crank*, where the Rev. Mr. *Wheelock*, a young Gentleman is lately settled: And there has been much of the same at *Durham*, under the Ministry of the Rev. Mr. *Chauncy*; and to appearance no small Ingathering of Souls there. And likewise amongst many of the young People in the first Precinct in *Stratford*, under the Ministry of the Rev. Mr. *Gould*; where the Work was much promoted by the remarkable Conversion of a young *Woman* that had been a great Company-Keeper, as it was here.

Something of this Work appeared in several other *Towns* in those Parts, as I was informed when I was there, the last *Fall*. And we have since been acquainted with something very remarkable of this nature at another Parish in *Stratford* call'd *Ripton*, under the pastoral Care of the Rev. Mr. *Mills*. And there was a considerable Revival of Religion last Summer at *New-Haven* old Town, as I was once and again informed by the Rev. Mr. *Noyes* the Minister there, and by others: And by a Letter which I very lately receiv'd from Mr. *Noyes*, and also by Information we have had otherwise, this flourishing of Religion still continues, and has lately much increased: Mr. *Noyes* writes, that *many this Summer have been added to the Church*, and particularly mentions several young Persons that belong to the principal Families of that Town.

There has been a degree of the same Work at a Part of *Guilford*; and very considerable at *Mansfield*, under the Ministry of the Rev. Mr. *Eleazer Williams*; and an unusual religious Concern at *Tolland*; and something of it at *Hebron*, and *Bolton*. There was also no small Effusion of the Spirit of God in the North Parish in *Preston*, in the eastern Part of *Connecticut*, which I was informed of, and saw something of it, when I was the last *Autumn* at the House, and in the Congregation of the Rev. Mr. *Lord*, the Minister there; who, with the Rev. Mr. *Owen* of *Groton*, came up hither in *May*, the last Year, on purpose to see the Work of God here; and having heard various and contradictory Accounts of it, were careful when they were here to inform, and satisfy themselves; and to that end particularly conversed with many of our People; which they declared to be entirely to their Satisfaction, and that the *one half had not been told them*, nor could be told them. Mr. *Lord* told me that, when he got home, he informed his Congregation of what he had seen, and that they were greatly affected with it, and that it proved the beginning of the same Work amongst them, which prevailed till there was a *general* Awakening, and many Instances of Persons, who seemed to be remarkably converted. I also have lately heard that there has been something of the same Work at *Woodbury*.

But this Shower of divine Blessing has been yet more *extensive*: There was no small Degree of it in some parts of the *Jerseys*; as I was informed when I was at *New-York*, (in a long Journey I took at that time of the Year for my Health,) by some People of the *Jerseys*, whom I saw: Especially the Rev. Mr. *William Tennent*, a Minister, who seemed to have such Things much at Heart, told me of a very great awakening of many in a Place called the *Mountains*, under the Ministry of one Mr. *Cross*; and of a very considerable Revival of Religion in another Place under the Ministry of his Brother the Rev. Mr. *Gilbert Tennent*; and also at another Place, under the Ministry of a very pious young Gentleman, a *Dutch Minister*, whose Name as I remember was *Freelinghousa*.

This seems to have been a very *extraordinary* Dispensation of Providence: God has in many Respects gone out of, and much beyond his usual, and *ordinary Way*. The Work in this Town, and some others about us, has been extraordinary on account of the *Universality* of it, affecting all sorts, sober and vicious, high and low, rich and poor, wise and unwise; it reach'd the most considerable Families and Persons, to all appearance, as much as others. In former stirrings of this nature, the Bulk of the *young* People have been greatly affected; but *old Men*, and *little Children* have been so now. Many of the *last* have, of their own accord, formed themselves into *religious Societies*, in different Parts of the Town: A loose careless Person could scarcely find a Companion in the whole Neighbourhood; and if there was *any one* that seemed to remain senseless or unconcerned, it would be spoken of as a *strange* Thing.

This Dispensation has also appeared very extraordinary in the *Numbers* of those, on whom we have reason to hope it has had a saving Effect: We have about six hundred and twenty *Communicants*, which include almost all our adult Persons. The Church was very *large* before; but Persons never *thronged* into it, as they did in the late extraordinary Time:—Our *Sacraments* are eight Weeks asunder, and I receiv'd into our Communion about an *hundred* before one Sacrament, and *fourscore* of them at one time, whose Appearance, when they presented themselves together to make an open explicit *Profession* of Christianity, was very affecting to the Congregation:—I took in near sixty before the next Sacrament Day: But it must be noted that it is not the Custom here, as it is in many other Churches in this Country, to make a credible Relation of their inward Experiences the ground of Admission to the Lord's Supper.

I am far from pretending to be able to determine how many have lately been the Subjects of such Mercy; but if I may be allowed to declare any thing that appears to me probable in a thing of this nature, I hope that more than three Hundred Souls were savingly brought home to *Christ*, in this Town, in the space of half a Year, (how many more I don't guess) and about the same Number of Males as Females; which, by what I have heard Mr. *Stoddard* say, was far from what has been usual in Years past, for he observed that in his Time, many more Women were converted than Men. Those of our young People, that are on other accounts most likely and considerable, are mostly, as I hope, truly Pious, and leading Persons in Ways of Religion. Those that were formerly looser young Persons, are generally to all Appearance, become true Lovers of God and *Christ*, and spiritual in their Dispositions. And I hope that by far the greater part of Persons in this Town, above 16 years of Age, are such as have the saving knowledge of *Jesus Christ*; and so by what I heard I suppose it is in some other Places, particularly at *Sunderland* and *South Hadley*.

This has also appeared to be a very extraordinary Dispensation, in that the Spirit of God has so much extended not only his *awakening*, but *regenerating* Influences both to *elderly* Persons, and also those that are *very young*. It has been a thing heretofore rarely to be heard of, that *any* were converted past middle Age; but now we have the same Ground to think, that *many such* have in this time been savingly changed, as that *others* have been so in more early Years. I suppose there were upwards of *fifty* Persons in this Town above 40 years of Age; and more than *twenty* of them above 50, and about *ten* of them above 60, and *two* of them above 70 years of Age.

It has heretofore been looked on as a strange Thing, when any have seem'd to be savingly wrought upon, and remarkably changed in their Childhood; but now I suppose, near *thirty* were to Appearance so wrought upon between 10 and 14 Years of Age, and *two* between 9 and 10, and *one* of about 4 years of Age; and because I suppose this last will be most difficultly believed, I will hereafter give a particular Account of it. The Influences of God's Spirit have also been very remarkable on Children in some other Places, particularly at *Sunderland* and *South-Hadley*, and the West part of *Suffield*. There are several Families in this Town that are all hopefully pious; yea, there are several numerous Families, in which, I think we have reason to hope that all the Children are truly godly, and most of them lately become so: And there are very few Houses in the whole Town, into which Salvation has not lately come, in one or more Instances. There are several Negroes, that from what was seen in them then, and what is discernable in them since, appear to have been truly born again in the late remarkable Season.

God has also seemed to have gone out of his usual way, in the *Quickness* of his Work, and the swift Progress his Spirit has made in his Operations on the Hearts of many: 'Tis wonderful that Persons should be so suddenly, and yet so greatly changed: Many have been taken from a loose and careless way of Living, and seized with strong Convictions of their Guilt and Misery, and in a very little time old Things have passed away, and all Things have become new with them.

God's Work has also appeared very extraordinary, in the *Degrees* of the Influences of his Spirit, both in the Degree of *Awakening* and *Conviction*, and also in the Degree of *saving Light*, and *Love*, and *Joy*, that many have experienced. It has also been very extraordinary in the *Extent* of it, and its being so swiftly propagated from Town to Town. In former Times of the pouring out of the Spirit of God on this Town, tho' in some of them it was very Remarkable, yet it reached no further than this Town, the neighbouring Towns all around continued unmoved.

The Work of God's Spirit seemed to be at its greatest Height in this Town, in the former part of the *Spring*, in *March* and *April*; at which time God's Work in the Conversion of Souls was carried on amongst us in so wonderful a manner, that so far as I, by looking back, can judge from the particular

Acquaintance I have had with Souls in this Work, it appears to me probable, to have been at the Rate, at least, of four Persons in a Day, or near thirty in a Week, take one with another, for five or six Weeks together: When God in so remarkable a manner took the Work into his own Hands, there was as much done in a Day or two, as at ordinary Times, with all Endeavours that Men can use, and with such a Blessing as we commonly have, is done in a Year.

I am very sensible how apt many would be, if they should see the Account I have here given, presently to think with themselves that I am very fond of making a great many Converts, and of magnifying and aggrandizing the matter; and to think that, for want of Judgment, I take every religious Pang, and enthusiastick Conceit, for saving Conversion; and I don't much wonder if they should be apt to think so: and for this reason I have forborn to publish an Account of this great Work of God, tho' I have often been put upon it; but having now as I thought a special Call to give an account of it, upon mature Consideration, I thought it might not be beside my Duty to declare this amazing Work, as it appear'd to me, to be indeed Divine, and to conceal no part of the Glory of it, leaving it with God to take care of the Credit of his own Work, and running the venture of any censorious Thoughts, which might be entertain'd of me to my disadvantage: But that distant Persons may be under as great Advantage as may be, to judge for themselves of this Matter, I would be a little more large, and particular.

I therefore proceed to give an Account of the *manner* of Persons being wrought upon; and here there is a *vast Variety*, perhaps as manifold as the Subjects of the Operation; but yet in many Things there is a *great Analogy* in all.

Persons are first awaken'd with a Sense of their miserable Condition by Nature, the Danger they are in of perishing eternally, and that it is of great Importance to them that they speedily escape, and get into a better State. Those that before were secure and senseless, are made sensible how much they were in the way to ruin in their former Courses. *Some* are more suddenly seized with Convictions; it may be, by the News of others' Conversion, or something they hear in publick, or in private Conference, their Consciences are suddenly smitten, as if their Hearts were pierced through with a Dart: *Others* have Awakenings that come upon them more gradually, they begin as first to be something more thoughtful and considerate, so as to come to a Conclusion in their Minds, that 'tis their best and wisest way to delay no longer, but to improve the present Opportunity; and have accordingly set themselves seriously to meditate on those Things that have the most awakening Tendency, on purpose to obtain *Convictions*; and so their Awakenings have increased, till a Sense of their Misery, by God's Spirit setting in therewith, has had fast hold of them. *Others* that, before this wonderful time, had been something religious and concern'd for their Salvation, have been awaken'd in a new manner, and made sensible that their slack and dull way of seeking was never like to attain their Purpose, and so have been roused up to a greater Violence for the Kingdom of Heaven.

These Awakenings when they have first seized on Persons have had two Effects: One was, that they have brought them immediately to quit their sinful Practices, and the looser Sort have been brought to forsake and dread their former Vices and Extravagancies. When once the Spirit of God began to be so wonderfully poured out in a general way thro' the Town, People had soon done with their old Quarrels, Backbitings, and intermeddling with other Men's Matters; the Tavern was soon left empty, and Persons kept very much at home; none went abroad unless on necessary Business, or on some religious Account, and every Day seemed in many respects like a Sabbath Day. And the *other* Effect was, that it put them on earnest Application to the means of Salvation, Reading, Prayer, Meditation, the Ordinances of God's House, and private Conference; their Cry was, *What shall we do to be saved*? The place of Resort was now altered, it was no longer the Tavern, but the Minister's House: that was thronged far more than ever the Tavern had been wont to be.

There is a very great variety as to the Degree of Fear and Trouble that Persons are exercised with, before they obtain any comfortable Evidences of Pardon and Acceptance with God: some are from the beginning carried on with abundantly more Encouragement and Hope than others: some have had *ten* times less trouble of Mind than others, in whom yet the Issue seems to be the same. Some have had such a Sense of the

Displeasure of God, and the great Danger they were in of Damnation, that they could not sleep at Nights; and many have said that when they have laid down, the Thoughts of sleeping in such a Condition have been frightful to them, and they have scarcely been free from Terrour while they have been asleep, and they have awaked with Fear, Heaviness, and Distress still abiding on their Spirits. It has been very common, that the deep and fixed Concern that has been on Persons Minds, has had a painful Influence on their Bodies, and had given Disturbance to animal Nature.

The awful Apprehensions Persons have had of their Misery, have for the most part been increasing, the nearer they have approached to Deliverance; tho' they often pass through many Changes, and Alterations in the Frame, and Circumstances of their Minds: Sometimes they think themselves wholly senseless, and fear that the Spirit of God has left them, and that they are given up to judicial Hardness; yet they appear very deeply exercised about that Fear, and are in great earnest to obtain *Convictions* again.

Together with those Fears, and that Exercise of Mind which is rational and which they have just ground for, they have often suffer'd many needless Distresses of Thought, in which *Satan* probably has a great hand, to entangle them, and block up their way; and sometimes the Distemper of Melancholy has been evidently mixed; of which when it happens, the Tempter seems to make great advantage, and puts an unhappy Bar in the way of any good Effect; One knows not how to deal with such Persons, they turn every Thing that is said to them the wrong way, and most to their own Disadvantage: And there is nothing that the Devil seems to make so great a handle of, as a melancholy Humour, unless it be the real Corruption of the Heart.

But it has been very remarkable, that there has been far less of this Mixture in this time of extraordinary Blessing, than there was wont to be in Persons under awakenings at other Times; for it is evident that many that before had been exceedingly involved in such Difficulties, seem'd now strangely to be set at liberty: Some Persons that had before, for a long time, been exceedingly entangled with peculiar Temptations, of one sort or other, and unprofitable and hurtful Distresses, were soon helped over former Stumbling Blocks, that hinder'd any Progress towards saving Good; and Convictions have wrought more kindly, and they have been successfully carried on in the way to Life. And thus *Satan* seemed to be restrain'd, till towards the latter end of this wonderful Time, when God's Spirit was about to withdraw.

Many times Persons under great Awakenings were concerned, because they thought they were not awaken'd, but miserable, hard-hearted, senseless, sottish Creatures still, and sleeping upon the brink of Hell: The sense of the Need they have to be awaken'd, and of their comparative Hardness, grows upon them with their Awakenings; so that they seem to themselves to be very *senseless*, when indeed most *sensible*. There have been some Instances of Persons that have had as great a Sense of their Danger and Misery, as their Natures could well subsist under, so that a little more would probably have destroyed them; and yet they have exprest themselves much amazed at their own Insensibility and Sottishness, in such an extraordinary Time as it then was.

Persons are sometimes brought to the Borders of Dispair, and it looks as black as Midnight to them a little before the Day dawns in their Souls; some few Instances there have been of Persons, who have had such a Sense of God's Wrath for Sin, that they have been overborn, and made to cry out under an astonishing Sense of their Guilt, wondering that God suffers such guilty Wretches to live upon Earth, and that he doth not immediately send them to Hell; and sometimes their Guilt does so glare them in the Face, that they are in exceeding Terrour for fear that God will instantly do it; but more commonly the Distresses under legal Awakenings have not been to such a Degree. In some these Terrours don't seem to be so sharp, when near Comfort, as before; their Convictions have not seem'd to work so much that way, but they seem to be led further down into their own Hearts, to a further Sense of their own universal Depravity, & Deadness in Sin.

The Corruption of the Heart has discover'd it self in various Exercises, in the time of legal Convictions; sometimes it appears in a great Struggle, like something roused by an Enemy, and *Satan* the old Inhabitant seems to exert himself, like a Serpent disturbed and enraged. Many in such Circumstances, have felt a great Spirit of Envy, towards the Godly, especially towards those that are thought to have been lately converted, and most of all towards Acquaintance and Companions, *when they* are thought to be converted: Indeed, some have felt many Heart-risings against God, and murmurings at his ways of Dealing with Mankind, and his Dealings with themselves in Particular. It has been much insisted on, both in publick and private, that Persons should have the utmost dread of such envious Thoughts, which if allowed tend exceedingly to quench the Spirit of God, if not to provoke him finally to forsake them. And when such a Spirit has much prevailed, and Persons have not so earnestly strove against it as they ought to have done, it has seem'd to be exceedingly to the hindrance of the Good of their Souls: but in some other Instances, where Persons have been much terrified at the Sight of such Wickedness in their Hearts, God has brought Good to them out of Evil; and made it a Means of convincing them of their own desperate Sinfulness, and bringing them off from all Self-confidence.

The drift of the Spirit of God in his *legal* strivings with Persons, has seem'd most evidently to be, to make way for, and to bring to, a Conviction of their absolute Dependance on his sovereign Power and Grace, and universal Necessity of a Mediator, by leading them more and more to a Sense of their exceeding Wickedness and Guiltiness in his sight; the Pollution and Insufficiency of their own Righteousness, that they can in no wise help themselves, and that God would be wholly just and righteous in rejecting them, and all that they do, and in casting them off for ever: Tho' there be a vast variety, as to the manner, and distinctness of Persons Convictions of these things.

As they are gradually more and more convinced of the Corruption and Wickedness of their Hearts, they seem to themselves to grow worse and worse, harder and blinder, and more desperately wicked, instead of growing better; they are ready to be discouraged by it, and oftentimes never think themselves so *far off* from Good as when they are *nearest*. Under the sense which the Spirit of God gives them of their Sinfulness, they often think that they differ from all others; their Hearts are ready to sink with the thought, that they are the worst of all, and that none ever obtained Mercy that were so wicked as they.

When Awakenings *first begin*, their Consciences are commonly most exercised about their outward vicious Course, or other Acts of Sin; but *afterwards* are much more burdened with a sense of Heart sins, the dreadful Corruption of their Nature, their Enmity against God, the Pride of their Hearts, their Unbelief, their Rejection of Christ, the Stubbornness and Obstinacy of their Wills; and the like. In many, God makes much use of their own Experience, in the course of their Awakenings and Endeavours after saving Good, to convince them of their own vile Emptiness and universal Depravity.

Very often under first Awakenings, when they are brought to reflect on the Sin of their past Lives, and have something of a terrifying sense of God's Anger, they set themselves to walk more strictly, and confess their Sins, and perform many religious Dutys, with a secret Hope of appeasing God's Anger and making up for the Sins they have committed: and oftentimes, at first setting out, their Affections are moved, and they are full of Tears, in their Confessions and Prayers, which they are ready to make very much of, as tho' they were some Attonement, and had Power to move correspondent Affections in God too: and hence they are for a while big with Expectation of what God will do for them; and conceive that they grow better apace, and shall soon be thoroughly converted. But these Affections are but short-lived, they quickly find that they fail, and then they think themselves to be grown worse again; they don't find such a Prospect of being soon converted, as they thought: instead of being *nearer*, they seem to be *farther off*; their Hearts they think are grown harder, and by this means their fears of perishing greatly increase. But tho' they are disappointed, they renew their Attempts again and again; and still as their Attempts are Multiplied, so are their Disappointments; all fails, they see no token of having inclin'd God's Heart to them, they don't see that he hears their Prayers at all, as they expected he would; and sometimes there have been great Temptations arising hence to leave off seeking, and to yield up the Case. But as they are still more terrify'd with Fears of perishing, and their former Hopes of prevailing on God to be merciful to them in a great measure fail; sometimes their religious Affections have turn'd into Heart-risings against God, because that he won't pity them, and seems to have little regard to their Distress, and piteous Cries, and to all the Pains that they take; They think of the Mercy that God has shown to others, how soon, and how easily others have obtained Comfort, and those too that were worse than they, and have not labour'd so much as they have done, and sometimes they have had even dreadful blasphemous Thoughts, in these Circumstances.

But when they reflect on these wicked Workings of Heart against God, if their Convictions are continued, and the Spirit of God is not provoked utterly to forsake them, they have more distressing Apprehensions of the Anger of God *towards those*, whose Hearts work after such a sinful manner *about him*; and it may be have great Fears that they have committed the unpardonable Sin, or that God will surely never shew Mercy to them that are such Vipers; and are often tempted to leave off in despair. But then perhaps by something they read or hear of the infinite Mercy of God, and All-sufficiency of *Christ* for the chief of Sinners; they have some Encouragement and Hope renewed; but think that as yet they are not fit to come to *Christ*; they are so wicked that *Christ* will never accept of them: and then it may be they set themselves upon a new Course of fruitless Endeavours in their own Strength to make themselves better, and still meet with new Disappointments: They are earnest to enquire what they shall do? They don't know but there is something else to be done, in order to their obtaining converting Grace, that they have never done yet. It may be they hope that they are something better than they were; but then the pleasing Dream all vanishes again. If they are told, that they trust too much to their own Strength and Righteousness, they go about to strive to bring themselves off from it, and it may be, think they have done it, when they only do the same thing under a new disguise, and still find no appearance of any Good, but all looks as dark as Midnight to them. Thus they wander about from Mountain to Hill, seeking rest, and finding none: when they are beat out of *one* Refuge they fly to *another*, till they are as it were debilitated, broken, and subdued with legal Humblings; in which God gives them a Conviction of their own utter Helplessness and Insufficiency, and discovers the true Remedy.

When they begin to seek Salvation, they are commonly profoundly ignorant of themselves; they are not sensible how blind they are, and how little they can do *towards* bringing themselves to see spiritual things aright, and *towards* putting forth gracious Exercises in their own Souls: they are not sensible how remote they are from Love to God, and other holy Dispositions, and how dead they are in Sin. When they see unexpected Pollution in their own Hearts, they go about to wash away their own Defilements and make themselves clean; and they weary themselves in vain, till God shows them that 'tis in vain, and that their help is not where they have sought it, but elsewhere.

But some Persons continue wandering in such a kind of Labyrinth, ten times as long as others, before their own Experience will convince them of their Insufficiency; and so it appears not to be their own Experience only, but the convincing Influence of God's Spirit with their Experience, that attains the Effect: and God has of late abundantly shown, that he don't need to wait to have Men convinced by long and often repeated fruitless Trials; for in multitudes of Instances he has made a shorter work of it: he has so awakened and convinced Persons Consciences, and made them so sensible of their exceeding great Vileness, and given 'em such a sense of his Wrath against Sin, as has quickly overcome all their vain Self-confidence, and born them down into the Dust before a holy and righteous God.

There have been some who have not had great Terrors, but have had a very quick Work. Some of those that han't had so deep a Conviction of these things before their Conversion, have, it may be, much more of it afterwards. God has appeared far from limiting himself to any certain Method in his Proceedings with Sinners under legal Convictions. In *some* Instances it seems easy for our reasoning Powers to discern the methods of divine Wisdom, in his Dealings with the Soul under awakenings: in *others* his Footsteps can't be traced, and his Ways are past finding out: and some that are *less distinctly* wrought upon, in what is preparatory to Grace, appear *no less eminent* in gracious experiences afterwards.

There is in nothing a greater Difference, in different Persons, than with respect to the *Time* of their being under Trouble;

some but a few Days, and others for Months or Years. There were many in this Town, that had been, before this Effusion of God's Spirit upon us, for Years, and some for many Years, concerned about their Salvation; tho' probably they were not thoroughly awaken'd, yet they were concern'd to such a Degree as to be very uneasy, so as to live an uncomfortable disquieted Life, and so as to continue in a way of taking considerable Pains about their Salvation, but had never obtained any comfortable Evidence of a good Estate, who now in this extraordinary time have received Light; but many of them were some of the last: They first saw Multitudes of others rejoicing, and with Songs of Deliverance in their Mouths, who seem'd wholly careless and at ease, and in pursuit of Vanity, while they had been bowed down with sollicitude about their Souls; yea some had lived licenciously, and so continued till a little before they were converted, and grew up to a holy Rejoicing in the infinite Blessings God had bestowed upon *them*.

And whatever Minister has the like Occasion to deal with Souls, in a Flock under such Circumstances as this was in the last Year, I can't but think he will soon find himself under a Necessity, greatly to insist upon it with them, that God is under no manner of Obligation to shew Mercy to any natural Man, whose Heart is not turn'd to God: and that a Man can challenge nothing, either in *absolute Justice*, or by *free Promise*, from any Thing he does before he has believed on *Jesus Christ*, or has true Repentance begun in him. It appears to me, that if I had taught those that came to me under Trouble, any other Doctrine, I should have taken a most direct Course utterly to have undone them; I should have directly cross'd what was plainly the Drift of the Spirit of God in his Influence upon them; for if they had believed what I said, it would either have promoted Self-flattery and Carelessness, and so put an End to their Awakenings; or cherished and established their Contention and Strife with God, concerning his Dealings with them and others, and block'd up their Way to that Humiliation before the Sovereign Disposer of Life and Death, whereby God is wont to prepare them for his Consolations. And yet those that have been under Awakenings, have oftentimes plainly stood in need of being encouraged, by being told of the infinite and all-sufficient Mercy of God in *Christ*; and that 'tis

God's Manner to succeed Diligence, and to bless his own Means, that so *Awakenings* and *Encouragements, Fear* and *Hope* may be duly mixed, and proportion'd to preserve their Minds in a just Medium between the two Extreams of *Self-flattery* and *Despondence*, both which tend to Slackness, and Negligence, and in the End to Security. I think I have found that no Discourses have been more remarkably blessed, than those in which the Doctrine of God's absolute Sovereignty with Regard to the Salvation of Sinners, and his just Liberty, with Regard to his answering the Prayers, or succeeding the Pains of natural Men, continuing such, have been insisted on. I never found so much immediate saving Fruit, in any Measure, of any Discourses I have offered to my Congregation, as some from those Words, Rom. 3. 19. *That every Mouth may be stopped*; endeavouring to shew from thence, that it would be just with God for ever to reject and cast off meer natural men.

In those in whom Awakenings seem to have a saving Issue, commonly the first Thing that appears after their legal Troubles, is a Conviction of the Justice of God in their Condemnation, in a Sense of their own exceeding Sinfulness, and the Vileness of all their Performances: In giving Account of this, they express'd themselves very variously; some, that God was Sovereign, and might receive others and reject them; some, that they were convinced, that God might justly bestow Mercy on every Person in the Town, and on every Person in the World, and damn themselves to all Eternity; some, that they see that God may justly have no Regard to all the Pains they have taken, and all the Prayers they have made; some, that they see that if they should seek, and take the utmost Pains, all their Lives, God might justly cast them into Hell at last, because all their Labours, Prayers, and Tears, cannot make an Atonement for the least Sin, nor merit any Blessing at the Hands of God; some have declared themselves to be in the Hands of God, that he can, and may dispose of them just as he pleases, some, that God may glorify himself in their Damnation, and they wonder that God has suffered them to live so long, and has not cast 'em into Hell long ago.

Some are brought to this Conviction by a great Sense of their Sinfulness, in general, that they are such vile wicked Creatures in Heart and Life: *Others* have the Sins of their Lives

in an extraordinary Manner set before them, Multitudes of
them coming just then fresh to their Memories, and being set
before them with their Aggravations; some have their Minds
especially fixed, on some particular wicked Practice, they have
indulged; some are especially convinced by a Sight of the Corruption and Wickedness of their Hearts; some, from a View
they have of the Horridness of some particular Exercises of
Corruption, which they have had in the Time of their Awakenings, whereby the Enmity of the Heart against God has been
manifested; some are convinced especially by a sense of the Sin
of Unbelief, the Opposition of their Hearts to the Way of Salvation by *Christ*, and their Obstinacy in rejecting him and his
Grace.

There is a great deal of difference as to Persons *Distinctness*
here; some, that han't so clear a Sight of God's Justice in their
Condemnation, yet mention things that plainly imply it. They
find a Disposition to acknowledge God to be just and righteous in his Threatnings, and that they are deserving of nothing: And many times, tho' they had not so particular a Sight of
it at the Beginning, they have very clear Discoveries of it soon
afterwards, with great Humblings in the Dust before God.

Commonly Persons Minds immediately before this Discovery of God's Justice are exceeding restless, and in a kind of
Struggle and Tumult, and sometimes in meer Anguish; but
generally, as soon as they have this Conviction, it immediately
brings their Minds to a Calm, and a before unexpected Quietness and Composure; and most frequently, tho' not always,
then the pressing weight upon their Spirits is taken away, and a
general Hope arises, that some time or other God will be gracious, even before any distinct and particular Discoveries of
Mercy; and often they then come to a Conclusion within
themselves, that they will lie at God's Feet, and wait his Time,
and they rest in that, not being sensible that the Spirit of God
has now brought them to a Frame whereby they are prepared
for Mercy: for 'tis remarkable that Persons, when they first
have this sense of the Justice of God, rarely in the time of it,
think any thing of its being that *Humiliation* that they have
often heard insisted on, and that others experience.

In many Persons, the first Conviction of the Justice of God
in their Condemnation, which they *take particular notice of*,

and probably the first distinct Conviction of it that they *have*, is of such a Nature, as seems to be above any thing meerly legal: Tho' it be after legal Humblings, and much of the sense of their own Helplessness and of the Insufficiency of their own Duties; yet it does not appear to be forced by meer legal Terrors and Convictions; but rather from an high Exercise of Grace, in saving Repentance, and evangelical Humiliation; for there is in it a sort of Complacency of Soul, in the *Attribute* of God's Justice, as display'd in his Threatnings of eternal Damnation to Sinners. Sometimes at the Discovery of it, they can scarcely forbear crying out, 'TIS JUST! 'TIS JUST! Some express themselves, that they see the Glory of God would *shine bright* in their own Condemnation; and they are ready to think that if they are damned, they could take part with God against themselves, and would glorify his Justice therein. And when it is thus, they commonly have some evident sense of free and all-sufficient Grace, tho' they give no distinct Account of it, but 'tis manifest, by that great degree of Hope and Encouragement that they then conceive, tho' they were never so sensible of their own Vileness and Ill deservings as they are at that time.

Some, when in such Circumstances, have felt that sense of the Excellency of God's Justice, appearing in the vindictive Exercises of it, against such Sinfulness as theirs was, and have had such a Submission of Mind in their *Idea* of this Attribute, and of those Exercises of it, together with an exceeding loathing of their own Unworthiness, and a kind of Indignation against themselves, that they have sometimes almost call'd it a *Willingness to be damned*; tho' it must be owned they had not clear and distinct Ideas of Damnation, nor does any Word in the Bible require such Self denial as this. But the truth is, as some have more clearly exprest it, that Salvation has appeared *too good for them, that they were worthy of nothing but Condemnation*, and they could *not tell how to think of Salvation's being bestowed upon them*, fearing it was *inconsistent with the Glory of God's Majesty, that they had so much contemned and affronted.*

That Calm of Spirit that some Persons have found after their legal Distresses, continues some time before any special and delightful Manifestation is made to the Soul of the Grace of God, as revealed in the Gospel; but very often some comfortable and sweet View of a merciful God, of a sufficient Redeemer, or of some great and joyful things of the Gospel, immediately follows, or in a very little time: And in some, the first Sight of their just Desert of Hell, and God's Sovereignty with respect to their Salvation, and a Discovery of all-sufficient Grace, are so near, that they seem to go as it were together.

These gracious Discoveries that are given, whence the first special Comforts are derived, are in many respects very various; more frequently *Christ* is distinctly made the Object of the Mind, in his All-sufficiency and Willingness to save Sinners: But some have their Thoughts more especially fixed on God, in some of his sweet and glorious Attributes manifested in the Gospel, and shining forth in the Face of *Christ*: Some view the All-sufficiency of the Mercy and Grace of God; some chiefly the infinite Power of God, and his Ability to save them, and to do all things for them; and some look most at the Truth and Faithfulness of God: In *some*, the Truth and Certainty of the Gospel in general is the first joyful Discovery they have; in *others*, the certain Truth of some particular Promises; in some, the Grace and Sincerity of God in his Invitations, very commonly in some particular Invitation in the Mind, and it now appears real to them that God does indeed invite them. Some are struck with the Glory and Wonderfulness of the dying Love of *Christ*; and some with the Sufficiency and Preciousness of his Blood, as offered to make an Atonement for Sin; and others with the Value and Glory of his Obedience and Righteousness. In some the Excellency and Loveliness of *Christ*, chiefly engages their Thoughts; in some his Divinity, that he is indeed *the Son of the living God*; and in others, the Excellency of the way of Salvation by *Christ*, and the Suitableness of it to their Necessities.

Some have an Apprehension of these things so given, that it seems more natural to them to express it by *Sight* or *Discovery*; *others* think what they experience better expressed by the *Realizing Conviction*, or a *lively* or *feeling Sense of Heart*; meaning, as I suppose, no other Difference but what is mearly circumstantial or gradual.

There is, often, in the Mind, some *particular* Text of Scripture, holding forth some evangelical ground of Consolation; sometimes a *Multitude* of Texts, gracious Invitations and Promises flowing in one after another, filling the Soul more and more, with Comfort and Satisfaction: and Comfort is first given to some, while *reading* some Portion of Scripture; but in some it is attended with *no particular Scripture* at all, either in *Reading* or *Meditation*. In *some, many divine things* seem to be discover'd to the Soul as it were at once; *others* have their Minds especially fixing on some *one thing* at first, and afterwards a sense is given of *others*; in *some* with a swifter, and *others* a slower Succession, and sometimes with Interruptions of much Darkness.

The way that Grace seems sometimes first to appear after legal Humiliation, is in earnest Longings of Soul after God and *Christ*, to know God, to love him, to be humbled before him, to have Communion with *Christ* in his Benefits, which Longings, as they express them, seem evidently to be of such a nature as can arise from nothing but a sense of the superlative Excellency of divine things, with a spiritual Taste and Relish of 'em, and an Esteem of 'em as their highest Happiness and best Portion. Such Longings as I speak of, are commonly attended with firm Resolutions to pursue this Good for ever, together with a hoping, waiting Disposition. When Persons have begun in such Frames, commonly other Experiences and Discoveries have soon followed, which have yet more clearly manifested a change of Heart.

It must needs be confest that *Christ* is not always *distinctly* and *explicitly* thought of in the first sensible Act of Grace, (tho' most commonly he is;) but sometimes he is the Object of the Mind only *implicitly*. Thus sometimes when Persons have seem'd evidently to be stript of all their own Righteousness, and to have stood self condemned as guilty of Death, they have been comforted with a joyful and satisfying View, that the Mercy and Grace of God is sufficient for them; that their Sins, tho' never so great, shall be no Hindrance to their being accepted; that there is Mercy enough in God for the whole World, and the like, when they give no Account of any particular or distinct Thought of *Christ*; but yet when the Account they give is duly weighed, and they are a little interrogated about it, it appears that the Revelation of the Mercy of God in the Gospel, is the Ground of this their Encouragement and Hope; and that it is indeed the Mercy of God thro' *Christ*, that is discovered to them, and that 'tis depended on *in him*, and not in any wise moved by any thing *in them*.

So sometimes disconsolate Souls amongst us, have been re-vived and brought to rest in God, by a sweet sense given of his Grace and Faithfulness, in some special Invitation or Promise, in which is no particular mention of *Christ*, nor is it accompa-nied with any distinct Thought of him, in their Minds; but yet it is not received as *out of Christ*, but as one of the Invitations or Promises made of God to poor Sinners *through* his Son *Jesus*, as it is indeed: and such Persons have afterwards had clear and distinct Discoveries of *Christ*, accompanied with lively and special Actings of Faith and Love towards him.

It has more frequently been so amongst us, that when Per-sons have first had the Gospel Ground of Relief for lost Sinners discovered to them, and have been entertaining their Minds with the sweet Prospect, they have thought nothing at that time of their being converted: To see that there is such an All-sufficiency in God, and such plentiful Provision made in *Christ*, after they have been borne down, and sunk with a sense of their Guilt and Fears of Wrath, exceedingly refreshes them; the View is joyful to them, as 'tis in its own nature glorious, and gives them quite new, and more delightful *Ideas* of God and *Christ*, and greatly encourages them to seek Conversion, and begets in them a strong Resolution to give up themselves, and devote their whole Lives to God and his Son, and patiently to wait till God Shall see fit to make all effectual; and very often they entertain a strong Persuasion, that he will in his own time do it for them.

There is wrought in them a holy Repose of Soul in God through *Christ*, and a secret Disposition to fear and love him, and to hope for Blessings from him in this Way: and yet they have no Imagination that they are now converted, it don't so much as come into their Minds: and very often the Reason is, that they don't see that they do *accept* of this sufficiency of Salvation, that they behold in *Christ*, having entertain'd a wrong Notion of *Acceptance*; not being sensible that the obe-dient and joyful Entertainment which their Hearts give to this Discovery of Grace, is a real Acceptance of it: They know not that the sweet Complacence they feel in the Mercy and com-plete Salvation of God, as it includes Pardon and Sanctifica-tion, and is held forth to them only through *Christ*, is a true receiving of this Mercy, or a plain Evidence of their receiving it. They expected I know not what Kind of Act of Soul, and perhaps they had no distinct *Idea* of it themselves.

And indeed it appears very plainly in some of them, that before their own Conversion they had very *imperfect Ideas* what Conversion was: It is all new and strange, and what there was no clear Conception of before. 'Tis most evident as they themselves acknowledge, that the Expressions that were used to describe Conversion, and the Graces of God's Spirit, such as *a spiritual Sight of Christ, Faith in Christ, Poverty of Spirit, Trust in God, Resignedness to God,* &c. were Expressions that did not convey those special and distinct *Ideas* to their Minds, which they were intended to signify, in some respects no more than the Names of Colours are to convey the *Ideas* to one that is blind from his Birth.

This Town is a Place where there has always been a great deal of Talk of Conversion, and spiritual Experiences; and therefore People in general had before form'd a Notion in their own Minds what these things were; but when they come to be the Subjects of them themselves, they find themselves much confounded in their Notions, and overthrown in many of their former Conceits. And it has been very observable, that Persons of the greatest Understanding, and that had studied most about things of this nature, have been more confounded than others. Some such Persons that have lately been converted, declare that all their former Wisdom is brought to nought, and that they appear to have been meer Babes, who knew nothing. It has appear'd that none have stood more in need of Enlightning and Instruction, even of their Fellow Christians, concerning their own Circumstances and Difficulties, than they: and it has seem'd to have been with delight, that they have seen themselves thus brought down and become *nothing*, that free Grace, and divine Power may be *exalted* in them.

It was very wonderful to see after what manner Persons Affections were sometimes moved and wrought upon, when God did as it were, suddenly open their Eyes and let into their Minds, a sense of the Greatness of his Grace, and Fulness of *Christ*, and his readiness to save, who before were broken with Apprehensions of divine Wrath, and sunk into an Abyss under a sense of Guilt, which they were ready to think was beyond the Mercy of God: their joyful Surprize has caused their Hearts as it were to leap, so that they have been ready to break forth into Laughter, Tears often at the same time issuing like a Flood, and intermingling a loud Weeping: and sometimes they han't been able to forbear crying out with a loud Voice, expressing their great Admiration. In some even the View of the Glory of God's Sovereignty in the Exercises of his Grace has surprized the Soul with such Sweetness, as to produce the same Effects. I remember an Instance of one, who, reading something concerning God's sovereign way of saving Sinners, as being self-moved, and having no regard to Men's own Righteousness as the Motive of his Grace, but as magnifying himself and abasing Man, or to that purpose, felt such a sudden Rapture of Joy and Delight in the Consideration of it: and yet then suspected himself to be in a Christless Condition, and had been long in great Distress for fear that God would not have mercy on him.

Many continue a long time in a Course of gracious Exercises and Experiences, and don't think themselves to be converted, but conclude themselves to be otherwise; and none knows how long they would continue so, were they not helped by particular Instruction. There are undoubted Instances of some that have lived in this way for many Years together; and a continuing in these Circumstances of being converted and not believing it, has had various consequences, with various Persons, and with the same Persons, at various Times; some continue in great Encouragement and Hope, that they shall obtain Mercy, in a stedfast Resolution to persevere in seeking it, and in an humble waiting for it at God's foot; but very often when the lively Sense of the Sufficiency of *Christ*, and the Riches of divine Grace begins to vanish, upon a withdraw of the Influences of the Spirit of God, they return to greater Distress than ever; for they have now a far greater Sense of the Misery of a natural Condition than before, being in a new manner sensible of the reality of eternal Things, and the greatness of God, and his Excellency, and how dreadful it is to be separated from him, and to be subject to his Wrath; so that they are sometimes swallowed up with Darkness and Amazement. *Satan* has a vast Advantage in such Cases to ply them with various Temptations, which he is not wont to neglect. In such a case Persons do very much need a Guide to lead them to an Understanding of what we are taught in the Word of God of the Nature of Grace, and to help them to apply it to themselves.

I have been much blamed and censured by many, that I should make it my Practice, when I have been satisfied concerning Persons good Estate, to signify it to them: Which Thing has been greatly misrepresented abroad, as innumerable other Things concerning us, to prejudice the Country against the whole Affair. But let it be noted, that what I have undertaken to judge of, has rather been Qualifications, and declared Experiences, than Persons: Not but that I have thought it my Duty as a Pastor to assist and instruct Persons in applying Scripture-Rules and Characters to their own Case, (in doing of which, I think many greatly need a Guide,) and have, where I thought the Case plain, used Freedom in signifying my Hope of them, to others: but have been far from doing this concerning all that I have had some hopes of; and I believe have used much more Caution than many have supposed. Yet I should account it a great Calamity to be deprived of the Comfort of Rejoicing with those of my Flock, that have been in great Distress, whose Circumstances I have been acquainted with, when there seems to be good Evidence that those that were dead are alive, and those that were lost are found. I am sensible the Practice would have been safer in the hands of one of a riper Judgment and greater Experience; but yet there has seemed to be an absolute Necessity of it on the forementioned Accounts; and it has been found to be that which God has most remarkably owned and blessed amongst us, both to the Persons themselves and others.

Grace in many Persons, through this Ignorance of their State, and their looking on themselves still as the Objects of God's Displeasure, has been like the Trees in Winter, or like Seed in the Spring suppressed under a hard Clod of Earth; and many in such Cases have laboured to their utmost to divert their Minds from the pleasing and joyful Views they have had, and to suppress those Consolations and gracious Affections that arose thereupon. And when it has once come into their Minds to enquire whether or no this was not true Grace, they have been much afraid lest they should be deceiv'd with common Illuminations and Flashes of Affection, and *eternally* undone with a false Hope. But when they have been better instructed, and so brought to allow of Hope, this has awaken'd the gracious Disposition of their Hearts into Life and Vigor, as the warm Beams of the Sun in the Spring, have quickened the Seeds and Productions of the Earth: Grace being now at liberty, and cherished with Hope, has soon flowed out to their abundant Satisfaction and Increase.

There is no one thing that I know of that God has made such a means of promoting his Work amongst us, as the News of others Conversion; in the awakening Sinners, and engaging them earnestly to seek the same Blessing, and in the quickening of Saints. Tho' I have thought that a Minister's declaring his Judgment about particular Persons Experiences might from these Things be justified, yet I am often signifying to my People how unable Man is to know another's Heart, and how unsafe it is depending meerly on the Judgment of Ministers, or others, and have abundantly insisted on it with them that a manifestation of Sincerity in *Fruits brought forth*, is better than any manifestation they can make of it in *Words* alone, can be; and that without this, all Pretences to spiritual Experiences are vain; as all my Congregation can witness. And the People in general, in this late extraordinary Time, have manifested an extraordinary Dread of being deceiv'd, being exceeding fearful lest they should build wrong, and some of them backward to receive Hope, even to a great Extreme.

Conversion is a great and glorious Work of God's Power, at once Changing the Heart, and infusing Life into the dead Soul; tho' that Grace that is then implanted does more gradually display it self in some than in others. But as to fixing on the *precise Time* when they put forth the very first Act of Grace, there is a great deal of difference in different Persons; in some it seems to be very discernable when the very Time of this was; but others are more at a loss. In *this respect* there are very many that don't know the Time, (as has been already observed) that when they have the first Exercises of Grace, don't know that *it is* the Grace of Conversion, and sometimes don't think it to be so till a long time after: And many, even when they come to entertain great Hope that they are converted, if they remember what they experienced in the first Exercises of Grace, they are at a loss whether it was any more than a common Illumination; or whether some other, more clear and remarkable Experience, that they had afterwards, was not the first that was of a saving nature. And the manner of God's Work on the Soul is (sometimes especially) very mysterious, and 'tis with the Kingdom of God as to its Manifestation in the Heart of a Convert, as is said, *Mark* iv 26, 27, 28. *So is the Kingdom of God, as if a Man should cast Seed into the Ground, and should sleep and rise Night and Day, and the Seed should spring, and grow up he knoweth not how; for the Earth bringeth forth of her self first the Blade, then the Ear, then the full Corn in the Ear.*

In *some*, converting Light is like a glorious Brightness suddenly shining in *upon* a Person, and all *around* him: They are in a remarkable manner brought *out of Darkness into marvellous Light.* In many *others* it has been like the dawning of the Day, when at first but a little Light appears, and it may be is presently hid with a Cloud; and then it appears again, and shines a little brighter, and gradually increases, with intervening Darkness, till at length, perhaps, it breaks forth more clearly from behind the Clouds. And many are, doubtless, ready to date their Conversion wrong, throwing by those lesser Degrees of Light that appeared at first dawning, and calling some more remarkable Experience, they had afterwards, their Conversions; which often in great measure arises from a wrong Understanding of what they have always been taught, that Conversion is a great Change, wherein *old Things are done away, and all Things become new*, or at least from a false arguing from that Doctrine.

Persons commonly at first Conversion, and afterwards, have had many Texts of Scripture brought to their Minds, that are exceeding suitable to their Circumstances, which often come with great Power, and as the Word of God or *Christ* indeed; and many have a multitude of sweet Invitations, Promises, and Doxologies flowing in one after another, bringing great Light and Comfort with them, filling the Soul brim full, enlarging the Heart, and opening the Mouth in Religion. And it seems to me necessary to suppose, that there is an immediate Influence of the Spirit of God, oftentimes in bringing Texts of Scripture to the Mind: Not that I suppose 'tis done in a way of immediate Revelation, without any manner of use of the Memory; but yet there seems plainly to be an immediate and extraordinary Influence, in leading their Thoughts to such and such Passages of Scripture, and exciting them *in the Memory*. Indeed in some God seems to bring Texts of Scripture to their Minds no otherwise than by leading them into such Frames and Meditations, as harmonize with those Scriptures; but in many Persons there seems to be something more than this.

Those that, while under legal Convictions, have had the greatest Terrors, have not always obtain'd the greatest Light and Comfort; nor have they always Light most suddenly communicated; but yet, I think, the time of Conversion has generally been most sensible in such Persons. Oftentimes, the first sensible Change after the Extremity of Terrors, is a Calmness, and then the Light gradually comes in; *small Glimpses* at first, after their midnight Darkness, and a *word or two of Comfort*, as it were softly spoken to 'em; they have a *little Taste* of the Sweetness of divine Grace, and the Love of a Saviour, when Terror and Distress of Conscience begins to be turned into an humble, meek Sense of their own Unworthiness before God; and there is felt inwardly, perhaps, some Disposition to praise God; and after a little while the Light comes in more clearly and powerfully. But yet, I think more frequently, great Terrors have been followed with more sudden and great Light, and Comfort; when the Sinner seems to be as it were subdued and brought to a Calm, from a kind of Tumult of Mind, then God lets in an extraordinary Sense of his great Mercy thro' a Redeemer.

The converting Influences of God's Spirit very commonly bring an extraordinary Conviction of the Reality and Certainty of the great Things of Religion; (tho' in some this is much greater, some time after Conversion, than at first:) they have that sight and taste of the Divinity, or divine Excellency, that there is in the Things of the Gospel, that is more to convince them, than reading many Volumes of Arguments without it. It seems to me that in many Instances amongst us, when the divine Excellency and Glory of the Things of Christianity have been set before Persons, and they have at the same time as it were seen, and tasted, and felt the Divinity of them, they have been as far from doubting of the Truth of them, as they are from doubting whether there be a Sun, when their Eyes are open upon it in the midst of a clear Hemisphere, and the strong Blaze of his

Light overcomes all Objections against his Being. And yet many of them, if we should ask them why they believed those Things to be true, would not be able well to express, or communicate a sufficient Reason, to satisfy the Enquirer, and perhaps would make no other Answer but that they see 'em to be true: But a Person might soon be satisfied, by a particular Conversation with 'em, that what they mean by such an Answer is, that they have intuitively beheld, and immediately felt, most illustrious Works, and powerful Evidence of Divinity in them.

Some are thus convinced of the Truth of the Gospel in general, and that the Scriptures are the Word of God: Others have their Minds more especially fixed on some particular great Doctrine of the Gospel, some particular Truths that they are *meditating* on; or are in a special manner convinced of the Divinity of the Things they are *reading* of, in some portion of Scripture. Some have such Convictions in a much more remarkable manner than others: And there are some that never had such a special Sense of the Certainty of divine Things, impressed upon them with such inward Evidence and Strength, have yet very clear Exercises of Grace; *i.e.* of Love to God, Repentance and Holiness. And if they be more particularly examined, they appear plainly to have an inward firm Persuasion of the Reality of divine Things, such as they don't use to have before their Conversion. And those that have the most clear Discoveries of divine Truth, in the manner that has been spoken of, can't have this always in view. When the Sense and Relish of the divine Excellency of these Things fades, on a withdraw of the Spirit of God, they han't the medium of the Conviction of their Truth at command: In a dull Frame they can't recall the *Idea*, and inward Sense they had, perfectly to mind; Things appear very dim to what they did before: And tho' there still remains an habitual strong Persuasion; yet not so as to exclude Temptations to Unbelief, and all possibility of Doubting, as before: But then at particular Times, by God's Help, the same Sense of Things revives again, like Fire that lay hid in Ashes.

I suppose the grounds of such a Conviction of the Truth of divine Things to be just and rational, but yet in some God makes use of their own Reason much more sensibly than in others. Oftentimes Persons have (so far as could be judged) receiv'd the first saving Conviction from reasoning, which they have heard *from the Pulpit*; and often in the course of Reasoning, which they are led into *in their own Meditations.*

The Arguments are the *same* that they have heard hundreds of times; but *the Force of the Arguments*, and *their Conviction by 'em*, is altogether new; they come with a new and before unexperienced Power: Before they *heard it* was so, and they *allow'd it* to be so; but now they *see it* to be so indeed. Things now look exceeding plain to 'em, and they wonder that they did not see 'em before.

They are so greatly taken with their new Discovery, and Things appear so plain, and so rational to 'em, that they are often at first ready to think they can convince others; and are apt to engage in talk with every one they meet with, *almost* to this End; and when they are disappointed, are ready to wonder that their Reasonings seem to make no more Impression.

Many fall under such a Mistake as to be ready to doubt of their good Estate, because there was so much use made of their own Reason in the Convictions they have receiv'd; they are afraid that they have no Illumination above the natural Force of their own Faculties: And many make that an Objection against the Spirituality of their Convictions, that 'tis so easy to see Things as they now see them. They have often heard that Conversion is a work of mighty Power, manifesting to the Soul what no Man nor Angel can give such a conviction of; but it seems to them that the Things that they see are so plain, and easy, and rational, that any body can see them: And if they are enquired of, why they never saw so before; they say, it seems to them it was because they never thought of it. But very often these Difficulties are soon removed by those of another nature; for when God withdraws, they find themselves as it were blind again, they for the present lose their realizing Sense of those Things that looked so plain to 'em, and by all that they can do they can't recover it, till God renews the Influences of his Spirit.

Persons after their Conversion often speak of Things of Religion as seeming *new* to them; that Preaching is a *new* thing; that it seems to them they never heard Preaching before; that the Bible is a *new* Book: They find there *new* Chapters, *new*

Psalms, *new* Histories, because they see them in a new Light. Here was a remarkable Instance of an aged Woman that had spent most of her Days under Mr. *Stoddard's* powerful Ministry; who reading in the New Testament, concerning *Christ*'s Sufferings for Sinners, seem'd to be surprized and astonished at what she read, as at a Thing that was real and very wonderful, but quite *new* to her, insomuch that at first, before she had time to turn her Thoughts, she wonder'd within her self that she had never heard of it before; but then immediately recollected her self, and thought that she had often heard of it, and read it, but never till now saw it as a thing real; and then cast in her Mind, how wonderful this was, that the Son of God should undergo such things for Sinners, and how she had spent her Time in ungratefully sinning against so good a God, and such a Saviour; tho' she was a Person, as to what was visible, of a very blameless and inoffensive Life. And she was so overcome by those Considerations, that her Nature was ready to fail under them: Those that were about her, and knew not what was the matter, were surprized, and thought she was a dying.

Many have spoken much of their Hearts being drawn out in Love to God and *Christ*; and their Minds being wrapt up in delightful Contemplation of the Glory, and wonderful Grace of God, and the Excellency, and dying Love of *Jesus Christ*; and of their Souls going forth in longing Desires *after God and Christ*. Several of our young Children have expressed much of this; and have manifested a Willingness to leave Father and Mother and all Things in the World, to go to be with *Christ*. Some Persons have had longing Desires after *Christ*, which have risen to that degree, as to take away their natural Strength. Some have been so overcome with a Sense of the dying Love of *Christ*, to such poor, wretched, and unworthy Creatures, as to weaken the Body. Several Persons have had so great a Sense of the Glory of God, and Excellency of *Christ*, that Nature and Life has seemed almost to sink under it; and in all probability, if God had shewed them a little more of himself, it would have dissolved their Frame. I have seen some, and been in Conversation with them in such Frames, who have certainly been perfectly sober, and very remote from any thing like enthusiastick Wildness: And have talk'd, when able to speak, of the Glory of God's Perfections, and the wonderfulness of his Grace in Christ, and their own Unworthiness, in such a manner that can't be perfectly expressed after them. Their Sense of their exceeding littleness and vileness, and their Disposition to abase themselves before God, has appeared to be great in proportion to their Light and Joy. Such Persons amongst us as have been thus distinguished with the most extraordinary Discoveries of God, have commonly in no wise appeared with the assuming, & self-conceited, and self-sufficient Airs of Enthusiasts, but exceedingly the contrary; and are eminent for a Spirit of Meekness, Modesty, Self diffidence, and low Opinion of themselves: No Persons seem to be so sensible of their need of Instruction, and so eager to receive it, as some of them; nor so ready to think others better than themselves. Those that have been thought to be converted amongst us have *generally* manifested a longing to lie low, and in the dust before God; withal complaining of their not being able to lie low enough. They very often speak much of their Sense of the Excellency of the way of Salvation, by free and sovereign Grace, through the Righteousness of *Christ* alone; and how it is with delight that they renounce their own Righteousness, and rejoice in having no Account made of it. Many have expressed themselves to this purpose, that it would lessen the Satisfaction they hope for in Heaven to have it by their own Righteousness, or in any other way than as bestowed by free Grace, and for *Christ*'s sake alone. They speak much of the *Inexpressibleness* of what they experience, how their Words fail, so that they can in no wise declare it: and particularly speak with exceeding Admiration of the superlative Excellency of that pleasure and delight of Soul, which they sometimes enjoy; how a little of it is sufficient to pay 'em for the Pains and Trouble they have gone through in seeking Salvation; and how far it exceeds all earthly Pleasures: And some express much of the Sense which these spiritual Views give 'em of the Vanity of earthly Enjoyments, how mean and worthless all these Things appear to 'em.

Many, while their Minds have been fill'd with spiritual Delights, have as it were forgot their Food; their bodily Appetite has fail'd, while their Minds have been entertain'd with *Meat to eat that* others *knew not of.* The Light and Comfort which some of them enjoy, gives a new relish to their common Blessings, and causes all Things about 'em to appear as it were beautiful, sweet and pleasant to them: All Things abroad, the Sun, Moon and Stars, the Clouds and Sky, the Heavens and Earth, appear as it were with a Cast of divine Glory and Sweetness upon them. The sweetest Joy that these good People amongst us express, is not that which consists in a Sense of the Safety of their own State, and that now they are out of danger of Hell; frequently, in times of their highest spiritual Entertainment, this seems to be as it were forgotten. The supreme Attention of their Minds is to the glorious Excellencies of God and *Christ*, which they have in view; not but that there is very often a ravishing Sense of God's Love accompanying a Sense of his Excellency, and they rejoice in a Sense of the Faithfulness of God's Promises, as they respect the future eternal Enjoyment of God.

The Joy that many of them speak of as that, to which none is to be parallel'd; is that which they find when they are lowest in the Dust, emptied most of themselves, and as it were annihilating themselves before God, when they are nothing, and God is all, are seeing their own Unworthiness, depending not at all on themselves, but alone on *Christ*, and ascribing all Glory to God: Then their Souls are most in the Enjoyment of satisfying Rest; excepting that, at such times, they apprehend themselves to be not sufficiently self-abased; for then above all times do they long to be lower. Some speak much of the exquisite Sweetness, and Rest of Soul that is to be found in the exercises of a Spirit of Resignation to God, and humble Submission to his Will. Many express earnest Longings of Soul to praise God; but at the same time complain that they can't praise him as they would do, and they want to have others help them in praising him: They want to have *every one* praise God, and are ready to call upon *every thing* to praise him. They express a longing Desire to live to God's Glory, and to do something to his Honour; but at the same time cry out of their Insufficiency and Barrenness, that they are *poor impotent Creatures, can do nothing of themselves, and are utterly insufficient to glorify their Creator and Redeemer.*

While God was so remarkably present amongst us by his Spirit, there was no Book so delighted in as the Bible; especially the Book of *Psalms*, the Prophecy of *Isaiah*, and the *New Testament*. Some by reason of their Esteem and Love to God's

Word, have at some times been greatly and wonderfully delighted and affected at the sight of a Bible; and *then* also, there was *no Time* so prized as the Lord's-Day, and *no Place* in this World so desired as God's House. Our Converts *then* remarkably appeared united in dear Affection to one another, and many have expressed much of that Spirit of Love which they felt toward all Mankind; and particularly to those that had been least friendly to them. Never, I believe, was so much done in confessing Injuries, and making up Differences as the last Year. Persons after their own Conversion, have commonly expressed an exceeding desire for the Conversion of others: Some have thought that they should be willing to die for the Conversion of any Soul, tho' of one of the meanest of their Fellow-Creatures, or of their worst Enemies; and many have indeed been in great Distress with Desires and Longings for it. This Work of God had also a good Effect to unite the People's Affections much to their Minister.

There are some Persons that I have been acquainted with, but more especially two, that belong to other Towns, that have been swallowed up exceedingly with a Sense of the awful Greatness and Majesty of God; and both of them told me to this purpose, that if they in the time of it, had had the least Fear that they were not at peace with this so great a God, they should instantly have died.

It is worthy to be remarked, that some Persons by their Conversion seem to be greatly helped as to their doctrinal Notions of Religion; it was particularly remarkable in one, who having been taken captive in his Childhood, was train'd up in *Canada*, in the *Popish* Religion; and some Years since returned to this his native Place, and was in a measure brought off from *Popery*: but seem'd very awkward and dull of receiving any true and clear Notion of the *Protestant* Scheme, till he was converted; and then he was remarkably altered in this respect.

There is a vast difference, as has been observ'd in the *Degree*, and also in the particular *Manner* of Persons Experiences, both *at*, and *after* Conversion; *some* have Grace working more sensibly in one way, *others* in another. *Some* speak more fully of a Conviction of the Justice of God in their Condemnation; *others* more of their consenting to the way of Salvation by *Christ*; some more of the Actings of Love to God and *Christ*:

Some more of Acts of Affiance, in a sweet and assured Conviction of the Truth and Faithfulness of God in his Promises; *others* more of their choosing and resting in God as their whole and everlasting Portion, and of their ardent and longing Desires after God, to have Communion with him; *others* more of their abhorrence of themselves for their past Sins, and earnest Longings to live to God's Glory for the time to come: *Some* have their Mind fixed more on God; *others* on *Christ*, as I have observed before, but it seems evidently to be the *same Work*, the *same Thing done*, the *same habitual Change* wrought in the Heart; it all tends the same way, and to the *same End*: and 'tis plainly the *same Spirit* that breathes and acts in *various* Persons. There is an endless *Variety* in the particular manner and circumstances in which Persons are wrought on, and an opportunity of seeing so much of such a Work of God, will shew that God is further from confining himself to certain Steps, and a particular Method, in his Work on Souls, than it may be some do imagine. I believe it has occasion'd some good People amongst us, that were before too ready to make their own Experiences a Rule to others, to be less censorious and more extended in their Charity. The Work of God has been glorious in its Variety, it has the more displayed the manifoldness and unsearchableness of the Wisdom of God, and wrought more Charity among his People.

There is a great Difference among those that are converted as to the Degree of *Hope and Satisfaction* that they have concerning their own *State*. Some have a high degree of Satisfaction in this Matter almost constantly: And yet it is rare that any do enjoy so full an Assurance of their Interest in *Christ*, that Self-Examination should seem needless to them; unless it be at particular Seasons, while in the actual enjoyment of some great Discovery, that God gives of his Glory and rich Grace in *Christ*, to the drawing forth of extraordinary acts of Grace. But the greater part, as they sometimes fall into dead Frames of Spirit, are frequently exercised with Scruples and Fears concerning their Condition.

They generally have an awful Apprehension of the Dreadfulness and undoing Nature of a false Hope; and there has been observable in most a great Caution, lest in giving an account of their Experiences, they should say too much, and use too strong Terms: And many after they have related their Experiences, have been greatly afflicted with Fears, lest they have play'd the Hypocrite, and used stronger Terms than their Case would fairly allow of; and yet could not find how they could correct themselves.

I think that the main ground of the Doubts and Fears that Persons, after their Conversion, have been exercised with about their own State, has been that they have found so much Corruption remaining in their Hearts. At first their Souls seem to be all alive, their Hearts are fixed, and their Affections flowing; they seem to live quite above the World, and meet with but little Difficulty in religious Exercises; and they are ready to think it will always be so: Tho' they are truly abased under a Sense of their Vileness by reason of former Acts of Sin, yet they are not then sufficiently sensible what Corruption still remains in their Hearts; and therefore are surprized when they find that they begin to be in dull and dead Frames, to be troubled with wandering Thoughts in the time of publick and private Worship, and to be utterly unable to keep themselves from 'em; also when they find themselves unaffected at Seasons in which, they think there is the greatest Occasion to be affected; and when they feel worldly Dispositions working in them, and it may be Pride, and Envy, and stirrings of Revenge, or some ill Spirit towards some Person, that has injured them, as well as other workings of indwelling Sin: Their Hearts are almost sunk with the Disappointment, and they are ready presently to think that all this they have met with is nothing, and that they are meer Hypocrites.

They are ready to argue, that if God had indeed done such great Things for them, as they hoped, such Ingratitude would be inconsistent with it: They cry out of the hardness and wickedness of their Hearts; and say there is so much Corruption, that it seems to them *impossible that there should be any Goodness there*: and many of them seem to be much more sensible how corrupt their Hearts are, than ever they were before they were converted; and some have been too ready to be impres'd with Fear, that instead of becoming better, they are grown much worse, and make it an Argument against the Goodness of their State. But in truth the Case seems plainly to be, that now they feel the pain of their own Wound; they have a watchful Eye upon their Hearts, that they don't use to have: They take more notice what Sin is there, and Sin is now more burdensome to 'em, they strive more against it, and feel more of the Strength of it.

They are somewhat surpriz'd that they should in this respect find themselves so different from the *Idea* that they generally had entertained of godly Persons; for tho' Grace be indeed of a far more excellent nature than they imagin'd; yet those that are godly have much less of it, and much more remaining Corruption, than they thought. They never realized it, that Persons were wont to meet with such Difficulties, after they were once converted. When they are thus exercised with Doubts about their State, through the Deadness of their Frames of Spirit, as long as these Frames last, they are commonly unable to satisfy themselves of the Truth of their Grace, by all their Self-examination. When they hear of the Signs of Grace laid down for 'em to try themselves by, they are often so clouded, that they don't know how to apply them: they hardly know whether they have such and such things in them or no, and whether they have experienced them or not: That which was sweetest, and best, and most distinguishing in their Experiences, they can't recover a sense or *Idea* of. But on a Return of the Influences of the Spirit of God, to revive the lively Actings of Grace, the Light breaks through the Cloud, and Doubting and Darkness soon vanish away.

Persons are often revived out of their dead and dark Frames, by religious Conversation: while they are talking of divine things, *or ever* they are *aware*, their *Souls* are carried away into holy Exercises with abundant Pleasure. And oftentimes, while they are relating their past Experiences to their Christian Brethren, they have a fresh sense of them revived, and the same Experiences in a Degree again renewed. Sometimes while Persons are exercised in Mind with several Objections against the Goodness of their State, they have Scriptures, one after another, coming to their Minds, to answer their Scruples, and unravel their Difficulties, exceeding apposite and proper to their Circumstances; by which means their Darkness is scattered; and often before the Bestowment of any new remarkable Comforts, especially after long continued Deadness and ill Frames, there are renewed Humblings, in a great sense of their own exceeding Vileness and Unworthiness, as before their first Comforts were bestowed.

Many in the Country have entertain'd a mean Thought of this great Work that there has been amongst us, from what they have heard of *Impressions* that have been made on Persons *Imaginations*. But there have been exceeding great Misrepresentations, and innumerable false Reports concerning that Matter. 'Tis not, that I know of, the Profession or Opinion of any one Person in the Town, that any weight is to be laid on any thing seen with the bodily Eyes: I know the contrary to be a receiv'd and established Principle amongst us. I cannot say that there have been no Instances of Persons that have been ready to give too much heed to vain and useless *Imaginations*; but they have been easily corrected, and I conclude it will not be wondered at, that a Congregation should need a Guide in such Cases, to assist them in distinguishing *Wheat* from *Chaff*. But such Impressions on the Imagination as have been more usual, seem to me, to be plainly no other, than what is to be expected in human Nature in such Circumstances, and what is the natural Result of the strong Exercise of the Mind, and Impressions on the Heart.

I do not suppose that they themselves imagined that they saw any thing with their bodily Eyes; but only have had within them *Ideas* strongly impress'd, and as it were, lively Pictures in their Minds: As for instance, some when in great Terrors, through fear of Hell, have had lively Ideas of a dreadful Furnace. Some, when their Hearts have been strongly impress'd, and their Affections greatly moved with a sense of the Beauty and Excellency of *Christ*, it has wrought on their Imaginations so, that together with a sense of his glorious spiritual Perfections, there has arisen in the Mind an *Idea* of one of glorious Majesty, and of a sweet and a gracious Aspect: So some when they have been greatly affected with *Christ*'s Death, have at the same time a lively *Idea* of *Christ* hanging upon the Cross, and of his Blood running from his Wounds; which things won't be wondred at by them that have observed how strong Affections about temporal Matters will excite lively *Ideas* and Pictures of different things in the Mind.

But yet the vigorous Exercise of the Mind, does doubtless more strongly impress it with imaginary *Ideas*, in some than others, which probably may arise from the difference of Constitution, and seems evidently in some, partly to arise from their peculiar Circumstances: When Persons have been exercised with extreme Terrors, and there is a sudden change to Light and Joy, the Imagination seems more susceptive of strong *Ideas*, and the inferior Powers, and even the Frame of the Body, is much more affected and wrought upon, than when the same Persons have as great spiritual Light and Joy afterwards; of which it might, perhaps, be easy to give a Reason. The forementioned Rev. Messi *Lord* and *Owen*, who I believe, are esteem'd Persons of Learning and Discretion where they are best known, declared that they found these *Impressions* on Persons *Imaginations*, quite different things from what Fame had before represented to them, and that they were what none need to wonder at, or be stumbled by, or to that purpose.

There have indeed been some few Instances, of *Impressions* on Persons *Imaginations*, that have been something mysterious to me, and I have been at a loss about them; for tho' it has been exceeding evident to me by many things that appear'd in them, both then (when they related them) and afterwards, that they indeed had a great sense of the spiritual Excellency of Divine Things accompanying them; yet I have not been able well to satisfy myself, whether their imaginary *Ideas* have been more than could naturally arise from their spiritual Sense of things. However, I have used the utmost Caution in such Cases; great Care has been taken both in publick and in private to teach Persons the difference between what is *spiritual* and what is merely *imaginary*. I have often warned Persons not to lay the stress of their Hope on any *Ideas* of any outward Glory, or any external thing whatsoever, and have met with no Opposition in such Instructions. But 'tis not strange if some weaker Persons, in giving an account of their Experiences, have not so prudently distinguished between the spiritual and imaginary Part; which some that have not been well affected to Religion, might take advantage of.

There has been much talk in many parts of the Country, as tho' the People have symbolized with the *Quakers*, and the *Quakers themselves* have been moved with such Reports; and came here, once and again, hoping to find good Waters to fish in; but without the least Success, and seem to be discouraged, and have left off coming. There have also been Reports spread about the Country, as tho' the first Occasion of so remarkable a Concern on People's Minds here, was an Apprehension that the World was near to an end, which was altogether a false Report: Indeed after this Stirring and Concern became so general and extraordinary, as has been related, the Minds of some were filled with Speculation, what so great a Dispensation of divine Providence might forebode: and some Reports were heard from abroad, as tho' certain Divines and others thought the Conflagration was nigh: but such Reports were never generally looked upon worthy of Notice.

The Work that has now been wrought on Souls is evidently the same that was wrought in my venerable Predecessor's Days; as I have had abundant Opportunity to know, having been in the Ministry here two Years with him, and so conversed with a considerable Number that my Grandfather thought to be savingly converted in that time; and having been particularly acquainted with the Experiences of many that were converted under his Ministry before. And I know no one of them, that in the least doubts of its being the same Spirit, and the same Work. Persons have now no otherwise been subject to Impressions on their Imaginations, than formerly: The Work is of the same nature, and has not been attended with any extraordinary Circumstances, excepting such as are analogous to the extraordinary degree of it before described. And God's People, that were formerly converted, have now partook of the same Shower of divine Blessing, in the *renewing, strengthening, edifying Influences* of the Spirit of God, that others have in his *converting Influences*; and the Work here has also been plainly the same with that, which has been wrought in those of other Places that have been mentioned, as partaking of the same Blessing. I have particularly conversed with Persons about their Experiences that belong to all parts of the County, and in various parts of *Connecticut*, where a religious Concern has lately appear'd; and have been inform'd of the Experiences of many others by their own Pastors.

'Tis easily perceived by the foregoing Account that 'tis very much the Practice of the People here, to converse freely one with another of their spiritual Experiences, which is a thing that many have been disgusted at. But however our People *may have*, in some respects, gone to extremes in it, yet 'tis doubtless a Practice that the Circumstances of this Town, and neighbouring Towns, has naturally led them into. Whatsoever People are in such Circumstances, where all have their Minds engaged to such a Degree, in the same Affair, that 'tis ever uppermost in their Thoughts; they will naturally make it the Subject of Conversation one with another when they get together, in which they will grow more and more free: Restraints will soon vanish; and they will not conceal from one another what they meet with. And it has been a Practice which, in the general, has been attended with many good Effects, and what God has greatly blessed amongst us: But it must be confest, there may have been some ill Consequences of it; which yet are rather to be laid to the indiscreet Management of it, than to the Practice it self; and none can wonder, if among such a multitude some fail of exercising so much Prudence in choosing the time, manner, and occasion of such Discourse, as is desireable.

But to give a clearer *Idea* of the Nature and Manner of the Operations of God's Spirit, in this wonderful Effusion of it, I would give an Account of two *particular Instances*. The first is an *Adult Person*, a young Woman whose Name was *Abigail Hutchinson*. I pitch upon her especially because she is now dead, and so it may be more fit to speak freely of her then of living Instances: tho' I am under far greater Disadvantages, on other accounts, to give a full and clear Narrative of her Experiences, than I might of some others; nor can any Account be given but what has been retain'd in the Memories of her near Friends, and some others, of what they have heard her express in her life time.

She was of a rational understanding Family: there could be nothing in her Education that tended to *Enthusiasm*, but rather to the contrary extreme. 'Tis in no wise the Temper of the Family to be ostentatious of Experiences, and it was far from being her Temper. She was before her Conversion, to the Observation of her Neighbours, of a sober and inoffensive Conversation; and was a still, quiet, reserv'd Person. She had long been infirm of Body, but her Infirmity had never been observed at all to incline her to be notional or fanciful, or to occasion any thing of religious Melancholy. She was under Awakenings scarcely a Week before there seem'd to be plain Evidence of her being savingly converted.

She was first awakened in the Winter Season, on *Monday*, by something she heard her Brother say of the Necessity of being in good earnest in seeking regenerating Grace, together with the News of the Conversion of the young Woman before mention'd, whose Conversion so generally affected most of the young People here. This News wrought much upon her, and stirr'd up a Spirit of Envy in her towards this young Woman, whom she thought very unworthy of being distinguished from others by such a Mercy; but withal it engaged her in a firm Resolution to do her utmost to obtain the same Blessing; and considering with herself what Course she should take, she thought, that she had not a sufficient Knowledge of the Principles of Religion, to render her capable of Conversion; whereupon she resolved thoroughly to search the Scriptures, and accordingly immediately began at the beginning of the Bible, intending to read it through. She continued thus till *Thursday*: and then there was a sudden Alteration by a great Increase of her Concern, in an extraordinary sense of her own Sinfulness, particularly the Sinfulness of her Nature, and Wickedness of her Heart, which came upon her (as she expressed it) as a Flash of Lightning, and struck her into an exceeding Terror. Upon which she left off reading the Bible in Course as she had begun, and turned to the New-Testament, to see if she could not find some relief there for her distressed Soul.

Her *great Terror* she said *was, that she had sin'd against God*: Her Distress grew more and more for three Days; until (as she said) she saw *nothing but Blackness of Darkness before her, and,* her *very Flesh trembled for fear of God's wrath:* she *wondred and was astonished at* herself, *that she had been so concerned for her Body, and had applied so often to Physicians to heal that, and* had *neglected* her *Soul*. Her Sinfulness appeared with a very awful Aspect to her, especially in three things (*viz*) her Original Sin, and her Sin in murmuring at God's Providence, in the Weakness and Afflictions she had been under, and in want of Duty to Parents, tho' others had look'd upon her to excel in Dutifulness. On *Saturday*, she was so earnestly engaged in reading the Bible and other Books, that she continued in it, searching for something to relieve her, till her Eyes were so dim, that she could not know the Letters. Whilst she was thus engaged in Reading, Prayer, and other religious Exercises, she thought of those Words of *Christ*, wherein he warns us not to be *as the Heathen*, that *think they shall be heard for their much speaking*; which, she said, led her to see that she had trusted to her own Prayers and religious Performances, and now she was put to a *nonplus*, and knew not which way to turn herself, or where to seek Relief.

While her Mind was in this Posture, her Heart, she said, seem'd to fly to the Minister for Refuge, hoping that he could give her some Relief. She came the same Day to her Brother, with the Countenance of a Person in distress, expostulating with him, why he had not told her more of her Sinfulness, and earnestly enquiring of him what she should do. She seem'd that Day to feel in herself an Enmity against the Bible, which greatly affrighted her. Her sense of her own exceeding Sinfulness continued increasing from *Thursday* till *Monday*; and she gave this account of it, that it had been an Opinion, which till now she had entertain'd, that she was not guilty of *Adam*'s Sin, nor any way concerned in it, because she was not active in it; but that now she saw she was guilty of that Sin, and all over defiled by it; and that the Sin which she brought into the World with her, was alone sufficient to condemn her.

On the *Sabbath day* she was so ill that her Friends thought it not best that she should go to publick Worship, of which she seem'd very desirous: But when she went to Bed on the *Sabbath day* Night, she took up a Resolution, that she would the next Morning go to the Minister, hoping to find some relief there. As she awaked on *Monday* Morning, a little before Day she wondred within herself at the Easiness and Calmness she felt in her Mind, which was of that kind which she never felt before; as she thought of this, such Words as these were in her Mind; *The Words of the Lord are pure Words, Health to* the Soul, *and Marrow to the Bones*: And then these Words came to her Mind, *the Blood of Christ cleanses from all Sin*; which were accompanied with a lively sense of the excellency of *Christ*, and his Sufficiency to satisfy for the Sins of the whole World. She then thought of that Expression; *'Tis a pleasant thing for the Eyes to behold the Sun*; which Words then seem'd to her to be very applicable to *Jesus Christ*. By these things her Mind was led into such Contemplations and Views of *Christ*, as fill'd her exceeding full of Joy. She told her Brother in the Morning that she had *seen* (*i e.* in realizing Views by Faith) *Christ the last Night*, and, that she had *really thought that she had not Knowledge enough to be converted*; but, says she, *God can make it quite easy*! On *Monday* she felt all day a constant Sweetness in her Soul. She had a Repetition of the same Discoverys of *Christ* three Mornings together, that she had on *Monday* Morning, and much in the same manner, at each time waking a little before day; but brighter and brighter every time.

At the last time on *Wednesday* Morning, while in the Enjoyment of a spiritual View of *Christ*'s Glory and Fulness, her Soul was filled with Distress for Christless Persons, to consider what a miserable Condition they were in: and she felt in herself a strong Inclination immediately to go forth to warn Sinners; and proposed it the next Day to her Brother to assist her in going from house to house; but her Brother restrain'd her, by telling her of the unsuitableness of such a Method. She told one of her Sisters that Day, that she loved *all Mankind, but especially the People of God*. Her Sister asked her why she loved all Mankind? She reply'd *because God had made them*. After this there happen'd to come into the Shop where she was at work, three Persons that were thought to have been lately converted; her seeing them as they step'd in one after another into the Door, so affected her, and so drew forth her love to them, that it overcame her, and she almost fainted: And when they began to talk of the things of Religion, it was more than she could bear; they were obliged to cease on that account. It was a very frequent thing with her to be overcome with a flow of Affection to them that she thought Godly, in Conversation with them, and sometimes only at the Sight of them.

She had many extraordinary Discoveries of the Glory of God and *Christ*; sometimes, in some particular Attributes, and sometimes in many. She gave an Account, that once, as those four Words passed thro' her Mind, *WISDOM, JUSTICE, GOODNESS, and TRUTH*, her Soul was fill'd with a sense of the Glory of each of these divine Attributes, but especially the last; *Truth*, said she, *sunk the deepest*! And therefore as these Words pass'd, this was repeated, *TRUTH, TRUTH*!

Her Mind was so swallowed up with a sense of the Glory of God's *Truth* and other Perfections, that she said, *it seem'd as tho' her Life was going*, and that she *saw it was easy with God to take away* her *Life by Discoveries of himself.* Soon after this she went to a private religious Meeting, and her Mind was full of a Sense and View of the Glory of God all the Time; and when the Exercise was ended, some asked her concerning what she had experienced: and she began to give them an Account; but as she was relating it, it revived such a Sense of the same Things, that her Strength fail'd, and they were oblig'd to take her, and lay her upon the Bed. Afterwards she was greatly affected, and rejoiced with these Words, *Worthy is the Lamb that was slain.*

She had several Days together a sweet sense of the Excellency and Loveliness of *Christ* in his *Meekness*, which disposed her continually to be repeating over these Words, which were sweet to her, *MEEK AND LOWLY IN HEART, MEEK AND LOWLY IN HEART.* She once express'd her self to one of her Sisters, to this purpose, that she had continued *whole days and whole Nights*, in a constant ravishing View of the Glory of God and *Christ, having enjoy'd as much as her Life could* bear. Once as her Brother was speaking of the dying Love of *Christ*, she told him that she had such a sense of it, that the meer Mentioning it was ready to overcome her.

Once, when she came to me, she told how that at such and such a time she thought she saw as much of God, and had as much Joy and Pleasure as was possible in this Life, and that yet afterwards God discover'd himself yet far more abundantly, and she saw the same things that she had seen before, yet more clearly, and in another and far more excellent and delightful manner, and was filled with a more exceeding Sweetness; she likewise gave me such an Account of the Sense she once had, from day to day, of the Glory of *Christ*, and of God, in his various Attributes, that it seem'd to me she dwelt for Days together in a kind of *beatific Vision* of God; and seem'd to have, as I thought, as immediate an Intercourse with him, as a Child with a Father: and at the same time, she appeared most remote from any high Thought of herself, and of her own Sufficiency; but was like a *little Child*, and expressed great Desire to be instructed, telling me that she longed very often to come to me for Instruction, and wanted to live at my House, that I might tell her her Duty.

She often expressed a sense of the Glory of God appearing in the Trees, and Growth of the Fields and other Works of God's Hands. She told her Sister that lived near the Heart of the Town, that she once thought it a pleasant thing to live in the middle of the Town, *but now*, says she, *I think it much more pleasant to sit and see the Wind blowing the Trees, and to behold what God has made.* She had sometimes the powerful Breathings of the Spirit of God on her Soul, while reading the Scripture, and would express a sense that she had of the certain Truth and Divinity thereof. She sometimes would appear with a pleasant Smile on her Countenance; and once when her Sister took notice of it, and asked why she smiled, she reply'd, *I am brim-full of a sweet feeling within!* She often used to express how *good and sweet it* was *to lie low before God, and the lower* (said she) *the better!* and that it was *pleasant to think of lying in the Dust all the Days of her Life, mourning for Sin.* She was wont to manifest a great sense of her own Meanness and De-pendance. She often express'd an exceeding Compassion, and pitiful Love, which she found in her Heart towards Persons in a Christless Condition; which was sometimes so strong, that as she was passing by such in the streets, or those that she fear'd were such, she would be overcome by the Sight of them. She once said, that she *longed to have the whole World saved*, she wanted, as it were, *to pull them all* to her; she could *not bear to have one lost.*

She had great Longings to die, that she might be with *Christ*; which increased 'till she thought she did not know how to be patient to wait till God's time should come. But once when she felt those Longings, she thought with herself, *If I long to die, why do I go to Physicians?* Whence she concluded that her Longings for Death were not well regulated. After this she often put it to herself, which she should choose, whether to live or to die, to be sick, or to be well; and she found she could not tell, till at last she found herself disposed to say these Words; *I am quite willing to live, and quite willing to die; quite willing to be sick, and quite willing to be well; and quite willing for any thing that God will bring upon me! And then*, said she, *I felt my self perfectly easy*, in a full Submission to the Will of

God. She then lamented much, that she had been so eager in her Longings for Death, as it argued want of such a Resignation to God, as ought to be. She seem'd henceforward to continue in this resigned Frame till Death.

After this her Illness increased upon her: and once after she had before spent the greater Part of the Night in extreme Pain, she waked out of a little sleep with these Words in her Heart and Mouth; *I am willing to suffer for Christ's sake, I am willing to spend and be spent for Christ's sake; I am willing to spend my Life, even my very Life for Christ's sake*! And tho' she had an extraordinary Resignation, with respect to Life or Death, yet the Thoughts of Dying were exceeding sweet to her. At a time when her Brother was reading in *Job*, concerning Worms feeding on the dead Body, she appear'd with a pleasant Smile; and being enquired of about it, she said, it was sweet to her to think of *her* being in such Circumstances. At another time, when her Brother mention'd to her the Danger there seem'd to be that the Illness she then labour'd under, might be an Occasion of her Death, it fill'd her with Joy that almost overcame her. At another time, when she met a Company following a Corpse to the Grave, she said, it was sweet to her to think, that they would in a little time follow her in like manner.

Her Illness in the latter part of it was seated much in her Throat; and swelling inward, fill'd up the Pipe, so that she could swallow nothing but what was perfectly liquid, and but very little of that, and with great and long Strugglings and Stranglings, that which she took in, flying out at her Nostrils, till she at last could swallow nothing at all: She had a raging Appetite to Food, so that she told her Sister, when talking with her about her Circumstances, that the worst Bit that she threw to her Swine, would be sweet to her: but yet when she saw that she could not swallow it, she seem'd to be as perfectly contented without it, as if she had no Appetite to it. Others were greatly moved to see what she underwent, and were fill'd with Admiration at her unexampled Patience. At a Time when she was striving in vain to get down a little Food, something liquid, and was very much spent with it; she look'd up on her Sister with a Smile, saying, *O Sister, this is for my Good*! At another time, when her Sister was speaking of what she underwent, she told her, that she *liv'd an Heaven upon Earth for all that*. She used sometimes to say to her Sister, under her extreme Sufferings, *It is good to be so*! Her Sister once asked her, why she said so, *why*, says she, *because God would have it so: It is best that things should be as God would have 'em: It looks best to me*. After her Confinement, as they were leading her from the Bed to the Door, she seem'd overcome by the Sight of things abroad, as shewing forth the Glory of the Being that had made them. As she lay on her Death-bed, she would often say these Words, *God is my Friend*! And once looking up on her Sister, with a Smile, said *O Sister! How good it is! How sweet and comfortable it is to consider, and think of heavenly things*! and used this Argument to persuade her Sister to be much in such Meditations.

She express'd on her Death Bed, an exceeding Longing, *both for Persons in a natural State, that they might be converted, and for the Godly that they might see and know more of God*. And when those that looked on themselves as in a Christless State came to see her, she would be greatly moved with compassionate Affection. One in particular that seem'd to be in a great distress about the State of her Soul, and had come to see her from time to time, she desired her Sister to persuade not to come any more, because the Sight of her so wrought on her Compassions, that it overcame her Nature. The same Week that she died, when she was in distressing Circumstances as to her Body, some of the Neighbours that came to see her, asked if she was willing to die? She reply'd, that she was *quite willing either to live or die; she was willing to be in pain; she was willing to be so always as she was then, if that was the Will of God*. She *willed what God willed*. They asked her whether she was willing to die that Night? She answer'd, *Yes, if it be God's Will*. And seem'd to speak all with that perfect composure of Spirit, and with such a chearful and pleasant Countenance, that it filled them with Admiration.

She was very weak a considerable time before she died, having pined away with Famine and Thirst, so that her Flesh seem'd to be dried upon her Bones; and therefore could say but little, and manifested her Mind very much by Signs. She said she had *Matter enough* to fill up *all her Time with Talk, if* she *had but Strength*. A few Days before her Death, some asked her, whether she *held* her *Integrity still*? Whether she was *not afraid of Death*? She answered to this purpose, that she had not the least Degree of fear of Death. They asked her *why* she would *be so confident?* She answered, *If I should say otherwise, I should speak contrary to what I know: there is,* says she, *indeed, a dark Entry that looks something dark, but on the other Side there appears such a bright shining Light, that I cannot be afraid!* She said not long before she died, that she *used to be afraid how* she *should grapple with Death; but,* says she, *God has shewed me that he can make it easy in great Pain.* Several Days before she died, she could scarcely say any thing but just *yes,* and *no,* to Questions that were asked her, for she seem'd to be dying for three Days together; but seem'd to continue in an admirable sweet Composure of Soul, without any Interruption, to the last, and died as a Person that went to sleep, without any struggling, about Noon, on *Friday, June* 27. 1735.

She had long been infirm, and often had been exercised with great Pain; but she died chiefly of Famine. It was, doubtless, partly owing to her bodily Weakness, that her Nature was so often overcome, and ready to sink with gracious Affection; but yet the truth was, that she had more Grace, and greater Discoveries of God and *Christ,* than the present frail State did well consist with. She wanted to be where strong Grace might have more Liberty, and be without the Clog of a weak Body; there she longed to be, and there she doubtless now is. She was looked upon amongst us, as a very eminent Instance of Christian Experience: but this is but a very broken and imperfect Account I have given of her; Her Eminency would much more appear, if her Experiences were fully related, as she was wont to express, and manifest them, while living. I once read this Account to some of her pious Neighbours, who were acquainted with her, who said, to this purpose, that the *Picture* fell much short of the *Life;* and particularly that it much fail'd of duly representing her Humility, and that admirable Lowliness of Heart, that at all times appeared in her. But there are (blessed be God!) many living Instances, of much the like nature, and in some Things no less extraordinary.

But I now proceed to the *other Instance* that I would give an Account of, which is of the *little Child* foremention'd. Her Name is *Phebe Bartlet,* Daughter of *William Bartlet.* I shall give the Account as I took it from the Mouths of her Parents, whose Veracity none that know them doubt of.

She was born in *March*, in the year 1731. About the latter
end of *April*, or beginning of *May*, 1735, she was greatly affected by the talk of her Brother, who had been hopefully
converted a little before, at about eleven years of Age, and
then seriously talked to her about the great Things of Religion.
Her Parents did not know of it at that time, and were not
wont, in the Counsels they gave to their Children, particularly
to direct themselves to her, by reason of her being so young,
and as they supposed not capable of Understanding: but after
her Brother had talked to her, they observed her very earnestly
to listen to the Advice they gave to the other Children; and she
was observed very constantly to retire, several times in a Day,
as was concluded, for secret Prayer; and grew more and more
engaged in Religion, and was more frequent in her Closet; till
at last she was wont to visit it five or six times in a Day: and was
so engaged in it, that nothing would at any Time divert her
from her stated Closet Exercises. Her Mother often observed
and watched her, when such Things occurr'd, as she thought
most likely to divert her, either by putting it out of her
Thoughts, or otherwise engaging her Inclinations; but never
could observe her to fail. She mention'd some very remarkable
Instances.

She once of her own accord spake of her Unsuccessfulness,
in that she could not find God, or to that purpose. But on
Thursday, the last Day of *July*, about the middle of the Day,
the Child being in the Closet, where it used to retire, its
Mother heard it speaking aloud; which was unusual, and never
had been observed before: And her Voice seemed to be as of
one exceeding importunate and engaged; but her Mother
could distinctly here only these Words, (spoken in her childish
Manner, but seemed to be spoken with extraordinary earnestness, and out of Distress of Soul,) *PRAY BLESSED LORD
give me Salvation! I PRAY BEG pardon all my Sins!* When the
Child had done Prayer she came out of the Closet, and came
and sat down by her Mother, and cried out aloud. Her Mother
very earnestly asked her several times, what the matter was,
before she would make any Answer; but she continued exceedingly crying, and wreathing her Body to and fro, like one in
anguish of Spirit. Her Mother then asked her, whether she was
afraid that God would not give her Salvation. She answered

yes, I am afraid I shall go to Hell! Her Mother then endeavoured to quiet her, and told her she *would not have* her *cry*, she *must be a good Girl, and pray every Day, and* she *hoped God would give her Salvation*. But this did not quiet her at all; but she continued thus earnestly crying, and taking on for some time, till at length she suddenly ceased crying, and began to smile, and presently said with a smiling Countenance, *Mother, the Kingdom of Heaven is come to me*! Her Mother was surprized at the sudden Alteration, and at the Speech; and knew not what to make of it, but at first said nothing to her. The Child presently spake again, and said, *there is another come to me, and there is another, there is three;* and being asked what she meant, she answered *one is, Thy will be done, and there is another, Enjoy him for ever*; by which it seems that when the Child said *there is three come to me*, she meant three Passages of its Catechism that came to her Mind.

After the Child had said this, she retired again into her Closet; and her Mother went over to her Brother's, who was next Neighbour; and when she came back, the Child, being come out of the Closet, meets her Mother with this chearful Speech, *I can find God now*! referring to what she had before complain'd of that she could not find God. Then the Child spoke again and said, *I love God*! Her Mother asked her, *how well* she loved God, whether she loved God *better than her Father and Mother*, she said *yes*. Then she asked her whether she loved God *better than her little Sister* Rachel? She answered *yes, better than any thing*! Then her eldest Sister, referring to her saying she could *find God now*, asked her where she could *find God*. She answered *in Heaven: Why*, said she, *have you been in Heaven? No*, said the Child. By this it seems not to have been any Imagination of any thing seen with bodily Eyes, that she called God, when she said I can find God now. Her Mother asked her whether she was *afraid of going to Hell*, and that had made her cry. She answered, *yes, I was; but now I shan't*. Her Mother asked her whether she thought that God had given her Salvation; She answered, *yes*. Her Mother asked her, *when*. She answered, *to day*. She appeared all that Afternoon exceeding chearful and joyful. One of the Neighbours asked her, how she felt her self? She answer'd, *I feel better than I did*. The Neighbour asked her, what made her feel better. She answered,

God makes me. That Evening as she lay a-bed, she called one of her little Cousins to her that was present in the Room, as having something to say to him; and when he came, she told him, that *Heaven* was *better than Earth*. The next Day being *Friday*, her Mother asking her her Catechism, asked her *what God made* her *for*: She answered *to serve him*, and added, *every body should serve God, and get an Interest in Christ*.

The same Day the elder Children, when they came home from School, seemed much affected with the extraordinary Change that seemed to be made in *Phebe*: And her Sister *Abigail* standing by, her Mother took occasion to counsel her, now to improve her Time, to prepare for another World: On which *Phebe* burst out in Tears, and cried out *Poor Nabby*! Her Mother told her she would not have her cry, she hoped that God would give *Nabby* Salvation; but that did not quiet her, but she continued earnestly crying for some time; and when she had in a measure ceased, her Sister *Eunice* being by her, she burst out again, and cried *Poor Eunice*! and cried exceedingly; and when she had almost done she went into another Room, and there looked up on her Sister *Naomi*: and burst out again, crying *Poor Amy*! Her Mother was greatly affected at such a Behaviour in the Child, and knew not what to say to her. One of the Neighbours coming in a little after, asked her what she had cried for. She seemed at first backward to tell the Reason; her Mother told her she might tell that Person, for he *had given* her *an Apple*: Upon which she said, she *cried because* she *was afraid they would go to Hell*.

At Night a certain Minister, that was occasionally in the Town, was at the House, and talked considerable with her, of the Things of Religion; and after he was gone she sat leaning on the Table, with Tears running out of her Eyes: And being asked what made her cry, she said it was *thinking about God*. The next Day, being *Saturday*, she seemed great part of the Day to be in a very affectionate Frame, had four turns of Crying, and seemed to endeavour to curb her self, and hide her Tears, and was very backward to talk of the occasion of it. On the *Sabbath* Day she was asked whether she believed in God; she answered *yes*: And being told that Christ was the Son of God, she made ready Answer, and said, *I know it*.

From this Time there has appeared a very remarkable abiding Change in the Child: She has been very strict upon the Sabbath; and seems to long for the Sabbath Day before it comes, and will often in the Week time be enquiring how long it is to the Sabbath Day, and must have the Days particularly counted over that are between, before she will be contented. And she seems to love God's House, is very eager to go thither: Her Mother once asked her why she had such a mind to go? whether it was not to see fine Folks? She said *no, it* was *to hear Mr* Edwards *preach.* When she is in the place of Worship, she is very far from spending her Time there as Children at her Age usually do, but appears with an Attention that is very extraordinary for such a Child. She also appears very desirous at all Opportunities to go to private religious Meetings; and is very still and attentive at Home, in Prayer time, and has appeared affected in time of Family Prayer. She seems to delight much in hearing religious Conversation: When I once was there with some others that were Strangers, and talked to her something of Religion, she seemed more than ordinarily attentive; and when we were gone, she looked out very wistly after us, and said, *I wish they would come again!* Her Mother asked her *why*: Says she, *I love to hear 'em talk!*

She seems to have very much of the Fear of God before her Eyes, and an extraordinary Dread of Sin against him; of which her Mother mention'd the following remarkable Instance. Some time in *August*, the last Year, she went with some bigger Children, to get some Plumbs, in a Neighbour's Lot, knowing nothing of any harm in what she did; but when she brought some of the Plumbs into the House, her Mother mildly reproved her, and told her that she *must not get Plumbs without leave, because it was Sin:* God had *commanded* her *not to steal.* The Child seemed greatly surprized, and burst out in Tears, and cryed out, *I won't have these Plumbs!* and turning to her Sister *Eunice*, very earnestly said to her *why did you ask me to go to that Plumb Tree? I should not have gone if you had not asked me.* The other Children did not seem to be much affected or concerned; but there was no pacifying *Phebe*. Her Mother told her she might go and ask leave, and then it would not be sin for her to eat them; and sent one of the Children to that end; and when she returned, her Mother told her that the Owner had given leave, now she might eat them, and it would not be

stealing. This still'd her a little while; but presently she broke
out again into an exceeding Fit of Crying: Her Mother asked
her *what* made her *cry again? Why* she cryed *now, since* they
had asked *leave? What* it was that troubled her now? And asked
her several times very earnestly, before she made any Answer;
but at last said, *it was BECAUSE IT WAS SIN.* She continued
a considerable time crying; and said she would not *go again if
Eunice* asked her *an hundred Times*; and she retain'd her Aversion to that Fruit for a considerable time, under the remembrance of her former Sin.

She at some times appears greatly affected, and delighted
with Texts of Scripture that come to her mind. Particularly,
about the beginning of *November*, the last Year, that Text came
to her mind, *Rev.* iii. 20. *Behold, I stand at the Door and knock:
If any Man hear my Voice, and open the Door, I will come in,
and sup with him, and he with me.* She spoke of it to those of
the Family, with a great appearance of Joy, a smiling Countenance, & Elevation of Voice, and afterwards she went into another Room, where her Mother overheard her talking very
earnestly to the Children about it, and particularly heard her
say to them, three or four times over, with an air of exceeding
Joy and Admiration, *Why it is to SUP WITH GOD.* At some
time about the middle of Winter, very late in the Night, when
all were a bed, her Mother perceived that she was awake, and
heard her, as tho' she was weeping. She called to her, and
asked her what was the matter. She answered with a low Voice,
so that her Mother could not hear what she said; but thinking
that it might be occasion'd by some spiritual Affection, said no
more to her; but perceived her to lie awake, and to continue in
the same Frame, for a considerable time. The next Morning,
she asked her whether she did not cry the last Night: The
Child answered *yes, I did cry a little, for I was thinking about
God and Christ, and they loved me.* Her Mother asked her
whether *to think of God and Christ's loving* her *made* her *cry*:
She answered *yes, it does sometimes.*

She has often manifested a great Concern for the good of
others Souls: and has been wont many times affectionately to
counsel the other Children. Once about the latter end of *September*, the last Year, when she and some others of the Children
were in a Room by themselves, a husking *Indian* Corn, the

Child, after a while, came out and sat by the Fire. Her Mother took notice that she appeared with a more than ordinary serious and pensive Countenance, but at last she broke silence, and said, I have been talking to *Nabby* and *Eunice*: Her Mother asked her what she had said to 'em. Why said she, I *told 'em they must pray, and prepare to die*, that they had *but a little while to live in this World, and* they *must be always ready*. When *Nabby* came out, her Mother asked her whether she had said that to them. *Yes* said she, *she said that, and a great deal more.* At other times, the Child took her Opportunities to talk to the other Children about the great Concern of their Souls, sometimes, so as much to affect them, and set them into Tears. She was once exceeding importunate with her Mother to go with her Sister *Naomi* to pray: Her Mother endeavoured to put her off; but she pulled her by the Sleeve, and seem'd as if she would by no means be denied. At last her Mother told her, that *Amy must go and pray her self; but*, says the Child, *she will not go*; and persisted earnestly to beg of her Mother to go with her.

She has discover'd an uncommon Degree of a Spirit of Charity; particularly on the following Occasion: A poor Man that lives in the Woods, had lately lost a Cow that the Family much depended on, and being at the House, he was relating his Misfortune, and telling of the Straits and Difficulties they were reduced to by it. She took much notice of it, and it wrought exceedingly on her Compassions: And after she had attentively heard him a while, she went away to her Father, who was in the Shop, and intreated him to give that Man a Cow: and told him that *the poor Man* had *no Cow!* that *the Hunters or something else* had *kill'd his Cow!* and entreated him to give him one of theirs. Her Father told her that they could not spare one. Then she entreated him to let him and his Family come and live at his House: And had much more talk of the same nature, whereby she manifested Bowels of Compassion to the Poor.

She has manifested great Love to her Minister: Particularly when I return'd from my long Journey for my Health, the last *Fall*, when she heard of it, she appear'd very joyful at the News, and told the Children of it, with an elevated Voice, as the most joyful Tidings, repeating it over and over, *Mr.* Edwards *is come home! Mr.* Edwards *is come home!* She still continues very constant in secret Prayer, so far as can be observed, (for she seems to have no Desire that others should observe her when she retires, but seems to be a Child of a reserved Temper) and every Night, before she goes to Bed, will say her Catechism, and will by no means miss of it: she never forgot it but once, and then after she was a bed, thought of it, and cryed out in Tears, *I han't said my Catechism!* and would not be quieted till her Mother asked her the Catechism as she lay in Bed. She sometimes appears to be in doubt about the Condition of her Soul, and when asked whether she thinks that she is prepared for Death, speaks something doubtfully about it: At other times seems to have no doubt, but when asked replies *yes* without hesitation.

In the former part of this great Work of God amongst us, till it got to its height, we seemed to be wonderfully smiled upon and blessed in all respects. *Satan* (as has been already observed,) seemed to be unusually restrain'd: Persons that before had been involved in Melancholy, seemed to be as it were waked up out of it; and those that had been entangled with extraordinary Temptations, seemed wonderfully to be set at liberty; and not only so, but it was the most remarkable time of Health, that ever I knew since I have been in the Town. We ordinarily have several Bills put up, every Sabbath, for Persons that are sick; but now we had not so much as one for many Sabbaths together. But after this it seemed to be otherwise, when this Work of God appear'd to be at its greatest Height, a poor weak Man that belongs to the Town, being in great spiritual Trouble, was hurried with violent Temptations to cut his own Throat, and made an Attempt; but did not do it effectually. He after this continued a considerable Time exceeding overwhelmed with Melancholy; but has now of a long time been very greatly deliver'd, by the Light of God's Countenance lifted up upon him, and has expressed a great Sense of his Sin in so far yielding to Temptation; and there are in him all hopeful Evidences of his having been made a Subject of saving Mercy.

In the latter part of *May*, it began to be very sensible that the Spirit of God was gradually withdrawing from us, and after this Time *Satan* seemed to be more let loose, and raged in a dreadful manner. The first Instance wherein it appear'd, was a Person's putting an end to his own Life, by cutting his Throat. He was a Gentleman of more than common Understanding, of strict Morals, religious in his Behaviour, and an useful honourable Person in the Town; but was of a Family that are exceeding prone to the Disease of Melancholy, and his Mother was killed with it. He had, from the beginning of this extraordinary Time, been exceedingly concern'd about the State of his Soul, and there were some Things in his Experience, that appeared very hopefully; but he durst entertain no Hope concerning his own good Estate. Towards the latter part of his Time, he grew much discouraged, and Melancholy grew amain upon him, till he was wholly overpower'd by it, and was in great measure past a Capacity of receiving Advice, or being reasoned with to any purpose: The Devil took the advantage, and drove him into despairing Thoughts. He was kept awake a-nights, meditating Terror; so that he had scarce any Sleep at all, for a long time together. And it was observed at last, that he was scarcely well capable of managing his ordinary Business, and was judged delirious by the Coroner's Inquest. The News of this extraordinarily affected the Minds of People here, and struck them as it were with Astonishment. After this, Multitudes in this, and other Towns, seemed to have it strongly suggested to 'em, and pressed upon 'em, to do as this Person had done. And many that seemed to be under no Melancholy, some pious Persons, that had no special Darkness, or Doubts about the goodness of their State, nor were under any special Trouble or Concern of Mind about any thing Spiritual or Temporal, yet had it urged upon 'em, as if somebody had spoke to 'em, *Cut your own Throat, now is a good Opportunity.* Now; now! So that they were oblig'd to fight with all their might to resist it, and yet no Reason suggested to 'em why they should do it.

About the same time, there were two remarkable Instances of Persons led away with strange Enthusiastick Delusions: one at *Suffield*, another at *South-Hadley*: That which has made the greatest noise in the Country was of the Man at *South-Hadley*, whose Delusion was, that he thought himself divinely instructed to direct a poor Man in melancholy and despairing

Circumstances, to say certain Words in Prayer to God, as recorded in *Psal.* cxvi. 4. for his own Relief. The Man is esteemed a pious Man: I have since this Error of his, had a particular Acquaintance with him; and I believe none would question his Piety, that had had such an Acquaintance. He gave me a particular Account of the Manner how he was deluded; which is too long to be here inserted. But in short, he was exceedingly rejoiced and elevated with this extraordinary Work, so carried on in this part of the Country; and was possessed with an Opinion that it was the beginning of the glorious Times of the Church spoken of in Scripture: And had read it as the Opinion of some Divines, that there would be many in these Times that should be endued with extraordinary Gifts of the Holy Ghost, and had embraced the Notion; tho' he had at first no Apprehensions that any besides Ministers would have such Gifts. But he since exceedingly laments the Dishonour he has done to God, and the Wound he has given Religion in it, and has lain low before God and Man for it.

After these things the Instances of Conversion were rare here in comparison of what they had before been, (tho' that remarkable Instance of the little Child was after this,) and the Spirit of God not long after this time, appear'd very sensibly withdrawing from all parts of the County; (tho' we have heard of its going on in some Places of *Connecticut*, and that it continues to be carried on even to this Day.) But Religion remain'd here, and I believe in some other Places, the main Subject of Conversation, for several Months after this. And there were some Turns, wherein God's Work seem'd something to revive, and we were ready to hope that all was going to be renewed again: yet in the main there was a gradual Decline of that general, engaged, lively Spirit in Religion, which had been before. Several things have happen'd since, that have diverted Peoples Minds, and turn'd their Conversation more to others Affairs, particularly his *Excellency* the Governour's coming up, and the *Committee* of *General Court*, on the Treaty with the *Indians*; and afterwards the *Springfield* Controversy; and since that, our People in this Town have been engaged in the building of a new Meeting-house: and some other Occurrences might be mentioned, that have seem'd to have this Effect. But as to those that have been thought to be converted among us, in this time, they generally seem to be Persons, that have had an abiding Change wrought on them: I have had particular acquaintance with many of them since, and they generally appear to be Persons that have a new Sense of Things, new Apprehensions and Views of God, of the divine Attributes, and *Jesus Christ*, and the great Things of the Gospel: They have a new Sense of the Truth of them, and they affect them in a new manner; tho' it is very far from being always alike with them, neither can they revive a Sense of things when they please. Their Hearts are often touched, and sometimes fill'd, with new Sweetnesses and Delights; there seems to be an inward Ardour and burning of Heart that they express, the like to which they never experienced before; sometimes, perhaps, occasioned only by the Mention of *Christ's* Name, or some one of the Divine Perfections: There are new Appetites, and a new kind of Breathings and Pantings of Heart, *and Groanings that cannot be uttered*. There is a new kind of inward Labour and Struggle of Soul towards Heaven and Holiness.

Some that before were very rough in their Temper and Manners, seem to be remarkably softned and sweeten'd. And some have had their Souls exceedingly filled, and overwhelmed with Light, Love, and Comfort, long since the Work of God has ceased to be so remarkably carried on in a general way: and some have had much greater Experiences of this nature than they had before. And there is still a great deal of religious Conversation continued in the Town, amongst young and old; a religious Disposition appears to be still maintain'd amongst our People, by their upholding frequent private religious Meetings; and all Sorts are generally worshipping God at such Meetings, on *Sabbath* Nights, and in the Evening after our publick Lecture. Many Children in the Town do still keep up such Meetings among themselves. I know of no one young Person in the Town that has returned to former ways of Looseness and Extravagancy in any respect; but we still remain a reformed People, and God has evidently made us a new People.

I can't say that there has been no Instance of any one Person that has carried himself so, that others should justly be stumbled concerning his Profession; nor am I so vain as to imagine that we han't been mistaken concerning any that we have entertain'd a good Opinion of, or that there are none pass amongst us for Sheep, that are indeed, Wolves in Sheep's cloathing; who probably may some time or other discover themselves by their Fruit. We are not so *pure*, but that we have great Cause to be humbled and asham'd, that we are so *impure*; nor so religious, but that those that watch for our Halting, may see things in us, whence they may take occasion to reproach us and Religion: but in the main, there has been a great and marvellous Work of Conversion and Sanctification among the People here; and they have paid all due Respects to those who have been blest of God to be the Instruments of it. Both old and young have shewn a Forwardness to hearken not only to my Counsels, but even to my Reproofs from the Pulpit.

A great part of the Country have not received the most favourable Thoughts of this Affair; and to this day many retain a Jealousy concerning it, and Prejudice against it: I have Reason to think that the meanness and weakness of the Instrument, that has been made use of in this Town, has prejudiced many against it; it don't appear to me strange that it should be so: But yet this Circumstance of this great Work of God, is analogous to other Circumstances of it: God has so ordered the manner of the Work in many Respects, as very signally and remarkably to shew it to be his own peculiar and immediate Work, and to secure the Glory of it wholly to his own Almighty Power, and Sovereign Grace. And whatever the Circumstances and Means have been, and tho' we are so unworthy, yet *so* hath it pleased God to work! And we are evidently a People blessed of the Lord! And here, *in this Corner of the World*, God dwells, and manifests his Glory.

Thus, *Rev. Sir*, I have given a *large* and *particular* Account of this remarkable Affair; and yet, considering how manifold God's Works have been amongst us, that are worthy to be written, 'tis but a very *brief* one. I should have sent it much sooner, had I not been greatly hindered by Illness in my Family, and also in myself. It is probably, much larger than you *expected*, and it may be than you *would have chosen*. I thought that the Extraordinariness of the Thing, and the innumerable Misrepresentations which have gone abroad of it, many of which have, doubtless, reached your Ears, made it necessary that I should be particular. But I would leave it entirely with your Wisdom to make what use of it you think best, to send a part of it to *England*, or all, or none if you think it not worthy; or otherwise to dispose of it as you may think most for God's Glory, and the Interest of Religion. If you are pleased to send any thing to the Revd. Dr. *Guyse*, I should be glad to have it signify'd to him as my humble Desire, that since he, and the Congregation to which he preach'd have been pleased to take so much notice of us, as they have, that they would also think of us at the Throne of Grace, and seek there for us, that God would not forsake us, but enable us to bring forth Fruit an-swerable to our Profession, and our Mercies, and that our *Light may shine before Men, that others seeing our good Works, may glorify* our *Father which is in Heaven.*

When I first heard of the Notice the Revd. Dr. *Watts* and Dr. *Guyse* took of God's Mercies to us, I took occasion to in-form our Congregation of it in a Discourse from these Words; *A City that is set upon an Hill cannot be hid.* And having since seen a particular Account of the Notice the Revd Dr. *Guyse*, and the Congregation he preached to, took of it, in a Letter you wrote to my Honoured Uncle *Williams*, I read that part of your Letter to the Congregation, and labour'd as much as in me lay to enforce their Duty from it. The Congregation were very sensibly moved and affected at both times.

I humbly request of you, *Rev Sir*, your Prayers, for *this County*, in its present melancholy Circumstances, into which it is brought by the *Springfield* Quarrel, which, doubtless, above all things that have happen'd, has tended to put a Stop to the glorious Work here, and to prejudice this Country against it, and hinder the Propagation of it. I also ask your Prayers for *this Town*, and would particularly beg an Interest in them for *him* who is,

> Honoured Sir,
> With humble Respect,
> Your Obedient Son and Servant,

Northampton, Nov. 6. 1736.

> *Jonathan Edwards*

THE
Diftinguifhing Marks

Of a Work of the

SPIRIT of GOD.

Applied to that uncommon Operation that has lately appeared on the Minds of many of the People of this Land :

With a particular Confideration of the extraordinary Circumftances with which this Work is attended.

A DISCOURSE

Delivered at *New-Haven*, *September* 10th 1741. Being the Day after the Commencement;

And now Publifhed at the earneft Defire of many Minifters and other Gentlemen that heard it; with great Enlargements.

By *Jonathan Edwards*, A. M.
Paftor of the Church of CHRIST at *Northampton*.

With a Preface by the Rev. Mr. COOPER of *Boston*.

JOHN 10. 4. 5 *And the Sheep follow him, for they know his Voice; and a Stranger will they not follow, but will flee from him, for they know not the Voice of Strangers.*

BOSTON: Printed and Sold by S. KNEELAND and T. GREEN, in Queenftreet, over againft the Prifon. 1741.

TO THE READER

THERE are several Dispensations, or Days of Grace, which the Church of God has been under from the beginning of Time. There is that under the ancient *Patriarchs*; that under the Law of *Moses*; and there is that of the *Gospel* of Jesus Christ, under which we now are. This is the brightest Day that ever shone, and exceeds the other for peculiar Advantages. To us who are so happy as to live under the *Evangelical Dispensation*, may those Words of our Saviour be directed, which he spake to his Disciples, when he was first setting up the *Messiah's* Kingdom in the World, and Gospel Light and Power began to spread abroad; *Blessed are the Eyes which see the Things that ye see. For I tell you, that many Prophets and Kings, have desired to see those Things which ye see, and have not seen them; and to hear those Things which ye hear, and have not heard them.**

The *Mosaic* Dispensation, tho' darkned with Types and Figures, yet far exceeded the former: But the Gospel Dispensation so much exceeds in Glory, that it doth eclipse the Glory of the Legal, as the Stars disappear when the Sun ariseth, and goeth forth in his Strength—And the chief Thing that renders the Gospel so glorious is, that it is *the Ministration of the* SPIRIT. Under the preaching of it the Holy Spirit was to be poured out in more plentiful Measures; not only in miraculous Gifts, as in the first Times of the Gospel; but in his internal saving Operations, accompanying the outward Ministry, to produce numerous Conversions to Christ, and give spiritual Life to Souls that were before dead in Trespasses and Sins, and so prepare them for Life eternal. Thus the *Apostle* speaks, when he runs a Comparison between the *old* Testament and the *new*, the Law of *Moses*, and the Gospel of *Jesus Christ*; *For the Letter killeth, but the Spirit giveth Life. But if the Ministration of Death, written and engraven in Stones was glorious, so that the Children of Israel could not stedfastly behold the Face of Moses, for the Glory of his Countenance, which Glory was to be done away; how shall not the Ministration of the Spirit be rather glorious?*†

*Luke 10. 23, 24.
†2 Cor. 3. 6, 7, 8.

This blessed Time of the Gospel, hath several other Denominations, which may raise our Esteem and Value for it. It is called by the evangelical Prophet,* *The acceptable Year of the Lord*. Or, as it may be read, the Year *of Liking*, or *of Benevolence*, or of *the good Will of the Lord*; because it would be the special Period in which he would display his Grace and Favour in an extraordinary Manner, and deal out spiritual Blessings with a full and liberal Hand.— It is also stiled by our Saviour, *The Regeneration*;† which may refer not only to that glorious Restitution of all Things, which is look'd for at the Close of the Christian Dispensation, but to the renewing Work of Grace in particular Souls, carried on from the Beginning to the End of it.

But few were renewed and sanctified under the former Dispensations, compared with the Instances of the Grace of God in Gospel Times. Such Numbers were bro't into the Gospel Church when it was first set up, as to give Occasion for that pleasing admiring Question, which was indeed a Prophecy of it,‡ *Who are these that fly as a Cloud? And as the Doves to their Windows? Then* the Power of the divine Spirit so accompanied the Ministry of the Word, as that *Thousands* were converted under one Sermon.—But notwithstanding this large Effusion of the Spirit, when Gospel Light first dawn'd upon the World, and that pleasant Spring of Religion which then appear'd on the Face of the Earth, there was a gradual Withdraw of his saving Light and Influences, and so the Gospel came to be less sucessful, and the State of Christianity withered in one Place and another.

Indeed at the Time of the Reformation from *Popery*, when Gospel Light broke in upon the Church, and dispell'd the Clouds of Antichristian Darkness that cover'd it, the Power of divine Grace so accompanied the Preaching of the Word, as that it had admirable Success in the Conversion and Edification of Souls, and the blessed Fruits thereof appear'd in the Hearts & Lives of it's Professors. That was one *of the Days of the Son of Man*, on which the exalted Redeemer, rode forth in his Glory & Majesty, on the *white Horse* of the pure Gospel,

*Isai. 61. 2.
†Matt. 19. 28.
‡Isai. 60. 8.

conquering and to conquer; and the Bow in his Hand, like that of *Jonathan's, returned not empty*.—

But what a dead and barren Time has it now been, for a great while, with all the Churches of the Reformation? The golden Showers have been restrain'd; the Influences of the Spirit suspended; and the Consequence has been, that the Gospel has not had any eminent Success: Conversions have been rare and dubious; few Sons & Daughters have been born to God; and the Hearts of Christians not so quickned, warm'd & refresh'd under the Ordinances, as they have been.

That this has been the sad State of Religion among us in this Land for many Years, (except one or two distinguish'd Places, who have at Times been visited with a Shower of Mercy, while other Towns and Churches have not been rained upon) will be acknowleg'd by all who have *spiritual Senses exercis'd*, as it has been lamented by faithful Ministers, and serious Christians. Accordingly it has been a constant Petition in our publick Prayers from Sabbath to Sabbath, "That God *would pour out his Spirit upon us, and revive his Work in the midst of the Years*". And besides our annual Fast-Days appointed by the Government, most of our Churches have set apart Days, wherein to seek the Lord by Prayer and Fasting, that he would *come and rain down Righteousness upon us.*

And now,—Behold! The Lord whom we have sought, has *suddenly come to his Temple*. The Dispensation of Grace we are now under, is certainly such as neither we nor our Fathers have seen; and in some Circumstances so wonderful, that I believe there has not been the like since the extraordinary pouring out of the Spirit immediately after our Lord's Ascension. The *Apostolical Times* seem to have return'd upon us: Such a Display has there been of the Power & Grace of the divine Spirit in the Assemblies of his People, & such Testimonies has he given to the Word of the Gospel.—

I remember a remarkable Passage of the late Reverend & Learned Mr. *How*, which I think it may be worth while to transcribe here. It is in his Discourse concerning *the prosperous State of the Christian Church before the End of Time, by a plentiful Effusion of the Holy Spirit, P. 80. "In such a Time*, says he, *when the Spirit shall be poured forth plentifully, sure Ministers shall have their proportionable Share. And when such a Time as*

that shall come, I believe you will hear much other Kind of Ser-
mons, (or they will who shall live to such a Time) than you are won't
to do now a Days: Souls will surely be dealt withal at another Kind
of Rate. It is plain, says He, *too sadly plain, There is a great Retrac-*
tion of the Spirit of God even from Us: We know not how to speak
living Sense into Souls; how to get within you: Our Words die in our
Mouths, or drop & die between you and us. We even faint when we
speak; long experienced Unsuccessfulness makes us despond: We speak
not as Persons that hope to prevail, that expect to make you serious,
heavenly, mindful of God, and to walk more like Christians. The
Methods of alluring & convincing Souls, even that some of us have
known, are lost from amongst us in a great Part. There have been
other Ways taken, than we can tell now how to fall upon, for the
mollifying of the Obdurate, and the awakening of the Secure, and
the convincing & perswading of the Obstinate, and the winning of
the Disaffected. Sure there will be a large Share, that will come
even to the Part of Ministers, when such an Effusion of the Spirit
shall be, as is expected: That they shall know how to speak to better
Purpose, with more Compassion, with more Seriousness, with more
Authority and Allurement, than we now find we can." Thus He.

Agreable to the just Expectation of this great and excellent
Man, we have found it in this remarkable Day. A number of
Preachers have appear'd among us, to whom God has given
such a large Measure of his Spirit, that we are ready sometimes
to apply to them the Character given of *Barnabas,** That *he*
was a good Man, and full of the Holy Ghost, and of Faith. They
preach the Gospel of the Grace of God from Place to Place,
with uncommon Zeal and Assiduity.—The *Doctrines* they insist on, are the Doctrines of the Reformation, under the Influence whereof the Power of Godliness so flourish'd in the last
Century. The Points on which their Preaching mainly turns,
are those important ones, of *Man's Guilt, Corruption, & Impo-*
tence; Super-natural Regeneration by the Spirit of God, and *free*
Justification by Faith in the Righteousness of Christ; and the
Marks of the new Birth.—The *Manner* of their preaching is not
with the enticing Words of Man's Wisdom: *Howbeit, they speak*
Wisdom among them that are perfect. An ardent Love to Christ
& Souls, warms their Breasts, and animates their Labours. God

*Acts II. 24.

has made these *his Ministers* active *Spirits, a Flame of Fire* in his Service: And his *Word* in their Mouths has been as *a Fire; and as a Hammer that breaketh the Rock in Pieces.* In most Places where they have labour'd, God has evidently wrought with them, and *confirm'd the Word by Signs following.* Such a Power & Presence of God in religious Assemblies, has not been known since God set up his Sanctuary amongst us: He has indeed *glorified the House of his Glory.*

This Work is truly extraordinary in Respect of the *Extent* of it. It is more or less in the several Provinces that measure many hundred Miles on this Continent. *He sendeth forth his Commandment upon Earth; his Word runneth very swiftly.* It has entred & spread in some of the most *populous Towns,* the chief Places of Concourse & Business. And,—Blessed be God! — It has visited the *Seats of Learning,* both here, and in a neighbouring Colony. O may the Holy Spirit constantly reside in them both, seize our devoted Youth, & form them *as polish'd Shafts* successfully to fight the Lord's Battles against the Powers of Darkness, when they shall be call'd out to Service!

It is extraordinary also with Respect to the *Numbers* that have been the Subjects of this Operation. Stupid Sinners have been awak'ned by *Hundreds*; And the Inquiry has been general in some Places, *What must I do to be saved?* I verily believe in this our *Metropolis,* there were the last Winter *some Thousands* under such religious Impressions as they never felt before.

The Work has been remarkable also for the *various Sorts of Persons* that have been under the Influence of it.— These have been of all *Ages.* Some *elderly* Persons have been snatch'd as Brands out of the burning, made Monuments of divine Mercy, & born to God, tho' out of due Time; as the *Apostle* speaks in his own Case.* But here with us it has lain mostly amongst the *Young.* Sprightly Youth have been made to bow like Willows to the Redeemer's Sceptre, & willingly to subscribe with their own Hands to the Lord. And out of the Mouths of *Babes,* some little Children, has God ordain'd to himself Praise, to still the Enemy and the Avenger.— Of all *Ranks & Degrees.* Some of the *great & rich*; but more of the *low & poor.*— Of other *Countries & Nations. Ethiopia* has stretched out her Hand:

---

*1 Cor. 15. 8.

Some poor *Negroes* have, I trust, been vindicated into the glorious Liberty of the Children of God.— Of all *Qualities & Conditions*. The most *ignorant*; the foolish Things of the World, Babes in Knowledge have been made wise unto Salvation, and taught those heavenly Truths, which have been hid from the wise & prudent. Some of the *learned* and *knowing* among Men, have had those Things revealed to them of the Father in Heaven, which Flesh and Blood do not teach: And of these, some who had gone into the modern Notions, and had no other than the polite Religion of the present Times, have had their Prejudices conquer'd, their carnal Reasonings overcome, and their Understandings made to bow to Gospel Mysteries; they now receive the Truth as it is in Jesus, and their Faith no longer *stands in the Wisdom of Man, but in the Power of God*. Some of the most *rude & disorderly*, are become regular in their Behaviour, & sober in all Things. The *Gay & Airy*, are become grave and serious. Some of the *greatest Sinners* have appear'd to be turned into real Saints. *Drunkards* have become temperate: *Fornicators & Adulterers* of a chast Conversation; *Swearers, & profane Persons*, have learn'd to fear that glorious and fearful Name, the Lord their God; and *carnal Worldlings* have been made to seek first the Kingdom of God and his Righteousness. Yea, *Deriders* and *Scoffers* at this Work and the Instruments of it, have come under its conquering Power. Some of this Stamp, who have gone to hear the Preacher, as some did *Paul; What will this Babler say?* Have not been able to resist the Power and the Spirit with which he spake; have sat trembling under the Word, and gone away from it weeping; and afterward did cleave unto the Preacher, as *Dionysius* the *Aropagite* did unto *Paul*.* Divers Instances of this Kind, have fallen under my Knowledge.—The *virtuous* and *civil* have been convinc'd that Morality is not to be relied on for Life; and so excited to seek after the new Birth, and a vital Union to Jesus Christ by Faith. The *formal Professor* likewise has been awakened out of his dead Formalities, and brought under the Power of Godliness; taken off from his false Rests, and bro't to build his Hopes only on the Mediator's

*Acts 17. 18. 34. compar'd.

Righteousness. At the same Time many of the *Children of God* have been greatly quickned & refreshed; have been awaken'd out of the sleepy Frames they were fallen into, and excited to give Diligence to make their Calling & Election sure; and have had precious reviving & sealing Times.— Thus *extensive & general* the divine Influence has been, at this glorious Season.

One Thing more is worthy Remark; and this is the *Uniformity* of the Work. By the Accounts I have received in Letters, and Conversation with Ministers and Others who live in different Parts of the Land where this Work is going on, It is the *same Work* that is carried on in one Place and another: The Method of the Spirit's Operation on the Minds of People is the same; tho' with some Variety of Circumstances as is usual at other Times: And the particular Appearances with which this Work is attended, that have not been so common at other Times, are also much the same. *These* are indeed objected by many against the Work: But tho' Conversion is the same Work, in the main Strokes of it, wherever it is wrought; yet it seems reasonable to suppose that at an extraordinary Season wherein God is pleas'd to carry on a Work of his Grace in a more observable and glorious Manner, in a Way which he would have to be taken Notice of by the World; at such a Time, I say, It seems reasonable to suppose, There may be some particular Appearances in the Work of Conversion, which are not common at other Times, when yet there are true Conversions wrought; or some Circumstances attending the Work may be carried to an unusual Degree and Height. If it were not *thus*, the Work of the Lord would not be so much regarded and spoken of; and so God would not have so much of the Glory of it: nor would the Work it self be like to spread so fast; for God has evidently made Use of Example & Discourse in the carrying of it on.

And as to the *Fruits* of this Work, (which we have been bid so often to wait for) Blessed be God! so far as there has been Time for Observation they appear to be *abiding*. I don't mean, That none have lost their Impressions, or that there are no Instances of Hypocrisy & Apostacy. Scripture and Experience lead us to expect these at such a Season. It is to me Matter of Surprize & Thankfulness that as yet there have been *no more*. But I mean, That a great Number of those who have been awakened are still seeking & striving to enter in at the strait Gate. The most of those who have been thought to be converted, continue to give Evidences of their being new Creatures, and seem to cleave to the Lord with full Purpose of Heart. To be sure a new Face of Things continues in this Town; tho' many Circumstances concur to render such a Work not so observable here, as in smaller & distant Places. Many Things not becoming the *Profession of the Gospel* are in a Measure reform'd. *Taverns, Dancing-Schools*, and such Meetings as have been call'd *Assemblies*, which have always prov'd unfriendly to serious Godliness, are much less frequented. Many have reduc'd their *Dress & Apparel*, so as to make them look more like the Followers of the humble Jesus. And it has been both surprizing and pleasant to see how some Younger People, and of that Sex too which is most fond of such Vanities, have put off the *Bravery of their Ornaments*, as the Effect & Indication of their seeking the inward Glories of *the King's Daughter*. Religion is now much more the Subject of Conversation at Friends Houses, than ever I knew it. The Doctrines of Grace are espous'd & relish'd. Private religious Meetings are greatly multiplied.—The publick Assemblies (especially *Lectures*) are much better attended: And our Auditories were never so attentive & serious. There is indeed an extraordinary Appetite after *the sincere Milk of the Word*.

It is more than a Twelve Month since an *Evening-Lecture* was set up in this Town; there are now several; two constantly on *Tuesday* and *Friday-Evenings*; when some of our most capacious Houses are well fill'd, with Hearers who by their Looks & Deportment seem to come to hear that their Souls might live. An Evening in God's Courts is now esteem'd better than many elsewhere. There is also great Resort to Ministers in private. Our Hands continue full of Work: And many Times we have more than we can discourse with distinctly and seperately—.

I have been thus large and particular, that Persons at a Distance, who are desirous to know the present State of Religion *here*, into whose Hands these Papers will come, may receive some Satisfaction.—

And now, Can any be at a Loss to what Spirit to ascribe this Work? To attribute it, as some do, to the Devil, is to make the *old Serpent*, like the *foolish Woman*, who plucketh down her House with her Hands.* Our Saviour has taught us to argue otherwise in such a Case as this: *Every Kingdom divided against it self, is bro't to Desolation; and every City or House divided against it self, shall not stand. And if Satan cast out Satan, he is divided against himself: How then shall his Kingdom stand?*†

That some entertain Prejudices against this Work, and others revile and reproach it, does not make it look less like a Work of God: It would else want one Mark of it's being so; for *the Spirit of this World*, and *the Spirit which is of God*, are contrary the one to the other. I don't wonder that Satan rages, and shews his Rage in some that are under his Influence, when his Kingdom is so shaken, and his Subjects desert him by *Hundreds*, I hope by *Thousands*.

The Prejudices of some, I make no doubt, are owing to the Want of Opportunity to be rightly informed, and their having received Misrepresentations from abroad. Others may be offended because they have not experienced any Thing like such a Work in themselves; and if these Things be so, they must begin again, and get another Foundation laid than that on which they have built: And this is what Men are hardly bro't to. And others, perhaps, may dislike the present Work, because it supports & confirms some Principles which they have not yet embraced, and against which such Prejudices hang about their Minds, as they cannot easily shake off: For 'tis certain these Fruits do not grow on *Arminian Ground*. I hope none dislike the Work because *they* have not been us'd as Instruments in it: For if we love our Lord Jesus Christ in Sincerity, we shall rejoyce to see *Him increase*, tho' *we* should *decrease*.

If any are *resolutely set* to disbelieve this Work, to reproach and oppose it, they must be left to the free sovereign Power & Mercy of God to enlighten and rescue them. These, if they have had Opportunity to be rightly inform'd, I am ready to think, would have been Disbelievers, & Opposers of the Miracles and Mission of our Saviour, had they liv'd in his Days. The Malignity which some of them have discover'd, to me approaches near to the unpardonable Sin; and they had need beware lest they indeed sin *the Sin which is unto Death*: For as I believe it can be

*Prov. 14. 1.
†Math. 12. 25, 26.

committed in these Days as well as in the Days of the Apostles, so I think Persons are now in more Danger of committing it than at other Times. (I hope these Words have dropt from my Pen not in an untemperate Zeal, but with due Caution, & some suitable Solemnity of Spirit) At least let them come under the Awe of that Word, Psal. 28. 5. *Because they regard not the Works of the Lord, nor the Operation of his Hands, he shall destroy them, and not build them up.*

But if any are dispos'd to receive Conviction, have a Mind open to Light, and are really willing to know of the present Work *whether it be of God*, it is with great Satisfaction and Pleasure I can recommend to them the following Sheets; in which they will find the distinguishing Marks of such a Work, as they are to be found in the Holy Scriptures, applied to the uncommon Operation that has been on the Minds of many in this Land. Here the Matter is tried by the infallible Touchstone of the holy Scriptures, and is weighed in the Ballances of the Sanctuary, with great Judgment and Impartiality.

A Performance of this Kind is seasonable and necessary; and I desire heartily to bless God who inclin'd this his Servant to undertake it, and has graciously assisted him in it. The *Reverend Author is* known to be a *Scribe instructed unto the Kingdom of Heaven*; the Place where he has been called to exercise his Ministry has been famous for experimental Religion; and he has had Opportunities to observe this Work in many Places where it has powerfully appear'd, and to converse with Numbers that have been the Subjects of it: These Things qualify him for this Undertaking above most. His Arguments in favour of the Work, are strongly drawn from *Scripture, Reason*, and *Experience*: And I believe every candid judicious Reader will say, he writes very free from an *Enthusiastic* or a *Party Spirit*. The Use of *human Learning* is asserted; a *methodical Way of Preaching*, the Fruit of Study as well as Prayer, is recommended; and the Exercise of *Charity* in judging Others press'd and urged: And those Things which are esteem'd the *Blemishes*, and are like to be the *Hindrances* of the Work, are with great Faithfulness caution'd and warn'd against.— Many I believe will be thankful for this Publication. Those who have already entertain'd favourable Thoughts of this Work, will be confirm'd by it; and the Doubting may be convinc'd & satisfied. But if there are any who cannot after all see the Signatures of a Divine Hand on the Work, 'tis to be hop'd they will be prevail'd on to spare their Censures, and stop their Oppositions, lest *haply they should be found even to fight against God*—

I had yet several Things to say, which I see I must suppress, or I shall go much beyond the Limits of a Preface: And I fear I need to ask Pardon, both of the *Reader* and the *Publishers*, for the Length I have run already. Only I can't help expressing my Wish, that those who have been conversant in this Work, in one Place and another, would transmit Accounts of it to such a Hand as the Reverend Author of *this* Discourse, to be compiled into a *Narrative*, like that of the Conversions at *Northampton* which was published a few Years ago: that so the World may know this surprizing Dispensation, in the Beginning, Progress, and various Circumstances of it. This, I apprehend, would be for the Honour of the HOLY SPIRIT, whose Work and Office has been treated so reproachfully in the Christian World: It would be an open Attestation to the Divinity of a despised Gospel: And it might have a happy Effect on other Places, where the Sound of this marvellous Work would by this Means be heard. I can't but think it would be one of the most useful Pieces of *Church History* the People of God are bless'd with. Perhaps it would come the nearest to the *Acts of the Apostles* of any Thing extant; and all the Histories in the World do not come up to *that: There* we have something as surprizing, as in the Book of *Genesis*; and a new Creation, of another Kind, seems to open to our View.—But I must forbear.—

I will only add my Prayer, That the worthy Author of this Discourse, may long be continued a burning and shining Light in the Golden Candlestick where *CHRIST* has plac'd him; and from thence diffuse his Light thro' these Provinces! That the divine *SPIRIT*, whose Cause is here espous'd, would accompany this, and the other valuable Publications of his Servant, with his powerful Influences: that they may promote the *REDEEMER's* Interest, serve the Ends of vital Religion, and so add to the Author's present Joy, and future Crown!

Boston, Nov. 20. 1741.

W. Cooper

The Marks of a Work of
the True Spirit

I JOHN IV. I.
*Beloved, believe not every Spirit, but try the Spirits
whether they are of GOD; because many false
Prophets are gone out into the World.*

THE apostolical Age, or the Age in which the Apostles lived
and preached the Gospel, was an Age of the greatest out-
pouring of the Spirit of God that ever was; and that both as to
the extraordinary Influences and Gifts of the Spirit, in Inspiration and Miracles, and also as to his ordinary Operations, in
convincing, converting, enlightening and sanctifying the Souls
of Men. But as the Influences of the true Spirit abounded, so
Counterfeits did also then abound: The Devil was abundant in
mimicking, both the ordinary and extraordinary Influences of
the Spirit of God, as is manifest by innumerable Passages of the
Apostles Writings. This made it very necessary that the Church
of Christ should be furnished with some certain Rules, and
distinguishing and clear Marks by which she might proceed
safely in judging of Spirits, and distinguish the true from the
false, without Danger of being imposed upon. The giving such
Rules is the plain Design of this Chapter, where we have this
Matter more expresly and fully treated of than any where else
in the Bible. The Apostle here, of set Purpose, undertakes to
supply the Church of God with such Marks of the true Spirit as
may be plain, & safe, and surely distinguishing, and well ac-
commodated to Use and Practice; and that the Subject might
be clearly and sufficiently handled, he insists upon it throughout the Chapter: Which makes it wonderful that what is said in
this Chapter, is no more taken notice of in this extraordinary
Day, when that which is so remarkable appears; such an uncommon Operation on the Minds of People, that is so extensive; and there is such a Variety of Opinions concerning it, and
so much Talk about the Work of the Spirit.

The Apostle is led to discourse on this Subject by an occasional
Mention of the indwelling of the Spirit, as the sure Evidence of

an Interest in Christ, in the last Verse of the foregoing Chapter, *And he that keepeth his Commandments dwelleth in him, and he in him; and hereby we know that he abideth in us, by the Spirit which he hath given us.* Whence we may infer, That the Design of the Apostle in this Chapter is not only to give Marks whereby to distinguish the true Spirit from false in his extraordinary Gifts of Prophecy & Miracles, but also in his ordinary Influences on the Minds of his People, in order to their Union to Christ, and being built up in him; which is also manifest from the Marks themselves that are given, which we shall hereafter take Notice of.

The Words of the Text are an Introduction to this Discourse, of the distinguishing Signs of the true and false Spirit. Before the Apostle proceeds to lay down these Signs, he exhorts the Christians he writes to, to Care in this Matter. And, 1. Here is the Duty of trying the Spirits urged, with a Caution annexed, against an over Creduloussness, and a Forwardness to admit every Thing as the Work of a true Spirit that has that Shew or Pretext; *Beloved, believe not every Spirit, but try the Spirits, whether they are of God.* 2. The Necessity of this Duty is shewn from this, That there were many Counterfeits; *because many false Prophets are gone out into the World.* The false Apostles, and false Prophets, that were in those Days, did not only pretend to have the Spirit of God in his extraordinary Gifts of Inspiration, but also to be the great Friends and Favorites of Heaven, and to be eminently holy Persons, and so to have much of the ordinary, saving, sanctifying Influences of the Spirit of God on their Hearts; and we are to look upon these Words as a Direction to examine and try their Pretences to the Spirit of God, in both these Respects.

After the Apostle had thus counsel'd & warn'd the Christians he wrote to, with Respect to the Trial of Spirits, he immediately proceeds to give them Rules, by which they may safely proceed in judging of every Thing that had the Pretext of being either the ordinary or extraordinary Work of the Spirit of God.

My Design therefore at this Time is to shew what are the true, certain, and distinguishing Evidences of a Work of the Spirit of God, by which we may proceed safely in judging of any Operation we find in our selves, or see in others.

And here I would observe that we are to take the Scriptures

as our Guide in such Cases: This is the great and standing Rule which God has given to his Church, to guide them in all Things relating to the great Concerns of their Souls; and 'tis an infallible and sufficient Rule. There are undoubtedly sufficient Marks given to guide the Church of God in this great Affair of judging of Spirits, without which it would lie open to woful Delusion, and would be remedilesly exposed to be imposed on and devoured by its Enemies: And what Rules soever we may find in the holy Scriptures to this end, we need not be afraid to trust to. Doubtless that Spirit that indited the Scriptures knew how to give us good Rules, by which to distinguish his Operations from all that is falsely pretended to be from him.

This, as I observed before, the Spirit of God has done of set purpose, in the Chapter wherein is the Text; and done it more particularly and fully than any where else: so that in my present Discourse, I shall go no where else for Rules or Marks for the Trial of Spirits, but shall confine my self to those that I find here.

But before I proceed particularly to speak to these, I would prepare my Way by first observing negatively, in some Instances, What are not Signs that we are to judge of a Work by, whether it be the Work of the Spirit of God or no; and especially, what are no Evidences that a Work that is wrought amongst a People, is not the Work of the Spirit of God.

I. Nothing can certainly be concluded from this, *That the Work that appears is carried on in a Way very unusual and extraordinary.* 'Tis no Sign that a Work is not the Work of the Spirit of God, that it is carried on in such a Way as the same Spirit of God heretofore has not been wont to carry on his Work, provided the Variety or Difference be such, as may still be comprehended within the Limits of those Rules which the Scriptures have given to distinguish a Work of the Spirit of God by. What we have been used to, or what the Church of God has been used to, is not a Rule by which we are to judge whether a Work be the Work of God, because there may be new and extraordinary Works of God. God has heretofore wrought in an extraordinary Manner; he has brought those Things to pass that have been new Things, strange Works; and has wrought in such a Manner as to surprize both Men and Angels: And as God has done thus in Times past, so we have no Reason to think but that he will do so still. The Prophecies of Scripture give us Reason to think that God has still new Things to accomplish, and Things to bring to pass that have never yet been seen. No Deviation from what has hitherto been usual, let it be never so great, is an Argument that a Work is not the Work of the Spirit of God, if it be no Deviation from the Rule that God has given, to judge of a Work of his Spirit by. The Spirit of God is sovereign in his Operations; and we know that he uses a great Variety; and we can't tell how great a Variety he may use, within the Compass of the Rules he himself has fixed. We ought not to limit God where he has not limited himself. If a Work be never so different from the Work of God's Spirit that has formerly been, yet if it only agrees in those Things that the Word of God has given us as the distinguishing Signs of a Work of his Spirit, that is sufficient to determine us intirely in its Favour.

Therefore 'tis not reasonable to determine that a Work is not the Work of God's Spirit, because of the extraordinary Degree in which the Minds of Persons are influenced and wrought upon. If they seem to have an extraordinary Conviction of the dreadful nature of Sin, and a very uncommon Sense of the Misery of a Christless Condition, or seem to have extraordinary Views of the certainty and glory of divine Things; and consequent on these Apprehensions, are proportionably moved with very extraordinary Affections of Fear and Sorrow, Desire, Love or Joy: Or if the Change that seems to be made in Persons, the Alteration in their Affections and Frames, be very sudden, and the Work that is wrought on People's Minds seems to be carried on with very unusual Swiftness, and the Persons that are thus strangely affected are very many, and many of them are very young; and also be very unusual in many other Circumstances, not infringing upon Scripture Marks of a Work of the Spirit; these Things are no Argument that the Work is not a Work of the Spirit of God.

The extraordinary and unusual Degree of Influence, and Power of Operation, if in its Nature it be agreable to the Rules and Marks given in the Scripture, is rather an Argument in it's Favour; for by how much the higher Degree that is in, which is in its Nature agreeable to the Rule, so much the more is there of Conformity to the Rule, and so much the more evident and manifest is that Conformity. When Things are in small Degrees, tho' they be really agreeable to the Rule, yet the Nature of them is more difficultly discerned, and 'tis not so easily seen whether it agrees with the Rule or no.

There is a great Aptness in Persons to doubt of Things that are Strange; especially it is difficult for elderly Persons, those that have lived a great while in the World, to think that to be right which they have been never used to in their Day, and have not heard of in the Days of their Fathers. But if it be a good Argument that a Work is not from the Spirit of God, that 'tis very unusual, then it always was so, and was so in the Apostles Days. The Work of the Spirit of God that was wrought then, was carried on in a Manner that, in very many Respects, was altogether new: There were such Things then that the Jews, then living, nor their Fathers, had never seen nor heard, yea such as never had been since the World stood: The Work was then carried on with more visible and remarkable Power than ever had been before; never were there seen before such mighty and wonderful Effects of the Spirit of God, in such sudden Changes, and such great Engagedness and Zeal in such Multitudes; such a great and sudden Alteration in Towns, Cities and Countries; such a swift Progress, and vast Extent of the Work; and many other extraordinary Circumstances might be mentioned. The great Unusualness of the Work surprized the Jews; they knew not what to make of it, but could not be lieve it to be the Work of God; many looked upon the Persons that were the Subjects of it as bereft of Reason; as you may see in *Acts* 2. 13. & 26. 24. & 1 Cor. 4. 10.

And we have Reason from Scripture Prophecy to suppose, That at the Commencement of that last and greatest Out-pouring of the Spirit of God, that is to be in the latter Ages of the World, the Manner of the Work will be very extraordinary, and such as never has yet been seen; so that there shall be Occasion then to say, as in Isai. 66. 8. *Who hath heard such a Thing? Who hath seen such Things? Shall the Earth be made to bring forth in one Day? Shall a Nation be born at once? for as soon as Zion travailed, she brought forth her Children.* It may be reasonably expected that the extraordinary Manner of the Work then, will bear some Proportion to the very extraordinary Events, and that glorious Change in the State of the World, God will be about to bring to pass by it.

2. A Work is not to be judged of by any *Effects on the Bodies of Men*; such as Tears, Trembling, Groans, loud Out-cries, Agonies of Body, or the failing of bodily Strength. The Influence the Minds of Persons are under, is not to be judged of one Way or the other, whether it be from the Spirit of God or no, by such Effects on the Body; and the Reason is, Because the Scripture no where gives us any such Rule. We can't conclude that Persons are under the Influence of the true Spirit, because we see such Effects upon their Bodies, because this is not given as a Mark of the true Spirit: nor on the other Hand, have we any Reason to conclude, from any such outward Appearances, that Persons are not under the Influence of the Spirit of God, because there is no Rule of Scripture given us to judge of Spirits by, that does, either expresly or indirectly, exclude such Effects on the Body; nor does Reason exclude them. 'Tis easily accounted for from the Consideration of the Nature of divine and eternal Things, and the Nature of Man, and the Laws of the Union between Soul and Body, how a right Influence, a true and proper Sense of Things, should have such Effects on the Body, even those that are of the most extraordinary Kind; such as taking away the bodily Strength, or throwing the Body into great Agonies, and extorting loud Outcries. There are none of us but what suppose, and would have been ready at any Time to say it, That the Misery of Hell is doubtless so dreadful, and Eternity so vast, that if a Person should have a clear Apprehension of that Misery as it is, it would be more than his feeble Frame could bear; and especially, if at the same Time he saw himself in great Danger of it, and to be utterly uncertain whether he should be delivered from it, yea, and to have no Security from it one Day or Hour. If we consider human Nature, we need not wonder that when Persons have a very great Sense of that which is so amazingly dreadful, and also have a great View of their own Wickedness and God's Anger, that Things seem to them to fore-bode speedy and immediate Destruction. We see the Nature of Man to be such, that when he is in Danger of some Calamity that is very terrible to him, and that he looks upon himself greatly exposed to, he is ready upon every Occasion to think that *now* it is coming: As when Persons Hearts are full of Fear, in Time of War, looking upon themselves eminently exposed; they are

ready to tremble at the shaking of a Leaf, and to expect the Enemy every Minute, and to say within themselves, *now* I shall be slain. If we should suppose that a Person saw himself hanging over a great Pit, full of fierce and glowing Flames, by a Thread that he knew to be very weak, and not sufficient long to bear his Weight, and knew that Multitudes had been in such Circumstances before, and that most of them had fallen and perish'd; and saw nothing within Reach, that he could take hold of to save him; What Distress would he be in? How ready to think that *now* the Thread was breaking; *now this Minute* he should be swallowed up in these dreadful Flames? And would not he be ready to cry out in such Circumstances? How much more those that see themselves in this Manner hanging over an infinitely more dreadful Pit, or held over it in the Hand of God, who at the same Time they see to be exceedingly provoked? No wonder they are ready to expect every Moment when this angry God will let them drop; and no Wonder they cry out of their Misery; and no Wonder that the Wrath of God when manifested but a little to the Soul, over-bears human Strength.

So it may be easily accounted for, that a true Sense of the glorious Excellency of the Lord Jesus Christ, and of his wonderful dying Love, and the Exercise of a truly spiritual Love and Joy, should be such as very much to over come the bodily Strength. We are all ready to own that no Man can see God and live; and that 'tis but a very small Part of that Apprehension of the Glory and Love of Christ, and Exercise of Love to him and Joy in him, which the Saints in Heaven are the Subjects of, that our present Frame can bear: Therefore 'tis not at all strange that God should sometimes give his Saints such Fore-tastes of Heaven, as to diminish their bodily Strength. If it was not unaccountable that the Queen of *Sheba* fainted, and had her bodily Strength taken away, when she came to see the Glory of *Solomon*, much less is it unaccountable that she who is the Anti-type of the Queen of *Sheba*, viz. the Church, that is brought as it were from the utmost Ends of the Earth, from being an Alien and Stranger, far off, in a State of Sin and Misery, should faint when she comes to see the Glory of Christ, who is the Anti-type of *Solomon*; and especially will be so in that prosperous, peaceful, glorious Kingdom, which he will set up in the World in it's latter Age.

Some object against such extraordinary Appearances, that we have no Instances of 'em recorded in the New Testament, in the Time of the extraordinary Effusions of the Spirit that were then. If this should be allowed, I can see no Force in the Objection, if neither Reason, nor any Rule of Scripture excludes such Things; especially considering what was observed under the foregoing Particular. I don't know that we have any express mention in the New Testament of any Person's weeping, or groaning, or sighing, thro' Fear of Hell, or a Sense of God's Anger; but is there any Body so foolish as from hence to argue, that in whomsoever these Things appear, their Convictions are not from the Spirit of God? And the Reason why we don't argue thus is, Because these are easily accounted for, from what we know of the Nature of Man, and from what the Scriptures do inform us in general concerning the Nature of eternal Things, and the Nature of the Convictions of God's Spirit; so that there is no need that any Thing should be said in particular concerning these external, circumstantial Effects. No Body supposes that there is any need of express Scripture for every external, accidental Manifestation of the inward Motion of the Mind: And tho' such Circumstances are not particularly recorded in sacred History, yet there is a great deal of Reason to think, from the general Accounts we have, that it could not be otherwise than that such Things must be in those Days. And there is also Reason to think that that great Outpouring of the Spirit that then was, was not wholly without those more extraordinary Effects on Persons Bodies. The *Jaylor* in particular, seems to have been an Instance of that Nature, when he, in the utmost Distress and Amazement, came trembling, and fell down before *Paul* and *Silas*: His falling down at that Time, don't seem to be a designed putting himself into a Posture of Supplication, or humble Address to *Paul* and *Silas*, for he seems not to have said any Thing to 'em then; but he first *brought them out*, and then he says to them, *Sirs, what must I do to be saved?* Act. 16. 29, 30. But his falling down, seems to be from the same Cause as his Trembling. The Psalmist gives an Account of his crying out aloud, and a great weakening of his Body under Convictions of Conscience, and a Sense of the Guilt of Sin, Psal. 32. 3, 4. *When I kept Silence my Bones waxed old, through my roaring all the Day long; for Day and Night thy Hand was heavy upon me, my Moisture is turned into the Drought of Summer.* We may at least argue so much from it, That such an Effect of Conviction of Sin, may well in some Cases be supposed: for if we should suppose any Thing of an *Auxesis* in the Expressions made use of, yet the Psalmist would not represent what was, by that which would be absurd, and which no Degree of that Exercise of Mind he spoke of, would have any Tendency to.

We read of the Disciples, *Math.* 14. 26, that when they saw Christ coming to them in the Storm, and took him for some terrible Enemy, threatning their Destruction in that Storm, *they cried out for Fear*: Why therefore should it be thought strange, that Persons should cry out for Fear, when God appears to them as their terrible Enemy, and they see themselves in great Danger of being swallowed up in the bottomless Gulf of eternal Misery?

The Spouse once and again speaks of her self as over-power'd with the Love of Christ, so as to weaken her Body, and make her ready to faint. Cant. 2. 5. *Stay me with Flaggons, comfort me with Apples, for I am sick of Love.* And Chap. 5. 8. *I charge you, O ye Daughters of Jerusalem, if ye find my Beloved, that ye tell him that I am sick of Love.* From whence we may at least argue, that such an Effect may well be supposed to arise from such a Cause in the Saints in some Cases, and that such an Effect will sometimes be seen in the Church of Christ.

'Tis a weak Objection, That the Impressions that Enthusiasts are under, have been won't to have a *great Effect on their Bodies.* That the *Quakers* used to tremble, is no Argument that *Saul*, afterwards *Paul*, and the *Jaylor*, did not tremble from real Convictions of Conscience. Indeed all such Objections from Effects on the Body, let them be greater or less, seem to be exceeding frivolous: they that argue from hence, are going in the Dark; they know not what Ground they go upon, nor what Rule they go by. The Root & Cause of Things is to be looked at, and the Nature of the Operations & Affections that Persons *Minds* are under, are what are to be inquired into, and examined by the Rule of God's Word, and not the Motions of the Blood and animal Spirits.

3. 'Tis no Argument that an Operation that appears on the Minds of a People, is not the Work of the Spirit of God, *That*

it occasions a great Ado, and a great deal of Noise about Religion. For tho' true Religion be of a contrary Nature to that of the *Pharisees,* that was ostentatious, and delighted to set it self forth to the View of Men, for their Applause; yet such is human Nature, that 'tis morally impossible that there should be a great Concern, and strong Affection, and Engagedness of Mind amongst a People, that should be general, and what most of them agree in, and yet there be but little said or done that should be publickly observable; or that it should not cause a notable, visible, and open Commotion and Alteration amongst that People.

Surely 'tis no Argument that the Minds of Persons are not under the Influence of God's Spirit, that they are very much moved: for indeed spiritual and eternal Things are so great, and of such vast and infinite Concern, that there is a great Absurdity in Men's being but moderately moved and affected by them; and 'tis no Argument that they are not moved by the Spirit of God, that they are affected with these Things properly, and in some Measure, as they deserve, or in some Proportion to their Importance. And when was there ever any such Thing, since the World stood, as a People in general being greatly affected, in any Affair whatsoever, without Noise or Stir? The Nature of Man will not allow it.

Indeed Christ says, Luk. 17. 20. *The Kingdom of God cometh not with Observation.* That is, it won't consist in what is outward and visible; it shall not be like the Kingdoms of earthly Kings, set up with outward Pomp, in some particular Place, which shall be especially the Royal City, and Seat of the Kingdom; as Christ explains himself in the Words next following, *Neither shall they say, lo here, or lo there; for behold the Kingdom of God is within you.* Not that the Kingdom of God shall be set up in the World, on the Ruins of Satan's Kingdom, without a very notable, observable, great Effect; a mighty Change in the State of Things; to the Observation and Astonishment of the whole World: For such an Effect as this is even held forth in the Prophecies of Scripture, and is so by Christ himself, in this very Place, and even in his own Explanation of those forementioned Words, ver. 24. *For as the Lightning, that lightneth out of one Part under Heaven, shineth unto the other Part under Heaven, so shall also the Son of Man be in his Day.* This is to distinguish Christ's coming to set up his Kingdom, from the coming of *false Christs*, which Christ tells us will be in a private Manner, *in the Deserts, and in the secret Chambers*; whereas this Event of setting up the Kingdom of God, should be open and publick, in the Sight of the whole World, with clear Manifestation, like Lightning that can't be hid, but glares in every ones Eyes, and shines from one Side of Heaven to the other.

And we find that when Christ's Kingdom came, by that remarkable pouring out of the Spirit in the Apostles Days, it occasioned a great Stir and Ado every where. What a mighty Opposition was there in *Jerusalem*, on Occasion of that great Effusion of the Spirit that was there? And so what a great Ado in *Samaria, Antioch, Ephesus*, and *Corinth*, and other Places? The Affair filled the World with Noise, and gave Occasion to some to say of the Apostles, that *they had turned the World upside down*, Act. 17. 6.

4. 'Tis no Argument that an Operation that appears on the Minds of a People, is not the Work of the Spirit of God, *That many that are the Subjects of it, have great Impressions on their Imaginations.* That Persons have many Impressions on their Imaginations, don't prove that they have nothing else. It is easy to be accounted for, that there should be much of this Nature amongst a People, where a great Multitude of all Kinds of Constitutions, have their Minds engaged with intense Thought and strong Affection about those Things that are invisible; yea, it would be Strange if there should not. Such is our Nature that we can't think of Things invisible, without a Degree of Imagination. I dare appeal to any Man, of the greatest Powers of Mind, Whether or no he is able to fix his Thoughts on God or Christ, or the Things of another World, without imaginary Ideas, attending his Meditations? And the more engaged the Mind is, and the more intense the Contemplation and Affection, still the more lively and strong will the imaginary Idea ordinarily be; especially when the Contemplation and Affection of the Mind is attended with any Thing of Surprize; as when the View a Person has is very new, and takes strong hold of the Passions, either Fear or Joy; and when the Change of the State and Views of the Mind is sudden, from a contrary Extreme, as from that which was extreamly dreadful, to that which is extreamly ravishing and delightful: And it is no Wonder that many Persons don't well distinguish between that

which is imaginary, and that which is intellectual and spiritual; and that they are apt to lay too much Weight on the imaginary Part, and are most ready to speak of *that* in the Account they give of their Experiences, especially Persons of less Understanding and Capacity of Distinction.

As God has given us such a Faculty as the Imagination, and has so made us that we can't think of Things spiritual and invisible, without some Exercise of this Faculty, so it appears to me that such is our State and Nature, that this Faculty is really subservient and helpful to the other Faculties of the Mind, when a proper Use is made of it; tho' oftentimes when the Imagination is too strong, and the other Faculties weak, it over-bears 'em, and much disturbs them in their Exercise. It appears to me manifest in many Instances I have been acquainted with, that God has really made Use of this Faculty to truly divine Purposes; especially in some that are more ignorant: God seems to condescend to their Circumstances, and deal with them as Babes; as of old he instructed his Church while in a State of Ignorance and Minority by Types and outward Representations. I can see nothing unreasonable in such a Supposition. Let others that have much Occasion to deal with Souls in spiritual Concerns, judge whether Experience don't confirm it.

It is no Argument that a Work is not the Work of the Spirit of God, that some that are the Subjects of it, have in some extraordinary Frames, been in a kind of Extasy, wherein they have been carried beyond themselves, and have had their Minds transported into a Train of strong and pleasing Imaginations, and kind of Visions, as tho' they were wrapt up even to Heaven, and there saw glorious Sights. I have been acquainted with some such Instances; and I see no Manner of Need of bringing in the Help of the Devil into the Account that we give of these Things; nor yet of supposing them to be of the same Nature with the Visions of the Prophets, or St. *Paul*'s Rapture into Paradise. Human Nature, under these vehement and intense Exercises and Affections of Mind, which some Persons are the Subjects of, is all that need be brought into the Account. If it may well be accounted for, that Persons under a true Sense of the glorious and wonderful Greatness and Excellency of divine Things, and Soul-ravishing Views of the Beauty and Love of Christ, should have the Strength of

Nature over-power'd, as I have already shewn that it may; then I think it is not at all strange, that amongst great Numbers that are thus affected and over-born, there should be some Persons of particular Constitutions that should have their Imaginations thus affected: When it is thus, the Effect is no other than what bears a Proportion and Analogy to other Effects of the strong Exercise of their Minds. 'Tis no Wonder that when the Thoughts are so fixed, and the Affections so strong, and the whole Soul so engaged and ravished and swallowed up, that all other Parts of the Body are so affected as to be deprived of their Strength, and the whole Frame ready to dissolve; I say, 'tis no Wonder that in such a Case, the Brain in particular, (especially in some Constitutions) which is a Part of the Body which we know is nextly and most especially affected by intense Contemplations and Exercises of Mind, should be over-born and affected, so that it's Strength and Spirits should for a season be diverted, and so taken off from Impressions made on the Organs of external Sense, and wholly imployed in a Train of pleasing delightful Imaginations, such as the Frame the Mind is then in disposes it to.

Some Persons are ready to interpret such Things wrong, and to lay too much Weight on them, as tho' they were prophetical Visions, and to look upon what they imagine they see or hear in them as divine Revelations, and sometimes Significations from Heaven of what shall come to pass; which the Issue, in some Instances I have known, has shown to be otherwise: But yet it appears to me that such Things are evidently sometimes, from the Spirit of God, tho' indirectly; that is, as that extraordinary Frame of Mind they are in, and that strong and lively Sense of divine Things that is the Occasion of them, is from his Spirit; and also as the Mind continues in it's holy Frame, and retains a divine Sense of the Excellency of spiritual Things, even in it's Rapture: which holy Frame and Sense is from the Spirit of God, tho' the Imaginations that attend it are but accidental, and therefore there is commonly something or other in them that is confused, improper and false.

5. 'Tis no Sign that a Work that appears, and is wrought on the Minds of People, is not from the Spirit of God, *That Example is made use of as a great Means of it*. 'Tis surely no Argument that an Effect is not from God, that Means are made use

of in producing it; for we know that 'tis God's Manner to make use of Means in carrying on his Work in the World: and 'tis no more an Argument against the Divinity of an Effect, that this Means is made use of, than if it was by any other Means. 'Tis agreable to Scripture that Persons should be influenced by one anothers good Example: The Scripture directs us to set good Examples to that End, *Math.* 5. 16. 1 *Pet.* 3. 1. 1 *Tim.* 4. 12. *Tit.* 2. 7. and also directs us to be influenced by the good Examples that others set, and to follow them, 2 *Cor.* 8. 1,–7. *Heb.* 6. 12. *Phil.* 3. 17. 1 *Cor.* 4. 16. *& Chap.* 11. 1. 2 *Thes.* 3. 9. 1 *Thes.* 1. 7. By which it appears that Example is one of God's Means; and certainly 'tis no Argument that a Work is not the Work of God, that God's own Means are made Use of to effect it.

And as 'tis a *scriptural* Way of carrying on God's Work, to carry it on by Example, so 'tis a *reasonable* Way. 'Tis no Argument that Men are not influenced by Reason, that they are influenced by Example. This Way of Persons holding forth Truth to one another, has a Tendency to enlighten the Mind, and to convince Reason. None will deny but that for Persons to signify Things one to another *by Words*, may rationally be supposed to tend to inlighten each others Minds; but the same Things may be signified *by Actions*, and signified much more fully and effectually. Words are of no Use any otherwise than as they convey our own Ideas to others; but Actions, in some Cases, may do it much more fully. There is a Language in Actions; and in some Cases, much more clear and convincing than in Words.

'Tis therefore no Argument against the Goodness of the Effect, that one affects and stirs up another; or that Persons are greatly affected by seeing others so; yea, tho' the Impression that is made upon them should be only by seeing the Tokens of great and extraordinary Affection in others in their Behaviour, taking for granted what they are affected with, without hearing them say one Word. There may be Language sufficient in such a Case in their Behaviour only, to convey their Minds to others, and to signify to them the Sense of Things they have, more than can possibly be done by Words only. If a Person should see another under some extreme bodily Torment, he might receive much clearer Ideas, and more convincing Evidence what he suffered by his Actions in his Misery, than he could do only by the Words of an unaffected indifferent Relator. In like Manner he might receive a greater Idea of any Thing that is excellent and very delightful, from the Behaviour of one that is in actual Enjoyment, or one that is sensible thro' Sight and Taste, than by the dull Narration of one that is unexperienced & insensible himself. I desire that this Matter may be examined by the strictest Reason.

And there is this Argument, that Effects that are produced in Persons Minds by Example are rational, that 'tis manifest that not only weak and ignorant People are much influenced by it, but nothing can be more evident to any one that observes the World of Mankind, than that all sorts of Persons, wise and unwise, and even those that make the greatest Boasts of Strength of Reason, are more influenced by Reason held forth in this Way than almost any other Way.

Indeed when religious Affections are raised by this Means, it is as when Persons affected in hearing the Word preached, or any other Means, the Affections of many prove flashy, and soon vanish, as Christ represents of the stony Ground Hearers; but the Affections of some that are thus moved by Example are abiding, and prove to be of saving Issue.

There never yet was a Time of remarkable pouring out of the Spirit, and great Revival of Religion, but that Example had a main Hand; so it was in the Time of the Reformation, and so it evidently was in that great Out-pouring of the Spirit that was in the Apostles Days, in *Jerusalem*, and *Samaria*, & *Ephesus*, and other Parts of the World, as will be most manifest to any one that attends to the Accounts we have in the Acts of the Apostles: As in these Days one Person was moved by another, so one City or Town was influenced by the Example of another, 1 Thes. 1. 7, 8. *So that ye were Ensamples to all that believe in* Macedonia, *and* Achaia; *for from you sounded out the Word of the Lord, not only in* Macedonia *and* Achaia, *but also in every Place your Faith to Godward is spread abroad.*

'Tis no valid Objection against Examples being made so much use of, that the Scripture speaks of the Word of God as the principal Means of carrying on God's Work; for the Word of God is the principal Means nevertheless, as that is the Means by which other Means operate, and are made effectual: The Sacraments have no Effect but by the Word. And so it is that

Example becomes effectual; for all that is visible to the Eye is unintelligible and vain, without the Word of God to instruct and guide the Mind: 'Tis the Word of God that is indeed held forth and applied by Example, as the Word of the Lord sounded forth to other Towns in *Macedonia* and *Achaia*, by the Example of those that believed in *Thessalonica*.

That Example should be a great Means of propagating the Church of God seems to be several Ways signified in Scripture: It is signified by *Ruth*'s following *Naomi* out of the Land of *Moab*, into the Land of *Israel*, when she resolved that she *would not leave her; but would go whether she went, and would lodge where she lodged*; and *that* Naomi*'s People should be her People, and* Naomi*'s God her God. Ruth* who was the Mother of *David* and of Christ, was undoubtedly a great Type of the Church; upon which Account her History is inserted in the Canon of the Scripture: In her leaving the Land of *Moab* and it's Gods, to come and put her Trust under the Shadow of the Wings of the God of *Israel*, we have a Type, not only of the Conversion of the Gentile Church, but the Conversion of every Sinner, that is naturally an Alien and Stranger, but in his Conversion forgets his own People, and Father's House, and is made nigh, and becomes a Fellow-Citizen with the Saints, and a true *Israelite*. The same seems to be signified in the Effect the Example of the Spouse, when she was *sick of Love*, has on the *Daughters of Jerusalem*, i.e. visible Christians, who are represented as being first awakened by seeing the Spouse in such extraordinary Circumstances, and then converted. See *Cant.* 5. 8, 9. *and* 6. 1. And this is undoubtedly one Way that *the Spirit and the Bride says, come*, Rev. 22. 17. i.e. the *Spirit* in the *Bride*. 'Tis foretold, that the Work of God should be carried on very much by this Means, in the last great Out-pouring of the Spirit, that should introduce the glorious Day of the Church, so often spoken of in Scripture. Zech. 8. 21, 22, 23. *And the Inhabitants of one City, shall go to another, saying, let us go speedily to pray before the Lord, and to seek the Lord of Hosts; I will go also. Yea many People, and strong Nations shall come to seek the Lord of Hosts in Jerusalem, and to pray before the Lord. Thus saith the Lord of Hosts, in those Days it shall come to pass, that ten Men shall take hold, out of all Languages of the Nations, even shall take hold of the Skirt of him that is a Jew,* *saying, we will go with you, for we have heard that God is with you.*

6. 'Tis no Sign that a Work that is wrought amongst a People is not from the Spirit of God, *That many that seem to be the Subjects of it, are guilty of great Imprudences & Irregularities in their Conduct.* We are to consider that the End for which God pours out his Spirit, is to make Men holy, and not to make them Politicians. 'Tis no Wonder at all, that in a mixt Multitude of all sorts, wise and unwise, young & old, of weak and strong natural Abilities, that are under strong Impressions of Mind, there are many that behave themselves imprudently. There are but few that know how to conduct them under vehement Affections of any Kind, whether they be of a temporal or spiritual Nature: to do so requires a great deal of Discretion, and strength & steadiness of Mind. A thousand Imprudences won't prove a Work not to be the Work of the Spirit of God; yea if there be not only Imprudences, but many Things prevailing that are irregular, and really contrary to the Rules of God's holy Word. That it should be thus may be well accounted for from the exceeding Weakness of human Nature, together with the remaining Darkness and Corruption of those that are yet the Subjects of the saving Influences of God's Spirit, and have a real Zeal for God.

We have a remarkable Instance in the New Testament, of a People that partook largely of that great Effusion of the Spirit there was in the Apostles Days, among whom, there nevertheless abounded Imprudences and great Irregularities; and that is the Church of the *Corinthians.* There is scarce any Church more celebrated in the New Testament for being blessed with large Measures of the Spirit of God, both in his ordinary Influences, in convincing and converting Sinners, and also in his extraordinary & miraculous Gifts; yet what manifold Imprudences, and great and sinful Irregularities, and strange Confusion did they run into, at the Lord's Supper, and in the Exercise of Church Discipline, and their indecent Manner of attending other Parts of publick Worship, and in Jarring and Contention about their Teachers, and even in the Exercise of their extraordinary Gifts of Prophecy, speaking with Tongues, and the like, wherein they spake and acted by the immediate Inspiration of the Spirit of God?

And if we see great Imprudences, and even sinful Irregularities in some that are improved as great Instruments to carry on
the Work, it won't prove it not to be the Work of God. The
Apostle *Peter* himself, that was a great & eminently holy and
inspired Apostle, and one of the chief Instruments of setting
up the Christian Church in the World, and one of the Chief of
the Apostles, when he was actually engaged in this Work, was
guilty of a great and sinful Error in his Conduct; of which the
Apostle *Paul* speaks, Gal. 2. 11, 12, 13. *But when* Peter *was come
to* Antioch, *I withstood him to the Face, because he was to be
blamed; for before that certain came from* James, *he did eat with
the Gentiles, but when they were come, he withdrew, and seperated himself, fearing them that were of the Circumcision; and the
other Jews dissembled likewise with him; insomuch that* Barnabas
also was carried away with their Dissimulation. If the great Pillar of the Christian Church, and he who was one of the Chief
of those that are the very Foundations on which, next to
Christ, the whole Church is said to be built, was guilty of such
an Irregularity; is it any Wonder if other lesser Instruments,
that have not that extraordinary Conduct of the divine Spirit
that he had, should be guilty of many Irregularities?

And here in particular, it is no Evidence that a Work is not
the Work of God, if many that are the Subjects of it, or are
improved as Instruments to carry it on, are guilty of too great
a forwardness *to censure others as Unconverted*, thro' Mistakes
they have embraced concerning the Marks by which they are
to judge of others Hypocrisy and Carnality; either not duly
apprehending the Latitude the Spirit of God uses in the Methods of his Operations, or for want of making due Allowance
for that Infirmity and Corruption that may be left in the
Hearts of the Saints; as well as thro' want of a due Sense of
their own Blindness and Weakness, and remaining Corruption,
whereby spiritual Pride may have a secret Vent, this Way, under
some Disguise, and not be discovered.

If we allow that truly pious Men may have a great deal of
remaining Blindness and Corruption, and may be liable to
Mistakes about the Marks of Hypocrisy, as undoubtedly all will
allow; then 'tis not unaccountable that they should sometimes
run into such Errors as these: 'Tis as easy, and upon some Accounts, more easy to be accounted for, why the remaining

Corruption of good Men should sometimes have an unobserved Vent this Way, then most other Ways, (tho' it be exceeding unhappy,) and without Doubt many holy Men have erred this Way.

Lukewarmness in Religion is abominable, and Zeal an excellent Grace; yet above all other Christian Vertues, it need to be strictly watched and searched; for 'tis that with which Corruption, and particularly Pride and human Passion, is exceeding apt to mix unobserved. And 'tis observable that there never was a Time of great Reformation, to cause a Revival of much of a Spirit of *Zeal* in the Church of God, but that it has been attended in some notable Instances, with Irregularity, running out some Way or other into an undue *Severity*. Thus in the Apostles Days, a great deal of Zeal was spent about unclean Meats, with heat of Spirit in Christians one against another, both Parties condemning and censuring one another, as not true Christians; when the Apostle had Charity for both, as influenced by a Spirit of real Piety: *He that eats*, says he, *to the Lord he eats, and giveth God Thanks; and he that eateth not, to the Lord he eateth not, and giveth God Thanks.* So in the Church of *Corinth*, they had got into a Way of extolling some Ministers, and censuring others, and were puffed up for one against another: but yet these Things were no Sign that the Work that was then so wonderfully carried on, was not the Work of God. And after this, when Religion was still greatly flourishing in the World, and a Spirit of eminent Holiness & Zeal prevailed in the Christian Church, the Zeal of Christians run out into a very improper and undue Severity, in the Exercise of Church Discipline towards Delinquents; in some Cases they would by no Means admit them into their Charity and Communion, tho' they appeared never so humble and penitent. And in the Days of *Constantine the Great*, the Zeal of Christians against Heathenism, run out into a Degree of Persecution. So in that glorious Revival of Religion, in the Time of the Reformation, Zeal in many Instances appeared in a very improper Severity, and even a Degree of Persecution; yea in some of the most eminent Reformers; as in the great *Calvin* in particular: and many in those Days of the flourishing of vital Religion, were guilty of severely censuring others that differed from them in Opinion in some Points of Divinity.

7. Nor are *many Errors in Judgment, and some Delusions of Satan intermix'd with the Work*, any Argument that the Work in general is not the Work of the Spirit of God. However great a pouring out of the Spirit there may be, 'tis not to be expected that the Spirit of God should be given now in the same Manner that it was to the Apostles, infallibly to guide them in Points of Christian Doctrine, so that what they taught might be relied on as a Rule to the Christian Church. And if many Delusions of Satan appear at the same Time that a great religious Concern prevails, it is not an Argument that the Work in general is not the Work of God, any more than it was an Argument in *Egypt* that there were no true Miracles wro't there, by the Hand of God, because *Jannes* and *Jambres* wrought false Miracles at the same Time by the Hand of the Devil. Yea the same Persons may be the Subjects of much of the Influences of the Spirit of God, and yet in some Things be led away by the Delusions of the Devil; and this be no more of a Paradox than many other Things that are true of real Saints, in the present State, where Grace dwells with so much Corruption, and the new Man and the old Man subsist together in the same Person; and the Kingdom of God and the Kingdom of the Devil remain for a while together in the same Heart. Many godly Persons have undoubtedly in this and other Ages, exposed themselves to woful Delusions, by an Aptness to lay too much Weight on Impulses and Impressions, as if they were immediate Revelations from God, to signify something future, or to direct them where to go and what to do.

8. If some such as were thought to be wrought upon, *fall away into gross Errors or scandalous Practices*, 'tis no Argument that the Work in general is not the Work of the Spirit of God. That there are some Counterfeits, is no Argument that nothing is true: such Things are always expected in a Time of Reformation. If we look into Church History, we shall find no Instance of great Revival of Religion, but what has been attended with many such Things: Instances of this Nature in the Apostles Days were innumerable, both of those that fell away into gross Heresies, and also vile Practices; that yet seemed to be the Subjects of that Work of the Spirit of God that was then, and were accepted for a while amongst those that were truly so, as their Brethren, and some of their Company, and

were not suspected not to be of them, till they went out from them: And they were not only private Christians, but Teachers and Officers, and eminent Persons in the Christian Church; and some that God had endowed with miraculous Gifts of the Holy Ghost; as appears by the Beginning of the 6 Chapter of *Hebrews*. An Instance of these was *Judas*, who was one of the twelve Apostles, and had long been constantly united to, and intimately conversant with a Company of truly experienced Disciples, without being discovered or suspected, 'till he discover'd himself by his scandalous Practice; and had been treated by Jesus himself, in all external Things, as if he had truly been a Disciple, even to the investing him with the Character of Apostle, and sending him forth to preach the Gospel, and induing him with miraculous Gifts of the Spirit: for tho' Christ knew him, yet he did not then cloath himself with the Character of Omniscient Judge, and Searcher of Hearts, but acted the Part of a Minister of the visible Church of God, (for he was his Father's Minister;) and therefore rejected him not, 'till he had discovered himself by his scandalous Practice; thereby giving an Example to other Guides and Rulers of the visible Church, not to take it upon them to act the Part of Searcher of Hearts, but to be influenced in their Administrations by what is visible and open.

There were some Instances then of such Apostates, not only in some that for a while were thought true Christians, but some that were esteemed eminently full of the Grace of God's Spirit: An Instance of this Nature was *Nicolas*, one of the seven Deacons; who was looked upon by the Christians in *Jerusalem*, in the Time of that extraordinary pouring out of the Spirit, as a Man full of the Holy Ghost, and was chosen out of the Multitude of Christians to that Office, for that Reason; as you may see in *Acts* 6. 3, 5. yet he afterwards fell away, and became the Head of a Set of vile Hereticks, of gross Practices, called from his Name the Sect of the *Nicolaitans*, Rev. 2. 6, & 15.

So in the Time of the Reformation from Popery, how great was the Number of those that for a while seemed to join with the Reformers, that fell away into the grossest and most absurd Errors, and abominable Practices.

And 'tis particularly observable that in Times of great pouring out of the Spirit to revive Religion in the World, a Number of those that for a while seemed to partake in it, have fallen off into whimsical and extravagant Errors, and gross Enthusiasm, boasting of high Degrees of Spirituality and Perfection, censuring and condemning others as Carnal. Thus it was with the *Gnosticks* in the Apostles Times; and thus it was with the several Sects of *Anabaptists* in the Time of the Reformation, as *Anthony Burgess* observes, in his Book called *Spiritual Refining*, Part I. Serm. 23. P. 132. "The first worthy Reformers, and glorious Instruments of God found a bitter Conflict herein, so that they were exercised not only with Formalists, and traditionary Papists on the one Side, but Men that pretended themselves to be more inlightned than the Reformers were, on the other Side: Hence they called those that did adhere to the Scripture, & would try Revelations by it, *Literists*, and *Vowelists*, as Men acquainted with the Words and Vowels of the Scripture, having nothing of the Spirit of God: And wheresoever, in any Town, the true Doctrine of the Gospel brake forth to the displacing of Popery, presently such Opinions arose, like Tares that came up among the good Wheat; whereby great Divisions were raised, and the Reformation made abominable and odious to the World; as if that had been the Sun to give Heat and Warmth to those Worms & Serpents to crawl out of the Ground. Hence they inveighed against *Luther*, and said he had only promulged a carnal Gospel." Some of the Leaders of those wild Enthusiasts, had been for a while, highly esteemed by the first Reformers, and peculiarly dear to them.

So in *England* at the Time when vital Religion did much prevail in the Days of King *Charles* I, the *Interregnum*, and *Oliver Cromwell*, such Things as these abounded. And so in the beginning of *New England*, in her purest Days, when vital Piety flourished, such Kind of Things as these broke out. Therefore the Devil's sowing such Tares is no Proof that a true Work of the Spirit of God is not gloriously carried on.

9. 'Tis no Argument that a Work is not from the Spirit of God, *That it seems to be promoted by Ministers insisting very much on the Terrors of God's holy Law, and that with a great deal of* Pathos *and Earnestness.* If there be really a Hell of such dreadful, and never ending Torments, as is generally supposed, that Multitudes are in great Danger of, and that the bigger Part of Men in Christian Countries do actually from Genera-

tion to Generation fall into, for want of a Sense of the Terrible-ness of it, and their Danger of it, and so for want of taking due Care to avoid it; then why is it not proper for those that have the Care of Souls, to take great Pains to make Men sensible of it? Why should not they be told as much of the Truth as can be? If I am in Danger of going to Hell, I should be glad to know as much as possibly I can of the Dreadfulness of it: If I am very prone to neglect due Care to avoid it, he does me the best Kindness, that does most to represent to me the Truth of the Case, that sets forth my Misery and Danger in the liveliest Manner.

I appeal to every one in this Congregation, whether this is not the very Course they would take in Case of Exposedness to any great temporal Calamity? If any of you that are Heads of Families, saw one of your Children in an House that was all on Fire over it's Head, and in eminent Danger of being soon consumed in the Flames, that seemed to be very insensible of it's Danger, and neglected to escape, after you had often spake to it, and called to it, would you go on to speak to it only in a cold and indifferent Manner? Would not you cry aloud, and call earnestly to it, and represent the Danger it was in, and it's own Folly in delaying, in the most lively Manner you was ca-pable of? Would not Nature it self teach this, and oblige you to it? If you should continue to speak to it only in a cold Manner, as you are won't to do in ordinary Conversation about indiffer-ent Matters, would not those about you begin to think you were bereft of Reason your self? This is not the Way of Man-kind, nor the Way of any one Person in this Congregation, in temporal Affairs of great Moment, that require earnest Heed and great Haste, and about which they are greatly concerned, to speak to others of their Danger, and warn them but a little; and when they do it at all, do it in a cold indifferent Manner: Nature teaches Men otherwise. If we that have the Care of Souls, knew what Hell was, had seen the State of the Damned, or by any other Means, become sensible how dreadful their Case was; and at the same Time knew that the bigger Part of Men went thither; and saw our Hearers in eminent Danger, and that they were not sensible of their Danger, and so after being often warned neglected to escape, it would be morally impossible for us to avoid abundantly and most earnestly setting before them the Dreadfulness of that Misery they were in Danger of, and their great Exposedness to it, and warning them to fly from it, and even to cry aloud to them.

When Ministers preach of Hell, and warn Sinners to avoid it, in a cold Manner, tho' they may say in Words that it is infinitely terrible; yet (if we look on Language as a Communication of our Minds to others) they contradict themselves; for Actions, as I observed before, have a Language to convey our Minds, as well as Words; and at the same Time that such a Preacher's Words represent the Sinner's State as infinitely dreadful, his Behaviour and Manner of speaking contradict it, and shew that the Preacher don't think so; so that he defeats his own Purpose; for the Language of his Actions, in such a Case, is much more effectual than the bare Signification of his Words.

Not that I think that the Law only should be preached: Ministers may preach other Things too little. The Gospel is to be preached as well as the Law, and the Law is to be preached only to make Way for the Gospel, and in order to an effectual preaching of that; for the main Work of Ministers of the Gospel is to preach the Gospel: it is the End of the Law; *Christ is the End of the Law for Righteousness*: So that a Minister would miss it very much if he should insist so much on the Terrors of the Law, as to forget his End, and neglect to preach the Gospel; but yet the Law is very much to be insisted on, and the preaching of the Gospel is like to be in vain without it.

And certainly such Earnestness and Affection in speaking is beautiful, as becomes the Nature and Importance of the Subject. Not but that there may be such a Thing as an indecent Boisterousness in a Preacher, that is something besides what naturally arises from the Nature of his Subject, and in which the Matter and Manner don't well agree together.

Some talk of it as an unreasonable Thing to think to fright Persons to Heaven; but I think it is a reasonable Thing to endeavour to fright Persons away from Hell, that stand upon the Brink of it, and are just ready to fall into it, and are senseless of their Danger: 'tis a reasonable Thing to fright a Person out of an House on Fire. The Word *Fright* is commonly used for sudden causless Fear, or groundless Surprize; but surely a just

Fear, that there is good Reason for, tho' it be very great, is not to be spoken against under any such Name.

Having thus shown, in some Instances, what are not Evidences that a Work that is wrought among a People, is not a Work of the Spirit of God,

I now proceed in the *Second Place*, as was proposed, to shew positively, What are the sure, distinguishing, Scripture Evidences and Marks of a Work of the Spirit of God, by which we may proceed in judging of any Operation we find in our selves, or see among a People, without Danger of being missed.

And in this, as I said before, I shall confine my self wholly to those Marks which are given us by the Apostle in the Chapter wherein is my Text, where this Matter is particularly handled, and more plainly and fully than any where else in the Bible. And in speaking to these Marks, I shall take them in the Order in which I find them in the Chapter.

1. When that Spirit that is at work amongst a People is observed to operate after such a Manner, as to raise their Esteem of that *Jesus* that was born of *the Virgin*, and was crucified without the Gates of *Jerusalem*; and seems more to confirm and establish their Minds in the Truth of what the Gospel declares to us of his being the Son of God, and the Saviour of Men; 'tis a sure Sign that that Spirit is the Spirit of God. This Sign the Apostle gives us in the 2d & 3d Verses, *Hereby know ye the Spirit of God; every Spirit that confesseth that Jesus Christ is come in the Flesh, is of God; and every Spirit that confesseth not that Jesus Christ is come in the Flesh, is not of God.* This implies a confessing, not only that there was such a Person that appeared in *Palestine*, and did and suffered those Things that are recorded of him, but that that Person was CHRIST, i.e. the Son of God, the Anointed of God to be Lord and Saviour, as the Name *Jesus Christ* implies. That thus much is implied in the Apostle's Meaning, is confirmed by the 15th *Verse*, where the Apostle is still on the same Subject of Signs of the true Spirit, *Whosoever shall confess that Jesus is the Son of God, God dwelleth in him, and he in God.*

And 'tis to be observed that the Word *confess*, as it is often used in the New Testament, signifies more than meerly *allowing*: It implies an establishing and confirming a Thing by Testimony, and declaring it with manifestation of Esteem and

Affection: so Math. 10. 32. *Whosoever therefore shall confess me before Men, him will I confess also before my Father which is in Heaven.* Rom. 15. 9. *I will confess to thee among the Gentiles, and sing unto thy Name.* And Phil. 2. 11. *That every Tongue shall confess that Jesus Christ is Lord, to the Glory of God the Father.* And that this is the Force of the Expression, as the Apostle *John* uses it in this Place, is confirmed by that other Place in the same Epistle, in the next Chapter, at the first Verse, *Whosoever believeth that Jesus is the Christ, is born of God; and every one that loveth him that begat, loveth him also that is begotten of him.* And by that parallel Place of the Apostle *Paul*, where we have the same Rule given to distinguish the true Spirit from all Counterfeits, 1 Cor. 12. 3. *Wherefore I give you to understand, that no Man speaking by the Spirit of God, calleth Jesus accursed,* (or will shew an ill or mean Esteem of him) *and that no Man can say that Jesus is the Lord, but by the Holy Ghost.*

So that if the Spirit that is at work among a People, is plainly observed to work after that Manner, as to convince them of Christ, and lead them to Christ; more to confirm their Minds in the Belief of the Story of Christ, as he appeared in the Flesh, and that he is the Son of God, and was sent of God to save Sinners, and that he is the only Saviour, and that they stand in great need of him; and seems to beget in them higher and more honourable Thoughts of him than they used to have, and to incline their Affections more to him; it is a sure Sign that it is the true and right Spirit; and that whether we can determine whether that Conviction and Affection be in that Manner, or to that Degree, as to be saving or no.

But the Words of the Apostle are remarkable; The Person that the Spirit gives Testimony to, and to whom he raises their Esteem and Respect, must be that *Jesus that appeared in the Flesh*, and not another Christ in his Stead; not any mystical, fantastical Christ; such as the *Light within*, which the Spirit of the *Quakers* extols, while it diminishes their Esteem of, and Dependance upon an outward Christ, or Jesus as he came in the Flesh, and leads them off from him; but the Spirit that gives Testimony for that Jesus, and leads to Him, can be no other than the Spirit of God.

The Devil has the most bitter and implacable Enmity against that Person, especially in his Character of the Saviour of Men;

he mortally hates the Story and Doctrine of his Redemption; he never would go about to beget in Men more honourable Thoughts of him, and so to incline them more to fear him, and lay greater Weight on his Instructions and Commands. The Spirit that inclines Mens Hearts to the Seed of the Woman, is not the Spirit of the Serpent, that has such an irreconcileable Enmity against him. He that heightens Mens Esteem of the glorious *Michael*, that Prince of the Angels, is not the Spirit of the *Dragon* that is at War with him.

2. When the Spirit that is at work *operates against the Interest of Satan's Kingdom, which lies in encouraging and establishing Sin, and cherishing Mens worldly Lusts*; this is a sure Sign that 'tis a true, and not a false Spirit. This Sign we have given us in the 4th & 5th Verses. *Ye are of God, little Children, and have overcome them; because greater is he that is in you, than he that is in the World. They are of the World, therefore speak they of the World, and the World heareth them.* Here is a plain *Antithesis*: 'Tis evident that the Apostle is still comparing those that are influenced by the two opposite Kinds of Spirits, the true and the false, and shewing the Difference; the one are of God, and overcome the Spirit of the World; the other are of the World, and speak and favour the Things of the World. The Spirit of the Devil is here called, *He that is in the World*. Christ says, *My Kingdom is not of this World*. But 'tis otherwise with Satan's Kingdom; he is *the God of this World*.

What the Apostle means by *the World*, or the Things that are *of the World*, we learn by his own Words, in the 2d Chapter of this Epistle 15th and 16th Verses: *Love not the World, neither the Things that are in the World: If any Man love the World, the Love of the Father is not in him: For all that is in the World, the Lust of the Flesh, and the Lust of the Eyes, and the Pride of Life, is not of the Father, but is of the World.* So that by *the World*, the Apostle evidently means every Thing that appertains to the Interest of Sin, and comprehends all the Corruptions and Lusts of Men, and all those Acts and Objects by which they are gratified. In these Things lies the Interest of his Kingdom, who is *the Spirit that is in the World*, and is the *God of the World*.

So that we may safely determine, from what the Apostle says, that the Spirit that is at work amongst a People, that is observed to work after such a Manner, as to lessen Mens

Esteem of the Pleasures, Profits & Honours of the World, and to take off their Hearts from an eager Pursuit after these Things; and to engage them in a deep Concern about a future and eternal Happiness in that invisible World, that the Gospel reveals; and puts them upon earnest seeking the Kingdom of God and his Righteousness; and convinces them of the Dreadfulness of Sin, the Guilt that it brings, and the Misery that it exposes to: I say, the Spirit that operates after such a Manner, must needs be the Spirit of God.

It is not to be supposed that Satan would go about to convince Men of Sin, and awaken the Conscience; it can no Way serve his End, to make that Candle of the Lord shine the brighter, and to open the Mouth of that Viceregent of God in the Soul: It is for his Interest, whatever he does, to lull Conscience asleep, and keep that quiet; to have that, with it's Eyes and Mouth open in the Soul, will tend to clog and hinder all his Designs of Darkness, and ever more to be disturbing his Affairs, and crossing his Interest in the Soul, and disquieting him, so that he can manage nothing to his Mind without Molestation. Would the Devil when he is about to establish Men in a Way and State of Sin, take such a Course, in the first Place to enlighten and awaken the Conscience to see the Dreadfulness of Sin, and make them exceedingly afraid of Sin, and sensible of their Misery by Reason of their past Sins, and their great Need of Deliverance from the Guilt of them, and more careful, inquisitive and watchful to discern what is sinful; and to avoid future Sins; and so more afraid of the Devil's Temptations, and careful to guard against them? What do those Men do with their Reason, that suppose that the Spirit that operates thus, is the Spirit of the Devil?

Possibly some may say, That the Devil may even awaken Mens Consciences to deceive them, and make them think they have been the Subjects of a saving Work of the Spirit of God, while they are indeed still in the Gall of Bitterness. But to this it may be replied, That the Man that has an awakened Conscience is the least likely to be deceived of any Man in the World: 'Tis the drowsy, insensible, stupid Conscience, that is most easily blinded. The more sensible Conscience is in a diseased Soul, the less easily is it quieted without a real Healing. The more sensible Conscience is made of the Dreadfulness of

Sin, & of the Greatness of a Man's own Guilt of it, the less likely is he to rest in his own Righteousness, or to be pacified with nothing but Shadows. A Man that has been thoroughly terrified with a Sense of his Danger and Misery, is not easily flattered and made to believe himself safe, without any good Grounds.

To awaken Conscience, and convince of the Evil of Sin, can't tend to establish Sin, but certainly tends to make Way for Sin & Satan's being cast out. Therefore this is a good Argument that the Spirit that operates thus, can't be the Spirit of the Devil; if Christ knew how to argue, who told the *Pharisees*, that supposed that the Spirit that he wro't by, was the Spirit of the Devil, *that Satan would not cast out Satan*, Math. 12. 25, 26.

And therefore if we see Persons made sensible of the dreadful Nature of Sin, and of the Displeasure of God against it, and of their own miserable Condition as they are in themselves, by Reason of Sin, and earnestly concerned for their eternal Salvation, and sensible of their Need of God's Pity and Help, and engaged to seek it in the Use of the Means that God has appointed, we may certainly conclude that it is from the Spirit of God, whatever Effects this Concern has on their Bodies; tho' it causes them to cry out aloud, or to shriek, or to faint, or tho' it throws them into Convulsions, or whatever other Way the Blood and Spirits are moved.

The Influence of the Spirit of God is yet more abundantly manifest, if Persons have their Hearts *drawn off* from the World, and *wean'd* from the Objects of their worldly Lusts, and taken off from worldly Pursuits, by the Sense they have of the Excellency of divine Things, and the Affection they have to those spiritual Enjoyments of another World, that are promised in the Gospel.

3. That Spirit that operates in such a Manner, as to *cause in Men a greater Regard to the holy Scriptures, and establishes them more in their Truth and Divinity*, is certainly the Spirit of God. This Rule the Apostle gives us in the 6th Verse: *We are of God; he that knoweth God heareth us: He that is not of God, heareth not us: Hereby know we the Spirit of Truth, and the Spirit of Error. We are of God*; that is, "We the Apostles, are sent forth of God, and appointed of him, to teach the World, and to deliver that Doctrine, those Instructions that are to be their Rule;

therefore *he that knoweth God, heareth us* &c.—" The Apostle's Argument in the Verse equally reaches all that in the same Sense *are of God*, that is, all those that God has appointed and inspired to deliver to his Church it's Rule of Faith and Practice; all the *Prophets* and *Apostles*, whose Doctrine God has made the Foundation on which he has built his Church, as in *Eph.* 2. 20; all the Penmen of the holy Scriptures. The Devil never would go about to beget in Persons a Regard to that divine Word, which God hath given to be the great and standing Rule for the Direction of his Church in all religious Matters and Concerns of their Souls, in all Ages. A Spirit of Delusion won't incline Persons to go to seek Direction at the Mouth of God. *To the Law and to the Testimony*, is never the Cry of those evil Spirits that *have no Light in them*; for 'tis God's own Direction to discover their Delusions, Isai. 8. 19, 20. *And when they shall say unto you, Seek unto them that have familiar Spirits, and unto Wizards that peep, and that mutter: should not a People seek unto their God? for the Living to the Dead? To the Law, and to the Testimony; if they speak not according to this Word, it is because there is no Light in them.* The Devil don't say the same as *Abraham* did, *They have Moses and the Prophets, let them hear them*: Nor the same that the Voice from Heaven did concerning Christ, *Hear ye him.* Would the Spirit of Error, in order to deceive Men, beget in them an high Opinion of the infallible Rule, and incline them to think much of it, and be very conversant with it? Would the Prince of Darkness, in order to promote his Kingdom of Darkness, lead Men to the Sun? The Devil has ever shewn a mortal Spite and Hatred towards that holy Book, the Bible: He has done all that has been in his Power to extinguish that Light, and to draw Men off from it: He knows that 'tis that Light by which his Kingdom of Darkness is to be overthrown. He has had for many Ages Experience of it's Power to defeat his Purposes, and baffle his Designs: It is his constant Plague: 'Tis the main Weapon which *Michael* uses in his War with him: 'Tis the Sword of the Spirit, that pierces him, and conquers him: 'Tis that *great, and sore, and strong Sword*, with which God *punishes Leviathan, that crooked Serpent*: 'Tis that sharp Sword that we read of, Rev. 19. 15. *that proceeds out of the Mouth of him that sat on the Horse*, with which he smites his Enemies. Every Text is a Dart to torment the old

Serpent: He has felt the stinging Smart thousands of Times; therefore he is enraged against the Bible, and hates every Word in it: And therefore we may be sure that he never will go about to raise Persons Esteem of it, or Affection to it. And accordingly we see it to be common in Enthusiasts, that they depreciate this written Rule, and set up the *Light within*, or some other Rule above it.

4. Another Rule to judge of Spirits may be drawn from those opposite Compellations given to the two opposite Spirits, in the last Words of the 6th Verse, *The SPIRIT OF TRUTH, and the SPIRIT OF ERROR*. These Words do exhibit the two opposite Characters of the Spirit of God, and other Spirits that counterfeit his Operations. And therefore, if by observing the Manner of the Operation of a Spirit that is at work among a People, we see that it operates as a *Spirit of Truth*, leading Persons to *Truth*, convincing them of those Things that are true, we may safely determine that 'tis a right and true Spirit. As for Instance, if we observe that the Spirit that is at work, makes Men more sensible than they used to be, that there is a God, and that he is a great God, and a Sin-hating God; and makes them more to realize it, that they must die, and that Life is short, and very uncertain; and confirms Persons in it that there is another World, that they have immortal Souls, and that they must give Account of themselves to God; and convinces them that they are exceeding sinful by Nature and Practice; and that they are helpless in themselves; and confirms them in other Things that are agreeable to sound Doctrine: The Spirit that works thus, operates as a Spirit of Truth: He represents Things as they are indeed: He brings Men to the Light; for whatever makes Truth manifest, is Light; as the Apostle *Paul* observes, Eph. 5. 13. *But all Things that are reproved* (or *discovered*, as it is in the Margin) *are made manifest by the Light; for whatsoever doth make manifest is Light*. And therefore we may conclude that 'tis not the Spirit of Darkness, that doth thus *discover*, and *make manifest* the Truth. Christ tells us that Satan *is a Liar, and the Father of Lies*; and his Kingdom is a *Kingdom of Darkness*. 'Tis upheld and promoted only by Darkness & Error: Satan has all his Power and Dominion by Darkness. Hence we read of *the Power of Darkness*, Luk. 22. 53. & Col. 1. 13. And Devils are called *the Rulers of the Darkness of*

this World. Whatever Spirit removes our Darkness, and brings us to the Light; undeceives us, and convinces us of the Truth; does us a Kindness. If I am brought to a Sight of Truth, and am made sensible of Things as they be, my Duty is immediately to thank God for it, without standing first to inquire by what Means I have such a Benefit.

5. If the Spirit that is at work among a People *operates as a Spirit of Love to God and Man*, 'tis a sure Sign that 'tis the Spirit of God. This Sign the Apostle insists upon from the 6th Verse to the End of the Chapter: *Beloved, let us love one another; for Love is of God, and every one that loveth is born of God, and knoweth God: He that loveth not, knoweth not God, for God is Love &c.* Here 'tis evident, that the Apostle is still comparing those two sorts of Persons that are influenced by the opposite Kinds of Spirits; and mentions *Love* as a Mark by which we may know who has the true Spirit: But this is especially evident by the 12th & 13th Verses, *If we love one another, God dwelleth in us, and his Love is perfected in us: Hereby know we that we dwell in him, and he in us, because he hath given us of his Spirit.* In these Verses *Love* is spoken of as if it were that wherein the very Nature of the Holy Spirit consisted; or as if divine Love dwelling in us, and the Spirit of God dwelling in us, were the same Thing; as it is also in the two last Verses of the foregoing Chapter; as also in the 16th Verse of this Chapter. Therefore this last Mark which the Apostle gives of the true Spirit, he seems to speak of as the most eminent; and so insists much more largely upon it, than upon all the rest; and speaks expresly of both Love to God and Men; of *Love to Men*, in the 7th, 11th and 12th Verses; and of *Love to God*, in the 17th, 18th & 19th Verses; and of both together, in the two last Verses; and of *Love to Men*, as arising from *Love to God*, in these two last Verses.

Therefore when the Spirit that is at work amongst a People, tends this Way, and brings many of them to high and exalting Thoughts of the divine Being, and his glorious Perfections; and works in them an admiring, delightful Sense of the Excellency of Jesus Christ; representing Him as the chief among ten Thousands, altogether lovely, and makes him precious to the Soul; winning and drawing the Heart with those Motives and Incitements to Love, which the Apostle speaks of in that Passage of Scripture we are upon, *viz.* the wonderful, free Love of

God in giving his only begotten Son to die for us, and the wonderful dying Love of Christ to us, who had no Love to him, but were his Enemies; as Ver. 9, 10. *In this was manifested the Love of God towards us, because that God sent his only begotten Son into the World, that we might live through him. Herein is Love; not that we loved God, but that he loved us, and sent his Son to be the Propitiation for our Sins.* And Ver. 16. *And we have known, and believed the Love that God hath to us.* And Ver. 19. *We Love him, because he first loved us.* The Spirit excites to Love on these Motives, and makes the Attributes of God as revealed in the Gospel, and manifested in Christ, delightful Objects of Contemplation; and makes the Soul to long after God and Christ, after their Presence and Communion, and Acquaintance with them, and Conformity to them; and to live so as to Please & Honour them: And also quells Contentions among Men, and gives a Spirit of Peace and Good-will, excites to Acts of outward Kindness, and earnest Desires of the Salvation of others Souls; and causes a Delight in those that appear as the Children of God, and Followers of Christ: I say when a Spirit operates after this Manner among a People, there is the highest Kind of Evidence of the Influence of a true and divine Spirit.

Indeed there is a Counterfeit of Love, that often appears amongst those that are led by a Spirit of Delusion: There is commonly in the wildest Enthusiasts a Kind of Union and Affection that appears in them one towards another, arising from Self-Love, occasioned by their agreeing one with another in those Things wherein they greatly differ from all others, and for which they are the Objects of the Ridicule of all the rest of Mankind; which naturally will cause them so much the more to prize the Esteem they observe in each other, of those Peculiarities that make them the Objects of others Contempt: So the ancient *Gnosticks* and the wild *Fanaticks*, that appeared in the Beginning of the Reformation, boasted of their great Love one to another: One Sect of them in particular, calling themselves the *Family of Love.* But this is quite another Thing than that Christian Love that I have just described; 'tis only the working of a natural Self-Love, and no true *Benevolence*, any more than the Union & Friendship which may be among a Company of Pirates, that are at War with all the rest of the World. There is sufficient said in this Passage of St. *John*, that we are upon, of the Nature and Motive of a truly Christian Love, thoroughly to distinguish it from all such Counterfeits. It is Love that arises from an Apprehension of the wonderful Riches of free Grace, and Sovereignty of God's Love to us, in Christ Jesus; being attended with a Sense of our own utter Unworthiness, as in our selves the Enemies and Haters of God & Christ, and with a Renunciation of all our own Excellency and Righteousness. See *Ver.* 9, 10, 11, & 19. The surest Character of true divine super-natural Love, distinguishing it from Counterfeits that do arise from a natural Self-Love, is that That Christian Vertue shines in it, that does above all others renounce and abase and annihilate Self, viz. *Humility.* Christian Love, or true Charity, is an humble Love, 1 Cor. 13. 4, 5. *Charity vaunteth not it self; is not puffed up, doth not behave it self unseemly, seeketh not her own, is not easily provoked.* When therefore we see Love in Persons attended with a Sense of their own Littleness, Vileness, Weakness, and utter Insufficiency; and so with Self-Diffidence, Self-Emptiness, Self-Renunciation, and Poverty of Spirit, there are the manifest Tokens of the Spirit of God: He that thus dwells in Love, dwells in God, and God in him. The Love the Apostle speaks of as a great Evidence of the true Spirit, is *God's Love*, or *Christ's Love*; as Ver. 12.—*His Love is perfected in us.* What Kind of Love that is, we may see best in what appeared in Christ, in the Example he set us, when he was here upon Earth. The Love that appeared in that Lamb of God, was not only a Love to Friends, but to Enemies, and a Love attended with a meek and humble Spirit. *Learn of me*, says he, *for I am meek and lowly in Heart.*

Love and Humility are two Things the most contrary to the Spirit of the Devil, of any Thing in the World; for the Character of that Evil Spirit, above all Things, consists in Pride and Malice.

Thus I have spoken particularly to the several Marks the Apostle gives us of a Work of the true Spirit. There are some of these Things the Devil would not do if he could: Thus, he would not awaken the Conscience, and make Men sensible of their miserable State by Nature, by Reason of Sin, and sensible of their great Need of a Saviour: And he would not confirm Men in a Belief that Jesus is the Son of God, and the Saviour of Sinners, or raise Mens Value and Esteem of Him: He would

not beget in Mens Minds an Opinion of the Necessity, Useful-
ness and Truth of the Holy Scriptures, or incline them to
hearken to them, or make much Use of them; nor would he go
about to shew Men the Truth, in Things that concern their
Souls Interest; to undeceive 'em, and lead 'em out of Darkness
into Light, and give 'em a View of Things as they are indeed.
And there are other Things that the Devil neither can nor will
do: He will not give Men a Spirit of Divine Love, or Christian
Humility and Poverty of Spirit; nor could he if he would: He
can't give those Things which he has not himself: These Things
are as contrary as possible to his Nature. And therefore when
there is an extraordinary Influence or Operation appearing on
the Minds of a People, if these Things are found in it, we are
safe in determining that 'tis the Work of God, whatever other
Circumstances it may be attended with, whatever Instruments
are improved, whatever Methods are taken to promote it;
whatever Means a sovereign God, whose Judgments are a
great Deep, makes Use of to carry it on; and whatever Motions there may be of the animal Spirits, whatever Effects may
be wrought on Mens Bodies. These Marks, that the Apostle
has given us, are sufficient to stand alone, and support themselves; and where-ever they be, they plainly shew the Finger of
God, and are sufficient to outweigh a Thousand such little
Objections, as many make from Oddities, Irregularities, and
Errors in Conduct, and the Delusions and Scandals of some
Professors.

Object. But here some may object against the Sufficiency of
the Marks given, what the Apostle *Paul* says, in the 2 Cor. 11.
13, 14. *For such are false Apostles, deceitful Workers, transforming themselves into the Apostles of Christ; and no Marvel, for
Satan himself is transformed into an Angel of Light.*

To which I Answer, That this can be no Objection against
the Sufficiency of these Marks to distinguish the true Spirit
from the false Spirit, in those *false Apostles* and *false Prophets*,
which the Apostle speaks of, in whom the Devil was *transformed into an Angel of Light*, because it is principally with a
View to them that the Apostle gives these Marks; as appears by
the Words of the Text, *Believe not every Spirit, but try the Spirits, whether they are of God*: And this is the Reason he gives,
Because many false Prophets are gone out into the World: "There

are many gone out into the World that are the Ministers of the Devil, that *transform themselves* into the Prophets of God, in whom the Spirit of the Devil *is transformed into an Angel of Light*; therefore try the Spirits by these Rules that I shall give you, that you may be able to distinguish the true Spirit from the false Spirit, under such a crafty Disguise." Those *false Prophets* the Apostle *John* speaks of, are doubtless the same Sort of Men with those *false Apostles*, and *deceitful Workers*, that the Apostle *Paul* speaks of, in that Place in the 2d of *Corinthians*, in whom *the Devil was transformed into an Angel of Light*: And therefore we may be sure that these Marks the Apostle gives, are especially adapted to distinguish between the true Spirit, and the Devil transformed into an Angel of Light, because they are given especially for that End; that is the Apostle's declared Purpose and Design, to give Marks by which the true Spirit may be distinguished from that Sort of Counterfeits.

And if we look over what is said about these *false Prophets*, and *false Apostles*, (as there is much said about them in the New Testament) and take Notice in what Manner the Devil was transformed into an Angel of Light in them, we shall not find any Thing that in the least injures the Sufficiency of these Marks to distinguish the true Spirit from such Counterfeits. The Devil transformed himself into an Angel of Light, as there was in them a Shew, and great Boasts of extraordinary Knowledge in divine Things; *Col.* 2. 8. 1 *Tim.* 1. 6, 7. and *Chap.* 6. 3, 4, 5. 2 *Tim.* 2. 14, 16, 17, 18. *Tit.* 1. 10, 16. Hence their Followers called themselves *Gnosticks*, from their great pretended Knowledge: And the Devil in them mimicked the miraculous Gifts of the Holy Spirit, in Visions, Revelations, Prophecies, Miracles, and the immediate Conduct of the Spirit in what they did: Hence they are called *false Apostles*, and *false Prophets*: See *Mat.* 24. 24. Again, there was a false Shew of, and lying Pretences to great Holiness and Devotion in Words: *Rom.* 16. 17, 18. *Eph.* 4. 14. Hence they are called *deceitful Workers*, and *Wells*, and *Clouds without Water.* 2 *Cor.* 11. 13. 2 *Pet.* 2. 17. *Jude* 12. There was also in them a Shew of extraordinary Piety and Righteousness in their superstitious Worship: *Col.* 2. 16, 17, 18, 21, 22, 23. So they had a false, proud, and bitter Zeal; *Gal.* 4. 17, 18. 1 *Tim.* 1. 6. *and Chap.* 6. 4, 5. And likewise a false *Shew of Humility*, in affecting an extraordinary outward Meanness and

Dejection, when indeed they were *vainly puffed up with their fleshly Mind*; and made a Righteousness of their Humility, and were exceedingly lifted up with their eminent Piety: *Col.* 2. 18, 23. But how do such Things as these, in the least injure those Things that have been mentioned as the distinguishing Evidences of the true Spirit?

Besides such vain Shews which may be from the Devil, there are common Influences of the Spirit, which are often mistaken for saving Grace: But these are out of the Question, because tho' they are not saving, yet are the Work of the true Spirit.

Having thus fulfil'd what I at first proposed, in considering what are the certain, distinguishing Marks, by which we may safely proceed in judging of any Work that falls under our Observation, whether it be the Work of the Spirit of God or no. I now proceed to the

APPLICATION

I. From what has been said, I will venture to draw this *Inference*, viz. *That that extraordinary Influence that has lately appeared on the Minds of the People abroad in this Land, causing in them an uncommon Concern and Engagedness of Mind about the Things of Religion, is undoubtedly, in the general, from the Spirit of God.* There are but two Things that need to be known in order to such a Work's being judged of, viz. *Facts* and *Rules.* The *Rules* of the Word of God we have had laid before us; and as to *Facts*, there are but two Ways that we can come at them, so as to be in a Capacity to compare them with the Rules, either by our own Observation, or by Information from others that have had Opportunity to observe.

As to this Work that has lately been carried on in the Land, there are many Things concerning it that are notorious, and known by every Body, (unless it be some that have been very much out of the Way of observing and hearing indeed) that unless the Apostle *John* was out in his Rules, are sufficient to determine it to be in general, the Work of God. 'Tis notorious that the Spirit that is at work, takes off Persons Minds from the Vanities of the World, and engages them in a deep Concern about a future and eternal Happiness in another World, and puts them upon earnestly seeking their Salvation, and convinces them of the Dreadfulness of Sin, and of their own guilty and miserable State as they are by Nature. It is notorious that it awakens Mens Consciences, and makes 'em sensible of the Dreadfulness of God's Anger, and causes in them a great Desire, and earnest Care and Endeavour to obtain his Favour. It is notorious, that it puts them upon a more diligent Improvement of the Means of Grace which God has appointed. It is also notorious, that, in general, it works in Persons a greater Regard to the Word of God, and desire of hearing and reading of it, and to be more conversant with the holy Scriptures than they used to be. And it is notoriously manifest that the Spirit that is at work, in general, operates as a Spirit of Truth, making Persons more sensible of what is really true, in those Things that concern their eternal Salvation: As that they must die, and that Life is very short and uncertain; that there is a Great, Sin-hating God, that they are accountable to, and will fix them in an eternal State in another World, and that they stand in great Need of a Saviour. It is furthermore notorious, that the Spirit that is at work makes Persons more sensible of the Value of that Jesus that was crucified, and their Need of him; and that it puts them upon earnestly seeking an Interest in him. It can't be but that these Things should be apparent to People in general through the Land: for these Things ben't done in a Corner; the Work that has been wrought has not been confined to a few Towns, in some remoter Parts of the Land, but has been carried on in many Places in all Parts of the Land, and in most of the principal, and most populous, & publick Places in it, (Christ in this Respect has wrought amongst us, in the same Manner that he wrought his Miracles in *Judea*) and has now been continued for a considerable Time; so that there has been a great deal of Opportunity to observe the Manner of the Work. And all such as have been much in the Way of observing the Work, & have been very conversant with those that have been the Subjects of it, do see a great deal more that, by the Rules of the Apostle, does clearly and certainly shew it to be the Work of God.

And here I would observe, That the Nature and Tendency of a Spirit that is at work, may be determined with much greater certainty, and less Danger of being imposed upon, when it is observed in a great Multitude of People of all Sorts, and in various different Places, than when it is only seen in a few, in some particular Place, that have been much conversant one with another. A few particular Persons may agree to put a Cheat upon others, by a false Pretence, and professing Things that they never were conscious to in their own Minds: But when the Work is spread over great Part of a Country, in Places distant one from another, among People of all Sorts, and all Ages, and in Multitudes of Persons, of sound Mind, good Understanding, and known Integrity; there would be the greatest Absurdity in supposing that, by all the Observation that can be made by all that is heard from them and seen in them, for many Months together, by those that are most intimate with them in these Affairs, and have long been acquainted with them, that yet it can't be determined what Kind of Influence the Operation they are under, has upon People's Minds, whether it tends to awaken their Consciences, or to stupify them; whether it tends to incline them more to seek their Salvation, or neglect it; whether it seems to confirm them in a Belief of the Scriptures, or to lead them to Deism; whether it makes them have more Regard to the great Truths of Religion, or less; and so in other Things. There is probably no particular Person here present, that thinks himself to have a Right to be treated as one of a sound Mind, and common Sense, and Veracity, but would think himself abused, if he should declare to others, that he had altered his Mind in these and those Particulars; he now found himself convinced of the Truth of this or that, that formerly he did not believe; and that he found in himself such and such Fears, that he don't use to have; or found a greater Aversion than he was won't to have, or a greater Esteem and Affection to such and such Things; and those that he made such a Profession to would not believe him, tho' they had long been conversant with him, and tho' he persisted in this Profession for many Months together, and nothing appeared in him but what agreed thereto. But much more unreasonable it would be, when such Professions are made, not by a particular Person only, but a great Part of a People in a Land, to suppose that they all agree in professing what indeed they do not feel in their Souls.

And here it is to be observed, That for Persons to profess that they are convinced of these or those divine Truths; or that they esteem and love such divine Things, in a saving Manner; and for them to profess, that they are more convinced or confirmed in the Truth of them, than they used to be, and find that they have a greater Regard to them than before they had, are two very different Things. Persons of Honesty and common Sense, have much greater Right to demand Credit to be given to the latter Profession, than to the former; (tho' in the former it is vastly less likely that a People in general should be deceived, than some particular Persons.) But whether Persons Convictions, and the Alteration in their Dispositions and Affections, be in a Degree & Manner that is saving, is beside the present Question. If there be such Effects on Peoples Judgments, Dispositions and Affections, as have been spoken of, whether they be in a Degree & Manner that is saving or no, it is nevertheless a Sign of the Influence of the Spirit of God. Scripture Rules serve to distinguish the common Influences of the Spirit of God, as well as those that are saving, from the Influence of other Causes.

And as I am One that, by the Providence of God, have for some Months past, been much amongst those that have been the Subjects of that Work, that has of late been carried on in the Land; and particularly, have been abundantly in the Way of seeing & observing those extraordinary Things that many Persons have been much stumbled at; such as Persons crying out aloud, shrieking, being put into great Agonies of Body, and deprived of their bodily Strength, and the like; and that in many different Towns; and have been very particularly conversant with great Numbers of such, both in the Time of their being the Subjects of such extraordinary Influences, and afterwards, from Time to Time, and have seen the Manner and Issue of such Operations, and the Fruits of them, for several Months together; many of them being Persons that I have long known, and have been intimately acquainted with them in Soul Concerns, before and since: So I look upon my self called on this Occasion to give my Testimony, that so far as the Nature and Tendency of such a Work is capable of falling under the Observation of a By-stander, to whom those that have been the Subjects of it have endcavour'd to open their *Hearts*, or can be come at by diligent and particular Inquiry, this Work has all those Marks that have been spoken of; in very many Instances, in every Article; and particularly in many of those that have been the Subjects of such extraordinary Operations, all those Marks have appeared in a very great Degree.

Those in whom have been these uncommon Appearances, have been of two Sorts; either those that have been in great Distress, in an Apprehension of their Sin and Misery; or those that have been overcome with a sweet Sense of the Greatness, Wonderfulness and Excellency of divine Things. Of the Multitude of those of the former sort, that I have had Opportunity to observe, and have been acquainted with, there have been very few, but that by all that could be observed in them, in the Time of it, or afterwards, their Distress has arisen from real, proper Conviction, and a being in a Degree sensible of that which was the Truth. And tho' I don't suppose, when such Things were observed to be common, that Persons have laid themselves under those violent Restraints, to avoid outward Manifestations of their Distress, that perhaps they otherwise would have done; yet there have been very few in whom there has been any Appearance of feigning or affecting such Manifestations, and very many for whom it would have been undoubtedly utterly impossible for 'em to avoid them. Generally those that have been in these Agonies have appeared to be in the perfect Exercise of their Reason; and those of them that have been able to speak, have been well able to give an Account of the Circumstances of their Minds, & the Cause of their Distress, in the Time of it, and well able to remember, and give an Account afterwards. I have known a very few Instances of those, that in their great Extremity, have for a short Space been deprived, in some Measure of the Use of Reason; but among the many Hundreds, and it may be Thousands, that have lately been brought to such Agonies, I never yet knew one, lastingly deprived of their Reason. In some that I have known, Melancholly has evidently been mixt; and when it is so, the Difference is very apparent; their Distresses are of another Kind, and operate quite after another Manner, than when their Distress is from meer Conviction: 'Tis not Truth only that distresses them, but many vain Shadows and Notions, that won't give Place either to Scripture or Reason. Some in their great Distress, have not been well able to give an Account of themselves, or to declare the Sense they have of Things, or to explain the Manner & Cause of their Trouble to others, that yet

I have had no Reason to think were not under proper Convictions, and in whom there has been manifested a good Issue. But this won't be at all wonder'd at, by those who have had much to do with Souls under spiritual Difficulties. Some Things that they are sensible of are altogether new to them, their Ideas and inward Sensations are new, and what they therefore knew not how to accommodate Language to, or to find Words to express. And some who on first Inquiry, say they know not what was the Matter with them, on being particularly Examined and Interrogated, have been able to represent their Case, tho' of themselves they could not find Expressions, and Forms of Speech to do it.

Some say they think that the Terrors that such Persons are in, that have such Effects on their Bodies, is only a *Fright*. But certainly there ought to be a Distinction made between a very great Fear, and extream Distress, arising from an Apprehension of some dreadful *Truth*, that is a Cause that is fully proportionable to such an Effect, and a needless causeless Fright: which is of two Kinds; either when Persons are terrified with that which is not the Truth; (of this I have seen very few Instances, unless in Case of Melancholy;) Or secondly, when Persons are under a childish Fright, only from some terrible outward Appearance and Noise, and a general Notion thence arising, that there is something or other Terrible, they know not what; without having in their Minds the Apprehension of any particular terrible Truth whatsoever; of such a Kind of Fright I have seen very little Appearance, either among Old or Young.

Those that are in such Extremity, commonly express a great Sense of their exceeding Wickedness, the Multitude and Aggravations of their actual Sins, and the dreadful Pollution, Enmity and Perverseness of their Hearts, and a dreadful Obstinacy and hardness of Heart; a Sense of their great Guilt in the Sight of God; and the Dreadfulness of the Punishment that Sin exposes to: Very often they have a lively Idea of the horrible Pit of eternal Misery; and at the same Time it appears to them, that a Great God that has them in his Hands, is exceeding Angry with them; his Wrath appears amazingly terrible to them: God appearing to them so much provoked, and his great Wrath so incensed, they are apprehensive of great Danger, that he will not bear with them any longer; but will now, forthwith, cut 'em off, and send them down to the dreadful Pit they have in View; at the same Time seeing no Refuge: They see more and more of the Vanity of every Thing they used to trust to, and flatter themselves in; 'till they are brought wholly to despair in all, and to see that they are at the Disposal of the meer Will of the God that is so angry with them. Very many, in the midst of their Extremity, have been brought to an extraordinary Sense of their fully deserving that Wrath & Destruction, which is then before their Eyes; and at the same Time, that they have feared every Moment, that it would be executed upon them, they have been greatly convinced that it would be altogether just that it should, and that God is indeed absolutely Sovereign: and very often, some Text of Scripture expressing God's Sovereignty, has been set home upon their Minds, whereby their Minds have been calm'd, and they have been brought as it were to lie at God's Foot; and after great Agonies, a little before Light has arisen, they have been composed and quiet, in a Kind of Submission to a Just and Sovereign God; but their bodily Strength much spent; and sometimes their Lives, to Appearance almost gone; and then Light has appeared, and a glorious Redeemer, with his wonderful, all-sufficient Grace, has been represented to them, often, in some sweet Invitation of Scripture. Sometimes the Light comes in suddenly, sometimes more gradually, filling their Souls with Love, Admiration, Joy & Self-Abasement; drawing forth their Hearts in Longing after the excellent lovely Redeemer, and Longings to lie in the Dust before him; and Longings that others might behold him, and embrace him, and be delivered by him; and Longings to live to his Glory: but sensible that they can do nothing of themselves; appearing Vile in their own Eyes, and having much of a Jealousy over their own Hearts. And all the Appearances of a real Change of Heart have followed; and Grace has acted, from Time to Time, after the same Manner that it used to act in those that were converted formerly, with the like Difficulties, Temptations, Buffetings, and like Comforts; excepting that in many, Light & Comfort has been in higher Degree than ordinary. Many very young Children have been thus wro't upon. There have been some Instances very much like those Demoniacks that we read of, *Mar.* 1. 26. and *Chap.* 9. 26. of whom we read, that *when the Devil had cried with a loud Voice, and rent them sore, he came out of them*. And probably those Instances were designed for a Type of such Things as these. Some have several Turns of great Agonies, before they are delivered: and some have been in such Distresses, and it has passed off, and no Deliverance at all has followed.

Some object against it, as great Confusion, when there is a Number together, in such Circumstances, making a Noise; and say, God can't be the Author of it, because he is the God of Order, not of Confusion. But let it be considered, what is the proper Notion of Confusion, but the breaking that Order of Things whereby they are properly disposed, and duly directed to their End, so that the Order and due Connection of Means being broken, they fail of their End; but Conviction and Conversion of Sinners is the obtaining the End of religious Means. Not but that I think that Persons that are thus extraordinarily moved shou'd endeavour to refrain from such outward Manifestations, what they well can, and should refrain to their utmost, in the Time of the solemn Worship. But if God is pleased to convince the Consciences of Persons, so that they can't avoid great outward Manifestations, even to the interrupting, and breaking off those publick Means they were attending, I don't think this is Confusion, or an unhappy Interruption, any more than if a Company should meet on the Field to pray for Rain, and should be broken off from their Exercise by a plentiful Shower. Would to God that all the publick Assemblies in the Land were broken off from their publick Exercises with such Confusion as this the next Sabbath Day! We need not be sorry for the breaking the Order of the Means, by obtaining the End to which that Order is directed: He that is going a Journey to fetch a Treasure, need not be sorry that he is stopped by meeting the Treasure in the midst of his Journey.

Besides those that are overcome with Conviction and Distress, I have seen many of late, that have had their bodily Strength taken away with a Sense of the glorious Excellency of the Redeemer, and the Wonders of his dying Love; with a very uncommon Sense of their own Littleness, and exceeding Vileness attending it, with all Expressions and Appearances of the greatest Abasement & Abhorrence of themselves: And not only new Converts, but many that were, as we hope, formerly converted, whose Love and Joy has been attended with a Flood of Tears, and a great Appearance of Contrition and Humiliation, especially for their having lived no more to God's Glory since their Conversion; with a far greater Sight of their Vileness, & the Evil of their Hearts than ever they had; with an exceeding Earnestness of Desire to live better for the Time to come, but attended with greater Self-Diffidence than ever: And many have been even overcome with Pity to the Souls of others, and longing for their Salvation.

And many other Things I might mention in this extraordinary Work, answering to every one of those Marks that have been insisted on. So that if the Apostle *John* knew how to give Signs of a Work of the true Spirit, this is such a Work.

Providence has cast my Lot in a Place where the Work of God has formerly been carried on: I had the Happiness to be settled in that Place two Years with the venerable STODDARD; and was then acquainted with a Number that, during that Season, were wro't upon, under his Ministry, and have been intimately acquainted with the Experiences of many others, that were wro't upon before under his Ministry, in a Manner agreeable to his Doctrine, and the Doctrine of all orthodox Divines; and of late that Work has been carried on there, with very much of these uncommon Opperations: but 'tis apparent to all to be the same Work, not only that was wro't there six or seven Years ago, but elder Christians there know it to be the same Work that was carried on there, in their former Pastor's Days, tho' there be some new Circumstances. And certainly we must throw by all the Talk of Conversion and Christian Experience; and not only so, but we must throw by our Bibles, and give up revealed Religion, if this be not in general the Work of God. Not that I suppose that the Degree of the Influence of the Spirit of God, is to be determined by the Degree of Effect on Men's Bodies, or that those are always the best Experiences, that have the greatest Influence on the Body.

And as to the Imprudences & Irregularities and Mixture of Delusion that have been; it is not at all to be wondered at that a Reformation, after a long continued, and almost universal Deadness, should at first when the Revival is new, be attended with such Things. In the first Creation God did not make a compleat World at once; but there was a great deal of Imperfection, Darkness, and Mixture of *Chaos* and Confusion, after God first said, *Let there be Light*, before the whole stood forth in perfect Form. When God at first began his great Work for the Deliverance of his People, after their long continued Bondage in *Egypt*, there were false Wonders mix'd with true, for a while; which harden'd the unbelieving *Egyptians*, and made 'em to doubt of the Divinity of the whole Work. When the Children of *Israel* first went about bringing up the Ark of God, after it had long been neglected, and had been long absent, they *sought not the Lord after the due Order*, 1 Chron. 15. 13. At the Time when the Sons of God came to present themselves before the Lord, *Satan came also among them*. And *Solomon*'s Ships when they *brought Gold and Silver and Pearls*, also brought *Apes and Peacocks*. When Day Light first appears, after a Night of Darkness, we must expect to have Darkness mixt with Light, for a while, and not to have perfect Day, and the Sun risen at once. The Fruits of the Earth are first green before they are ripe, and come to their proper Perfection gradually; and so Christ tells us, *is the Kingdom of God*. Mark 4. 26, 27, 28. *So is the Kingdom of God; as if a Man should cast Seed into the Ground, and should Sleep, and rise Night and Day; and the Seed should spring and grow up, he knoweth not how: for the Earth bringeth forth Fruit of her self; first the Blade; then the Ear; then the full Corn in the Ear.*

The Imprudences and Errors that have attended this Work, are the less to be wonder'd at, if it be considered, that it is chiefly young Persons that have been the Subjects of it, who have less Steadiness and Experience, and are in the Heat of Youth, and much more ready to run to Extreams. Satan will keep Men secure as long as he can; but when he can do that no longer, he often endeavours to drive them to Extreams, and so to dishonour God, and wound Religion that Way. And doubtless it has been one Occasion of much of the Misconduct there has been, that in many Places, People that are the Subjects of this Work of God's Spirit, see plainly that their Ministers have an ill Opinion of the Work; and therefore with just Reason, durst not apply themselves to 'em as their Guides in this Work; and so are without Guides: and no Wonder that when a People are as Sheep without a Shepherd, they wander out of the Way.

A People, in such Circumstances especially, stand in great and continual Need of Guides, and their Guides stand in continual Need of much more Wisdom than they have of their own. And if a People have Ministers that favour the Work, and rejoyce in it, yet 'tis not to be expected that, either People or Ministers should know so well how to conduct themselves in such an extraordinary State of Things, while it is new, and what they never had any Experience of before, as they may, after they have had Experience, and Time to see the Tendency, Consequences and Issue of Things. The happy Influence of Experience is very manifest at this Day, in the People among whom God has settled my Abode. The Work of God that has been carried on there this Year, has been much purer than that which was wrought there six Years before: It has seem'd to be more purely spiritual; freer from natural and corrupt Mixtures, and any Thing favouring of enthusiastick Wildness & Extravagance: It has wrought more by deep Humiliation and Abasement before God and Men; and they have been much freer from Imprudences and Irregularities. And particularly there has been a remarkable Difference in this Respect, That whereas many before, in their Comforts and Rejoycings, did too much forget their Distance from God, and were ready in their Conversation together of the Things of God, and of their own Experiences, to talk with too much of an Air of Lightness, and something of Laughter; now they seem to have no Disposition to it, but rejoyce with a more solemn, reverential, humble Joy; as God directs the Princes of the Earth, *Psal.* 2. 11. 'Tis not because the Joy is not as great, and in many of them much greater: There are many among us, that were wro't upon in that former Season, that have now had much greater Communications from Heaven than they had then; but their Rejoycing operates in another Manner: it only abases and solemnizes them; breaks their Hearts, and brings them into the Dust: Now when they speak of their Joys, it is not with Laughter, but a Flood of Tears. Thus those that laughed before, weep now; and yet, by their united Testimony, their Joy is vastly purer and sweeter than that which before did more raise their animal Spirits. They are now more like *Jacob*, when God appeared to him at *Bethel*, when he saw the Ladder that reached to Heaven, and said, *How dreadful is this Place*; and like *Moses*, when God shewed him his Glory on the Mount, when *he made haste, and bowed himself unto the Earth.*

II. Let us all be hence warned, *by no Means to oppose, or do any Thing, in the least to clog or hinder that Work that has lately been carried on in the Land, but on the contrary, to do our utmost to promote it.* Now Christ is come down from Heaven into this Land, in a remarkable & wonderful Work of his Spirit, it becomes all his professed Disciples to acknowlege him, and give him Honour.

The Example of the Jews in Christ's and the Apostles Times, is enough to beget in those that don't acknowlege this Work, a great Jealousy of themselves, and to make them exceeding cautious of what they say or do. Christ then *was in the World, and the World knew him not: He came to his own* professing People, *and his own received him not.* That coming of Christ had been much spoken of in the Prophecies of Scripture that they had in their Hands, and had been long expected; and yet because Christ came in a Manner that they did not expect, and that was not agreeable to their carnal Reason, they would not own him, but opposed him, counted him a Madman, and the Spirit that he wrought by the Spirit of the Devil. They stood and wondered at the great Things that were done, and knew not what to make of 'em; but yet they met with so many stumbling Blocks, that they finally could not acknowlege him. And when the Spirit of God came to be so wonderfully poured out in the Apostles Days, they looked upon it to be Confusion and Distraction. They were astonished by what they saw and heard, but not convinced. And especially was the Work of God then rejected by those that were most conceited of their own Understanding & Knowlege, agreeable to Isai. 29. 14. *Therefore behold, I will proceed to do a marvellous Work amongst this People, even a marvellous Work and a Wonder; for the Wisdom of their wise Men shall perish, and the Understanding of their prudent Men shall be hid.* And many of them that had been in Reputation for Religion & Piety, had a great Spite against the Work, because they saw it tended to diminish their Honour, and to reproach their Formality and Lukewarmness. Some upon these Accounts, maliciously and openly opposed and reproached the Work of the Spirit of God, and called it the Work of the Devil, against inward Conviction; and so were guilty of the unpardonable Sin against the Holy Ghost.

There is another Coming of Christ, a spiritual Coming, to set up his Kingdom in the World, that is as much spoken of in Scripture Prophecy, as that first Coming of Christ was, and that has been long expected by the Church of God; that we have Reason to think, from what is said of it, will be, in many Respects, parallel with the other. And certainly, that low State that the visible Church of God has lately been sunk into, is very parallel with the State of the Jewish Church, when Christ came: and therefore no Wonder at all, that when Christ comes, his Work should appear a strange Work to most; yea, it would be a Wonder if it should be otherwise. Whether the Work that is now wro't, be the Beginning of that great Coming of Christ to set up his Kingdom, that is so much spoken of, or no; yet it is evident from what has been said, that it is a Work of the same Spirit, and of the same Nature. And there is no Reason to doubt but that, for Persons to continue long to refuse to ac-knowlege Christ in the Work, especially those that are set to be Teachers in his Church, will be in like Manner provoking to God, as it was in the Jews of old to refuse to acknowlege Christ; and that notwithstanding what they may plead of the great stumbling Blocks that are in the Way, and the Cause they have to doubt of the Work. The Teachers of the Jewish Church found innumerable stumbling Blocks, that were to them insu-perable: there were many Things appeared in Christ, and in the Work of the Spirit after his Ascension, that were exceeding strange to 'em; they were assured that they had just Cause for their Scruples: Christ and his Work were to the Jews a stum-bling Block: *But blessed is he*, says Christ, *whosoever shall not be offended* (or *stumbled*) *in me*. As strange and as unexpected as the Manner of Christ's Appearance was, yet he had not been long in *Judea*, working Miracles, before all those that had Op-portunity to observe, and yet refused to acknowlege him, brought fearful Guilt upon themselves in the Sight of God; and Christ condemned them, that tho' *they could discern the Face of the Sky, and of the Earth, yet they could not discern the Signs of these Times: and why,* says he, *Even of your selves, judge ye not what is right?* Luk. 12. at the latter End.

'Tis not to be supposed that the great JEHOVAH has bowed the Heavens and come down into this Land, and appeared here now for so long a Time, in such a glorious Work of his Power and Grace, in so extensive a Manner, in the most publick Places of the Land, and almost all Parts of it, without giving such Evidences of his Presence, that great Numbers, and even many Teachers in his Church, can remain guiltless in his Sight, without ever receiving and acknowledging him, and giving him Honour, and appearing to rejoyce in his gracious Presence; or without so much as once giving him Thanks for so glorious and blessed a Work of his Grace, wherein his Goodness does more appear, than if he had bestowed on us all the temporal Blessings that the World affords. A long continued Silence in such a Case is undoubtedly provoking to God; especially in Ministers: it is a secret Kind of Opposition, that really tends to hinder the Work: such silent Ministers stand in the Way of the Work of God; as Christ said of old, *He that is not with us is against us.* Those that stand wondering at this strange Work of God, not knowing what to make of it, and refusing to receive it, and ready it may be sometimes to speak contemptibly of it, as it was with the Jews of old, would do well to consider and tremble at St. *Paul*'s Words to them, Act. 13. 40, 41. *Beware therefore least that come upon you, which is spoken of in the Prophets, Behold ye Despisers, and wonder, and perish; for I work a Work in your Days, which you shall in no wise believe, tho' a Man declare it unto you.* And those that can't believe the Work to be true, because of the extraordinary Degree and Manner of it, should consider how it was with the unbelieving Lord in *Samaria*, who said, *Behold, if the Lord would make Windows in Heaven, might this Thing be?* To whom *Elisha* said, *Behold thou shalt see it with thine Eyes, but shall not eat thereof.* Let all to whom this Work is a Cloud and Darkness, as the Pillar of Cloud & Fire was to the *Egyptians*, take heed that it ben't their Destruction, as that was theirs, while it gave Light to God's Israel.

I would pray those that quiet themselves with that, that they proceed on a Principle of Prudence, and are waiting to see what the Issue of Things will be, and what Fruits those that are the Subjects of this Work will bring forth in their Lives and Conversations, would consider, whether this will justify a long refraining from acknowleging Christ when he appears so wonderfully and graciously present in the Land. 'Tis probable that many of those that are thus waiting, know not what they are waiting for: If they wait to see a Work of God without Difficulties & stumbling Blocks, that will be like the Fool's waiting at the River Side to have the Water all run by. A Work of God without stumbling Blocks is never to be expected: *It must needs be that Offences come.* There never yet was any great Manifestation that God made of himself to the World, without many Difficulties attending it. It is with the Works of God, as 'tis with the Word of God; they are full of those Things that seem strange and inconsistent and difficult to the carnal unbelieving Hearts of Men. Christ and his Work always was, and always will be a Stone of Stumbling, and Rock of Offence; a Gin and a Snare to many. The Prophet *Hosea*, in the last Chap. of his Prophecy, speaking of a glorious Revival of Religion in God's Church, when God *would be as the Dew unto Israel, and he should grow as the Lilly, and cast forth his Roots as Lebanon, his Branches should spread, &c.* concludes all thus, in the last Verse, *Who is wise? and he shall understand these Things; prudent? and he shall know them. For the Ways of the Lord are right, and the Just shall walk in them, but the Transgressors shall fall therein.*

'Tis probable that the stumbling Blocks that now attend this Work, will in some Respects be increased, and not diminished. Particularly, we probably shall see more Instances of Apostacy & gross Iniquity among Professors. And if one Kind of stumbling Blocks are removed, 'tis to be expected that others will come. 'Tis with Christ's Works, as it was with his Parables: Things that are difficult to Men's dark Minds, are ordered of purpose, for the Trial of Person's Dispositions and spiritual Sense, and that Persons of corrupt Minds, and of an unbelieving, perverse, cavelling Spirit, *seeing might see and not understand*. Those that are now waiting to see the Issue of this Work, think they shall be better able to determine by and by; but they are probably, many of them, mistaken. The Jews that saw Christ's Miracles, waited to see better Evidences of his being the Messiah; they wanted a Sign from Heaven; but they waited in vain; their stumbling Blocks did not diminish, but increase; they found no End to 'em; and so were more and more hardened in their Unbelief. Many have been praying for that glorious Reformation spoken of in Scripture, that knew not what they have been praying for, (as it was with the Jews when they prayed for the Coming of Christ) if it should come, they would not acknowlege or receive it.

This pretended Prudence of Persons, in waiting so long before they acknowlege this Work, will probably in the End prove the greatest Imprudence, in this Respect, that hereby they will fail of any Share of so great a Blessing, and will miss the most precious Opportunity of obtaining divine Light, Grace and Comfort, and heavenly and eternal Benefits, that ever God gave in *New England*: While the glorious Fountain is set open in so wonderful a Manner, and Multitudes flock to it, and receive a rich Supply of the Wants of their Souls, they stand at a Distance doubting and wondring, and receive nothing, and are like to continue thus till the precious Season is past.

It is to be wondered at, that those that have doubted of the Work that has been attended with such uncommon external Appearances, should be easy in their Doubts, without taking thorough Pains to inform themselves, by going where such Things have been to be seen, and narrowly observing them, and diligently inquiring into them; not contenting themselves only with observing two or three Instances, nor resting till they were fully informed by their own Observation. I don't doubt but that if this Course had been taken, it would have convinced all whose Minds are not shut up against Conviction, in a great Degree indeed. How greatly have they erred, who only from the uncertain Reports of others, have ventured to speak slightily of these Things? That Caution of an unbelieving Jew might teach them more Prudence, Act. 5. 38, 39. *Refrain from these Men, and let them alone; for if this Counsel, or this Work be of Men, it will come to nought; but if it be of God, ye cannot overthrow it: lest haply ye be found to fight against God.* Whether what has been said in this Discourse be enough to convince all that have heard it, that the Work that is now carried on in the Land, is the Work of God, or not, yet I hope that for the future, they will at least hearken to the Caution of *Gamaliel* that has been now mentioned; for the future not to oppose it, or say any Thing against it, or any Thing that has so much as an indirect Tendency to bring it into Discredit, least they should be found to be Opposers of the Holy Ghost. There is no Kind of Sins so hurtful and dangerous to the Souls of Men, as those that are committed against the Holy Ghost. We had better speak against God the Father, or the Son, than to speak against the Holy Spirit in his gracious Operations on the Hearts of Men: nothing will so much tend for ever to prevent our having any Benefit of his Operations in our own Souls.

If there are any that will still resolutely go on to speak contemptibly of these Things, I would beg of them to take heed that they ben't guilty of the unpardonable Sin against the Holy Ghost. A Time when the Holy Spirit is much poured out, and Mens Lusts, Lukewarmness and Hypocrisy reproached by it's powerful Operations, is the most likely Time of any whatsoever, for this Sin to be committed. If the Work goes on, 'tis well if among the many that shew an Enmity against it, and reproach it, some ben't guilty of this Sin, if none have been already. Those that maliciously oppose and reproach this Work, and call it the Work of the Devil, want but one Thing of the unpardonable Sin, and that is doing it against inward Conviction. And tho' some are so prudent, as not openly to oppose and reproach the Work, yet 'tis to be feared, at this Day when the Lord is going forth so gloriously against his Enemies, that many that are silent and unactive, especially Ministers, will bring that Curse of the Angel of the Lord upon themselves, Judg. 5. 23. *Curse ye Meroz, said the Angel of the Lord: curse ye bitterly the Inhabitants thereof, because they came not to the Help of the Lord, to the Help of the Lord against the Mighty.*

Since the Great God has come down from Heaven, and manifested himself in so wonderful a Manner in this Land, it is in vain for any of us to expect any other, than to be greatly affected by it in our spiritual State and Circumstances, respecting the Favour of God, one Way or the other. Those that don't become more happy by it, will become far more guilty and miserable. It is always so: such a Season that proves an *acceptable Year*, and a Time of great Grace & Favour to them that will accept it and improve it, proves a *Day of Vengeance* to others. *Isai.* 61. 2. When God sends forth his *Word* it shall not return to him void; much less his *Spirit.* When Christ was upon Earth in *Judea*, many slighted and neglected him; but it proved in the Issue to be no Matter of Indifference to them: God made all that People to feel that Christ had been among them; those that did not feel it to their Comfort, felt it to their Sorrow with a Witness. When God only sent the Prophet *Ezekiel* to the Children of Israel, he declared *that whether they would hear, or whether they would forbear*, yet *they should know that there had been a Prophet among them*. How much more may we suppose that when God has appeared so wonderfully in this Land, that he will make every one to know that the great JEHOVAH has been in *New England*.

I come now in the

III. and last Place, to apply my self to those that are the Friends of this Work, and have been Partakers of it, and are zealous to promote it. Let me earnestly exhort such *to give diligent heed to themselves to avoid all Errors & Misconduct, and whatsoever may darken and obscure the Work, and give Occasion to those that stand ready to reproach it.* The Apostle was careful *to cut off Occasion from those that desired Occasion.* The same Apostle exhorts *Titus,* to maintain that strict Care and Watch over himself, that both his Preaching and Behaviour might be such as *could not be condemned; that he that was of the contrary Part might be ashamed, having no evil Thing to say of them,* Tit. 2. 7, 8. We had need to be wise as Serpents and harmless as Doves. 'Tis of no small Consequence that we should at this Day behave our selves innocently and prudently. We must expect that the great Enemy of this Work will especially try his utmost *with us*; and he will especially triumph if he can prevail against any of us, in any Thing to blind and mislead us: He knows it will do more to further his Purpose and Interest, than if he prevailed against an hundred others. We had need to watch and pray, for we are but little Children; this roaring Lion is too strong for us, and this old Serpent too subtil for us.

Humility and Self-Diffidence, and an intire Dependance on our Lord Jesus Christ, will be our best Defence. Let us therefore maintain the strictest Watch against spiritual Pride, or a being lifted up with extraordinary Experiences & Comforts, and high Favours of Heaven that any of us may have received. We had need after such Favours, in a special Manner to keep a strict & jealous Eye upon our own Hearts, least there should arise Self-exalting Reflections upon what we have received, and high Thoughts of our selves as being now some of the most eminent of Saints and peculiar Favourites of Heaven, and that the Secret of the Lord is especially with us, and that we above all are fit to be improved as the great Instructors and Censors of this evil Generation: And in an high Conceit of our own Wisdom and Discerning, should as it were naturally assume to our selves the Airs of Prophets or extraordinary Ambassadors of Heaven. When we have great Discoveries of God made to our Souls, we should not shine bright in our own Eyes. *Moses* when he had been conversing with God in the Mount, tho' his Face shone so as to dazzle the Eyes of *Aaron* and the People, yet he did not shine in his own Eyes; *he wist not that his Face shone.* Let none think themselves out of Danger of this spiritual Pride, even in their best Frames. God saw that the Apostle *Paul,* (tho' probably the most eminent Saint that ever lived.) was not out of Danger of it, no not when he had just been conversing with God in the third Heaven: See 2 *Cor.* 12. 7. Pride is the worst Viper that is in the Heart; it is the first Sin that ever entred into the Universe, and it lies lowest of all in the Foundation of the whole Building of Sin, and is the most secret, deceitful and unsearchable in its Ways of working, of any Lust whatsoever: it is ready to mix with every Thing; and nothing is so hateful to God, and contrary to the Spirit of the Gospel, or of so dangerous Consequence; and there is no one Sin that does so much let in the Devil into the Hearts of the Saints, and expose them to his Delusions. I have seen it in many Instances, and that in eminent Saints. The Devil has come in at this Door presently after some eminent Experience and extraordinary Communion with God, and has wofully deluded and led 'em astray, 'till God has mercifully open'd their Eyes and delivered them; and they themselves have afterwards been made sensible that it was Pride that betrayed them.

Some of the true Friends of the Work of God's Spirit have err'd in giving too much heed to Impulses and strong Impressions on their Minds, as tho' they were immediate Significations from Heaven, to them, of something that should come to pass, or something that it was the Mind & Will of God that they should do, which was not signified or revealed any where in the Bible without those Impulses. These Impressions, if they are truly from the Spirit of God, are of a quite different Nature from the *gracious Influences* of the Spirit of God on the Hearts of the Saints; they are of the Nature of the *extraordinary Gifts* of the Spirit, and are properly *Inspiration*, such as the Prophets and Apostles, and others had of old; which the Apostle distinguishes from the Grace of the Spirit, in the 13th Chap. of the first of *Corinthians.*

One Reason why some have been ready to lay Weight on such Impulses, is an Opinion they have had, That the Glory of the approaching happy Days of the Church would partly consist in restoring those extraordinary Gifts of the Spirit: which Opinion I believe arises partly thro' Want of duly considering & comparing the Nature and Value of those two Kinds of Influences of the Spirit, *viz.* his ordinary gracious Influences, and his extraordinary Influences in Inspiration and miraculous Gifts. The former are by far the most excellent and glorious; as the Apostle largely shews in the first of *Corinthians* beginning, with the 31st Verse of the 12th Chapter; speaking of the extraordinary Gifts of the Spirit, he says, *But covet earnestly the best Gifts; and yet I shew you a more excellent Way.* i.e. a more excellent Way of the Influence of the Spirit: And then he goes on in the next Chapter, to shew what that more excellent Way is, even that which is in the Grace of the Spirit, which summarily consists in *Charity*, or divine *Love.* And thro'out that Chapter he shews the great Preference of that above Inspiration. God communicates himself in his own Nature more to the Soul in saving Grace in the Heart, than in all miraculous Gifts: The blessed Image of God consists in that, and not in these: The Excellency, Happiness and Glory of the Soul, does immediately consist in that, and not in those: That is a Root that bears infinitely more excellent Fruit: Salvation and the eternal Enjoyment of God is promised to divine Grace, but not to Inspiration: A Man may have those extraordinary Gifts, and yet be abominable to God, and go to Hell: The spiritual and eternal Life of the Soul don't consist in the extraordinary Gifts of the Spirit, but the Grace of the Spirit: This, and not those, is that Influence of the Spirit of God which God bestows only on his Favourites and dear Children: He has sometimes thrown out the other to Dogs and Swine, as he did to *Balaam, Saul,* and *Judas*; and some that in the primitive Times of the Christian Church committed the unpardonable Sin, as *Heb.* 6. Many wicked Men at the Day of Judgment will plead, *Have we not prophesied in thy Name, and in thy Name cast out Devils, and in thy Name done many wonderful Works*. The greatest Privilege of the Prophets and Apostles, was not their being inspired and working Miracles, but their eminent Holiness. The Grace that was in their Hearts, was a thousand Times more their Dignity and Honour, than their miraculous Gifts. The Things that we find *David* comforting himself in, in the Book of Psalms, are not his being a King, or a Prophet, but the holy Influences of the Spirit of God in his Heart, communicating to him divine Light, Love & Joy. The Apostle *Paul* abounded in Visions and Revelations and miraculous Gifts, above all the Apostles; but yet he esteems all Things but Loss for the Excellency of the spiritual Knowlege of Christ. It was not the Gifts but the Grace of the Apostles, that was the proper Evidence of their Names being written in Heaven, which Christ directs them to rejoyce in, much more, than in the Devils being subject to them. To have Grace in the Heart is an higher Privilege than the blessed Virgin her self had, in having the Body of the second Person in the Trinity conceived in her Womb, by the Power of the Highest overshadowing her; Luk. 11. 27, 28. *And it came to pass as he spake these Things, a certain Woman of the Company lift up her Voice, and said unto them, Blessed is the Womb that bear thee, and the Paps that thou hast sucked! But he said, yea, rather blessed are they that hear the Word of God, and keep it.* See also to the same Purpose, *Math.* 12. 47, *&c.*

The Influence of the Holy Spirit, or divine Charity in the Heart, is the very greatest Privilege and Glory of the highest Arch-Angel in Heaven; yea, this is the very Thing by which the Creature has Fellowship with God himself, with the Father and the Son, in their Beauty & Happiness, and are made Partakers of the divine Nature, and have Christ's Joy fulfilled in themselves.

The ordinary sanctifying Influences of the Spirit of God are the End of all extraordinary Gifts, as the Apostle shews, *Eph.* 4. 11, 12, 13. They are good for nothing, any further than as they are subordinate to this End; they will be so far from profiting any without it, that they will only aggravate their Misery.

This is as the Apostle observes, the most excellent Way of God's communicating his Spirit to his Church; 'tis the greatest Glory of the Church in all Ages. This Glory is what makes the State of the Church on Earth most like the State of the Church in Heaven, where Prophecy and Tongues, and other miraculous Gifts cease, and are vanished away, and God communicates his Spirit only in that more excellent Way that the Apostle speaks of, *viz. Charity*, or divine *Love*, which never faileth. Therefore the Glory of the approaching happy State of the Church don't at all require these extraordinary Gifts. As that State of the Church will be the nearest of any to its perfect State in Heaven, so I believe it will be like it in this, that all extraordinary Gifts shall have ceased and vanished away; and all those Stars and Moon, with the reflected Light they gave in the Night, or a more dark Season, shall be swallowed up in the Sun of divine Love. The Apostle speaks of those Gifts of Inspiration as childish Things, in comparison of the Influence of the Spirit in divine Love, Things given to the Church only to support it in its Minority, 'till the Church should have a compleat, standing Rule established, and all the ordinary Means of Grace should be settled; but as Things that should cease, as the Church advanced above it's childish State, and should intirely vanish when the Church should come to the State of Manhood; which will be in the approaching glorious Times, above any other State of the Church on Earth. 1 Cor. 13. 11. *When I was a Child, I spake as a Child, I understood as a Child, I thought as a Child: but when I became a Man, I put away childish Things*: Compared with the three preceeding Verses.

When the Apostle in this Chapter, speaks of Prophecies, Tongues and Revelations ceasing and vanishing away in the Church, when the Christian Church should be advanced from a State of Minority to a State of Manhood, he seems to have Respect to it's coming to an adult State in this World as well as in Heaven; for he speaks of such an adult State, or State of Manhood, wherein those three Things, *Faith, Hope*, and *Charity*, should *abide* or remain after Miracles and Revelations had ceased; as you may see in the last Verse, *And now abideth* (μένει *remaineth*) *Faith, Hope, Charity; these three*. The Apostle's Manner of speaking here shews an evident Reference to what he had just been saying before; and here is a manifest *Antithesis* between that *remaining* spoken of here, and that *failing, ceasing*, and *vanishing away*, spoken of in the 8th Verse. The Apostle had been shewing how that all those Gifts of Inspiration, that were the Leading-Strings of the Christian Church in it's Infancy, should vanish away, when the Church came to a State of Manhood; and when he has done, then he returns to observe, what Things remain after those had fail'd and ceased; and he observes that those three Things shall remain in the Church, *Faith, Hope*, and *Charity*: And therefore the adult State of the Church he speaks of, is the more perfect State which it shall arrive at in this World, which will be above all in that glorious State it shall be bro't to in the latter Ages of the World. And this was the more properly observed to the Church of the *Corinthians*, upon two Accounts; Because the Apostle had before observed to that Church that they were in a State of Infancy, *Chap.* 3. 1, 2. And because that Church seems above all others to have abounded with miraculous Gifts.— When the expected glorious State of the Church comes, the increase of Light shall be so great, that it will in some Respect answer what is said *ver.* 12. of *seeing Face to Face.* See *Isai.* 24. 23, & 25. 7.

Therefore I don't expect a Restoration of these miraculous Gifts in the approaching glorious Times of the Church, nor do I desire it: It appears to me that it would add nothing to the Glory of those Times, but rather diminish from it. For my Part, I had rather enjoy the sweet Influences of the Spirit, shewing Christ's spiritual divine Beauty, and infinite Grace, and dying Love, drawing forth the holy Exercises of Faith, and divine Love, and sweet Complacence, and humble Joy in God, one Quarter of an Hour, than to have prophetical Visions and Revelations for a whole Year. It appears to me much more probable that God should give immediate Revelations to his Saints in the dark Times of Popery, than now in the Approach of the most glorious & perfect State of his Church on Earth. It don't appear to me that there is any Need of those extraordinary Gifts, to introduce this happy State, and set up the Kingdom of God thro' the World: I have seen so much of the Power of God in *a more excellent Way*, as to convince me that God can easily do it without.

I would therefore intreat the People of God to be very

cautious how they give Heed to such Things. I have seen 'em fail in very many Instances; and know by Experience that Impressions being made with great Power, and upon the Minds of true Saints, yea eminent Saints; and presently after, yea in the midst of, extraordinary Exercises of Grace, and sweet Communion with God, and attended with Texts of Scripture strongly impress'd on the Mind, are no sure Signs of their being Revelations from Heaven: for I have known such Impressions fail, and prove vain by the Event, in some Instances attended with all these Circumstances. I know that they that leave the sure Word of Prophecy, that God has given us to be a Light shining in a dark Place, to follow such Impressions and Impulses, leave the Guidance of the Pole Star, to follow *a Jack with a Lanthorn*. And no wonder therefore that sometimes they are led a dreadful Dance, and into woful Extravagancies.

And seeing Inspiration is not to be expected, let us not despise human Learning. They that say human Learning is of little or no Use in the Work of the Ministry, don't consider what they say; if they did, they would not say it. By human Learning I mean, and suppose others mean, that Improvement of that common Knowlege which Men have, by human and outward Means. And therefore to say that human Learning is of no Use, is as much as to say that the Education of a Child, or that the common Knowlege that a grown Man has, more than a little Child, is of no Use; and so that a Child of four Years old is as fit for a Teacher in the Church of God, with the same Degree of Grace, and capable of doing as much to advance the Kingdom of Christ, by his Instruction, as a very understanding knowing Man of thirty Years of Age. If adult Persons have greater Ability and Advantage to do Service, because they have more human Knowlege than a little Child, then doubtless if they have more human Knowlege still, with the same Degree of Grace, they would have still greater Ability and Advantage to do Service. An increase of Knowlege, without doubt, increases a Man's Advantage either to do Good or Hurt, according as he is disposed. 'Tis too manifest to be denied, that God made great Use of human Learning in the Apostle *Paul*, as he also did in *Moses* & *Solomon*.

And if Knowlege, obtain'd by human Means, is not to be despised, then it will follow that the Means of obtaining it are not to be neglected, *viz.* Study; and that this is of great Use in order to a Preparation for a publick instructing others. And tho' undoubtedly, an having the Heart full of the powerful Influences of the Spirit of God, may at some Times enable Persons to speak profitably, yea very excellently, without Study; yet this will not warrant us needlesly to cast our selves down from the Pinnacle of the Temple, depending upon it that the Angel of the Lord will bear us up, and keep us from dashing our Foot against a Stone, when there is another Way to go down, tho' it ben't so quick. And I would pray that *Method* in publick Discourses, which tends greatly to help both the Understanding and Memory, mayn't be wholly neglected.

And another Thing I would beg the dear Children of God more fully to consider of, is; How far, and upon what Grounds, the Rules of the holy Scriptures will truly justify their passing Censures upon others that are professing Christians, as Hypocrites and ignorant of any Thing of real Religion. We all know that there is a *judging* and censuring of some Sort or other, that the Scripture very often, and very strictly forbids. I desire that those Rules of Scripture may be looked into, and thoroughly weighed; and that it may be considered whether or no a taking it upon us to discern the State of the Souls of others, and to pass Sentence upon them as wicked Men, that are professing Christians, and of a good visible Conversation, be not really forbidden by Christ in the New Testament: If it be, then doubtless the Disciples of Christ ought to avoid it, however sufficient they may think themselves for it; or however needful, or of good Tendency, they may think it. 'Tis plain that *that* Sort of Judging is forbidden, that God claims as his Prerogative, whatever that be. We know that there is a certain Judging of the Hearts of the Children of Men, that is often spoken of as the great Prerogative of God, and which belongs only to him; as in 1 Kin. 8. 39. *Forgive, and do, and give to every Man according to his Ways, whose Heart thou knowest: for thou, even thou only, knowest the Hearts of all the Children of Men.* And if we examine, we shall find that *that* Judging of Hearts that is spoken of as God's Prerogative, is not only the judging of the Aims and Disposition of Mens Hearts in particular Actions, but chiefly a judging the State of the Hearts of the Professors of Religion, with Regard to that Profession.

This will appear very manifest, by looking over the following Scriptures; 1 *Chron.* 28. 9. *Psal.* 7. 9, 10, 11. *Psal.* 26. *thro'out.* *Prov.* 16. 2. & 17. 3. & 21. 2. *Joh.* 2. 23, 24, 25. *Rev.* 2. 22, 23. That Sort of Judging which is God's proper business, is forbidden, as Rom. 14. 4. *Who art thou that judgest another Man's Servant? to his own Master he standeth or falleth.* Jam. 4. 12. *There is one Lawgiver that is able to save and to destroy; who art thou that judgest another?* 1 Cor. 4. 3, 4. *But with me it is a very small Thing, that I should be judged of you, or of Man's Judgment; yea I judge not mine own self; but he that judgeth me is the Lord.*

Again; Whatsoever Kind of Judging is the proper Work and Business of the Day of Judgment, is a Judging that we are forbidden, as in 1 Cor. 4. 5. *Therefore judge nothing before the Time, until the Lord come; who both will bring to Light the hidden Things of Darkness, and will make manifest the Counsels of the Hearts; and then shall every Man have Praise of God.* But to distinguish Hypocrites, that have the Form of Godliness, and the visible Conversation of godly Men, from true Saints; to seperate the Sheep from Goats, is the proper Business of the Day of Judgment; yea, is represented as the main Business and End of that great Day. They therefore do greatly err that take it upon them positively to determine who are sincere, and who not, and to draw the dividing Line between true Saints and Hypocrites, and to seperate between Sheep and Goats, setting the one on the Right and the other on the Left, and to distinguish and gather out the Tares from amongst the Wheat: Many of the Servants of the Owner of the Field are very ready to think themselves sufficient for this, and are forward to offer their Service to this End; but their Lord says *Nay, least while ye gather up the Tares, ye root up the Wheat also: Let both grow together until the Harvest; and in the Time of the Harvest I will* take Care to see a thorough Seperation made; as *Mat.* 13. 28, 29, 30. Agreably to that foremention'd Prohibition of the Apostle, 1 Cor. 4. 5. *Judge nothing before the Time.* In this Parable by the Servants that have the Care of the Fruit of the Field, is doubtless meant the same with the Servants that have the Care of the Fruit of the Vineyard, *Luke* 20. and those that are elsewhere represented as Servants of the Lord of the Harvest, that are appointed as Labourers in his Harvest, which we know are Ministers of the Gospel. *Now* that Parable in the 13th of *Math.* is fulfilled; *While Men slept,* (during that long sleepy, dead Time that has been in the Church,) *the Enemy has sowed Tares*; and now is the Time *when the Blade is sprung up*, and Religion is reviving; now some of the Servants that have the Care of the Field, say, *Let us go and gather up the Tares.*— I know by Experience that there is a great Aptness in Men, that think they have had some Experience of the Power of Religion, to think themselves sufficient to discern and determine the State of others Souls, by a little Conversation with them; and Experience has taught me that 'tis an Error. I once did not imagine that the Heart of Man had been so unsearchable as I find it is. I am less charitable, and less uncharitable than once I was. I find more Things in wicked Men that may Counterfeit, and make a fair Shew of Piety, and more Ways that the remaining Corruption of the Godly may make them appear like carnal Men, Formalists and dead Hypocrites, than once I knew of. The longer I live, the less I wonder that God challenges it as his Prerogative to try the Hearts of the Children of Men, and has directed that this Business should be let alone *till the Harvest*. I find that God is wiser than Men. I desire to adore the Wisdom of God, and his Goodness to me and my fellow Creatures, that he has not committed this great Business into the Hands of such poor, weak, dim-sighted a Creature as I am; of so much Blindness, Pride, Partiality, Prejudice, and Deceitfulness of Heart; but has committed it into the Hands of one infinitely fitter for it, and has made it his Prerogative.

The Talk of some Persons, and the Account they give of their Experiences is exceeding satisfying, and such as forbids and banishes the least Thought of their being any other, than the precious Children of God; it obliges and as it were forces full Charity: But yet we must allow the Scriptures to stand good, that speak of every Thing in the Saint, that belongs to the spiritual and divine Life, as hidden. *Their Life* is said to be *hidden*, Col. 3. 3, 4. Their Food is the *hidden Manna*; they *have Meat to eat that others know not of; a Stranger intermeddles not with their Joys*: The Heart in which they possess their divine distinguishing Ornaments, *is the hidden Man*, and *in the Sight of God* only, 1 *Pet.* 3. 4. Their *new Name*, that Christ has given them, *No Man knows but he that receives it*, Rev. 2. 17. *The*

Praise of the true *Israelites, whose Circumcision is that of the Heart, is not of Men but of God*, Rom. 2. 29. that is; they can be certainly known and discerned to be *Israelites*, so as to have the Honour that belongs to such, only of God; as appears by the Use of the like Expression by the same Apostle, 1 *Cor.* 4. 5. speaking there of it's being God's Prerogative to judge who are upright Christians, and that which he will do at the Day of Judgment, he adds, *and then shall every Man have Praise of God.*

The Instance of *Judas* is remarkable; who tho' he had been so much amongst the rest of the Disciples, who were all Persons of true Experience, yet never seem'd to have entertain'd a Thought of his being any other than a true Disciple, till he discover'd himself by his scandalous Practice.

And the Instance of *Achitophel* is also very remarkable; whom *David* did not discern, tho' he was so wise and holy a Man, a Person of such great Experience, and so great a Divine, and had such great Acquaintance with the Scriptures, and *knew more than all his Teachers*, and *more than the Ancients*; and was grown old in Experience, and was in the greatest Ripeness of his Judgment, and was a great Prophet; and tho' he was so intimately acquainted with *Achitophel*, he being his familiar Friend, and most intimate Companion in religious and spiritual Concerns: yet *David* not only never discovered him to be an Hypocrite, but *relied upon him* as a true Saint, thought he relished and felt his religious Discourse, it was sweet to him, and he counted him an eminent Saint; so that he made him above any other Man his Guide and Counseller in Soul Matters: but yet he was not only, no Saint, but a notoriously wicked Man, a murderous, vile Wretch. Psal. 55. 11, 12, 13, 14. *Wickedness is in the midst thereof; Deceit and Guile depart not from her Streets: For it was not an Enemy that reproached me, then I could have born it; neither was it he that hated me that did magnify himself against me, then I would have hid my self from him: But it was thou, a Man mine Equal, my Guide and mine Acquaintance: We took sweet Counsel together, and walked unto the House of God in Company.*

To suppose that Men have Ability and Right to determine the State of the Souls of visible Christians, and so to make an open Separation between Saints and Hypocrites, that true Saints may be of one visible Company, and Hypocrites of another, separated by a Partition that Men make, carries in it an Inconsistency: for it supposes that God has given Men Power to make another visible Church, within his visible Church; for by visible Christians, or those that are of God's visible Church, can be understood nothing else, than that Company that are Christians or Saints, visibly so; i.e. that have a Right to be received as such, in the Eye of a publick Charity. None can have Right to exclude any one of this visible Church, but in the Way of that regular ecclesiastical Proceeding, which God has established in his visible Church.

I beg of those that have a true Zeal for promoting this Work of God, that God has begun in the Land, well to consider these Things. I am perswaded that as many of them as have much to do with Souls, if they don't hearken to me now, yet will be of the same Mind when they have had more Experience.

And another Thing that I would intreat the zealous Friends of this glorious Work of God to avoid, is managing the Controversy with Opposers with too much Heat, and Appearance of an angry Zeal; and particularly insisting very much in publick Prayer and Preaching, on the Persecution of Opposers. If their Persecution were ten Times so great as it is, methinks it would not be best to say so much about it. It becomes Christians to be like Lambs, not to be apt to complain and cry when they are hurt; to be dumb and not open their Mouth, after the Example of our dear Redeemer; and not to be like Swine, that are apt to scream aloud when they are touch'd. We should not be ready presently to think and speak of Fire from Heaven, when the *Samaritans* oppose us, and won't receive us into their Villages. God's zealous Ministers would do well to think of the Direction the Apostle *Paul* gave to a zealous Minister, 2 Tim. 2. 24, 25, 26. *And the Servant of the Lord must not strive, but be gentle unto all Men, apt to teach, patient; in meekness instructing those that oppose themselves, if God peradventure will give them Repentance, to the acknowledging of the Truth. And that they may recover themselves out of the Snare of the Devil, who are taken Captive by him at his Will.*

And another Thing that I would humbly recommend to those that Love the Lord Jesus Christ, and would advance his Kingdom, is a good Attendance to that excellent Rule of

Prudence Christ has left us, Math. 9. 16, 17. *No Man putteth a Piece of new Cloth into an old Garment; for that which is put in to fill it up, taketh from the Garment, and the Rent is made worse. Neither do Men put new Wine into old Bottles; else the Bottles break, and the Wine runneth out, and the Bottles perish. But they put new Wine into new Bottles, and both are preserved.* I am afraid that the Wine is now running out in some Parts of this Land, for want of attending to this Rule. For tho' I believe we have confined our selves too much to a certain stated Method & Form in the Management of our religious Affairs; which has had a Tendency to cause all our Religion to degenerate into meer Formality; yet whatsoever has the Appearance of a great Innovation, that tends much to shock and surprize Peoples Minds, and to set them a talking and disputing, tends greatly to hinder the Progress of the Power of Religion, by raising the Opposition of some, and diverting the Minds of others, and perplexing the Minds of many with Doubts & Scruples, and causing People *to swerve* from their great Business, *and turn aside to vain Jangling.* Therefore that which is very much beside the common Practice, unless it be a Thing in it's own Nature of considerable Importance, had better be avoided. Herein we shall follow the Example of one, who had the greatest Success in propagating the Power of Religion in the World, of any Man that ever lived, that he himself gives us an Account of, 1 Cor. 9. 20, 21, 22, 23. *Unto the Jews, I became as a Jew, that I might gain the Jews: to them that are under the Law, as under the Law, that I might gain them that are under the Law: To them that are without Law, (being not without Law to God, but under Law to Christ,) that I might gain them that are without Law: To the weak, became I as weak, that I might gain the weak: I am made all Things to all Men, that I might by all Means, save some. And this I do for the Gospel's sake, that I might be partaker thereof with you.*

FINIS

Some Thoughts

Concerning the prefent

Revival of Religion

IN

NEW-ENGLAND,

And the Way in which it ought to be
acknowledged and promoted,
Humbly offered to the Publick, in a

TREATISE on that Subject.

In Five Parts;

PART I. Shewing that the Work that has of late been going on in this Land, is a glorious Work of God.

PART II. Shewing the Obligations that all are under, to acknowlege, rejoice in and promote this Work, and the great Danger of the contrary.

PART III. Shewing in many Inftances, where-in the Subjects, or zealous Promoters, of this Work have been injurioufly blamed.

PART IV. Shewing what Things are to be corrected or avoided, in promoting this Work, or in our Behaviour under it.

PART V. Shewing pofitively what ought to be done to promote this Work.

By *JONATHAN EDWARDS*, A. M.
Paftor of the Church of CHRIST at *Northampton*.

Ifai. 40. 3. *Prepare ye the Way of the Lord, make ftrait in the Defart a high-Way for our God*

BOSTON: Printed and Sold by S. *Kneeland* and *T. Green*, in *Queen-Street*, 1742.

THE PREFACE

In the ensuing Treatise, I condemn Ministers assuming, or taking too much upon them, and appearing as tho' they supposed that they were the Persons, to whom it especially belonged to dictate, direct and determine; but perhaps shall be thought to be very guilty of it my self: And some when they read this Treatise, may be ready to say that I condemn this in others, that I may have the Monopoly of it.—I confess that I have taken a great deal of Liberty freely to express my Thoughts, concerning almost every Thing appertaining to the wonderful Work of GOD that has of late been carried on in the Land, and to declare what has appeared to me to be the Mind of GOD, concerning the Duty and Obligations of all Sorts of Persons, and even those that are my Superiours and Fathers, Ministers of the Gospel, and Civil Rulers: But yet I hope the Liberty I have taken is not greater than can be justified. In a free Nation, such Liberty of the Press is allowed, that every Author takes Leave without Offence, freely to speak his Opinion concerning the Management of publick Affairs, and the Duty of the Legislature, and those that are at the Head of the Administration, tho' vastly his Superiours. As now at this Day, private Subjects offer their Sentiments to the Publick, from the Press, concerning the Management of the War with *Spain*; freely declaring what they think to be the Duty of the Parliament, and the principal Ministers of State, &c. We in *New-England* are at this Day engaged in a more important War: And I'm sure, if we consider the sad Jangling and Confusion that has attended it, we shall confess that it is highly requisite that some Body should speak his Mind, concerning the Way in which it ought to be managed: And that not only a few of the many Particulars, that are the Matter of Strife in the Land, should be debated, on the one Side and the other, in Pamphlets; (as has of late been done, with Heat and Fierceness enough;) which don't tend to bring the Contention in general to an End, but rather to inflame it, and increase the Uproar: But that something should be published, to bring the Affair in general, and the many Things that attend it, that are the

167

Subjects of Debate, under a particular Consideration. And certainly it is high Time that this was done. If private Persons may speak their Minds without Arrogance; much more may a Minister of the Kingdom of CHRIST speak freely about Things of this Nature, which do so nearly concern the Interest of the Kingdom of his Lord and Master, at so important a Juncture. If some elder Minister had undertaken this, I acknowledge it would have been more proper; but I have heard of no such Thing a doing, or like to be done. I hope therefore I shall be excused for undertaking such a Piece of Work. I think that nothing that I have said can justly be interpreted, as tho' I would impose my Thoughts upon any, or did not suppose that others have equal Right to think for themselves, with my self. We are not accountable one to another for our Thoughts; but we must all give an Account to him who searches our Hearts, and has doubtless his Eye especially upon us at such an extraordinary Season as this. If I have well confirmed my Opinion concerning this Work, and the Way in which it should be acknowledged and promoted, with Scripture and Reason, I hope others that read it will receive it, as a Manifestation of the Mind and Will of GOD. If others would hold forth further Light to me in any of these Particulars, I hope I should thankfully receive it. I think I have been made in some Measure sensible, and much more of late than formerly, of my Need of more Wisdom than I have. I make it my Rule to lay hold of Light and embrace it, where-ever I see it, tho' held forth by a Child or an Enemy. If I have assumed too much in the following Discourse, and have spoken in a Manner that savours of a Spirit of Pride, no Wonder that others can better discern it than I my self. If it be so I ask Pardon, and beg the Prayers of every Christian Reader, that I may have more Light, Humility and Zeal; and that I may be favoured with such Measures of the Divine Spirit, as a Minister of the Gospel stands in Need of, at such an extraordinary Season.

Part I

Shewing that the extraordinary WORK that has of
late been going on in this Land, is a glorious
WORK OF GOD.

The Error of those who have had ill Thoughts of the great
religious Operation on the Minds of Men, that has been carried on of late in *New-England*, (so far as the Ground of such
an Error has been in the Understanding, and not in the Disposition,) seems fundamentally to lie in three Things; *First*, in
judging of this Work *a priori*. *Secondly*, in not taking the Holy
Scriptures as an whole Rule whereby to judge of such Operations. *Thirdly*, in not justly separating and distinguishing the
good from the bad.

I. They have greatly err'd in the Way in which they have
gone about to try this Work, whether it be a Work of the Spirit
of God or no, *viz.* in judging of it *a priori*; from the Way that
it began, the Instruments that have been employed, the Means
that have been made Use of, and the Methods that have been
taken and succeeded, in carrying it on. Whereas, if we duly
consider the Matter, it will evidently appear that such a Work is
not to be judged of *a priori*, but *a posteriori*: We are to observe
the Effect wrought; and if, upon Examination of that, it be
found to be agreeable to the Word of God, we are bound
without more ado to rest in it as God's Work; and shall be like
to be rebuked for our Arrogance, if we refuse so to do 'till
God shall explain to us how he has brought this Effect to pass,
or why he has made Use of such and such Means in doing of
it. Those Texts are enough to cause us with trembling to forbear
such a Way of proceeding in judging of a Work of God's Spirit,
Isai. 40. 13, 14. *Who hath directed the Spirit of the LORD, or
being his Counsellor hath taught him? With whom took he Counsel? and who instructed him, and who taught him in the Path of
Judgment, and taught him Knowledge, and shewed to him the
Way of Understanding?* Joh. 3. 8. *The Wind bloweth where it
listeth; and thou hearest the Sound thereof; but canst not tell
whence it cometh, and whether it goeth.* We hear the sound, we
perceive the Effect, and from thence we judge that the Wind

does indeed blow; without waiting, before we pass this Judgment, first to be satisfied what should be the Cause of the Wind's blowing from such a Part of the Heavens, and how it should come to pass that it should blow in such a Manner, at such a Time. To judge *a priori*, is a wrong Way of judging of any of the Works of GOD. We are not to resolve that we will first be satisfied how GOD brought this or the other Effect to pass, and why he hath made it thus, or why it has pleased him to take such a Course, and to use such and such Means, before we will acknowledge his Work, and give him the Glory of it. This is too much for the *Clay* to take upon it with respect to the *Potter. GOD gives not Account of his Matters: His Judgments are a great Deep: He hath his Way in the Sea, and his Path in the great Waters, and his Footsteps are not known; and who shall teach GOD Knowledge, or enjoin him his Way, or say unto him what doest thou? We know not what is the Way of the Spirit, nor how the Bones do grow in the Womb of her that is with Child; even so we know not the Works of GOD who maketh all.* No wonder therefore if those that go this forbidden Way to work, in judging of the present wonderful Operation, are perplexed and confounded. We ought to take heed that we don't expose our selves to the Calamity of those who pried into the Ark of GOD, when GOD mercifully returned it to *Israel*, after it had departed from them.

Indeed GOD has not taken that Course, nor made Use of those Means, to begin and carry on this great Work, which Men in their Wisdom, would have thought most adviseable, if he had asked their Counsel; but quite the contrary. But it appears to me that the great GOD has wrought like Himself, in the Manner of his carrying on this Work; so as very much to show his own Glory, and exalt his own Sovereignty, Power and All-sufficiency, and pour Contempt on all that human Strength, Wisdom, Prudence and Sufficiency, that Men have been won't to trust, and to glory in; and so as greatly to cross, rebuke and chastize the Pride and other Corruptions of Men; in a Fulfilment of that Isai. 2. 17. *And the Loftiness of Man shall be bowed down, and the Haughtiness of Men shall be made low, and the LORD alone shall be exalted in that Day.* GOD doth thus, in intermingling in his Providence so many Stumbling-blocks with this Work; in suffering so much of human Weakness and

Infirmity to appear; and in ordering so many Things that are mysterious to Men's Wisdom: in pouring out his Spirit chiefly on the common People, and bestowing his greatest and highest Favours upon them, admitting them nearer to himself than the great, the honourable, the rich and the learned, agreeable to that Prophecy, Zech. 12. 7. *The LORD also shall save the Tents of Judah first, that the Glory of the House of David, and the Glory of the Inhabitants of Jerusalem, do not magnify themselves against Judah.* Those that dwelt in the Tents of *Judah* were the common People, that dwelt in the Country, and were of inferiour Rank. The Inhabitants of *Jerusalem* were their Citizens, their Men of Wealth and Figure: And *Jerusalem* also was the chief Place of the Habitation or Resort of their Priests, and Levites, and their Officers and Judges; there sat the great *Sanhedrim.* The House of *David* were the highest Rank of all, the Royal Family, and the great Men that were round about the King.—'Tis evident by the Context, that this Prophecy has Respect to something further than the saving the People out of the Babylonish Captivity.

GOD in this Work has begun at the lower End, and he has made Use of the weak and foolish Things of the World to carry on his Work. The Ministers that have been chiefly improved, some of them have been meer Babes in Age and Standing, and some of them such as have not been so high in Reputation among their Fellows as many others; and GOD has suffered their Infirmities to appear in the Sight of others, so as much to displease them; and at the same Time it has pleased GOD to improve them, and greatly to succeed them, while he has not so succeeded others that are generally reputed vastly their Superiours. Yea, there is Reason to think that it has pleased GOD to make Use of the Infirmities and Sins of some that he has improved and succeeded; as particularly their imprudent and rash Zeal and censorious Spirit, to chastize the Deadness, Negligence, Earthly-mindedness and Vanity, that have been found among Ministers, in the late Times of general Declension and Deadness, wherein wise Virgins and foolish, Ministers and People have sunk into such a deep Sleep. These Things in Ministers of the Gospel, that go forth as the Ambassadors of CHRIST, and have the Care of immortal Souls, are extremely abominable to GOD; vastly more hateful in his Sight than all

the Imprudence, and intemperate Heats, Wildness and Distraction (as some call it) of these zealous Preachers. A supine
Carelesness, and a vain, carnal, worldly Spirit, in a Minister of
the Gospel, is the worst Madness and Distraction in the Sight
of GOD. GOD may also make Use at this Day, of the unchristian
Censoriousness of some Preachers, the more to humble and
purify some of his own Children and true Servants, that have
been wrongfully censured, to fit them for more eminent Service, and future Honour that he designs them for.

II. Another Foundation-Error of those that don't acknowledge the Divinity of this Work, is not taking the Holy Scriptures
as an *whole*, and in it self a sufficient Rule to judge of such
Things by. They that have one certain consistent Rule to judge
by, are like to come to some clear Determination; but they that
have half a Dozen different Rules to make the Thing they would
judge of agree to, no Wonder that instead of justly and clearly
determining, they do but perplex and darken themselves and
others. They that would learn the true Measure of any Thing,
and will have many different Measures to try it by, and find in it
a Conformity to, have a Task that they will not accomplish.

Those that I am speaking of, will indeed make some Use of
Scripture, so far as they think it serves their Turn; but don't
make Use of it *alone*, as a Rule sufficient by it self, but make as
much, and a great deal more Use of other Things, diverse and
wide from it, to judge of this Work by. As particularly,

1. Some make *Philosophy* instead of the Holy Scriptures, their
Rule of judging of this Work; particularly the Philosophical
Notions they entertain of the Nature of the Soul, its Faculties
and Affections. Some are ready to say, "There is but little sober
solid Religion in this Work: it is little else but Flash and Noise.
Religion now-a-Days all runs out into Transports and high
Flights of the Passions and Affections." In their Philosophy,
the Affections of the Soul are something diverse from the Will,
and not appertaining to the noblest Part of the Soul, but the
meanest Principles that it has, that belong to Men as partaking
of animal Nature, and what he has in common with the Brute
Creation, rather than any Thing whereby he is conformed to
Angels and pure Spirits. And tho' they acknowledge that there
is a good Use may be made of the Affections in Religion, yet

they suppose that the substantial Part of Religion don't consist in them, but that they are rather to be looked upon as something adventitious and accidental in Christianity.

But I can't but think that these Gentlemen labour under great Mistakes, both in their Philosophy and Divinity. 'Tis true, Distinction must be made in the Affections or Passions. There's a great deal of Difference in high and raised Affections, which must be distinguished by the Skill of the Observer. Some are much more solid than others. There are many Exercises of the Affections that are very flashy, and little to be depended on; and oftentimes there is a great deal that appertains to them, or rather that is the Effect of them, that has its Seat in animal Nature, and is very much owing to the Constitution and Frame of the Body; and that which sometimes more especially obtains the Name of Passion, is nothing solid or substantial. But it is false Philosophy to suppose this to be the Case with all Exercises of Affection in the Soul, or with all great and high Affections; and false Divinity to suppose that religious Affections don't appertain to the Substance and Essence of Christianity: On the contrary, it seems to me that the very Life and Soul of all true Religion consists in them.

I humbly conceive that the Affections of the Soul are not properly distinguished from the Will, as tho' they were two Faculties in the Soul. All Acts of the Affections of the Soul are in some Sense Acts of the Will, and all Acts of the Will are Acts of the Affections. All Exercises of the Will are in some Degree or other, Exercises of the Soul's Appetition or Aversion; or which is the same Thing, of its Love or Hatred. The Soul wills one Thing rather than another, or chuses one Thing rather than another, no otherwise than as it loves one Thing more than another; but Love and Hatred are Affections of the Soul: and therefore all Acts of the Will are truly Acts of the Affections; tho' the Exercises of the Will don't obtain the Name of Passions, unless the Will, either in its Aversion or Opposition, be exercised in a high Degree, or in a vigorous and lively Manner.

All will allow that true Vertue or Holiness has its Seat chiefly in the Heart, rather than in the Head: It therefore follows from what has been said already, that it consists chiefly in holy *Affections*. The Things of Religion take Place in Men's Hearts, no further than they are *affected* with them. The informing of the

Understanding is all vain, any farther than it *affects* the Heart; or, which is the same Thing, has Influence on the *Affections*.

Those Gentlemen that make light of these raised Affections in Religion, will doubtless allow that true Religion and Holiness, as it has its Seat in the Heart, is capable of very high Degrees, and high Exercises in the Soul. As for Instance; They will doubtless allow that the Holiness of the Heart or Will, is capable of being raised to an hundred Times as great a Degree of Strength as it is in the most eminent Saint on Earth, or to be exerted in an hundred Times so strong and vigorous Exercises of the Heart; and yet be true Religion or Holiness still, but only in an high Degree. Now therefore I would ask them, By what Name they will call these high and vigorous Exercises of the Will or Heart? Ben't they high Affections? What can they consist in, but in high Acts of Love; strong and vigorous Exercises of Benevolence and Complacence; high, exalting and admiring Thoughts of GOD and his Perfections; strong Desires after GOD, *&c.*—? And now what are we come to but high and raised Affections? Yea, those very same high and raised Affections that before they objected against, or made light of, as worthy of little Regard?

I suppose furthermore that all will allow that there is nothing but solid Religion in Heaven: But that there, Religion and Holiness of Heart is raised to an exceeding great Height, to strong, high, exalted Exercises of Heart. Now what other Kinds of such exceeding strong and high Exercises of the Heart, or of Holiness as it has its Seat in their Hearts, can we devise for them, but only holy Affections, high Degrees of Actings of Love to GOD, rejoicing in GOD, admiring of GOD, *&c.*—? Therefore these Things in the Saints and Angels in Heaven, are not to be despised and cashier'd by the Name of great Heats and Transports of the Passions.

And it will doubtless be yet further allowed, that the more eminent the Saints are on Earth, and the stronger their Grace is, and the higher its Exercises are, the more they are like the Saints in Heaven. *i.e.* (by what has been just now observed,) the more they have of high or raised Affections in Religion.

Tho' there are false Affections in Religion, and Affections that in some Respects are raised high, that are flashy, yet undoubtedly there are also true, holy and solid Affections; and

the higher these are raised, the better: and if they are raised to
an exceeding great Height, they are not to be thought meanly
of or suspected, meerly because of their great Degree, but on
the contrary to be esteemed and rejoiced in. Charity, or divine
Love, is in Scripture represented as the Sum of all the Religion
of the Heart; but this is nothing but an holy *Affection*: And
therefore in Proportion as this is firmly fixed in the Soul, and
raised to a great Height, the more eminent a Person is in Holiness. Divine Love or Charity is represented as the Sum of all
the Religion of Heaven, and that wherein mainly the Religion
of the Church in its more perfect State on Earth shall consist,
when Knowledge, and Tongues, and Prophesyings shall cease;
and therefore the higher this holy Affection is raised in the
Church of GOD, or in a gracious Soul, the more excellent and
perfect is the State of the Church, or a particular Soul.

If we take the Scriptures for our Rule, then the greater and
higher are the Exercises of Love to GOD, Delight and Complacence in GOD, Desires and Longings after GOD, Delight in the
Children of GOD, Love to Mankind, Brokenness of Heart,
Abhorrence of Sin, and Self-abhorrence for Sin; and the Peace
of GOD which passeth all Understanding, and Joy in the Holy
Ghost, Joy unspeakable and full of Glory; admiring Thoughts
of GOD, exulting and glorying in GOD; so much the higher is
CHRIST's Religion, or that Vertue which he and his Apostles
taught, raised in the Soul.

It is a Stumbling to some that religious Affections should
seem to be so powerful, or that they should be so violent (as
they express it,) in some Persons: They are therefore ready to
doubt whether it can be the Spirit of GOD, or whether this
Vehemence ben't rather a Sign of the Operation of an evil
Spirit. But why should such a Doubt arise from no other
Ground than this? What is represented in Scripture, as more
powerful in its Effects, than the Spirit of GOD? which is therefore called *the Power of the highest*, Luk. 1. 35. And its saving
Effect in the Soul called *the Power of Godliness*. So we read of
the *Demonstration of the Spirit, and of Power*, 1 Cor. 2. 4. And
it is said to operate in the Minds of Men with the *exceeding
Greatness of Divine Power*, and *according to the working of
GOD's mighty Power*, Eph. 1. 19. So we read of *the effectual
working of his Power*, Eph. 3. 7. *And of the Power that worketh*

in Christians, v. 20. And of the *Glorious Power* of GOD in the Operations of the Spirit, *Col.* I. II. And of *the Work of Faith*, its being wrought *with Power*, 2 Thes. I. II. and in 2 Tim. I. 7. The Spirit of GOD is called *the Spirit of Power, and Love, and of a sound Mind*. So the Spirit is represented by a mighty Wind, and by Fire, Things most powerful in their Operation.

2. Many are guilty of not taking the holy Scriptures as a sufficient and whole Rule, whereby to judge of this Work, whether it be the Work of GOD, in that they judge by those Things which the Scripture don't give as any Signs or Marks whereby to judge one Way or the other, and therefore do in no wise belong to the Scripture-Rule of judging, *viz.* The Effects that religious Exercises and Affections of Mind have upon the Body. Scripture Rules respect the State of the Mind, and Persons moral Conduct, and voluntary Behaviour, and not the physical State of the Body. The Design of the Scripture is to teach us Divinity, and not Physick and Anatomy. Ministers are made the Watchmen of Men's Souls, and not their Bodies; and therefore the great Rule which GOD has committed into their Hands, is to make them Divines, and not Physicians. CHRIST knew what Instructions and Rules his Church would stand in Need of better than we do; and if he had seen it needful in order to the Churches Safety, he doubtless would have given Ministers Rules to judge of Bodily Effects, and would have told 'em how the Pulse should beat under such and such religious Exercises of Mind; when Men should look pale, and when they should shed Tears; when they should tremble, and whether or no they should ever be faint or cry out; or whether the Body should ever be put into Convulsions: He probably would have put some Book into their Hands, that should have tended to make them excellent Anatomists and Physicians: But he has not done it, because he did not see it to be needful. He judged, that if Ministers thoroughly did their Duty as Watchmen and Overseers of the State and Frame of Men's Souls, and of their voluntary Conduct, according to the Rules he had given, his Church would be well provided for, as to its Safety in these Matters. And therefore those Ministers of CHRIST and Overseers of Souls, that busy themselves, and are full of Concern about the involuntary Motions of the Fluids and Solids of Men's Bodies, and from thence full of Doubts and Suspicions

of the Cause, when nothing appears but that the State and Frame of their Minds, and their voluntary Behaviour is good, and agreeable to GOD's Word; I say, such Ministers go out of the Place that CHRIST has set them in, and leave their proper Business, as much as if they should undertake to tell who are under the Influence of the Spirit by their Looks, or their Gate. I can't see which Way we are in Danger, or how the Devil is like to get any notable Advantage against us, if we do but thoroughly do our Duty with Respect to those two Things, *viz.* The State of Persons Minds, and their moral Conduct, seeing to it that they be maintain'd in an Agreeableness to the Rules that CHRIST has given us. If Things are but kept right in these Respects, our Fears and Suspicions arising from extraordinary bodily Effects seem wholly groundless.

The most specious Thing that is alledged against these extraordinary Effects on the Body, is that the Body is impaired and Health wronged; and that it's hard to think that GOD, in the merciful Influences of his Spirit on Men, would wound their Bodies, and impair their Health. But if it were so pretty commonly or in multiplied Instances, (which I don't suppose it is,) that Persons received a lasting Wound to their Health by extraordinary religious Impressions made upon their Minds, yet 'tis too much for us to determine that GOD shall never bring an outward Calamity, in bestowing a vastly greater spiritual and eternal Good. *Jacob* in doing his Duty in wrestling with GOD for the Blessing, and while GOD was striving with him, at the same Time that he received the Blessing from GOD, suffer'd a great outward Calamity from his Hand; GOD impaired his Body so that he never got over it as long as he lived: He gave him the Blessing, but sent him away halting on his Thigh, and he went lame all his Life after. And yet this is not mentioned as if it were any Diminution of the great Mercy of GOD to him, when GOD blessed him, and he received his Name *Israel*, because as a Prince he had Power with GOD, and had prevailed.

But, say some, The Operations of the Spirit of GOD are of a benign Nature; nothing is of a more kind Influence on human Nature than the merciful Breathings of GOD's own Spirit. But it has been a Thing generally supposed and allowed in the Church of GOD, till now, that there is such a Thing as being

sick of Love to CHRIST, or having the bodily Strength weak'ned
by strong and vigorous Exercises of Love to him. And however
kind to human Nature the Influences of the Spirit of GOD are,
yet no Body doubts but that divine and eternal Things, as they
may be discovered, would overpower the Nature of Man in its
present weak State; and that therefore the Body in its present
Weakness, is not fitted for the Views and Pleasures and Employments of Heaven: and that if GOD did discover but a little
of that which is seen by the Saints and Angels in Heaven, our
frail Natures would sink under it. Indeed I know not what
Persons may deny now, to defend themselves in a Cause they
have had their Spirits long engaged in; but I know these
Things don't use to be denied, or doubted of.—Let us rationally consider what we profess to believe of the infinite Greatness of the Things of GOD, the divine Wrath, the divine Glory,
and the divine infinite Love and Grace in JESUS CHRIST, and
the Vastness and infinite Importance of the Things of Eternity;
and how reasonable is it to suppose that if it pleases GOD a
little to withdraw the Vail, and let in Light into the Soul, and
give something of a View of the great Things of another
World in their transcendent and infinite Greatness, That
human Nature, that is as the Grass, a shaking Leaf, a weak
withering Flower, should totter under such a Discovery? Such
a Bubble is too weak to bear the Weight of a View of Things
that are so vast. Alass! What is such Dust and Ashes, that it
should support it self under the View of the awful Wrath or
infinite Glory and Love of JEHOVAH! No Wonder therefore
that it is said, *No Man can see me and live*, and *Flesh and Blood
cannot inherit the Kingdom of GOD*. That external Glory &
Majesty of CHRIST which *Daniel* saw, when *there remained no
Strength in him, and his Comeliness was turned in him into Corruption*, Dan. 10. 6, 7, 8. And which the Apostle *John* saw,
when he fell at his Feet as dead; was but an Image or Shadow
of that spiritual Glory and Majesty of CHRIST, which will be
manifested in the Souls of the Saints in another World, and
which is sometimes, in some Degree, manifested to the Soul in
this World, by the Influences of the Spirit of GOD. And if the
beholding the Image, and external Representation of this spiritual Majesty and Glory, did so overpower human Nature, is it

unreasonable to suppose that a Sight of the spiritual Glory it self, which is the Substance, of which that was but the Shadow, should have as powerful an Effect? The Prophet *Habakkuk*, speaking of the awful Manifestations GOD made of his Majesty and Wrath, at the Red Sea, and in the Wilderness, and at Mount *Sinai*, where he gave the Law; and of the merciful Influence, and strong Impression GOD caused it to have upon him, to the End that he might be saved from that Wrath, and rest in the Day of Trouble; says, Hab. 3. 16. *When I heard my Belly trembled, my Lips quivered at the Voice, Rottenness entered into my Bones, I trembled in my self, that I might rest in the Day of Trouble.* Which is much such an Effect as the Discovery of the same Majesty and Wrath, in the same awful Voice from Mount *Sinai*, has had upon many in these Days; and to the same Purposes, *viz.* to give 'em *Rest in the Day of Trouble*, and save 'em from that Wrath. The Psalmist also speaks of very much such an Effect as I have often seen on Persons under religious Affections of late, *Psal.* 119. 131. *I opened my Mouth and panted, for I longed for thy Commandments.*

GOD is pleased sometimes in dealing forth spiritual Blessings to his People, in some Respect to exceed the Capacity of the Vessel, in its present Scantiness, so that he don't only fill it full, but he makes their *Cup to run over*; agreeable to *Psal.* 23. 5. And pours out a Blessing, sometimes, in such a Manner and Measure that there is not Room enough to receive it, *Mal.* 3. 10. and gives 'em Riches more than they can carry away; as he did to *Jehoshaphat*, and his People in a Time of great Favour, by the Word of his Prophet *Jehaziel* in Answer to earnest Prayer, when the People blessed the Lord in the Valley of *Berachah*, 2 Chron. 20. 25, 26. It has been with the Disciples of CHRIST, for a long Time, a Time of great Emptiness upon spiritual Accounts; They have gone hungry, and have been toiling in vain, during a dark Season, a Time of Night with the Church of GOD; as it was with the Disciples of old, when they had toiled all Night for something to eat and caught nothing, *Luk.* 5. 5. and *Joh.* 21. 3. But now, the Morning being come, JESUS appears to his Disciples, and takes a compassionate Notice of their Wants, and says to 'em, *Children have ye any Meat?* And gives some of them such abundance of Food, that they are not able to draw their Net; yea, so that their Net breaks, and their Vessel is overloaded, and begins to sink; as it was with the Disciples of old, *Luk.* 5. 6, 7. and *Joh.* 21. 6.

We can't determine that GOD never shall give any Person so much of a Discovery of himself, not only as to weaken their Bodies, but to take away their Lives. 'Tis supposed by very learned and judicious Divines, that *Moses*'s Life was taken away after this Manner; and this has also been supposed to be the Case with some other Saints. Yea, I don't see any solid sure Grounds any have to determine, that GOD shall never make such strong Impressions on the Mind by his Spirit, that shall be an Occasion of so impairing the Frame of the Body, and particularly that Part of the Body, the Brain, that Persons shall be deprived of the Use of Reason. As I said before, it is too much for us to determine, that GOD will not bring an outward Calamity in bestowing spiritual and eternal Blessings: so it is too much for us to determine, how great an outward Calamity he will bring. If GOD gives a great Increase of Discoveries of himself, and of Love to him, the Benefit is infinitely greater than the Calamity, tho' the Life should presently after be taken away; yea tho' the Soul should not immediately be taken to Heaven, but should lie some Years in a deep Sleep, and then be taken to Heaven: Or, which is much the same Thing, if it be deprived of the Use of its Faculties, and be unactive and unserviceable, as if it lay in a deep Sleep for some Years, and then should pass into Glory. We cannot determine how great a Calamity Distraction is, when considered with all its Consequences, and all that might have been consequent, if the Distraction had not happen'd; nor indeed whether, (thus considered) it be any Calamity at all, or whether it be not a Mercy, by preventing some great Sin, or some more dreadful Thing, if it had not been. 'Tis a great Fault in us to limit a sovereign all-wise GOD, whose Judgments are a great Deep, and his Ways past finding out, where he has not limited himself, and in Things, concerning which, he has not told us what his Way shall be.—'Tis remarkable, considering in what Multitudes of Instances, and to how great a Degree, the Frame of the Body has been over-powered of late, that Persons Lives have notwithstanding been preserved, and that the Instances of those that have been deprived of Reason have been so very few, and those, perhaps, all of them, Persons under the peculiar Disadvantage of a weak, vapoury Habit of Body. A merciful and careful divine Hand is very manifest in it, that in so many Instances where the Ship has begun to sink, yet it has been upheld, and has not totally sunk.—The Instances of such as have been deprived of Reason are so few, that certainly they are not enough to cause us to be in any Fright, as tho' this Work that has been carried on in the Country, was like to be of baneful Influence; unless we are disposed to gather up all that we can to darken it, and set it forth in frightful Colours.

There is one particular Kind of Exercise and Concern of Mind, that many have been over-powered by, that has been especially stumbling to some; and that is the deep Concern and Distress that they have been in for the Souls of others. I am sorry that any put us to the Trouble of doing that which seems so needless, as defending such a Thing as this. It seems like meer trifling in so plain a Case, to enter into a formal and particular Debate, in order to determine whether there be any thing in the Greatness and Importance of the Case that will answer, and bear a Proportion to the Greatness of the Concern that some have manifested. Men may be allowed, from no higher a Principle than common Ingenuity and Humanity, to be very deeply concerned, and greatly exercised in Mind, at the seeing others in great Danger, of no greater a Calamity than drowning, or being burnt up in an House on Fire. And if so, then doubtless it will be allow'd to be equally reasonable, if they saw them in Danger of a Calamity ten Times greater, to be still much more concern'd; & so much more still, if the Calamity was still vastly greater. And why then should it be thought unreasonable, and looked upon with a very suspicious Eye, as if it must come from some bad Cause, when Persons are extremely concerned at seeing others in very great Danger of suffering the Fierceness and Wrath of Almighty GOD, to all Eternity? And besides it will doubtless be allowed that those that have very great Degrees of the Spirit of GOD, that is a Spirit of Love, may well be supposed to have vastly more of Love and Compassion to their Fellow-Creatures, than those that are influenced only by common Humanity. Why should it be thought strange that those that are full of the Spirit of CHRIST, should be proportionably, in their Love to Souls, like to CHRIST? who had so strong a Love to them and Concern for them, as to be willing to drink the Dregs of the Cup of GOD's Fury for them; and at the same Time that he offered up his Blood for Souls, offered up also, as their High Priest, strong Crying and Tears, with an extreme Agony, wherein the Soul of CHRIST was as it were in Travail for the Souls of the Elect; and therefore in saving them he is said to see of the *Travail* of his Soul. As such a Spirit of Love to, and Concern for Souls was the Spirit of CHRIST, so it is the Spirit of the Church; and therefore the Church, in desiring and seeking that CHRIST might be brought forth in the World, and in the Souls of Men, is represented, Rev. 12. as a *Woman crying, travailing in Birth, and pained to be delivered.* The Spirit of those that have been in Distress for the Souls of others, so far as I can discern, seems not to be different from that of the Apostle, who travailed for Souls, and was ready to *wish himself accursed from CHRIST* for others. And that of the Psalmist, *Psal.* 119. 53. *Horror hath taken hold upon me, because of the Wicked that forsake thy Law.* And v. 136. *Rivers of Waters run down mine Eyes, because they keep not thy Law.* And that of the Prophet *Jeremiah*, Jer. 4. 19. *My Bowels! my Bowels! I am pained at my very Heart! My Heart maketh a Noise in me! I cannot hold my Peace! Because thou hast heard, O my Soul, the Sound of the Trumpet, the Alarm of War!* And so Chap. 9. 1. and 13. 17. and 14. 17. and *Isa.* 22. 4. We read of *Mordecai*, when he saw his People in Danger of being destroyed with a temporal Destruction, *Esth.* 4. 1. *That he rent his Clothes, and put on Sackcloth with Ashes, and went out into the midst of the City, and cried with a loud and bitter Cry.* And why then should Persons be thought to be distracted, when they can't forbear crying out, at the Consideration of the Misery of those that are going to eternal Destruction?

3. Another Thing that some make their Rule to judge of this Work by, instead of the Holy Scriptures, is History, or former Observation. Herein they err two Ways; *First*, If there be any Thing new and extraordinary in the Circumstances of this Work, that was not observed in former Times, that is a Rule with them to reject this Work as not the Work of GOD. Herein they make that their Rule, that GOD has not given them for their Rule; and limit GOD, where he has not limited himself. And this is especially unreasonable in this Case: For whosoever

has well weighed the wonderful and mysterious Methods of
Divine Wisdom, in carrying on the Work of the New Creation,
or in the Progress of the Work of Redemption, from the first
Promise of the Seed of the Woman to this Time, may easily
observe that it has all along been GOD's Manner to open new
Scenes, and to bring forth to View Things new and wonderful,
such as Eye had not seen, nor Ear heard, nor entered into the
Heart of Man or Angels, to the Astonishment of Heaven and
Earth, not only in the Revelations he makes of his Mind and
Will, but also in the Works of his Hands. As the old Creation
was carried on through six Days, and appeared all compleat,
settled in a State of Rest on the seventh; so the New Creation,
which is immensely the greatest and most glorious Work, is
carried on in a gradual Progress, from the Fall of Man, to the
Consummation of all Things, at the End of the World. And as
in the Progress of the Old Creation, there were still new
Things accomplished; new Wonders appeared every Day in the
Sight of the Angels, the Spectators of that Work; while those
Morning Stars sang together, new Scenes were opened or
Things that they had not seen before, 'till the whole was finished; so it is in the Progress of the New Creation. So that that
Promise, Isa. 64. 4. *For since the beginning of the World, Men
have not heard, nor perceived by the Ear, neither hath the Eye
seen, O GOD, besides thee, what he hath prepared for him that
waiteth for him.* Tho' it had a glorious Fulfilment in the Days
of CHRIST and the Apostles, as the Words are applied, 1 *Cor.* 2. 9.
Yet it always remains to be fulfilled, in Things that are yet behind, 'till the New Creation is finished, at CHRIST's delivering
up the Kingdom to the Father. And we live in those latter
Days, wherein we may be especially warranted to expect that
Things will be accomplished, concerning which it will be said,
Who hath heard such a Thing? Who hath seen such Things?

And besides those Things in this Work that have been chiefly
complained of as new, are not so new as has been generally
imagined: Tho' they have been much more frequent lately, in
Proportion to the uncommon Degree, Extent and Swiftness,
and other extraordinary Circumstances of the Work, yet they
are not new in their Kind; but are Things of the same Nature
as have been found and well approved of in the Church of
GOD before, from Time to Time.

We have a remarkable Instance in Mr. *Bolton*, that noted Minister of the Church of *England*, who being awaken'd by the preaching of the famous Mr. *Perkins*, Minister of CHRIST in the University of *Cambridge*, was subject to such Terrors as threw him to the Ground, and caused him to roar with Anguish; and the Pangs of the New-Birth in him were such, that he lay pale and without Sense, like one dead; as we have an Account in the *Fulfilling of the Scripture*, the 5th Edition, p. 103, 104. We have an Account in the same Page of another, whose Comforts under the Sun-shine of GOD's Presence were so great, that he could not forbear crying out in a Transport, and expressing in Exclamations, the great Sense he had of forgiving Mercy and his Assurance of GOD's Love. And we have a remarkable Instance in the Life of Mr. *George Trosse*, written by himself (who, of a notoriously vicious profligate Liver, became an eminent Saint and Minister of the Gospel,) of Terrors occasion'd by Awakenings of Conscience, so overpowering the Body, as to deprive, for some Time, of the Use of Reason.

Yea, such extraordinary external Effects of inward Impressions have not only been to be found in here and there a single Person, but there have also before now been Times wherein many have been thus affected, in some particular Parts of the Church of GOD, & such Effects have appeared in Congregations, in many at once. So it was in the Year 1625, in the West of *Scotland*, in a Time of great Out-pouring of the Spirit of GOD. It was then a frequent Thing for many to be so extraordinarily seized with Terror in the hearing of the Word, by the Spirit of GOD convincing them of Sin, that they fell down, and were carried out of the Church, who afterwards proved most solid and lively Christians; as the Author of the *Fulfilling of the Scripture* informs us, p. 185. The same Author in the preceding Page, informs of many in *France* that were so wonderfully affected with the Preaching of the Gospel, in the Time of those famous Divines *Farel* and *Viret*, that for a Time, they could not follow their secular Business. And p. 186. of many in *Ireland*, in a Time of great Out-pouring of the Spirit there, in the Year 1628, that were so filled with Divine Comforts, and a Sense of GOD, that they made but little Use of either Meat, Drink or Sleep, and professed that they did not feel the Need thereof. The same Author gives an Account of very much such

Things in Mrs. *Catherine Brettergh* of *Lancashire* in *England*, (p. 391. 392.) as have been cried out of, here amongst us, as wild and distracted: how that after great Distress, which very much affected her Body, the Sweat sometimes bursting out upon her, GOD did so break in upon her Mind with Light and Discoveries of himself, that she was forced to burst out, crying, "O the Joys, the Joys, the Joys, that I feel in my Soul! O they be wonderful, they be wonderful! The Place where I now am is sweet and pleasant! How comfortable is the Sweetness I feel, that delights my Soul! The Taste is precious; do you not feel it? Oh so sweet as it is!" And at other Times, "O my sweet Saviour, shall I be one with thee, as thou art one with the Father? And dost thou so love me that am but Dust, to make me Partaker of Glory with CHRIST? O how wonderful is thy Love! And Oh that my Tongue and Heart were able to sound forth thy Praises as I ought." At another Time she burst forth thus; "Yea Lord, I feel thy Mercy, and I am assured of thy Love! And so certain am I thereof, as thou art that GOD of Truth: even so certainly do I know my self to be thine, O LORD my GOD; and this my Soul knoweth right well!" Which last Words she again doubled. To a grave Minister, one Mr. *Harrison*, then with her, she said, "My Soul hath been compassed with the Terrors of Death, the Sorrows of Hell were upon me, and a Wilderness of Woe was in me; but blessed, blessed, blessed be the LORD my GOD! he hath brought me to a Place of Rest, even to the sweet running Waters of Life. The Way I now go in is a sweet and easy Way, strowed with Flowers; he hath brought me into a Place more sweet than the Garden of *Eden*. O the Joy, the Joy, the Delights and Joy that I feel! O how wonderful!"

Great Out-Cries under Awakenings were more frequently heard of in former Times in the Country than they have been of late, as some aged Persons now living do testify: Particularly I think fit here to insert a Testimony of my honoured Father, of what he remembers formerly to have heard.

"I well remember that one Mr. *Alexander Allyn*, a Scots Gentleman of good Credit, that dwelt formerly in this Town, shewed me a Letter that came from *Scotland*, that gave an Account of a Sermon preached in the City of *Edinburgh*, (as I remember) in the Time of the sitting of the general Assembly of Divines in that Kingdom, that so affected the People, that there was a great and loud Cry made throughout the Assembly. I have also been credibly informed, & how often I cannot now say, that it was a common Thing, when the famous Mr. *John Rogers* of *Dedham* in *England* was preaching, for some of his Hearers to cry out; and by what I have heard, I conclude that it was usual for many that heard that very awakening and rousing Preacher of GOD's Word, to make a great Cry in the Congregation."

Windsor, May 5. 1742.

TIMOTHY EDWARDS.

Mr. *Flavel* gives a remarkable Instance of a Man that he knew, that was wonderfully overcome with divine Comforts; which it is supposed he knew, as the Apostle *Paul* knew the Man that was caught up to the Third Heaven. He relates,

That "As the Person was travelling alone, with his Thoughts closely fixed on the great and astonishing Things of another World, his Thoughts began to swell higher and higher, like the Water in *Ezekiel*'s Vision, 'till at last they became an overflowing Flood: Such was the Intenseness of his Mind, such the ravishing Tastes of heavenly Joys, and such his full Assurance of his Interest therein, that he utterly lost all Sight & Sense of this World, & the Concernments thereof; and for some Hours, knew not where he was, nor what he was about: But having lost a great Quantity of Blood at the Nose, he found himself so faint, that it brought him a little more to himself. And after he had washed himself at a Spring, and drank of the Water for his Refreshment, he continued to the End of his Journey, which was Thirty Miles; and all this while was scarce sensible: And says he had several Trances of considerable Continuance. The same blessed Frame was preserved all that Night, and in a lower Degree, great Part of the next Day: The Night passed without one Wink of Sleep; and yet he declares he never had a sweeter Night's Rest in all his Life. Still *adds the Story*, The Joy of the Lord overflowed him, and he seem'd to be an Inhabitant of another World. And he used for many Years after to call that Day one of the Days of Heaven; and profess'd that he understood more of the Life of

Heaven by it, than by all the Books he ever read, or Discourses he ever entertain'd about it."

There have been Instances before now, of Persons crying
out in Transports of divine Joy in *New-England*. We have an
Instance in Capt. *Clap*'s Memoirs, published by the Rev. Mr.
Prince, not of a silly Woman or Child, but a Man of solid Understanding, that in a high Transport of spiritual Joy, was made
to cry out aloud on his Bed. His Words p. 9. are, "GOD's holy
Spirit did witness, (I do believe) together with my Spirit; that I
was a Child of GOD, and did fill my Heart and Soul with such
full Assurance that CHRIST was mine, that it did so transport
me, as to make me cry out upon my Bed, with a loud Voice,
He is come, He is come!"

There has, before now, been both crying out and falling down,
in this Town, under Awakenings of Conscience, and in the Pangs
of the New-Birth, and also in some of the Neighbour Towns. In
one of them, more than seven Years ago, was a great Number
together that cried out and fell down, under Convictions; in most
of which, by good Information, was a hopeful and abiding good
Issue. And the Rev. Mr. *Williams* of *Deerfield* gave me an Account
of an aged Man in that Town, many Years before that, that being
awaken'd by his Preaching, cried out aloud in the Congregation.
There have been many Instances in this and some Neighbour
Towns, before now, of Persons fainting with joyful Discoveries
made to their Souls: once several together in this Town. And
there also formerly have been several Instances here, of Person's
Flesh waxing cold and benumb'd, and their Hands clinch'd, yea
their Bodies being set into Convulsions, being over-power'd with
a strong Sense of the astonishingly great and excellent Things of
GOD and the Eternal World.

Secondly, Another Way that some err in making History and
former Observation their Rule to judge of this Work, instead
of the Holy Scripture, is in comparing some external, accidental Circumstances of this Work, with what has appear'd sometimes in Enthusiasts; and as they find an Agreement in some
such Things, so they reject the whole Work, or at least the
Substance of it, concluding it to be Enthusiasm. So, great Use
has been made to this Purpose of many Things that are found
amongst the *Quakers*; however totally and essentially different

in its Nature this Work is, and the Principles it is built upon, from the whole Religion of the *Quakers*. So, to the same Purpose, some external Appearances that were found amongst the *French Prophets*, and some other Enthusiasts in former Times, have been of late trump'd up with great Assurance and Triumph.

4. I would propose it to be consider'd, Whether or no, some instead of making the Scriptures their only Rule to judge of this Work, don't make their own Experience the Rule, and reject such and such Things as are now professed and experienced, because they never felt 'em themselves. Are there not many, that chiefly on this Ground, have entertained and vented Suspicions, if not peremptory Condemnations of those extreme Terrors, and those great, sudden & extraordinary Discoveries of the glorious Perfections of GOD, and of the Beauty and Love of CHRIST; and such vehement Affections, such high Transports of Love and Joy, such Pity and Distress for the Souls of others, and Exercises of Mind that have such great Effects on Persons Bodies, meerly, or chiefly, because they knew nothing about 'em by Experience? Persons are very ready to be suspicious of what they han't felt themselves. 'Tis to be fear'd many good Men have been guilty of this Error; which yet don't make it the less unreasonable. And perhaps there are some that upon this Ground don't only reject these extraordinary Things, but all such Conviction of Sin, and such Discoveries of the Glory of GOD, and Excellency of CHRIST, and inward Conviction of the Truth of the Gospel, by the immediate Influence of the Spirit of GOD, that are now supposed to be necessary to Salvation.

These Persons that thus make their own Experiences their Rule of Judgment, instead of bowing to the Wisdom of GOD, and yielding to his Word as an infallible Rule, are guilty of casting a great Reflection upon the Understanding of the most High.

III. Another Foundation-Error of those that reject this Work, is their not duly distinguishing the Good from the Bad, and very unjustly judging of the Whole by a Part; and so rejecting the Work in general, or in the main Substance of it, for the sake of some Things that are accidental to it, that are evil.

They look for more in Men that are divinely influenced, because subject to the Operations of a good Spirit, than is justly to be expected from them for that Reason, in this imperfect State, and dark World, where so much Blindness and Corruption remains in the best. When any profess to have received Light and Influence and Comforts from Heaven, and to have had sensible Communion with GOD, many are ready to expect that now they appear like Angels, and not still like poor, feeble, blind and sinful Worms of the Dust. There being so much Corruption left in the Hearts of GOD's own Children, and its prevailing as it sometimes does, is indeed a mysterious Thing, and always was a Stumbling-Block to the World; but won't be so much wondred at by those that are well versed in, and duly mindful of, two Things, viz. *First*, the Word of GOD, which teaches us the State of true Christians in this World, and *Secondly*, their own Hearts, at least if they have any Grace, and have Experience of its Conflicts with Corruption. They that are true Saints are most inexcuseable in making a great Difficulty of a great deal of Blindness, and many sinful Errors in those that profess Godliness. If all our Conduct, both open and secret, should be known, and our Hearts laid open to the World, how should we be even ready to fly from the Light of the Sun, and hide ourselves from the View of Mankind! And what great Allowances would it be found that we should need, that others should make for us? perhaps much greater than we are willing to make for others.

The great Weakness of the bigger Part of Mankind, in any Affair that is new and uncommon, appears in not distinguishing, but either approving or condemning all in the Lump. They that highly approve of the Affair in general, can't bear to have any Thing at all found Fault with; and on the other Hand, those that fasten their Eyes upon some Things in the Affair that are amiss, and appear very disagreeable to them, at once reject the whole. Both which Errors oftentimes arise from want of Persons due Acquaintance with themselves. It is rash and unjust when we proceed thus in judging either of a particular Person, or a People, or of such an Affair as the present wonderful Influence on the Minds of the People of this Land. Many if they see any Thing very ill in a particular Person, a Minister or private Professor, will at once brand him as an

Hypocrite. And if there be two or three of a People or Society that behave themselves very irregularly, the whole must bear the Blame of it. And if there be a few, tho' it may be not above One in an Hundred, that professed, and had a Shew of being the happy Partakers of what are called the saving Benefits of this Work, that prove naught, and give the World just Grounds to suspect 'em, the whole Work must be rejected on their Account; and those in general, that make the like Profession must be condemned for their Sakes.

So careful are some Persons lest this Work should be defended, that now they will hardly allow that the Influences of the Spirit of GOD on the Heart, can so much as indirectly, and accidentally, be the Occasion of the Exercise of Corruption, and Commission of Sin.—Thus far is true, That the Influence of the Spirit of GOD in his saving Operations, won't be an Occasion of the Increase of the Corruption of the Heart in general, but on the contrary, of the weakening of it: But yet there is nothing unreasonable in supposing, that at the same Time that it weakens Corruption in general, it may be an Occasion of the turning what is left into a new Channel, and so of there being more of some certain Kinds of the Exercise of Corruption than there was before; as that which tends to hinder and stop the Course of a Stream, if it don't do it wholly, may give a new Course to so much of the Water as gets by the Obstacle. The Influences of the Spirit, for Instance, may be an Occasion of new Ways of the Exercise of *Pride*, as has been acknowledged by orthodox Divines in general. That spiritual Discoveries and Comforts may, through the Corruption of the Heart, be an Occasion of the Exercises of spiritual Pride, don't use to be doubted of, 'till now it is found to be needful to maintain the War against this Work.

They that will hardly allow that a Work of the Spirit of GOD can be a remote Occasion of any sinful Behaviour or unchristian Conduct, I suppose will allow that the truly gracious Influences of the Spirit of GOD, yea and an high Degree of Love to GOD, is consistent with these two Things, *viz.* A considerable Degree of remaining Corruption, and also many Errors in Judgment in Matters of Religion, and in Matters of Practice. And this is all that need to be allowed, in order to its being most demonstratively evident, that a high Degree of Love to

GOD may accidentally move a Person to that which is very wrong, and contrary to the Mind and Will of GOD. For a high Degree of Love to GOD will strongly move a Person to do that which he believes to be agreeable to GOD's Will; and therefore, if he be mistaken, and be perswaded that That is agreeable to the Will of GOD, which indeed is very contrary to it, then his Love will accidentally, but strongly, incline him to that, which is indeed very contrary to the Will of GOD.

They that are studied in Logick have learned that the Nature of the Cause is not to be judged of by the Nature of the Effect, nor the Nature of the Effect from the Nature of the Cause, when the Cause is only *Causa sine quâ non*, or an occasional Cause; yea, that in such a Case, oftentimes the Nature of the Effect is quite contrary to the Nature of the Cause.

True Disciples of CHRIST may have a great deal of false Zeal, such as the Disciples had of old, when they would have Fire called for from Heaven to come down on the *Samaritans*, because they did not receive them. And even so eminently holy, and great, and divine a Saint as *Moses*, who conversed with GOD from Time to Time, as a Man speaks with his Friend, and concerning whom GOD gives his Testimony, that he *was very meek, above any Man upon the Face of the Earth*, yet may be rash and sinful in his Zeal, when his Spirit is stirred by the Hard-heartedness and Opposition of others, so as to speak very unadvisedly with his Lips, and greatly to offend GOD, and shut himself out from the Possession of the good Things that GOD is about to accomplish for his Church on Earth; as *Moses* was excluded *Canaan*, tho' he had brought the People out of *Egypt*, Psal. 106. 32, 33. And Men, even in those very Things wherein they are influenced by a truly pious Principle, yet, through Error and want of due Consideration and Caution, may be very rash with their Zeal. It was a truly good Spirit that animated that excellent Generation of *Israel* that was in *Joshua*'s Time, in that Affair that we have an Account of in the 22d Chapter of *Joshua*; and yet they were rash and heady with their Zeal, to go about to gather all *Israel* together to go up so furiously to War with their Brethren of the two Tribes and half, about their building the Altar *Ed*, without first enquiring into the Matter, or so much as sending a Messenger to be informed. So the Christians that were of the Circumcision, with Warmth and Contention condemned *Peter* for receiving *Cornelius*, as we have Account, *Act.* 11. This their Heat and Censure was unjust, and *Peter* was wronged in it; but there is all Appearance in the Story that they acted from a real Zeal and Concern for the Will and Honour of GOD. So the primitive Christians, from their Zeal for, and against unclean Meats, censured and condemned one another: This was a bad Effect, and yet the Apostle bears them Witness, or at least expresses his Charity towards them, that both Sides acted from a good Principle, and true Respect to the Lord, *Rom.* 14. 6. The Zeal of the *Corinthians* with Respect to the incestuous Man, tho' the Apostle highly commends it, yet at the same Time saw that they needed a Caution, lest they should carry it too far, to an undue Severity, and so as to fail of Christian Meekness and Forgiveness, 2 *Cor.* 2. 6, 7, 8, 9, 10, 11. and Chap. 7. 11. to the End.—*Luther* that great Reformer had a great deal of Bitterness with his Zeal.

It surely cannot be wonder'd at by considerate Persons, that at a Time when Multitudes all over the Land have their Affections greatly moved, that great Numbers should run into many Errors and Mistakes with Respect to their Duty, and consequently into many Acts and Practices that are imprudent and irregular. I question whether there be a Man in *New-England*, of the strongest Reason and greatest Learning, but what would be put to it to keep Master of himself, thoroughly to weigh his Words, and consider all the Consequences of his Behaviour, so as to behave himself in all Respects prudently, if he were so strongly impressed with a Sense of divine and eternal Things, and his Affections so exceedingly moved, as has been frequent of late among the common People.—How little do they consider Human Nature, who look upon it so insuperable a Stumbling-Block, when such Multitudes of all Kinds of Capacities, natural Tempers, Educations, Customs and Manners of Life, are so greatly and variously affected, that Imprudences and Irregularities of Conduct should abound; especially in a State of Things so uncommon, and when the Degree, Extent, Swiftness and Power of the Operation is so very extraordinary, and so new, that there has not been Time and Experience enough to give Birth to Rules for People's Conduct, and so unusual in Times past, that the Writings of Divines don't afford Rules to direct us in such a State of Things?

A great deal of Noise and Tumult, Confusion and Uproar, and Darkness mixed with Light, and Evil with Good, is always to be expected in the beginning of something very extraordinary, and very glorious in the State of Things in human Society, or the Church of GOD. As after Nature has long been shut up in a cold dead State, in Time of Winter, when the Sun returns in the Spring, there is, together with the Increase of the Light and Heat of the Sun, very dirty and tempestuous Weather, before all is settled calm and serene, and all Nature rejoices in its Bloom and Beauty. It is in the New-Creation as it was in the Old, the Spirit of GOD first moved upon the Face of the Waters, which was an Occasion of great Uproar and Tumult, and Things were gradually brought to a settled State, 'till at length all stood forth in that beautiful, peaceful Order, when the Heavens and the Earth were finished, and GOD saw every Thing that he had made, and behold it was very good. When GOD is about to bring to pass something great and glorious in the World, Nature is in a Ferment and Struggle, and the World as it were in Travail. As when GOD was about to introduce the *Messiah* into the World, and that new and glorious Dispensation that he set up, he *shook the Heavens and the Earth, and shook all Nations.* There is nothing that the Church of GOD is in Scripture more frequently represented by than Vegetables; as a Tree, a Vine, Corn, *&c.*—which gradually bring forth their Fruit, and are first green before they are ripe. A great Revival of Religion is expressly compared to this gradual Production of Vegetables, Isa. 61. 11. *As the Earth bringeth forth her Bud, and as the Garden causeth the Things that are sown in it to spring forth; so the Lord God will cause Righteousness and Praise to spring forth before all the Nations.* The Church is in a special Manner compared to a Palm-Tree, *Cant.* 7. 7, 8. *Exod.* 15. 27. 1 *King.* 6. 29. *Psal.* 92. 12. Of which Tree this peculiar Thing is observed, That the Fruit of it, tho' it be very sweet and good when it is ripe, yet, before it has had Time to ripen, has a Mixture of Poison.

The Weakness of human Nature has always appeared in Times of great Revival of Religion, by a Disposition to run to Extreams and get into Confusion; and especially in these three Things, Enthusiasm, Superstition, and intemperate Zeal. So it appeared in the Time of the Reformation, very remarkably;

and also in the Days of the Apostles; many were then exceedingly disposed to lay Weight on those Things that were very Notional and Chimerical, giving Heed to Fables and Whimsies, as appears by 1 *Tim*. 1. 4. and 4. 7. 2 *Tim*. 2. 16. and v. 23. and *Tit*. 1. 14. and 3. 9. Many, as Ecclesiastical History informs us, fell off into the most wild Enthusiasm, and extravagant Notions of Spirituality, and extraordinary Illumination from Heaven beyond others; and many were prone to Superstition, Will-Worship and a voluntary Humility, giving Heed to the Commandments of Men, being fond of an unprofitable bodily Exercise, as appears by many Passages in the Apostles Writings: And what a Proneness then appeared among Professors to swerve from the Path of Duty, and the Spirit of the Gospel, in the Exercises of a rash indiscreet Zeal, censuring and condemning Ministers and People; one saying, I am of *Paul*, another I of *Apollos*, another I of *Cephas*; judging one another for Differences of Opinion about smaller Matters, unclean Meats, holy Days and holy Places, and their different Opinions and Practices respecting civil Intercourse and Communication with their Heathen Neighbours? And how much did vain Jangling and Disputing and Confusion prevail through undue Heat of Spirit, under the Name of a religious Zeal? 1 *Tim*. 6. 4, 5. 2 *Tim*. 2. 16. and *Tit*. 3. 9. And what a Task had the Apostles to keep them within Bounds, and maintain good Order in the Churches? How often are they mentioning their Irregularities? The prevailing of such like Disorders seems to have been the special Occasion of writing many of their Epistles. The Church in that great Effusion of the Spirit that was then, and the strong Impressions that GOD's People were then under, was under the Care of infallible Guides, that watched over them Day and Night; but yet so prone were they, through the Weakness and Corruption of human Nature, to get out of the Way, that Irregularity and Confusion rose in some Churches, where there was an extraordinary Out-pouring of the Spirit, to a very great Height, even in the Apostles Lifetime, and under their Eye. And tho' some of the Apostles liv'd long to settle the State of Things, yet presently after they were dead, the Christian Church ran into many Superstitions and childish Notions and Practices, and in some Respects into a great Severity in their Zeal. And let any wise Person that han't, in the midst of the

Disputes of the present Day, got beyond the Calmness of Consideration, impartially consider to what Lengths, we may reasonably suppose, many of the primitive Christians, in their Heat of Zeal, and under their extraordinary Impressions, would soon have gone, if they had had no inspired Guides; and whether or no 'tis not probable that the Church of *Corinth* in particular, by an Increase of their Irregularities and Contentions, would not in a little Time have broke to Pieces, and dissolved in a State of the utmost Confusion? and yet this would have been no Evidence that there had not been a most glorious and remarkable Out-pouring of the Spirit in that City. But as for us, we have no infallible Apostle to guide and direct us, to rectify Disorders, and reclaim us when we are wandring; but every one does what is right in his own Eyes; and they that err in Judgment, and are got into a wrong Path, continue to wander, till Experience of the mischievous Issue convinces them of their Error.

If we look over this Affair, and seriously weigh it in its Circumstances, it will appear a Matter of no great Difficulty to account for the Errors that have been gone into, supposing the Work in general to be from a very great Out-pouring of the Spirit of GOD. It may easily be accounted for, that many have run into great Errors, and into just such Errors as they have. It is known, that some that have been improved as great Instruments to promote this Work, have been very young; and how natural is it for such as are themselves newly 'waked out of Sleep, and bro't out of that State of Darkness, Insensibility and spiritual Death, which they had been in ever since they were born; and have a new and wonderful Scene opened to them; and have in View the Reality, the Vastness, and infinite Importance, and Nearness of spiritual & eternal Things; and at the same Time are surprized to see the World asleep about them; and han't the Advantage of Age and Experience, and have had but little Opportunity to study Divinity, or to converse with aged experienced Christians and Divines; I say, how natural is it for such to fall into many Errors with Respect to the State of Mankind, with which they are so surprized, and with Respect to the Means and Methods of their Relief? Is it any Wonder that they han't at once learned how to make all the Allowances that are to be made, and that they don't at once find out that

Method of dealing with the World, that is adapted to the mysterious State and Nature of Mankind? Is it any Wonder that they can't at once foresee what the Consequences of Things will be, what Evils are to be guarded against, and what Difficulties are like to arise, that are to be provided for?

We have long been in a strange Stupor; the Influences of the Spirit of GOD upon the Heart have been but little felt, and the Nature of them but little taught; so that they are in many Respects new to great Numbers of those that have lately fallen under them. And is it any Wonder that they that never before had Experience of the supernatural Influence of the Divine Spirit upon their Souls, and never were instructed in the Nature of these Influences, don't so well know how to distinguish one extraordinary new Impression from another, and so (to themselves insensibly) run into Enthusiasm, taking every strong Impulse or Impression to be divine? How natural is it to suppose, that among the Multitudes of illiterate People (most of which are in their Youth) that find themselves so wonderfully changed, and brought into such new, and before (to them) almost unheard of Circumstances, that many should pass wrong, and very strange Judgments of both Persons and Things that are about them; and that now they behold them in such a new Light, they in their Surprize should go further from the Judgment that they were wont to make of them than they ought, & in their great Change of Sentiments, should pass from one Extreme to another? And why should it be thought strange, that those that scarce ever heard of any such Thing as an Out-pouring of the Spirit of GOD before; or if they did, had no Notion of it; don't know how to behave themselves in such a new and strange State of Things? And is it any Wonder that they are ready to hearken to those that have instructed them, that have been the Means of delivering them from such a State of Death and Misery as they were in before, or have a Name for being the happy Instruments of promoting the same Work among others? Is it unaccountable that Persons in these Circumstances are ready to receive every Thing they say, and to drink down Error as well as Truth from them? And why should there be all Indignation and no Compassion towards those that are thus misled?

When these Persons are extraordinarily affected with a new

Sense, and recent Discovery they have received, of the Greatness and Excellency of the divine Being, the Certainty and infinite Importance of eternal Things, the Preciousness of Souls,
and the dreadful Danger and Madness of Mankind, together
with a great Sense of GOD's distinguishing Kindness and Love
to them; no Wonder that now they think they must exert
themselves, and do something extraordinary for the Honour
of GOD and the Good of the Souls of their Fellow-Creatures,
and know not how to sit still, and forbear speaking and acting
with uncommon Earnestness and Vigour. And in these Circumstances, if they ben't Persons of more than common
Steadiness & Discretion, or han't some Person of Wisdom to
direct them, 'tis a Wonder if they don't proceed without due
Caution, and do Things that are irregular, and that will, in the
Issue, do much more Hurt than Good.

Censuring others is the worst Disease with which this Affair
has been attended: But yet such a Time as this is indeed a Time
of great Temptation to this sinful Error. When there has been
such a Time of great and long continued Deadness, and many
are brought out of a State of Nature into a State of Grace, in so
extraordinary a Manner, and filled with such uncommon Degrees of Light, 'tis natural for such to form their Notions of a
State of Grace wholly from what they experience; many of them
know no other Way; for they never have been taught much
about a State of Grace, and the different Degrees of Grace, and
the Degrees of Darkness and Corruption that Grace is consistent with, nor concerning the Manner of the Influences of the
Spirit in converting a Soul, and the Variety of the Manner of his
Operations: They therefore forming their Idea of a State of Grace
only by their own Experience, no Wonder that it appears an insuperable Difficulty to them to reconcile such a State, of which
they have this Idea, with what they observe in Professors that are
about them. 'Tis indeed in it self a very great Mystery, that
Grace should be consistent with so much and such kind of Corruption as sometimes prevails in the truly godly; and no Wonder
that it especially appears so to uninstructed new Converts, that
have been converted in an extraordinary Manner.

Tho' Censoriousness be a Thing that is very sinful, and is
most commonly found in Hypocrites and Persons of a pharisa-
ical Spirit, yet it is not so inconsistent with true Godliness as

some imagine. We have remarkable Instances of it in those holy Men that we have an Account of in the Book of *Job*: Not only were *Job*'s three Friends, that seem to have been eminently holy Men, guilty of it, in very unreasonably censuring the best Man on Earth, very positively determining that he was an unconverted Man; But *Job* himself, that was not only a Man of true Piety, but excelled all Men in Piety, and particularly excelled in a humble, meek and patient Spirit, was guilty of bitterly censuring his three Friends, as wicked, vile Hypocrites. *Job* 16. 9, 10, 11. *He teareth me in his Wrath who hateth me, he gnasheth upon me with his Teeth; mine Enemy sharpeneth his Eyes upon me: They have gaped upon me with their Mouth.—GOD hath delivered me to the ungodly, and turned me over into the Hands of the Wicked.* So he is very positive in it that they are Hypocrites, and shall be miserably destroyed as such, in the next Chapter, v. 2, 3, 4. *Are there not Mockers with me? And doth not mine Eye continue in their Provocation? Lay down now, put me in Surety with thee; who is he that will strike Hands with me? For thou hast hid their Heart from Understanding: therefore shalt thou not exalt them.* And again, v. 8, 9, 10. *Upright Men shall be astonished at this, and the Innocent shall stir up himself against the Hypocrite: The Righteous also shall hold on his Way, and he that hath clean Hands shall be stronger and stronger. But as for you all, do you return and come now: for I cannot find one wise Man* (i.e. one good Man) *among you.*

Thus I think the Errors and Irregularities that attend this Work, may be accounted for, from the Consideration of the Infirmity and Weakness and common Corruption of Mankind, together with the Circumstances of the Work, tho' we should suppose it to be the Work of GOD. And it would not be a just Objection in any to say, if these powerful Impressions and great Affections are from the Spirit of GOD, why don't the same Spirit give Strength of Understanding and Capacity in Proportion, to those Persons that are the Subjects of them; so that strong Affections may not, through their Error, drive them to an irregular and sinful Conduct? For I don't know that GOD has any where obliged himself to do it. The End of the Influences of GOD's Spirit is to make Men spiritually knowing, wise to Salvation, which is the most excellent Wisdom; and he has also appointed Means for our gaining such Degrees of other

Knowledge as we need, to conduct our selves regularly, which
Means should be carefully used: But the End of the Influence of
the Spirit of GOD is not to increase Men's natural Capacities, nor
has GOD obliged himself immediately to increase civil Prudence
in Proportion to the Degrees of spiritual Light.

If we consider the Errors that attend this Work, not only as
from Man, and his Infirmity, but also as from GOD, and by his
Permission and Disposal, they are not strange, upon the Supposition of its being, as to the Substance of it, a Work of GOD. If
GOD intends this great Revival of Religion to be the dawning,
or a Forerunner of an happy State of his Church on Earth, it
may be an Instance of the divine Wisdom, in the beginning of
it, to suffer so many Irregularities and Errors in Conduct, to
which he knew Men, in their present weak State, were most
exposed, under great religious Affections, and when animated
with great Zeal. For it will be very likely to be of excellent
Benefit to his Church, in the Continuance and Progress of the
Work afterwards: Their Experience in the first setting out, of
the mischievous Consequences of these Errors, and smarting
for them in the Beginning, may be an happy Defence to them
afterwards, for many Generations, from these Errors, which
otherwise they might continually be exposed to. As when *David*
and all *Israel* went about to bring back the Ark into the midst
of the Land, after it had been long absent, first in the Land of
the *Philistines*, and then in *Kirjathjearim*, in the utmost Borders of the Land; they at first sought not the LORD after the
due Order, and they smarted for their Error; but this put them
upon studying the Law, and more thoroughly acquainting
themselves with the Mind and Will of GOD, and seeking and
serving him with greater Circumspection; and the Consequence was glorious, *viz.* their seeking GOD in such a Manner
as was accepted of him; and the Ark of GOD's ascending into
the Heights of *Zion*, with those great and extraordinary Rejoicings of the King and all the People, without any Frown or
Rebuke from GOD intermixed; and GOD's dwelling thenceforward in the midst of the People, to those glorious Purposes
that are expressed in the 68th Psalm.

And 'tis very analogous to the Manner of GOD dealing with his
People, to permit a great deal of Error, and suffer the infirmity of
his People much to appear, in the beginning of a glorious Work

of his Grace for their Felicity, to teach them what they be, to humble them, and fit them for that glorious Prosperity he is about to advance them to, and the more to secure to himself the Honour of such a glorious Work: For by Man's exceeding Weakness appearing in the beginning of it, 'tis evident that GOD don't lay the Foundation of it in Man's Strength or Wisdom.

And as we need not wonder at the Errors that attend this Work, if we look at the Hand of Men that are guilty of them, and the Hand of GOD in permitting them, so neither shall we see Cause to wonder at them, if we consider them with Regard to the Hand that Satan has in them. For as the Work is much greater than any other Out-pouring of the Spirit that ever has been in *New-England*, so no Wonder that the Devil is more alarmed and enraged, and exerts himself more vigorously against it, and does more powerfully endeavour to tempt and mislead those that are the Subjects of it, or are its Promoters.

Whatever Imprudences there have been, and whatever sinful Irregularities; whatever Vehemence of the Passions, and Heats of the Imaginations, Transports and Extacies; and whatever Error in Judgment, and indiscreet Zeal; and whatever Outcries, and Faintings, and Agitations of Body; yet it is manifest and notorious, that there has been of late a very uncommon Influence upon the Minds of a very great Part of the Inhabitants of *New-England*, from one End of the Land to the other, that has been attended with the following Effects; *viz.* a great Increase of a Spirit of Seriousness, and sober Consideration of the Things of the eternal World; a Disposition to hearken to any Thing that is said of Things of this Nature, with Attention and Affection; a Disposition to treat Matters of Religion with Solemnity, and as Matters of great Importance; a Disposition to make these Things the Subject of Conversation; and a great Disposition to hear the Word of GOD preached, and to take all Opportunities in order to it; and to attend on the publick Worship of GOD, and all external Duties of Religion in a more solemn and decent Manner; so that there is a remarkable and general Alteration in the Face of *New-England* in these Respects: Multitudes in all Parts of the Land, of vain, thoughtless, regardless Persons are quite changed, and become serious and considerate: There is a vast Increase of Concern for the Salvation of the precious Soul, and of that Inquiry, *What shall I do to be saved*? The Hearts of Multitudes have been greatly taken off from the Things of the World, its Profits, Pleasures and Honours; and there has been a great Increase of Sensibleness and Tenderness of Conscience: Multitudes in all Parts have had their Consciences awaken'd, and have been made sensible of the pernicious Nature and Consequences of Sin, and what a dreadful Thing it is to lie under Guilt and the Displeasure of GOD, and to live without Peace and Reconciliation with him: They have also been awakened to a Sense of the Shortness and Uncertainty of Life, and the Reality of another World and future Judgment, and of the Necessity of an Interest in CHRIST: They are more afraid of Sin, more careful and inquisitive that they may know what is contrary to the Mind and Will of GOD, that they may avoid it, and what he requires of them, that they may do it; more careful to guard against Temptations, more watchful over their own Hearts, earnestly desirous of being informed what are the Means that GOD has directed to, for their Salvation, and diligent in the Use of the Means that GOD has appointed in his Word, in order to it. Many very stupid, senseless Sinners, and Persons of a vain Mind, have been greatly awakened. There is a strange Alteration almost all over *New-England* amongst young People: By a powerful, invisible Influence on their Minds, they have been brought to forsake those Things in a general Way, as it were at once, that they were extremely fond of, and greatly addicted to, and that they seem'd to place the Happiness of their Lives in, and that nothing before could induce them to forsake; as their Frolicking, vain Company-keeping, Night-walking, their Mirth and Jollity, their impure Language, and lewd Songs: In vain did Ministers preach against those Things before, and in vain were Laws made to restrain them, and in vain was all the Vigilance of Magistrates and Civil Officers; but now they have almost every where dropped them as it were of themselves. And there is a great Alteration amongst Old and Young as to Drinking, Tavern-haunting, profane speaking, and Extravagance in Apparel. Many notoriously vicious Persons have been reformed, and become externally quite New-Creatures: Some that are wealthy, and of a fashionable, gay Education; some great Beaus and fine Ladies, that seem'd to have their Minds swallowed up with nothing but the vain Shews and Pleasures of the World,

have been wonderfully altered, and have relinquished these
Vanities, and are become serious, mortified and humble in
their Conversation. 'Tis astonishing to see the Alteration that
is in some Towns, where before was but little Appearance of
Religion, or any Thing but Vice and Vanity: and so remote was
all that was to be seen or heard amongst them from any Thing
that savour'd of vital Piety or serious Religion, or that had any
Relation to it, that one would have thought, if they had judged
only by what appeared in them, that they had been some other
Species from the serious and religious, that had no Concern
with another World, and whose Natures were not made capable
of those Things that appertain to Christian Experience, and
pious Conversation; especially was it thus among young Persons: And now they are transformed into another sort of People; their former vain, worldly and vicious Conversation and
Dispositions seem to be forsaken, and they are as it were, gone
over to a new World: Their Thoughts, and their Talk, and their
Concern, Affections and Enquiries are now about the Favour
of GOD, an Interest in CHRIST, a renewed sanctified Heart,
and a spiritual Blessedness, and Acceptance and Happiness in a
future World. And through the greater Part of *New-England*,
the Holy Bible is in much greater Esteem and Use than it used
to be; The great Things that are contained in it are much more
regarded, as Things of the greatest Consequence, and are
much more the Subjects of Meditation and Conversation; and
other Books of Piety that have long been of established Reputation, as the most excellent, and most tending to promote
true Godliness, have been abundantly more in Use: The Lord's-
Day is more religiously and strictly observed: And abundance
has been lately done at making up Differences, and confessing
Faults one to another, and making Restitution; probably more
within this two Years, than was done in Thirty Years before: It
has been so undoubtedly in many Places. And surprizing has
been the Power of that Spirit that has been poured out on the
Land, in many Instances, to destroy old Grudges, and make up
long continued Breaches, and to bring those that seemed to be
in a confirm'd irreconcileable Alienation, to embrace each
other in a sincere and entire Amity. Great Numbers under this
Influence have been brought to a deep Sense of their own
Sinfulness and Vileness; the Sinfulness of their Lives, the

Heinousness of their Disregard of the Authority of the great GOD, and the Heinousness of their living in Contempt of a Saviour: they have lamented their former Negligence of their Souls, and neglecting and losing precious Time. Their Sins of Life have been extraordinarily set before them: and they have also had a great Sense of their Sins of Heart; their hardness of Heart, and Enmity against that which is Good, and Proneness to all Evil; and also of the Worthlessness of their own religious Performances, how unworthy their Prayers, Praises, and all that they did in Religion, was to be regarded of GOD: And it has been a common Thing that Persons have had such a Sense of their own Sinfulness, that they have thought themselves to be the worst of all, and that none ever was so vile as they: And many seem to have been greatly convinced that they were utterly unworthy of any Mercy at the Hands of GOD, however miserable they were, and tho' they stood in extreme Necessity of Mercy; and that they deserved nothing but eternal Burnings: and have been sensible that GOD would be altogether just and righteous in inflicting endless Damnation upon them, at the same Time that they have had an exceeding affecting Sense of the Dreadfulness of such endless Torments, and have apprehended themselves to be greatly in Danger of it. And many have been deeply affected with a Sense of their own Ignorance and Blindness, and exceeding Helplessness, and so of their extreme Need of the divine Pity and Help. And so far as we are worthy to be credited one by another, in what we say, (and Persons of good Understanding and sound Mind, and known and experienced Probity, have a Right to be believ'd by their Neighbours, when they speak of Things that fall under their Observation and Experience,) Multitudes in *New-England* have lately been brought to a new and great Conviction of the Truth and Certainty of the Things of the Gospel; to a firm Perswasion that CHRIST JESUS is the Son of GOD, and the great and only Saviour of the World; and that the great Doctrines of the Gospel touching Reconciliation by his Blood, and Acceptance in his Righteousness, and eternal Life and Salvation through him, are Matters of undoubted Truth; together with a most affecting Sense of the Excellency and Sufficiency of this Saviour, and the glorious Wisdom and Grace of GOD shining in this Way of Salvation; and of the Wonders of CHRIST's

dying Love, and the Sincerity of CHRIST in the Invitations of
the Gospel, and a consequent Affiance and sweet Rest of Soul in
CHRIST, as a glorious Saviour, a strong Rock and high Tower,
accompanied with an admiring and exalting Apprehension of
the Glory of the divine Perfections, GOD's Majesty, Holiness,
sovereign Grace, &c—; with a sensible, strong and sweet Love
to GOD, and Delight in him, far surpassing all temporal Delights, or earthly Pleasures; and a Rest of Soul in him as a
Portion and the Fountain of all Good, attended with an Abhorrence of Sin, and Self-loathing for it, and earnest longings
of Soul after more Holiness and Conformity to GOD, with a
Sense of the great Need of GOD's Help in order to Holiness of
Life; together with a most dear Love to all that are supposed to
be the Children of GOD, and a Love to Mankind in general,
and a most sensible and tender Compassion for the Souls of
Sinners, and earnest Desires of the Advancement of CHRIST's
Kingdom in the World. And these Things have appear'd to be
in many of them abiding now for many Months, yea, more
than a Year and half; with an abiding Concern to live an holy
Life, and great Complaints of remaining Corruption, longing
to be more free from the Body of Sin and Death. And not only
do these Effects appear in new Converts, but great Numbers
of those that were formerly esteemed the most sober and pious
People, have, under the Influence of this Work, been greatly
quicken'd, and their Hearts renewed with greater Degrees of
Light, renewed Repentance and Humiliation, and more lively
Exercises of Faith, Love and Joy in the LORD. Many as I am
well knowing, have of late been remarkably engaged to watch,
and strive, and fight against Sin, and cast out every Idol, and
sell all for CHRIST, and give up themselves entirely to GOD,
and make a Sacrifice of every worldly and carnal Thing to the
Welfare and Prosperity of their Souls. And there has of late
appeared in some Places an unusual Disposition to bind themselves to it in a solemn Covenant with GOD. And now instead
of Meetings at Taverns and drinking Houses, and Meetings of
young People in Frolicks and vain Company, the Country is
full of Meetings of all Sorts and Ages of Persons, Young and
Old, Men, Women and little Children, to read and pray, and
sing Praises, and to converse of the Things of GOD and another
World. In very many Places the main of the Conversation in all

Companies turns on Religion, and Things of a spiritual Nature. Instead of vain Mirth amongst young People, there is
now either mourning under a Sense of the Guilt of Sin, or holy
rejoicing in CHRIST JESUS; and instead of their lewd Songs, are
now to be heard from them Songs of Praise to GOD, and the
Lamb that was slain to redeem them by his Blood. And there has
been this Alteration abiding on Multitudes all over the Land,
for a Year and half, without any Appearance of a Disposition to
return to former Vice and Vanity. And under the Influences of
this Work, there have been many of the Remains of those
wretched People and Dregs of Mankind, the poor *Indians*,
that seemed to be next to a State of Brutality, and with
whom, till now, it seemed to be to little more Purpose to use
Endeavours for their Instruction and Awakening, than with
the Beasts; whose Minds have now been strangely opened to
receive Instruction, and have been deeply affected with the
Concerns of their precious Souls, and have reformed their
Lives, and forsaken their former stupid, barbarous & brutish
Way of living; & particularly that Sin to which they have been
so exceedingly addicted, their Drunkenness; & are become
devout & serious Persons; & many of them to Appearance
bro't truly and greatly to delight in the Things of GOD, and to
have their Souls very much engaged and entertained with the
great Things of the Gospel. And many of the poor *Negroes* also
have been in like Manner wrought upon and changed. And the
Souls of very many little Children have been remarkably
enlighten'd, and their Hearts wonderfully affected and enlarged, and their Mouths open'd, expressing themselves in a
Manner far beyond their Years, and to the just Astonishment
of those that have heard them; and some of them from Time
to Time, for many Months, greatly and delightfully affected
with the Glory of divine Things, and the Excellency and Love
of the Redeemer, with their Hearts greatly filled with Love to
and Joy in him, and have continued to be serious and pious in
their Behaviour.

The divine Power of this Work has marvellously appeared in
some Instances I have been acquainted with, in supporting
and fortifying the Heart under great Trials, such as the Death
of Children, and extreme Pain of Body; wonderfully maintaining
the Serenity, Calmness and Joy of the Soul, in an immoveable

Rest in GOD, and sweet Resignation to him. There also have been Instances of some that have been the Subjects of this Work, that under the blessed Influences of it have, in such a calm, bright and joyful Frame of Mind, been carried through the Valley of the Shadow of Death.

And now let us consider—; Is it not strange that in a Christian, orthodox Country, and such a Land of Light as this is, there should be many at a Loss whose Work this is, whether the Work of GOD or the Work of the Devil? Is it not a Shame to *New-England* that such a Work should be much doubted of here? Need we look over the Histories of all past Times, to see if there ben't some Circumstances and external Appearances that attend this Work, that have been formerly found amongst Enthusiasts? Whether the *Montanists* had not great Transports of Joy, and whether the *French Prophets* had not Agitations of Body? Blessed be GOD! He don't put us to the Toil of such Inquiries. We need not say, Who shall ascend into Heaven, to bring us down something whereby to judge of this Work? Nor does GOD send us beyond the Seas, nor into past Ages, to obtain a Rule that shall determine and satisfy us. But we have a Rule near at Hand, a sacred Book that GOD himself has put into our Hands, with clear and infallible Marks, sufficient to resolve us in Things of this Nature; which Book I think we must reject, not only in some particular Passages, but in the Substance of it, if we reject such a Work as has now been described, as not being the Work of GOD. The whole Tenor of the Gospel proves it; all the Notion of Religion that the Scripture gives us confirms it.

I suppose there is scarcely a Minister in this Land, but from Sabbath to Sabbath used to pray that GOD would pour out his Spirit, and work a Reformation and Revival of Religion in the Country, and turn us from our Intemperance, Profaneness, Uncleanness, Worldliness and other Sins; and we have kept from Year to Year Days of publick Fasting and Prayer to GOD, to acknowledge our Backslidings, and humble our selves for our Sins, and to seek of GOD Forgiveness & Reformation: and now when so great and extensive a Reformation is so suddenly and wonderfully accomplished, in those very Things that we have sought to GOD for, shall we not acknowledge it? Or when we do, do it with great Coldness, Caution and Reserve, and scarcely take any Notice of it in our publick Prayers & Praises, or mention it but slightly and cursorily, and in such a Manner as carries an Appearance as tho' we would contrive to say as little of it as ever we could, and were glad to pass from it? And that because, (altho' indeed there be such a Work attended with all these glorious Effects, yet) The Work is attended with a Mixture of Error, Imprudences, Darkness and Sin; because some Persons are carried away with Impressions, and are indiscreet, and too censorious with their Zeal; and because there are high Transports of religious Affection; and because of some Effects on Persons Bodies that we don't understand the Reason of?

I have been particularly acquainted with many Persons that have been the Subjects of the high and extraordinary Transports of the present Day; and in the highest Transports of any of the Instances that I have been acquainted with, and where the Affections of Admiration, Love and Joy, so far as another could judge, have been raised to a higher Pitch than in any other Instances I have observed or been informed of, the following Things have been united, *viz.* a very frequent dwelling, for some considerable Time together, in such Views of the Glory of the divine Perfections, and CHRIST's Excellencies, that the Soul in the mean Time has been as it were perfectly overwhelmed, and swallowed up with Light and Love and a sweet Solace, Rest and Joy of Soul, that was altogether unspeakeable; and more than once continuing for five or six Hours together, without any Interruption, in that clear and lively View or Sense of the infinite Beauty and Amiableness of CHRIST's Person, and the heavenly Sweetness of his excellent and transcendent Love; so that (to use the Person's own Expressions) the Soul remained in a kind of heavenly Elysium, and did as it were swim in the Rays of CHRIST's Love, like a little Mote swimming in the Beams of the Sun, or Streams of his Light that come in at a Window; and the Heart was swallowed up in a kind of Glow of CHRIST's Love, coming down from CHRIST's Heart in Heaven, as a constant Stream of sweet Light, at the same Time the Soul all flowing out in Love to him; so that there seem'd to be a constant flowing and reflowing from Heart to Heart: The Soul dwelt on high, and was lost in GOD, and seemed almost to leave the Body; dwelling in a pure Delight that fed and satisfied the Soul; enjoying Pleasure without the least Sting, or any Interruption; a Sweetness that the Soul was lost in; so that (so far as the Judgment, and Word of a Person of Discretion may be taken, speaking upon the most deliberate Consideration,) what was enjoyed in each single Minute of the whole Space, which was many Hours, was undoubtedly worth more than all the outward Comfort and Pleasure of the whole Life put together; and this without being in any Trance, or being at all deprived of the Exercise of the Bodily Senses: And the like heavenly Delight and unspeakable Joy of Soul, enjoyed from Time to Time, for Years together; tho' not frequently so long together, to such an height: Extraordinary Views of divine Things, and religious Affections, being frequently attended with very great Effects on the Body, Nature often sinking under the Weight of divine Discoveries, the Strength of the Body taken away, so as to deprive of all Ability to stand or speak; sometimes the Hands clinch'd, and the Flesh cold, but Senses still remaining; animal Nature often in a great Emotion and Agitation, and the Soul very often, of late, so overcome with great Admiration, and a kind of omnipotent Joy, as to cause the Person (wholly unavoidably,) to leap with all the Might, with Joy and mighty Exultation of Soul; the Soul at the same Time being so strongly drawn towards GOD and CHRIST in Heaven, that it seem'd to the Person as tho' Soul and Body would, as it were of themselves, of Necessity mount up, leave the Earth and ascend thither. These Effects on the Body did not begin now in this wonderful Season, that they should be owing to the Influence of the Example of the Times, but about seven Years ago; and began in a much higher Degree, and greater Frequency, near three Years ago, when there was no such enthusiastical Season, as many account this, but it was a very dead Time through the Land: They arose from no Distemper catched from Mr. *Whitefield*, or Mr. *Tennent*, because they began before either of them came into the Country; They began as I said, near three Years ago, in a great Increase, upon an extraordinary Self-Dedication, and Renunciation of the World, and Resignation of all to GOD, made in a great View of GOD's Excellency, and high Exercise of Love to him, and Rest and Joy in him; since which Time they have been very frequent; and began in a yet higher Degree, and greater Frequency, about a Year and half ago, upon another new Resignation of all to GOD, with a yet greater Fervency and Delight of Soul; since which Time the Body has been very often fainting, with the Love of CHRIST; and began in a much higher Degree still, the last Winter, upon another Resignation and Acceptance of GOD, as the only Portion and Happiness of the Soul, wherein the whole World, with the dearest Enjoyments in it, were renounced as Dirt and Dung, and all that is pleasant and glorious, and all that is terrible in this World, seemed perfectly to vanish into nothing, and nothing to be left but GOD, in whom the Soul was perfectly swallowed up, as in an infinite Ocean of Blessedness: Since which Time there have often been great Agitations of Body, and an unavoidable leaping for Joy; and the Soul as it were dwelling almost without Interruption, in a kind of Paradise; and very often, in high Transports, disposed to speak of those great and glorious Things of GOD and CHRIST, and the eternal World, that are in View, to others that are present, in a most earnest Manner, and with a loud Voice, so that it is next to impossible to avoid it: These Effects on the Body not arising from any bodily Distemper or Weakness, because the greatest of all have been in a good State of Health. This great Rejoicing has been a rejoicing with trembling, *i.e.* attended with a deep and lively Sense of the Greatness and Majesty of GOD, and the Person's own exceeding Littleness and Vileness: Spiritual Joys in this Person never were attended, either formerly or lately, with the least Appearance of any Laughter or Lightness of Countenance, or Manner of speaking; but with a peculiar Abhorrence of such Appearances in spiritual Rejoicings, especially since Joys have been greatest of all: These high Transports when they have been past, have had abiding Effects in the Increase of the Sweetness, Rest and Humility that they have left upon the Soul; and a new Engagedness of Heart to live to GOD's Honour, and watch and fight against Sin. And these Things not in one that is in the giddy age of Youth, nor in a new Convert, and unexperienced Christian, but in one that was converted above Twenty-seven Years ago; and neither converted, nor educated in that enthusiastical Town of *Northampton*, (as some may be ready to call it,) but in a Town and Family that none that I know of suspected of Enthusiasm; and in a Christian that has been long, in an uncommon Manner, growing in Grace, and rising,

by very sensible Degrees, to higher Love to GOD, and
Weanedness from the World, and Mastery over Sin and Temptation, through great Trials and Conflicts, and long continued
struggling and fighting with Sin, and earnest and constant
Prayer and Labour in Religion, and Engagedness of Mind in
the Use of all Means, attended with a great Exactness of Life:
Which Growth has been attended, not only with a great Increase of religious Affections, but with a wonderful Alteration
of outward Behaviour, in many Things, visible to those who
are most intimately acquainted, so as lately to have become as
it were a new Person; and particularly in living so much more
above the World, and in a greater Degree of Stedfastness and
Strength in the Way of Duty and Self-denial, maintaining the
Christian Conflict against Temptations, and conquering from
Time to Time under great Trials; persisting in an unmoved,
untouched Calm and Rest, under the Changes and Accidents
of Time. The Person had formerly in lower Degrees of Grace,
been subject to Unsteadiness, and many ups and downs, in the
Frame of Mind; The Mind being under great Disadvantages,
thro' a vapoury Habit of Body, and often subject to Melancholy, and at Times almost over-born with it, it having been so
even from early Youth: but Strength of Grace, and divine Light
has of a long Time, wholly conquered these Disadvantages,
and carried the Mind in a constant Manner, quite above all
such Effects of Vapours. Since that Resignation spoken of before, made near three Years ago, every Thing of that Nature
seems to be overcome and crushed by the Power of Faith and
Trust in GOD, and Resignation to him; the Person has remained in a constant uninterrupted Rest, and humble Joy in
GOD, and Assurance of his Favour, without one Hour's Melancholy or Darkness, from that Day to this; Vapours have had
great Effects on the Body, such as they used to have before,
but the Soul has been always out of their Reach. And this
Stedfastness and Constancy has remained thro' great outward
Changes and Trials; such as Times of the most extreme Pain,
and apparent Hazard of immediate Death. What has been felt
in late great Transports is known to be nothing new in Kind,
but to be of the same Nature with what was felt formerly,
when a little Child of about five or six Years of Age; but only in
a vastly higher Degree. These transporting Views and rapturous

Affections are not attended with any enthusiastick Disposition, to follow Impulses, or any supposed prophetical Revelations; nor have they been observed to be attended with any Appearance of spiritual Pride, but very much of a contrary Disposition, an Increase of a Spirit of Humility and Meekness, and a Disposition in Honour to prefer others: And 'tis worthy to be remark'd, that at a Time remarkably distinguished from all others, wherein Discoveries and holy Affections were evidently at the greatest Height that ever happen'd, the Greatness and Clearness of divine Light being overwhelming, and the Strength and Sweetness of divine Love altogether over-powering, which began early in the Morning of the holy Sabbath, and lasted for Days together, melting all down in the deepest Humility and Poverty of Spirit, Reverence and Resignation, and the sweetest Meekness, and universal Benevolence; I say, 'tis worthy to be observed, that there were these two Things in a remarkable Manner felt at that Time, *viz.* a peculiar sensible Aversion to a judging others that were professing Christians of good standing in the visible Church, that they were not converted, or with respect to their Degrees of Grace; or at all intermeddling with that Matter, so much as to determine against and condemn others in the Thought of the Heart; it appearing hateful, as not agreeing with that Lamb-like Humility, Meekness, Gentleness & Charity, which the Soul then, above other Times, saw the Beauty of, and felt a Disposition to. The Disposition that was then felt was, on the contrary, to prefer others to Self, and to hope that they saw more of GOD and loved him better; tho' before, under smaller Discoveries, and feebler Exercises of divine Affection, there had been felt a Disposition to censure and condemn others. And another Thing that was felt at that Time, was a very great Sense of the Importance of moral social Duties, and how great a Part of Religion lay in them: There was such a new Sense and Conviction of this, beyond what had been before, that it seemed to be as it were a clear Discovery then made to the Soul: But in general, there has been a very great Increase of a Sense of these two Things, as divine Views and divine Love have increased.

The Things already mention'd have been attended also with the following Things, *viz.* an extraordinary Sense of the awful Majesty and Greatness of GOD, so as oftentimes to take away the bodily Strength; a Sense of the Holiness of GOD, as of a Flame infinitely pure and bright, so as sometimes to overwhelm Soul and Body; a Sense of the piercing all-seeing Eye of GOD, so as sometimes to take away the bodily Strength; and an extraordinary View of the infinite Terribleness of the Wrath of GOD, which has very frequently been strongly impress'd on the Mind, together with a Sense of the ineffable Misery of Sinners that are exposed to this Wrath, that has been over-bearing: Sometimes the exceeding Pollution of the Person's own Heart, as a Sink of all manner of Abomination, and a Nest of Vipers, and the Dreadfulness of an eternal Hell of GOD's Wrath, open'd to View both together; with a clear View of a Desert of that Misery, without the least Degree of divine Pity, and that by the Pollution of the best Duties; yea, only by the Pollution and Irreverence, and want of Humility that attended once speaking of the holy Name of GOD, when done in the best Manner that ever it was done; the Strength of the Body very often taken away with a deep mourning for Sin, as committed against so holy and good a GOD, sometimes with an affecting Sense of actual Sin, sometimes especially indwelling Sin, sometimes the Consideration of the Sin of the Heart as appearing in a particular Thing, as for Instance, in that there was no greater Forwardness and Readiness to Self-denial for GOD and CHRIST, that had so denied himself for us; yea, sometimes the Consideration of Sin that was in only speaking one Word concerning the infinitely great and holy GOD, has been so affecting as to overcome the Strength of Nature: A very great Sense of the certain Truth of the great Things revealed in the Gospel; an over-whelming Sense of the Glory of the Work of Redemption, and the Way of Salvation by JESUS CHRIST; the glorious Harmony of the divine Attributes appearing therein, as that wherein Mercy and Truth are met together, and Righteousness and Peace have kissed each other; a Sight of the Fulness and glorious Sufficiency of CHRIST, that has been so affecting as to overcome the Body: A constant immoveable Trust in GOD through CHRIST, with a great Sense of his Strength and Faithfulness, the Sureness of his Covenant, and the Immutability of his Promises, so that the everlasting Mountains and perpetual Hills have appeared as meer Shadows to these Things: Sometimes the Sufficiency and Faithfulness of GOD as the Cov-

enant GOD of his People, appearing in these Words, I AM
THAT I AM, in so affecting a Manner as to overcome the
Body: A Sense of the glorious, unsearchable, unerring Wisdom
of GOD in his Works, both of Creation and Providence, so as
to swallow up the Soul, & overcome the Strength of the Body:
A sweet rejoicing of Soul at the Thoughts of GOD's being infinitely and unchangeably happy, and an exulting gladness of
Heart that GOD is Self-sufficient, and infinitely above all Dependence, and reigns over all, and does his Will with absolute and
uncontroulable Power and Sovereignty; a Sense of the Glory of
the Holy Spirit, as the great Comforter, so as to overwhelm both
Soul and Body; only mentioning the Word the COMFORTER, has
immediately taken away all Strength; that Word, as the Person
expressed it, seem'd great enough to fill Heaven and Earth: A
most vehement and passionate Desire of the Honour and Glory
of GOD's Name; a sensible, clear and constant Preference of it
not only to the Person's own temporal Interest, but spiritual
Comfort in this World; and a Willingness to suffer the hidings of
GOD's Face, and to live and die in Darkness and Horror if GOD's
Honour should require it, and to have no other Reward for it
but that GOD's Name should be glorified, altho' so much of the
Sweetness of the Light of GOD's Countenance had been experienced: A great lamenting of Ingratitude, and the lowness of the
Degree of Love to GOD, so as to deprive of bodily Strength; and
very often vehement Longings and Faintings after more Love to
Christ, and greater Conformity to him; especially longing after
these two Things, *viz.* To be more perfect in *Humility*, and *Ado-
ration*; the Flesh and Heart, seems often to cry out for a lying
low before GOD, and adoring him with greater Love and Humility: The Thoughts of the perfect Humility with which the
Saints in Heaven worship GOD, and fall down before his Throne,
have often overcome the Body, and set it into a great Agitation.
A great Delight in singing Praises to GOD and JESUS CHRIST, and
longing that this present Life may be, as it were, one continued
Song of Praise to GOD; longing, as the Person expressed it, to
sit and sing this Life away; and an overcoming Pleasure in the
Thoughts of spending an Eternity in that Exercise: A living by
Faith to a great Degree; a constant and extraordinary Distrust
of own Strength and Wisdom; a great Dependence on GOD for
his Help, in order to the Performance of any Thing to GOD's

Acceptance, and being restrain'd from the most horrid Sins, and running upon GOD, even on his Neck, and on the thick Bosses of his Bucklers: Such a Sense of the black Ingratitude of true Saints Coldness and Deadness in Religion, and their setting their Hearts on the Things of this World, as to overcome the bodily Frame: A great longing that all the Children of GOD might be lively in Religion, fervent in their Love, and active in the Service of GOD; and when there have been Appearances of it in others, rejoicing so in beholding the pleasing Sight, that the Joy of Soul has been too great for the Body: Taking Pleasure in the Thoughts of watching and striving against Sin, and fighting through the Way to Heaven, and filling up this Life with hard Labour, and bearing the Cross for CHRIST, as an Opportunity to give GOD Honour; not desiring to rest from Labours 'till arrived in Heaven, but abhorring the Thoughts of it, and seeming astonished that GOD's own Children should be backward to strive and deny themselves for GOD: Earnest Longings that all GOD's People might be cloathed with Humility and Meekness, like the Lamb of GOD, and feel nothing in their Hearts but Love and Compassion to all Mankind; and great Grief when any Thing to the contrary seems to appear in any of the Children of GOD, as any Bitterness, or fierceness of Zeal, or Censoriousness, or reflecting uncharitably on others, or disputing with any Appearance of Heat of Spirit; a deep Concern for the Good of others Souls; a melting Compassion to those that look'd on themselves as in a State of Nature, and to Saints under Darkness, so as to cause the Body to faint: An universal Benevolence to Mankind, with a longing as it were to embrace the whole World in the Arms of Pity and Love; Ideas of suffering from Enemies, the utmost conceiveable Rage and Cruelty, with a Disposition felt to fervent Love and Pity in such a Case, so far as it could be realized in Thought; Fainting with Pity to the World that lies in Ignorance and Wickedness; sometimes a Disposition felt to a Life given up to mourning alone in a Wilderness over a lost and miserable World; Compassion towards them being often to that Degree, that would allow of no Support or Rest, but in going to GOD, and pouring out the Soul in Prayer for them; earnest Desires that the Work of GOD, that is now in the Land, may be carried on, and that with greater Purity, and Freedom from all bitter Zeal,

Censoriousness, spiritual Pride, hot Disputes, &c—; a vehe-
ment and constant Desire for the setting up of CHRIST's
Kingdom thro' the Earth, as a Kingdom of Holiness, Purity,
Love, Peace and Happiness to Mankind: The Soul often enter-
tained with unspeakable Delight, and bodily Strength over-
born, at the Thoughts of Heaven, as a World of Love, where
Love shall be the Saints eternal Food, and they shall dwell in the
Light of Love, and swim in an Ocean of Love, and where the very
Air and Breath will be nothing but Love; Love to the People of
GOD, or GOD's true Saints, as such that have the Image of
CHRIST, and as those that will in a very little Time shine in his
perfect Image, that has been attended with that Endearment
and Oneness of Heart, and that Sweetness and Ravishment of
Soul, that has been altogether inexpressible; The Strength very
often taken away with Longings that others might love GOD
more, and serve GOD better, and have more of his comfortable Presence, than the Person that was the Subject of these
Longings, desiring to follow the whole World to Heaven, or
that every one should go before, and be higher in Grace and
Happiness, not by this Person's Diminution, but by others Increase: A Delight in conversing of Things of Religion, and in
seeing Christians together, talking of the most spiritual and
heavenly Things in Religion, in a lively and feeling Manner,
and very frequently overcome with the Pleasure of such Conversation: A great Sense often expressed, of the Importance of
the Duty of Charity to the Poor, and how much the generality
of Christians come short in the Practice of it: A great Sense of
the Need GOD's Ministers have of much of the Spirit of GOD,
at this Day especially; and most earnest Longings and Wres-
tlings with GOD for them, so as to take away the bodily
Strength: The greatest, fullest, longest continued, and most
constant Assurance of the Favour of GOD, and of a Title to
future Glory, that ever I saw any Appearance of in any Person,
enjoying, especially of late, (to use the Person's own Expression) *The Riches of full Assurance*: Formerly longing to die
with something of Impatience, but lately, since that Resignation fore-mentioned about three Years ago, an uninterrupted
entire Resignation to GOD with Respect to Life or Death,
Sickness or Health, Ease or Pain, which has remained unchanged
and unshaken, when actually under extreme and violent Pains,

and in Times of Threatnings of immediate Death; But tho'
there be this Patience and Submission, yet the Thoughts of
Death and the Day of Judgment are always exceeding sweet to
the Soul: This Resignation is also attended with a constant Resignation of the Lives of dearest earthly Friends, and sometimes
when some of their Lives have been imminently threaten'd;
often expressing the Sweetness of the Liberty of having wholly
left the World, and renounced all for GOD, and having nothing but GOD, in whom is an infinite Fulness. These Things
have been attended with a constant sweet Peace and Calm and
Serenity of Soul, without any Cloud to interrupt it; a continual
rejoicing in all the Works of GOD's Hands, the Works of Nature, and GOD's daily Works of Providence, all appearing with
a sweet Smile upon them; a wonderful Access to GOD by
Prayer, as it were seeing him, and sensibly immediately conversing with him, as much oftentimes, (to use the Person's own Expressions,) as if Christ were here on Earth, sitting on a visible
Throne, to be approached to and conversed with; frequent,
plain, sensible and immediate Answers of Prayer; all Tears wiped
away; all former Troubles and Sorrows of Life forgotten, and all
Sorrow and Sighing fled away, excepting Grief for past Sins, and
for remaining Corruption, and that CHRIST is loved no more,
and that GOD is no more honoured in the World, and a compassionate Grief towards Fellow-Creatures; a daily sensible doing
and suffering every Thing for GOD, for a long Time past, eating
for GOD, and working for GOD, and sleeping for GOD, and
bearing Pain and Trouble for GOD, and doing all as the Service
of Love, and so doing it with a continual, uninterrupted Cheer-
fulness, Peace and Joy. Oh how good, said the Person once, is it
to work for GOD in the Day-time, and at Night to lie down
under his Smiles! High Experiences and religious Affections in
this Person have not been attended with any Disposition at
all to neglect the necessary Business of a secular Calling, to
spend the Time in Reading and Prayer, and other Exercises of
Devotion; but worldly Business has been attended with great
Alacrity, as Part of the Service of GOD: The Person declaring
that it being done thus, 'tis found to be as good as Prayer.
These Things have been accompanied with an exceeding Concern and Zeal for moral Duties, and that all Professors may with
them adorn the Doctrine of GOD their Saviour; and an un-

common Care to perform relative and social Duties, and a noted Eminence in them; a great Inoffensiveness of Life and Conversation in the Sight of others; a great Meekness, Gentleness and Benevolence of Spirit and Behaviour; and a great Alteration in those Things that formerly used to be the Person's Failings; seeming to be much overcome and swallowed up by the late great Increase of Grace, to the Observation of those that are most conversant and most intimately acquainted: In Times of the brightest Light and highest Flights of Love and Joy, finding no Disposition to any Opinion of being now perfectly free from Sin, (agreable to the Notion of the *Wesleys* and their Followers, and some other high Pretenders to Spirituality in these Days;) but exceedingly the contrary: at such Times especially, seeing how loathsome and polluted the Soul is, Soul and Body and every Act and Word appearing like Rotenness and Corruption in that pure and holy Light of GOD's Glory: not slighting Instruction or Means of Grace any more for having had great Discoveries; on the contrary, never more sensible of the Need of Instruction than now. And one Thing more may be added, *viz.* That these Things have been attended with a particular Dislike of placing Religion much in Dress, and spending much Zeal about those Things that in themselves are Matters of Indifference, or an affecting to shew Humility and Devotion by a mean Habit, or a demure and melancholy Countenance, or any Thing singular and superstitious.

Now if such Things are Enthusiasm, and the Fruits of a distemper'd Brain, Let my Brain be evermore possess'd of that happy Distemper! If this be Distraction, I pray GOD that the World of Mankind may be all seized with this benign, meek, beneficent, beatifical, glorious Distraction! If Agitations of Body were found in the *French Prophets*, and Ten Thousand Prophets more, 'tis little to their Purpose who bring it as an Objection against such a Work as this, unless their Purpose be to disprove the whole of the Christian Religion. The great Affections and high Transports that others have lately been under, are in general of the same Kind with those in the Instance that has been given, tho' not to so high a Degree, and many of them, not so pure and unmixed, and so well regulated. I have had Opportunity to observe many Instances here and elsewhere; and tho' there are some Instances of great Affections in which there has been a great Mixture of Nature with Grace, and in some, a sad degenerating of religious Affections; yet there is that Uniformity observable, that 'tis easy to be seen that in general 'tis the same Spirit from whence the Work in all Parts of the Land has originated. And what Notions have they of Religion, that reject what has been described as not true Religion? What shall we find to answer those Expressions in Scripture, *The Peace of GOD that passes all Understanding;—Rejoicing with Joy unspeakable & full of Glory, in believing in and loving an unseen Saviour;—All Joy & Peace in believing;—GOD's shining into our Hearts, to give the Light of the Knowledge of the Glory of GOD, in the Face of Jesus Christ; with open Face, beholding as in a Glass, the Glory of the Lord, and being changed into the same Image, from Glory to Glory, even as by the Spirit of the Lord;—Having the Love of GOD shed abroad in our Hearts, by the Holy Ghost given to us;—Having the Spirit of GOD, and of Glory rest upon us;—A being called out of Darkness into marvellous Light; and having the Day-Star arise in our Hearts:*—I say, if those Things that have been mentioned, don't answer these Expressions, what else can we find out that does answer them? Those that don't think such Things as these to be the Fruits of the true Spirit, would do well to consider what Kind of Spirit they are waiting and praying for, and what Sort of Fruits they expect he should produce when he comes. I suppose it will generally be allow'd that there is such a Thing as a glorious Out-pouring of the Spirit of GOD to be expected, to introduce very joyful and glorious Times upon religious Accounts; Times wherein holy Love and Joy will be raised to a great Height in true Christians: But if those Things that have been mentioned be rejected, what is left that we can find wherewith to patch up a Notion, or form an Idea, of the high, blessed, joyful Religion of these Times? What is that any have a Notion of, that is very sweet, excellent and joyful, of a religious Nature, that is entirely of a different Nature from these Things?

Those that are waiting for the Fruits in order to determine whether this be the Work of GOD or no, would do well to consider two Things; 1. What they are waiting for: Whether it ben't this; To have this wonderful religious Influence that is on the Minds of People over and past, and then to see how they will behave themselves? That is, to have Grace subside, and the Acting of it in a great Measure to cease, and to have Persons grow cold and dead, and then to see whether after that, they will behave themselves with that Exactness and Brightness of Conversation, that is to be expected of lively Christians, or those that are in the vigorous Exercises of Grace. There are many that will not be satisfied with any Exactness or Laboriousness in Religion now, while Persons have their Minds much moved, and their Affections are high; for they lay it to their Flash of Affection, and Heat of Zeal, as they call it; they are waiting to see whether they will carry themselves as well when these Affections are over: That is, they are waiting to have Persons sicken and lose their Strength, that they may see whether they will then behave themselves like healthy strong Men. I would desire that they would also consider whether they ben't waiting for more than is reasonably to be expected, supposing this to be really a great Work of GOD, and much more than has been found in former great Out-pourings of the Spirit of GOD, that have been universally acknowledged in the Christian Church? Don't they expect fewer Instances of Apostacy, and Evidences of Hypocrisy in Professors, and those that for the present seem to be under the Influences of the Spirit, than were after that great Out-pouring of the Spirit in the Apostles Days, or that which was in the Time of the Reformation? And don't they stand prepared to make a mighty Argument of it against this Work, if there should be *half* so many? And 2. They would do well to consider how *long* they will wait to see the good Fruit of this Work, before they will determine in Favour of it. Is not their Waiting unlimited? The visible Fruit that is to be expected of a pouring out of the Spirit of GOD on a Country, is a visible Reformation in that Country: What Reformation has lately been brought to pass in *New-England*, by this Work, has been before observed: And has it not continued long enough already, to give reasonable Satisfaction? If GOD can't work on the Hearts of a People after such a Manner, as to shew his Hand so plainly, as reasonably to expect it should be acknowledged in a Year & half, or two Years Time; yet surely it is unreasonable, that our Expectations and Demands should be unlimited, and our Waiting without any Bounds.

As there is the clearest Evidence, from those Things that have been observed, that this is the Work of GOD, so it is evident that it is a very great and wonderful, and exceeding glorious Work of

GOD. This is certain that it is a great and wonderful Event, a strange Revolution, an unexpected, surprizing Overturning of Things, suddenly brought to pass; such as never has been seen in *New-England*, and scarce ever has been heard of in any Land. Who that saw the State of Things in *New-England* a few Years ago, the State that it was settled in, and the Way that we had been so long going on in, would have thought that in so little a Time there would be such a Change? This is undoubtedly either a very great Work of GOD, or a great Work of the Devil, as to the main Substance of it. For tho' undoubtedly, GOD and the Devil may work together at the same Time, and in the same Land; and when GOD is at work, especially if he be very remarkably at Work, Satan will do his utmost endeavour to intrude, and by intermingling his Work, to darken and hinder GOD's Work; yet GOD and the Devil don't work together in producing the same Event, and in effecting the same Change in the Hearts and Lives of Men: But 'tis apparent that there are some Things wherein the main Substance of this Work consists, a certain Effect that is produced, and Alteration that is made in the Apprehensions, Affections, Dispositions and Behaviour of Men, in which there is a Likeness and Agreement every where: Now this I say, is either a wonderful Work of GOD, or a mighty Work of the Devil; and so is either a most happy Event, greatly to be admired and rejoiced in, or a most awful Calamity. Therefore if what has been said before, be sufficient to determine it to be as to the Main, the Work of GOD, then it must be acknowledged to be a very wonderful and glorious Work of GOD.

Such a Work is in its Nature and Kind, the most glorious of any Work of GOD whatsoever; and is always so spoken of in Scripture. It is the Work of Redemption, (The great End of all other Works of GOD, and of which the Work of Creation was but a Shadow,) in the Event, Success and End of it: It is the Work of New-Creation, that is infinitely more glorious than the Old. I am bold to say, that the Work of GOD in the Conversion of one Soul, considered together with the Source, Foundation and Purchase of it, and also the Benefit, End and eternal Issue of it, is a more glorious Work of GOD than the Creation of the whole material Universe: It is the most glorious of GOD's Works, as it above all others manifests the Glory of GOD: It is spoken of in Scripture as that which shews *the exceeding Greatness of GOD's Power*, and *the Glory and Riches of divine Grace*, and wherein CHRIST has the most glorious Triumph over his Enemies, and wherein GOD is mightily exalted: And it is a Work above all others glorious, as it concerns the Happiness of Mankind; more Happiness, and a greater Benefit to Man, is the Fruit of each single Drop of such a Shower, than all the temporal Good of the most happy Revolution in a Land or Nation amounts to, or all that a People could gain by the Conquest of the World.

And as this Work is very glorious in its Nature, so it is in its Degree and Circumstances. It will appear very glorious if we consider the Unworthiness of the People that are the Subjects of it; what Obligations GOD has laid us under by the special Priviledges we have enjoyed for our Souls Good, and the great Things GOD did for us at our first Settlement in the Land; and how he has followed us with his Goodness to this Day, and how we have abused his Goodness; how long we have been revolting more and more, (as all confess,) and how very corrupt we were become at last; in how great a Degree we had cast off GOD, and forsaken the Fountain of living Waters: how obstinate we have been under all Manner of Means that GOD has used with us to reclaim us; how often we have mocked GOD with hypocritical Pretences of Humiliation, as in our annual Days of publick Fasting, and other Things, while instead of reforming, we only grew worse and worse; how dead a Time it was every where before this Work began: If we consider these Things, we shall be most stupidly ungrateful, if we don't acknowledge GOD's visiting of us as he has done, as an Instance of the glorious Triumph of free and sovereign Grace.

The Work is very glorious if we consider the Extent of it; being in this Respect vastly beyond any former Out-pouring of the Spirit that ever was known in *New-England*. There has formerly sometimes been a remarkable Awakening and Success of the Means of Grace, in some particular Congregation; and this used to be much taken Notice of, and acknowledged to be glorious, tho' the Towns and Congregations round about continued dead: But now GOD has bro't to pass a new Thing, he has wrought a great Work of this Nature, that has extended from one End of the Land to the other, besides what has been wrought in other British Colonies in *America*.

The Work is very glorious in the great Numbers that have to Appearance, been turned from Sin to GOD, and so delivered from a wretched Captivity to Sin and Satan, saved from everlasting Burnings, and made Heirs of eternal Glory. How high an Honour, and great Reward of their Labours, have some eminent Persons, of Note in the Church of GOD, signified that they should esteem it, if they should be made the Instruments of the Conversion and eternal Salvation of but *one* Soul? And no greater Event than that is tho't worthy of great Notice in Heaven, among the Hosts of glorious Angels, who rejoice and sing on such an Occasion: and when there are many Thousands of Souls thus converted and saved, shall it be esteemed worth but little Notice, and be mentioned with Coldness and Indifference here on Earth, by those among whom such a Work is wrought?

The Work has been very glorious and wonderful in many Circumstances and Events of it, that have been extraordinary, wherein GOD has in an uncommon Manner made his Hand visible, and his Power conspicuous; as in the extraordinary Degrees of Awakening, the Suddenness of Conversions in innumerable Instances, in whom tho' the Work was quick, yet the Thing wro't is manifestly durable. How common a Thing has it been for great Part of a Congregation to be at once moved, by a mighty invisible Power; and for six, eight or ten Souls to be converted to GOD, (to all Appearance,) in an Exercise, in whom the visible Change still continues? How great an Alteration has been made in some Towns; yea, some populous Towns; the Change still abiding? And how many very vicious Persons have been wrought upon, so as to become visibly New-Creatures? GOD has also made his Hand very visible, and his Work glorious, in the Multitudes of little Children that have been wrought upon: I suppose there have been some Hundreds of Instances of this Nature of late, any one of which formerly would have been looked upon so remarkable, as to be worthy to be recorded, and published thro' the Land. The Work is very glorious in its Influences and Effects on many that have been very ignorant and barbarous, as I before observed of the Indians and Negroes.

The Work is also exceeding glorious in the high Attainments of Christians, in the extraordinary Degrees of Light, Love and spiritual Joy, that GOD has bestowed upon great Multitudes. In this Respect also, The Land in all Parts has abounded with such Instances, any one of which, if they had happen'd formerly, would have been thought worthy to be taken Notice of by GOD's People, throughout the *British* Dominions. The *New-Jerusalem* in this Respect has begun to come down from Heaven, and perhaps never were more of the Prelibations of Heaven's Glory given upon Earth.

There being a great many Errors and sinful Irregularities mixed with this Work of GOD, arising from our Weakness, Darkness and Corruption, don't hinder this Work of GOD's Power & Grace from being very glorious. Our Follies and Sins that we mix, do in some Respects manifest the Glory of it: The Glory of divine Power & Grace is set off with the greater Lustre, by what appears at the same Time of the Weakness of the earthen Vessel. 'Tis GOD's Pleasure that there should be something remarkably to manifest the Weakness and Unworthiness of the Subject, at the same Time that he displays the Excellency of his Power and Riches of his Grace. And I doubt not but some of those Things that make some of us here on Earth to be out of Humour, and to look on this Work with a sour displeased Countenance, do heighten the Songs of the Angels, when they praise GOD and the Lamb for what they see of the Glory of GOD's All-sufficiency, and the Efficacy of CHRIST's Redemption. And how unreasonable is it that we should be backward to acknowledge the Glory of what GOD has done, because withal, the Devil, and we in hearkening to him, have done a great deal of Mischief.

Part II

Shewing the Obligations that all are under, to acknowledge, rejoice in, and promote this WORK, and the great Danger of the contrary.

THERE are many Things in the Word of GOD, that shew that when GOD remarkably appears in any great Work for his Church, and against his Enemies, it is a most dangerous Thing, and highly provoking to GOD, to be slow and backward to acknowledge and honour GOD in the Work, and to lie still and not to put to an helping Hand. CHRIST's People are in Scripture represented as his Army; he is the LORD OF HOSTS or Armies: He is the Captain of the Host of the Lord, as he call'd himself when he appear'd to *Joshua*, with a Sword drawn in his Hand, *Joshua* 5. 13, 14, 15. He is the Captain of his People's Salvation; and therefore it may well be highly resented if they don't resort to him when he orders his Banner to be displayed; or if they refuse to follow him when he blows the Trumpet, and gloriously appears going forth against his Enemies. GOD expects that every living Soul should have his Attention roused on such an Occasion, and should most chearfully yield to the Call, and heedfully and diligently obey it; Isai. 18. 3. *All ye In-habitants of the World, and Dwellers on the Earth, see ye when he lifteth up an Ensign on the Mountains; And when he bloweth the Trumpet, hear ye.* Especially should all *Israel* be gathered after their Captain, as we read they were after *Ehud*, when he blew the Trumpet in Mount *Ephraim*, when he had slain *Eglon* King of *Moab, Judg.* 3. 27, 28. How severe is the martial Law in such a Case, when any of an Army refuses to obey the Sound of the Trumpet, and follow his General to the Battel? GOD at such a Time appears in peculiar Manifestations of his Glory, and therefore not to be affected and animated, and to lie still, and refuse to follow God, will be resented as an high Contempt of him. If a Subject should stand by, and be a Spectator of the solemnity of his Prince's Coronation, and should appear silent and sullen, when all the Multitude were testifying their Loyalty and Joy, with loud Acclamations; how greatly would he expose himself to be treated as a Rebel, and quickly to perish by the Authority of the Prince that he refuses to honour?

At a Time when GOD manifests himself in such a great Work for his Church, there is no such Thing as being Neuters; there is a Necessity of being either for or against the King that then gloriously appears: As when a King is crown'd, and there are public Manifestations of Joy on that Occasion, there is no such Thing as standing by as an indifferent Spectator; all must appear as loyal Subjects, and express their Joy on that Occasion, or be accounted Enemies: So it always is when GOD, in any great Dispensation of his Providence, does remarkably set his

King on his holy Hill of *Zion*, and Christ in an extraordinary Manner comes down from Heaven to the Earth, and appears in his visible Church in a great Work of Salvation for his People: So it was when Christ came down from Heaven in his Incarnation, and appeared on Earth in his human Presence; there was no such Thing as being Neuters, neither on his Side nor against him: those that sat still and said nothing, and did not declare for him, and come and join with him, after he, by his Word and Works, had given sufficient Evidence who he was, were justly looked upon as his Enemies; as CHRIST says, Math. 12. 30. *He that is not with me is against me; and he that gathereth not with me, scattereth abroad.* So it is in a time when CHRIST is remarkably spiritually present, as well as when he is bodily present; and when he comes to carry on the Work of Redemption in the Application of it, as well as in the Revelation and Purchase. If a King should come into one of his Provinces, that had been oppress'd by it's Foes, where some of his Subjects had fallen off to the Enemy, and join'd with them against their lawful Sovereign and his loyal Subjects; I say, if the lawful Sovereign himself should come into the Province, and should ride forth there against his Enemies, and should call upon all that were on his Side to come and gather themselves to him; there would be no such Thing, in such a Case, as standing neuter: they that lay still and staid at a Distance would undoubtedly be looked upon and treated as Rebels. So in the Day of Battle, when two Armies join, there is no such Thing for any present as being of neither Party, all must be on one Side or the other; and they that ben't found with the Conqueror in such a Case, must expect to have his Weapons turned against them, and to fall with the rest of his Enemies.

When God manifests himself with such glorious Power in a Work of this Nature, he appears especially determined to put Honour upon his Son, and to fulfill his Oath that he has sworn to him, that he would make every Knee to bow, and every Tongue to confess to him. God hath had it much on his Heart, from all Eternity, to glorify his dear and only begotten Son; and there are some special Seasons that he appoints to that End, wherein he comes forth with omnipotent Power to fulfil his Promise and Oath to him: And these Times are Times of remarkable pouring out of his Spirit, to advance his Kingdom;

such a Day is a Day of his Power, wherein his People shall be made willing, and he shall rule in the midst of his Enemies; these especially are the Times wherein God declares his firm Decree that his Son shall Reign on his holy Hill of *Zion*: and therefore those that at such a Time don't kiss the Son, as he then manifests himself, and appears in the Glory of his Majesty and Grace, expose themselves to *perish from the Way*, and to be *dash'd in Pieces with a Rod of Iron*.

As such a Time is a Time wherein God eminently *sets his King on his holy Hill of* Zion, so it is a Time wherein he remarkably fulfils that in Isai. 28. 16. *Therefore thus saith the Lord God, behold, I lay in Zion for a Foundation, a Stone, a tried Stone, a precious Corner Stone, a sure Foundation*. Which the two Apostles *Peter* and *Paul*, (1 *Pet.* 2. 6, 7, 8. and *Rom.* 9. 33.) join with that Prophecy, Isai. 8. 14, 15. *And he shall be for a Sanctuary; but for a Stone of Stumbling, and for a Rock of Offence to both the Houses of Israel, for a Gin and for a Snare to the Inhabitants of Jerusalem: and many among them shall stumble and fall, and be broken, and be snared, and taken*. As signifying that both are fulfilled together. Yea both are joined together by the Prophet *Isaiah* himself; as you may see in the Context of that formention'd, Isai. 28. 16. In Ver. 13. preceeding it is said, *But the Word of the Lord was unto them Precept upon Precept, Precept upon Precept; Line upon Line, Line upon Line; here a little and there a little, that they might go, and fall backward, and be broken, and snared and taken*. And accordingly it always is so, that when Christ is in a peculiar and eminent Manner manifested and magnified, by a glorious Work of God in his Church, as a Foundation and a Sanctuary for some, he is remarkably a Stone of Stumbling and a Rock of Offence, a Gin and a Snare to others. They that continue long to stumble, and be offended and ensnared in their Minds, at such a great & glorious Work of Christ, in God's Account, stumble at Christ, and are offended in him; for the Work is that by which he makes Christ manifest, and shows his Glory, and by which he makes *the Stone that the Builders refused, to become the Head of the Corner*. This shows how dangerous it is to continue always stumbling at such a Work, for ever doubting of it, and forbearing fully to acknowledge it, and give God the Glory of it: Such Persons are in Danger *to go, and fall backward, and be broken, and snared and taken*, and to have Christ *a Stone of Stumbling* to them, that shall be an Occasion of their Ruin; while he is to others, *a Sanctuary*, and a *sure Foundation*.

The Prophet *Isaiah, Isai.* 29. 14. speaks of God's Proceeding to do a marvellous Work and a Wonder, which should stumble and confound the Wisdom of the wise and prudent; which the Apostle in *Acts* 13. 41. applies to the glorious Work of Salvation wrought in those Days by the Redemption of Christ, and that glorious Out-pouring of the Spirit to apply it that followed; the Prophet in the Context of that Place in *Isai.* 29. speaking of the same Thing, and of the Prophets and Rulers and Seers, those wise and prudent whose Eyes God had closed, says to them, Verse 9. *Stay your selves and wonder.* In the Original it is, *be ye slow and wonder.* I leave it to others to consider whether it ben't natural to interpret it thus, "wonder at this *marvellous Work*; let it be a strange Thing, a great Mystery that you know not what to make of, and that you are very slow and backward to acknowledge, long delaying to come to a Determination concerning it." And what Persons are in Danger of, that wonder, and are thus slow to acknowledge God in such a Work, we learn by that of the Apostle in that foremention'd Acts 13. 41. *Behold ye Despisers, and wonder and perish; for I work a Work in your Days, a Work which you shall in no wise believe, tho' a Man declare it unto you.*

The Church of Christ is called upon greatly to rejoice, when at any Time Christ remarkably appears, coming to his Church, to carry on the Work of Salvation, to enlarge his own Kingdom, and to deliver poor Souls out of the Pit wherein there is no Water, in Zech. 9. 9, 10, 11. *Rejoice greatly O Daughter of Zion, shout O Daughter of Jerusalem; behold thy King cometh unto thee; he is just and having Salvation,—His Dominion shall be from Sea to Sea,—as for thee also, by the Blood of thy Covenant, I have sent forth thy Prisoners out of the Pit wherein is no Water.* Christ was pleased to give a notable typical or symbolical Representation of such a great Event as is spoken of in that Prophecy, in his solemn Entry into the literal *Jerusalem*, which was a Type of the Church or Daughter of *Zion*, there spoken of; probably intending it as a Figure and Prelude of that great actual Fulfillment of this Prophecy, that was to be after his Ascension, by the pouring out of the Spirit in the Days of the Apostles, and that more full Accomplishment that should be in the latter Ages of the Christian Church. We have an Account, that when Christ made this his solemn Entry into *Jerusalem*, and the whole Multitude of the Disciples were rejoicing and praising God, with loud Voices, for all the mighty Works that they had seen, the Pharisees from among the Multitude said to Christ, *Master, rebuke thy Disciples*; but we are told, Luke 19. 39, 40. Christ *answered and said unto them, I tell you, that if these should hold their Peace, the Stones would immediately cry out.* Signifying that if Christ's professing Disciples should be unaffected on such an Occasion, and should not appear openly to acknowledge and rejoice in the Glory of God therein appearing, it would manifest such fearful Hardness of Heart, so exceeding that of the Stones, that the very Stones would condemn them. Should not this make those consider, who have held their Peace so long, since Christ has come to our *Zion* having Salvation, and so wonderfully manifested his Glory in this mighty Work of his Spirit, and so many of his Disciples have been *rejoicing and praising God with loud Voices*?

It must be acknowledged that so great and wonderful a Work of God's Spirit, is a Work wherein God's Hand is remarkably *lifted up*, and wherein he displays his *Majesty*, and shows great *Favour* and Mercy to Sinners, in the glorious Opportunity he gives them; and by which he makes our Land to become much more a *Land of Uprightness*: therefore that Place, *Isai.* 26. 10, 11. shows the great Danger of not seeing God's Hand, and acknowledging his Glory and Majesty in such a Work: *Let Favour be shewed to the Wicked, yet will he not learn Righteousness; In the Land of Uprightness he will deal unjustly, and will not behold the Majesty of the Lord. Lord, when thy Hand is lifted up, they will not see; but they shall see, and be ashamed for their Envy at the People; yea the Fire of thine Enemies shall devour them.*

'Tis not unlikely that this Work of God's Spirit, that is so extraordinary and wonderful, is the dawning, or, at least, a Prelude of that glorious Work of God, so often foretold in Scripture, which in the Progress and Issue of it, shall renew the World of Mankind. If we consider how long since, the Things foretold, as what should preceed this great Event, have been accomplished; and how long this Event has been expected by the Church of God, and thought to be nigh by the most eminent Men of God in the Church: and withal consider what the State of Things now is, and has for a considerable Time been, in the Church of God, and World of Mankind, we cant reasonably think otherwise, than that the Beginning of this great Work of God must be near. And there are many Things that make it probable that this Work will begin in *America*. 'Tis signified that it shall begin in some very remote Part of the World, that the rest of the World have no Communication with but by Navigation, in Isai. 60. 9. *Surely the Isles shall wait for me, and the Ships of* Tarshish *first, to bring my Sons from far.* It is exceeding manifest that this Chapter is a Prophecy of the Prosperity of the Church, in its most glorious State on Earth, in the latter Days; and I can't think that any Thing else can be here intended but *America* by the Isles that are far off, from whence the First-born Sons of that glorious Day shall be brought. Indeed, By *the Isles,* in Prophecies of Gospel-Times, is very often meant *Europe*: It is so in Prophecies of that great spreading of the Gospel that should be soon after Christ's Time, because it was far separated from that Part of the World where the Church of GOD had 'till then been, by the Sea. But this Prophecy can't have Respect to the Conversion of *Europe*, in the Time of that great Work of GOD, in the primitive Ages of the Christian Church; for it was not fulfilled then: The Isles and Ships of *Tarshish*, thus understood, did not wait for GOD first; that glorious Work did not begin in *Europe*, but in *Jerusalem*, and had for a considerable Time, been very wonderfully carried on in *Asia*, before it reach'd *Europe*. And as it is not that Work of GOD that is chiefly intended in this Chapter, but that more glorious Work that should be in the latter Ages of the Christian Church, therefore some other Part of the World is here intended by the Isles, that should be as *Europe* then was, far separated from that Part of the World where the Church had before been, by the Sea, and with which it can have no Communication but by the Ships of *Tarshish*. And what is chiefly intended is not the *British* Isles, nor any Isles near the other Continent; for they are spoken of as at a great Distance from that Part of the World where the Church had 'till then been. This Prophecy therefore seems plainly to point out *America*, as the first Fruits of that glorious Day.

GOD has made as it were two Worlds here below, The old and the new, (according to the Names they are now called by,) two great habitable Continents, far separated one from the other; The latter is but newly discover'd, it was formerly wholly unknown, from Age to Age, and is as it were now but newly created: It has been, 'till of late, wholly the Possession of *Satan*, the Church of GOD having never been in it, as it has been in the other Continent, from the beginning of the World. This new World is probably now discovered, that the new and most glorious State of GOD's Church on Earth might commence there; That GOD might in it begin a new World in a spiritual Respect, when he creates the *new Heavens* and *new Earth*.

GOD has already put that Honour upon the other Continent, that CHRIST was born there literally, and there made the *Purchase of Redemption*: So, as Providence observes a Kind of equal Distribution of Things, 'tis not unlikely that the great spiritual Birth of CHRIST, and the most glorious *Application of Redemption* is to begin in this: As the elder Sister brought forth *Judah*, of whom came CHRIST, and so she was the Mother of CHRIST; But the younger Sister, after long Barenness, brought forth *Joseph* and *Benjamin*, the beloved Children. *Joseph*, that had the most glorious Apparel, the Coat of many Colours, who was separated from his Brethren, and was exalted to such Glory out of a dark Dungeon, and fed and saved the World, when ready to perish with Famine, and was as a fruitful Bough by a Well, whose Branches ran over the Wall, and was blessed with all Manner of Blessings and precious Things, of Heaven and Earth, through the good Will of him that dwelt in the Bush; and was, as by the Horns of a Unicorn, to push the People together, to the Ends of the Earth, *i.e.* conquer the World. See *Gen.* 49. 22, *&c.* and *Deut.* 33. 13, *&c.* And *Benjamin*, whose Mess was five Times so great as that of any of his Brethren, and to whom *Joseph*, that Type of Christ, gave Wealth and Rayment far beyond all the rest. *Gen.* 45. 22.

The other Continent hath slain Christ, and has from Age to Age shed the Blood of the Saints and Martyrs of Jesus, and has often been as it were deluged with the Churches Blood: GOD has therefore probably reserved the Honour of building the glorious Temple to the Daughter, that has not shed so much

Blood, when those Times of the Peace and Prosperity and Glory of the Church shall commence, that were typified by the Reign of *Solomon*.

The Gentiles first received the true Religion from the Jews: GOD's Church of ancient Times, had been among them, and Christ was of them: but that there might be a Kind of Equality in the Dispensations of Providence, GOD has so ordered it, that when the Jews come to be admitted to the Benefits of the evangelical Dispensation, and to receive their highest Priviledges of all, they should receive the Gospel from the *Gentiles*: Tho' CHRIST was of them, yet they have been guilty of crucifying him; it is therefore the Will of GOD, that that People should not have the Honour of communicating the Blessings of the Kingdom of GOD in its most glorious State, to the *Gentiles*, but on the contrary they shall receive the Gospel in the Beginning of that glorious Day, from the *Gentiles*. In some Analogy to this, I apprehend GOD's Dealings will be with the two Continents. *America* has received the true Religion of the old Continent; the Church of ancient Times has been there, and CHRIST is from thence: but that there may be an Equality, and inasmuch as that Continent has crucified CHRIST, they shall not have the Honour of communicating Religion in its most glorious State to us, but we to them.

The old Continent has been the Source and Original of Mankind, in several Respects. The first Parents of Mankind dwelt there; and there dwelt *Noah* and his Sons; and there the second *Adam* was born, and was crucified and rose again: and 'tis probable that, in some Measure to balance these Things, the most glorious Renovation of the World shall originate from the new Continent, and the Church of GOD in that Respect be from hence. And so 'tis probable that that will come to pass in Spirituals, that has in Temporals, with Respect to *America*; that whereas, 'till of late, the World was supplied with its Silver and Gold and earthly Treasures from the old Continent, now it's supplied chiefly from the new, so the Course of Things in spiritual Respects will be in like Manner turn'd.

And 'tis worthy to be noted that *America* was discovered about the Time of the Reformation, or but little before: Which Reformation was the first Thing that GOD did towards the glorious Renovation of the World, after it had sunk into the

Depths of Darkness and Ruin, under the great Antichristian Apostacy. So that as soon as this new World is (as it were) created, and stands forth in View, GOD presently goes about doing some great Thing to make Way for the Introduction of the Churches Latter-Day Glory, that is to have its first Seat in, and is to take its Rise from that new World.

It is agreeable to GOD's Manner of Working, when he accomplishes any glorious Work in the World, to introduce a new and more excellent State of his Church, to begin his Work where his Church had not been till then, and where was no Foundation already laid, that the Power of GOD might be the more conspicuous; that the Work might appear to be entirely GOD's, and be more manifestly a Creation out of nothing; agreable to Hos. 1. 10. *And it shall come to pass that in the Place where it was said unto them, ye are not my People, there it shall be said unto them, ye are the Sons of the living God.* When GOD is about to turn the Earth into a Paradice, he don't begin his Work where there is some good Growth already, but in a Wilderness, where nothing grows, and nothing is to be seen but dry Sand and barren Rocks; that the Light may shine out of Darkness, and the World be replenished from Emptiness, and the Earth watered by Springs from a droughty Desart; agreable to many Prophecies of Scripture, as Isai. 32. 15. *Until the Spirit be poured from on high, and the Wilderness become a fruitful Field.* And Chap. 41. 18, 19. *I will open Rivers in high Places, and Fountains in the Midst of the Valleys; I will make the Wilderness a Pool of Water, and the dry Land Springs of Water: I will plant in the Wilderness the Cedar, the Shittah Tree, and the Myrtle and Oyl Tree: I will set in the Desart the Fir Tree, and the Pine, and the Box Tree together*; and Ch. 43. 20. *I will give Waters in the Wilderness, and Rivers in the Desart, to give Drink to my People, my Chosen.* And many other parrallel Scriptures might be mentioned.

I observed before, that when GOD is about to do some great Work for his Church, his Manner is to begin at the lower End; so when he is about to renew the whole Habitable Earth, 'tis probable that he will begin in this utmost, meanest, youngest and weakest Part of it, where the Church of GOD has been planted last of all; and so the First shall be last, and the Last first; and that will be fulfil'd in an eminent Manner in Isai. 24. 16.

From the uttermost Part of the Earth have we heard Songs, even Glory to the Righteous.

There are several Things that seem to me to argue, that when the Sun of Righteousness, the Sun of the new Heavens and new Earth, comes to rise, and *comes forth as the Bridegroom* of his Church, *rejoicing as a strong Man to run his Race, having his going forth from the End of Heaven, and his Circuit to the End of it, that nothing may be hid from the Light and Heat of it.** That the Sun shall rise in the West, contrary to the Course of this World, or the Course of Things in the old Heavens and Earth. The Course of God's Providence shall in that Day be so wonderfully alter'd in many Respects, that God will as it were change the Course of Nature, in answer to the Prayers of his Church; as God chang'd the Course of Nature, and caused the Sun to go from the West to the East, when *Hezekiah* was healed, & God promised to do such great Things for his Church, to deliver it out of the Hand of the King of *Assyria*, by that mighty Slaughter by the Angel; which is often used by the Prophet *Isaiah*, as a Type of the glorious Deliverance of the Church from her Enemies in the latter Days: The Resurrection of *Hezekiah*, the King & Captain of the Church, (as he is called 2 *Kin.* 20. 5.) as it were from the Dead, is given as an Earnest of the Churches Resurrection & Salvation, *Isai.* 38. 6. and is a Type of the Resurrection of Christ. At the same Time there is a Resurrection of the Sun, or coming back and rising again from the West, whether it had gone down; which is also a Type of the Sun of Righteousness. The Sun was bro't back ten Degrees; which probably brought it to the Meridian. The Sun of Righteousness has long been going down from East to West; and probably when the Time comes of the Churches Deliverance from her Enemies, so often typified by the *Assyrians*, the Light will rise in the West, 'till it shines through the World, like the Sun in its meridian Brightness.

*'Tis evident that the Holy Spirit in those Expressions in *Psal* 19. 4, 5, & 6 *Verses*, has Respect to something else besides the natural Sun; and that an Eye is had to the Sun of Rightcousness, that by his Light converts the Soul, makes wise the Simple, inlightens the Eyes, & rejoyces the Heart; and by his preached Gospel enlightens & warms the World of Mankind. By the Psalmist's own Application in *ver* 7. and the Apostles Application of *ver* 4. in *Rom.* 10. 18.

The same seems also to be represented by the Course of the Waters of the Sanctuary, *Ezek.* 47. which was from West to East; which Waters undoubtedly represent the Holy Spirit, in the Progress of his saving Influences, in the latter Ages of the World: for 'tis manifest that the whole of those last Chapters of *Ezekiel*, are concerning the glorious State of the Church that shall then be.

And if we may suppose that this glorious Work of God shall begin in any Part of *America*, I think, if we consider the Circumstances of the Settlement of *New-England*, it must needs appear the most likely of all *American* Colonies, to be the Place whence this Work shall principally take it's Rise.

And if these Things are so, it gives us more abundant Reason to hope that what is now seen in *America*, and especially in *New-England*, may prove the Dawn of that glorious Day: And the very uncommon & wonderful Circumstances and Events of this Work, seem to me strongly to argue that God intends it as the Beginning or Forerunner of some Thing vastly great.

I have thus long insisted on this Point, because if these Things are so, it greatly manifests how much it behoves us to encourage and promote this Work, and how dangerous it will be to forbear so to do.

It is very dangerous for God's professing People to lie still, and not to come to the Help of the Lord, whenever he remarkably pours out his Spirit, to carry on the Work of Redemption in the Application of it; but above all, when he comes forth in that last and greatest Out-pouring of his Spirit, to introduce that happy Day of GOD's Power & Salvation, so often spoken of. That is especially the appointed Season of the Application of the Redemption of CHRIST: 'Tis the proper Time of the Kingdom of Heaven upon Earth, the appointed Time of CHRIST's Reign: The Reign of Satan as God of this World lasts 'till then: This is the proper Time of actual Redemption, or new Creation, as is evident by *Isai.* 65. 17, 18. & 66. 12. & *Rev.* 21. 1. All the Out-pourings of the Spirit of GOD that are before this, are as it were by Way of Anticipation.

There was indeed a glorious Season of the Application of Redemption, in the first Ages of the Christian Church, that began at *Jerusalem*, on the Day of *Pentecost*; but that was not the proper Time of Ingathering; it was only as it were the Feast of the first Fruits; the Ingathering is at the End of the Year, or in the last Ages of the Christian Church, as is represented, *Rev.* 14. 14, 15, 16. and will probably as much exceed what was in the first Ages of the Christian Church, tho' that fill'd the *Roman* Empire, as that exceeded all that had been before, under the old Testament, confined only to the Land of *Judea.*

The great Danger of not appearing openly to acknowledge, rejoyce in, and promote that great Work of GOD, in bringing in that glorious Harvest, is represented in Zech. 14. 16, 17, 18, 19. *And it shall come to pass, that every one that is left, of all the Nations, which came against Jerusalem, shall even go up, from Year to Year, to worship the King, the Lord of Hosts, and to keep the Feast of Tabernacles. And it shall be, that whoso will not come up, of all the Families of the Earth, unto* Jerusalem, *to worship the King, the Lord of Hosts, even upon them shall be no Rain. And if the Family of* Egypt *go not up, and come not, that have no Rain, there shall be the Plague wherewith the Lord will smite the Heathen, that come not up to keep the Feast of Tabernacles. This shall be the Punishment of* Egypt, *and the Punishment of all Nations that come not up to keep the Feast of Tabernacles.* 'Tis evident by all the Context, that the glorious Day of the Church of God in the latter Ages of the World, is the Time spoken of: The *Feast of Tabernacles* here seems to signify that glorious spiritual Feast, which GOD shall then make for his Church, the same that is spoken of *Isai.* 25. 6. and the great spiritual Rejoycings of GOD's People at that Time. There were three great Feasts in *Israel,* at which all the Males were appointed to go up to *Jerusalem*; the Feast of the *Passover*; and the Feast of the *first Fruits,* or the Feast of *Pentecost*; and the Feast of *Ingathering,* at the End of the Year, or the Feast of *Tabernacles.* In the first of these, viz. *The Feast of the Passover,* was represented the *Purchase* of Redemption by Jesus Christ, the Paschal Lamb, that was slain at the Time of that Feast. The other two that followed it, were to represent the two great Seasons of the *Application* of the purchased Redemption: In the former of them, viz. *the Feast of the first Fruits,* which was called the Feast of *Pentecost,* was represented that Time of the Out-pouring of the Spirit, that was in the first Ages of the Christian Church, for the bringing in the *first Fruits* of Christ's Redemption, which began at *Jerusalem*, on the Day of *Pentecost*: The other, which was the *Feast of Ingathering*, at the End of the Year, which the Children of Israel were appointed to keep on Occasion of their gathering in their Corn and their Wine, and all the Fruit of their Land, and was called the *Feast of Tabernacles*, represented the other more joyful and glorious Season of the Application of Christ's Redemption, which is to be in the latter Days; the great Day of Ingathering of the Elect, the proper and appointed Time of gathering in God's Fruits, when the Angel of the Covenant shall thrust in his Sickle, and gather the Harvest of the Earth; and the Clusters of the Vine of the Earth shall also be gathered. This was upon many Accounts the greatest Feast of the three: There were much greater Tokens of Rejoycing in this Feast, than any other: The People then dwelt in Booths of green Boughs, and were commanded to take Boughs of goodly Trees, Branches of Palm-Trees, and the Boughs of thick Trees, and Willows of the Brook, and to rejoyce before the Lord their GOD: Which represents the flourishing, beautiful, pleasant State the Church shall be in, rejoycing in GOD's Grace & Love, triumphing over all her Enemies, at the Time typified by this Feast. The Tabernacle of GOD was first set up among the Children of *Israel*, at the Time of the *Feast of Tabernacles*; but in that glorious Time of the Christian Church, GOD will above all other Times set up his Tabernacle amongst Men. Rev. 21. 3. *And I heard a great Voice out of Heaven, saying, The Tabernacle of God is with Men, and he will dwell with them, and they shall be his People, and God himself shall be with them, and be their God.* The World is supposed to have been created about the Time of Year wherein the *Feast of Tabernacles* was appointed; so in that glorious Time, God will create a new Heaven, and a new Earth. The Temple of *Solomon* was dedicated at the Time of the *Feast of Tabernacles*, when GOD descended in a Pillar of Cloud, and dwelt in the Temple; so at this happy Time, the Temple of GOD shall be gloriously built up in the World, and GOD shall in a wonderful Manner come down from Heaven to dwell with his Church. Christ is supposed to have been born at the Feast of Tabernacles; so at the Commencement of that glorious Day, Christ shall be born; then above all other Times shall *the Woman cloathed with the Sun, with the Moon under her Feet, that is in Travail, and*

pained to be delivered, bring forth her Son, to Rule all Nations,
Rev. 12. at the Beginning. The *Feast of Tabernacles,* was the last
Feast that Israel had in the whole Year, before the Face of the
Earth was destroyed by the Winter; presently after the Rejoycings of that Feast were past, a tempestuous Season began. Act.
27. 9. *Sailing was now dangerous, because the Feast was now already past.* So this great Feast of the Christian Church will be
the last Feast she shall have on Earth: soon after it is past, this
lower World will be destroyed. At the Feast of Tabernacles, *Israel* left their Houses to dwell in Booths or green Tents, which
signifies the great Weanedness of GOD's People from the
World, as Pilgrims and Strangers on the Earth, and their great
Joy therein. Israel were prepared for the *Feast of Tabernacles,*
by the *Feast of Trumpets,* and the Day of Atonement both on
the same Month; so Way shall be made for the Joy of the
Church of GOD, in its glorious State on Earth, by the extraordinary preaching of the Gospel, and deep Repentance and
Humiliation for past Sins, and the great and long continued
Deadness and Carnality of the visible Church. Christ at the
great *Feast of Tabernacles,* stood in *Jerusalem,* and *cried, saying, If any Man thirst, let him come unto me & drink: He that
believeth on me, as the Scripture hath said, out of his Belly shall
flow Rivers of living Waters*: Signifying the extraordinary Freedom and Riches of divine Grace towards Sinners, at that Day,
and the extraordinary Measures of the Holy Spirit that shall be
then given; agreable to *Rev.* 21. 6. *&* 22. 17.

It is threatned here in this 14th Chap. of *Zech.* that those
who at that Time shall not come to keep this Feast; i.e. that
shall not acknowlege GOD's glorious Works, and praise his
Name, and rejoyce with his People, but should stand at a Distance, as unbelieving and disaffected; *upon them shall be no
Rain*; and that this shall be the Plague wherewith they shall all
be smitten: that is, they shall have no Share in that Shower of
divine Blessing that shall then descend on the Earth, that spiritual Rain spoken of, *Isai.* 44. 3. But God would give them
over to Hardness of Heart and Blindness of Mind.

The Curse is yet in a more awful Manner denounced against
such as shall appear as Opposers at that Time, Ver. 12. *And this
shall be the Plague, wherewith the Lord shall smite all the People
that have fought against* Jerusalem, *Their Flesh shall consume*

away while they stand upon their Feet, and their Eyes shall consume away in their Holes, and their Tongue shall consume away in their Mouth. Here also in all probability it is a spiritual Judgment, or a Plague and Curse from GOD upon the Soul, rather than upon the Body, that is intended; that such Persons, who at that Time shall oppose GOD's People in his Work, shall in an extraordinary Manner be given over to a State of spiritual Death & Ruin, that they shall remarkably appear dead while alive, and shall be as walking rotten Corpses, while they go about amongst Men.

The great Danger of not joining with GOD's People at that glorious Day is also represented, Isai. 60. 12. *For the Nation and Kingdom that will not serve thee shall perish; yea, those Nations shall be utterly wasted.*

Most of the great temporal Deliverances that were wro't for *Israel* of old, as Divines and Expositors observe, were typical of the great spiritual Works of GOD for the Salvation of Men's Souls, and the Deliverance and Prosperity of his Church, in the Days of the Gospel; and especially did they represent that greatest of all Deliverances of GOD's Church, and Chief of GOD's Works of actual Salvation, that shall be in the latter Days; which as has been observed is above all others, the appointed Time, and proper Season of actual Redemption of Men's Souls. But it may be observed that if any appeared to oppose GOD's Work in these great temporal Deliverances; or if there were any of his professing People, that on such Occasions lay still, and stood at a Distance, and did not arise and acknowlege GOD in his Work, and appear to promote it; it was what in a remarkable Manner incensed GOD's Anger, and brought his Curse upon such Persons.

So when GOD wrought that great Work of bringing the Children of Israel out of *Egypt*, (which was a Type of GOD's delivering his Church out of the spiritual *Egypt*, at the Time of the Fall of *Antichrist*, as is evident by *Rev.* 11. 8. *and* 15. 3.) How highly did GOD resent it, when the *Amalekites* appeared as Opposers in that Affair? and how dreadfully did he curse them for it? Exod. 17. 14, 15, 16. *And the Lord said unto* Moses, *Write this for a Memorial in a Book, and rehearse it in the Ears of* Joshua; *for I will utterly put out the Remembrance of* Amalek *from under Heaven. And* Moses *built an Altar, and called the Name of it* Jehovah-Nissi; *For he said, because the Lord will have War with* Amalek, *from Generation to Generation.* And accordingly we find that God remembered it a long Time after, 1 *Sam.* 15. 3. And how highly did GOD resent it in the *Moabites* and *Ammonites,* that they did not lend an helping Hand, and encourage and promote the Affair? Deut. 23. 3, 4. *An* Ammonite *or* Moabite *shall not enter into the Congregation of the Lord; even to their tenth Generation, shall they not enter into the Congregation of the Lord forever; because they met you not with Bread and with Water, in the Way when ye came forth out of* Egypt. And how were the Children of *Reuben,* and the Children of *Gad,* and the half Tribe of *Manasseh* threatned, if they did not go and help their Brethren in their Wars against the *Canaanites,* Numb. 32. 20, 21, 22, 23. *And* Moses *said unto them, If ye will do this Thing, if ye will go armed before the Lord to War, and will go all of you armed over* Jordan, *before the Lord, until he hath driven out his Enemies from before him, and the Land be subdued before the Lord, then afterward ye shall return and be guiltless before the Lord, & before* Israel, *and this Land shall be your Possession before the Lord: But if ye will not do so, behold ye have sinned against the Lord, and be sure your Sin will find you out.*

That was a glorious Work of GOD that he wro't for *Israel,* when he deliver'd them from the *Canaanites,* by the Hand of *Deborah* & *Barak:* almost every Thing about it shewed a remarkable Hand of GOD. It was a Prophetess, one immediately inspir'd by GOD, that called the People to the Battle, and conducted them in the whole Affair: The People seem to have been miraculously animated and encouraged in the Matter, when they willingly offered themselves, and gathered together to the Battle; they jeoparded their Lives in the high Places of the Field, without being pressed or hired; when one would have thought they should have but little Courage for such an Undertaking; for what could a Number of poor, weak, defenceless Slaves do, without *a Shield or Spear to be seen among forty Thousand of 'em,* to go against a great Prince, with his mighty Host, and nine Hundred Chariots of Iron. And the Success did wonderfully shew the Hand of GOD; which makes *Deborah* exultingly to say, Judg. 5. 21. *O my Soul, thou hast trodden down Strength!* CHRIST with his heavenly Host was engaged in that Battle; and therefore 'tis said, Ver. 20. *They fought from Heaven, the Stars in their Courses fought against* Sisera. The Work of GOD therefore in this Victory and Deliverance that CHRIST and his Host wrought for *Israel*, was a Type of that Victory and Deliverance which he will accomplish for his Church in that great Battle, that last Conflict that the Church shall have with her open Enemies, that shall introduce the Churches Latter-Day Glory; as appears by Rev. 16. 16. (speaking of that great Battle,) *And he gathered them together into a Place, called in the Hebrew Tongue*, Armageddon, i.e. the Mountain of *Megiddo*; alluding, as is supposed by Expositors, to the Place where the Battle was fought with the Host of *Sisera*, Judg. 5. 19. *The Kings came and fought, the Kings of* Canaan, *in* Taanach, *by the Waters of* Megiddo. Which can signify nothing else, than that this Battle, which Christ & his Church shall have with their Enemies, is the Antitype of the Battle that was fought there. But what a dreadful Curse from Christ, did some of GOD's professing People *Israel*, bring upon themselves, by lying still at that Time, and not putting to an helping Hand? Judg. 5. 23. *Curse ye* Meroz, *said the Angel of the Lord, curse ye bitterly the Inhabitants thereof, because they came not to the Help of the Lord, to the Help of the Lord against the Mighty.* The Angel of the Lord was the Captain of the Host; he that had led *Israel*, and fought for them in that Battle, who is very often called *the Angel of the Lord*, in Scripture; the same that appeared to *Joshua* with a Sword drawn in his Hand, and told him that *he was come as the Captain of the Host of the Lord*; and the same glorious Captain that we have an Account of, as leading forth his Hosts to that Battle, of which this was the Type, *Rev.* 19. 11, *&c.* It seems the Inhabitants of *Meroz* were unbelieving concerning this great Work, nor would they hearken to *Deborah*'s Pretences, nor did it enter into them that such a poor defenceless Company, should ever prevail against those that were so Mighty; they did not acknowlege the Hand of GOD, and therefore stood at a Distance, and did nothing to promote the Work: but what a bitter Curse from GOD, did they bring upon themselves by it!

'Tis very probable that one great Reason why the Inhabitants of *Meroz* were so unbelieving concerning this Work, was that they argued *a Priori*; they did not like the Beginning of it, it being a Woman that first led the Way, and had the chief Conduct in the Affair; nor could they believe that such despicable Instruments, as a Company of unarmed Slaves, were ever like to effect so great a Thing; and Pride and Unbelief wro't together, in not being willing to follow *Deborah* to the Battle.

It was another glorious Work of GOD that he wro't for *Israel*, in the Victory that was obtained by *Gideon* over the *Midianites* and *Amalekites*, and the Children of the East, when they came up against *Israel* like Grashoppers, a Multitude that could not be numbered. This also was a remarkable Type of the Victory of CHRIST and his Church over his Enemies, by the pouring out of the SPIRIT with the preached Gospel, as is evident by the Manner of it, which *Gideon* was immediately directed to of GOD; which was not by human Sword or Bow, but only by blowing of Trumpets, and by Lights in earthen Vessels. We read that on this Occasion, *Gideon* called the People together to help in this great Affair; and that accordingly, great Numbers resorted to him, and came to the Help of the Lord, *Judg.* 7. 23, 24. But there were some also at that Time, that were unbelieving, and would not acknowledge the Hand of GOD in that Work, tho' it was so great and wonderful, nor would they join to promote it; and they were the Inhabitants of *Succoth* and *Penuel: Gideon* desired their Help, when he was pursuing after *Zebah* and *Zalmunna*; but they despised his Pretences, and his Confidence of the LORD's being on his Side, to deliver those two great Princes into the Hands of such a despicable Company, as he and his three Hundred Men, and would not own the Work of GOD, nor afford *Gideon* any Assistance: GOD proceeded in this Work in a Way that was exceeding cross to their Pride. And they also refused to own the Work, because they argued *a Priori*; they could not believe that GOD would do such great Things by such a despicable Instrument; one of such a poor, mean Family in *Manasseh*, and he the least in his Father's House; and the Company that was with him appeared very wretched, being but three Hundred Men, and they weak & faint: But we see how they suffered for their Folly, in not acknowleging, and appearing to promote this Work of GOD. *Gideon* when he returned from the Victory, *took them, and taught them with the Briers and Thorns of the Wilderness, and beat down the Tower of* Penuel, (he brought down their Pride, and their false Confidence,) *and slew the Men of the City*, Judg. Chap. 8. This, in all probability *Gideon* did, as moved & directed by the Angel of the LORD, that is CHRIST, that first called him, and sent him forth in this Battle, and instructed & directed him, in the whole Affair.

The Return of the Ark of GOD to dwell in *Zion*, in the midst of the Land of *Israel*, after it had been long absent, first in the Land of the *Philistines*, and then in *Kirjath-jearim*, in the utmost Borders of the Land, did livelily represent the Return of GOD to a professing People, in the spiritual Tokens of his Presence, after long Absence from them; as well as the Ark's ascending up into a Mountain, typified CHRIST's Ascension into Heaven. 'Tis evident by the Psalms that were penn'd on that Occasion, especially the 68th *Psalm*, that the exceeding Rejoycings of Israel on that Occasion, represented the Joy of the Church of CHRIST, on his returning to it, after it has been in a low and dark State, to revive his Work, bringing his People *back*, as it were *from* Bashan, *and from the Depth of the Sea*, scattering their spiritual Enemies, and causing that *tho' they had lien among the Pots, yet they should be as the Wings of a Dove, covered with Silver, and her Feathers with yellow Gold*; and giving the blessed Tokens of his Presence in his House, that his People may *see the Goings of God their King in his Sanctuary*; and that the Gifts which *David*, with such royal Bounty, distributed amongst the People on that Occasion (2 *Sam.* 6. 18, 19. & 1 *Chron.* 16. 2, 3.) represent spiritual Blessings, that CHRIST liberally sends down on his Church, by the Outpourings of his Spirit. See *Psal.* 68. 1, 3, 13, 18, 19, 20, 21, 22, 23, 24. And we have an Account how that all the People, from *Shihor* of *Egypt*, even unto the entring in of *Hemath*, gathered together, and appeared to join and assist in that great Affair; and that all Israel *brought up the Ark of the Covenant of the Lord, with Shouting, and with sound of the Cornet, and with Trumpets, and with Cymbals, making a Noise with Psalteries and Harps*, 1 Chron. 13. 2, 5. & 15. 28. And not only the Men, but the Women of *Israel*, the Daughters of *Zion* appeared as publickly joining in the Praises & Rejoycings that were on that Occasion, 2 *Sam.* 6. 19. But we read of one of *David*'s Wives, even *Michal, Saul*'s Daughter, whose Heart was not engaged in the Affair, and did not appear with others to rejoyce and Praise GOD on this Occasion, but kept away, and stood at a Distance, as disaffected, and disliking the Managements; she despised and ridiculed the Transports, and extraordinary Manifestations of Joy that then were; and the Curse that she brought upon herself by it, was that, of being barren to the Day of her Death.—Let this be a Warning to us: Let us take Heed, in this Day of the bringing up of the Ark of GOD, that while we are in Visibility and Profession the Spouse of the spiritual *David*, we don't shew our selves to be indeed the Children of false-hearted and rebellious *Saul*, by our standing aloof, and not joining in the Joy and Praises of the Day, and disliking and despising the Joys & Affections of GOD's People, because they are to so high a Degree, and so bring the Curse of perpetual Barrenness upon our Souls.

Let us take Heed that we ben't like the Son of the Bond-Woman, that was born after the Flesh, that persecuted him that was born after the Spirit, and mocked at the Feasting and Re-joicings that were made for *Isaac* when he was weaned; lest we should be cast out of the Family of *Abraham*, as he was. *Gen.* 21. 8, 9. That Affair contain'd spiritual Mysteries, and was typical of Things that come to pass in these Days of the Gospel; as is evident by the Apostles Testimony, *Gal.* 4. 22. to the End. And particularly it seems to have been typical of two Things. 1. The Weaning of the Church from it's Milk of carnal Ordi-nances, Ceremonies, Shadows, and beggarly Elements, upon the Coming of CHRIST, and pouring out of the Spirit in the Days of the Apostles. The Church of CHRIST, in the Times of the Old-Testament, was in it's Minority, and was a Babe; and the Apostle tells us that Babes must be fed with Milk, and not with strong Meat; but when GOD weaned his Church from these carnal Ordinances, on the ceasing of the legal Dispensa-tion, a glorious Gospel Feast was provided for Souls, and GOD fed his People with spiritual Dainties, and fill'd them with the Spirit, and gave 'em Joy in the Holy Ghost. *Ishmael*, in mock-ing at the Time of *Isaac*'s Feast, by the Apostles Testimony, represented the carnal *Jews*, the Children of the literal *Jerusa-lem*, who when they beheld the Rejoicings of Christians, in their spiritual and evangelical Priviledges, were filled with Envy, deriding, contradicting and blaspheming. *Act.* 2. 13. and

Chap. 13. 45. and 18. 6. And therefore were cast out of the Family of *Abraham*, and out of the Land of *Canaan*, to wander through the Earth. 2. This Weaning of *Isaac*'s seems also to represent the Conversion of Sinners, which is several Times represented in Scripture by the weaning of a Child; as in *Psal.* 131. and *Isai.* 28. 9. Because in Conversion, the Soul is weaned from the Enjoyments of the World, which are as it were the Breast of our Mother Earth; and is also wean'd from the Covenant of our first Parents, which we as naturally hang upon, as a Child on it's Mother's Breasts: And the great Feast that *Abraham* made on that Occasion, represents the spiritual Feast, the heavenly Priviledges, and holy Joys and Comforts, which GOD gives Souls at their Conversion. Now is a Time when GOD is in a remarkable Manner bestowing the Blessings of such a Feast. Let every one take Heed that he don't now shew himself to be the Son of the Bond-Woman, and born after the Flesh, by standing and deriding, with mocking *Ishmael*; lest they be cast out as he was, and it be said concerning them, these Sons of the Bond-Woman, shall not be Heirs with the Sons of the Free-Woman. Don't let us stumble at the Things that have been, because they are so great and extraordinary; for if we have run with the Foot-Men, and they have wearied us, how shall we contend with Horses? There is doubtless a Time coming when GOD will accomplish Things vastly greater and more extraordinary than these.

And that we may be warned not to continue doubting and unbelieving, concerning this Work, because of the extraordinary Degree of it, and the Suddenness and Swiftness of the Accomplishment of the great Things that pertain to it. Let us consider the Example of the unbelieving Lord in *Samaria*; who could not believe so extraordinary a Work of GOD to be accomplished so suddenly as was declared to him: The Prophet *Elisha* foretold that the great Famine in *Samaria* should very suddenly, even in one Day, be turned into an extraordinary Plenty; but the Work was too great, and too sudden for him to believe; says he, *If the Lord should make Windows in Heaven, might this Thing be?* And the Curse that he brought upon himself by it, was that he saw it with his Eyes, and did not eat thereof, but miserably perished, and was trodden down as the Mire of the Streets, when others were feasting and rejoicing. 2 *Kings, Chap.* 7.

When GOD redeemed his People from their *Babylonish* Captivity, and they rebuilt *Jerusalem*, it was, as is universally own'd, a remarkable Type of the spiritual Redemption of GOD's Church; and particularly, was an eminent Type of the great Deliverance of the Christian Church from spiritual *Babylon*, & their re-building the spiritual *Jerusalem*, in the latter Days; and therefore they are often spoken of under one by the Prophets: and this probably was the main Reason that it was so ordered in Providence, and particularly noted in Scripture, that the Children of *Israel*, on that Occasion, kept the greatest *Feast of Tabernacles*, that ever had been kept in *Israel*, since the Days of *Joshua*, when the People were first settled in *Canaan*; (*Neh.* 8. 16, 17.) because at that Time happen'd that Restoration of *Israel*, that had the greatest Resemblance of that great Restoration of the Church of GOD, of which the *Feast of Tabernacles* was the Type, of any that had been since *Joshua* first bro't the People out of the Wilderness, and settled them in the good Land. But we read of some that opposed the *Jews* in that Affair, and weaken'd their Hands, and ridiculed GOD's People, and the Instruments that were improved in that Work, and despised their Hope, and made as tho' their Confidence was little more than a Shadow, and would utterly fail 'em: *What do these feeble Jews?* (say they,) *Will they fortify themselves? Will they sacrifice? Will they make an End in a Day? Will they revive the Stones out of the Heaps of the Rubbish which are burn't? Even that which they build, if a Fox go up, he shall even break down their Stone Wall.* Let not us be in any Measure like them, lest it be said to us, as *Nehemiah* said to them, Neh. 2. 20. *We his Servants will arise and build; but you have no Portion, nor Right, nor Memorial in* Jerusalem. And least we bring *Nehemiah's* Imprecation upon us, Chap. 4. 5. *Cover not their Iniquity, and let not their Sin be blotted out from before thee; for they have provoked thee to Anger, before the Builders.*

As Persons will greatly expose themselves to the Curse of GOD, by opposing, or standing at a Distance, and keeping Silence at such a Time as this; so for Persons to arise, and readily to acknowledge GOD, and honour him in such a Work, and chearfully and vigorously to exert themselves to promote it, will be to put themselves much in the Way of the divine Blessing. What a Mark of Honour does GOD put upon those in

Israel, that willingly offered themselves, and came to the Help of the Lord against the Mighty, when the Angel of the Lord led forth his Armies, and they fought from Heaven against *Sisera? Judg.* 5. 2, 9, 14, 15, 17, 18. And what a great Blessing is pronounc'd on *Jael*, the Wife of *Heber*, the *Kenite*, for her appearing on the Lord's Side, and for what she did to promote this Work? *Ver.* 24. Which was no less than the Curse pronounced in the preceeding Verse, against *Meroz*, for lying still: *Blessed above Women, shall* Jael, *the Wife of* Heber, *the* Kenite *be, blessed shall she be above Women, in the Tent.* And what a Blessing is pronounced on those which shall have any Hand in the Destuction of *Babylon*, which was the Head City of the Kingdom of *Satan*, and of the Enemies of the Church of GOD? Psal. 137. 9, *Happy shall he be, that taketh, and dasheth thy little ones against the Stones.* What a particular and honourable Notice is taken, in the Records of God's Word, of those that arose, and appear'd as *David's* Helpers, to introduce him into the Kingdom of *Israel*, in the 12 Chap. of 1 *Chron.* The Host of those that thus came to the Help of the Lord, in that Work of his, and glorious Revolution in *Israel*, by which the Kingdom of that great Type of the *Messiah* was set up in *Israel*, is compared to the Host of God, Ver. 22. *At that Time, Day by Day, there came to* David, *to help him, until it was a great Host, like the Host of God.* And doubtless it was intended to be a Type of that Host of God, that shall appear with the spiritual *David*, as his Helpers, when he shall come to set up his Kingdom in the World; the same Host that we read of, *Rev.* 19. 14. The Spirit of GOD then pronounced a special Blessing on *David*'s Helpers, as those that were Co-workers with God, Ver. 18. *Then the Spirit came upon* Amasai, *who was chief of the Captains, and he said, Thine are we* David, *and on thy Side, thou Son of* Jesse; *Peace, Peace be unto thee, and Peace be to thine Helpers, for thy God helpeth thee.* So we may conclude that God will much more give his Blessing to such as come to the Help of the Lord, when he sets his own dear Son as King on his holy Hill of *Zion*; and they shall be received by CHRIST, and he will put peculiar Honour upon them, as *David* did on those his Helpers; as we have an Account, in the following Words, Ver. 18. *Then* David *received them, and made them Captains of the Band.* 'Tis particularly noted of those that came to *David* to

Hebron, ready armed to the War, to turn the Kingdom of *Saul* to him, according to the Word of the Lord, that *they were Men that had understanding of the Times, to know what* Israel *ought to do.* Ver. 23. & 32. Herein they differed from the *Pharisees* and other *Jews*, that did not come to the Help of the Lord, at the Time that the great Son of *David* appeared to set up his Kingdom in the World, whom CHRIST condems, that they had not *Understanding of those Times*, Luke 12. 56. *Ye Hypocrites, ye can discern the Face of the Sky, and of the Earth; but how is it, that ye do not discern these Times?* So it always will be, when CHRIST remarkably appears on Earth, on a Design of setting up his Kingdom here, there will be many that will not understand the Times, nor what *Israel* ought to do, and so will not come to turn about the Kingdom to *David*.

The favourable Notice that GOD will take of such as appear to promote the Work of GOD, at such a Time as this, may also be argued from such a very particular Notice being taken in the sacred Records, of those that helped in rebuilding the Wall of *Jerusalem*, upon the Return from the *Babylonish* Captivity. *Nehem.* Chap. 3.

At such a Time as this, when GOD is setting his King on his holy Hill of *Zion*, or establishing his Dominion, or shewing forth his regal Glory from thence, he expects that his visible People, without Exception, should openly appear to acknowledge him in such a Work, and bow before him, & join with him. But especially does he expect this of civil Rulers: GOD's Eye is especially upon them, to see how they behave themselves on such an Occasion. If a new King comes to the Throne, when he comes from Abroad, and enters into his Kingdom, and makes his solemn Entry into the royal City, it is expected that all Sorts should acknowledge him; but above all others is it expected that the great Men, and public Officers of the Nation should then make their Appearance, and attend on their Sovereign, with suitable Congratulations, and Manifestations of Respect and Loyalty: If such as these stand at a Distance, at such a Time, it will be much more taken Notice of, and will awaken the Princes Jealousy and Displeasure much more, than such a Behaviour in the common People. And thus it is, when that eternal Son of GOD, and Heir of the World, by whom Kings reign, and Princes decree Justice, whom his Father has appointed to be King of Kings, comes as it were from far, and in the spiritual Tokens of his Presence, enters into the royal City *Zion*; GOD has his Eye at such a Time, especially upon those Princes, Nobles and Judges of the Earth, spoken of Prov. 8. 16. to see how they behave themselves, whether they bow to him, that he has made the Head of all Principality & Power. This is evident by the 2d. Psal. Ver. 6, 7, 10, 11, 12. *Yet have I set my King, upon my holy Hill of* Zion. *I will declare the Decree; the Lord hath said unto me, thou art my Son, this Day have I begotten thee.—Be wise now therefore, O ye Kings, be instructed ye Judges of the Earth; serve the Lord with Fear, and rejoice with Trembling; kiss the Son, lest he be angry, and ye perish from the Way, when his Wrath is kindled but a little.* There seems to be in the Words, an Allusion to a new King's coming to the Throne, and making his solemn Entry into the royal City; (as *Zion* was the royal City in *Israel*,) when it is expected that all, especially Men in publick Office and Authority, should manifest their Loyalty, by some open and visible Token of Respect, *by the Way*, as he passes along; and those that refuse or neglect it are in Danger of being immediately struck down, and perishing *from the Way*, by which the King goes in solemn Procession.

The Day wherein God does in an eminent Manner send forth the Rod of CHRIST's Strength out of *Zion*, that he may rule in the midst of his Enemies, the Day of his Power wherein his People shall be made willing, is also eminently a Day of his Wrath, especially to such Rulers as oppose him, or won't bow to him; a Day wherein he *shall strike through Kings, and fill the Places with the dead Bodies, and wound the Heads over many Countries.* Psal. 110. And thus it is, that when the Son of God *girds his Sword upon his Thigh, with his Glory and his Majesty, and in his Majesty rides prosperously, because of Truth, Meekness and Righteousness, his right Hand teaches him terrible Things.* It was the Princes of *Succoth* especially, that suffered Punishment, when the Inhabitants of that City refused to come to the Help of the Lord, when *Gideon* was pursuing after *Zebah* and *Zalmunna*; we read that *Gideon* took the *Elders* of the City, and Thorns of the Wilderness, and Briers, and with them he taught the Men of *Succoth*. 'Tis especially taken Notice of that the Rulers, and chief Men of *Israel*, were called upon to assist in the Affair of bringing up the Ark of GOD; they were chiefly consulted, and were principal in the Management of the Affair. I Chro. 13. I. *And* David *consulted with the Captains of Thousands and Hundreds, and with every Leader.* And Chap. 15. 25. *So* David *and the Elders of* Israel, *and the Captains over Thousands, went to bring up the Ark of the Covenant of the Lord, out of the House of* Obed-Edom, *with Joy.* So 2 *Sam.* 6. 1. And so it was when the Ark was brought into the Temple, 1 *King.* 8. 1, 3. *&* 2 *Chro.* 5. 2, 4.

And as Rulers, by neglecting their Duty at such a Time, will especially expose themselves to GOD's great Displeasure, so by fully acknowledging GOD in such a Work, and by chearfully and vigorously exerting themselves to promote it, they will especially be in the Way of receiving peculiar Honours and Rewards at GOD's Hands. 'Tis noted of the Princes of *Israel,* that *they* especially appeared to honour GOD with their princely Offering, on Occasion of the setting up the Tabernacle of GOD, in the Congregation of *Israel*: (which I have observed already was done at the Time of the Feast of Tabernacles, and was a Type of the Tabernacle of GOD's being with Men, and his dwelling with Men in the latter Days,) and with what abundant particularity, is it noted of each Prince, how much he offered to GOD on that Occasion, for their everlasting Honour, in the 7th Chap. of *Numb?* And so with how much Favour and Honour does the Spirit of GOD take Notice of those Princes in *Israel,* that came to the Help of the Lord, in the War against *Sisera?* Judg. 5. 9. *My Heart is towards the Governours of* Israel, *that offered themselves willingly among the People.* And Ver. 14. *Out of* Machir *came down Governours.* Ver. 15. *And the Princes of* Issachar *were with* Deborah. And in the Account that we have of the re-building the Wall of *Jerusalem,* in the 3d Chap. of *Nehem.* It is particularly noted, what an Hand one and another of the Rulers had in this Affair; we have an Account that such a Part of the Wall was repaired by the Ruler of the half Part of *Jerusalem,* and such a Part by the Ruler of the other Half Part of *Jerusalem,* and such a Part by the Ruler of Part of *Beth-haccerem,* and such a Part by the Ruler of Part of *Mizpah,* and such a Part by the Ruler of the Half Part of *Beth-zur*; and such a Part by the Ruler of *Mizpah,* Ver. 9, 12, 14, 15, 16, 19. And there it is particularly noted of the Rulers of one of the Cities, that they put not their Necks to the Work of the Lord, tho' the common People did; and they are stigmatized for it, in the sacred Records, to their everlasting Reproach, Ver. 5. *And next unto them, the* Tekoites *repaired; but their Nobles put not their Necks to the Work of the Lord.* So the Spirit of GOD, with special Honour, takes Notice of Princes and Rulers of several Tribes, that assisted in bringing up the Ark, *Psal.* 68. 27.

And I humbly desire that it may be considered, Whether we han't Reason to fear that GOD is provoked with this Land, that no more Notice has been taken of this glorious Work of the Lord, that has been lately carried on, by the civil Authority; that there has no more been done by them, as a public Acknowledgment of GOD in this Work, and no more Improvement of their Authority to promote it, either by appointing a Day of public Thanksgiving to GOD, for so unspeakable a Mercy, or a Day of Fasting and Prayer, to humble ourselves before GOD, for our past Deadness and Unprofitableness under the Means of Grace, and to seek the Continuance and Increase of the Tokens of his Presence; or so much as to enter upon any public Consultation, what should be done to advance the present Revival of Religion, and great Reformation that is begun in the Land. Is there not Danger that such a Behaviour, at such a Time, will be interpreted by GOD, as a Denial of Christ? If but a new Governour comes into a Province, how much is there done, especially by those that are in Authority, to put Honour upon him, to arise, and appear publicly, and go forth to meet him, to address and congratulate him, and with great Expence to attend upon him, and aid him? If the Authority of the Province, on such an Occasion, should all sit still, and say & do nothing, and take no Notice of the Arrival of their new Governour, would there not be Danger of its being interpreted by him, and his Prince that sent him, as a Denial of his Authority, or a refusing to receive him, and honour him as their Governour? And shall the Head of the Angels, and Lord of the Universe, come down from Heaven, in so wonderful a Manner, into the Land, and shall all stand at a Distance, and be silent and unactive on such an Occasion? I would humbly recommend it to our Rulers, to consider whether GOD don't now say to them, *Be wise now ye Rulers, be instructed ye Judges of* New-England; *Kiss the Son, lest he be angry, and ye perish from the Way.*

'Tis prophesied *Zech.* 12. 8. That in the glorious Day of the

Christian Church, the House of *David*, or the Rulers in GOD's *Israel, shall be as GOD, as the Angel of the LORD, before his People.* But how can such Rulers expect to have any Share in this glorious Promise, that don't so much as openly acknowledge GOD in the Work of that Spirit, by which the Glory of that Day is to be accomplished? The Days are coming, so often spoken of, when the Saints shall reign on Earth, and all Dominion and Authority shall be given into their Hands: But if our Rulers would partake of this Honour, they ought at such a Day as this, to bring their Glory and Honour into the spiritual *Jerusalem*, agreable to *Rev.* 21. 24.

But above all others, is GOD's Eye upon Ministers of the Gospel, as expecting of them, that they should arise, and acknowledge, and honour him in such a Work as this, and do their utmost to encourage and promote it: For to promote such a Work, is the very Business which they are called and devoted to; 'tis the Office to which they are appointed, as Co-workers with Christ, and as his Ambassadors and Instruments, to awaken and convert Sinners, and establish, build up and comfort Saints; 'tis the Business they have been solemnly charged with, before GOD, Angels and Men, and that they have given up themselves to, by the most sacred Vows. These especially, are the Officers of CHRIST's Kingdom, that above all other Men upon Earth, do represent his Person, into whose Hands CHRIST has committed the sacred Oracles, and holy Ordinances, and all his appointed Means of Grace, to be administred by them; they are the Stewards of his Houshold, into whose Hands he has committed its Provision; the immortal Souls of Men are committed to them, as a Flock of Sheep are committed to the Care of a Shepherd, or as a Master commits a Treasure to the Care of a Servant, of which he must give an Account: 'Tis expected of them, above all others, that they should have Understanding of the Times, and know what *Israel* ought to do; for 'tis their Business to acquaint themselves with Things pertaining to the Kingdom of GOD, and to teach and enlighten others in Things of this Nature. We that are employed in the sacred Work of the Gospel-Ministry, are the Watchmen over the City, to whom GOD has committed the Keys of the Gates of *Zion*; and if when the rightful King of *Zion* comes, to deliver his People from the Enemy that oppresses them, we refuse to open the Gates to him, how greatly shall we expose our selves to his Wrath? We are appointed to be the Captains of the Host in this War: And if a General will highly resent it in a private Soldier, if he refuses to follow him when his Banner is display'd, and his Trumpet blown; how much more will he resent it in the Officers of his Army? The Work of the Gospel-Ministry, consisting in the Administration of GOD's Word and Ordinances, is the principal Means that GOD has appointed, for carrying on his Work on the Souls of Men; and 'tis his revealed Will, that when ever that glorious Revival of Religion, and Reformation of the World, so often spoken of in his Word, is accomplished, it should be principally by the Labours of his Ministers; and therefore how heinous will it be in the Sight of GOD, if when a Work of that Nature is begun, we appear unbelieving, slow, backward and disaffected? There was no sort of Persons among the *Jews* that was in any Measure treated with such Manifestations of GOD's great Displeasure, and severe Indignation, for not acknowledging CHRIST, and the Work of his Spirit, in the Days of Christ and his Apostles, as the Ministers of Religion: See how CHRIST deals with them for it, in the 23d Chapter of *Matthew*; with what Gentleness did CHRIST treat Publicans and Harlots, in Comparison of them?

When the Tabernacle was erected in the Camp of *Israel*, and GOD came down from Heaven to dwell in it, the Priests were above all others concerned, and busily employed in the solemn Transactions of that Occasion, *Levit.* Chap. 8. and 9. And so it was at the Time of the Dedication of the Temple of *Solomon*, 1 *King.* Chap. 8. and 2 *Chron.* Chap. 5. and 6. and 7. which was at the Time of the Feast of Tabernacles, at the same Time that the Tabernacle was erected in the Wilderness: And the *Levites* were primarily, and most immediately concerned in bringing up the Ark into Mount *Zion*; the Business properly belonged to them, and the Ark was carried upon their Shoulders. 1 *Chron.* 15. 2. *Then* David *said, None ought to carry the Ark of GOD but the Levites; for them hath the LORD chosen to carry the Ark of GOD, and to minister unto him for ever.* And v. 11, 12. *And* David *called for* Zadok *and* Abiathar *the Priests, and for the* Levites, *for* Uriel, Asaiah, *and* Joel, Shemaiah, *and* Eliel, *and* Aminadab, *and said unto them, Ye are the chief of the Fathers of the* Levites; *sanctify your selves, both ye, and your Brethren, that you may bring up the Ark of the Lord God of* Israel, *unto the Place that I have prepared for it.* So we have an Account that the Priests led the Way, in rebuilding the Wall of *Jerusalem*, after the *Babylonish* Captivity, *Neh.* 3. at the beginning.

If Ministers preach never so good Doctrine, and are never so painful and laborious in their Work, yet, if at such a Day as this, they shew to their People, that they are not well affected to this Work, but are very doubtful and suspicious of it, they will be very likely to do their People a great deal more Hurt than Good: For the very Fame of such a great and extraordinary Work of GOD, if their People were suffered to believe it to be his Work, and the Example of other Towns, together with what Preaching they might hear occasionally, would be likely to have a much greater Influence upon the Minds of their People, to awaken them and animate them in Religion, than all their Labours with them: And besides their Ministers Opinion won't only beget in them a Suspicion of the Work they hear of abroad, whereby the mighty Hand of GOD that appears in it, loses its Influence upon their Minds, but it will also tend to create a Suspicion of every Thing of the like Nature, that shall appear among themselves, as being something of the same Distemper that is become so Epidemical in the Land; and that is, in Effect, to create a Suspicion of all vital Religion, and to put the People upon talking against it, and discouraging it, where-ever it appears, and knocking it in the Head, as fast as it rises. And we that are Ministers, by looking on this Work, from Year to Year, with a displeased Countenance, shall effectually keep the Sheep from their Pasture, instead of doing the Part of Shepherds to them, by feeding them; and our People had a great deal better be without any settled Minister at all, at such a Day as this.

We that are in this sacred Office, had Need to take Heed what we do, and how we behave our selves at this Time: A less Thing in a Minister will hinder the Work of GOD, than in others. If we are very silent, or say but little about the Work, in our publick Prayers and Preaching, or seem carefully to avoid speaking of it in our Conversation, it will, and justly may be interpreted by our People, that we who are their Guides, to whom they are to have their Eye for spiritual Instruction, are suspicious of it; and this will tend to raise the same Suspicions in them; and so the fore-mentioned Consequences will follow. And if we really hinder, and stand in the Way of the Work of GOD, whose Business above all others it is to promote it, how can we expect to partake of the glorious Benefits of it? And by keeping others from the Benefit of it, we shall keep them out of Heaven; therefore those awful Words of CHRIST to the *Jewish* Teachers, should be considered by us, *Matth.* 23. 13. *Wo unto you, for you shut up the Kingdom of Heaven;—for ye neither go in your selves, neither suffer ye them that are entring, to go in.* If we keep the Sheep from their Pasture, how shall we answer it to the great Shepherd, that has bought the Flock with his precious Blood, and has committed the Care of them to us? I would humbly desire of every Minister that has thus long remain'd disaffected to this Work, and has had contemptible Thoughts of it, to consider whether he has not hitherto been like *Michal*, without any Child, or at least in a great Measure barren and unsuccessful in his Work: I pray GOD it may not be a perpetual Barrenness as her's was.

The Times of CHRIST's remarkably appearing, in Behalf of his Church, and to revive Religion, and advance his Kingdom in the World, are often spoken in the Prophecies of Scripture, as Times wherein he will remarkably execute Judgments on such Ministers or Shepherds, as don't feed the Flock, but hinder their being fed, and so deliver his Flock from them, as *Jer.* 23. throughout, and *Ezek.* 34. throughout, and *Zech.* 10. 3. and *Isai.* 56. 7, 8, 9, *&c.* I observed before that CHRIST's solemn, magnificent Entry into *Jerusalem*, seems to be designed, as a Representation of his glorious coming into his Church, the spiritual *Jerusalem*; and therefore 'tis worthy to be noted, to our present Purpose, that CHRIST at that Time, cast out all them that sold and bought in the Temple, and overthrew the Tables of the Money-Changers, and the Seats of them that sold Doves; signifying that when he should come to set up his Kingdom on Earth, he would cast out those out of his House, who, instead of being faithful Ministers, officiated there only for worldly Gain: Not that I determine that all Ministers that are suspicious of this Work, do so; but I mention these Things to shew that it is to be expected, that a Time of a glorious Out-pouring of the Spirit of GOD to revive Religion, will be a

Time of remarkable Judgments on those Ministers that don't serve the End of their Ministry.

The Example of the unbelieving Lord in *Samaria*, should especially be for the Warning of Ministers and Rulers: At the Time when GOD turned an extreme Famine into a great Plenty, by a wonderful Work of his, the King appointed this Lord to have the Charge of the Gate of the City; where he saw the common People, in Multitudes, entring with great Joy and Gladness, loaden with Provision, to feed and feast their almost famished Bodies; but he himself, tho' he saw it with his Eyes, never had one Taste of it, but being weak with Famine, sunk down in the Crowd, and was trodden to Death, as a Punishment of GOD, for his not giving Credit to that great and wonderful Work of GOD, when sufficiently manifested to him, to require his Belief.—Ministers are those, that the King of the Church has appointed to have the Charge of the Gate, at which his People enter into the Kingdom of Heaven, there to be entertain'd and satisfy'd with an eternal Feast; Ministers have the Charge of the House of GOD, which is the Gate of Heaven.

Ministers should especially take Heed of a Spirit of Envy towards other Ministers, that GOD is pleased to make more Use of to carry on this Work, than they; and that they don't, from such a Spirit, reproach some Preachers, that have the true Spirit, as tho' they were influenced by a false Spirit, or were bereft of Reason, and were mad, and were proud, false Pretenders, and deserved to be put in Prison or the Stocks, as Disturbers of the Peace; lest they expose themselves to the Curse of *Shemaiah*, the *Nehelamite*, who envied the Prophet *Jeremiah*, and in this Manner reviled him, in his Letter to *Zephaniah* the Priest, *Jer.* 29. 26, 27. *The Lord hath made thee Priest, in the Stead of* Jehoiada *the Priest, that ye should be Officers in the House of the LORD, for every Man that is mad, and maketh himself a Prophet, that thou shouldst put him in Prison, and in the Stocks. Now therefore, Why hast thou not reproved* Jeremiah *of* Anathoth, *which maketh himself a Prophet* to you? His Curse is denounced in the 32d v. *Therefore, thus saith the LORD, Behold, I will punish* Shemaiah *the* Nehelamite, *and his Seed; He shall not have a Man to dwell among his People, neither shall he behold the Good that I will do for my People, saith the*

LORD, because he hath taught Rebellion against the LORD. All those that are others Superiors or Elders, should take Heed, that at this Day they ben't like the elder Brother, who could not bear it, that the Prodigal should be made so much of, and should be so sumptuously entertained, and would not join in the Joy of the Feast; was like *Michal, Saul*'s Daughter, offended at the Musick and Dancing that he heard; the Transports of Joy displeased him; it seem'd to him to be an unseemly and unseasonable Noise and Ado, that was made; and therefore stood at a Distance, sullen, and much offended, and full of Invectives against the young Prodigal.

'Tis our wisest and best Way, fully, and without Reluctance, to bow to the great GOD in this Work, and to be entirely resign'd to him, with Respect to the Manner in which he carries it on, and the Instruments he is pleased to make Use of, and not to shew our selves out of Humour, and sullenly to refuse to acknowledge the Work, in the full Glory of it, because we han't had so great a Hand in promoting it, or han't shared so largely in the Blessings of it, as some others; and not to refuse to give all that Honour, that belongs to others, as Instruments, because they are young, or are upon other Accounts, much inferiour to our selves, and many others, and may appear to us very unworthy, that GOD should put so much Honour upon them. When GOD comes to accomplish any great Work for his Church, and for the Advancement of the Kingdom of his Son, he always fulfills that Scripture, Isai. 2. 17. *And the Loftiness of Man shall be bowed down, and the Haughtiness of Men shall be made low, and the Lord alone shall be exalted in that Day.* If GOD has a Design of carrying on this Work, every one, whether he be great or small, must either bow to it, or be broken before it: It may be expected that GOD's Hand will be upon every Thing that is high, and stiff, and strong in Opposition, as in Isai. 2. 12, 13, 14, 15. *For the Day of the Lord of Hosts, shall be upon every one that is proud & lofty, and upon every one that is lifted up, and he shall be brought low; and upon all the Cedars of* Lebanon, *that are high and lifted up, and upon all the Oaks of* Bashan, *and upon all the high Mountains, and upon all the Hills that are lifted up, and upon every high Tower, and upon every fenced Wall.*

Not only Magistrates and Ministers, but every living Soul, is now obliged to arise, and acknowledge GOD in this Work, and put to his Hand to promote it, as they would not expose themselves to GOD's Curse. All Sorts of Persons, throughout the whole Congregation of *Israel*, Great and Small, Rich and Poor, Men and Women, helped to build the Tabernacle in the Wilderness; some in one Way, others in another; each one according to his Capacity: Every one whose Heart stirred him up, and every one whom his Spirit made willing; all Sorts contributed, and all Sorts were employed in that Affair, in Labours of their Hands, both Men and Women: Some brought Gold and Silver, others Blue, Purple and Scarlet, and fine Linnen; others offered an Offering of Brass; others, with whom was found Shittim Wood, brought it an Offering to the LORD: The Rulers brought Onyx Stones, and Spice, and Oyl; and some brought Goats Hair; and some Rams Skins, and others Badgers Skins. See Exod. 35. 20, &c. And we are told Ver. 29. *The Children of* Israel *brought a willing Offering unto the Lord, every Man and Woman, whose Heart made them willing.* And thus it ought to be in this Day of building the Tabernacle of GOD; with such a willing and cheerful Heart, ought every Man, Woman, and Child, to do something to promote this Work: Those that have not Onyx Stones, or are not able to bring Gold or Silver, yet may bring Goats Hair.

As all Sorts of Persons were employed in building the Tabernacle in the Wilderness, so the whole Congregation of *Israel* were called together to set up the Tabernacle in *Shiloh*, after they came into *Canaan*, Josh. 18. 1. And so again, the whole Congregation of *Israel* were gathered together, to bring up the Ark of GOD, from *Kirjath-jearim*; and again, they were all assembled to bring it up, out of the House of *Obed-Edom into Mount Zion*; so again, all *Israel* met together to assist in the great Affair of the Dedication of the Temple, and bringing the Ark into it: So we have an Account, how that all Sorts assisted in the Re-building the Wall of *Jerusalem*, not only the proper Inhabitants of *Jerusalem*, but those that dwelt in other Parts of the Land; not only the Priests & Rulers, but the *Nethinims* and Merchants, Husbandmen and Mechanicks, and Women. *Neh.* 3. 5, 12, 26, 31, 32. And we have an Account of one and another, that he repaired over against his House, *Ver.* 10. & 23, 28. and of one that repaired over against his Chamber, *Ver.* 30. So now, at this Time of the Re-building the Walls of *Jerusalem*, every one ought to promote the Work of GOD within his own Sphere, and by doing what belongs to him, in the Place in which GOD has set him: Men in a private Capacity, may repair over against their Houses: and even those that have not the Government of Families, and have but Part of an House belonging to them, should repair, each one over against his Chamber: And every one should be engaged to do the utmost that lies in his Power, labouring with the utmost Watchfulness, Care and Diligence, with united Hearts, and united Strength, and the greatest Readiness, to assist one another in this Work: as GOD's People re-built the Wall of *Jerusalem*; who were so diligent in the Work, that they wro't from break of Day, 'till the Stars appeared, and did not so much as put off their Cloaths in the Night; and wrought with that Care & Watchfulness, that with one Hand they wrought in the Work, and with the other Hand held a Weapon; besides the Guard they set to defend them; and were so well united in it, that they took Care, that one should stand ready, with a Trumpet in his Hand, that if any were assaulted in one Part, those in the other Parts, at the sound of the Trumpet, might resort to 'em, & help 'em, *Neh.* 4. at the latter End.

Great Care should be taken that the Press should be improved to no Purpose contrary to the Interest of this Work. We read that when GOD fought against *Sisera*, for the Deliverance of his oppressed Church, *They that handle the Pen of the Writer* came to the Help of the LORD in that Affair, *Jud.* 5. 14. Whatever Sort of Men in *Israel* they were that were intended, yet as the Words were Indited by a Spirit, that had a perfect View of all Events to the End of the World, and had a special Eye on this Song, to that great Event of the Deliverance of GOD's Church, in the latter Days, of which this Deliverance of *Israel* was a Type, 'tis not unlikely that they have Respect to Authors, those that should fight against the Kingdom of *Satan*, with their Pens. Those therefore that publish Pamphlets, to the Disadvantage of this Work, and tending either directly or indirectly to bring it under Suspition, and to discourage or hinder it, would do well thoroughly to consider whether this be not indeed the Work of GOD; and whether if it be, 'tis not likely that GOD will go forth as Fire, to consume all that stands in his Way, and so burn up those Pamphlets; and whether there be not Danger that the Fire that is kindled in them, will scorch the Authors.

When a People oppose CHRIST in the Work of his Holy SPIRIT, it is because it touches 'em, in something that is dear to their carnal Minds; and because they see the Tendency of it is to cross their Pride, and deprive them of the Objects of their Lusts. We should take Heed that at this Day we be not like the *Gadarenes*, who when CHRIST came into their Country, in the Exercise of his glorious Power and Grace, triumphing over a Legion of Devils, and delivering a miserable Creature, that had long been their Captive, were all alarmed, because they lost their Swine by it, and the whole Multitude of the Country came, and besought him to depart out of their Coasts: they loved their filthy Swine, better than Jesus Christ; and had rather have a Legion of Devils in their Country, with their Herd of Swine, than JESUS CHRIST without them.

This Work may be opposed, not only by directly speaking against the whole of it: Persons may say that they believe there is a good Work carried on the Country; and may sometimes bless GOD, in their publick Prayers, in general Terms, for any Awakenings or Revivals of Religion, there have lately been in any Parts of the Land; and may pray that GOD would carry on his own Work, and pour out his Spirit more and more; and yet, as I apprehend, be in the Sight of GOD, great Opposers of his Work: Some will express themselves after this Manner, that are so far from acknowledging & rejoycing in the infinite Mercy, and glorious Grace of GOD, in causing so happy a Change in the Land, that they look upon the religious State of the Country, take it in the Whole of it, much more sorrowful than it was ten Years ago; and whose Conversation, to those that are well acquainted with 'em, evidently shews, that they are more out of Humour with the State of Things, and enjoy themselves less, than they did before ever this Work began. If it be manifestly thus with us, and our Talk and Behaviour with Respect to this Work, be such as has, (tho' but) an indirect Tendency, to beget ill Thoughts and Suspicions in others concerning it, we are Opposers of the Work of God.

Instead of coming to the Help of the Lord, we shall actually fight against him, if we are abundant in insisting on, and setting forth the Blemishes of the Work, so as to manifest that we rather choose, and are more forward to take Notice of what is amiss, than what is good and glorious in the Work. Not but that the Errors that are committed, ought to be observed and lamented, and a proper Testimony born against them, and the most probable Means should be used to have 'em amended; but an insisting much upon 'em, as tho' it were a pleasing Theme, or speaking of them with more Appearance of Heat of Spirit, or with Ridicule, or an Air of Contempt, than Grief for them, has no Tendency to correct the Errors; but has a Tendency to darken the Glory of GOD's Power and Grace, appearing in the Substance of the Work, and to beget Jealousies and ill Thoughts in the Minds of others, concerning the whole of it. Whatever Errors many zealous Persons have ran into, yet if the Work, in the Substance of it, be the Work of GOD, then it is a joyful Day indeed; 'tis so in Heaven, and ought to be so, among GOD's People on Earth, especially in that Part of the Earth, where this glorious Work is carried on. 'Tis a Day of great Rejoicing with Christ himself, the good Shepherd, when he finds his Sheep that was lost, lays it on his Shoulders rejoicing, and calls together his Friends and Neighbours, saying rejoyce with me: If we therefore are CHRIST's Friends, now it should be a Day of great Rejoicing with us. If we view'd Things in a just Light, so great an Event as the Conversion of such a Multitude of Sinners, would draw and engage our Attention, much more than all the Imprudences and Irregularities that have been; our Hearts would be swallowed up with the Glory of this Event, and we should have no great Disposition to attend to any Thing else. The Imprudences and Errors of poor feeble Worms, don't hinder or prevent great Rejoicing, in the Presence of the Angels of GOD, over so many poor Sinners that have repented; and it will be an Argument of something very ill in us, if they prevent our Rejoicing.

Who loves in a Day of great Joy & Gladness, to be much insisting on those Things that are uncomfortable? Would it not be very improper, on a King's Coronation Day, to be much in taking Notice of the Blemishes of the Royal Family? Or would it be agreeable to the Bridegroom, on the Day of his Espousals, the Day of the Gladness of his Heart, to be much insisting on the Blemishes of his Bride? We have an Account, how that at the Time of that joyful Dispensation of Providence, the Restoration of the Church of *Israel*, after the *Babylonish* Captivity, and at the Time of the Feast of Tabernacles, many wept at the Faults that were found amongst the People, but were reproved for taking so much Notice of the Blemishes of that Affair, as to overlook the Cause of Rejoicing. *Neh.* 8. 9, 10, 11, 12. *And* Nehemiah, *which is the* Tirshatha, *and* Ezra *the Priest, the Scribe, and the* Levites, *that taught the People, said unto all the People, This Day is holy unto the Lord your GOD, mourn not nor weep; for all the People wept, when they heard the Words of the Law. Then he said unto them, Go your Way, eat the Fat, and drink the Sweet, and send Portions unto them, for whom nothing is prepared; for this Day is holy unto our Lord; neither be you sorry, for the Joy of the Lord is your Strength. So the* Levites *stilled all the People, saying, Hold your Peace, for the Day is holy, neither be ye grieved. And all the People went their Way, to eat, and to drink, and to send Portions, and to make great Mirth, because they had understood the Words that were declared unto them.*

GOD doubtless now expects, that all Sorts of Persons in *New-England*, Rulers, Ministers and People, high and low, rich and poor, old & young, should take great Notice of his Hand, in this mighty Work of his Grace, and should appear to acknowledge his Glory in it, and greatly to rejoice in it, every one doing his utmost, in the Place that GOD has set them in, to promote it. And GOD, according to his wonderful Patience, seems to be still waiting, to give us Opportunity, thus to acknowledge and honour him. But if we finally refuse, there is not the least Reason to expect any other, than that his awful Curse will pursue us, and that the Pourings out of his Wrath will be proportionable to the despised Out-pourings of his Spirit and Grace.

Part III

Shewing, in many Instances, wherein the Subjects, or zealous Promoters of this WORK, have been injuriously blamed.

THIS Work that has lately been carried on in the Land, is the Work of GOD, and not the Work of Man. It's beginning has not been of Man's Power or Device, and it's being carried on, depends not on our Strength or Wisdom; but yet GOD expects of all, that they should use their utmost Endeavours to promote it, and that the Hearts of all should be greatly engaged in this Affair, and that we should improve our utmost Strength in it, however vain human Strength is without the Power of GOD; and so he no less requires that we should improve our utmost Care, Wisdom and Prudence, tho' human Wisdom, of it self, be as vain as human Strength. Tho' GOD is won't to carry on such a Work, in such a Manner, as many Ways, to shew the Weakness and Vanity of Means and human Endeavours, in themselves; yet at the same Time, he carries it on in such a Manner, as to encourage Diligence and Vigilance, in the Use of proper Means and Endeavours, and to punish the Neglect of them. Therefore in our Endeavours to promote this great Work, we ought to use the utmost Caution, Vigilance and Skill, in the Measures we take in order to it. A great Affair should be managed with great Prudence: This is the most important Affair that ever *New-England* was called to be concerned in. When a People are engaged in War with a powerful and crafty Nation, it concerns them to manage an Affair of such Consequence with the utmost Discretion. Of what vast Importance then must it be, that we should be vigilant and prudent, in the Management of this great War that *New-England* now has, with so great a Host of such subtle and cruel Enemies, wherein we must either conquer or be conquered, and the Consequence of the Victory, on one Side, will be our eternal Destruction, in both Soul and Body in Hell, and on the other Side, our obtaining the Kingdom of Heaven, and reigning in it in eternal Glory? We had Need always to stand on our Watch, and to be well versed in the Art of War, and not to be ignorant of the Devices of our Enemies, and to take Heed lest by any Means we be beguiled through their Subtilty.

Tho' the Devil be strong, yet in such a War as this, he depends more on his Craft than his Strength: And the Course he has chiefly taken, from Time to Time, to clog, hinder and overthrow Revivals of Religion in the Church of GOD, has been by his subtle, deceitful Management, to beguile and mislead those that have been engaged therein; and in such a Course GOD has been pleased, in his holy and sovereign Providence, to suffer him to succeed, oftentimes, in a great

Measure, to overthrow that, which in its Beginning appear'd most hopeful and glorious. The Work that is now begun in *New-England*, is, as I have shown, eminently glorious, and if it should go on and prevail, would make *New-England* a kind of Heaven upon Earth: Is it not therefore a thousand Pities, that it should be overthrown, through wrong and improper Management, that we are led into by our subtle Adversary, in our Endeavours to promote it?

In treating of the Methods that ought to be taken to promote this Work, I would, I. Take Notice, in some Instances, wherein Fault has been found with the Conduct of those that have appear'd to be the Subjects of it, or have been zealous to promote it, (as I apprehend,) beyond just Cause. II. I would shew what Things ought to be corrected or avoided. III. I would shew positively, what ought to be done to promote this glorious Work of GOD.

I. I would take Notice of some Things, at which Offence has been taken without, or beyond just Cause.

One Thing that has been complained of, is Ministers addressing themselves, rather to the Affections of their Hearers, than to their Understandings, and striving to raise their Passions to the utmost Height, rather by a very affectionate Manner of speaking, and a great Appearance of Earnestness, in Voice and Gesture, than by clear Reasoning, and informing their Judgment: By which Means, it is objected, that the Affections are moved, without a proportionable enlightening of the Understanding.

To which I would say, I am far from thinking that it is not very profitable, for Ministers in their Preaching, to endeavour clearly and distinctly to explain the Doctrines of Religion, and unravel the Difficulties that attend them, and to confirm them with Strength of Reason and Argumentation, and also to observe some easy and clear Method and Order, in their Discourses, for the Help of the Understanding and Memory; and 'tis very probable that these Things have been of late, too much neglected, by many Ministers; yet, I believe that the Objection that is made, of Affections raised without enlightening the Understanding, is in a great Measure built on a Mistake, and confused Notions that some have about the Nature and Cause of the Affections, and the Manner in which they depend on the Understanding. All Affections are raised either by Light *in the Understanding*, or by some Error and Delusion *in the Understanding*; for all Affections do certainly arise from some Apprehension in the Understanding; and that Apprehension must either be agreeable to Truth, or else be some Mistake or Delusion; if it be an Apprehension or Notion that is agreeable to Truth, then it is *Light in the Understanding*. Therefore the Thing to be enquired into is, Whether the Apprehensions or Notions of divine and eternal Things, that are raised in Peoples Minds, by these affectionate Preachers, whence their Affections are excited, be Apprehensions that are agreeable to Truth, or whether they are Mistakes. If the former, then the Affections are raised the Way they should be, *viz.* By informing the Mind, or conveying Light to the Understanding. They go away with a wrong Notion, that think that those Preachers can't affect their Hearers, by enlightning their Understandings, that don't do it by such a distinct, and learned handling of the doctrinal Points of Religion, as depends on human Discipline, or the Strength of natural Reason, and tends to enlarge their Hearers Learning, and speculative Knowledge in Divinity. The Manner of Preaching without this, may be such as shall tend very much to set divine and eternal Things, in a right View, and to give the Hearers such Ideas and Apprehensions of them as are agreeable to Truth, and such Impressions on their Hearts, as are answerable to the real Nature of Things: And not only the Words that are spoken, but the Manner of speaking, is one Thing that has a great Tendency to this. I think an exceeding affectionate Way of Preaching about the great Things of Religion, has in it self no Tendency to beget false Apprehensions of them; but on the contrary a much greater Tendency to beget true Apprehensions of them, than a moderate, dull, indifferent Way of speaking of 'em. An Appearance of Affection and Earnestness, in the Manner of Delivery, if it be very great indeed, yet if it be agreeable to the Nature of the Subject, and ben't beyond a Proportion to its Importance, and Worthiness of Affection, and there be no Appearance of its being feigned or forced, has so much the greater Tendency to beget true Ideas or Apprehensions in the Minds of the Hearers, of the Subject spoken of, and so to enlighten the Understanding: And that for this Reason, That such a Way or Manner of speaking of these Things, does in Fact, more truly represent them, than a more cold and indifferent Way of speaking of them. If the Subject be in its own Nature, worthy of very great Affection, then a speaking of it with very great Affection, is most agreeable to the Nature of that Subject, or is the truest Representation of it, and therefore has most of a Tendency to beget true Ideas of it, in the Minds of those, to whom the Representation is made. And I don't think Ministers are to be blamed, for raising the Affections of their Hearers too high, if that which they are affected with, be only that which is worthy of Affection, and their Affections are not raised beyond a Proportion to their Importance, or Worthiness of Affection. I should think my self in the Way of my Duty, to raise the Affections of my Hearers as high as possibly I can, provided that they are affected with nothing but Truth, and with Affections that are not disagreeable to the Nature of what they are affected with. I know it has long been fashionable to despise a very earnest and pathetical Way of Preaching; And they, and they only have been valued as Preachers, that have shown the greatest Extent of Learning, and Strength of Reason, and Correctness of Method and Language: but I humbly conceive it has been for want of Understanding, or duly considering human Nature, that such Preaching has been tho't to have the greatest Tendency to answer the Ends of Preaching; and the Experience of the present and past Ages abundently confirms the same. Tho', as I said before, Clearness of Distinction & Illustration, & Strength of Reason, and a good Method, in the doctrinal Handling of the Truths of Religion, is many Ways needful and profitable, and not to be neglected, yet an Increase in speculative Knowledge in Divinity, is not what is so much needed by our People, as something else. Men may abound in this Sort of Light and have no Heat: How much has there been of this Sort of Knowledge, in the Christian World, in this Age? Was there ever an Age, wherein Strength and Penetration of Reason, Extent of Learning, Exactness of Distinction, Correctness of Style, and Clearness of Expression, did so abound? And yet was there ever an Age, wherein there has been so little Sense of the Evil of Sin, so little Love to GOD, heavenly Mindedness, and Holiness of Life, among the Professors of the true Religion? Our People don't so much need to have their Heads stored, as to have their Hearts touched;

and they stand in the greatest Need of that Sort of Preaching, that has the greatest Tendency to do this.

Those Texts, Isai. 58. 1. *Cry aloud, spare not, lift up thy Voice like a Trumpet, and shew my People their Transgression, and the House of* Jacob *their Sins.* And Ezek. 6. 11. *Thus saith the Lord God, smite with thine Hand, and stamp with thy Foot, and say, alass, for all the evil Abominations of the House of* Israel! I say these Texts, (however the Use that some have made of them has been laughed at,) will fully justify, a great Degree of *Pathos*, and Manifestation of Zeal & Fervency in preaching the Word of GOD: They may indeed be abused, to justify that which would be odd and unnatural, amongst us, not making due Allowance for Difference of Manners and Custom, in different Ages and Nations; but let us interpret them how we will, they at least imply, that a most affectionate and earnest Manner of Delivery, in many Cases, becomes a Preacher of GOD's Word.

Preaching of the Word of GOD, is commonly spoken of in Scripture, in such Expressions, as seem to import a loud and earnest Speaking; as in Isai. 40. 2. *Speak ye comfortably to* Jerusalem, *and cry unto her, that her Iniquity is pardoned.* And Ver. 3. *The Voice of him that crieth in the Wilderness, prepare ye the Way of the Lord,*—Verse 6. *The Voice said Cry: And he said, what shall I cry? All Flesh is Grass, and all the Goodliness thereof, as the Flower of the Field.* Jer. 2. 2. *Go and cry in the Ears of* Jerusalem, *saying, thus saith the Lord,* &c. Jonah 1. 2. *Arise, go to* Ninevah, *that great City, and cry against it.* Isai. 61. 1, 2. *The Spirit of the Lord God is upon me, because the Lord hath anointed me, to preach good Tidings to the Meek,—to proclaim Liberty to the Captives, and the opening of the Prison to them that are bound, to proclaim the acceptable Year of the Lord, and the Year of Vengeance of our God.* Isai. 62. 11. *Behold, the Lord hath proclaimed unto the End of the World, say ye to the Daughter of* Zion, *behold thy Salvation cometh* &c. Rom. 10. 18. *Their Sound went into all the Earth, and their Words to the End of the World.* Jer. 11. 6. *Proclaim all these Words in the Cities of* Judah, *& in the Streets of* Jerusalem, *saying, Hear ye the Words of this Covenant, and do them.* So Chap. 19. 2. *& 7. 2.* Prov. 8. 1. *Doth not Wisdom cry, and Understanding put forth her Voice?* Ver. 3, 4. *She crieth at the Gates, at the Entry of the City, at the coming in at the Doors; unto you, O Men, I call, and my Voice is to the Sons* *of Men!* And Chap. 1. 20. *Wisdom crieth without, she uttereth her Voice in the Streets.* Chap. 9. 3. *She hath sent forth her Maidens, she crieth upon the high Places of the City.* John 7. 37. *In the last Day, that great Day of the Feast,* Jesus *stood and cried, saying, if any Man thirst, let him come unto me and drink.*

It seems to be foretold, that the Gospel should be especially preached in a loud and earnest Manner, at the Introduction of the Prosperous State of Religion, in the latter Days. Isai. 40. 9. *O* Zion, *that bringeth good Tidings, get thee up into the high Mountain! O* Jerusalem, *that bringeth good Tidings, lift up thy Voice with Strength! lift up, and be not afraid! Say unto the Cities of* Judah, *Behold your God!* Isai. 52. 7, 8. *How beautiful upon the Mountains, are the Feet of him that bringeth good Tidings!— Thy Watchmen shall lift up the Voice.—*Isai. 27. 13. *And it shall come to pass, in that Day, that the great Trumpet shall be blown, and they shall come which were ready to perish.—*And this will be one Way, that the Church of God will cry at that Time, like a travailing Woman, when CHRIST mystical is going to be brought forth; as Rev. 12. at the Beginning. It will be by Ministers, that are her Mouth: And it will be this Way, that CHRIST will then cry like a travailing Woman, as in Isai. 42. 14. *I have long Time holden my Peace: I have been still, and refrained my self; now will I cry, like a travailing Woman.* CHRIST cries by his Ministers, and the Church cries by her Officers. And 'tis worthy to be noted, that the Word commonly used in the New-Testament, that we translate *preach,* properly signifies to *proclaim aloud like a Crier.*

Another Thing that some Ministers have been greatly blamed for, and I think unjustly, is speaking Terror to them, that are already under great Terrors, instead of comforting them. Indeed, if Ministers in such a Case, go about to terrify Persons with that which is not true, or to affright 'em by representing their Case worse than it is, or in any respect otherwise than it is, they are to be condemned; but if they terrify 'em only by still holding forth more Light to them, and giving them to understand more of the Truth of their Case, they are altogether to be justified. When Sinners Consciences are greatly awaken'd by the Spirit of GOD, it is by Light imparted to the Conscience, enabling them to see their Case to be, in some Measure, as it is; and if more Light be let in, it will terrify 'em still more: but

Ministers are not therefore to be blamed that they endeavour
to hold forth more Light to the Conscience, and don't rather
alleviate the Pain they are under, by intercepting and obstruct-
ing that Light that shines already. To say any Thing to those
who have never believed in the LORD JESUS CHRIST, to represent their Case any otherwise than exceeding terrible, is not to
preach the Word of GOD to 'em; for the Word of GOD reveals
nothing but Truth, but this is to delude them. Why should we
be afraid to let Persons, that are in an infinitely miserable Condition, know the Truth, or bring 'em into the Light, for fear it
should terrify them? 'Tis Light that must convert them, if ever
they are converted. The more we bring Sinners into the Light,
while they are miserable, and the Light is terrible to them, the
more likely it is, that by and by, the Light will be joyful to
them. The Ease, Peace & Comfort, that natural Men enjoy,
have their Foundation in Darkness and Blindness; therefore as
that Darkness vanishes, and Light comes in, their Peace vanishes, and they are terrified: but that is no good Argument,
why we should endeavour to hold their Darkness, that we may
uphold their Comfort. The Truth is, that as long as Men reject
CHRIST, and don't savingly believe in him, however they may
be awaken'd, and however strict, and consciencious, and laborious they may be in Religion, they have the Wrath of GOD
abiding on them, they are his Enemies, and the Children of
the Devil, (as the Scripture calls all that ben't savingly converted, *Mat.* 13. 38. 1 *John* 3. 10.) and 'tis uncertain whether
they shall ever obtain Mercy: GOD is under no Obligation to
shew 'em Mercy, nor will he be, if they fast and pray and cry
never so much; and they are then especially provoking GOD,
under those Terrors, that they stand it out against CHRIST, and
won't accept of an offered SAVIOUR, tho' they see so much
Need of him: And seeing this is the Truth, they should be told
so, that they may be sensible what their Case indeed is.

To blame a Minister, for thus declaring the Truth to those
who are under Awakenings, and not immediately administring
Comfort to them, is like blaming a Surgeon, because when he
has begun to thrust in his Lance, whereby he has already put
his Patient to great Pain, and he shrinks and cries out with
Anguish, he is so cruel that he won't stay his Hand, but goes
on, to thrust it in further, 'till he comes to the Core of the

Wound. Such a compassionate Physician, who as soon as his Patient began to flinch, should withdraw his Hand, and go about immediately to apply a Plaister, to skin over the Wound, and leave the Core untouch'd, would be one that would heal the Hurt slightly, crying Peace, Peace, when there is no Peace.

Indeed something else besides Terror, is to be preached to them, whose Consciences are awaken'd: The Gospel is to be preached to them: They are to be told that there is a SAVIOUR provided, that is excellent and glorious, who has shed his precious Blood for Sinners, and is every Way sufficient to save 'em, that stands ready to receive 'em, if they will heartily embrace him; for this is also the Truth, as well as that they now are in an infinitely dreadful Condition: This is the Word of GOD. Sinners at the same Time that they are told how miserable their Case is, should be earnestly invited to come and accept of a SAVIOUR, and yield their Hearts unto him, with all the winning, encouraging Arguments, for 'em so to do, that the Gospel affords: but this is to induce 'em to escape from the Misery of the Condition that they are now in: but not to make 'em think their present Condition less miserable than it is, or at all to abate their Uneasiness and Distress, while they are in it; that would be the Way to quiet them, and fasten them in it, and not to excite 'em to fly from it. Comfort, in one Sense, is to be held forth, to Sinners under Awakenings of Conscience, i.e. Comfort is to be offered to 'em in CHRIST, on Condition of their flying *from their present miserable State,* to Him: but Comfort is not to be administred to 'em, *in their present State,* as any Thing that they have now any Title to, while out of CHRIST. No Comfort is to be administred to 'em, from any Thing in *them,* any of their Qualifications, Prayers or other Performances, past, present or future; but Ministers should, in such Cases, strive to their utmost to take all such Comforts from 'em, tho' it greatly increases their Terror. A Person that sees himself ready to sink into Hell, is ready to strive, some Way or other, to lay GOD under some Obligation to him; but he is to be beat off from every Thing of that Nature, tho' it greatly increases his Terror, to see himself wholly destitute, on every Side, of any Refuge, or any Thing of his own to lay hold of; as a Man that sees himself in Danger of drowning, is in Terror, and endeavours to catch hold on every Twig within his Reach, and he that pulls away those Twigs from him, increases his Terror; yet if they are insufficient to save him, and by being in his Way, prevent his looking to that which will save him, to pull them away, is necessary to save his Life.

If Sinners are in any Distress, from any Error that they embrace, or Mistake they are under, that is to be removed: For Instance, if they are in Terror, from an Apprehension that they have committed the unpardonable Sin, or that those Things have happen'd to 'em that are certain Signs of Reprobation, or any other Delusion, such Terrors have no Tendency to do them any Good; for these Terrors are from Temptation, and not from Conviction: But that Terror which arises from Conviction, or a Sight of Truth, is to be increased; for those that are most awakened, have great remaining Stupidity, they have a Sense of but little of that which is; and 'tis from remaining Blindness and Darkness, that they see no more; and that remaining Blindness is a Disease, that we ought to endeavour to remove. I am not afraid to tell Sinners, that are most sensible of their Misery, that their Case is indeed as miserable as they think it to be, and a thousand Times more so; for this is the Truth. Some may be ready to say that tho' it be the Truth, yet the Truth is not to be spoken at all Times, and seems not to be seasonable then: But it seems to me, such Truth is never more seasonable than at such a Time, when Christ is beginning to open the Eyes of Conscience. Ministers ought to act as Co-Workers with him; to take that Opportunity, and to the utmost to improve that Advantage, and strike while the Iron is hot, and when the Light has begun to shine, then to remove all Obstacles, and use all proper Means, that it may come in more fully, and the Work be done thoroughly then. And Experience abundantly shews, that to take this Course, is not of an hurtful Tendency, but very much the contrary: I have seen, in very many Instances, the happy Effects of it, and oftentimes a very speedy happy Issue, and never knew any ill Consequence, in Case of real Conviction, and when Distress has been only from thence.

I know of but one Case, wherein the Truth ought to be witheld from Sinners in Distress of Conscience, and that is the Case of Melancholy: And 'tis not to be witheld from them then, because the Truth tends to do 'em hurt, but because if we speak the Truth to them, sometimes they will be deceived,

and led into Error by it, through that strange Disposition
there is in them, to take Things wrong. So that, that which as
it is spoken, is Truth, as it is heard and received, and applied by
them, is Falshood; as it will be, unless the Truth be spoken
with Abundance of Caution and Prudence, and Consideration
of their Disposition and Circumstances. But the most awful
Truths of GOD's Word, ought not to be witheld from public
Congregations, because it may happen that some such melancholick Persons may be in it: any more, than the Bible is to be
witheld from the Christian World, because it is manifest that
there are a great many melancholick Persons in Christendom,
that exceedingly abuse the awful Things contained in the
Scripture, to their own wounding. Nor do I think that to be of
Weight, which is made use of by some, as a great and dreadful
Objection against the terrifying Preaching that has of late been
in *New-England, viz.* That there have been some Instances of
melancholick Persons that have so abused it, that the Issue has
been the Murder of themselves. The Objection from hence is
no stronger against awakening Preaching, than it is against the
Bible it self: There are Hundreds, and probably Thousands of
Instances, might be produced, of Persons that have murdered
themselves, under religious Melancholy: These Murders, probably never would have been, if it had not been for the Bible, or
if the World had remain'd in a State of heathenish Darkness.
The Bible has not only been the Occasion of these sad Effects,
but of Thousands, and I suppose Millions, of other cruel Murders, that have been committed, in the Persecutions that have
been raised, that never would have been, if it had not been for
the Bible: Many whole Countrys have been, as it were deluged
with innocent Blood, which would not have been, if the Gospel never had been preached in the World. 'Tis not a good
Objection against any Kind of Preaching, that some Men
abuse it greatly to their Hurt. It has been acknowledged by all
Divines, as a Thing common in all Ages, and all Christian
Countrys, that a very great Part of those that set under the
Gospel, do so abuse it, that it only proves an Occasion of their
far more aggravated Damnation, and so of Men's eternally
murdering their Souls; which is an Effect infinitely more terrible than the Murder of their Bodies. 'Tis as unjust to lay the
Blame of these Self-Murders, to those Ministers who have

declared the awful Truths of God's Word, in the most lively and affecting Manner they were capable of, as it would be to lay the Blame of hardening Men's Hearts, and blinding their Eyes, and their more dreadful eternal Damnation, to the Prophet *Isaiah*, or JESUS CHRIST, because this was the Consequence of their Preaching, with respect to many of their Hearers. *Isai*. 6. 10. *Joh*. 9. 39. *Math*. 13. 14. Tho' a very few have abused the awakening Preaching that has lately been, to so sad an Effect as to be the Cause of their own temporal Death; yet it may be, to one such Instance, there have been Hundreds, yea Thousands, that have been saved, by this Means, from eternal Death.

What has more especially given Offence to many, and raised a loud Cry against some Preachers, as tho' their Conduct were intolerable, is their frighting poor innocent Children, with talk of Hell-Fire, and eternal Damnation. But if those that complain so loudly of this, really believe, what is the general Profession of the Country, *viz*. That all are by Nature the Children of Wrath, and Heirs of Hell; and that every one that has not been born again, whether he be young or old, is exposed, every Moment, to eternal Destruction, under the Wrath of Almighty God; I say, if they really believe this, then such a Complaint and Cry as this, bewrays a great deal of Weakness and Inconsideration. As innocent as Children seem to be to us, yet, if they are out of Christ, they are not so in GOD's Sight, but are young Vipers, and are infinitely more hateful than Vipers, and are in a most miserable Condition, as well as grown Persons; and they are naturally very senseless and stupid, being *born as the wild Asses Colt*, and need much to awaken them. Why should we conceal the Truth from them? Will those Children that have been dealt tenderly with, in this Respect, and lived and died insensible of their Misery, 'till they come to feel it in Hell, ever thank Parents, and others, for their Tenderness, in not letting them know what they were in Danger of. If Parents Love towards their Children was not blind, it would affect 'em much more to see their Children, every Day, exposed to eternal Burnings, and yet senseless, than to see 'em suffer the Distress of that Awakening, that is necessary in Order to their Escape from them, & that tends to their being eternally happy, as the Children of GOD. A Child that has a dangerous Wound, may need the painful Lance, as well as grown Persons; and that would be a foolish Pity, in such a Case, that should hold back the Lance, and throw away the Life.—I have seen the happy Effects of dealing plainly, and thoroughly with Children, in the Concerns of their Souls, without sparing them at all, in many Instances; and never knew any ill Consequence of it, in any one Instance.

Another Thing, that a great deal has been said against, is having so frequent religious Meetings, and spending so much Time in Religion. And indeed, there are none of the Externals of Religion, but what are capable of Excess: And I believe it is true, that there has not been a due Proportion observed in Religion of late. We have placed Religion too much in the external Duties of the first Table; we have abounded in religious Meetings, and in praying, reading, hearing, singing, and religious Conference; and there has not been a proportionable Increase of Zeal for Deeds of Charity, and other Duties of the second Table; (tho' it must be acknowledged that they are also much increased.) But yet it appears to me, that this Objection of Persons spending too much Time in Religion, has been in the general groundless. Tho' worldly Business must be done, and Persons ought not to neglect the Business of their particular Callings, yet 'tis to the Honour of GOD, that a People should be so much in outward Acts of Religion, as to carry in it, a visible, publick Appearance, of a great Engagedness of Mind in it, as the main Business of Life: And especially is it fit, that at such an extraordinary Time, when GOD appears unusually present with a People, in wonderful Works of Power and Mercy, that they should spend more Time than usual in religious Exercises, to put Honour upon that GOD that is then extraordinarily present, and to seek his Face; as it was with the Christian Church in *Jerusalem*, on Occasion of that extraordinary pouring out of the Spirit, soon after CHRIST's Ascension. Act. 2. 46. *And they continued daily, with one Accord, in the Temple, and breaking Bread, from House to House.* And so it was at *Ephesus*, at a Time of great Out-pouring of the Spirit there; the Christians there attended publick religious Exercises, every Day, for two Years together, Act. 19. 8, 9, 10. *And he went into the Synagogue, and spake boldly, for the Space of three Months, disputing and persuading the Things concerning the Kingdom of God: But when divers were harden'd, and believed not; but spake Evil of that Way, before the Multitude, he departed from them, and separated the Disciples, disputing daily, in the School of one* Tyrannus; *and this continued, by the Space of two Years; so that all they which dwelt in* Asia, *hear'd the Word of the Lord, both* Jews *and* Greeks. And as to the grand Objection, of *six Days shalt thou Labour*, all that can be understood by it, and all that the very Objectors themselves understand by it, is that we *may* follow our secular Labours in those six Days, that are not the Sabbath, and *ought* to be diligent in them: Not but that sometimes, we may turn from them, even within those six Days, to keep a Day of Fasting, or Thanksgiving, or to attend a Lecture; and that more frequently or rarely, as GOD's Providence, and the State of Things, shall call us, according to the best Judgment of our Discretion.

Tho' secular Business, as I said before, ought not to be neglected, yet I can't see how it can be maintain'd, that Religion ought not to be attended, so as in the least to injure our temporal Affairs, on any other Principles than those of Infidelity. None objects against injuring one temporal Affair for the Sake of another temporal Affair of much greater Importance; and therefore, if eternal Things are as real as temporal Things, and are indeed of infinitely greater Importance; then why may we not voluntarily suffer, in some Measure, in our temporal Concerns, while we are seeking eternal Riches, and immortal Glory? 'Tis looked upon no Way improper for a whole Nation, to spend considerable Time, and much of their outward Substance, on some extraordinary temporal Occasions, for the Sake only of the Ceremonies of a public Rejoicing; and it would be thought dishonourable to be very exact, about what we spend, or careful lest we injure our Estates, on such an Occasion: and why should we be exact only with Almighty GOD, so that it should be a Crime to be otherwise than scrupulously careful, lest we injure ourselves in our temporal Interest, to put Honour upon Him, and seek our own eternal Happiness? We should take Heed that none of us be in any wise like *Judas*, who greatly complain'd of needless Expence, and Waste of outward Substance, to put Honour upon Christ, when *Mary* broke her Box, and poured the precious Ointment on his Head: He had Indignation within himself on that Account, and crys out, *Why was this Waste of the Ointment made? For it might have been sold for more than three*

Hundred Pence, and have been given to the Poor. Mark 14. 3, 4, 5, *&c.* And *Joh.* 12. 4, 5, *&c.*

And besides, if the Matter be justly considered and examined, I believe it will be found, that the Country has lost no Time from their temporal Affairs, by the late Revival of Religion, but have rather gained Time; and that more Time has been saved from Frolicking, & Tavern-haunting, Idleness, unprofitable Visits, vain Talk, fruitless Pastimes, and needless Diversions, that has lately been spent in extraordinary Religion; and probably five Times as much has been saved in Persons Estates, at the Tavern, and in their Apparel, as has been spent by religious Meetings.

The great Complaint that is made against so much Time spent in Religion, can't be in general from a real Concern that GOD may be honoured, and his Will done, and the best Good of Men promoted; as is very manifest from this, that now there is a much more earnest and zealous Out-cry made in the Country, against this extraordinary Religion, than was before, against so much Time spent in Tavern-haunting, vain Company-keeping, Night-walking, & other Things, which wasted both our Time and Substance, and injured our moral Vertue.

The frequent Preaching that has lately been, has in a particular Manner been objected against as unprofitable and prejudicial. 'Tis objected that when Sermons are heard so very often, one Sermon tends to thrust out another; so that Persons loose the Benefit of all: They say, two or three Sermons in a Week is as much as they can remember and digest. Such Objections against frequent Preaching, if they ben't from an Enmity against Religion, are for Want of duly considering the Way that Sermons usually profit an Auditory. The main Benefit that is obtain'd by Preaching, is by Impression made upon the Mind in the Time of it, and not by any Effect that arises afterwards by a Remembrance of what was delivered. And tho' an after Remembrance of what was heard in a Sermon, is oftentimes very profitable; yet, for the most Part, that Remembrance is from an Impression the Words made on the Heart in the Time of it; and the Memory profits, as it renews and increases that Impression; and a frequent inculcating the more important Things of Religion in preaching, has no Tendency to rase out such Impressions, but to increase them, and fix them deeper and deeper in the Mind, as is found by Experience. It never used to be objected against, that Persons, upon the Sabbath, after they have heard two Sermons that Day, should go home, and spend the remaining Part of the Sabbath in reading the Scriptures, and printed Sermons; which, in Proportion as it has a Tendency to affect the Mind at all, has as much of a Tendency to drive out what they have heard, as if they heard another Sermon preach'd. It seems to have been the Practice of the Apostles to preach every Day, in Places where they went; yea tho' sometimes they continued long in one Place, *Acts* 2. 42. & 46. *Acts* 19. 8, 9, 10. They did not avoid preaching one Day, for Fear they should thrust out of the Minds of their Hearers what they had delivered the Day before; nor did Christians avoid going every Day to hear, for Fear of any such bad Effect, as is evident by *Acts* 2. 42, 46.

There are some Things in Scripture that seem to signify as much, as that there should be Preaching in an extraordinary Frequency, at the Time when God should be about to introduce that flourishing State of Religion that should be in the latter Days; as that in Isai. 62. at the Beginning: *For* Zion*'s Sake will I not hold my Peace, for* Jerusalem*'s Sake, I will not rest; until the Righteousness thereof go forth as Brightness, and the Salvation thereof, as a Lamp that burneth: And the Gentiles shall see thy Righteousness, and all Kings thy Glory.* And Ver. 5, 6. *For as a young Man marrieth a Virgin, so shall thy Sons marry thee; & as the Bridegroom rejoiceth over the Bride, so shall thy God rejoice over thee. I have set Watchmen upon thy Walls, O* Jerusalem, *which shall never hold their Peace, Day nor Night.* The Destruction of the City of *Jericho*, is evidently, in all its Circumstances, intended by GOD, as a great Type of the Overthrow of Satan's Kingdom; the Priests blowing with Trumpets at that Time, represents Ministers preaching the Gospel; the People compassed the City seven Days, the Priests blowing the Trumpets; but when the Day was come that the Walls of the City were to fall, the Priests were more frequent and abundant in blowing their Trumpets; there was as much done in one Day then, as had been done in seven Days before; they compassed the City seven Times that Day, blowing their Trumpets, 'till at Length it come to one long and perpetual Blast, and then the Walls of the City fell down flat. The extraordinary Preaching that shall be at the Beginning of that glorious Jubilee of the Church, is represented by the extraordinary Sounding of Trumpets, throughout the Land of *Canaan*, at the Beginning of the Year of Jubilee; and by the reading of the Law, before all *Israel*, in the Year of Release, at the Feast of Tabernacles. And the Crowing of the Cock, at break of Day, which brought *Peter* to Repentance, seems to me to be intended to signify, the Awakening of GOD's Church out of their Lethergy, wherein they had denied their Lord, by the extraordinary Preaching of the Gospel, that shall be at the Dawning of the Day of the Churches Light and Glory. And there seems at this Day to be an uncommon Hand of divine Providence, in animating, enabling, and upholding some Ministers, in such abundant Labours.

Another Thing, wherein I think some Ministers have been injured, is in being very much blamed for making so much of Out-Cries, Faintings, and other bodily Effects; speaking of them as Tokens of the Presence of GOD, and Arguments of the Success of Preaching; seeming to strive to their utmost to bring a Congregation to that pass, and seeming to rejoyce in it, yea even blessing GOD for it, when they see these Effects.

Concerning this I would observe, in the *first* Place, That there are many Things, with Respect to Cryings out, Falling down &c. that are charged on Ministers, that they are not guilty of. Some would have it, that they speak of these Things as certain Evidences of a Work of the SPIRIT of GOD on the Hearts of their Hearers, or that they esteem these bodily Effects themselves to be the Work of GOD, as tho' the Spirit of GOD took hold of, and agitated the Bodies of Men; and some are charged with making these Things essential, and supposing that Persons can't be converted without them; whereas I never yet could see the Person that held either of these Things.

But for speaking of such Effects as probable Tokens of GOD's Presence, and Arguments of the Success of Preaching, it seems to me they are not to be blamed; because I think they are so indeed: and therefore when I see them excited by preaching the important Truths of GOD's Word, urged and inforced by proper Arguments and Motives, or are consequent on other Means that are good, I don't scruple to speak of them, and to rejoyce in them, and bless GOD for them as such; and that for this, (as I think) good Reason, *viz*. That from

Time to Time, upon proper Inquiry and Examination, and Observation of the Consequence and Fruits, I have found that there are all Evidences that the Persons in whom these Effects appear, are under the Influences of GOD's Spirit, in such Cases. Cryings out, in such a Manner, and with such Circumstances, as I have seen them from Time to Time, is as much an Evidence to me, of the general Cause it proceeds from, as Language: I have learned the Meaning of it, the same Way that Persons learn the Meaning of Language, *viz.* by Use and Experience. I confess that when I see a great Crying out in a Congregation, in the Manner that I have seen it, when those Things are held forth to 'em that are worthy of their being greatly affected by, I rejoyce in it, much more than meerly in an Appearance of solemn Attention, and a Shew of Affection by Weeping; and that because when there have been those Out-cries, I have found from Time to Time, a much greater and more excellent Effect. To rejoyce that the Work of GOD is carried on calmly, without much ado, is in Effect to rejoyce that 'tis carried on with less Power, or that there is not so much of the Influence of GOD's Spirit: for tho' the Degree of the Influence of the Spirit of GOD, on *particular Persons*, is by no Means to be judged of by the Degree of external Appearances, because of the different Constitution, Tempers, and Circumstances of Men; yet if there be a very powerful Influence of the Spirit of GOD on a mix'd Multitude, it will cause some Way or other, a great visible Commotion.

And as to Ministers aiming at such Effects, and striving by all Means to bring a Congregation to that Pass, that there should be such an Uproar among them; I suppose none aim at it any otherwise, than as they strive to raise the Affections of their Hearers to such an Height, as very often appears in these Effects; and if it be so, that those Affections are commonly good, and it be found by Experience that such a Degree of them commonly has a good Effect, I think they are to be justified in so doing.

Again, some Ministers have been blam'd for keeping Persons together, that have been under great Affections, which have appeared in such extraordinary outward Manifestations. Many think this promotes Confusion, that Persons in such Circumstances do but discompose each others Minds, and disturb the Minds of others; and that therefore 'tis best they should be dispersed, and that when any in a Congregation are strongly seized, that they can't forbear outward Manifestations of it, they should be removed that others Minds may not be diverted.

But I can't but think that those that thus object go upon quite wrong Notions of Things: For tho' Persons ought to take Heed that they don't make an Ado without Necessity; for this will be the Way in Time, to have such Appearances lose all their Effect; yet the unavoidable Manifestations of strong religious Affections tend to an happy Influence on the Minds of By-standers, and are found by Experience to have an excellent and durable Effect; and so to contrive and order Things, that others may have Opportunity and Advantage to observe them, has been found to be blessed, as a great Means to promote the Work of GOD; and to prevent their being in the Way of Observation, is to prevent the Effect of that, which GOD makes use of, as a principal Means of carrying on his Work, at such an extraordinary Time, *viz.* Example; which is often spoken of in Scripture, as one of the chief Means by which GOD would carry on his Work, in the Time of the Prosperity of Religion in the latter Days: I have mentioned some Texts already to this Purpose, in what I published before, of *the Marks of a Work of the true Spirit*; but would here mention some others. In *Zech.* 9. 15, 16. Those that in the latter Days should be fill'd, in an extraordinary Manner with the Holy Spirit, so as to appear in outward Manifestations, and making a Noise, are spoken of as those that GOD, in these uncommon circumstances, will set up to the View of others, as a Prize or Ensign, by their Example and the Excellency of their Attainments, to animate and draw others, as Men gather about an Ensign, and run for a Prize, a Crown and precious Jewels, set up in their View. The Words are; *And they shall drink, and make a Noise, as thro' Wine; and they shall be filled like Bowls, and as the Corners of the Altar: and the Lord their God shall save them, in that Day, as the Flock of his People; for they shall be as the Stones of a Crown, lifted up as an Ensign upon his Land.* (But I shall have Occasion to say something more of this Scripture afterwards.) Those that make the Objection I am upon, instead of suffering this Prize or Ensign to be in publick View, are for having it removed, and hid in some Corner. To the like Purpose is that, Isai. 62. 3. *Thou shalt be a Crown of Glory, in the Hand of the Lord, and a royal*

Diadem, in the Hand of thy God. Here it is observable, that 'tis not said, thou shalt be a Crown *upon the Head*, but *in the Hand* of the Lord. i.e. held forth, in thy Beauty and Excellency, as a Prize, to be bestowed upon others that shall behold thee, and be animated by the Brightness and Lustre which GOD shall endow thee with. The great Influence of the Example of GOD's People, in their bright and excellent Attainments, to propagate Religion, in those Days, is farther signified, in Isai. 60. 3. *And the Gentiles shall come to thy Light, and Kings to the Brightness of thy rising.* With Ver. 22. *A little One shall become a Thousand, and a small One a strong Nation.* And Zech. 10. 8, 9. *And they shall increase, as they have increased; and I will sow them among the People.* And Hos. 2. 23. *And I will sow her unto me in the Earth.* So Jer. 31. 27.

Another Thing that gives great Disgust to many, is the Disposition that Persons shew, under great Affections, to speak so much, and, with such Earnestness and Vehemence, to be setting forth the Greatness and Wonderfulness and Importance of divine & eternal Things; and to be so passionately warning, inviting and intreating others.

Concerning which I would say, That I am far from thinking that such a Disposition should be wholly without any Limits or Regulation, (as I shall more particularly shew afterwards;) and I believe some have erred, in setting no Bounds, and indulging and encouraging this Disposition without any kind of Restraint or Direction: But yet, it seems to me, that such a Disposition in general, is what both Reason & Scripture will justify. Those that are offended at such Things, as tho' they were unreasonable, are not just: upon Examination it will probably be found, that they have one Rule of reasoning about temporal Things, and another about spiritual Things. They won't at all wonder, if a Person on some very great and affecting Occasion, of extraordinary Danger or great Joy, that eminently and immediately concerns him and others, is disposed to speak much, and with great Earnestness, especially to those to whom he is united, in the Bonds of dear Affection, and great Concern for their Good. And therefore, if they were just, why would not they allow it in spiritual Things? and much *more* in them, agreeably to the vastly greater Importance, and more affecting Nature of spiritual Things, and the Concern which true Religion causes in Mens Minds for the Good of others, and the Disposition it gives and excites to speak GOD's Praises, to shew forth his infinite Glory, and talk of all his glorious Perfections and Works?

That a very great Sense, of the right Kind, of the Importance of the Things of Religion, and the Danger Sinners are in, should sometimes cause an almost insuperable Disposition to speak and warn others, is agreeable to Jer. 6. 10, 11. *To whom shall I speak, and give Warning, that they may hear? Behold, their Ear is uncircumcised, and they cannot hearken: behold the Word of the Lord is unto them, a Reproach; they have no Delight in it. Therefore I am full of the Fury of the Lord; I am weary with holding in; I will pour it out upon the Children abroad, and upon the Assembly of the young Men together; for even the Husband with the Wife shall be taken, the aged, with him that is full of Days.* And that true Christians, when they come to be as it were waked out of Sleep, and to be filled with a sweet and joyful Sense of the excellent Things of Religion, by the preaching of the Gospel, or by other Means of Grace, should be disposed to be much in speaking of divine Things, tho' before they were dumb, is agreeable to what CHRIST says to his Church, Cant. 7. 9. *And the Roof of thy Mouth is like the best Wine, for my Beloved, that goeth down sweetly, causing the Lips of those that are asleep to speak.* The Roof of the Churches Mouth, is the Officers in the Church, that preach the Gospel; their Word is to CHRIST's Beloved, like the best Wine, that goes down sweetly; extraordinarily refreshing & enlivening the Saints, causing them to speak, tho' before they were mute and asleep. 'Tis said by some, that the People that are the Subjects of this Work, when they get together, talking loud and earnestly, in their pretended great Joys, several in a Room, talking at the same Time, make a Noise just like a Company of drunken Persons. On which I would observe, that it is foretold that GOD's People should do so, in that forementioned Place, *Zech.* 9. 15, 16, 17. which I shall now take more particular Notice of: the Words are as follows; *The Lord of Hosts shall defend them; and they shall devour and subdue with sling Stones; and they shall drink, and make a Noise, as through Wine, and they shall be filled like Bowls, and as the Corners of the Altar: And the Lord their God shall save them in that Day, as the Flock of his People; for they shall be as the Stones of a Crown, lifted up, as an Ensign, upon his Land: For how great is his Goodness! and how great is his Beauty! Corn shall make the young Men cheerful, and new Wine the Maids.* The Words are very remarkable: Here it is foretold, that at the Time when CHRIST shall set up an universal Kingdom upon Earth, (*Ver.* 10.) The Children of *Zion* shall drink, 'till they are filled like the Vessels of the Sanctuary: and if we would know what they shall be thus filled with, the Prophecy does, in Effect, explain it self: They shall be filled, as the Vessels of the Sanctuary that contain'd the Drink-Offering, which was Wine; and yet the Words imply, that it shall not literally be Wine that they shall drink, and be filled with, because it is said, They shall drink, and make a Noise, *as through Wine*, as if they had drank Wine: which implies that they had not literally done it; and therefore we must understand the Words, that they shall drink into that, and be filled with that, which the Wine of the Drink-Offering represented, or was a Type of, which is the Holy SPIRIT, as well as the Blood of CHRIST, that new Wine that is drank in our heavenly Father's Kingdom: They shall be filled with the Spirit, which the Apostle sets in Opposition to a being drunk with Wine, *Eph.* 5. 18. This is the new Wine spoken of, *Ver.* 17. 'Tis the same with that *best Wine*, spoken of in *Canticles, that goes down sweetly, causing the Lips of those that are asleep to speak.* 'Tis here foretold, that the Children of *Zion*, in the latter Days, should be filled with that which should make 'em cheerful, and cause 'em to make a Noise as thro' Wine, and by which these joyful happy Persons that are thus filled, shall be as the Stones of a Crown, lifted up as an Ensign upon GOD's Land, being made joyful, in the extraordinary Manifestations of the Beauty and Love of CHRIST: as it follows, *How great is his Goodness! And how great is his Beauty!* And 'tis further remarkable that 'tis here foretold, that it should be thus especially amongst young People; *Corn shall make the young Men cheerful, and new Wine the Maids.* It would be ridiculous to understand this of literal Bread and Wine: without doubt, the same spiritual Blessings are signified by Bread &

Wine here, which were represented by *Melchizedeck*'s Bread and Wine, and are signified by the Bread & Wine in the Lord's Supper. One of the marginal Readings is, *shall make the young Men to speak*; which is agreeable to that in *Canticles*, of the *best Wine's causing the Lips of those that are asleep to speak.*

We ought not to be, in any Measure, like the unbelieving *Jews*, in CHRIST's Time, who were disgusted both with crying out with Distress, and with Joy. When the poor blind Man cried out, before all the Multitude, JESUS, *thou Son of* David, *have Mercy on me*! and continued instantly thus doing, the Multitude rebuked him, and charged him that he should hold his Tongue, *Mark* 10. 46, 47, 48. and *Luke* 18. 38, 39. They looked upon it to be a very indecent Noise that he made; a Thing very ill becoming him to cause his Voice to be heard, so much, and so loud, among the Multitude. And when CHRIST made his solemn and triumphant Entry into *Jerusalem*, (which, I have before observed, was a Type of the Glory and Triumph of the latter Days,) the whole Multitude of the Disciples, of all Sorts, especially young People, began to rejoyce and praise GOD, with a loud Voice, for all the mighty Works that they had seen, saying, *Blessed be the King that cometh in the Name of the LORD! Peace in Heaven, and Glory in the highest*! The *Pharisees* said to CHRIST, *Master, Rebuke thy Disciples.* They did not understand such great Transports of Joy; it seem'd to them a very unsuitable and indecent Noise and Clamour that they made, a confused Uproar, many crying out together, as tho' they were out of their Wits; they wondered that CHRIST would tolerate it. But what says CHRIST? *I tell you, that if these should hold their Peace, the Stones would immediately cry out.* The Words seem to intimate as much, as that there was Cause enough to constrain those whose Hearts were not harder than the very Stones, to cry out, and make a Noise; which is something like that other Expression, of *causing the Lips of those that are asleep to speak.*

When many under great religious Affections, are earnestly speaking together, of divine Wonders, in various Parts of a Company, to those that are next to 'em; some attending to what one says, and others to another, there is something very beautiful in it, provided they don't speak so many as to drown each others Voices, that none can hear what any say; there is a greater and more affecting Appearance of a joint Engagedness of Heart, in the Love & Praises of GOD. And I had rather see it, than to see one speaking alone, and all attending to what he says; it has more of the Appearance of Conversation. When a Multitude meets on any Occasion of temporal Rejoycing, freely and cheerfully to converse together, they ben't won't to observe the Ceremony, of but one speaking at a Time, while all the Rest, in a formal Manner, set themselves to attend to what he says; that would spoil all Conversation, and turn it into the Formality of set Speeches, and the solemnity of Preaching. It is better for Lay-Persons, when they speak one to another of the Things of GOD, when they meet together, to speak after the Manner of Christian Conversation, than to observe the Formality of but one speaking at a Time, the whole Multitude silently and solemnly attending to what he says; which would carry in it too much of the Air, of the Authority and Solemnity of Preaching. What the Apostle says, 1 Cor. 14. 29, 30, 31. *Let the Prophets speak, two, or three, and let the other judge: if any Thing be revealed to another that sitteth by, let the first hold his Peace: for ye may all prophecy, one by one, that all may learn, and all may be comforted*, I say, this don't reach this Case; because what the Apostle is speaking of, is the solemnity of their religious Exercises, in publick Worship, and Persons speaking in the Church, by immediate Inspiration, and in the Use of the Gift of Prophecy, or some Gift of Inspiration, in the Exercise of which, they acted as extraordinary Ministers of CHRIST.

Another Thing that some have found Fault with, is abounding so much in singing, in religious Meetings. Objecting against such a Thing as this, seems to arise from a Suspicion already established of this Work: They doubt of the pretended extraordinary Love and Joys that attend this Work, and so find Fault with the Manifestations of them. If they thought Persons were truly the Subjects of an extraordinary Degree of divine Love, and heavenly rejoycing in GOD, I suppose they would not wonder at their having a Disposition to be much in Praise. They won't object against the Saints & Angels in Heaven singing Praises and *Hallelujahs* to GOD, without ceasing, Day or Night; and therefore doubtless will allow that the more the Saints on Earth are like 'em in their Dispositions, the more they will be disposed to do like 'em. They will readily own that the generality of Christians have great Reason to be ashamed that they have so little Thankfulness, and are no more in praising GOD, whom they have such infinite Cause to Praise. And why therefore, should Christians be found Fault with, for shewing a Disposition to be much in praising GOD, and manifesting a Delight in that heavenly Exercise? To complain of this, is to be too much like the *Pharisees*, who were disgusted when the Multitude of the Disciples began to rejoyce, and, with loud Voices, to praise GOD, and cry *Hosanna*, when CHRIST was en-tring into *Jerusalem*.

There are many Things in Scripture, that seem to intimate that praising GOD, both in Speeches and Songs, will be what the Church of GOD will very much abound in, in the ap-proaching glorious Day. So on the seventh Day of compassing the Walls of *Jericho*, when the Priests blew with the Trumpets, in an extraordinary Manner, the People shouted with a great Shout, and the Wall of the City fell down flat. So the Ark was brought back from its Banishment, with extraordinary shout-ing and singing of the whole Congregation of *Israel*. And the Places in the Prophecies of Scripture, that signify that the Church of GOD, in that glorious *Jubilee* that is foretold, shall greatly abound in singing & shouting forth the Praises of GOD, are too many to be mentioned. And there will be Cause enough for it: I believe it will be a Time wherein both Heaven and Earth, will be much more full of Joy and Praise, than ever they were before.

But what is more especially found Fault with in the singing that is now practised, is making use of Hymns of humane Composure. And I am far from thinking that the Book of Psalms should be thrown by in our publick Worship, but that it should always be used in the Christian Church, to the End of the World: But I know of no Obligation we are under to confine our selves to it. I can find no Command or Rule of GOD's Word, that does any more confine us to the Words of the Scripture in our singing, than it does in our praying; we speak to GOD in both: and I can see no Reason why we should limit our selves to such particular Forms of Words, that we find in the Bible, in speaking to him by Way of Praise, in Metre, and with Musick, than when we speak to him in Prose, by Way of

Prayer and Supplication. And 'tis really needful that we should have some other Songs besides the Psalms of *David*: 'Tis unreasonable to suppose that the Christian Church, should for ever, and even in Times of her greatest Light in her Praises of GOD & the Lamb, be confined only to the Words of the old Testament, wherein all the greatest and most glorious Things of the Gospel, that are infinitely the greatest Subjects of her Praise, are spoken of under a Veil, and not so much as the Name of our glorious Redeemer, ever mention'd, but in some dark Figure, or as hid under the Name of some Type. And as to our making use of the Words of others, and not those that are conceived by our selves, 'tis no more than we do in all our publick Prayers; the whole worshipping Assembly, excepting one only, makes use of the Words that are conceived by him that speaks for the rest.

Another Thing that many have disliked, is the religious Meetings of Children, to read and pray together, and perform religious Exercises by themselves. What is objected is Childrens want of that Knowledge and Discretion, that is requisite, in order to a decent and profitable Management of religious Exercises. But it appears to me the Objection is not sufficient: Children, as they have the Nature of Men, are inclined to Society; and those of them that are capable of Society one with another, are capable of the Influences of the Spirit of GOD, in its active Fruits; and if they are inclined by a religious Disposition, that they have from the Spirit of GOD, to improve their Society one with another, in a religious Manner, and to religious Purposes, who should forbid them? If they han't Discretion to observe Method in their religious Performances, or to speak Sense in all that they say in Prayer, they may notwithstanding have a good Meaning, and GOD understands 'em, and it don't spoil or interrupt their Devotion one with another. We that are grown Persons, have Defects in our Prayers, that are a thousand Times worse in the Sight of GOD, and are a greater Confusion, and more absurd Nonsense in his Eyes, than their childish Indiscretions. There is not so much Difference before GOD, between Children & grown Persons, as we are ready to imagine; we are all poor, ignorant, foolish Babes, in his Sight: Our adult Age don't bring us so much nearer to

GOD, as we are apt to think. GOD in this Work has shewn a remarkable Regard to little Children; never was there such a glorious Work amongst Persons in their Childhood, as has been of late, in *New England*: He has been pleased in a wonderful Manner to perfect Praise out of the Mouths of Babes and Sucklings; and many of them have more of that Knowledge and Wisdom, that pleases him, and renders their religious Worship acceptable, than many of the great and learned Men of the World: 'Tis they, in the Sight of GOD, are the ignorant and foolish Children: These are grown Men, and an hundred Years old, in Comparison with them; and 'tis to be hoped that the Days are coming, prophesyed of Isai. 65. 20. when *the Child shall die an hundred Years old.*

I have seen many happy Effects of Childrens religious Meetings; and GOD has seem'd often remarkably to own them in their Meetings, and really descended from Heaven to be amongst them: I have known several probable Instances of Childrens being converted at such Meetings. I should therefore think, that if Children appear to be really moved to it, by a religious Disposition, and not meerly from a childish Affectation of imitating grown Persons, they ought by no Means to be discouraged or discountenanced: but yet 'tis fit that Care should be taken of them, by their Parents, and Pastors, to instruct and direct them, and to correct imprudent Conduct and Irregularities, if they are perceived; or any Thing by which the Devil may pervert and destroy the Design of their Meetings. All should take Heed that they don't find Fault with, and despise the Religion of Children, from an evil Principle, lest they should be like the chief Priests and Scribes, who were sore displeased at the religious Worship and Praises of little Children, and the Honour they gave CHRIST in the Temple. We have an Account of it, and of what CHRIST said upon it, in Mat. 21. 15, 16. *And when the chief Priests & Scribes saw the wonderful Things that he did, and the Children crying in the Temple, and saying,* Hosanna *to the Son of* David, *they were sore displeased, and said unto him, Hearest thou what these say? And* JESUS *saith unto them, yea; have ye never read, Out of the Mouths of Babes and Sucklings, thou hast perfected Praise?*

Part IV

Shewing what Things are to be corrected or
avoided, in promoting this WORK, or in our
Behaviour under it.

HAVING thus observed, in some Instances, wherein the Conduct of those that have appeared to be the Subjects of this
Work, or have been zealous to promote it, has been objected
against or complained of, without or beyond just Cause, I
proceed now in the

II. Place, to shew what Things ought to be corrected or
avoided.

Many that are zealous for this glorious WORK of GOD, are
heartily sick of the great Noise there is in the Country, about
Imprudences and *Disorders*: they have heard it so often from
the Mouths of Opposers that they are prejudiced against the
Sound; and they look upon it that That which is called a being
prudent and *regular*, which is so much insisted on, is no other
than being asleep, or cold and dead in Religion, and that the
great Imprudence that is so much cried out of, is only a being
alive, and engaged in the Things of GOD: and they are therefore
rather confirmed in any Practice, than brought off from it, by
the Clamour they hear against it, as imprudent and irregular.
And to tell the Truth, the Cry of Irregularity and Imprudence
has been much more in the Mouths of those that have been
Enemies to the Main of the Work than others; for they have
watched for the Halting of the Zealous, and eagerly catched at
any Thing that has been wrong, and have greatly insisted on it,
made the most of it, and magnified it; especially have they
watched for Errors in zealous Preachers, that are much in reproving and condemning the Wickedness of the Times: They
would therefore do well to consider that Scripture, Isai. 29.
20, 21. *The Scorner is consumed, and all that watch for Iniquity
are cut off, that make a Man an Offender for a Word, and lay a
Snare for him that reproveth in the Gate, and turn aside the Just
for a Thing of nought.* They han't only too much insisted on,
and magnified real Errors, but have very injuriously charged

them as guilty, in Things wherein they have been innocent, and have done their Duty. This has so prejudiced the Minds of some, that they have been ready to think that all that has been said about Errors and Imprudences, was injurious and from an ill Spirit; and has confirmed them in it, that there is no such Thing as any prevailing Imprudences; and it has made 'em less cautious and suspicious of themselves, lest they should err. Herein the Devil has had an Advantage put into his Hands, and has taken the Advantage; and, doubtless, has been too subtil for some of the true Friends of Religion. That would be a strange Thing indeed, if in so great a Commotion and Revolution, and such a new State of Things, wherein so many have been engaged, none have been guilty of any Imprudence; it would be such a Revival of Religion, as never was yet, if among so many Men, not guided by infallible Inspiration, there had not been prevailing a pretty many notable Errors in Judgment and Conduct; our young Preachers, and young Converts, must in general vastly exceed *Luther*, the Head of the Reformation, who was guilty of a great many Excesses, in that great Affair, in which GOD made him the chief Instrument.

If we look back into the History of the Church of GOD in past Ages, we may observe that it has been a common Device of the Devil, to overset a Revival of Religion, when he finds he can keep Men quiet and secure no longer, then to drive 'em to Excesses and Extravagances. He holds them back as long as he can, but when he can do it no longer, then he'll push 'em on, and if possible, run 'em upon their Heads. And it has been by this Means chiefly, that he has been successful, in several Instances, to overthrow most hopeful and promising Beginnings: yea, the principal Means by which the Devil was successful, by Degrees, to overset that grand religious Revival of the World, that was in the primitive Ages of Christianity, and in a Manner, to overthrow the Christian Church thro' the Earth, and to make Way for, and bring on the great antichristian Apostacy, that Master-Piece of all the Devil's Works, was to improve the indiscreet Zeal of Christians, to drive them into those three Extremes, of *Enthusiasm, Superstition*, and *Severity towards Opposers*, which should be enough for an everlasting Warning to the Christian Church.

Tho' the Devil will do his Diligence to stir up the open Enemies of Religion, yet he knows what is for his Interest so well, that in a Time of Revival of Religion, his main Strength shall be tried with the Friends of it, and he'll chiefly exert himself in his Attempts upon them, to mislead them. One truly zealous Person, in the Time of such an Event, that seems to have a great Hand in the Affair, and draws the Eyes of many upon him, may do more, (thro' Satan's being too subtil for him,) to hinder the Work, than an hundred great, and strong, and open Opposers.

In the Time of a great *Work* of CHRIST, his Hands, with which he *works*, are often wounded in the House of his Friends; and his Work hindred chiefly by them: So that if any one inquires, as in Zech. 13. 6. *What are those Wounds in thine Hands?* He may answer, *Those, with which I was wounded in the House of my Friends.*

The Errors of the Friends of the Work of God, and especially of the great Promoters of it, give vast Advantage to the Enemies of such a Work. Indeed there are many Things that are no Errors, but are only Duties faithfully and thoroughly done, that wound the Minds of such Persons more, and are more cross to 'em, than real Errors: but yet one real Error gives Opposers as much Advantage, and hinders and clogs the Work, as much as ten that are only supposed ones. Real Errors don't fret and gaul the Enemies of Religion, so much as those Things that are strictly right; but they encourage 'em more; they give 'em Liberty, and open a Gap for 'em; so that some that before kept their Enmity burning in their own Bowels, and durst not show themselves, will on such an Occasion take Courage, and give themselves Vent, and their Rage will be like that of an Enemy let loose; and those that lay still before, having nothing to say, but what they would be ashamed of, (agreeable to *Tit.* 2. 8.) when they have such a Weapon put into their Hands, will fight with all Violence. And indeed the Enemies of Religion would not know what to do for Weapons to fight with, were it not for the Errors of the Friends of it; and so must soon fall before them. And besides, in real Errors, Things that are truly disagreeable to the Rules of GOD's Word, we can't expect the divine Protection, and that GOD will appear on our Side, as if our Errors were only supposed ones.

Since therefore the Errors of the Friends & Promoters of such a glorious Work of GOD, are of such dreadful Conse-

quence; and seeing the Devil, being sensible of this, is so as-
siduous, and watchful and subtil in his Attempts with them,
and has thereby been so successful to overthrow Religion
heretofore, certainly such Persons ought to be exceeding
circumspect and vigilant, diffident and jealous of themselves,
and humbly dependent on the Guidance of the good Shepherd.
I Pet. 4. 7. *Be sober, and watch unto Prayer.* And Chap. 5. 8. *Be
sober, be vigilant; because your Adversary the Devil, as a roaring
Lion, walketh about,*—For Persons to go on resolutely, in a
Kind of Heat and Vehemence, despising Admonition and Correction, being confident that they must be in the Right, because
they are full of the Spirit, is directly contrary to the Import of
these Words, be *sober*, be *vigilant*.

'Tis a Mistake, I have observed in some, by which they have
been greatly exposed, to their Wounding, that they think they
are in no Danger of going astray, or being misled by the Devil,
because they are near to GOD; and so have no jealous Eye
upon themselves, and neglect Vigilance and Circumspection,
as needless in their Case. They say, they don't think that GOD
will leave them to dishonour him, and wound Religion, as
long as they keep near to him: And I believe so too, as long as
they keep near to GOD in that Respect, that they maintain an
universal & diligent Watch, and Care to do their Duty, and
avoid Sin and Snares, with Diffidence in themselves, and
humble Dependence and Prayerfulness: but not meerly because they are near to GOD, in that Respect, that they now are
receiving blessed Communications from GOD, in refreshing
Views of him; if at the same Time they let down their Watch,
and are not jealous over their own Hearts, by Reason of it's
remaining Blindness and Corruption, and a subtil Adversary.
'Tis a grand Error, for Persons to think they are out of Danger
of the Devil, and a corrupt, deceitful Heart, even in their highest Flights, and most raised Frames of spiritual Joy. For Persons
in such a Confidence, to cease to be jealous of themselves, and
to neglect Watchfulness and Care, is a Presumption by which I
have known many wofully ensnared. However highly we may
be favoured with divine Discoveries and Comforts, yet as long
as we are in the World, we are in the Enemies Country; and
therefore that Direction of CHRIST to his Disciples is never out
of Date in this World, Luke 21. 36. *Watch and pray always, that*

ye may be accounted worthy to escape all these Things, and to stand before the Son of Man. It was not out of Date with the Disciples, to whom it was given, after they came to be filled so full of the Holy Ghost and out of their Bellies flowed Rivers of living Water, by that great Effusion of the Spirit upon them, that began on the Day of *Pentecost*. And tho' GOD stands ready to protect his People, especially those that are near to him, yet he expects great Care and Labour of all; and that we should put on the whole Armour of GOD, that we may stand in the evil Day: and whatever spiritual Priviledges we are raised to, we have no Warrant to expect Protection in any other Way; for GOD has appointed this whole Life, as a State of Labour, to be all, as a Race or a Battle; the State of Rest, wherein we shall be so out of Danger, as to have no Need of Watching and Fighting, is reserved for another World. I have known it in Abundance of Instances, that the Devil has come in very remarkably, even in the midst of the most exalted, and upon some Accounts excellent Frames: It may seem a great Mystery that it should be so; but 'tis no greater Mystery, than that CHRIST should be taken Captive by the Devil, and carried into the Wilderness, immediately after the Heavens had been open'd to him, and the Holy Ghost descended like a Dove upon him, and he heard that comfortable, joyful Voice from the Father, saying, *This is my beloved Son, in whom I am well pleased*. In like Manner Christ in the Heart of a Christian, is oftentimes as it were taken by the Devil, and carried Captive into a Wilderness, presently after Heaven has been, as it were open'd to the Soul, and the Holy Ghost has descended upon it like a Dove, and GOD has been sweetly owning the Believer, and testifying his Favour to him as his beloved Child.

'Tis therefore a great Error, and Sin in some Persons, at this Day, that they are fix'd in their Way, in some Things that others account Errors, and won't hearken to Admonition and Counsel, but are confident that they are in the right of it, in those Practices that they find themselves disposed to, because GOD is much with them, and they have great Degrees of the Spirit of GOD. There were some such in the Apostles Days: The Apostle *Paul*, writing to the Corinthians, was sensible that some of them would not be easily convinced that they had been in any Error, because they looked upon themselves *Spiritual*, or full of the Spirit of GOD. I Cor. 14. 37, 38. *If any Man think himself to be a Prophet, or* spiritual, *let him acknowledge that the Things that I write unto you, are the Commandment of the Lord; but if any Man be ignorant, let him be ignorant.*

And altho' those that are spiritual amongst us, have no infallible Apostle to admonish them, yet let me intreat them, by the Love of CHRIST, calmly and impartially to weigh what may be said to them, by One that is their hearty and fervent Friend, (tho' an inferiour Worm) in giving his humble Opinion, concerning the Errors that have been committed, or that we may be exposed to, in Methods or Practices that have been, or may be fallen into, by the zealous Friends or Promoters of this great Work of GOD.

In speaking of the Errors that have been, or that we are in Danger of, I would in the

First Place, take Notice of the Causes whence the Errors that attend a great Revival of Religion usually arise; and as I go along, take Notice of some particular Errors that arise from each of those Causes.

Secondly, Observe some Errors, that some have lately gone into, that have been owing to the Influence of several of those Causes conjunctly.

As to the first of these, the Errors that attend a great Revival of Religion, usually arise from these three Things. 1. Undiscerned spiritual Pride. 2. Wrong Principles. 3. Ignorance of Satan's Advantages and Devices.

The first, and the worst Cause of Errors, that prevail in such a State of Things, is *spiritual Pride*. This is the main Door, by which the Devil comes into the Hearts of those that are zealous for the Advancement of Religion. 'Tis the chief Inlet of Smoke from the bottomless Pit, to darken the Mind, and mislead the Judgment: This is the main Handle by which the Devil has hold of religious Persons, and the chief Source of all the Mischief that he introduces, to clog and hinder a Work of GOD. This Cause of Error is the main Spring, or at least the main Support of all the rest. 'Till this Disease is cured, Medicines are in vain applied to heal other Diseases. 'Tis by this that the Mind defends it self in other Errors, and guards it self against Light, by which it might be corrected and reclaimed. The spiritually proud Man is full of Light already, he don't

need Instruction, and is ready to despise the Offer of it. But if
this Disease be healed, other Things are easily rectified. The
humble Person is like a little Child, he easily receives Instruction; he is jealous over himself, sensible how liable he is to go
astray; and therefore if it be suggested to him that he does so,
he is ready most narrowly and impartially to enquire. Nothing
sets a Person so much out of the Devil's reach, as Humility,
and so prepares the Mind for true divine Light, without Darkness, and so clears the Eye to look on Things, as they truly are.
Psal. 25. 9. *The Meek will he guide in Judgment, and the Meek he
will teach his Way.* Therefore we should fight, neither with
small nor with great, but with the King of *Israel*: Our first
Care should be to rectify the Heart, and pull the Beam out of
our Eye, and then we shall see clearly.

I know that a great many Things at this Day, are very injuriously laid to the Pride of those that are zealous in the Cause of
GOD. When any Person appears, in any Respect, remarkably
distinguished in Religion from others, if he professes those
spiritual Comforts and Joys that are greater than ordinary, or if
he appears distinguishingly zealous in Religion, if he exerts
himself more than others do, in the Cause of Religion, or if he
seems to be distinguished with Success, ten to one, but it will
immediately awaken the Jealousy of those that are about him;
and they'll suspect, (whether they have Cause or no) that he is
very proud of his Goodness, and that he affects to have it
thought that no Body is so good as he; and all his Talk is heard,
and all his Behaviour beheld, with this Prejudice. Those that
are themselves cold and dead, and especially such as never had any
Experience of the Power of Godliness on their own Hearts, are
ready to entertain such Thoughts of the best Christians; which
arises from a secret Enmity against vital & fervent Piety.

But then those that are zealous Christians should take heed
that this Injuriousness of those that are cold in Religion, dont
prove a Snare to them, and the Devil don't take Advantage
from it, to blind their Eyes from beholding what there is indeed of this Nature in their Hearts, and make 'em think, because they are charged with Pride wrongfully, and from an ill
Spirit, in many Things, that therefore it is so in every Thing.
Alas, how much Pride have the best of us in our Hearts! 'Tis
the worst Part of the Body of Sin and Death: 'Tis the first Sin

that ever entred into the Universe, and the last that is rooted out; 'Tis God's most stubborn Enemy!

The Corruption of Nature may all be resolved into two Things, *Pride* and *Worldly-mindedness*, the *Devil* and the *Beast*, or *Self* and the *World*. These are the two Pillars of *Dagon*'s Temple, on which the whole House leans. But the former of these is every Way, the worst Part of the Corruption of Nature; 'tis the first born Son of the Devil, and his Image in the Heart of Man chiefly consists in it; 'tis the last Thing in a Sinner that is over-born by Conviction, in order to Conversion; and here is the Saints hardest Conflict; 'tis the last Thing that he obtains a good Degree of Conquest over, & Liberty from; 'tis that which most directly militates against God, and is most contrary to the Spirit of the Lamb of God; and 'tis most like the Devil its Father, in a serpentine Deceitfulness and Secrecy; it lies deepest, and is most active, is most ready secretly to mix it self with every Thing.

And of all Kinds of Pride, spiritual Pride is upon many Accounts the most hateful; 'tis most like the Devil; 'tis most like the Sin that he committed in an Heaven of Light and Glory, where he was exalted high in divine Knowledge, Honour, Beauty and Happiness. Pride is much more difficultly discerned than any other Corruption, for that Reason, that the Nature of it does very much consist in a Person's having too high a Thought of himself: but no Wonder that he that has too high a Thought of himself, don't know it; for he necessarily thinks that the Opinion he has of himself, is what he has just Grounds for, and therefore not too high; if he thought such an Opinion of himself was without just Grounds, he would therein cease to have it. But of all Kinds of Pride, spiritual Pride is the most hidden, and difficultly discovered; and that for this Reason, Because those that are spiritually proud, their Pride consists much in an high Conceit of those two Things, *viz.* Their *Light*, and their *Humility*; both which are a strong Prejudice against a Discovery of their Pride. Being proud of their *Light*, that makes 'em not jealous of themselves; he that thinks a clear Light shines around him, is not suspicious of an Enemy lurking near him, unseen: And then being proud of their *Humility*, that makes 'em least of all jealous of themselves in that Particular, *viz.* as being under the Prevalence of Pride. There are many

Sins of the Heart that are very secret in their Nature, and difficultly discerned. The Psalmist says, Psal. 19. 12. *Who can understand his Errors? Cleanse thou me from secret Faults.* But
spiritual Pride is the most secret of all Sins. The Heart is so
deceitful and unsearchable in nothing in the World, as it is in
this Matter, and there is no Sin in the World, that Men are so
confident in, and so difficultly convinced of: The very Nature
of it is to work Self-Confidence, and drive away Self-Diffidence,
and Jealousy of any Evil of that Kind. There is no Sin so much
like the Devil, as this, for Secrecy and Subtilty, and appearing
in a great many Shapes, undiscerned and unsuspected, and
appearing as an Angel of Light: It takes Occasion to arise from
every Thing; it perverts and abuses every Thing, and even the
Exercises of real Grace, and real Humility, as an Occasion to
exert it self: It is a Sin that has, as it were many Lives; if you kill
it, it will live still; if you mortify and suppress it in one Shape,
it rises in another; if you think it is all gone, yet it is there still:
There are a great many Kinds of it, that lie in different Forms
and Shapes, one under another, and encompass the Heart like
the Coats of an Onion; if you pull off one there is another underneath. We had need therefore to have the greatest Watch
imaginable, over our Hearts, with respect to this Matter, and
to cry most earnestly to the great Searcher of Hearts, for his
help. He that trusts his own Heart is a Fool.

God's own People should be the more jealous of themselves,
with respect to this Particular, at this Day, because the Temptations that many have to this Sin are exceeding great: The
great and distinguishing Priviledges to which God admits
many of his Saints, and the high Honours that he puts on
some Ministers, are great Trials of Persons in this Respect. 'Tis
true that great Degrees of the spiritual Presence of God tends
greatly to mortify Pride and all Corruption; but yet, tho' in the
Experience of such Favours there be much to restrain Pride
one Way, there is much to tempt and provoke it another; and
we shall be in great Danger thereby without great Watchfulness and Prayerfulness. There was much in the Circumstances
that the Angels that fell, were in, in Heaven, in their great
Honours & high Priviledges, in beholding the Face of GOD,
and View of his infinite Glory, to cause in them Exercises of
Humility, and to keep 'em from Pride; yet through want of

Watchfulness in them, their great Honour and heavenly Priviledge proved to be to them, an undoing Temptation to Pride,
tho' they had no Principle of Pride in their Hearts to expose
'em. Let no Saint therefore, however eminent, and however
near to GOD, think himself out of Danger of this: He that
thinks himself most out of Danger, is indeed most in Danger.
The Apostle *Paul*, who doubtless was as eminent a Saint as any
are now, was not out of Danger, even just after he was admitted to see GOD in the third Heavens, by the Information he
himself gives us, 2 *Cor.* 12. Chap. And yet doubtless, what he
saw in Heaven of the ineffable Glory of the divine Being, had
a direct Tendency to make him appear exceeding little and vile
in his own Eyes.

Spiritual Pride in its own Nature is so secret, that it is not so
well discerned by immediate Intuition on the Thing it self, as by
the Effects and Fruits of it; some of which, I would mention,
together with the contrary Fruits of pure Christian Humility.

Spiritual Pride disposes to speak of other Persons Sins, their
Enmity against GOD and his People, the miserable Delusion of
Hypocrites and their Enmity against vital Piety, and the Deadness of some Saints, with Bitterness, or with Laughter and
Levity, and an Air of Contempt; whereas pure Christian Humility rather disposes, either to be silent about 'em, or to speak
of them with Grief and Pity.

Spiritual Pride is very apt to suspect others; whereas an
humble Saint is most jealous of himself, he is so suspicious of
nothing in the World as he is of his own Heart. The spiritually
proud Person is apt to find Fault with other Saints, that they
are low in Grace, and to be much in observing how cold and
dead they be, and crying out of them for it, and to be quick to
discern and take Notice of their Deficiences: But the eminently
humble Christian has so much to do at Home, and sees so
much Evil in his own Heart, and is so concerned about it, that
he is not apt to be very busy with others Hearts; he complains
most of himself, and cries out of his own Coldness and Lowness in Grace, and is apt to esteem others better than himself,
and is ready to hope that there is no Body but what has more
Love and Thankfulness to GOD than he, and can't bare to
think that others should bring forth no more Fruit to GOD's
Honour than he. Some that have spiritual Pride mix'd with

high Discoveries and great Transports of Joy, that dispose 'em in an earnest Manner to talk to others, are apt, in such Frames, to be calling upon other Christians that are about them, and sharply reproving them for their being so cold and lifeless. And there are some others that behave themselves very differently from these, who in their Raptures are over-whelmed with a Sense of their own Vileness; and when they have extraordinary Discoveries of GOD's Glory, are all taken up about their own Sinfulness; and tho' they also are disposed to speak much and very earnestly, yet it is very much in Crying out of themselves, and exhorting Fellow Christians, but in a charitable and humble Manner. Pure Christian Humility disposes a Person to take Notice of every Thing that is in any Respect good in others, and to make the best of it, and to diminish their Failings; but to have his Eye chiefly on those Things that are bad in himself, and to take much Notice of every Thing that aggravates them.

In a Contrariety to this, it has been the Manner in some Places, or at least the Manner of some Persons, to speak of almost every Thing that they see amiss in others, in the most harsh, severe and terrible Language. 'Tis frequent with them to say of others Opinions or Conduct or Advice, or of their Coldness, their Silence, their Caution, their Moderation, and their Prudence, and many other Things that appear in them, that they are from the Devil, or from Hell; that such a Thing is devilish or hellish or cursed, and that such Persons are serving the Devil or the Devil is in them, that they are Soul-Murtherers and the like; so that the Words *Devil* and *Hell* are almost continually in their Mouths. And such Kind of Language they will commonly use, not only towards wicked Men, but towards them that they themselves allow to be the true Children of GOD, and also towards Ministers of the Gospel and others that are very much their Superiours. And they look upon it a Vertue and high Attainment thus to behave themselves. *Oh*, say they, *we must be plain hearted and bold for Christ, we must declare War against Sin wherever we see it, we must not mince the Matter in the Cause of God and when speaking for Christ.* And to make any Distinction in Persons, or to speak the more tenderly, because that which is amiss is seen in a Superiour, they look upon as very mean for a Follower of CHRIST when speaking in the Cause of his Master.

What a strange Device of the Devil is here, to over-throw all
Christian Meekness and Gentleness, and even all Shew and
Appearance of it, and to defile the Mouths of the Children of
God, and to introduce the Language of common Sailors
among the Followers of CHRIST, under a Cloak of high Sanc-
tity and Zeal and Boldness for CHRIST! And it is a remarkable
Instance of the Weakness of the human Mind, and how much
too cunning the Devil is for us!

The grand Defence of this Way of Talking is, that they say
no more than what is true; they only speak the Truth without
mincing the Matter; and that true Christians that have a great
Sight of the Evil of Sin, and Acquaintance with their own
Hearts know it to be true, and therefore won't be offended to
hear such harsh Expressions made Use of concerning them
and their Sins; 'tis only (say they) Hypocrites, or cold and dead
Christians, that are provoked and feel their Enmity rise on
such an Occasion.

But 'tis a grand Mistake to think that we may commonly use
concerning one another all such Language as represents the
worst of each other, according to strict Truth. 'Tis really true,
that every Kind of Sin, & every Degree of it, is devilish and
from Hell, and is cursed, hellish, and condemned or damned:
And if Persons had a full Sight of their Hearts they would
think no Terms too bad for them; they would look like Beasts,
like Serpents and like Devils to themselves; they would be at a
loss for Language to express what they see in themselves, the
worst Terms they could think of would seem as it were faint to
represent what they see in themselves. But shall a Child therefore, from Time to Time, use such Language concerning an
excellent & eminently holy Father or Mother, as that the Devil
is in them, that they have such and such devilish, cursed Dispositions, that they commit every Day Hundreds of hellish,
damn'd Acts, and that they are cursed Dogs, Hell-Hounds and
Devils? And shall the meanest of the People be justified, in
commonly using such Language concerning the most excellent Magistrates, or their most eminent Ministers? I hope no
Body has gone to this Height: but the same Pretences of Boldness, Plain-heartedness, and declared War against Sin, will as
well justify these Things as the Things they are actually made
Use of to justify. If we proceed in such a Manner, on such

Principles as these, what a Face will be introduced upon the Church of CHRIST, the little beloved Flock of that gentle Shepherd the Lamb of GOD? What a Sound shall we bring into the House of GOD, into the Family of his dear little Children? How far off shall we soon banish that lovely Appearance of Humility, Sweetness, Gentleness, mutual Honour, Benevolence, Complacence, and an Esteem of others above themselves, which ought to clothe the Children of GOD all over? Not but that Christians should watch over one another, and in any wise reprove one another, and be much in it and do it plainly and faithfully; but it don't thence follow that dear Brethren in the Family of GOD, in rebuking one another, should use worse Language than *Michael* the Arch-angel durst use when rebuking the Devil himself.

Christians that are but Fellow-Worms ought at least to treat one another with as much Humility and Gentleness as CHRIST that is infinitely above them treats them. But how did CHRIST treat his Disciples when they were so cold towards him and so regardless of him, at the Time when his Soul was exceeding sorrowful even unto Death, and he in a dismal Agony was crying and sweating Blood for them, and they would not watch with him and allow him the Comfort of their Company one Hour in his great Distress, tho' he once and again desired it of them: One would think that then was a proper Time if ever to have reproved 'em for a devilish, hellish, cursed and damned Slothfulness and Deadness. But after what Manner does CHRIST reprove them? Behold his astonishing Gentleness! Says he, *What, could ye not watch with me one Hour? The Spirit indeed is willing, but the Flesh is weak.* And how did he treat *Peter* when he was ashamed of his Master, while he was made a Mocking-Stock and a Spitting-Stock for him? Why he looked upon him with a Look of Love, and melted his Heart.

And tho' we read that CHRIST once *turned and said unto* Peter, on a certain Occasion, *get thee behind me* Satan; and this may seem like an Instance of Harshness and Severity in reproving *Peter*; yet I humbly conceive that this is by many taken wrong, and that this is indeed no Instance of CHRIST's Severity in his Treatment of *Peter*, but on the contrary, of his wonderful Gentleness and Grace, distinguishing between *Peter* and the Devil in him, not laying the Blame of what *Peter* had then said, or imputing it to him, but to the Devil that influenced him. CHRIST saw the Devil then present, secretly influencing *Peter* to do the Part of a Tempter to his Master; and therefore CHRIST turned him about to *Peter*, in whom the Devil then was, and spake to the Devil, and rebuked him. Thus the Grace of CHRIST don't behold Iniquity in his People, imputes not what is amiss in 'em to them, but to Sin that dwells in them, and to *Satan* that influences them.

But to return,

Spiritual Pride often disposes Persons to Singularity in external Appearance, to affect a singular Way of Speaking, to use a different Sort of Dialect from others, or to be singular in Voice, or Air of Countenance or Behaviour: but he that is an eminently humble Christian, tho' he will be firm to his Duty, however singular he is in it; he'll go in the Way that leads to Heaven alone, tho' all the World forsakes him; yet he delights not in Singularity for Singularity's Sake, he don't affect to set up himself to be viewed and observed as one distinguished, as desiring to be accounted better than others, or dispising their Company, or an Union and Conformity to them; but on the contrary is disposed to become all Things to all Men, and to yield to others, and conform to them and please 'em, in every Thing but Sin. Spiritual Pride commonly occasions a certain Stiffness and Inflexibility in Persons, in their own Judgment and their own Ways; whereas the eminently humble Person, tho' he be inflexible in his Duty, and in those Things wherein GOD's Honour is concerned; and with Regard to Temptation to those Things he apprehends to be sinful, tho' in never so small a Degree, he is not at all of a yieldable Spirit, but is like a Brazen Wall; yet in other Things he is of a pliable Disposition, not disposed to set up his own Opinion, or his own Will; he is ready to pay Deference to others Opinions, and loves to comply with their Inclinations, and has a Heart that is tender and flexible, like a little Child.

Spiritual Pride disposes Persons to affect Separation, to stand at a Distance from others, as better than they, and loves the Shew and Appearance of the Distinction: But on the contrary the eminently humble Christian is ready to look upon himself as not worthy that others should be united to him, to think himself more brutish than any Man, and worthy to be cast out of human Society, and especially unworthy of the Society of GOD's Children; and tho' he will not be a Companion with one that is visibly CHRIST's Enemy, and delights most in the Company of lively Christians, will choose such for his Companions, and will be most intimate with them, & don't at all delight to spend away much Time in the Company of those that seem to relish no Conversation but about worldly Things; yet he don't love the Appearance of an open Separation from visible Christians, as being a Kind of distinct Company from them, that are one visible Company with him by CHRIST Appointment, and will as much as possible shun all Appearances of a Superiority, or distinguishing himself as better than others: His universal Benevolence delights in the Appearance of Union with his fellow Creatures, and will maintain it as much as he possibly can, without giving open Countenance to Iniquity, or wounding his own Soul; and herein he follows the Example of his meek & lowly Redeemer, who did not keep up such a Separation and Distance as the Pharisees, but freely eat with Publicans and Sinners, that he might win them.

The eminently humble Christian is as it were cloathed with Lowliness, Mildness, Meekness, Gentleness of Spirit and Behaviour, & with a soft, sweet, condescending, winning Air and Deportment; these Things are just like Garments to him, he is cloathed all over with them. 1 Pet. 5. 5. *And be cloathed with Humility.* Col. 3. 12. *Put on therefore, as the elect of God, holy and beloved, Bowels of Mercies, Kindness, Humbleness of Mind, Meekness, Long-suffering.*

Pure Christian Humility has no such Thing as Roughness, or Contempt, or Fierceness, or Bitterness in its Nature; it makes a Person like a little Child, harmless and innocent, and that none need to be afraid of; or like a Lamb, destitute of all Bitterness, Wrath, Anger and Clamour, agreeable to *Eph.* 4. 31.

With such a Spirit as this ought especially zealous Ministers of the Gospel to be cloathed, and those that GOD is pleased to improve as Instruments in his Hands of promoting his Work: they ought indeed to be thorough in preaching the Word of GOD, without mincing the Matter at all; in handling the Sword of the SPIRIT, as the Ministers of the Lord of Hosts, they ought not to be mild and gentle; they are not to be gentle and moderate in searching & awakening the Conscience but should be Sons of Thunder: The Word of GOD, which is in it self sharper

than any two-edged Sword, ought not to be sheathed by its
Ministers, but so used that its sharp Edges may have their full
Effect, even to the dividing asunder Soul and Spirit, Joints and
Marrow; (provided they do it without judging particular Persons, leaving it to Conscience and the Spirit of GOD to make
the particular Application;) But all their Conversation should
savour of nothing but Lowliness and good Will, Love and Pity
to all Mankind; so that such a Spirit should be like a sweet
Odour diffused around 'em wherever they go, or like a Light
shining about 'em, their Faces should as it were shine with it;
they should be like Lions to guilty Consciences, but like Lambs
to Men's Persons. This would have no Tendency to prevent
the Awakening of Men's Consciences, but on the contrary
would have a very great Tendency to awaken them; it would
make Way for the sharp Sword to enter; it would remove the
Obstacles, and make a naked Breast for the Arrow. Yea the
amiable, Christ-like Conversation of such Ministers, in it self
would terrify the Consciences of Men, as well as their terrible
Preaching; both would co-operate one with another, to subdue the hard, and bring down the proud Heart. If there had
been, constantly and universally observable such a Behaviour
as this in Itinerant Preachers, it would have terrified the Consciences of Sinners, ten Times as much as all the Invectives,
and the censorious Talk there has been concerning particular
Persons, for their Opposition, Hypocrisy, Delusion, Pharisa-
ism, &c.—These Things in general have rather stupified Sinners Consciences; they take 'em up, and make Use of 'em as a
Shield, wherewith to defend themselves from the sharp Arrows
of the Word, that are shot by these Preachers: The Enemies of
the present Work have been glad of these Things with all their
Hearts. Many of the most bitter of them are probably such as
in the Beginning of this Work had their Consciences something gauled & terrified with it; but these Errors of awakening
Preachers are the Things they chiefly make Use of as Plaisters
to heal the Sore that was made in their Consciences.

Spiritual Pride takes great Notice of Opposition and Injuries
that are received, and is apt to be often speaking of them, and
to be much in taking Notice of the Aggravations of 'em, either
with an Air of Bitterness or Contempt: Whereas pure, unmixed
Christian Humility, disposes a Person rather to be like his

blessed Lord, when reviled, dumb, not opening his Mouth, but committing himself in Silence to him that judgeth righteously. The eminently humble Christian, the more clamorous and furious the World is against him, the more silent and still will he be; unless it be in his Closet, and there he will not be still. Our Blessed Lord Jesus seems never to have been so silent, as when the World compassed him round, reproaching, buffetting and spitting on him, with loud and virulent Outcries, and horrid Cruelties.

There has been a great deal too much Talk of late, among many of the true and zealous Friends of Religion, about Opposition and Persecution. It becomes the Followers of the Lamb of GOD, when the World is in an Uproar about them, and full of Clamour against them, not to raise another Noise to answer it, but to be still and quiet: 'Tis not beautiful, at such a Time, to have Pulpits and Conversation ring with the sound, *Persecution, Persecution*, or with abundant Talk about Pharisees, carnal Persecutors, and the Seed of the Serpent.

Meekness and Quietness among GOD's People, when opposed & reviled, would be the surest Way to have GOD remarkably to appear for their Defence. 'Tis particularly observed of *Moses*, on the Occasion of *Aaron* and *Miriam* their envying him, & rising up in Opposition against him, that he *was very meek, above all Men upon the Face of the Earth*, Num. 12. 3. Doubtless because he remarkably shew'd his Meekness on that Occasion, being wholly silent under the Abuse. And how remarkable is the Account that follows of GOD's being as it were suddenly roused to appear for his Vindication? And what high Honour did he put upon *Moses*? And how severe were his Rebukes of his Opposers? The Story is very remarkable, and worth every One's observing. Nothing is so effectual to bring GOD down from Heaven in the Defence of his People, as their Patience and Meekness under Sufferings. When CHRIST *girds his Sword upon his Thigh, with his Glory and Majesty, and in his Majesty rides prosperously, his right Hand teaching him terrible Things, it is because of Truth & MEEKNESS & Righteousness.* Psal. 45. 3, 4. *God will cause Judgment to be heard from Heaven; the Earth shall fear and be still, and God will arise to Judgment,* to save all the MEEK of the Earth. Psal. 76. 8, 9. *He will lift up the* Meek, *and cast the Wicked down to the Ground.* Psal. 147. 6.

He will reprove with Equity, for the Meek of the Earth, *and will smite the Earth with the Rod of his Mouth, and with the Breath of his Lips will he slay the Wicked.* Isai. 11. 4. The great Commendation that CHRIST gives the Church of *Philadelphia,* is that, *Thou hast kept the Word of my Patience,* Rev. 3. 10. And we may see what Reward he promises her, in the preceeding Verse, *Behold, I will make them of the Synagogue of Satan, which say they are Jews and are not, but do lie; behold, I will make them to come and worship at thy Feet, and to know that I have loved thee.* And thus it is, that we might expect to have CHRIST appear for us, if under all Reproaches we are loaded with, we behaved ourselves with a Lamb-like Meekness and Gentleness; but if our Spirits are raised, and we are vehement and noisy with our Complaints under Colour of Christian Zeal, this will be to take upon us our own Defence, and GOD will leave it with us, to vindicate our Cause as well as we can: Yea if we go on in a Way of Bitterness, and high Censuring, it will be the Way to have him rebuke us, and put us to Shame before our Enemies.

Here some may be ready to say, "'Tis not in our own Cause, that we are thus vehement, but it is in the Cause of GOD; and the Apostle directed the primitive Christians to contend earnestly for the Faith once delivered to the Saints." But how was it that the primitive Christians contended earnestly for the Faith? They defended the Truth with Arguments, and a holy Conversation; but yet gave their Reasons with Meekness & Fear: They contended earnestly for the Faith, by fighting violently against their own Unbelief, and the Corruptions of their Hearts, yea they resisted unto Blood striving against Sin; but the Blood that was shed in this earnest Strife, was their own Blood, and not the Blood of their Enemies. It was *in the Cause of God,* that *Peter* was so fierce, and drew his Sword, and began to smite with it; but Christ bids him put up his Sword again, telling him that they that take the Sword shall perish by the Sword; and while *Peter* wounds, CHRIST heals. They contend the most violently, and are the greatest Conquerors in a Time of Persecution, who bear it with the greatest Meekness and Patience.

Great Humility improves even the Reflections and Reproaches of Enemies, to put upon serious Self-Examination, whether or no there be not some just Cause, whether they han't in some Respect given Occasion to the Enemy to speak reproachfully: Whereas spiritual Pride improves such Reflections to make 'em the more bold and confident, and to go the greater Lengths in that for which they are found fault with. I desire it may be consider'd whether there has been nothing amiss of late, among the true Friends of vital Piety in this Respect; and whether the Words of *David*, when reviled by *Michal*, han't been mis-interpreted and misapplied to justify them in it, when he said I will be yet more vile, and will be base in mine own Sight. The Import of his Words is that he would humble himself yet more before GOD, being sensible that he was far from being sufficiently abased; and he signifies this to *Michal*, and that he longed to be yet lower, and had designed already to abase himself more in his Behaviour: not that he would go the greater Length, to shew his Regardlesness of her Revilings; that would be to exalt himself, and not more to abase himself, as more vile in his own Sight.

Another Effect of spiritual Pride is a certain unsuitable and self-confident Boldness before GOD and Men. Thus some in their great Rejoicings before GOD, han't paid a sufficient Regard to that Rule, in *Psal.* 2. 11. They han't rejoiced with a reverential Trembling, in a proper Sense of the awful Majesty of GOD, and the awful Distance between GOD and them. And there has also been an improper Boldness before Men, that has been encouraged & defended, by a Misapplication of that Scripture, Prov. 29. 25. *The Fear of Man bringeth a Snare.* As tho' it became all Persons, high and low, Men, Women & Children, in all religious Conversation, wholly to divest themselves of all Manner of Shamefacedness, Modesty or Reverence towards Man; which is a great Error, and quite contrary to Scripture. There is a Fear of Reverence that is due to some Men. Rom. 13. 7. *Fear, to whom Fear; Honour, to whom Honour.* And there is a Fear of Modesty and Shamefacedness, in Inferiours towards Superiours, that is amiable, and required by Christian Rules. 1 Pet. 3. 2. *While they behold your chaste Conversation, coupled with Fear.* And 1 Tim. 2. 9. *In like Manner also, that Women adorn themselves, in modest Apparel, with Shamefacedness and Sobriety.* And the Apostle means that this Vertue shall have Place, not only in civil Communication, but also in spiritual Communication, and in our religious Concerns and Behaviour, as is evident by what follows. Ver. 11, 12. *Let the Women learn in Silence, with all Subjection. But I suffer not a Woman to teach, nor to usurp Authority over the Man, but to be in Silence.* Not that I would hence infer that Women's Mouths should be shut up from Christian Conversation; but all that I mean from it at this Time is, that Modesty, or Shamefacedness, and Reverence towards Men, ought to have some Place, even in our religious Communication one with another. The same is also evident by 1 Pet. 3. 15. *Be ready always to give an Answer, to every Man that asketh you a Reason of the Hope that is in you, with Meekness and Fear.* 'Tis well if that very Fear and Shame-facedness, which the Apostle recommends, han't sometimes been condemned, under the Name of a *cursed Fear* of *Man.*

'Tis beautiful for Persons when they are at Prayer as the Mouth of others, to make GOD only their Fear and their Dread, and to be wholly forgetful of Men that are present, who let 'em be great or small, are nothing in the Presence of the great GOD. And 'tis beautiful for a Minister, when he speaks in the Name of the Lord of Hosts, to be bold, and put off all Fear of Men. And 'tis beautiful in private Christians, tho' they are Women and Children, to be bold in professing the Faith of CHRIST, and in the Practice of all Religion, and in owning GOD's Hand in the Work of his Power and Grace, without any Fear of Men, tho' they should be reproached as Fools and Madmen, and frowned upon by great Men, and cast off by Parents & all the World. But for private Christians, Women and others, to instruct, rebuke and exhort, with a like Sort of Boldness as becomes a Minister when preaching, is not beautiful.

Some have been bold in some Things that have really been Errors; and have gloried in their Boldness in practicing them, tho' cried out of as odd and irregular. And those that have gone the greatest Lengths in these Things, have been by some most highly esteemed, as those that come out, and appear bold for the Lord Jesus Christ, and fully on his Side; and others that have profess'd to be godly, that have condemned such Things, have been spoken of as Enemies of the Cross of CHRIST, or at least very cold and dead; and many that of themselves, were not inclined to such Practices, have by this Means been driven on, being asham'd to be behind, and accounted poor Soldiers for CHRIST.

308 SOME THOUGHTS

Another Effect of spiritual Pride is *Assuming*: It oftentimes makes it natural to Persons so to act and speak, as tho' it in a special Manner belong'd to them to be taken Notice of and much regarded. It is very natural to a Person that is much under the Influence of spiritual Pride, to take all that Respect that is paid him: If others shew a Disposition to submit to him, and yield him the Deference of a Preceptor, he is open to it, and freely admits it; yea, 'tis natural for him to expect such Treatment, and to take much Notice of it if he fails of it, and to have an ill Opinion of others that don't pay him that which he looks upon as his Prerogative: He is apt to think that it belongs to him to speak, and to clothe himself with a judicial and dogmatical Air in Conversation, and to take it upon him as what belongs to him, to give forth his Sentence, and to determine and decide: Whereas pure Christian Humility *vaunteth not it self, doth not behave it self unseemly*, and is apt to *prefer others in Honour*. One under the Influence of spiritual Pride is more apt to instruct others, than to enquire for himself, and naturally puts on the Airs of a Master: Whereas one that is full of pure Humility, naturally has on the Air of a Disciple; his Voice is, "What shall I do? What shall I do that I may live more to GOD's Honour? What shall I do with this wicked Heart?" He is ready to receive Instruction from any Body, agreable to *Jam.* I. 19. *Wherefore, my beloved Brethren, let every Man be swift to hear, slow to speak.* The eminently humble Christian thinks he wants Help from every Body, whereas he that is spiritually proud thinks that every Body wants his Help. Christian Humility, under a Sense of others Misery, intreats and beseeches; spiritual Pride affects to command, and warn with Authority.

There ought to be the utmost Watchfulness against all such Appearances of spiritual Pride, in all that profess to have been the Subjects of this Work, and especially in the Promoters of it, but above all in Itinerant Preachers: The most eminent Gifts, and highest Tokens of GOD's Favour and Blessing, will not excuse them: Alas! What is Man at his best Estate! What is the most highly favoured Christian, or the most eminent and successful Minister, that he should now think he is sufficient for something, and some-body to be regarded, and that he should go forth, and act among his Fellow Creatures, as if he were wise and strong and good!

Ministers that have been the principal Instruments of carrying on this glorious Revival of Religion, and that GOD has made Use of, as it were to bring up his People out of *Egypt*, as he did of *Moses*, should take Heed that they don't provoke GOD as *Moses* did, by assuming too much to themselves, and by their intemperate Zeal, to shut them out from seeing the good Things that GOD is going to do for his Church in this World. The Fruits of *Moses*'s Unbelief, which provoked GOD to shut him out of *Canaan*, and not to suffer him to partake of those great Things GOD was about to do for *Israel* on Earth, were chiefly these two Things; *First*, His mingling Bitterness with his Zeal: he had a great Zeal for GOD, and he could not bear to see the intolerable Stiff-neckedness of the People, that they did not acknowledge the Work of GOD, and were not convinced by all his Wonders that they had seen: But human Passion was mingled with his Zeal. *Psal.* 106. 32, 33. *They angred him also at the Waters of Strife; so that it went ill with* Moses *for their Sakes: Because they provoked his Spirit, so that he spake unadvisedly with his Lips. Hear now ye Rebels*, says he, with Bitterness of Language. *Secondly*, He behaved himself, and spake with an assuming Air: He assumed too much to himself; *Hear now ye Rebels, must WE fetch Water out of this Rock?* Spiritual Pride wrought in *Moses* at that Time: His Temptations to it were very great, for he had had great Discoveries of GOD, and had been priviledged with intimate and sweet Communion with him, and GOD had made him the Instrument of great Good to his Church; and tho' he was so humble a Person, and, by GOD's own Testimony, meek above all Men upon the Face of the whole Earth, yet his Temptations were too strong for him: Which surely should make our young Ministers, that have of late been highly favoured, and have had great Success, exceeding careful, and distrustful of themselves. Alas! how far are we from having the Strength of holy, meek, aged *Moses*! The Temptation at this Day is exceeding great, to both those Errors that *Moses* was guilty of; there is great Temptation to Bitterness and corrupt Passion with Zeal; for there is so much unreasonable Opposition made against this glorious Work of GOD, and so much Stiff-neckedness manifested in Multitudes of this Generation, notwithstanding all the great & wonderful Works in which GOD has passed before them, that it greatly tends to provoke the Spirits of such as have the Interest of this Work at Heart, so as to move 'em to speak unadvisedly with their Lips. And there is also great Temptation to an assuming Behaviour in some Persons: When a Minister is greatly succeeded, from Time to Time, and so draws the Eyes of the Multitude upon him, and he sees himself flocked after, and resorted to as an Oracle, and People are ready to adore him, and to offer Sacrifice to him, as it was with *Paul* and *Barnabas*, at *Lystra*, it is almost impossible for a Man to avoid taking upon him the Airs of a Master, or some extraordinary Person; a Man had Need to have a great Stock of Humility, and much divine Assistance, to resist the Temptation. But the greater our Dangers are, the more ought to be our Watchfulness & Prayerfulness, and Diffidence of our selves, lest we bring our selves into Mischief. Fishermen that have been very successful, and have caught a great many Fish, had Need to be careful that they don't at Length begin to burn Incense to their Net. And we should take Warning by *Gideon*, who after GOD had highly favoured and exalted him, and made him the Instrument of working a wonderful Deliverance for his People, at Length made a God of the Spoils of his Enemies, which became a Snare to him and to his House, so as to prove the Ruin of his Family.

All young Ministers in this Day of the bringing up the Ark of GOD, should take Warning by the Example of a young *Levite* in *Israel*, viz. *Uzza* the Son of *Abinadab*. He seem'd to have a real Concern for the Ark of GOD, and to be zealous and engaged in his Mind, on that joyful Occasion of bringing up the Ark, and GOD made him an Instrument to bring the Ark out of its long continued Obscurity in *Kirjath-jearim*, & he was succeeded to bring it a considerable Way towards Mount *Zion*; but for his Want of Humility, Reverence and Circumspection, and assuming to himself, or taking too much upon him, GOD broke forth upon him, and smote him for his Error, so that he never lived to see, and partake of the great Joy of his Church, on Occasion of the carrying up the Ark into Mount *Zion*, and the great Blessings of Heaven upon *Israel*, that were consequent upon it. Ministers that have been improved to carry on this Work have been chiefly of the younger Sort, who have doubtless, (as *Uzza* had,) a real Concern for

the Ark; and 'tis evident that they are much animated and engaged in their Minds, (as he was) in this joyful Day of bringing
up the Ark; and they are afraid what will become of the Ark
under the Conduct of its Ministers, (that are sometimes in
Scripture compared to Oxen;) They see the Ark shakes, and
they are afraid these blundering Oxen will throw it; and some
of 'em it is to be fear'd, have been over officious on this Occasion, and have assumed too much to themselves, and have
been bold to put forth their Hand to take hold of the Ark, as
tho' they were the only fit and worthy Persons to defend it.

If young Ministers had great Humility, without a Mixture, it
would dispose 'em especially to treat aged Ministers with Respect and Reverence, as their Fathers, notwithstanding that a
sovereign GOD may have given them greater Assistance and
Success, than they have had. 1 Pet. 5. 5. *Likewise ye younger,*
submit your selves unto the elder; yea all of you, be subject one to
another; and be clothed with Humility; for God resisteth the
Proud, and giveth Grace to the Humble. Lev. 19. 32. *Thou shalt*
rise up before the hoary Head, and honour the Face of the old
Man, and fear thy GOD; I am the LORD.

As spiritual Pride disposes Persons to assume much to themselves, so it also disposes 'em to treat others with Neglect: On
the contrary, pure Christian Humility disposes Persons to
honour all Men, agreeable to that Rule, 1 *Pet.* 2. 17.

There has been in some, that I believe are true Friends of
Religion, too much of an Appearance of this Fruit of spiritual
Pride, in their Treatment of those that they looked upon to be
carnal Men; and particularly in refusing to enter into any Discourse or Reasoning with them. Indeed to spend a great deal
of Time in Jangling and warm Debates about Religion, is not
the Way to propagate Religion, but to hinder it; and some are
so dreadfully set against this Work, that it is a dismal Talk to
dispute with them, all that one can say is utterly in vain, I have
found it so by Experience; and to go to enter into Disputes
about Religion, at some Times, is quite unseasonable, as particularly in Meetings for religious Conference, or Exercises of
Worship. But yet we ought to be very careful that we don't
refuse to discourse with Men, with any Appearance of a super-
cilious Neglect, as tho' we counted 'em not worthy to be regarded; on the contrary we should condescend to carnal Men,

as CHRIST has condescended to us, to bear with our Unteach-ableness and Stupidity, and still to follow us with Instructions, Line upon Line, and Precept upon Precept, saying, Come let us reason together; setting Light before us, and using all Manner of Arguments with us, and waiting upon such dull Scholars, as it were hoping that we should receive Light. We should be ready with Meekness and Calmness, without hot disputing, to give our Reasons, why we think this Work is the Work of GOD, to carnal Men when they ask us, and not turn them by as not worthy to be talk'd with; as the Apostle directed the primitive Christians to be ready to give a Reason of the Christian Faith and Hope to the Enemies of Christianity, 1 Pet. 3. 15. *Be ready always to give an Answer to every Man that asketh you a Reason of the Hope that is in you, with Meekness and Fear.* And we ought not to condemn all Reasoning about Things of Religion under the Name of carnal Reason. For my Part, I desire no better than that those that oppose this Work, should come fairly to submit to have the Cause betwixt us tried by strict Reasoning.

One Qualification that the Scripture speaks of once and again, as requisite in a Minister is, that he should be διδακτικος apt to teach, 1 *Tim.* 3. 2. And the Apostle seems to explain what he means by it, in 2 *Tim.* 2. 24, 25. Or at least he ex-presses one Thing he intends by it, *viz.* That a Minister should be ready, meekly to condescend to, and instruct Opposers. *And the Servant of the Lord must not strive, but be gentle unto all Men, apt to teach, patient, in Meekness instructing those that oppose themselves, if God peradventure will give them Repen-tance, to the acknowledging of the Truth.*

Secondly, Another Thing from whence Errors in Conduct, that attend such a Revival of Religion, do arise, is *wrong Principles.*

And one erroneous Principle, than which scarce any has proved more mischievous to the present glorious Work of GOD, is a Notion that 'tis GOD's Manner, now in these Days, to guide his Saints, at least some that are more eminent, by Inspiration, or immediate Revelation, and to make known to 'em what shall come to pass hereafter, or what it is his Will that they should do, by Impressions that he by his Spirit makes upon their Minds, either with, or without Texts of Scripture; whereby something is made known to them, that is not taught in the Scripture as the Words lie in the Bible. By such a Notion the Devil has a great Door opened for him; and if once this Opinion should come to be fully yielded to, and established in the Church of GOD, Satan would have Opportunity thereby to set up himself as the Guide and Oracle of God's People, & to have *his* Word regarded as their infallible Rule, & so to lead 'em where he would, & to introduce what he pleas'd, and soon to bring the Bible into Neglect and Contempt:—Late Experience in some Instances, has shown that the Tendency of this Notion is to cause Persons to esteem the Bible as a Book that is in a great Measure useless.

This Error will defend and support all Errors. As long as a Person has a Notion that he is guided by immediate Direction from Heaven, it makes him incorrigible and impregnable in all his Misconduct: For what signifies it, for poor blind Worms of the Dust, to go to argue with a Man, and endeavour to convince him and correct him, that is guided by the immediate Counsels & Commands of the great JEHOVAH?

This great Work of GOD has been exceedingly hindered by this Error; and 'till we have quite taken this Handle out of the Devil's Hands, the Work of GOD will never go on without great Clogs & Hindrances. But Satan will always have a vast Advantage in his Hands against it, and as he has improved it hitherto, so he will do still: And 'tis evident that the Devil knows the vast Advantage he has by it, that makes him exceeding loth to let go his Hold.

'Tis strange what a Disposition there is in many well disposed and religious Persons, to fall in with and hold fast this Notion. 'Tis enough to astonish one that such multiplied, plain Instances of the failing of such supposed Revelations, in the Event, don't open every one's Eyes. I have seen so many Instances of the failing of such Impressions, that would almost furnish an History: I have been acquainted with them when made under all Kinds of Circumstances, and have seen 'em fail in the Event, when made with such Circumstances as have been fairest and brightest, and most promising; as when they have been made upon the Minds of such, as there was all Reason to think were true Saints, yea eminent Saints, and at the very Time when they have had great divine Discoveries, and have been in the high Exercise of true Communion with

GOD, and made with great Strength, and with great Sweetness accompanying, and I have had Reason to think, with an excellent heavenly Frame of Spirit, yet continued, and made with Texts of Scripture, that seem'd to be exceeding apposite, yea many Texts following one another, extraordinarily and wonderfully bro't to the Mind, and with great Power and Majesty, and the Impressions repeated over and over, after Prayers to be directed; and yet all has most manifestly come to nothing, to the full Conviction of the Persons themselves. And GOD has in so many Instances of late in his Providence, covered such Things with Darkness, that one would think it should be enough quite to blank the Expectations of such as have been ready to think highly of such Things; it seems to be a Testimony of GOD, that he has no Design of reviving Revelations in his Church, and a Rebuke from him to the groundless Expectations of it.

It seems to me that That Scripture, *Zech.* 13. 5. is a Prophecy concerning Ministers of the Gospel, in the latter, & glorious Day of the Christian Church, which is evidently spoken of in this and the foregoing Chapters; The Words are, *I am no Prophet; I am an Husbandman: For Man taught me to keep Cattle from my Youth.* The Words, I apprehend, are to be interpreted in a spiritual Sense; *I am an Husbandman*: The Work of Ministers is very often in the New-Testament, compared to the Business of the Husbandman, that take Care of GOD's Husbandry, to whom he lets out his Vineyard, and sends 'em forth to labour in his Field, where one plants and another waters, one sows and another reaps; so Ministers are called Labourers in GOD's Harvest. And as it is added, *Man taught me to keep Cattle from my Youth.* So the Work of a Minister is very often in Scripture represented by the Business of a Shepherd or Pastor. And whereas it is said, *I am no Prophet; but Man taught me from my Youth.* 'Tis as much as to say, I don't pretend to have received my Skill, whereby I am fitted for the Business of a Pastor or Shepherd in the Church of GOD, by immediate Inspiration, but by Education, by being train'd up to the Business by human Learning, and Instructions I have received from my Youth or Childhood, by ordinary Means.

And why can't we be contented with the divine Oracles, that holy, pure Word of GOD, that we have in such Abundance,

and such Clearness, now since the Canon of Scripture is compleated? Why should we desire to have any Thing added to
them by Impulses from above? Why should not we rest in that
standing Rule that GOD has given to his Church, which the
Apostle teaches us is surer than a Voice from Heaven? And why
should we desire to make the Scripture speak more to us than it
does? Or why should any desire any higher Kind of Intercourse
with Heaven, than that which is by having the holy Spirit given
in his sanctifying Influences, infusing and exciting Grace and
Holiness, Love and Joy, which is the highest Kind of Intercourse
that the Saints and Angels in Heaven have with GOD, and the
chief Excellency of the glorified Man CHRIST JESUS?

Some that follow Impulses and Impressions go away with a
Notion that they do no other than follow the Guidance of
GOD's Word, and make the Scripture their Rule, because the
Impression is made with a Text of Scripture, that comes to
their Mind, tho' they take that Text as it is impressed on their
Minds, and improve it as a new Revelation, to all Intents and
Purposes, or as the Revelation of a particular Thing, that is
now newly made, while the Text in it self, as it is in the Bible,
implies no such Thing, and they themselves do not suppose
that any such Revelation was contained in it before. As for Instance, suppose that Text should come into a Person's Mind
with strong Impression, *Act.* 9. 6. *Arise, and go into the City;
and it shall be told thee what thou must do.* And he should interpret it as an immediate Signification of the Will of GOD, that
he should now, forthwith go to such a Neighbour Town, and
as a Revelation of that future Event, *viz.* That there he should
meet with a further Discovery of his Duty. If such Things as
these are revealed by the Impression of these Words, 'tis to all
Intents, a new Revelation, not the less because certain Words
of Scripture are made Use of in the Case: Here are Propositions or Truths entirely new, that are supposed now to be revealed, that those Words do not contain in themselves, and
that 'till now there was no Revelation of any where to be found
in Heaven or Earth. These Propositions, That 'tis GOD's Mind
and Will that such a Person by Name, should arise at such a
Time, and go from such a Place to such a Place, and that there
he should meet with Discoveries, are entirely new Propositions, wholly different from the Propositions contain'd in that

Text of Scripture, no more contain'd, or consequentially implied in the Words themselves, without a new Revelation, than it is implied that he should arise and go to any other Place, or that any other Person should arise and go to that Place. The Propositions supposed to be now revealed, are as really different from those contained in that Scripture, as they are from the Propositions contain'd in that Text, *Gen.* 5. 6. *And Seth lived an hundred and five Years, & begat Enos.*

This is quite a different Thing from the Spirit's enlightening the Mind to understand the Precepts or Propositions of the Word of GOD, and know what is contained and revealed in them, and what Consequences may justly be drawn from them, and to see how they are applicable to our Case and Circumstances; which is done without any new Revelation, only by enabling the Mind to understand and apply a Revelation already made.

Those Texts of Scripture that speak of the Children of GOD as *led by the Spirit*, have been by some, brought to defend a being guided by such Impulses; as particularly, those *Rom.* 8. 14. *For as many as are led by the Spirit of God, they are the Sons of God*: And Gal. 5. 18. *But if ye are led by the Spirit, ye are not under the Law.* But these Texts themselves confute them that bring them; for 'tis evident that the leading of the Spirit that the Apostle speaks of is a gracious Leading, or what is peculiar to the Children of GOD, & that natural Men cannot have; for he speaks of it as a sure Evidence of their being the Sons of GOD, and not under the Law: But a leading or directing a Person, by immediately revealing to him where he should go, or what shall hereafter come to pass, or what shall be the future Consequence of his doing thus or thus, if there be any such Thing in these Days, is not of the Nature of the gracious leading of the Spirit of GOD, that is peculiar to GOD's Children; 'tis no more than a common Gift; there is nothing in it but what natural Men are capable of, and many of them have had in the Days of Inspiration: A Man may have ten Thousand such Revelations and Directions from the Spirit of GOD, and yet not have a Jot of Grace in his Heart: 'Tis no more than the Gift of Prophecy, which immediately reveals what will be, or should be hereafter; but this is but a common Gift, as the Apostle expresly shews, I *Cor.* 13. 2, 8. If a Person has any

Thing revealed to him from God, or is directed to any Thing, by a Voice from Heaven, or a Whisper, or Words immediately suggested and put into his Mind, there is nothing of the Nature of Grace, meerly in this; 'tis of the Nature of a common Influence of the Spirit, and is but Dross and Dung, in Comparison of the Excellency of that gracious leading of the Spirit that the Saints have. Such a Way of being directed where one shall go, and what he shall do, is no more than what *Balaam* had from GOD, who from Time to Time revealed to him what he should do, and when he had done one Thing, then directed him what he should do next; so that he was in this Sense led by the Spirit, for a considerable Time. There is *a more excellent Way* that the Spirit of GOD leads *the Sons of God*, that natural Men cannot have, and that is, by inclining them to do the Will of GOD, and go in the shining Path of Truth and Christian Holiness, from an holy heavenly Disposition, which the Spirit of GOD gives them, & enlivens in them which inclines 'em, and leads 'em to those Things that are excellent, & agreable to GOD's Mind, whereby they *are transformed, by the renewing of their Minds, and prove what is that good, and acceptable, and perfect Will of God*, as in *Rom.* 12. 2. And so the Spirit of GOD does in a gracious Manner teach the Saints their Duty; and teaches 'em in an higher Manner than ever *Balaam*, or *Saul*, or *Judas* were taught, or any natural Man is capable of while such. The Spirit of GOD enlightens 'em with Respect to their Duty, by making their Eye single and pure, whereby the whole Body is full of Light. The sanctifying Influence of the Spirit of GOD rectifies the Taste of the Soul, whereby it savours those Things that are of GOD, and naturally relishes and delights in those Things that are holy and agreeable to GOD's Mind, and like one of a distinguishing Taste, chuses those Things that are good and wholesom, and rejects those Things that are evil; for the sanctified Ear tries Words, and the sanctified Heart tries Actions, as the Mouth tastes Meat. And thus the Spirit of GOD leads and guides the Meek in his Way, agreeable to his Promises; he enables them to understand the Commands and Counsels of his Word, and rightly to apply them. CHRIST blames the *Pharisees* that they had not this holy distinguishing Taste, to discern and distinguish what was right and wrong. *Luk.* 12. 57. *Yea, and why, even of your own selves, judge ye not what is right?*

The leading of the Spirit which GOD gives his Children, which is peculiar to them, is that teaching them his Statutes, and causing them to understand the Way of his Precepts, which the Psalmist so very often prays for, especially in the 119th Psalm; and not in giving of them *new Statutes*, and *new Precepts*: He graciously gives them Eyes to see, and Ears to hear, and Hearts to understand; he causes them to understand the Fear of the Lord, and so brings the Blind by a Way they knew not, and leads them in Paths that they had not known, and makes Darkness Light before them, & crooked Things strait.

So the Assistance of the Spirit in Praying and Preaching seems by some to have been greatly misunderstood, and they have sought after a miraculous Assistance of Inspiration, by immediate suggesting of Words to them, by such Gifts and Influences of the Spirit, in Praying and Teaching, as the Apostle speaks of, 1 *Cor.* 14. 14, 26. (which many natural Men had in those Days.) Instead of a gracious holy Assistance of the Spirit of GOD, which is the far *more excellent Way*; (as 1 *Cor.* 12. 31. & 13. 1.) The gracious, and most excellent kind Assistance of the Spirit of God in Praying and Preaching, is not by immediate suggesting of Words to the Apprehension, which may be with a cold dead Heart, but by warming the Heart, and filling it with a great Sense of those Things that are to be spoken of, and with holy Affections, that that Sense and those Affections may suggest Words. Thus indeed the Spirit of GOD may be said, indirectly and mediately to suggest Words to us, to indite our Petitions for us, & to teach the Preacher what to say; he fills the Heart, and that fills the Mouth; as we know that when Men are greatly affected in any Matter, and their Hearts are very full, it fills them with Matter for Speech, and makes 'em eloquent upon that Subject; and much more have spiritual Affections this Tendency, for many Reasons that might be given. When a Person is in an holy and lively Frame in secret Prayer, it will wonderfully supply him with Matter, and with Expressions, as every true Christian knows; and so it will fill his Mouth in Christian Conversation, and it has the like Tendency to enable a Person in publick Prayer and Preaching. And if he has these holy Influences of the Spirit on his Heart in an high Degree, nothing in the World will have so great a Tendency to make both the Matter and Manner of his publick Performances excellent and profitable. But since there is no immediate suggesting of Words from the Spirit of GOD to be expected or desired, they who neglect and despise Study and Pre-meditation, in order to a Preparation for the Pulpit, in such an Expectation, are guilty of Presumption; tho' doubtless it may be lawful for some Persons, in some Cases, (and they may be called to it,) to preach with very little Study; and the Spirit of GOD, by the heavenly Frame of Heart that he gives them, may enable them to do it to excellent Purpose.

Besides this most excellent Way of the Spirit of GOD his assisting Ministers in publick Performances, which (consider'd as the Preacher's Priviledge) far excels Inspiration. There is a common Assistance which natural Men may have in these Days, and which the godly may have intermingled with a gracious Assistance, which is also very different from Inspiration, and that is his assisting natural Principles; as his assisting the natural Apprehension, Reason, Memory, Conscience and natural Affection.

But to return to the Head of Impressions and immediate Revelations; many lay themselves open to a Delusion by expecting Direction from Heaven in this Way, and waiting for it: In such a Case it is easy for Persons to imagine that they have it. They are perhaps at a Loss concerning something, undetermined what they shall do, or what Course they should take in some Affair, and they pray to GOD to direct them, and make known to 'em his Mind and Will; and then, instead of expecting to be directed, by being assisted in Consideration of the Rules of GOD's Word, and their Circumstances, and GOD's Providence, and enabled to look on Things in a true Light, and justly to weigh them, they are waiting for some secret immediate Influence on their Minds, unaccountably swaying their Minds, and turning their Tho'ts or Inclinations that Way that GOD would have them go, and are observing their own Minds, to see what arises there, whether some Texts of Scripture don't come into the Mind, or whether some Ideas, or inward Motions and Dispositions don't arise in something of an unaccountable Manner, that they may call a divine Direction. Hereby they are exposed to two Things, *First*, They lay themselves open to the Devil, and give him a fair Opportunity to lead them where he pleases; for they stand ready to follow the first extraordinary Impulse that they shall have, groundlesly concluding it is from GOD. And *Secondly*, They are greatly exposed to be deceived by their own Imaginations; for such an Expectation awakens and quickens the Imagination; and that oftentimes is called an uncommon Impression, that is no such Thing; and they ascribe that to the Agency of some invisible Being, that is owing only to themselves.

Again, another Way that many have been deceived, is by drawing false Conclusions from true Premises. Many true and eminent Saints have been led into Mistakes and Snares, by arguing too much from that, that they have prayed in Faith; and that oftentimes when the Premises are true, they have indeed been greatly assisted in Prayer for such a particular Mercy, and have had the true Spirit of Prayer in Exercise in their asking it of GOD; but they have concluded more from these Premises than is a just Consequence from them: That they have thus prayed is a sure Sign that their Prayer is accepted and heard, and that GOD will give a gracious Answer, according to his own Wisdom, and that the particular Thing that was asked shall be given, or that which is equivalent; this is a just Consequence from it; but it is not infer'd by any new Revelation now made, but by the Revelation that is made in GOD's Word, the Promises made to the Prayer of Faith in the holy Scriptures: But that GOD will answer them in that individual Thing that they ask, if it ben't a Thing promised in GOD's Word, or they don't certainly know that it is that which will be most for the Good of God's Church, and the Advancement of CHRIST's Kingdom and Glory, nor whether it will be best for them, is more than can be justly concluded from it.—If GOD remarkably meets with one of his Children while he is praying for a particular Mercy of great Importance, for himself, or some other Person, or any Society of Men, & does by the Influences of his Spirit greatly humble him, & empty him of himself in his Prayer, and manifests himself remarkably in his Excellency, Sovereignty and his All-sufficient Power and Grace in JESUS CHRIST, and does in a remarkable Manner enable the Person to come to him for that Mercy, poor in Spirit, and with humble Resignation to God, and with a great Degree of Faith in the divine Sufficiency, and the Sufficiency of CHRIST's Mediation, that Person has indeed a great deal the more Reason to hope that God will grant that Mercy, than otherwise he would have; the greater Probability is justly infer'd from That, agreeable to the Promises of the holy Scripture, that the Prayer is accepted and heard; and it is much more probable that a Prayer that is heard will be returned with the particular Mercy that is asked, than one that is not heard. And there is no Reason at all to doubt, but that God does some Times especially enable to the Exercises of Faith, when the Minds of his Saints are engaged in Tho'ts of, and Prayer for some particular Blessing they greatly desire; i.e. GOD is pleased especially to give 'em a believing Frame, a Sense of his Fulness, and a Spirit of humble Dependence on him, at such Times as when they are thinking of and praying for that Mercy, more than for other Mercies; he gives 'em a particular Sense of his Ability to do that Thing, and of the Sufficiency of his Power to overcome such and such Obstacles, and the Sufficiency of his Mercy, and of the Blood of CHRIST for the Removal of the Guilt that is in the Way of the Bestowment of such a Mercy, in particular. When this is the Case, it makes the Probability still much greater, that God intends to bestow the particular Mercy sought, in his own Time, and his own Way. But here is nothing of the Nature of a Revelation in the Case, but only a drawing rational Conclusions from the particular Manner and Circumstances of the ordinary gracious Influences of GOD's Spirit. And as GOD is pleased sometimes to give his Saints particular Exercises of Faith in his Sufficiency, with Regard to particular Mercies they seek, so he is sometimes pleas'd to make Use of his Word in order to it, and helps the Actings of Faith with Respect to such a Mercy, by Texts of Scripture that do especially exhibit the Sufficiency of GOD's Power or Mercy, in such a like Case, or speak of such a Manner of the Exercise of GOD's Strength & Grace. The strengthening of their Faith in GOD's Sufficiency in this Case, is therefore a just Improvement of such Scriptures; it is no more than what those Scriptures, as they stand in the Bible, do hold forth just Cause for. But to take them as new Whispers or Revelations from Heaven, is not making a just Improvement of them.—If Persons have thus a Spirit of Prayer remarkably given them, concerning a particular Mercy, from Time to Time, so as evidently to be assisted to act Faith in GOD, in that

Particular, in a very distinguishing Manner, the Argument in some Cases, may be very strong that GOD does design to grant that Mercy, not from any Revelation now made of it, but from such a Kind and Manner of the ordinary Influence of his Spirit, with respect to that Thing.

But here a great deal of Caution and Circumspection must be used in drawing Inferences of this Nature: There are many Ways Persons may be misled and deluded. The Ground on which some expect that they shall receive the Thing they have asked for, is rather a strong Imagination, than any true humble Faith in the divine Sufficiency. They have a strong Perswasion that the Thing asked shall be granted, (which they can give no Reason for,) without any remarkable Discovery of that Glory and Fulness of GOD and CHRIST, that is the Ground of Faith. And sometimes the Confidence that Persons have that their Prayers shall be answered, is only a Self-righteous Confidence, and no true Faith: They have a high Conceit of themselves as eminent Saints, and special Favourites of GOD, and have also a high Conceit of the Prayers they have made, because they were much enlarged and affected in them; and hence they are positive in it that the Thing will come to pass. And sometimes when once they have conceived such a Notion, they grow stronger and stronger in it; and this they think is from an immediate divine Hand upon their Minds to strengthen their Confidence; whereas it is only by their dwelling in their Minds on their own Excellency, and high Experiences, and great Assistances, whereby they look brighter and brighter in their own Eyes. Hence 'tis found by Observation and Experience, that nothing in the World exposes so much to Enthusiasm as spiritual Pride and Self-righteousness.

In order to drawing a just Inference from the supposed Assistance we have had in Prayer for a particular Mercy, and judging of the Probability of the Bestowment of that individual Mercy, many Things must be considered. We must consider the Importance of the Mercy sought, and the Principle whence we so earnestly desire it; how far it is good, and agreeable to the Mind and Will of GOD; the Degree of Love to GOD that we exercised in our Prayer; the Degree of Discovery that is made of the divine Sufficiency, and the Degree in which our Assistance is manifestly distinguishing with respect to that

Mercy. And there is nothing of greater Importance in the Argument than the Degree of Humility, Poverty of Spirit, Selfemptiness and Resignation to the holy Will of GOD, which GOD gives us the Exercise of in our seeking that Mercy: Praying for a particular Mercy with much of these Things, I have often been blessed with a remarkable Bestowment of the particular Thing asked for.

From what has been said, we may see which Way GOD may, only by the ordinary gracious Influences of his Spirit, sometimes give his Saints special Reason to hope for the Bestowment of a particular Mercy they desire and have prayed for, and which we may suppose he oftentimes gives eminent Saints, that have great Degrees of Humility, and much Communion with GOD. And here, I humbly conceive, some eminent Servants of JESUS CHRIST that have appear'd in the Church of GOD, that we read of in Ecclesiastical Story, have been led into a Mistake; and through Want of distinguishing such Things as these from immediate Revelations, have thought that GOD has favoured 'em, in some Instances, with the same Kind of divine Influences that the Apostles and Prophets had of old.

Another erroneous Principle that some have embraced, that has been a Source of many Errors in their Conduct, is, That Persons ought always to do whatsoever the Spirit of GOD (tho' but indirectly,) inclines them to. Indeed the Spirit of GOD in it self is infinitely perfect, and all his immediate Actings, simply considered, are perfect, and there can be nothing wrong in them; and therefore all that the Spirit of GOD inclines us to directly and immediately, without the Intervention of any other Cause that shall pervert and misimprove what is from the Spirit of GOD, ought to be done; but there may be many Things that we may be disposed to do, which Disposition may indirectly be from the Spirit of GOD, that we ought not to do: The Disposition in general may be good, and be from the Spirit of GOD, but the particular Determination of that Disposition, as to particular Actions, Objects and Circumstances, may be ill, and not from the Spirit of GOD, but may be from the Intervention or Interposition of some Infirmity, Blindness, Inadvertence, Deceit or Corruption of ours; so that altho' the Disposition in general ought to be allowed & promoted, and all those Actings of it that are simply from GOD's

Spirit, yet the particular ill Direction or Determination of that Disposition, which is from some other Cause, ought not to be followed.

As for Instance, The Spirit of GOD may cause a Person to have a dear Love to another, and so a great Desire of, and Delight in his Comfort, Ease and Pleasure: This Disposition in general is good, and ought to be followed; but yet through the Intervention of Indiscretion, or some other bad Cause, it may be ill directed, and have a bad Determination, as to particular Acts; and the Person indirectly, through that real Love that he has to his Neighbour, may kill him with Kindness; he may do that out of sincere good Will to him, that may tend to ruin him.—A good Disposition may through some Inadvertence or Delusion, strongly incline a Person to that, which if he saw all Things as they are, would be most contrary to that Disposition. The true Loyalty of a General, and his Zeal for the Honour of his Prince, may exceedingly animate him in War; but yet this that is a good Disposition, thro' Indiscretion and Mistake, may push him forward to those Things that give the Enemy great Advantage, and may expose him and his Army to Ruin, and may tend to the Ruin of his Master's Interest.

The Apostle does evidently suppose that the Spirit of GOD in his extraordinary, immediate and miraculous Influences on Men's Minds, may in some Respect excite Inclinations in Men, that if gratified, would tend to Confusion, and therefore must sometimes be restrained, and in their Exercise, must be under the Government of Discretion. 1 *Cor.* 14. 31, 32, 33. *For ye may all prophecy, one by one, that all may learn, and all may be comforted. And the Spirits of the Prophets are subject to the Prophets; for God is not the Author of Confusion, but of Peace, as in all the Churches of the Saints.* Here by *the Spirits of the Prophets,* according to the known Phraseology of the Apostle, is meant the Spirit of GOD acting in the Prophets, according to those special Gifts, with which each one was endow'd. And here it is plainly implied that the Spirit of GOD, thus operating in them, may be an Occasion of their having, sometimes an Inclination to do that, in the Exercise of those Gifts, which it was not proper, decent or profitable that they should; and that therefore the Inclination, tho' indirectly from the Spirit of GOD, should be restrain'd, and that it ought to be subject to the Discretion of the Prophets, as to the particular Time and Circumstances of its Exercise.

I can make no Doubt but that it is possible for a Minister to have given him by the Spirit of GOD, such a Sense of the Importance of eternal Things, and of the Misery of Mankind, that are so many of them exposed to eternal Destruction, together with such a Love to Souls, that he might find in himself a Disposition to spend all his Time, Day and Night, in warning, exhorting and calling upon Men, and so that he must be obliged as it were to do Violence to himself ever to refrain, so as to give himself any Opportunity to eat, drink or sleep. And so I believe there may be a Disposition in like Manner, indirectly excited in Lay-Persons, through the Intervention of their Infirmity, to do what only belongs to Ministers. Yea to do those Things that would not become either Ministers or People: Through the Influence of the Spirit of GOD, together with want of Discretion, and some remaining Corruption, Women & Children might feel themselves inclined to break forth and scream aloud, to great Congregations, warning & exhorting the whole Multitude, and to go forth & hallow and scream in the Streets, or to leave the Families they belong to, and go from House to House, earnestly exhorting others; but yet it would by no Means follow that it was their Duty to do these Things, or that they would not have a Tendency to do ten Times as much Hurt as Good.

Another wrong Principle from whence have arisen Errors in Conduct, is, that whatsoever is found to be of present and immediate Benefit, may and ought to be practised, without looking forward to future Consequences. Some Persons seem to think that it sufficiently justifies any Thing that they say or do, that it is found to be for their present Edification, and the Edification of those that are with them; it assists and promotes their present Affection, and therefore they think they should not concern themselves about future Consequences, but leave them with GOD. Indeed in Things that are in themselves our Duty, being required by moral Rules, or absolute positive Commands of GOD, they must be done, and future Consequences must be left with GOD; our Election and Discretion takes no Place here: But in other Things we are to be governed by Discretion, and must not only look at the present Good, but our View must be extensive, and we must look at the Consequences of Things. 'Tis the Duty of Ministers especially to exercise this Discretion: In Things wherein they are not determined by an absolute Rule, and that are not enjoin'd them by a Wisdom superior to their own, CHRIST has left them to their own Discretion, with that general Rule, that they should exercise the utmost Wisdom they can obtain, in pursuing that, which upon the best View of the Consequences of Things they can get, will tend most to the Advancement of his Kingdom. This is implied in those Words of CHRIST to his Disciples, when he sent 'em forth to preach the Gospel, *Mat.* 10. 16. *Be ye wise as Serpents.* The Scripture always represents the Work of a Gospel-Minister by those Employments that do especially require a wise Foresight of, and Provision for future Events and Consequences. So it is compared to the Business of a Steward, that is a Business that in an eminent Manner requires Forecast, and a wise laying in of Provision, for the Supply of the Needs of the Family, according to its future Necessities; and a good Minister is called a wise Steward: So 'tis compared to the Business of an Husbandman, that almost wholly consists in those Things that are done with a View to the future Fruits & Consequences of his Labour: The Husbandman's Discretion and Forecast is eloquently set forth in *Isa.* 28. 24, 25, 26. *Doth the Plowman plow all Day to sow? Doth he open and break the Clods of his Ground? When he hath made plain the Face thereof, doth he not cast abroad the Fitches, and scatter the Cummin, and cast in the principal Wheat, and the appointed Barly, and the Rye, in their Place? For his God doth instruct him to Discretion, and doth teach him.* So the Work of the Ministry is compared to that of a wise Builder or Architect, who has a long Reach, and comprehensive View; and for whom it is necessary, that when he begins a Building, he should have at once a View of the whole Frame, and all the future Parts of the Structure, even to the Pinnacle, that all may fitly be fram'd together. So also it is compar'd to the Business of a Trader or Merchant, who is to gain by trading with the Money that he begins with: This also is a Business that exceedingly requires Forecast, and without it, is never like to be followed with any Success, for any long Time: So 'tis represented by the Business of a Fisherman, which depends on Craft and

Subtilty: 'Tis also compar'd to the Business of a Soldier that goes to War, which is a Business that perhaps, above any other secular Business, requires great Foresight, and a wise Provision for future Events and Consequences.

And particularly Ministers ought not to be careless how much they discompose & ruffle the Minds of those that they esteem natural Men, or how great an Uproar they raise in the carnal World, and so lay Blocks in the Way of the Propagation of Religion. This certainly is not to follow the Example of that zealous Apostle *Paul*, who tho' he would not depart from his enjoin'd Duty to please carnal Men, yet wherein he might with a good Conscience, did exceedingly lay out himself to please them, and if possible to avoid raising in the Multitude, Preju-dices, Oppositions and Tumults against the Gospel; and look'd upon it that it was of great Consequence that it should be, if possible, avoided. 1 *Cor.* 10. 32, 33. *Give none Offence, neither to the Jews, nor to the Gentiles, nor to the Church of God: Even as I please all Men, in all Things, not seeking mine own Profit, but the Profit of many, that they may be saved.* Yea, he declares that he laid himself out so much for this, that he made himself a Kind of a Servant to all Sorts of Men, conforming to their Customs and various Humours, in every Thing wherein he might, even in Things that were very burdensom to him, that he might not fright Men away from Christianity, and cause them to stand as it were braced and armed against it, but on the contrary, if possible, might with Condescention and Friendship win and draw them to it; as you may see, 1 *Cor.* 9. 19, 20, 21, 22, 23. And agreable hereto, are the Directions he gives to others, both Ministers and People: So he directs the Christian *Romans, not to please themselves, but every one please his Neighbour, for his Good, to Edification*, Rom. 15. 1, 2. *And to follow after the Things that make for Peace*, Chap. 14. 19. And he presses it in Terms exceeding strong, *Rom.* 12. 18. *If it be possible, as much as lieth in you, live peaceably with all Men.* And he directs Ministers, to endeavour if possible, to gain Opposers by a meek condescending Treatment, avoiding all Appearance of Strife or Fierceness, 2 *Tim.* 2. 24, 25, 26. To the like Pur-pose, the same Apostle directs Christians to *walk in Wisdom, towards them that are without*, Col. 4. 5. And to avoid giving Offence to others, if we can, *that our Good mayn't be evil spoken of*, Rom. 14. 16. So that 'tis evident that the great and most zealous and most successful Propagator of vital Religion that ever was, looked upon it to be of great Consequence to endeavour, as much as possible, by all the Methods of lawful Meekness and Gentleness, to avoid raising the Prejudice and Opposition of the World against Religion.—When we have done our utmost there will be Opposition enough against vital Religion, against which the carnal Mind of Man has such an Enmity; (we should not therefore needlesly increase and raise that Enmity) as in the Apostles Days, tho' he took so much Pains to please Men, yet because he was faithful and thorough in his Work, Persecution almost every where was raised against him.

A Fisherman is careful not needlessly to ruffle and disturb the Water, least he should drive the Fish away from his Net; but he'll rather endeavour if possible to draw them into it. Such a Fisherman was the Apostle. 2 *Cor*. 12. 15, 16. *And I will very gladly spend and be spent for you; though the more abundantly I love you, the less I be loved. But be it so, I did not burden you, nevertheless, being crafty, I caught you with Guile.*

The Necessity of suffering Persecution, in order to being a true Christian, has undoubtedly by some been carried to an Extreme, and the Doctrine has been abused. It has been look'd upon necessary to uphold a Man's Credit amongst others as a Christian, that he should be persecuted. I have heard it made an Objection against the Sincerity of particular Persons, that they were no more hated and reproached. And the Manner of glorying in Persecution, or the Cross of CHRIST, has in some been very wrong, so as has had too much of an Appearance of lifting up themselves in it, that they were very much hated and reviled, more than most, as an Evidence of their excelling others, in being good Soldiers of JESUS CHRIST. Such an Improvement of the Doctrine of the Enmity between the Seed of the Woman & the Seed of the Serpent, and of the Necessity of Persecution, becoming credible and customary, has a direct Tendency to cause those that would be accounted true Christians, to behave themselves so towards those that are not well affected to Religion, as to provoke their Hatred, or at least to be but little careful to avoid it, and not very studiously and earnestly to strive, (after the Apostle's Example and Precepts,) to please them to their Edification, and by Meekness & Gentleness to win them, and by all possible Means to live peaceably with them.

I believe that Saying of our Saviour, *I came not to send Peace on Earth, but Division*, has been abused; as tho' when we see great Strife and Division arise about Religion, and violent Heats of Spirit against the truly pious, and a loud Clamour and Uproar against the Work of GOD, it was to be rejoiced in, because it is that which CHRIST came to send. It has almost been laid down as a Maxim by some, that the more Division and Strife, the better Sign; which naturally leads Persons to seek it and provoke it, or leads 'em to, and encourages 'em in such a Manner of Behaviour, such a Roughness and Sharpness, or such an affected Neglect, as has a natural Tendency to raise Prejudice and Opposition; instead of striving, as the Apostle did to his utmost, by all Meekness, Gentleness and Benevolence of Behaviour, to prevent or asswage it.—CHRIST came to send a Sword on Earth, and to cause Division, no otherwise than he came to send Damnation; for CHRIST that is set for the glorious Restoration of some, is set for the Fall of others, and to be a Stone of Stumbling and Rock of Offence to them, and an Occasion of their vastly more aggravated and terrible Damnation; and this is always the Consequence of a great Outpouring of the Spirit and Revival of vital Religion, it is the Means of the Salvation of some, and the more aggravated Damnation of others. But certainly this is no just Argument that Men's Exposedness to Damnation is not to be lamented, or that we should not exert our selves to our utmost, in all the Methods that we can devise, that others might be saved, & to avoid all such Behaviour towards 'em as tends to lead 'em down to Hell.

I know there is naturally a great Enmity in the Heart of Man against vital Religion; and I believe there would have been a great deal of Opposition against this glorious Work of GOD in *New-England* if the Subjects & Promoters of it had behaved themselves never so agreeably to Christian Rules; and I believe if this Work goes on and spreads much in the World, so as to begin to shake Kingdoms and Nations, it will dreadfully stir up the Rage of Earth & Hell, and will put the World into the greatest Uproar that ever it was in since it stood; I believe Satan's dying Struggles will be the most violent: But yet I believe a great deal might be done to restrain this Opposition, by a good Conformity to that of the Apostle *James*, Jam. 3. 13. *Who is a wise Man, and endued with Knowledge? Let him shew out of a good Conversation, his Works, with Meekness of Wisdom.* And I also believe that if the Rules of Christian Charity, Meekness, Gentleness and Prudence had been duly observed by the Generality of the zealous Promoters of this Work, it would have made three Times the Progress that it has; *i.e.* if it had pleased GOD in such a Case, to give a Blessing to Means in Proportion as he has done.

Under this Head of Carelesness of the future Consequences of Things, it may be proper to say something of introducing Things new & strange, and that have a Tendency by their Novelty to shock and surprize People. Nothing can be more evident from the New-Testament, than that such Things ought to be done with great Caution and Moderation, to avoid the Offence that may be thereby given, and the Prejudices that might be raised, to clog & hinder the Progress of Religion: Yea, that it ought to be thus in Things that are in themselves good and excellent, and of great Weight, provided they are not Things that are of the Nature of absolute Duty, which tho' they may appear to be Innovations, yet can't be neglected without Immorality or Disobedience to the Commands of GOD. What great Caution and Moderation did the Apostles use in introducing Things that were new, and abolishing Things that were old in their Day? How gradually were the Ceremonial Performances of the Law of *Moses* removed and abolished among the Christian Jews? And how long did even the Apostle *Paul* himself conform to those Ceremonies which he calls weak and beggarly Elements? Yea even to the Rite of Circumcision, (*Acts* 16. 3.) that he speaks so much in his Epistles of the Worthlesness of, that he might not prejudice the *Jews* against Christianity? So it seems to have been very gradually that the *Jewish* Sabbath was abolished, and the Christian Sabbath introduced, for the same Reason. And the Apostles avoided teaching the Christians in those early Days, at least for a great while, some high and excellent divine Truths, because they could not bear 'em yet. 1 *Cor.* 3. 1, 2. *Heb.* 5. 11. to the End. Thus strictly did the

Apostles observe the Rule that their blessed Master gave
them, of not putting new Wine into old Bottles, lest they
should burst the Bottles, and lose the Wine. And how did
CHRIST himself, while on Earth, forbear so plainly to teach
his Disciples the great Doctrines of Christianity, concerning
his Satisfaction, and the Nature and Manner of a Sinner's
Justification & Reconciliation with God, and the particular
Benefits of his Death, Resurrection & Ascension, because in
that infant State the Disciples were then in, their Minds were
not prepared for such Instructions; and therefore the more
clear and full Revelation of these Things was reserved for the
Time when their Minds should be further enlighten'd and
strengthen'd by the Out-pouring of the Spirit after his Ascension. Joh. 16. 12, 13. *I have yet many Things to say unto you,
but ye cannot bear them now: Howbeit, when he, the Spirit of
Truth is come, he will guide you into all Truth.* And Mark. 4. 33.
*And with many such Parables spake he the Word unto them, as
they were able to bear it.*—These Things might be enough to
convince any one, that don't think himself wiser than CHRIST
and his Apostles, that great Prudence and Caution should be
used in introducing Things into the Church of GOD, that are
very uncommon, tho' in themselves they may be very excellent, least by our Rashness & imprudent Haste we hinder
Religion, much more than we help it.

Persons that are influenced by an indiscreet Zeal are always
in too much Haste; they are impatient of Delays, and therefore
are for jumping to the uppermost Step first, before they have
taken the preceeding Steps; whereby they expose themselves
to fall and break their Bones: It is a Thing very taking with
them to see the Building rise very high, and all their Endeavour and Strength is employed in advancing the Building in
Height, without taking Care withal proportionably to enlarge
the Bottom; whereby the whole is in Danger of coming to
the Ground; or they are for putting on the Cupola and Pinnacle before they are come to it, or before the lower Parts of
the Building are done; which tends at once to put a Stop to the
Building, and hinder its ever being a compleat Structure. Many
that are thus imprudent and hasty with their Zeal, have a real
eager Appetite for that which is good; but are like Children,
that are impatient to wait for the Fruit 'till the proper Season

of it, and therefore snatch it before it is ripe: Oftentimes in their Haste they overshoot their Mark, and frustrate their own End; they put that which they would obtain further out of Reach than it was before, and establish and confirm that which they would remove. Things must have Time to ripen: The prudent Husbandman waits 'till he has received the former and the latter Rain, and 'till the Harvest is ripe, before he reaps. We are now just as it were beginning to recover out of a dreadful Disease that we have been long under; and to feed a Man recovering from a Fever with strong Meat at once, is the ready Way to kill him. The Reformation from Popery was much hinder'd by this hasty Zeal: Many were for immediately rectifying all Disorders by Force, which were condemned by *Luther*, and were a great Trouble to him. See *Sleiden*'s Hist. of the Reformation, pag. 52. *&c.* and Book V. throughout. It is a vain Prejudice that some have lately imbibed against such Rules of Prudence and Moderation: They will be forced to come to 'em at last; they'll find themselves that they are not able to maintain their Cause without 'em; and if they won't hearken before, Experience will convince 'em at last, when it will be too late for them to rectify their Mistake.

Another Error, that is of the Nature of an erroneous Principle, that some have gone upon, is a wrong Notion that they have of an Attestation of divine Providence to Persons or Things. We go too far when we look upon the Success that GOD gives to some Persons, in making them the Instruments of doing much Good, as a Testimony of GOD's Approbation of those Persons and all the Courses they take. It is a main Argument that has been made Use of to defend the Conduct of some of those Ministers, that have been blamed as imprudent & irregular, that GOD has smiled upon them and blessed them, and given them great Success, and that however Men charge them as guilty of many wrong Things, yet 'tis evident that GOD is with them, and then who can be against them? And probably some of those Ministers themselves, by this very Means, have had their Ears stopp'd against all that has been said to convince 'em of their Misconduct. But there are innumerable Ways that Persons may be misled, in forming a Judgment of the Mind and Will of GOD, from the Events of Providence. If a Person's Success be a Reward of something that GOD sees in him, that

he approves of, yet 'tis no Argument that he approves of every
Thing in him. Who can tell how far the divine Grace may go in
greatly rewarding some small Good that he sees in a Person, a
good Meaning, something good in his Disposition, while he at
the same Time, in sovereign Mercy, hides his Eyes from a great
deal that is bad, that 'tis his Pleasure to forgive, and not to
mark against the Person, tho' in it self it be very ill? GOD has
not told us after what Manner he will proceed in this Matter,
and we go upon most uncertain Grounds when we undertake
to determine. It is an exceeding difficult Thing to know how
far Love or Hatred are exercised towards Persons or Actions,
by all that is before us. GOD was pleased in his Sovereignty to
give such Success to *Jacob* in that, which from Beginning to
End, was a deceitful, lying Contrivance and Proceeding of his,
that in that Way, he obtain'd that Blessing that was worth infinitely more than the Fatness of the Earth, and the Dew of
Heaven, that was given to *Esau*, in his Blessing, yea worth
more than all that the World can afford. GOD was for a while
with *Judas*, so that he by GOD's Power accompanying him,
wrought Miracles and cast out Devils; but this could not justly
be interpreted as GOD's Approbation of his Person, or his
Thievery, that he lived in at the same Time.

The Dispensations and Events of Providence, with their
Reasons, are too little understood by us, to be improved by us
as our Rule, instead of GOD's Word; *God has his Way in the
Sea, and his Path in the mighty Waters, and his Footsteps are not
known, and he gives us no Account of any of his Matters*; and
therefore we can't safely take the Events of his Providence as a
Revelation of his Mind concerning a Person's Conduct and
Behaviour, we have no Warrant so to do, GOD has never appointed those Things, but something else to be our Rule; we
have but one Rule to go by, and that is his holy Word, and
when we join any Thing else with it as having the Force of a
Rule, we are guilty of that which is strictly forbidden, *Deut.* 4. 2.
Prov. 30. 6. & *Rev.* 22. 18. They who make what they imagine is pointed forth to 'em in Providence, their Rule of Behaviour, do err, as well as those that follow Impulses and
Impressions: We should put nothing in the Room of the Word
of GOD. It is to be feared that some have been greatly confirmed and emboldened by the great Success that GOD has

given them, in some Things that have really been contrary to the Rules of GOD's holy Word. If it has been so, they have been guilty of Presumption, and abusing God's Kindness to them, and the great Honour he has put upon them: They have seen that God was with them, and made them victorious in their Preaching; and this it is to be feared has been abused by some to a Degree of Self-confidence; it has much taken off all Jealousy of themselves; they have been bold therefore to go great Lengths, in a Presumption that GOD was with them, and would defend them, & finally baffle all that found Fault with them.

Indeed there is a Voice of GOD in his Providence, that may be interpreted and well understood by the Rule of his Word; and Providence may to our dark Minds and weak Faith, confirm the Word of GOD, as it fulfils it: But to improve divine Providence thus, is quite a different Thing from making a Rule of Providence. There is a good Use may be made of the Events of Providence, of our own Observation and Experience, and human Histories, and the Opinion of the Fathers, & other eminent Men; but finally all must be brought to *one Rule, viz.* the Word of GOD, and that must be regarded as our *only Rule*.

Nor do I think that they go upon sure Ground, that conclude that they have not been in an Error in their Conduct, because that at the Time of their doing a Thing, for which they have been blamed and reproached by others, they were favour'd with special Comforts of GOD's Spirit. GOD's bestowing special spiritual Mercies on a Person at such a Time, is no Sign that he approves of every Thing that he sees in him at that Time. *David* had very much of the Presence of GOD while he lived in Polygamy: And *Solomon* had some very high Favours, and peculiar Smiles of Heaven, and particularly at the Dedication of the Temple, while he greatly multiplied Wives to himself, and Horses, and Silver and Gold; all contrary to the most express Command of GOD to the King, in the Law of *Moses*, Deut. 17. 16, 17. We can't tell how far GOD may hide his Eyes from beholding Iniquity in *Jacob*, and seeing Perverseness in *Israel*. We can't tell what are the Reasons of GOD's Actions any further than he interprets for himself. GOD sometimes gave some of the primitive Christians, the extraordinary

Influence of his Spirit, when they were out of the Way of their
Duty; and continued it, while they were abusing it; as is plainly
implied, 1 *Cor.* 14. 31, 32, 33.

Yea, if a Person has done a Thing for which he is reproached,
and that Reproach be an Occasion of his feeling sweet Exercises of Grace in his Soul, and that from Time to Time, I don't
think that is a certain Evidence that GOD approves of the
Thing he is blamed for. For undoubtedly a Mistake may be the
Occasion of stirring up the Exercise of Grace, in a Man that
has Grace. If a Person, through Mistake, thinks he has received
some particular great Mercy, that Mistake may be the Occasion of stirring up the sweet Exercises of Love to GOD, and
true Thankfulness and Joy in GOD. As for Instance, if one that
is full of Love to GOD should hear credible Tidings, concerning a remarkable Deliverance of a Child, or other dear Friend,
or of some glorious Thing done for the City of GOD, no
Wonder if, on such an Occasion, the sweet Actings of Love to
GOD, and Delight in GOD should be excited, tho' indeed
afterwards it should prove a false Report that he heard. So if
one that loves GOD, is much maligned and reproached for
doing that which he thinks GOD required and approves, no
Wonder that it is sweet to such an one to think that GOD is his
Friend, tho' Men are his Enemies; no Wonder at all, that this is
an Occasion of his, as it were, leaving the World, and sweetly
betaking himself to GOD, as his sure Friend, and finding sweet
Complacence in GOD; tho' he be indeed in a Mistake, concerning that which he thought was agreeable to GOD's Will. As
I have before shewn that the Exercise of a truly good Affection, may be the Occasion of Error, and may indirectly incline
a Person to do that which is wrong; so on the other Hand,
Error, or a doing that which is wrong, may be an Occasion of
the Exercise of a truly good Affection. The Reason of it is this,
that however all Exercises of Grace be from the Spirit of GOD,
yet the Spirit of GOD dwells and acts in the Hearts of the
Saints, in some Measure after the Manner of a vital, natural
Principle, a Principle of new Nature in them; whose Exercises
are excited by Means, in some Measure as other natural Principles are. Tho' Grace ben't in the Saints, as a *meer natural
Principle*, but as a sovereign Agent, and so its Exercises are not
tied to Means, by an immutable Law of Nature, as in meer

natural Principles; yet GOD has so constituted, that Grace should dwell so in the Hearts of the Saints, that its Exercises should have some Degree of Connection with Means, after the Manner of a Principle of Nature.

Another erroneous Principle that there has been something of, and that has been an Occasion of some Mischief and Confusion, is that external Order in Matters of Religion, and Use of the Means of Grace, is but little to be regarded: 'Tis spoken lightly of, under the Names of Ceremonies & dead Forms, &c. And is probably the more despised by some because their Opposers insist so much upon it, and because they are so continually hearing from them the Cry of *Disorder and Confusion*.—'Tis objected against the Importance of external Order that GOD don't look at the outward Form, he looks at the Heart: But that is a weak Argument against its Importance, that true Godliness don't consist in it; for it may be equally made Use of against all the outward Means of Grace whatsoever. True Godliness don't consist in Ink and Paper, but yet that would be a foolish Objection against the Importance of Ink and Paper in Religion, when without it we could not have the Word of GOD. If any external Means at all are needful, any outward Actions of a publick Nature, or wherein GOD's People are jointly concerned in publick Society, without Doubt external Order is needful: The Management of an external Affair that is publick, or wherein a Multitude is concerned without Order, is in every Thing found impossible. Without Order there can be no general Direction of a Multitude to any particular designed End, their Purposes will cross one another, and they won't help but hinder one another. A Multitude can't act in Union one with another without Order; Confusion separates and divides them, so that there can be no Concert or Agreement. If a Multitude would help one another in any Affair, they must unite themselves one to another in a regular Subordination of Members, in some Measure as it is in the natural Body; by this Means they will be in some Capacity to act with united Strength: And thus CHRIST has appointed that it should be in the visible Church as 1 *Cor.* 12. 14. to the End, and *Rom.* 12. 4, 5, 6, 7, 8. Zeal without Order will do but little, or at least it will be effectual but a little while. Let a Company that are very zealous against the Enemy, go forth to War, without any

Manner of Order, every one rushing forward as his Zeal shall drive him, all in Confusion, if they gain something at first Onset, by surprizing the Enemy, yet how soon do they come to nothing, and fall an easy helpless Prey to their Adversaries? Order is one of the most necessary of all external Means of the spiritual Good of GOD's Church; and therefore it is requisite even in Heaven it self, where there is the least Need of any external Means of Grace; Order is maintained amongst the glorious Angels there. And the Necessity of it in order to the carrying on any Design, wherein a Multitude are concerned, is so great, that even the Devils in Hell are driven to something of it, that they may carry on the Designs of their Kingdom. And 'tis very observable, that those Kinds of irrational Creatures, for whom it is needful that they should act in Union and join a Multitude together, to carry on any Work for their Preservation, they do by a wonderful Instinct that GOD has put into them, observe and maintain a most regular and exact Order among themselves; such as Bees and some others. And Order in the visible Church is not only necessary to the carrying on the Designs of CHRIST's Glory and the Church's Prosperity, but it is absolutely necessary to its Defence; without it, it's like a City without Walls, and can be in no Capacity to defend it self from any Kind of Mischief: And so however it be an external Thing, yet is not to be despised on that Account; for tho' it ben't the Food of Souls, yet it is in some Respect their Defence.—The People of *Holland* would be very foolish to despise the Dikes that keep out the Sea from overwhelming them, under the Names of dead Stones and vile Earth, because the Matter of which they are built is not good to eat.

It seems to be partly on the Foundation of this Notion of the Worthlesness of external Order, that some have seem'd to act on that Principle, that the Power of judging & openly censuring others should not be reserved in the Hands of particular Persons, or Consistories appointed thereto, but ought to be left at large, for any Body that pleases to take it upon them, or that think themselves fit for it, But more of this afterwards—

On this Foundation also, an orderly attending on the stated Worship of GOD in Families, has been made too light of; and it has been in some Places too much of a common & customary Thing to be absent from Family Worship, & to be abroad late in the Night at religious Meetings, or to attend religious Conversation. Not but that this may be, on certain extraordinary Occasions; I have seen the Case to be such in many Instances, that I have thought did afford sufficient Warrant for Persons to be absent from Family Prayer, and to be from Home 'till very late in the Night: But we should take Heed that this don't become a Custom or common Practice; if it should be so, we shall soon find the Consequences to be very ill.

It seems to be on the same Foundation, of the supposed Unprofitableness of external Order, that it has been thought by some, that there is no Need that such and such religious Services and Performances should be limited to any certain Office in the Church; (of which more afterwards.) And also that those Offices themselves, as particularly that of the Gospel-Ministry, need not be limited as it used to be, to Persons of a liberal Education; but some of late have been for having others that they have supposed to be Persons of eminent Experience, publickly licensed to preach, yea and ordained to the Work of the Ministry; and some Ministers have seem'd to favour such a Thing: But how little do they seem to look forward, and consider the unavoidable Consequences of opening such a Door? If once it should become a Custom, or a Thing generally approved and allowed of, to admit Persons to the Work of the Ministry that have had no Education for it, because of their remarkable Experiences, and being Persons of good Understanding, how many Lay-Persons would soon appear as Candidates for the Work of the Ministry? I doubt not but that I have been acquainted with Scores that would have desired it. And how shall we know where to stop? If one is admitted because his Experiences are remarkable, another will think his Experiences also remarkable; and we perhaps, shall not be able to deny but that they are near as great: If one is admitted because besides Experiences, he has good natural Abilities, another by himself, and many of his Neighbours, may be thought equal to him. It will be found of absolute Necessity that there should be some certain, visible Limits fixed, to avoid bringing Odium upon ourselves, and breeding Uneasiness and Strife amongst others; and I know of none better, and indeed no other that can well be fix'd, than those that the Prophet *Zechariah* fixes, *viz.* That those only should be appointed to be Pastors or

Shepherds in GOD's Church, that *have been taught to keep Cattle from their Youth*, or that have had an Education for that Purpose. Those Ministers that have a Disposition to break over these Limits, if they should do so, and make a Practice of it, would break down that Fence, which they themselves after a while, after they have been wearied with the ill Consequences, would be glad to have some Body else build up for them. Not but that there may probably be some Persons in the Land, that have had no Education at College, that are in themselves better qualified for the Work of the Ministry than some others that have taken their Degrees, and are now ordained. But yet I believe the breaking over those Bounds that have hitherto been set, in ordaining such Persons, would in its Consequences be a greater Calamity, than the missing such Persons in the Work of the Ministry. The opening a Door for the Admission of unlearned Men to the Work of the Ministry, tho' they should be Persons of extraordinary Experience, would on some Accounts be especially prejudicial at such a Day as this; because such Persons, for want of an extensive Knowledge, are oftentimes forward to lead others into those Things, which a People are in Danger of at such a Time, above all other Times, *viz.* Impulses, vain Imaginations, Superstition, indiscreet Zeal, and such like Extremes; instead of defending them from them, for which a People especially need a Shepherd, at such an extraordinary Season.

Another erroneous Principle that it seems to me some have been, at least, in Danger of, is, that Ministers, because they speak as CHRIST's Ambassadors, may assume the same Style, and speak as with the same Authority that the Prophets of old did, yea that JESUS CHRIST himself did in the 23d of Matthew, *Ye Serpents, ye Generation of Vipers*, &c. and other Places; and that not only when they are speaking to the People, but also to their Brethren in the Ministry. Which Principle is absurd, because it makes no Difference in the different Degrees and Orders of Messengers that GOD has sent into the World, tho' God has made a very great Difference: For tho' they all come in some Respect in the Name of GOD, and with something of his Authority, yet certainly there is a vast Difference in the Degree of Authority with which GOD has invested them. JESUS CHRIST was one that was sent into the World as GOD's

Messenger, and so was one of his Apostles, and so also is an ordinary Pastor of a Church; but yet it don't follow, that because JESUS CHRIST and an ordinary Minister are both Messengers of GOD, that therefore an ordinary Minister in his Office, is vested with an equal Degree of Authority, that CHRIST was, in his. As there is a great Difference in their Authority, and as CHRIST came as GOD's Messenger, in a vastly higher Manner, so another Style became him, more authoritative than is proper for us Worms of the Dust, tho' we also are Messengers of inferiour Degree. It would be strange if GOD, when he has made so great a Difference in the Degree in which he has invested different Messengers with his Authority, should make no Difference as to the outward Appearance and Shew of Authority, in Style and Behaviour, which is proper and fit to be seen in them. Tho' GOD has put great Honour upon Ministers, and they may speak as his Ambassadors, yet he never intended that they should have the same outward Appearance of Authority and Majesty, either in their Behaviour or Speech, that his Son shall have, when he comes to Judgment, at the last Day; tho' both come, in different Respects and Degrees, in the Name of the Lord: Alas! Can any Thing ever make it enter into the Hearts of Worms of the Dust, that it is fit and suitable that it should be so?

Thus I have considered the two first of those three Causes of Error in Conduct that were mention'd; I come now to the

Third and last Cause of the Errors of those that have appear'd to be the Subjects or zealous Promoters of this Work, *viz.* a being ignorant or unobservant of some particular Things, by which the Devil has special Advantage.

And here I would particularly take Notice 1. Of some Things with Respect to the inward Experiences of Christians themselves. And 2. Something with Regard to the external Effects of Experiences.

There are three Things I would take Notice of with Regard to the Experiences of Christians, by which the Devil has many Advantages against us.

1. The first Thing is the *Mixture* there oftentimes is in the Experiences of true Christians; whereby when they have truly gracious Experiences, and divine and spiritual Discoveries and Exercises, they have something else mix'd with them, besides

what is spiritual: There is a Mixture of that which is natural, and that which is corrupt, with that which is divine. This is what Christians are liable to in the present exceeding imperfect State: The great Imperfection of Grace, and Feebleness and Infancy of the new Nature, and the great Remains of Corruption, together with the Circumstances we are in in this World, where we are encompassed all round with what tends to pollute us, exposes to this. And indeed it is not to be supposed that Christians ever have any Experiences in this World that are wholly pure, entirely spiritual, without any Mixture of what is natural and carnal: The Beam of Light, as it comes from the Fountain of Light upon our Hearts, is pure, but as it is reflected thence, it is mixt: The Seed as sent from Heaven and planted in the Heart, is pure, but as it springs up out of the Heart, is impure; yea there is commonly a much greater Mixture, than Persons for the most Part seem to have any Imagination of; I have often thought that the Experiences of true Christians are very frequently as it is with some Sorts of Fruits, that are invelop'd in several Coverings of thick Shells or Pods, that are thrown away by him that gathers the Fruit, and but a very small Part of the whole Bulk is the pure Kernel, that is good to eat.

The Things, of all which there is frequently some Mixture with gracious Experiences, yea with very great and high Experiences, are these three, *Human, or natural Affection and Passion; Impressions on the Imagination*; and a Degree of *Self-righteousness* or *spiritual Pride*. There is very often with that which is spiritual a great Mixture of that Affection or Passion which arises from natural Principles; so that Nature has a very great Hand in those vehement Motions and Flights of the Passions that appear. Hence the same Degrees of divine Communications from Heaven, shall have vastly different Effects, in what outwardly appears, in Persons of different natural Tempers. The great Mixture of that which is natural with that which is spiritual, is very manifest in the peculiar Effects that divine Influences have in some certain Families, or Persons of such a Blood, in a distinguishing Manner of the operating of the Passions and Affections, and the Manner of the outward Expressions of 'em. I know some remarkable Instances of this. The same is also evident by the different Effects of divine

Communications on the same Person at different Times, and in different Circumstances: The Novelty of Things, or the sudden Transition from an opposite Extreme, and many other Things that might be mentioned, greatly contribute to the raising of the Passions. And sometimes there is not only a Mixture of that which is common and natural with gracious Experience, but even that which is animal, that which is in a great Measure from the Body, and is properly the Result of the animal Frame. In what true Christians feel of Affections towards GOD, all is not always purely holy and divine; every Thing that is felt in the Affections don't arise from spiritual Principles, but common and natural Principles have a very great Hand; an improper Self-Love may have a great Share in the Effect: GOD is not loved for his own Sake, or for the Excellency and Beauty of his own Perfections as he ought to be; nor have these Things in any wise, that Proportion in the Effect that they ought to have. So in that Love that true Christians have one to another, very often there is a great Mixture of what arises from common and natural Principles, with Grace; & Self-Love has a great Hand: The Children of GOD ben't loved purely for Christ's Sake, but there may be a great Mixture of that natural Love that many Sects of Hereticks have boasted of, who have been greatly united one to another, because they were of their Company, on their Side, against the rest of the World; yea, there may be a Mixture of natural Love to the opposite Sex, with Christian and divine Love. So there may be a great Mixture in that Sorrow for Sin that the godly have; and also in their Joys; natural Principles may greatly contribute to what is felt, a great many Ways, as might easily be shown, would it not make my Discourse too lengthy. There is nothing that belongs to Christian Experience that is more liable to a corrupt Mixture than Zeal; tho' it be an excellent Virtue, a heavenly Flame, when it is pure: but as it is exercised in those who are so little sanctified, and so little humbled, as we are in the present State, 'tis very apt to be mix'd with human Passion, yea with corrupt hateful Affections, Pride and uncharitable Bitterness, and other Things that are not from Heaven but from Hell.

Another Thing that is often mixed with what is spiritual in the Experiences of Christians, are, Impressions on the Imagina-

tion; whereby godly Persons, together with a spiritual understanding of divine Things, and Conviction of their Reality and
Certainty, and a strong and deep Sense of their Excellency or
great Importance upon their Hearts, have strongly impress'd
on their Minds external Ideas or Images of Things. A Degree
of Imagination in such a Case, as I have observ'd elsewhere, is
unavoidable, and necessarily arises from human Nature, as
constituted in the present State; and a Degree of Imagination
is really useful, and often is of great Benefit; but when it is in
too great a Degree it becomes an impure Mixture that is prejudicial. This Mixture very often arises from the Constitution of
the Body. It commonly greatly contributes to the other Kind
of Mixture mentioned before, *viz.* of natural Affections & Passions; it helps to raise them to a great Height.

Another Thing that is often mix'd with the Experiences of
true Christians, which is the worst Mixture of all, is a Degree
of Self-righteousness or spiritual Pride. This is often mix'd with
the Joys of Christians; the Joy that they have is not purely the
Joy of Faith, or a Rejoicing in Christ Jesus, but is partly a rejoicing in themselves; There is oftentimes in their Elevations a
looking upon themselves, and a viewing their own high Attainments; they rejoice partly because they are taken with their
own Experiences and great Discoveries, which makes 'em in
their own Apprehensions so to excel; and this heightens all
their Passions, and especially those Effects that are more
External.

There is a much greater Mixture of these Things in the Experiences of some Christians than others; in some the Mixture
is so great, as very much to obscure and hide the Beauty of
Grace in them, like a thick Smoke that hinders all the Shining
of the Fire.

These Things we ought to be well aware of, that we mayn't
take all for Gold that glisters, and that we may know what to
countenance and encourage, and what to discourage; otherwise Satan will have a vast Advantage against us, for he works
in the corrupt Mixture. Sometimes for want of Persons distinguishing the Oar from the pure Metal, those Experiences are
most admired by the Persons themselves that are the Subjects
of them, and by others, that are not the most excellent. The
great external Effects, and Vehemence of the Passions, & violent

Agitations of the animal Spirits, is sometimes much owing to the corrupt Mixture; (as is very apparent in some Instances) tho' it be not always so. I have observed a great Difference among those that are under high Affections, and seem disposed to be earnestly talking to those that are about them; some insist much more, in their Talk, on what they behold in GOD and CHRIST, the Glory of the divine Perfections, CHRIST's Beauty and Excellency, and wonderful Condescension and Grace, and their own Unworthiness, and the great and infinite Obligations that they themselves and others are under to love and serve GOD; some insist almost wholly on their own high Priviledges, their Assurance of GOD's Love and Favour, and the Weakness and Wickedness of Opposers, and how much they are above their Reach. The latter may have much of the Presence of GOD, but their Experiences don't appear to be so solid and unmix'd as the former. And there is a great deal of Difference in Persons Earnestness in their Talk and Behaviour; in some it seems to come indeed from the Fulness of their Hearts, and from the great Sense they have of Truth, a deep Sense of the Certainty and infinite Greatness, Excellency and Importance of divine and eternal Things, attended with all Appearances of great Humility; in others their Earnestness seems to arise from a great Mixture of human Passion, and an undue and intemperate Agitation of the Spirits, which appears by their Earnestness and Vehemence not being proportion'd to the Nature of the Subject they insist on, but they are violent in every Thing they say, as much when they are talking of Things of smaller Importance, as when speaking of Things of greater Weight. I have seen it thus in an Instance or two, in which this Vehemence at length issued in Distraction. And there have been some few Instances of a more extraordinary Nature still, even of Persons finding themselves disposed earnestly to talk and cry out, from an unaccountable Kind of bodily Pressure, without any extraordinary View of any Thing in their Minds, or Sense of any Thing upon their Hearts; wherein probably there was the immediate Hand of the Devil.

2. Another Thing by which the Devil has great Advantage, is, the unheeded *Defects* there sometimes are in the Experiences of true Christians, and those high Affections wherein there is much that is truly good.

What I now have Respect to is something diverse from that Defect, or Imperfection of Degree, which is in every holy Disposition and Exercise in this Life, in the best of the Saints. What I aim at is Experiences being especially defective in some particular Thing, that ought to be in them; which tho' it ben't an essential Defect, or such a Defect as is in the Experiences of Hypocrites, which renders them utterly vain, monstrous, and altogether abominable to GOD, yet is such a Defect as maims and deforms the Experience; the Essence of truly Christian Experiences is not wanting, but yet that is wanting that is very needful in order to the proper Beauty of the image of Christ in such a Person's Experiences; but Things are very much out of a due Proportion: There is indeed much of some Things, but at the same Time there is so little of some other Things that should bear a Proportion, that the Defect very much deforms the Christian, and is truly odious in the Sight of GOD.

What I observed before was something that deform'd the Christian, as it was *too much*, something mix'd, that is not belonging to the Christian as such; what I speak of now is something that deforms the Christian the other Way, *viz.* By their *not* being *enough*, something wanting, that does belong to the Christian as such: The one deforms the Christian as a monstrous Excrescence, the other as thereby the new Creature is maimed, and some Member in a great Measure wanting, or so small and withering as to be very much out of due Proportion. This is another spiritual Calamity that the Saints are liable to through the great Imperfection of Grace in this Life; like the Chicken in the Egg, in the beginning of its Formation, in which, tho' there are indeed the Rudiments or Lineaments of all the Parts, yet some few Parts are plain to be seen, when others are hid, so that without a Microscope it appears very monstrous.

When this Deficiency & Disproportion is great, as sometimes it is in real Saints, it is not only a great Deformity in it self, but has many ill Consequences; it gives the Devil great Advantage, and leaves a Door open for Corruption, & exposes to very deformed and unlovely Actions, and issues oftentimes in the great wounding of the Soul.

For the better understanding of this Matter, we may observe that GOD in the Revelation that he has made of himself to the

World by Jesus Christ, has taken Care to give a proportionable Manifestation of two Kinds of Excellencies or Perfections of his Nature, *viz.* Those that especially tend to possess us with Awe and Reverence, and to search and humble us, and those that tend to win and draw and encourage us: By *the one*, he appears as an infinitely great, pure, holy and Heart-searching Judge; by *the other*, as a gentle and gracious Father and a loving Friend: By the one he is a pure, searching & burning Flame; by the other a sweet, refreshing Light. These two Kinds of Attributes are as it were admirably tempered together in the Revelation of the Gospel: There is a proportionable Manifestation of Justice and Mercy, Holiness and Grace, Majesty & Gentleness, Authority and Condescension. GOD hath thus ordered that his diverse Excellencies, as he reveals himself in the Face of JESUS CHRIST, should have a proportionable Manifestation, herein providing for our Necessities; he knew it to be of great Consequence that our Apprehensions of these diverse Perfections of his Nature should be duely proportion'd one to another; a Defect on the one Hand, *viz.* Having much of a Discovery of his Love and Grace, without a proportionable Discovery of his awful Majesty, and his holy and searching Purity, would tend to spiritual Pride, carnal Confidence and Presumption; and a Defect on the other Hand, *viz.* Having much of a Discovery of his holy Majesty, without a proportionable Discovery of his Grace, tends to Unbelief, a sinful Fearfulness and Spirit of Bondage. And therefore herein chiefly consists that Deficiency of Experiences that I am now speaking of: The Revelation GOD has made of himself in his Word, and the Provision made for our spiritual Welfare in the Gospel is perfect, but yet the actual Light and Communications we have, are not perfect, but many Ways exceeding imperfect and maimed. And Experience plainly shews that Christians may have high Experiences in some Respects, and yet their Circumstances may be unhappy in this Regard, that their Experiences and Discoveries are no more general. There is a great Difference among Christians in this Respect, some have much more general Discoveries than others, who are upon many Accounts the most amiable Christians. Christians may have Experiences that are very high, and yet there may be very much of this Deficiency and Disproportion: Their high Experiences are truly from the Spirit of GOD, but Sin comes in by the Defect; (as indeed all Sin is originally from a defective, privative Cause;) and in such a Case high Discoveries, at the same Time that they are enjoyed, may be, and sometimes are the Occasion, or *Causa sine qua non* of Sin; Sin may come in at that back Door, the Gap that is left open; as spiritual Pride often does: And many Times the Spirit of GOD is quenched by this Means, and GOD punishes the Pride and Presumption that rises, by bringing such Darkness, and suffering such awful Consequences and horrid Temptations, as are enough to make one's Hair stand an End to hear them. Christians therefore should diligently observe their own Hearts as to this Matter, and should pray to GOD that he would give 'em Experiences in which one Thing may bear a Proportion to another, that GOD may be honoured and their Souls edified thereby; and Ministers should have an Eye to this, in their private Dealings with the Souls of their People.

'Tis chiefly from such a Defect of Experiences that some Things have arisen that have been pretty common among true Christians of late, that have been supposed by many to have risen from a good Cause; as particularly talking of divine and heavenly Things, and expressing divine Joys with Laughter or a light Behaviour. I believe in many Instances such Things have arisen from a good Cause, as their *Causa sine qua non*; that high Discoveries and gracious joyful Affections have been the Occasion of them: but the proper Cause has been Sin, even that odious Defect in their Experience, whereby there has been wanting a Sense of the awful and holy Majesty of GOD as present with them, and their Nothingness and Vileness before him, proportionable to the Sense they have had of GOD's Grace and the Love of CHRIST. And the same is true in many Cases of Persons unsuitable Boldness, their Disposition to speak with Authority, intemperate Zeal, and many other Things that sometimes appear in true Christians, under great religious Affections.

And sometimes the Vehemence of the Motion of the animal Spirits, under great Affections, is owing in considerable Measure, to Experiences being thus partial. I have known it in several Instances, that Persons have been greatly affected with the dying Love of CHRIST, and the Consideration of the

Happiness of the Enjoyment of him in Heaven, and other Things of that Nature, and their animal Spirits at the same Time have been in a great Emotion, but in the midst of it have had given 'em a deep Sense of the awful, holy Majesty of GOD, and it has at once composed them, and quieted animal Nature, without diminishing their Comfort, but only has made it of a better, and more solid Nature; when they have had a Sense both of the Majesty & Grace of GOD, one Thing has as it were ballanced another, & caused a more happy Sedateness and Composure of Body & Mind.

From these Things we may learn how to judge of Experiences, and to estimate their Goodness. Those are not always the best Experiences, that are attended with the most violent Affections, and most vehement Motions of the animal Spirits, or that have the greatest Effects on the Body; nor are they always the best, that do most dispose Persons to abound in Talk to others, and to speak in the most vehement Manner; (tho' these Things often arise from the Greatness of spiritual Experiences;) But those are the most excellent Experiences that are qualified as follows; 1. That have the least Mixture, or are the most purely spiritual. 2. That are the least deficient and partial, in which the diverse Things that appertain to Christian Experience are proportionable one to another. And 3. That are raised to the highest Degree: 'Tis no Matter how high they are raised if they are qualified as before mentioned, the higher the better. Experiences thus qualified, will be attended with the most amiable Behaviour, and will bring forth the most solid and sweet Fruits, and will be the most durable, and will have the greatest Effect on the abiding Temper of the Soul.

If GOD is pleased to carry on this Work, and it should prove to be the Dawning of a general Revival of the Christian Church, it may be expected that the Time will come before long, when the Experiences of Christians shall be much more generally thus qualified. We must expect green Fruits before we have ripe ones. 'Tis probable that hereafter the Discoveries which the Saints shall have of divine Things, will be in a much higher Degree than yet have been; but yet shall be so ordered of an infinitely wise and all-sufficient GOD, that they shall not have so great an Effect, in Proportion, on the Body, and will be less oppressive to Nature; and that the outward Manifestations will

rather be like those that were in *Stephen*, when he was full of
the Holy Ghost, when *all that sat in the Council, looking stedfastly on him, saw his Face, as it had been the Face of an Angel.*
Their inward Fulness of the Spirit of GOD, in his divine, amiable
and sweet Influences shall as it were shine forth in an heavenly
Aspect, and Manner of Speech and Behaviour.   But

3. There is another Thing concerning Experiences of Christians, of which it is of yet greater Importance that we should
be aware, than either of the preceding, and that is the *degenerating of Experiences.* What I mean is something diverse from
the meer Decay of Experiences, or their gradually vanishing,
by Persons losing their Sense of Things; 'Tis Persons Experiences growing by Degrees worse and worse in their Kind,
more and more partial and deficient, in which Things are more
out of due Proportion; and also have more and more of a corrupt Mixture, the spiritual Part decreases, and the other useless
and hurtful Parts greatly increase. There is such a Thing, and it
is very frequent, as Experience abundantly evidences: I have
seen it in very many Instances; and great are the Mischiefs that
have risen through want of being more aware of it.

There is commonly, as I observed before, in high Experiences, besides that which is spiritual, a Mixture of three
Things, *viz.* Natural or common Affections and Workings of
the Imagination, and a Degree of Self-righteousness or spiritual Pride. Now it often comes to pass, that through Persons
not distinguishing the Wheat from the Chaff, and for want of
Watchfulness and humble Jealousy of themselves, and laying
great Weight on the natural and imaginary Part, and yielding
to it, & indulging of it, that Part grows & increases, and the
spiritual Part decreases; the Devil sets in, and works in the corrupt Part, and cherishes it to his utmost; 'till at length the Experiences of some Persons, who began well, come to but little
else, but violent Motions of carnal Affections, with great Heats
of the Imagination, and a great Degree of Enthusiasm, and
swelling of spiritual Pride; very much like some Fruits which
bud, blossom and kernel well, but afterwards are blasted
with an Excess of Moisture; so that tho' the Bulk is mon-
strously great, yet there is little else in it but what is useless
and unwholsome. It appears to me very probable, that many
of the Heresies that have arisen, & Sects that have appeared

in the Christian World, in one Age and another, with wild enthusiastical Notions and Practices, began at first by this Means,
that it was such a Degenerating of Experiences that first gave
Rise to 'em, or at least led the Way to 'em.

There is nothing in the World that does so much expose to
this degenerating of Experiences, as an unheeded spiritual
Pride & Self-Confidence, and Persons being conceited of their
own Stock, without an humble, daily & continual Dependance
on GOD. And this very Thing seems to be typified of old, by
the corrupting of the *Manna*. Some of the Children of *Israel*,
because they had gathered a Store of *Manna*, trusted in it,
there being, as they apprehended, sufficient in the Store they
had gather'd and laid up, without humbly looking to Heaven,
and stooping to the Earth for daily Supplies; and the Consequence was, that their *Manna* bred Worms and stank, *Exod.*
16. 20. Pride above all Things promotes this Degeneracy of
Experiences, because it grieves & quenches the Spirit of the
Lamb of GOD, and so kills the spiritual Part; and it cherishes
the natural Part, it inflames the carnal Affections, and heats the
Imagination.

The unhappy Person that is the Subject of such a Degeneracy
of Experiences, for the most Part, is not sensible of his own
Calamity; but because he finds himself still violently moved,
and greater Heats of Zeal, and more vehement Motions of his
animal Spirits, thinks himself fuller of the Spirit of GOD than
ever. But indeed it is with him, as the Apostle says of the *Galatians*, Gal. 3. 3. *Having begun in the Spirit, they are made perfect
by the Flesh.*

By the Mixture there is of common Affection with Love to
GOD, the Love of true Christians is liable to degenerate, and
to be more and more built on the Foundation of a Supposition
of being his high and peculiar Favourites, and less and less on
an Apprehension of the Excellency of GOD's Nature, as he is in
himself. So the Joy of Christians, by Reason of the Mixture
there is with spiritual Joy, is liable to degenerate, and to come
to that at last, as to be but little else but Joy in Self, Joy in a
Person's own supposed Eminency, and Distinction from others
in the Favour of GOD. So Zeal, that at first might be in great
Part spiritual, yet through the Mixture there is, in a long Continuance of Opposition and Controversy, may degenerate

more and more into human and proud Passion, and may come to Bitterness, and even a Degree of Hatred. And so Love to the Brethren may by Degrees come to little else but Fondness, and Zeal for a Party; yea, thro' a Mixture of a natural Love to the opposite Sex, may degenerate more and more, 'till it issues in that which is criminal and gross. And I leave it with those who are better acquainted with Ecclesiastical History, to enquire whether such a Degeneracy of Affections as this, might not be the first Thing that led the Way, and gave Occasion to the Rise of the abominable Notions of some Sects that have arisen, concerning the Community of Women. However that is, yet certainly the mutual Embraces and Kisses of Persons of different Sexes, under the Notion of Christian Love & holy Kisses, are utterly to be disallowed and abominated, as having the most direct Tendency quickly to turn Christian Love into unclean & bruitish Lust, which won't be the better, but ten Times the worse, for being christen'd by the Name of *Christian Love*. I should also think it adviseable, That Meetings of young People, of both Sexes, in the Evening, by themselves, without a Minister, or any elder People amongst them, for religious Exercises, should be avoided: For tho' for the present, while their Minds are greatly solemnized with lively Impressions, & a deep Sense of divine Things, there may appear no ill Consequence; yet we must look to the further End of Things, and guard against future Dangers & Advantages that Satan might gain against us. As a lively, solemn Sense of divine Things on the Minds of young Persons may gradually decay, so there will be Danger that an ill Improvement of these Meetings may gradually prevail; if not in any unsuitable Behaviour while together in the Meeting, yet when they break up to go Home, they may naturally consort together in Couples, for other than religious Purposes; and it may at last come to That, that young Persons may go to such Meetings, chiefly for the Sake of such an Opportunity for Company-keeping.

The *Defect* there sometimes is in the Experiences of Christians exposes 'em to degenerate, as well as the Mixture that they have. Deficient maimed Experiences do sometimes become more and more so: The Mind being wholly intent upon those Things that are in View, and those that are most wanting being neglected, there is less and less of them, and so the Gap for Corruption to come in grows wider and wider. And commonly both these Causes of the degenerating of Experiences operate together.

We had need to be jealous over our selves with a godly Jealousy, as the Apostle was over the Christian *Corinthians*, lest by any Means, as the Serpent beguiled *Eve* thro' his Subtilty, so our Minds should be corrupted from the Simplicity that is in CHRIST. GOD indeed will never suffer his true Saints totally and finally to fall away, but yet may punish their Pride and Self-Confidence, by suffering them to be long led into a dreadful Wilderness, by the subtle Serpent, to the great wounding of their own Souls, and the Interest of Religion.

And before I dismiss this Head of the Degenerating of Experiences, I would mention one Thing more that tends to it; and that is Person's aiming in their Experience to go beyond the Rule of GOD's Word, *i.e.* aiming at that, *which is indeed*, in some Respect, beyond the Rule. Thus some Persons have endeavoured utterly to root out and abolish all natural Affection, or any special Affection or Respect to their near Relations, under a Notion that no other Love ought to be allowed, but spiritual Love, and that all other Love is to be abolished as carnal, and that it becomes Christians to love none upon the Account of any Thing else, but the Image of GOD; and that therefore Love should go out to one and another only in that Proportion in which the Image of GOD is seen in them. They might as well argue that a Man ought utterly to disallow of, and endeavour to abolish all Love or Appetite to their daily Food, under a Notion that it is a carnal Appetite, and that no other Appetite should be tolerated but spiritual Appetites. Why should the Saints strive after that, as an high Attainment in Holiness, which the Apostle in *Rom.* i. 31. mentions as one Instance wherein the Heathen had got to the most horrid Pass in Wickedness, *viz. A being without natural Affection?*

Some have doubted whether they might pray for the Conversion and Salvation of the Souls of their Children, any more than for the Souls of others; because the Salvation of the Souls of others would be as much to GOD's Glory, as the Salvation of their Children; and they have supposed that to pray most for their own, would shew a selfish Disposition. So they have been afraid to tolerate a compassionate Grief and Concern for their nearest Friends, for Fear it would be an Argument of want of Resignation to GOD.

And 'tis true, there is great Danger of Persons setting their Hearts too much upon their earthly Friends; our Love to earthly Friends ought to be under the Government of the Love of GOD, and should be attended with a Spirit of Submission and Resignation to his Will, and every Thing should be subordinated to his Glory: But that is no Argument that these Affections should be entirely abolished, which the Creator of the World has put within Mankind, for the Good of Mankind, and because he saw they would be needful for them, as they must be united in Society, in the present State, and are of great Use, when kept in their proper Place; and to endeavour totally to root them out, would be to reproach and oppose the Wisdom of the Creator. Nor is the Being of these natural Inclinations, if well regulated, inconsistent with any Part of our Duty to GOD, or any Argument of a sinful Selfishness, any more than the natural Abhorrence that there is in the human Nature of Pain, and natural Inclination to Ease that was in the Man CHRIST JESUS himself.

'Tis the Duty of Parents to be more concern'd, and to pray more for the Salvation of their Children, than for the Children of their Neighbours; as much as it is the Duty of a Minister to be more concerned for the Salvation of the Souls of his Flock, and to pray more for them, than those of other Congregations, because they are committed to his Care; so our near Friends are more committed to our Care than others, and our near Neighbours, than those that live at a great Distance; and the People of our Land and Nation are more in some Sense, committed to our Care than the People of *China*, and we ought to pray more for them, and to be more concerned that the Kingdom of CHRIST should flourish among them, than in another Country, where it would be as much, and no more for the Glory of GOD. Compassion ought to be especially exercised towards Friends, *Job.* 6. 14. CHRIST did not frown upon a special Affection and Compassion for near Friends, but countenanced and encouraged it, from Time to Time, in those that in the Exercise of such an Affection and Compassion, applied to him for Relief for their Friends; as in the Instance of the Woman of *Canaan, Jairus, Mary* and *Martha*, the Centurion, the Widow of *Nain*, and many others. The Apostle *Paul*, tho' a Man as much resigned and devoted to GOD, and under the Power of his Love, perhaps as any meer Man that ever lived, yet had a peculiar Concern for his Countrymen the *Jews*, the rather on that Account, that they were his *Brethren and Kinsmen according to the Flesh*; he had a very high Degree of compassionate Grief for them, insomuch that he tells us he had great Heaviness and continual Sorrow of Heart for them, and could wish himself accursed from CHRIST for them.

There are many Things that are proper for the Saints in Heaven, that are not suitable to the State GOD has set us in, in this World: And for Christians, in these and other Instances, to affect to go beyond the present State of Mankind, and what GOD has appointed as fit for it, is an Instance of that which the wise Man calls *a being righteous over-much*, and has a Tendency to open a Door for Satan, and to cause religious Affections to degenerate into something very unbecoming of Christians.

Thus I have, as I proposed, taken Notice of some Things with Regard to the inward Experiences of Christians, by which *Satan* has an Advantage. I now proceed in the

2d. Place, to take Notice of something with Regard to the external Effects of Experiences, which also gives *Satan* an Advantage. What I have Respect to, is the secret and unaccountable Influence that Custom has upon Persons, with respect to the external Effects and Manifestations of the inward Affections of the Mind. By Custom I mean, both a Person's being accustomed to a Thing in himself, in his own common, allowed and indulged Practice, and also the Countenance and Approbation of others amongst whom he dwells, by their general Voice and Practice. It is well known, & appears sufficiently by what I have said already in this Treatise and elsewhere, that I am far from ascribing all the late uncommon Effects and outward Manifestations of inward Experiences to Custom & Fashion, as some do; I know it to be otherwise, if it be possible for me to know any Thing of this Nature by the most critical Observation, under all Manner of Opportunities of observing. But yet, this also is exceeding evident by Experience, that Custom has a strange Influence in these Things: I know it by the different Manners and Degrees of external Effects & Manifestations of great Affections and high Discoveries, in different Towns, according to what Persons are gradually led into, and insensibly habituated to, by Example and Custom; and also in the same Place, at different Times, according to the Conduct that they have: If some Person is among them to conduct them, that much countenances & encourages such Kind of outward Manifestations of great Affections, they naturally and insensibly prevail, & grow by Degrees unavoidable; but when afterwards they come under another Kind of Conduct, the Manner of external Appearances will strangely alter: And yet it seems to be without any proper Design or Contrivance of those in whom there is this Alteration; 'tis not properly affected by them, but the Influence of Example and Custom is secret and insensible to the Persons themselves. These Things have a vast Influence in the Manner of Persons manifesting their Joys, whether with Smiles & an Air of Lightness, or whether with more Solemnity and Reverence; and so they have a great Influence as to the Disposition Persons have under high Affections to abound in Talk; and also as to the Manner of their speaking, the Loudness and Vehemence of their Speech; (Tho' it would be exceeding unjust, & against all the Evidence of Fact and Experience, and the Reason of Things, to lay all Dispositions Persons have to be much in speaking to others, and to speak in a very earnest Manner, to Custom.) 'Tis manifest that Example and Custom has some Way or other, a secret and unsearchable Influence on those Actions that are involuntary, by the Difference that there is in different Places, and in the same Places at different Times, according to the diverse Examples and Conduct that they have.

Therefore, tho' it would be very unreasonable, and prejudicial to the Interest of Religion, to frown upon all these extraordinary external Effects and Manifestations of great religious Affections, (for a Measure of them is natural, necessary and beautiful, and the Effect in no wise disproportion'd to the spiritual Cause, and is of great Benefit to promote Religion;) yet I think they greatly err who think that these Things should be wholly unlimited, and that all should be encouraged in going in these Things to the utmost Length that they feel themselves inclined to: The Consequence of this will be very bad: There ought to be a gentle Restraint held upon these

Things, and there should be a prudent Care taken of Persons in such extraordinary Circumstances, and they should be moderately advised at proper Seasons, not to make more Ado than there is Need of, but rather to hold a Restraint upon their Inclinations; otherwise extraordinary outward Effects will grow upon them, they will be more and more natural and unavoidable, and the extraordinary outward Show will increase, without any Increase of the internal Cause; Persons will find themselves under a Kind of Necessity of making a great Ado, with less and less Affection of Soul, 'till at length almost any slight Emotion will set them going, and they will be more and more violent and boisterous, and will grow louder and louder, 'till their Actions and Behaviour becomes indeed very absurd. These Things Experience proves.

Thus I have taken Notice of the more general Causes whence the Errors that have attended this great Revival of Religion have risen, & under each Head have observed some particular Errors that have flowed from these Fountains. I now proceed as I proposed in the

Second Place, to take Notice of some particular Errors that have risen from several of these Causes: in some perhaps they have been chiefly owing to one, and in others to another, and in others to the Influence of several, or all conjunctly. And here the

1st Thing I would take Notice of is censuring others that are professing Christians, in good Standing in the visible Church, as unconverted. I need not repeat what I have elsewhere said to shew this to be against the plain and frequent and strict Prohibitions of the Word of GOD: It is the worst Disease that has attended this Work, most contrary to the Spirit and Rules of Christianity, & of worst Consequences. There is a most unhappy Tincture that the Minds of many, both Ministers & People, have received that Way. The Manner of many has been, when they first enter into Conversation with any Person, that seems to have any Shew or make any Pretences to Religion, to discern him, or to fix a Judgment of him, from his Manner of talking of Things of Religion, whether he be converted, or experimentally acquainted with vital Piety or not, and then to treat him accordingly, & freely to express their Thoughts of him to others, especially those that they have a good Opinion of as true Christians, and accepted as Brethren and Companions in CHRIST; or if they don't declare their Minds expresly, yet by their Manner of speaking of them, at least to their Friends, they'll show plainly what their Thoughts are. So when they have heard any Minister pray or preach, their first Work has been to observe him on a Design of discerning him, whether he be a converted Man or no; whether he prays like one that feels the saving Power of GOD's Spirit in his Heart, & whether he preaches like one that knows what he says. It has been so much the Way in some Places, that many new Converts don't know but it is their Duty to do so, they know no other Way. And when once Persons yield to such a Notion, and give in to such a Humour, they'll quickly grow very discerning in their own Apprehension, they think they can easily tell a Hypocrite: And when once they have pass'd their Censure, every Thing seems to confirm it, they see more and more in the Person that they have censured, that seems to them to shew plainly that he is an unconverted Man. And then, if the Person censured be a Minister, every Thing in his publick Performances seems dead and sapless, and to do them no Good at all, but on the contrary to be of deadning Influence, and poisonous to the Soul; yea it seems worse and worse to them, his Preaching grows more & more intolerable: which is owing to a secret, strong Prejudice, that steals in more and more upon the Mind, as Experience plainly and certainly shows. When the Spirit of GOD was wonderfully poured out in this Place, more than seven Years ago, and near thirty Souls in a Week, take one with another, for five or six Weeks together, were to Appearance bro't Home to CHRIST, and all the Town seem'd to be alive and full of GOD, there was no such Notion or Humour prevailing here; when Ministers preached here, as very many did at that Time, young and old, our People did not go about to discern whether they were Men of Experience or not: They did not know that they must: Mr. *Stoddard* never brought 'em up in that Way; it did not seem natural to 'em to go about any Thing of that Nature, nor did any such Thing enter into their Hearts; but when any Minister preached, the Business of every one was to listen and attend to what he said, and apply it to his own Heart, and make the utmost Improvement of it. And 'tis remarkable, that never did their appear such a Disposition in

the People, to relish, approve of, and admire Ministers preaching as at that Time: Such Expressions as these were frequent in
the Mouths of one and another, on Occasion of the preaching
of Strangers here, viz. *That they rejoyced that there were so many*
such eminent Ministers in the Country; and they wonder'd they
never heard the Fame of 'em before: They were thankful that other
Towns had so good Means; and the like. And scarcely ever did
any Minister preach here, but his preaching did some remarkable Service; as I had good Opportunity to know, because at
that Time I had particular Acquaintance, with most of the
Persons in the Town, in their Soul Concerns. That it has been
so much otherwise of late in many Places in the Land, is another Instance of the secret and powerful Influence of Custom
and Example.

There has been an unhappy Disposition in some Ministers
toward their Brethren in the Ministry in this Respect, which
has encouraged and greatly promoted such a Spirit among
some of their People. A wrong Improvement has been made of
CHRIST's scourging the Buyers and Sellers out of the Temple;
it has been expected by some, that CHRIST was now about
thus to purge his House of unconverted Ministers, and this has
made it more natural to them to think that they should do
CHRIST Service, and act as Co-workers with him, to put to
their Hand, and endeavour by all Means to cashier those Ministers that they thought to be unconverted. Indeed it appears
to me probable that the Time is coming, when awful Judgments will be executed on unfaithful Ministers, and that no
Sort of Men in the World will be so much exposed to divine
Judgments; but then we should leave that Work to CHRIST,
who is the Searcher of Hearts, and to whom Vengeance belongs; and not without Warrant, take the Scourge out of his
Hand into our own. There has been too much of a Disposition
in some, as it were to give Ministers over as Reprobates, that
have been look'd upon as Wolves in Sheep's Clothing; which
has tended to promote and encourage a Spirit of Bitterness
towards them, and to make it natural to treat them too much
as if they knew GOD hated them. If GOD's Children knew that
others were Reprobates, it would not be required of them to
love them; we may hate those that we know GOD hates; as 'tis
lawful to hate the Devil, and as the Saints at the Day of

Judgment will hate the Wicked.—Some have been too apt to look for Fire from Heaven upon particular Ministers; and this has naturally excited that Disposition to call for it, that CHRIST rebuked in his Disciples at *Samaria*. For my Part, tho' I believe no Sort of Men on Earth are so exposed to spiritual Judgments as wicked Ministers, yet I feel no Disposition to treat any Minister as if I supposed that he was finally rejected of GOD; for I can't but hope that there is coming a Day of such great Grace, a Time so appointed for the magnifying the Riches and Sovereignty of divine Mercy, beyond what ever was, that a great Number of unconverted Ministers will obtain Mercy. There was no Sort of Persons in CHRIST's Time that were so guilty, and so harden'd, and towards whom CHRIST manifested such great Indignation, as the Priests and Scribes, and there were no such Persecutors of CHRIST and his Disciples as they; and yet in that great Out-pouring of the Spirit that began on the Day of *Pentecost*, tho' it began with the common People, yet in the Progress of the Work, after a-while, *a great Company of Priests in* Jerusalem *were obedient to the Faith*, Act. 6. 7. And *Saul*, one of the most violent of all the persecuting Pharisees, became afterwards the greatest Promoter of the Work of GOD that ever was. I hope we shall yet see in many Instances a Fulfilment of that in *Isa.* 29. 24. *They also that erred in Spirit shall come to Understanding, and they that murmured shall learn Doctrine.*

Nothing has been gain'd by this Practice. The End that some have aim'd at in it has not been obtain'd, nor is ever like to be. Possibly some have openly censured Ministers, and encouraged their People's Uneasiness under them, in Hopes that it would soon come to That, that the Uneasiness would be so general, and so great, that unconverted Ministers in general would be cast off, and that then Things would go on happily: but there is no Likelihood of it. The Devil indeed has obtain'd his End; this Practice has bred a great deal of Unhappiness among Ministers and People, has spoil'd Christians Enjoyment of Sabbaths, and made 'em their most uneasy, uncomfortable and unprofitable Days, and has stir'd up great Contention, and set all in a Flame; and in one Place & another where there was a glorious Work of GOD's Spirit begun, it has in a great Measure knock'd all in the Head, and their Ministers hold their

Places. Some have aim'd at a better End in censuring Ministers; they have supposed it to be a likely Means to awaken them: Whereas indeed, there is no one Thing has had so great a Tendency to prevent the Awakening of disaffected Ministers in general: And no one Thing has actually had such Influence to lock up the Minds of Ministers against any good Effect of this great Work of GOD in the Land, upon their Minds, in this Respect: I have known Instances of some that seem'd to be much moved by the first Appearance of this Work, but since have seem'd to be greatly deaden'd by what has appear'd of this Nature. And if there be one or two Instances of Ministers that have been awaken'd by it, there are ten to one on whom it has had a contrary Influence. The worst Enemies of this Work have been inwardly eased by this Practice; they have made a Shield of it to defend their Consciences, and have been glad that it has been carried to so great a Length; at the same Time that they have look'd upon it, and improv'd it, as a Door open'd for 'em to be more bold in opposing the Work in general.

There is no such dreadful Danger of natural Men's being undone by our forbearing thus to censure them, and carrying it towards them as visible Christians; it will be no bloody, Hell-peopling Charity, as some seem to suppose, when it is known that we don't treat 'em as Christians, because we have taken it upon us to pass a Judgment on their State, on any Trial, or Exercise of our Skill in examining and discerning them, but only as allowing them to be worthy of a publick Charity, on their Profession and good external Behaviour; any more than *Judas* was in Danger of being deceived, by CHRIST's treating him a long Time as a Disciple, and sending him forth as an Apostle, (because he did not then take it upon him to act as the Judge and Searcher of Hearts, but only as the Head of the visible Church.) Indeed such a Charity as this may be abused by some, as every Thing is, and will be, that is in its own Nature proper, and of never so good Tendency. I say nothing against dealing thoroughly with Conscience, by the most convincing & searching Dispensation of the Word of GOD: I don't desire that that Sword should be sheath'd, or gently handled by Ministers; but let it be used as a two-edged Sword, to pierce, even to the dividing asunder Soul and Spirit, Joints and Marrow; let Conscience be dealt with, without any Complements; let Ministers handle it in flaming Fire, without having any more Mercy on it, than the Furnace has on those Metals that are tried in it. But let us let Men's Persons alone: Let the Word of GOD judge them, but don't let us take it upon us 'till we have Warrant for it.

Some have been ready to censure Ministers because they seem, in Comparison of some other Ministers, to be very cold and lifeless in their ministerial Performances. But then it should be considered that for ought we know, GOD may hereafter raise up Ministers of so much more excellent and heavenly Qualifications, and so much more spiritual & divine in their Performances, that there may appear as great a Difference between them, and those that now seem the most lively, as there is now between them, and others that are called dead and sapless; and those that are now called lively Ministers may appear to their Hearers, when they compare them with others that shall excel them, as wretchedly mean, and their Performances poor, dead, dry Things; and many may be ready to be prejudiced against them, as accounting them good for nothing, and it may be calling them Soul-Murderers. What a poor Figure may we suppose, the most lively of us, and those that are most admired by the People, do make in the Eyes of one of the Saints of Heaven, any otherwise than as their Deadness, Deformity & Rottenness is hid by the Veil of Christ's Righteousness?

Another Thing that has been supposed to be sufficient Warrant for openly censuring Ministers as unconverted, is their opposing this Work of GOD that has lately been carried on in the Land. And there can be no Doubt with me but that Opposition against this Work may be such, as to render either Ministers or People, truly scandalous, and expose 'em to publick Ecclesiastical Censure; and that Ministers hereby may utterly defeat the Design of their Ministry, (as I observed before;) and so give their People just Cause of Uneasiness: I should not think that any Person had Power to oblige me, constantly to attend the Ministry of one, who did from Time to Time, plainly pray and preach against this Work, or speak reproachfully of it frequently in his publick Performances, after all

Christian Methods had been used for a Remedy, and to no Purpose.

But as to determining how far opposing this Work is consistent with a State of Grace, or how far, and for how long Time, some Persons of good Experience in their own Souls, through Prejudices they have receiv'd from the Errors that have been mix'd with this Work, or through some peculiar Disadvantages they are under to behold Things in a right View of them, by Reason of the Persons they converse with, or their own cold and dead Frames, is, as Experience shows, a very difficult Thing; I have seen that which abundantly convinces me that the Business is too high for me; I am glad that GOD has not committed such a difficult Affair to me; I can joyfully leave it wholly in his Hands, who is infinitely fit for it, without meddling at all with it my self.—We may represent it as exceeding dangerous to oppose this Work, for this we have good Warrant in the Word of GOD; but I know of no Necessity we are under to determine whether it be possible for these that are guilty of it to be in a State of Grace or no.

GOD seems so strictly to have forbidden this Practice, of our judging our Brethren in the visible Church, not only because he knew that we were too much of Babes, infinitely too weak, fallible and blind, to be well capacitated for it, but also because he knew that it was not a Work suited to our proud Hearts; that it would be setting us vastly too high, and making us too much of Lords over our Fellow-Creatures. Judging our Brethren and passing a condemnatory Sentence upon them, seems to carry in it an Act of Authority, especially in so great a Case, to sentence them with respect to that State of their Hearts, on which depends their Liableness to eternal Damnation; as is evident by such Interrogations as those, (to hear which from GOD's Mouth, is enough to make us shrink into Nothing with Shame and Confusion, and Sense of our own Blindness and Worthlesness) Rom. 14. 4. *Who art thou that judgest another Man's Servant? To his own Master he standeth or falleth.* And Jam. 4. 12. *There is one Lawgiver that is able to save and to destroy; who are thou that judgest another?* Our wise and merciful Shepherd has graciously taken Care not to lay in our Way such a Temptation to Pride; he has cut up all such Poison out of our Pasture; and therefore we should not desire to have it restored.

Blessed be his Name, that he has not laid such a Temptation in the Way of my Pride! I know that in order to be fit for this Business, I must not only be vastly more knowing, but more humble than I am.

Tho' I believe some of GOD's own Children have of late been very guilty in this Matter, yet by what is said of it in the Scripture, it appears to me very likely, that before these Things which GOD has lately begun, have an End, GOD will awfully rebuke that Practice; may it in sovereign and infinite Mercy be prevented, by the deep and open Humiliation of those that have openly practised it.

As this Practice ought to be avoided, so should all such open, visible Marks of Distinction & Separation that imply it; as particularly, distinguishing such as we have judged to be in a converted State with the Compellations of *Brother* or *Sister*; any further than there is a visible Ecclesiastical Distinction. In those Places where it is the Manner to receive such, and such only to the Communion of the visible Church, as recommend themselves by giving a satisfying Account of their inward Experiences, there Christians may openly distinguish such Persons, in their Speech and ordinary Behaviour, with a visible Separation, without being inconsistent with themselves: And I don't now pretend to meddle with that Controversy, whether such an Account of Experience be requisite to Church-Fellowship: But certainly, to admit Persons to Communion with us as Brethren in the visible Church, & then visibly to reject them, and to make an open Distinction between them and others, by different Names or Appellations, is to be inconsistent with our selves; 'tis to make a visible Church within a visible Church, and visibly to divide between Sheep and Goats, setting one on the right Hand, and the other on the left.

This bitter Root of Censoriousness must be totally rooted out, as we would prepare the Way of the Lord. It has nourished and upheld many other Things contrary to the Humility, Meekness and Love of the Gospel. The Minds of many have receiv'd an unhappy Turn, in some Respects, with their Religion: There is a certain Point or Sharpness, a Disposition to a Kind of Warmth, that does not savour of that meek, Lamblike, sweet Disposition that becomes Christians: Many have now been so long habituated to it, that they don't know how to get out of it; but we must get out of it; the Point & Sharpness must be blunted, and we must learn another Way of manifesting our Zeal for GOD.

There is a Way of reflecting on others, and censuring them in open Prayer, that some have; which tho' it has a fair Shew of Love, yet is indeed the boldest Way of reproaching others imaginable, because there is implied in it an Appeal to the most high GOD, concerning the Truth of their Censures and Reflections.

And here I would also observe by the Way, that some have a Way of joining a Sort of Imprecations with their Petitions for others, tho' but conditional ones, that appear to me wholly needless and improper: They pray that others may either be converted or removed. I never heard nor read of any such Thing practiced in the Church of GOD 'till now, unless it be with Respect to some of the most visibly and notoriously abandon'd Enemies of the Church of GOD. This is a Sort of cursing Men in our Prayers, adding a Curse with our Blessing; whereas the Rule is *Bless and curse not*. To pray that GOD would kill another, is to curse him with the like Curse wherewith *Elisha* cursed the Children that came out of *Bethel*. And the Case must be very great and extraordinary indeed to warrant it, unless we were Prophets, and did not speak our own Words, but Words indited by the immediate Inspiration of the Spirit of GOD. 'Tis pleaded that if GOD has no Design of converting others, 'tis best for them, as well as best for others, that they should be immediately taken away and sent to Hell before they have contracted more Guilt. To which I would say, that so it was best that those Children that met *Elisha*, seeing GOD had no Design of converting them, should die immediately as they did; but yet *Elisha*'s imprecating that sudden Death upon them, was cursing them; and therefore would not have been lawful for one that did not speak in the Name of the LORD as a Prophet.

And then if we give Way to such Things as these, where shall we stop? A Child that suspects he has an unconverted Father and Mother, may pray openly that his Father and Mother may either be converted, or taken away and sent to Hell now quickly, before their Guilt is greater. (For unconverted Parents are as likely to poison the Souls of their Family in their Manner of training them up, as unconverted Ministers are to poison their People.) And so it might come to That, that it might be a common Thing all over the Country, for Children to pray after this Manner concerning their Parents, and Brethren and Sisters concerning one another, & Husbands concerning their Wives, and Wives concerning Husbands; and so for Persons to pray concerning all their unconverted Friends and Neighbours; and not only so, but we may also pray concerning all those Saints that are not lively Christians, that they may either be enliven'd or taken away; if that be true that is often said by some at this Day, that these cold dead Saints do more Hurt than natural Men, and lead more Souls to Hell, and that it would be well for Mankind if they were all dead.

How needless are such Petitions or Imprecations as these? What Benefit is there of them? Why is it not sufficient for us to pray that GOD would provide for his Church, and the Good of Souls, and take Care of his own Flock, and give it needful Means and Advantages for its spiritual Prosperity? Does GOD need to be directed by us in what Way he shall do it? What need we ask of GOD to do it by killing such and such Persons, if he don't convert them? Unless we delight in the Thoughts of GOD's answering us in such terrible Ways, and with such awful Manifestations of his Wrath to our Fellow-Creatures.

And why don't Ministers direct Sinners to pray for themselves, that GOD would either convert them or kill them, and send them to Hell now, before their Guilt is greater? In this Way we should lead Persons in the next Place to Self-Murther: For many probably would soon begin to think that That which they may pray for, they may seek, and use the Means of.

Some with whom I have discoursed about this Way of praying, have said, that the Spirit of GOD, as it were, forces them to utter themselves thus, as it were forces out such Words from their Mouths, when otherwise they should not dare to utter them. But such a Kind of Impulse don't look like the Influence of the Spirit of GOD. The Spirit of GOD sometimes strongly inclines Men to utter Words; but not by putting Expressions into the Mouth, and urging to utter them; but by filling the Heart with a Sense of divine Things, and holy Affections; and those Affections and that Sense inclines the Mouth to speak.

That other Way of Men's being urged to use certain Expressions, by an unaccountable Force, is very probably from the
Influence of the Spirit of the Devil.

2. Another Thing I would take Notice of, in the Manage-
ment of which there has been much Error and Misconduct, is
Lay-Exhorting; about which there has been abundance of
Disputing, Jangling, and Contention.

In the midst of all the Disputes that have been, I suppose
that all are agreed as to these two Things, *viz.* 1. That all exhorting one another of Laymen is not unlawful or improper,
but on the contrary, that some Exhorting is a Christian Duty.
And 2. I suppose also, all will allow that there is something
that is proper only for Ministers; that there is some Kind or
Way of Exhorting & Teaching or other, that belongs only to
the Office of Teachers. All will allow, that GOD has appointed
such an Office as that of *Teachers* in the Christian Church, and
therefore doubtless will allow that something or other is
proper and peculiar to that Office, or some Business of *Teaching* that belongs to it, that don't belong as much to others as
to them.

If there be any Way of Teaching that is peculiar to that Office, then for others to take that upon them, is to invade the
Office of a Minister; which doubtless is very sinful, and is often
so represented in Scripture. But the great Difficulty is to settle
the Bounds, and to tell exactly, how far Lay-men may go, and
when they exceed their Limits; which is a Matter of so much
Difficulty, that I don't wonder if many in their Zeal have
transgress'd. The two Ways of Teaching & Exhorting, the one of
which ought ordinarily to be left to Ministers, and the other
of which may and ought to be practised by the People, may be
express'd by those two Names of *Preaching*, and *Exhorting* in a
Way of *Christian Conversation*. But then a great deal of Difficulty & Controversy arises to determine what is *Preaching*,
and what is *Christian Conversation*. However I will humbly
offer my Thoughts concerning this Subject of Lay-Exhorting,
as follows.

1. The common People in exhorting one another ought not
to cloath themselves with the like Authority with that which is
proper for Ministers. There is a certain Authority that Ministers have, and should exercise in teaching, as well as governing

the Flock. Teaching is spoken of in Scripture as an Act of Authority, 1 *Tim.* 2. 12. In order to a Man's preaching, special Authority must be committed to him. Rom. 10. 15. *How shall they preach, except they be sent?* Ministers in this Work of Teaching & Exhorting are cloath'd with Authority, as Christ's Messengers, (*Mal.* 2. 7.) and as representing him, and so speaking in his Name, and in his Stead, 2 *Cor.* 5. 18, 19, 20. And it seems to be the most honourable Thing that belongs to the Office of a Minister of the Gospel, that to him is committed the Word of Reconciliation, and that he has Power to preach the Gospel, as Christ's Messenger, and speaking in his Name. The Apostle seems to speak of it as such, 1 *Cor.* 1. 16, 17. Ministers therefore in the Exercise of this Power, may cloath themselves with Authority in speaking, or may teach others in an authoritative Manner. Tit. 2. 15. *These Things speak and exhort, and rebuke with all Authority: Let no Man despise thee.* But the common People in exhorting one another, ought not thus to exhort in an authoritative Manner. There is a great deal of Difference between teaching as a *Father* amongst a Company of Children, & counselling in a *brotherly* Way, as the Children may kindly counsel and admonish one another. Those that are meer Brethren, ought not to assume Authority in exhorting, tho' one may be better, and have more Experience than another. Lay-men ought not to exhort as tho' they were the Ambassadors or Messengers of Christ, as Ministers do; nor should they exhort and warn and charge *in his Name*, according to the ordinary Import of such an Expression, when applied to Teaching. Indeed in one Sense, a Christian ought to do every Thing he does in Religion in the Name of Christ, i.e. He ought to act in a Dependance on him as his Head and Mediator, and do all for his Glory: But the Expression as it is usually understood, when applied to Teaching or Exhorting, is speaking in Christ's Stead, & as having a Message from him.

Persons may cloath themselves with Authority in speaking, either by the authoritative Words they make Use of, or in the Manner, and authoritative Air of their speaking: Tho' some may think that this latter is a Matter of Indifferency, or at least of small Importance, yet there is indeed a great deal in it: a Person may go much out of his Place, and be guilty of a great Degree of Assuming, in the Manner of his speaking those

Words, which as they might be spoken, might be proper for him: The same Words spoken in a different Manner, may express what is very diverse: Doubtless there may be as much Hurt in the Manner of a Person's speaking, as there may in his Looks; but the wise Man tells us, that *an high Look is an Abomination to the Lord*, Prov. 21. 4. Again, a Man may cloath himself with Authority, in the Circumstances under which he speaks; as for Instance, if he sets himself up as a *publick Teacher*. Here I would have it observed, that I don't suppose that a Person is guilty of this, meerly because he speaks in the Hearing of many: Persons may speak, and speak only in a Way of Conversation, and yet speak in the Hearing of a great Number, as they often do in their common Conversation about temporal Things, at Feasts and Entertainments, where Women as well as others, do converse freely together about worldly Things, in the hearing of a considerable Number; and it may happen to be in the Hearing of a great Number, and yet without Offence: And if their Conversation on such Occasions should turn on spiritual Things, & they should speak as freely and openly, I don't see why it would not be as harmless. Nor do I think, that if besides a great Number's being present, Persons speak with a very earnest and loud Voice, this is for them to set up themselves as publick Teachers, if they do it from no Contrivance or premeditated Design, or as purposely directing themselves to a Congregation or Multitude, and not speaking to any that are composed to the Solemnity of any publick Service; but speaking in the Time of Conversation, or a Time when all do freely converse one with another, they express what they then feel, directing themselves to none but those that are near 'em, and fall in their Way, speaking in that earnest and pathetical Manner, to which the Subject they are speaking of, and the affecting Sense of their Souls naturally leads them, and as it were constrains them: I say, that for Persons to do thus, tho' many happen to hear them, yet it don't appear to me to be a setting themselves up as publick Teachers: Yea, if this be added to these other Circumstances, that all this happens to be in a Meeting-House; I don't think that meerly its being in such a Place, much alters the Case, provided the Solemnity of publick Service and divine Ordinances be over, and the solemn Assembly broke up, and some stay in the

House for mutual religious Conversation; provided also that they speak in no authoritative Way, but in an humble Manner, becoming their Degree & Station, tho' they speak very earnestly and pathetically.

Indeed Modesty might in ordinary Cases, restrain some Persons, as Women, and those that are young, from so much as speaking, when a great Number are present; at least, when some of those present are much their Superiours, unless they are spoken to: And yet the Case may be so extraordinary, as fully to warrant it. If something very extraordinary happens to Persons, or if they are in extraordinary Circumstances: as if a Person be struck with Lightning, in the midst of a great Company, or if he lies a dying, it appears to none any Violation of Modesty, for him to speak freely, before those that are much his Superiours. I have seen some Women and Children in such Circumstances, on religious Accounts, that it has appear'd to me no more a transgressing the Laws of Humility and Modesty, for them to speak freely, let who will be present, than if they were dying.

But then may a Man be said to set up himself as a publick Teacher, when he in a set Speech, of Design, directs himself to a Multitude, either in the Meeting-House or elsewhere, as looking that they should compose themselves to attend to what he has to say; and much more when this is a contrived & premeditated Thing, without any thing like a Constraint, by any extraordinary Sense or Affection that he is then under; and more still, when Meetings are appointed on Purpose to hear Lay-Persons exhort, and they take it as their Business to be Speakers, while they expect that others should come, and compose themselves, and attend as Hearers; when private Christians take it upon them in private Meetings, to act as the Masters or Presidents of the Assembly, and accordingly from Time to Time to teach and exhort the rest, this has the Appearance of authoritative Teaching.

When private Christians, that are no more than meer Brethren, exhort and admonish one another, it ought to be in an humble Manner, rather by Way of Intreaty, than with Authority; and the more, according as the Station of Persons is lower. Thus it becomes Women, and those that are young, ordinarily to be at a greater Distance from any Appearance of Authority in speaking than others: Thus much at least is evident by that in 1 *Tim.* 2. 9, 11, 12.

That Lay-Persons ought not to exhort one another as cloathed with Authority, is a general Rule, but it can't justly be supposed to extend to Heads of Families in their own Families. Every Christian Family is a little Church, and the Heads of it are its authoritative Teachers and Governours. Nor can it extend to School-Masters among his Scholars; and some other Cases might perhaps be mention'd, that ordinary Discretion will distinguish, where a Man's Circumstances do properly cloath him with Authority, and render it fit and suitable for him to counsel and admonish others in an authoritative Manner.

2. No Man but only a Minister that is duely appointed to that sacred Calling, ought to follow Teaching and Exhorting *as a Calling*, or so as to neglect that which is his *proper Calling*. An having the Office of a Teacher in the Church of God implies two Things, 1. A being invested with the *Authority* of a Teacher; and 2. A being called to the *Business* of a Teacher, to make it the Business of his Life. Therefore that Man that is not a Minister, that takes either of these upon him, invades the Office of a Minister. Concerning assuming the Authority of a Minister I have spoken already. But if a Lay-man don't assume Authority in his Teaching, yet if he forsakes his proper Calling, or doth so at least in a great Measure, & spends his Time in going about from House to House, to counsel and exhort, he goes beyond his Line, and violates Christian Rules. Those that have the Office of Teachers or Exhorters, have it for their Calling, and should make it their Business, as a Business proper to their Office; and none should make it their Business but such. Rom. 12. 3, 4, 5, 7, 8. *For I say, through the Grace given unto me, to every Man that is among you, not to think of himself more highly than he ought to think; but to think soberly, according as GOD hath dealt to every Man the Proportion of Faith. For as we have many Members, in one Body, and all Members have not the same Office; so we being many, are one Body in Christ.—He that teacheth, let him wait on Teaching, or he that exhorteth, on Exhortation.* 1 Cor. 12. 29. *Are all Apostles? Are all Prophets? Are all Teachers?* 1 Cor. 7. 20. *Let every Man abide in the same Calling wherein he was called.* 1 Thes. 4. 11. *And that ye study to be*

*quiet, and to do your own Business, and to work with your own
Hands, as we commanded you.*

It will be a very dangerous Thing for Lay-men, in either of
these Respects, to invade the Office of a Minister; if this be
common among us we shall be in Danger of having a Stop put
to the Work of GOD, and the Ark's turning aside from us, before
it comes to Mount *Zion*, and of GOD's making a Breach upon
us; as of old there was an unhappy Stop put to the Joy of the
Congregation of *Israel*, in bringing up the Ark of GOD, because
others carried it besides the *Levites*: And therefore *David*, when
the Error was found out, says, 1 Chron. 15. 2. *None ought to
carry the Ark of GOD, but the* Levites *only; for them hath the Lord
chosen to carry the Ark of God, and to minister unto him for ever.*
And because one presumed to touch the Ark that was not of the
Sons of *Aaron*, therefore the Lord made a Breach upon them,
and covered their Day of Rejoicing with a Cloud in his Anger.

Before I dismiss this Head of Lay-Exhorting, I would take
Notice of three Things relating to it, upon which there ought
to be a Restraint.

1. Speaking in the Time of the solemn Worship of GOD, as
publick Prayer, Singing, or Preaching, or Administration of the
Sacrament of the Holy Supper; or any Duty of social Worship:
This should not be allowed. I know it will be said, that in some
Cases, when Persons are exceedingly affected, they cannot help
it; and I believe so too: but then I also believe, and know by
Experience, that there are several Things that contribute to
that Inability, besides meerly and absolutely the Sense of divine
Things they have upon their Hearts. Custom and Example, or
the Thing's being allowed, have such an Influence, that they
actually help to make it impossible for Persons under strong
Affections to avoid speaking. If it was disallowed, and Persons
at the Time that they were thus disposed to break out, had this
Apprehension, that it would be a very unbecoming, shocking
Thing for 'em so to do, it would be a Help to 'em, as to their
Ability to avoid it: Their Inability arises from their strong and
vehement Disposition; and so far as that Disposition is from a
good Principle, it would be weaken'd by the coming in of this
Tho't to their Minds, *viz.* "What I am going to do, will be for
the Dishonour of CHRIST and Religion: And so that inward

Vehemence, that pushed 'em forward to speak, would fall, and they would be enabled to avoid it. This Experience confirms.

2. There ought to be a moderate Restraint on the Loudness of Persons talking under high Affections; for if there be not, it will grow natural and unavoidable for Persons to be louder and louder, without any Increase of their inward Sense; 'till it becomes natural to 'em, at last, to scream and hallow to almost every one they see in the Streets, when they are much affected: But this is certainly a Thing very improper, and what has no Tendency to promote Religion. The Man CHRIST JESUS when he was upon Earth, had doubtless as great a Sense of the infinite Greatness and Importance of eternal Things, and the Worth of Souls, as any have now-a-days; but there is not the least Appearance in his History, of his taking any such Course, or Manner of exhorting others.

3. There should also be some Restraint on the abundance of Persons Talk, under strong Affections; for if Persons give themselves an unbounded Liberty, to talk just so much as they feel an Inclination to, they will increase and abound more and more in Talk, beyond the Proportion of their Sense or Affection; 'till at length it will become ineffectual on those that hear them, and by the Commonness of their abundant Talk, they will defeat their own End.

One Thing more I would take Notice of before I conclude this Part, is the Mismanagement that has been in some Places of the Duty of singing Praises to GOD. I believe it to have been one Fruit of the extraordinary Degrees of the sweet and joyful Influences of the Spirit of GOD that have been lately given, that there has appear'd such a Disposition to abound in that Duty, & frequently to fall into this divine Exercise; not only in appointed solemn Meetings, but when Christians occasionally meet together at each other's Houses. But the Mismanagement I have Respect to, is the getting into a Way of performing it, without almost any Appearance of that Reverence and Solemnity with which all visible, open Acts of divine Worship ought to be attended; it may be two or three in a Room singing Hymns of Praise to GOD, others that are present talking at the same Time, others about their Work, with little more Appearance of Regard to what is doing, than if some were only singing a common Song, for their Amusement and Diversion.

There is Danger, if such Things are continued, of its coming to that by Degrees, that a meer Nothing be made of this Duty, to the great Violation of the third Commandment. Let Christians abound as much as they will in this holy, heavenly Exercise, in GOD's House and in their own Houses; but when it is performed, let it be performed as an holy Act, wherein they have immediately and visibly to do with GOD. When any social open Act of Devotion, or solemn Worship of GOD is performed, GOD should be reverenced as visibly present, by those that are present. As we would not have the Ark of GOD depart from us, nor provoke GOD to make a Breach upon us, we should take Heed that we handle the Ark with Reverence.

With Respect to Companies singing in the Streets, going to, or coming from the Place of publick Worship, I would humbly offer my Thoughts in the following Particulars.

I. The Rule of CHRIST concerning *putting new Wine into old Bottles*, does undoubtedly take Place in Things of this Nature, supposing it to be a Thing that in it self is good, but not essential, and not particularly enjoin'd or forbidden. For Things, so very new & uncommon, and of so open and publick a Nature, to be suddenly introduced and set up & practised, in many Parts of the Country, without the Matter's being so much as first proposed to any publick Consideration, or giving any Opportunity for the People of GOD to weigh the Matter, or to consider any Reasons that might be offered to support it, is putting new Wine into old Bottles with a Witness; as if it were with no other Design than to burst them directly. Nothing else can be expected to be the Consequence of this, than Uproar and Confusion, and great Offence, and unhappy mischievous Disputes, even among the Children of GOD themselves: Not that that which is good in it self, and is new, ought to be forborn, 'till there is no Body that will dislike it; but it ought to be forborn 'till the visible Church of GOD is so prepared for it, at least, that there is a Probability that it will not do more Hurt than Good, or hinder the Work of GOD more than promote it; as is most evident from CHRIST's Rule, and the Apostles Practice. If it be brought in, when the Country is so unprepared, that the Shock and Surprize on Persons Minds, and the Contention and Prejudice against Religion, that it is like to be an Occasion of, will do more to hinder Religion, than the Practice of it is like to do to promote it, then the Fruit is pick'd before 'tis ripe. And indeed, such an hasty Endeavour to introduce such an Innovation, supposing it to be good in it self, is the likeliest Way to retard the effectual Introduction of it; it will hinder its being extensively introduced, much more than it will promote it, and so will defeat its own End.   But

2. As to the Thing it self, If a considerable Part of a Congregation have Occasion to go in Company together to a Place of publick Worship, and they should join together in singing Praises to GOD, as they go, I confess, that after long Consideration, and endeavouring to view the Thing every Way, with the utmost Deligence and Impartiality I am capable of, I cannot find any valid Objection against it. As to the common Objection from Mat. 6. 5. *And when thou prayest, thou shalt not be as the Hypocrites are; for they love to pray standing in the Synagogues, and in the Corners of the Streets, that they may be seen of Men.* It is strong against a single Person's singing in the Streets, or in the Meeting-House, by himself, as offering to GOD personal Worship; but as it is brought against a considerable Company, their thus publickly worshipping GOD, it appears to me to have no Weight at all; to be sure it is of no more Force against a Company's thus praising GOD in the Streets, than against their praising him in the Synagogue or Meeting-House, for the Streets & the Synagogues are both put together in these Words of our Saviour, as Parallel in the Case that he had Respect to. 'Tis evident that CHRIST speaks of personal, and not publick Worship. If to sing in the Streets be ostentatious, then it must be because it is a publick Place, and it can't be done there without being very open; but it is no more publick than the Synagogue or Meeting-House is when full of People. Some Worship is in its Nature private, as that which is proper to particular Persons, or Families, or private Societies, & has Respect to their particular Concerns: But that which I now speak of, is performed under no other Notion than a Part of GOD's publick Worship, without any Relation to any private, separate Society, or any chosen or pick'd Number, and in which every visible Christian has equal Liberty to join, if it be convenient for him, and he has a Disposition, as in the Worship that is perform'd in the Meeting-House. When Persons are going to the House of publick Worship, to serve GOD

there with the Assembly of his People, they are upon no other
Design than that of putting publick Honour upon GOD, that
is the Business they go from Home upon, and even in their
walking the Streets on this Errand, they appear in a publick
Act of Respect to GOD; and therefore if they go in Company
with publick Praise, 'tis not a being publick when they ought
to be private. 'Tis one Part of the Beauty of publick Worship,
that it be *very publick*; the more publick it is, the more open
Honour it puts upon GOD; and especially is it beautiful in that
Part of publick Worship, *viz. publick Praise*; For the very Notion of publick praising of GOD, is to declare abroad his Glory,
to publish his Praise, to make it known, and proclaim it aloud,
as is evident by innumerable Expressions of Scripture. 'Tis fit
that GOD's Honour should not be concealed, but made known
in the great Congregation, and proclaimed before the Sun,
and upon the House-Tops, before Kings, and all Nations, and
that his Praises should be heard to the utmost Ends of the
Earth.

I suppose none will condemn singing GOD's Praises, meerly
because 'tis performed in the open Air, and not in a close
Place: And if it may be performed by a Company in the open
Air, doubtless they may do it moving, as well as standing still.
So the Children of *Israel* praised GOD, when they went to
Mount *Zion*, with the Ark of GOD; and so the Multitude
praised CHRIST, when they entred with him into *Jerusalem*, a
little before his Passion; and so the Children of *Israel* were
wont, from Year to Year, to go up to *Jerusalem*, when they
went in Companies, from all Parts of the Land, three Times in
the Year, when they often used to manifest the Engagedness of
their Minds, by travelling all Night, and manifested their Joy
and Gladness, by singing Praises, with great Decency and
Beauty, as they went towards GOD's holy Mountain; as is evident by Isa. 30. 29. *Ye shall have a Song, as in the Night, when a
holy Solemnity is kept, and Gladness of Heart; as when one goeth
with a Pipe, to come into the Mountain of the Lord, to the mighty
One of Israel.* And Psal. 42. 4. *When I remember these Things, I
pour out my Soul in me; for I had gone with the Multitude, I
went with them to the House of God, with the Voice of Joy and
Praise, with a Multitude that kept holy Day.* Psal. 100. 4. *Enter
into his Gates with Thanksgiving, and into his Courts with*

Praise. When GOD's People are going to his House, the Occasion is so joyful to a Christian in a lively Frame, (the Language of whose Heart is, *Come, let us go up to the House of the Lord*, and who is glad when it is so said to him,) that the Duty of singing Praises seems to be peculiarly beautiful on such an Occasion. So that if the State of the Country was ripe for it, and it should be so that there should be frequent Occasions for a considerable Part of a Congregation to go together to the Places of publick Worship, and there was in other Respects a proportionable Appearance of Fervency of Devotion, it appears to me that it would be ravishingly beautiful, if such Things were practised all over the Land, and would have a great Tendency to enliven, animate and rejoice the Souls of GOD's Saints, and greatly to propagate vital Religion. I believe the Time is coming when the World will be full of such Things.

3. It seems to me to be requisite that there should be the Consent of the governing Part of the worshipping Societies, to which Persons have join'd themselves, and of which they own themselves a Part, in order to the introducing of Things in publick Worship, so new & uncommon, and not essential, nor particularly commanded, into the Places where those worshipping Societies belong: The Peace and Union of such Societies seems to require it; seeing they have voluntarily united themselves to these worshipping Societies, to that End, that they might be one in the Affairs of GOD's publick Worship, and obliged themselves in Covenant to act as Brethren & mutual Assistants, and Members of one Body, in those Affairs, & all are hereby naturally and necessarily led to be concern'd with one another, in Matters of Religion and GOD's Worship; and seeing that this is a Part of the publick Worship, & Worship that must be perform'd from Time to Time in the View of the whole, being performed at a Time when they are meeting together for mutual Assistance in Worship, and therefore that which all must unavoidably be in some Measure concerned in, so at least as to shew their Approbation & Consent, or open Dislike and Separation from them in it; I say it being thus, Charity and a Regard to the Union and Peace of such Societies, seems to require a Consent of the governing Part, in order to the introducing any Thing of this Nature; (unless they think those Societies unworthy that they should be join'd to them

any longer, and so first renounce them, as the worshipping Societies of which they are Members.) Certainly if we are of the Spirit of the Apostle *Paul*, and have his Discretion, we shall not set up any such Practice without it: He for the Sake of Peace, conformed, in Things wherein he was not particularly forbidden, to the *Jews*, when among them; and so when among those that were without the Law, conformed to them, wherein he might.—To be sure those go much beyond proper Limits, who coming from abroad, do immediately of their own Heads, in a strange Place, set up such a new and uncommon Practice among a People.

In introducing any Thing of this Nature among a People, their Minister especially ought to be consulted, and his Voice taken, as long as he is own'd for their Minister. Ministers are Pastors of worshipping Societies, & their Heads & Guides in the Affairs of publick Worship. They are called in Scripture, *those that rule over them*, and their People are commanded *to obey them, because they watch for their Souls, as those that must give Account.* If it belongs to these Shepherds & Rulers to direct and guide the Flock in any Thing at all, it belongs to 'em so to do, in the Circumstantials of their publick Worship.

Thus I have taken particular Notice of many of those Things that have appeared to me to be amiss, in the Management of our religious Concerns, relating to the present Revival of Religion, and have taken Liberty freely to express my Thoughts upon them. Upon the whole it appears manifest to me, that Things have as yet, never been set a-going in their right Channel; if they had, and Means had been bless'd in Proportion as they have been now, this Work would have so prevailed, as before this Time to have carried all afore it, and have triumph'd over *New-England* as its Conquest.

The Devil in driving Things to these Extremes, besides the present Hindrance of the Work of GOD, has, I believe, had in View, a two-fold Mischief hereafter, in the Issue of Things; one with Respect to those that are more cold in Religion; to carry Things to such an Extreme, that People in general, at length, having their Eyes open'd, by the great Excess, & seeing that Things must needs be wrong, he might take the Advantage to tempt them entirely to reject the whole Work, as being all nothing but Delusion and Distraction. And another is with

Respect to those that have been very warm and zealous, of
GOD's own Children, that have been out of the Way, to sink
them down in Unbelief and Darkness. The Time is coming I
doubt not, when the bigger Part of them will be convinced of
their Errors; and then probably the Devil will take Advantage
to lead them into a dreadful Wilderness, & to puzzle and
confound them about their own Experiences, and the Experiences of others; and to make them to doubt of many Things
that they ought not to doubt of, and even to tempt them with
atheistical Thoughts. I believe if all true Christians all over the
Land, should now at once have their Eyes open'd, fully to see all
their Errors, it would seem for the present to damp Religion:
The dark Thoughts, that it would at first be an Occasion of,
and the inward Doubts, Difficulties and Conflicts that would
rise in their Souls, would deaden their lively Affections and
Joys, and would cause an Appearance of a present Decay of
Religion. But yet it would do GOD's Saints great Good in their
latter End; it would fit them for more spiritual and excellent
Experiences, more humble and heavenly Love, and unmix'd
Joys, and would greatly tend to a more powerful, extensive
and durable Prevalence of vital Piety.

I don't know but we shall be in Danger by and by, after our
Eyes are fully open'd to see our Errors, to go to contrary Extremes. The Devil has driven the *Pendulum* far beyond its
proper Point of Rest; and when he has carried it to the utmost
Length that he can, and it begins by its own Weight to swing
back, he probably will set in, and drive it with the utmost Fury
the other Way; and so give us no Rest; and if possible prevent
our settling in a proper Medium. What a poor, blind, weak and
miserable Creature is Man, at his best Estate! We are like poor
helpless Sheep; the Devil is too subtle for us: What is our
Strength! What is our Wisdom! How ready are we to go astray!
How easily are we drawn aside, into innumerable Snares, while
we in the mean Time are bold and confident, and doubt not
but that we are right and safe! We are foolish Sheep, in the
midst of subtle Serpents and cruel Wolves, and don't know it.
Oh! how unfit are we to be left to our selves! And how much
do we stand in Need of the Wisdom, the Power, the Condescension, Patience, Forgiveness and Gentleness of our good
Shepherd!

Part V

Shewing positively, what ought to be done to promote this WORK.

In considering of Means and Methods for promoting this glorious Work of God, I have already observed, in some Instances wherein there has been needless objecting and complaining, and have also taken Notice of many Things amiss, that ought to be amended: I now proceed in the

Third and last Place, to shew positively, what ought to be done, or what Courses (according to my humble Opinion) ought to be taken to promote this Work. The Obligations that all are under, with one Consent, to do their utmost, and the great Danger of neglecting it, were observed before. I hope that some, upon reading what was said under that Head, will be ready to say, What shall we do? To such Readers I would now offer my Thoughts, in Answer to such an Enquiry.

And that which I think we ought to set our selves about in the first Place, is to remove Stumbling-blocks. When God is revealed, as about to come, gloriously to set up his Kingdom in the World, this is proclaimed, *Prepare ye the Way of the Lord, make strait in the Desert an high Way for our God*, Isai. 40. 3. And again, Isai. 57. 14. *Cast ye up, Cast ye up; prepare the Way; take up the Stumbling-block out of the Way of my People.* And Chap. 62. 10. *Go through, go through the Gates; prepare you the Way of the People; Cast up, Cast up the High-way; gather out the Stones.*

And in order to this, there must be a great deal done at confessing of Faults, on both Sides: For undoubtedly many and great are the Faults that have been committed, in the Jangling and Confusions, and Mixtures of Light and Darkness, that have been of late. There is hardly any Duty more contrary to our corrupt Dispositions, and mortifying to the Pride of Man; but it must be done. Repentance of Faults is, in a peculiar Manner, a proper Duty, when the Kingdom of Heaven is at Hand, or when we especially expect or desire that it should come; as appears by *John* the *Baptist*'s Preaching. And if God does now loudly call upon us to repent, then he also calls upon us to make proper Manifestations of our Repentance. I am perswaded that those that have openly opposed this Work, or have from Time to Time spoken lightly of it, cannot be excused in the Sight of GOD, without openly confessing their Fault therein; especially if they be Ministers. If they have any Way, either directly or indirectly, opposed the Work, or have so behaved, in their publick Performances or private Conversation, as has prejudiced the Minds of their People against the Work, if hereafter they shall be convinced of the Goodness and Divinity of what they have opposed, they ought by no Means to palliate the Matter, and excuse themselves, and pretend that they always thought so, and that it was only such & such Imprudences that they objected against, but they ought openly to declare their Conviction, and condemn themselves for what they have done; for 'tis CHRIST that they have spoken against, in speaking lightly of, and prejudicing others against this Work; yea, worse than that, 'tis the Holy Ghost. And tho' they have done it ignorantly, and in Unbelief, yet when they find out who it is that they have opposed, undoubtedly GOD will hold them bound publickly to confess it.

And on the other Side, if those that have been zealous to promote the Work, have in any of the fore-mentioned Instances, openly gone much out of the Way, and done that which is contrary to Christian Rules, whereby they have openly injur'd others, or greatly violated good Order, and so done that which has wounded Religion, they must publickly confess it, and humble themselves, as they would gather out the Stones, and prepare the Way of GOD's People. They who have laid great Stumbling-blocks in others Way, by their *open Transgression*, are bound to remove them, by their *open Repentance*.

Some probably will be ready to object against this, that the Opposers will take Advantage by this to behave themselves insolently, and to insult both them and Religion. And indeed, to the Shame of some, they have taken Advantage by such Things; as of the good Spirit that Mr. *Whitefield* shewed in his Retractions, and some others. But if there are some imbitter'd Enemies of Religion, that stand ready to improve every Thing to its Disadvantage, yet that ought not to hinder doing an enjoin'd Christian Duty; tho' it be in the Manifestation of

Humility and Repentance, after a Fault openly committed. To stand it out, in a visible Impenitence of a real Fault, to avoid such an Inconvenience, is to do Evil, to prevent Evil. And besides, the Danger of an evil Consequence is much greater on the other Side: To commit Sin, and then stand in it, is what will give the Enemy the greatest Advantage. For Christians to act like Christians, in openly humbling themselves, when they have openly offended, in the End brings the greatest Honour to CHRIST and Religion; and in this Way are Persons most likely to have GOD appear for them.

Again, At such a Day as this, GOD does especially call his People to the Exercise of extraordinary Meekness and mutual Forbearance: For at such a Time, CHRIST appears as it were coming in his Kingdom, which calls for great Moderation in our Behaviour towards all Men; as is evident Phil. 4. 5. *Let your Moderation be known unto all Men: the Lord is at Hand.* The Awe of the divine Majesty that appears present or approaching, should dispose us to it, and deter us from the contrary. For us to be judging one another, and behaving with Fierceness and Bitterness, one towards another, when he who is the Searcher of all Hearts, to whom we must all give an Account, appears so remarkably present, is exceeding unsuitable. Our Business, at such a Time, should be at Home, searching our selves, and condemning our selves, and taking Heed to our own Behaviour. If there be glorious Prosperity to the Church of GOD approaching, those that are the most meek, will have the largest Share in it: For when CHRIST *rides forth, in his Glory and his Majesty*, it is *because of Truth, Meekness and Righteousness*, Psal. 45. 3, 4. And when GOD remarkably *arises, to execute Judgment*, it is *to save all the Meek of the Earth*, Psal. 76. 9. And 'tis *the Meek*, that *shall increase their Joy in the Lord*, Isa. 29. 19. And when the Time comes, that GOD will give this lower World into the Hands of his Saints, it is *the Meek that shall inherit the Earth*, Psal. 37. 11. and Matth. 5. 5. *But with the froward, God will shew himself unsavoury.*

Those therefore, that have been zealous for this Work, and have greatly err'd and been injurious with their Zeal, ought not to be treated with Bitterness. There is abundant Reason to think, that most of them are the dear Children of GOD, for whom CHRIST died; and therefore that they will see their

Error. As to those Things, wherein we see them to be in an Error, we have Reason to say of 'em as the Apostle, Philip. 3. 15. *If any are otherwise minded, God shall reveal this unto them.* Their Errors should not be made Use of by us, so much to excite Indignation towards them, but should influence all of us, that hope that we are the Children of GOD, to humble our selves, and become more entirely dependent on the LORD JESUS CHRIST, when we see those, that are GOD's own People, so ready to go astray. And those Ministers that have been judged, and injuriously dealt with, will do the Part of CHRIST's Disciples, not to judge and revile again, but to receive such Injuries with Meekness and Forbearance, and making a good Improvement of them, more strictly examining their Hearts & Ways, and committing themselves to GOD. This will be the Way to have GOD vindicate them in his Providence, if they belong to him. We han't yet seen the End of Things; nor do we know who will be most vindicated, and honoured of GOD, in the Issue. Eccles. 7. 8. *Better is the End of a Thing, than the Beginning thereof; and the patient in Spirit, is better than the proud in Spirit.*

Contrary to this mutual Meekness, is each Party's stigmatizing one another with odious Names; as is done in many Parts of *New-England*: which tends greatly to widen and perpetuate the Breach. Such distinguishing Names of Reproach, do as it were divide us into two Armies, separated, and drawn up in Battle-Array, ready to fight one with another; which greatly hinders the Work of GOD.

And as such an extraordinary Time as this, does especially require of us the Exercise of a great deal of Forbearance, *one towards another*; so there is peculiarly requisite in GOD's People, the Exercise of great Patience, in waiting *on GOD*, under any special Difficulties and Disadvantages they may be under, as to the Means of Grace. The beginning of a Revival of Religion will naturally and necessarily be attended with a great many Difficulties of this Nature; many Parts of the reviving Church will, for a while, be under great Disadvantages, by Reason of what remains of the old Disease, of a general Corruption of the visible Church. We can't expect that, after a long Time of Degeneracy and Depravity, in the State of Things in the Church, Things should all come to Rights at once; it must be a Work of Time: And for God's People to be over-hasty and violent, in such a Case, being resolved to have every Thing rectified at once, or else forcibly to deliver themselves, by Breaches and Separations, is the Way to hinder Things coming to Rights, as they otherwise would, and to keep 'em back, and the Way to break all in Pieces. Not but that the Case may be such, the Difficulty may be so intolerable, as to allow of no Delay, and GOD's People can't continue in the State wherein they were, without Violations of absolute Commands of GOD. But otherwise, tho' the Difficulty may be very great, another Course should be taken. GOD's People should have their Recourse directly to the Throne of Grace, to represent their Difficulties before the great Shepherd of the Sheep, that has the Care of all the Affairs of his Church; and when they have done, they should wait patiently upon him: If they do so, they may expect that in his Time, he will appear for their Deliverance: But if instead of that, they are impatient, and take the Work into their own Hands, they will bewray their Want of Faith, and will dishonour GOD, and can't have such Reason to hope that CHRIST will appear for them, as they have desired, but have Reason to fear, that he will leave 'em to manage their Affairs for themselves, as well as they can: When otherwise, if they had waited on CHRIST patiently, continuing still instant in Prayer, they might have had him appearing for them, much more effectually to deliver them. *He that believeth shall not make haste*; and 'tis for those that are found patiently waiting on the Lord, under Difficulties, that he will especially appear, when he comes to do great Things for his Church, as is evident by *Isa.* 30. 18. and Chap. 40. at the latter End, and 49. 23. and *Psal.* 37. 9. and many other Places.

I have somewhere, not long since, met with an Exposition of those Words of the Spouse, that we have several Times repeated in the Book of *Canticles, I charge you, O Daughters of* Jerusalem, *that ye stir not up, nor awake my Love, 'till he please*, which is the only satisfying Exposition that ever I met with; which was to this Purpose, *viz.* That when the Church of GOD is under great Difficulties, and in Distress, and CHRIST don't appear for her Help, but seems to neglect her, as tho' he were asleep, GOD's People, or the Daughters of *Jerusalem*, in such a Case, should not shew an hasty Spirit; and not having Patience to wait for Christ to awake for their Help, 'till his Time comes, take indirect Courses for their own Deliverance, and use violent Means for their Escape, before Christ appears to open the Door for them; and so as it were, *stir up, and awake Christ*, before his Time. When the Church is in Distress, and GOD seems not to appear for her in his Providence, he is very often represented in Scripture, as being asleep; as CHRIST was asleep in the Ship, when the Disciples were tossed by the Storm, & the Ship covered with Waves: And GOD's appearing afterwards for his People's Help, is represented as his awaking out of Sleep. *Psal.* 7. 6. and 35. 23. and 44. 23. and 59. 4. and 73. 20. CHRIST has an appointed Time for his thus awaking out of Sleep: And his People ought to wait upon him; and not, in an impatient Fit, stir him up, before his Time. 'Tis worthy to be observed how strict this Charge is, given to the Daughters of *Jerusalem*, which is repeated three Times over in the Book of *Canticles*, Chap. 2. 7. and 3. 5. and 8. 4. In the 2d Chapter and six first Verses, is represented the Supports CHRIST gives his Church, while she is in a suffering State, *as the Lilly among Thorns*: In the 7th Verse is represented her Patience in waiting for CHRIST, to appear for her Deliverance, when she charges the Daughters of *Jerusalem*, not to stir up, nor awake her Love 'till he please, *by the Roes, and the Hinds of the Field*; which are Creatures of a gentle, harmless Nature, are not Beasts of Prey, do not devour one another, don't fight with their Enemies, but fly from them; and are of a pleasant, loving Nature, *Prov.* 5. 19. In the next Verse, we see the Church's Success, in this Way of waiting under Sufferings, with Meekness & Patience; CHRIST soon awakes, speedily appears, and swiftly comes; *The Voice of my Beloved! Behold, he cometh, leaping upon the Mountains, skipping upon the Hills!*

What has been mentioned hitherto, has Relation to the Behaviour we are obliged to, as we would prevent the Hindrances of the Work, but besides these, there are Things that must be done, more directly to advance it. And here, it concerns every one, in the first Place, to look into his own Heart, and see to it that he be a Partaker of the Benefits of the Work himself, and that it be promoted in his own Soul. Now is a most glorious Opportunity for the Good of Souls. 'Tis manifestly, with respect to a Time of great Revival of Religion in the World, that we have that gracious, earnest and moving Invitation proclaimed, in the 55th of Isai. *Ho, every one that thirsteth!* &c. as is evident by what preceeds in the foregoing Chapter, and what follows in the Close of this. Here, in the 6th Verse it is said, *Seek ye the Lord, while he may be found; call upon him, while he is near.* And 'tis with special Reference to such a Time, that CHRIST proclaims as he does, Rev. 21. 6. *I will give unto him that is athirst, of the Fountain of the Water of Life freely.* And Chap. 22. 17. *And the Spirit and the Bride say, Come; and let him that heareth say, Come; and let him that is athirst come; and whosoever will, let him take the Water of Life freely.* And it seems to be with Reference to such a Time, which is typified by the *Feast of Tabernacles,* that JESUS, at that Feast, stood and cried, as we have an Account, Joh. 7. 37, 38. *In the last Day, that great Day of the Feast, Jesus stood and cried, saying, If any Man thirst, let him come unto me and drink. He that believeth on me, out of his Belly shall flow Rivers of living Water.* And 'tis with special Reference to GOD's Freeness and Readiness to bestow Grace at such a Time, that it is said in Isa. 60. 11. of the spiritual *Jerusalem, Thy Gates shall be open continually, they shall not be shut, Day nor Night.*

And tho' I judge not those that have opposed this Work, and would not have others judge them, yet, if any such shall happen to read this Treatise, I would take the Liberty to intreat them to leave off concerning themselves so much about others, and look into their own Souls, and see to it that they are the Subjects of a true, saving Work of the Spirit of GOD. If they have Reason to think they never have been, or it be but a very doubtful Hope that they have, then how can they have any Heart to be busily and fiercely engaged about the Mistakes, and the supposed false Hopes of others? And I would now beseech those that have hitherto been something inclining to *Arminian* Principles, seriously to weigh the Matter with Respect to this Work, and consider, whether, if the Scriptures are the Word of God, the Work that has been described in the first Part of this Treatise, must not needs be, as to the Substance of it, the Work of GOD, and the Flourishing of that Religion, that is taught by CHRIST and his Apostles; and whether any good Medium can be found, where a Man can rest, with any Stability, between owning this Work, and being a Deist; and also to consider whether or no, if it be indeed so, that this be the Work of God, it don't entirely overthrow their Scheme of Religion; and therefore whether it don't infinitely concern 'em, as they would be Partakers of eternal Salvation, to relinquish their Scheme. Now is a good Time for *Arminians* to change their Principles. I would now, as one of the Friends of this Work, humbly invite 'em to come and join with us, and be on our Side; and if I had the Authority of *Moses,* I would say to them as he did to *Hobab,* Num. 10. 29. *We are journeying unto the Place, of which the Lord said, I will give it you; come thou with us; and we will do thee Good: For the Lord hath spoken Good concerning* Israel.

As the Benefit and Advantage of the good Improvement of such a Season, is extraordinary great; so the Danger of neglecting, and misimproving it, is proportionably great. 'Tis abundantly evident by the Scripture, that as a Time of great Out-pouring of the Spirit, is a Time of great Favour to those that are Partakers of the Blessing; so it is always a Time of remarkable Vengeance to others. So in Isai. 61. 2. the same that is called, *the acceptable Year of the Lord,* is called also, *the Day of Vengeance of our God.* So it was amongst the Jews, in the Apostles Days: The Apostle in 2 Cor. 6. 2. says of that Time, that it was *the accepted Time, and Day of Salvation*; And Christ says of the same Time, Luk. 21. 22. *These are the Days of Vengeance.* At the same Time that the Blessings of the Kingdom of Heaven were given to some, there was an *Ax laid at the Root of the Trees, that those that did not bear Fruit, might be hewn down, and cast into the Fire,* Matth. 3. 9, 10, 11. Then was glorified, both the Goodness & Severity of GOD, in a remarkable Manner. *Rom.* 11. 22. The Harvest and the Vintage go together: At the same Time that the Earth is reaped, and GOD's Elect are gathered into the Garner of GOD, *the Angel that has Power over Fire, thrusts in his Sickle, and gathers the Cluster of the Vine of the Earth, and casts it into the great Wine-Press of the Wrath of God,* Rev. 14. at the latter End. So it is foretold, that at the Beginning of the glorious Times of the Christian Church, at the same Time that *the Hand of the Lord is known, towards his Servants, so shall his Indignation, towards his Enemies,* Isa. 66. 14. So when that glorious Morning shall appear, wherein *the Sun of Righteousness shall arise, to the Elect, with Healing in his*

Wings, the Day shall burn as an Oven to the Wicked, Mal. 4. 1, 2, 3. There is no Time like such a Time, for the Increase of Guilt, and treasuring up Wrath, and desperate hardening of the Heart, if Men stand it out; which is the most awful Judgment, and Fruit of divine Wrath, that can be inflicted on any Mortal. So that a Time of great Grace, and pouring out of the Spirit, and the Fruits of divine Mercy, is evermore also, a Time of great Out-pouring of something else, *viz.* Divine Vengeance, on those that neglect and misimprove such a Season.

The State of the present Revival of Religion, has an awful Aspect upon those that are advanced in Years. The Work has been chiefly amongst those that are young; and comparatively, but few others have been made Partakers of it. And indeed, it has commonly been so, when GOD has begun any great Work, for the Revival of his Church; he has taken the young People, and has cast off the old & stiff-necked Generation. There was a remarkable Out-pouring of the Spirit of GOD, on the Children of *Israel* in the Wilderness, on the younger Generation, *their little ones, that they said, should be a Prey,* the Generation that entred into *Canaan,* with *Joshua;* which is evident by many Things in Scripture. That Generation seems to have been the most excellent Generation that ever was in the Church of *Israel.* There is no Generation, of which there is so much Good, and so little Hurt spoken in Scripture; as might be shewn, if it would not be too long. In that Generation, that were under twenty Years, when they went out of *Egypt,* was that *Kindness of Youth,* and *Love of Espousals,* spoken of, Jer. 2. 2, 3. But the old Generation were passed by, and remained obstinate and stiff-necked, were always murmuring, and would not be convinced by all GOD's wondrous Works that they beheld. GOD by his awful Judgments that he executed in the Wilderness, and the Affliction that the People suffered there, convinced and humbled the younger Generation, and fitted them for great Mercy; as is evident by *Deut.* 2. 16. but he destroyed the old Generation; *he swore in his Wrath, that they should not enter into his Rest, and their Carcases fell in the Wilderness*: When it was a Time of great Mercy, and pouring out of GOD's Spirit on their Children, it was remarkably a Day of Vengeance unto them; as appears by the 90 Psalm. Let the old Generation in this Land, take Warning from hence, and take Heed that they don't refuse to be convinced, by all GOD's Wonders that he works before their Eyes, and that they don't continue forever objecting, murmuring & cavailling against the Work of GOD, least while GOD is bringing their Children into a Land flowing with Milk and Honey, he should swear in his Wrath concerning them, that their Carcases shall fall in the Wilderness.

So when GOD had a Design of great Mercy to the *Jews*, in bringing 'em out of the *Babylonish* Captivity, and returning them to their own Land, there was a blessed Out-pouring of the Spirit upon them in *Babylon*, to bring 'em to deep Conviction and Repentance, and to a Spirit of Prayer, to cry earnestly to GOD for Mercy; which is often spoken of by the Prophets: But it was not upon the old Generation, that were carried Captive. The Captivity continued just long enough, for that perverse Generation to waste away and die in their Captivity; at least those of them that were adult Persons, when carried Captive. The old Generation, and Heads of Families, were exceeding obstinate, and would not hearken to the earnest repeated Warnings of the Prophet *Jeremiah*; but he had greater Success among the young People; as appears by Jer. 6. 10, 11. *To whom shall I speak and give Warning, that they may hear? Behold their Ear is uncircumcised, and they cannot hearken: Behold, the Word of the Lord is unto them a Reproach; they have no Delight in it. Therefore I am full of the Fury of the Lord; I am weary with holding in; I will pour it out upon the Children abroad, and upon the Assembly of the young Men together; for even the Husband with the Wife* (i.e. The Heads of Families, and Parents of these Children) *shall be taken, the aged, with him that is full of Days.* Blessed be GOD! There are some of the elder People, that have been made Partakers of this Work: And those that are most awakened, by these Warnings of GOD's Word, and the awful Frowns of his Providence, will be most likely to be made Partakers hereafter. It infinitely concerns them to take Heed to themselves, that they may be Partakers of it; for how dreadful will it be to go to Hell, after having spent so many Years in doing nothing, but treasuring up Wrath.

But above all others whatsoever, does it concern us that are Ministers, to see to it that we are Partakers of this Work, or that we have Experience of the saving Operations of the same

Spirit, that is now poured out on the Land. How sorrowful and melancholy is the Case, when it is otherwise? For one to stand at the Head of a Congregation of GOD's People, as representing CHRIST and speaking in his Stead, and to act the Part of a Shepherd and Guide to a People, in such a State of Things, when many are under great Awakenings, and many are converted, & many of GOD's Saints are filled with divine Light, Love and Joy, and to undertake to instruct and lead 'em all, under all these various Circumstances, and to be put to it, continually to play the Hypocrite, and force the Airs of a Saint in Preaching, and from Time to Time, in private Conversation, & particular dealing with Souls, to undertake to judge of their Circumstances, to try to talk with those that come to him, as if he knew what they said; to try to talk with Persons of Experience, as if he knew how to converse with them, and had Experience as well as they; to make others believe that he rejoices when others are converted, and to force a pleased and joyful Countenance and Manner of Speech, when there is nothing in the Heart, what sorrowful Work is here! Oh! how miserably must such a Person feel! What a wretched Bondage and Slavery is this! What Pains, and how much Art must such a Minister use to conceal himself! And how weak are his Hands! Besides the infinite Provocation of the most high GOD, and Displeasure of his Lord & Master, that he incurs, by continuing a secret Enemy to him in his Heart, in such Circumstances. I think there is a great deal of Reason, from the Scripture, to conclude, that no Sort of Men in the World, will be so low in Hell, as ungodly Ministers: Every thing that is spoken of in Scripture, as that which aggravates Guilt, and heightens divine Wrath, meets in them; however some particular Persons, of other Sorts, may be more guilty than some of these.

And what great Disadvantages are unconverted Ministers under, to oppose any Irregularities, or Imprudences, or intemperate Zeal, that they may see in those that are the Children of GOD, when they are conscious to themselves, that they have no Zeal at all? If Enthusiasm and Wildness comes in like a Flood, what poor weak Instruments are such Ministers to withstand it? With what Courage can they open their Mouths, when they look inward, and consider how it is with them?

We that are Ministers, not only have Need of some true

Experience of the saving Influence of the Spirit of GOD upon our Heart, but we need a double Portion of the Spirit of GOD at such a Time as this; we had need to be as full of Light, as a Glass is, that is held out in the Sun; and with Respect to Love and Zeal, we had need at this Day, to be like the Angels, that are a Flame of Fire. The State of the Times extremely requires a Fulness of the divine Spirit in Ministers, and we ought to give our selves no Rest 'till we have obtain'd it. And in order to this, I should think Ministers, above all Persons, ought to be much in secret Prayer and Fasting, and also much in Praying and Fasting one with another. It seems to me it would be becoming the Circumstances of the present Day, if Ministers in a Neighbourhood would often meet together, and spend Days in Fasting, and fervent Prayer, among themselves, earnestly seeking for those extraordinary Supplies of divine Grace from Heaven, that we need at this Day: And also if, on their occasional Visits one to another, instead of spending away their Time in sitting & smoking, and in diverting, or worldly, unprofitable Conversation, telling News, & making their Remarks on this & the other trifling Subject, they would spend their Time in praying together, and singing Praises, & religious Conference. How much do many of the common People shame many of us that are in the Work of the Ministry, in these Respects? Surely we do not behave our selves so much like Christian Ministers, & the Disciples and Ambassadors of Christ, as we ought to do. And while we condemn zealous Persons for their doing so much at censuring Ministers at this Day, it ought not to be without deep Reflections upon, & great Condemnation of our selves: For indeed, we do very much to provoke Censoriousness, and lay a great Temptation before others, to the Sin of Judging: And if we can prove, that those that are guilty of it, do transgress the Scripture Rule, yet our Indignation should be chiefly against our selves.

Ministers, at this Day in a special Manner, should act as Fellow-helpers, in their great Work. It should be seen that they are animated & engag'd, and exert themselves with one Heart & Soul, and with united Strength, to promote the present glorious Revival of Religion: And to that End should often meet together, & act in Concert. And if it were a common Thing in the Country, for Ministers to join in publick Exercises, and second one another, in their Preaching, I believe it would be of great Service. I mean that Ministers having consulted one another, as to the Subjects of their Discourses, before they go to the House of GOD, should there speak, two or three of them going, in short Discourses, as seconding each other, and earnestly enforcing each other's Warnings & Counsels. Only such an Appearance of united Zeal in Ministers, would have a great Tendency to awaken Attention, & much to impress & animate the Hearers; as has been found by Experience, in some Parts of the Country.

Ministers should carefully avoid weakening one another's Hands. And therefore every Thing should be avoided, by which their Interest with their People might be diminished, or their Union with them broken. On the contrary, if Ministers han't forfeited their Acceptance in that Character, in the visible Church, by their Doctrine or Behaviour, their Brethren in the Ministry ought studiously to endeavour to heighten the Esteem and Affection of their People towards them, that they may have no Temptation to repent their admitting other Ministers to come & preach in their Pulpits.

Two Things, that are exceeding needful in Ministers, as they would do any great Matters, to advance the Kingdom of Christ, are *Zeal* & *Resolution*. The Influence and Power of these Things, to bring to pass great Effects, is greater than can well be imagined: A Man of but an ordinary Capacity, will do more with them, than one of ten Times the Parts & Learning, without them: More may be done with them, in a few Days, or at least Weeks, than can be done without them, in many Years. Those that are possessed of these Qualities, commonly carry the Day, in almost all Affairs. Most of the great Things that have been done in the World of Mankind, the great Revolutions that have been accomplished in the Kingdoms and Empires of the Earth, have been chiefly owing to these Things. The very Sight or Appearance of a thoroughly engaged Spirit, together with a fearless Courage & unyielding Resolution, in any Person, that has undertaken the managing any Affair amongst Mankind, goes a great Way towards accomplishing the Effect aimed at. 'Tis evident that the Appearance of these Things in *Alexander*, did three Times as much towards his conquering the World, as all the Blows that he struck. And how much were the great

Things that *Oliver Cromwel* did, owing to these Things? And
the great Things that Mr. *Whitefield* has done, every where, as
he has run through the *British* Dominions, (so far as they are
owing to Means) are very much owing to the Appearance of
these Things, which he is eminently possess'd of. When the
People see these Things apparently in a Person, and to a great
Degree, it awes them, & has a commanding Influence upon
their Minds; it seems to them that they must yield; they naturally fall before them, without standing to contest or dispute
the Matter; they are conquered as it were by Surprize. But
while we are cold & heartless, & only go on in a dull Manner,
in an old formal Round, we shall never do any great Matters.
Our Attempts, with the Appearance of such Coldness and
Irresolution, won't so much as make Persons think of yielding:
They will hardly be sufficient to put it into their Minds; and if
it be put into their Minds, the Appearance of such Indifference
and Cowardice, does as it were call for, & provoke Opposition.—Our Misery is Want of Zeal and Courage; for not only
thro' Want of them, does all fail that we seem to attempt, but
it prevents our attempting any Thing very remarkable, for the
Kingdom of CHRIST. Hence, oftentimes it has been, that when
any Thing very considerable, that is new, is proposed to be
done, for the Advancement of Religion, or the publick Good,
many Difficulties are found out, that are in the Way, and a
great many Objections are started, and it may be, it is put off
from one to another; but no Body does any Thing. And after
this Manner good Designs or Proposals have oftentimes failed,
& have sunk as soon as proposed. Whenas, if we had but Mr.
Whitefield's Zeal and Courage, what could not we do, with
such a Blessing as we might expect?

Zeal and Courage will do much in Persons of but an ordinary Capacity; but especially would they do great Things, if
join'd with great Abilities. If some great Men, that have appear'd
in our Nation, had been as eminent in Divinity, as they were in
Philosophy, and had engaged in the Christian Cause, with as
much Zeal and Fervour, as some others have done, & with a
proportionable Blessing of Heaven, they would have conquered all *Christendom*, & turn'd the World upside down. We
have many Ministers in the Land that don't want for Abilities,
they are Persons of bright Parts and Learning; they should

consider how much is expected, and will be required of them, by their Lord & Master, and how much they might do for Christ, and what great Honour, and how glorious a Reward they might receive, if they had in their Hearts an heavenly Warmth, and divine Heat, proportionable to their Light.

With Respect to Candidates for the Ministry, I won't undertake particularly to determine, what Kind of Examination or Trial they should pass under, in order to their Admission to that sacred Work: But I think this is evident from the Scripture, that another Sort of Trial, with Regard to their Vertue & Piety, is requisite, than is required in order to Persons being admitted into the visible Church. The Apostle directs, *that Hands be laid suddenly on no Man*; but that they should *first be tried*, before they are admitted to the Work of the Ministry: But 'tis evident that Persons were suddenly admitted, by Baptism, into the visible Church, from Time to Time, on their Profession of their Faith in Christ, without such Caution & Strictness in their Probation. And it seems to me, those would act very unadvisedly, that should enter on that great and sacred Work, before they had comfortable Satisfaction concerning themselves, that they have had a saving Work of God on their Souls.

And tho' it may be thought, that I go out of my proper Sphere, to intermeddle in the Affairs of the Colleges, yet I will take the Liberty of an Englishman, (that speaks his Mind freely, concerning publick Affairs) & the Liberty of a Minister of Christ, (who doubtless may speak his Mind as freely about Things that concern the Kingdom of his Lord and Master) to give my Opinion, in some Things, with Respect to those Societies; the Original and main Design of which is to train up Persons, & fit them for the Work of the Ministry. And I would say in general, that it appears to me that Care should be taken, some Way or other, that those Societies should be so regulated, that they should, in Fact, be Nurseries of Piety. Otherwise, they are fundamentally ruin'd & undone, as to their main Design, and most essential End. They ought to be so constituted, that Vice and Idleness should have no Living there: They are intolerable in Societies, whose main Design is, to train up Youth in Christian Knowledge & eminent Piety, to fit them to be Pastors of the Flock of the blessed Jesus. I have heretofore had some Acquaintance with the Affairs of a College, and Experience of what belonged to its Tuition & Government; and I can't but think that it is practicable enough, so to constitute such Societies, that there should be no being there, without being vertuous, serious and diligent. It seems to me to be a Reproach to the Land, that ever it should be so with our Colleges, that instead of being Places of the greatest Advantages for true Piety, one can't send a Child thither, without great Danger of his being infected, as to his Morals; as it has certainly, sometimes been with these Societies: 'Tis perfectly intolerable; and any Thing should be done, rather than it should be so. If we pretend to have any Colleges at all, under any Notion of training up Youth for the Ministry, there should be some Way found out, that should certainly prevent its being thus. To have Societies for bringing Persons up to be Ambassadors of Jesus Christ, and to lead Souls to Heaven, & to have 'em Places of so much Infection, is the greatest Nonsense and Absurdity imaginable.

And, as thorough and effectual Care should be taken that Vice & Idleness ben't tolerated in these Societies, so certainly, the Design of 'em requires, that extraordinary Means should be used in them, for training up the Students in vital Religion, and experimental & practical Godliness; so that they should be holy Societies, the very Place should be as it were sacred: They should be, in the midst of the Land, Fountains of Piety and Holiness. There is a great deal of Pains taken, to teach the Scholars human Learning; there ought to be as much, and more Care, thoroughly to educate 'em in Religion, & lead 'em to true & eminent Holiness. If the main Design of these Nurseries, is to bring up Persons to teach CHRIST, then it is of greatest Importance that there should be Care and Pains taken, to bring those that are there educated, to the Knowledge of Christ. It has been common in our publick Prayers, to call these Societies, *the Schools of the Prophets*; and if they are Schools, to train up young Men to be *Prophets*, certainly there ought to be extraordinary Care there taken, to train 'em up to be *Christians*.

And I can't see, why it is not on all Accounts fit & convenient, for the Governours & Instructors of the Colleges, particularly, singly and frequently to converse with the Students, about the State of their Souls. As is the Practice of the Rev. Dr. *Doddridge*, one of the most noted of the present dissenting Ministers in

England, who keeps an Academy at *Northampton*, as he himself informs the Rev. Mr. *Wadsworth* of *Hartford*, in *Connecticut*, in a Letter, dated at *Northampton*, March 6. 1740, 41. The Original of which Letter I have seen, and have by me an Extract of it, sent to me, by Mr. *Wadsworth*; which is as follows;

"Thro' the divine Goodness, I have every Year, the Pleasure to see some Plants taken out of my Nursery, & set in neighbouring Congregations; where they generally settle with a unanimous Consent, and that to a very remarkable Degree, in some very large, and once divided Congregations. A Circumstance, in which, I own and adore the Hand of a wise & gracious God; and can't but look upon it as a Token for Good. I have at present, a greater Proportion of pious and ingenious Youth under my Care, than I ever before had. So that I hope the Church may reasonably expect some considerable Relief from hence, if GOD spare their Lives a few Years, & continue to them those gracious Assistances, which he has hitherto mercifully imparted.—I will not, Sir, trouble you at present, with a large Account of my Method of accademical Education: Only would observe, that I think it of vast Importance, to instruct them carefully in the Scriptures; & not only endeavour to establish them in the great Truths of Christianity, but to labour to promote their practical Influence on their Hearts. For which Purpose, I frequently converse with each of them alone, & conclude the Conversation with Prayer. This does indeed take up a great deal of Time; but, I bless GOD, it's amply repaired, in the Pleasure I have, in seeing my Labour is not in vain in the LORD."

There are some that are not Ministers, nor are concern'd immediately in those Things that appertain to their Office, or in the Education of Persons for it, that are under great Advantages to promote such a glorious Work as this. Some Lay-men, tho' it be not their Business publickly to exhort & teach, yet are in some Respects, under greater Advantage to encourage and forward this Work, than Ministers. As particularly great Men, or Men that are high in Honour and Influence. How much might such do, to encourage Religion, & open the Way for it to have free Course, & bear down Opposition, if they were but inclin'd? There is commonly a certain unhappy Shyness, in great Men, with Respect to Religion, as tho' they were asham'd of it, or at least, asham'd to do very much at it; whereby they dishonour, & doubtless, greatly provoke the King of Kings, and very much wound Religion among the common People. They are careful of their Honour, and seem to be afraid of appearing openly forward and zealous in Religion, as tho' it were what would debase their Character, & expose 'em to Contempt. But in this Day of bringing up the Ark, they ought to be like *David*, that great King of *Israel*, who *made himself vile* before the Ark; and as he was the highest in Honour and Dignity, among GOD's People, so thought it became him to appear foremost, in the Zeal & Activity he manifested on that Occasion; thereby animating & encouraging the whole Congregation to praise the Lord, and rejoice before him, with all their Might: And tho' it diminished him in the Eyes of scoffing *Michal*, yet it did not at all abate the Honour and Esteem of the Congregation of *Israel*, but advanced it; as appears by 2 *Sam.* 6. 22.

Rich Men have a Talent in their Hands, in the Disposal and Improvement of which, they might very much promote such a Work as this, if they were so disposed. They are far beyond others under Advantage to do Good, and lay up for themselves Treasures in Heaven. What a thousand Pities is it, that for Want of a Heart, they commonly have no Share at all there, but Heaven is peopled mostly with the Poor of this World? One would think that our rich Men, that call themselves Christians, might devise some notable Things, to do with their Money, to advance the Kingdom of their professed Redeemer, and the Prosperity of the Souls of Men, at this Time of such extraordinary Advantage for it. It seems to me, that in this Age, most of us have but very narrow, penurious Notions of Christianity, as it respects our Use and Disposal of our temporal Goods. The primitive Christians had not such Notions: They were train'd up by the Apostles in another Way.—GOD has greatly distinguished some of the Inhabitants of *New-England*, from others, in the Abundance that he has given 'em of the good Things of this Life. If they could now be persuaded to lay out some considerable Part of that which GOD has given 'em for the Honour of GOD, and lay it up in Heaven, instead of spending it for their own Honour, or laying it up for their Posterity, they would not repent of it afterwards. How liberally did the Heads of the Tribes contribute of their Wealth, at the setting up the Tabernacle, tho' it was in a barren Wilderness? These are the Days of the erecting the Tabernacle of GOD amongst us. We have a particular Account how the Goldsmiths & the Merchants helped to rebuild the Wall of *Jerusalem*, Neh. 3. 32. The Days are coming spoken of in Scripture, and I believe not very far off, when the Sons of *Zion shall come from far, bringing their Silver and their Gold with them, unto the Name of the Lord their God, and to the holy One of* Israel; and when the Merchants of the Earth, shall trade for CHRIST, more than for themselves, & *their Merchandize and Hire shall be Holiness to the Lord, and shall not be treasured, or laid up for Posterity, but shall be for them that dwell before the Lord, to eat sufficiently, and for durable Clothing*; and when *the Ships of* Tarshish *shall bring* the Wealth of the distant Parts of the Earth, *to the Place of God's Sanctuary, and to make the Place of his Feet glorious*; and *the abundance of the Sea shall be converted to the Use of God's Church, and she shall suck the Milk of the Gentiles, and suck the Breasts of Kings.* The Days are coming, when the great and rich Men of the World, *shall bring their Honour and Glory into the Church*, and shall, as it were, strip themselves, to spread their Garments under CHRIST's Feet, as he enters triumphantly into *Jerusalem*; & when those that won't do so shall have no Glory, & their Silver & Gold shall be canker'd, and their Garments Moth-eaten; for the Saints shall then inherit the Earth, & they shall reign on Earth, and those that honour GOD he will honour, and those that despise him shall be lightly esteemed.

If some of our rich Men would give one Quarter of their Estates to promote this Work, they would act a little, as if they were design'd for the Kingdom of Heaven, & a little as rich Men will act by and by, that shall be Partakers of the spiritual Wealth and Glories of that Kingdom.

Great Things might be done for the Advancement of the Kingdom of CHRIST, at this Day, by those that have Ability, by establishing Funds, for the Support and Propagation of Religion; by supporting some that are eminently qualified with Gifts and Grace, in preaching the Gospel in certain Parts of the Country, that are more destitute of the Means of Grace; in searching out Children, of promising Abilities, & their Hearts full of Love to CHRIST, but of poor Families, (as doubtless there are such now in the Land) & bringing them up for the Ministry; & in distributing Books, that are remarkably fitted to promote vital Religion, and have a great Tendency to advance this Work; or if they would only bear the Trouble, Expence & Loss of sending such Books into various Parts of the Land, to be sold, it might be an Occasion that ten Times so many of those Books should be bought, as otherwise would be; and in establishing and supporting Schools, in poor Towns & Villages; which might be done on such a Foundation, as not only to bring up Children in common Learning, but also, might very much tend to their Conviction & Conversion, and being train'd up in vital Piety; and doubtless something might be done this Way, in old Towns, and more populous Places, that might have a great Tendency to the Flourishing of Religion, in the rising Generation.

But I would now proceed to mention some Things, that ought to be done, at such a Day as this, that concern all in general.

And here, the first Thing I shall mention, is *Fasting and Prayer*. It seems to me, that the Circumstances of the present Work do loudly call God's People to abound in this; whether they consider the Experience GOD has lately given 'em, of the Worth of his Presence, & of the blessed Fruits of the Effusions of his Spirit, to excite them to pray for the Continuance & Increase, & greater Extent of such Blessings; or whether they consider the great Encouragement GOD has lately given 'em, to pray for the Out-pourings of his Spirit, & the carrying on this Work, by the great Manifestations he has lately made, of the Freeness & Riches of his Grace; and how much there is, in what we have seen of the glorious Works of GOD's Power & Grace, to put us in Mind of the yet greater Things of this Nature, that he has spoken of in his Word, & to excite our Longings for those Things, & Hopes of their Approach; or whether we consider the great Opposition that *Satan* makes against this Work, and the many Difficulties with which it is clog'd, and the distressing Circumstances that some Parts of GOD's Church in this Land are under at this Day, on one Account and another.

So is GOD's Will, thro' his wonderful Grace, that the Prayers of his Saints should be one great and principal Means of carrying on the Designs of CHRIST's Kingdom in the World. When GOD has something very great to accomplish for his Church, 'tis his Will, that there should precede it, the extraordinary Prayers of his People; as is manifest by Ezek. 36. 37. *I will yet, for this, be enquired of, by the House of* Israel, *to do it for them*; together with the Context. And 'tis revealed that, when GOD is about to accomplish great Things for his Church, he will begin by remarkably pouring out the Spirit of Grace & Supplication. *Zech.* 12. 10. If we are not to expect that the Devil should go out of a particular Person, that is under a bodily Possession, without extraordinary Prayer, *or Prayer and Fasting*; how much less, should we expect to have him cast out of the Land, & the World, without it.

I am sensible that considerable has been done in Duties of this Nature, in some Places; but I don't think so much as GOD, in the present Dispensations of his Providence calls for. I should think the People of GOD in this Land, at such a Time as this is, would be in the Way of their Duty, to do three Times so much at Fasting and Prayer as they do; not only, nor principally, for the pouring out of the Spirit on those Towns or Places where they belong; but that GOD would appear for his Church, and in Mercy to miserable Men, to carry on his Work in the Land, & in the World of Mankind, and to fulfil the Things that he has spoken of in his Word, that his Church has been so long wishing & hoping & waiting for. *They that make Mention of the Lord*, at this Day, ought not *to keep Silence*, and should *give God no Rest, 'till he establish, and 'till he make* Jerusalem *a Praise in the Earth*, agreeable to *Isa.* 62. 6, 7. Before the first great Out-pouring of the Spirit of GOD, on the Christian Church, which began at *Jerusalem*, the Church of GOD gave themselves to incessant Prayer, *Act.* 1. 13, 14. There is a Time spoken of, wherein GOD will remarkably & wonderfully appear, for the Deliverance of his Church from all her Enemies, and when he will *avenge his own Elect*: And CHRIST reveals that this will be in Answer to their incessant Prayers, or *crying Day and Night*, Luk. 18. 7. In *Israel*, the *Day of Attonement*, which was their great Day of Fasting & Prayer, preceeded & made Way for the glorious and joyful *Feast of Tabernacles*. When CHRIST is mystically born into the World, to rule over all Nations, it is represented in the 12 Chap. of *Rev.* as being in

Consequence of the Church's *crying, and travailing in Birth, and being pained to be delivered.* One Thing here intended, doubtless is, her crying and agonizing in Prayer.

GOD seems now, at this very Time, to be waiting for this from us. When GOD is about to bestow some great Blessing on his Church, it is often his Manner, in the first Place, so to order Things in his Providence, as to shew his Church their great Need of it, & to bring 'em into Distress for Want of it, and so put 'em upon crying earnestly to him for it. And let us consider GOD's present Dispensations towards his Church in this Land: A glorious Work of his Grace has been begun & carried on; and GOD has, of late, suffer'd innumerable Difficulties to arise, that do in a great Measure clog and hinder it, and bring many of GOD's dear Children into great Distress; & yet don't wholly forsake the Work of his Hand; there are remarkable Tokens of his Presence still to be seen, here and there; as tho' he was not forward to forsake us, and (if I may so say) as tho' he had a Mind to carry on his Work; but only was waiting for something that he expected in us, as requisite in order to it. And we have a great deal of Reason to think, that one Thing at least is, that we should further acknowledge the Greatness and Necessity of such a Mercy, & our Dependence on GOD for it, in earnest and importunate Prayers to him. And by the many Errors that have been run into, & the Wounds we have thereby given our selves & the Cause that we would promote, and the Mischief & Confusion we have thereby made, GOD has hitherto been remarkably shewing us our great & universal Dependence on him, & exceeding Need of his Help and Grace: which should engage our Cries to him for it.

There is no Way that Christians in a private Capacity can do so much to promote the Work of GOD, and advance the Kingdom of CHRIST, as by Prayer. By this even Women, Children and Servants may have a publick Influence. Let Persons be never so weak, & never so mean, & under never so poor Advantages to do much for Christ, and the Souls of Men, otherwise; yet, if they have much of the Spirit of Grace & Supplication, in this Way, they may have Power with him that is infinite in Power, & has the Government of the whole World: And so a poor Man in his Cottage may have a blessed Influence all over the World. GOD is, if I may so say, at the

Command of the Prayer of Faith; and in this Respect is, as it were, under the Power of his People; *as Princes, they have Power with God, and prevail*: Tho' they may be private Persons, their Prayers are put up in the Name of a Mediator, that is a publick Person, being the Head of the whole Church, and the Lord of the Universe: And if they have a great Sense of the Importance of eternal Things, & Concern for the precious Souls of Men, yet they need not regret it, that they are not Preachers; they may go in their Earnestness and Agonies of Soul, and pour out their Souls before One that is able to do all Things; before him they may speak as freely as Ministers; they have a great High-Priest, through whom they may come boldly at all Times, & may vent themselves before a Prayer-hearing Father, without any Restraint.

If the People of GOD, at this Day, instead of spending Time in fruitless Disputing, and talking about Opposers, and judging of them, and animadverting upon the Unreasonableness of their Talk and Behaviour, and its Inconsistence with true Experience, would be more silent in this Way, and open their Mouths much more before GOD, and spend more Time in Fasting & Prayer, they would be more in the Way of a Blessing. And if some Christians in the Land, that have been complaining of their Ministers, and struggling in vain to deliver themselves, from the Difficulties they have complain'd of, under their Ministry, had said and acted less before Men, and had applied themselves with all their Might to cry to GOD for their Ministers, had as it were risen, and storm'd Heaven with their humble, fervent and incessant Prayers for them, they would have been much more in the Way of Success.

GOD in his Providence, appearing in the present State of Things, does especially call on his People in *New-England* to be very much in praying to him for the pouring out of the Spirit upon *Ministers* in the Land. For tho' it is not for us to determine, concerning particular Ministers, how much they have of the Spirit of GOD; yet in the general, it is apparent, that there is, at this Day, Need of very great Degrees of the Presence of GOD with the Ministry in *New-England*, much greater Degrees of it than has hitherto been granted; they need it for themselves, & the Church of God stands in extreme Need of it.

In Days of Fasting & Prayer, wherein the whole Church or

Congregation is concern'd, if the whole Day, besides what is spent in our Families, was not spent in the Meeting-House, but Part of it in particular praying Companies or Societies, it would have a Tendency to animate & engage Devotion, more than if the whole Day were spent in publick, where the People are no Way active themselves in the Worship, any otherwise than as they join with the Ministers. The Inhabitants of many of our Towns are now divided into particular praying Societies, most of the People, young & old, have voluntarily associated themselves, in distinct Companies, for mutual Assistance, in social Worship, in private Houses: What I intend therefore is, that Days of Prayer should be spent partly in these distinct praying Companies. Such a Method of keeping a Fast as *this*, has several Times been proved, *viz.* In the Forenoon, after the Duties of the Family & Closet, as early as might be, all the People of the Congregation have gather'd in their particular religious Societies; Companies of Men by themselves, and Companies of Women by themselves; young Men by themselves, and young Women by themselves; & Companies of Children, in all Parts of the Town, by themselves, as many as were capable of social religious Exercises; the Boys by themselves, and Girls by themselves: And about the middle of the Day, at an appointed Hour, all have met together in the House of GOD, to offer up publick Prayers, and to hear a Sermon suitable to the Occasion: And then, they have retir'd from the House of God again, into their private Societies, and spent the remaining Part of the Day in praying together there, excepting so much as was requisite for the Duties of the Family and Closet, in their own Houses.—And it has been found to be of great Benefit, to assist and engage the Minds of the People in the Duties of the Day.

I have often thought it would be a Thing very desireable, and very likely to be follow'd with a great Blessing, if there could be some Contrivance, that there should be an Agreement of all GOD's People in *America*, that are well affected to this Work, to keep a Day of Fasting & Prayer to God; wherein we should all unite on the same Day, in humbling our selves before GOD for our past long continued Lukewarmness & Unprofitableness; not omitting Humiliation for the Errors that so many of GOD's People that have been zealously affected towards this Work, through their Infirmity & remaining Blindness and Corruption, have run into; and together with Thanksgivings to GOD, for so glorious and wonderful a Display of his Power and Grace, in the late Out-pourings of his Spirit, to address the Father of Mercies, with Prayers & Supplications, and earnest Cries, that he would guide and direct his own People, and that he would continue, and still carry on this Work, & more abundantly & extensively pour out his Spirit; and particularly that he would pour out his Spirit upon Ministers; & that he would bow the Heavens and come down, and erect his glorious Kingdom thro' the Earth.—Some perhaps may think that its being all on the same Day, is a Circumstance of no great Consequence; but I can't be of that Mind: Such a Circumstance makes the Union and Agreement of God's People in his Worship the more visible, and puts the greater Honour upon God, & would have a great Tendency to assist & enliven the Devotions of Christians: It seems to me, it would mightily encourage and animate God's Saints, in humbly & earnestly seeking to God, for such Blessings which concerns them all; and that it would be much for the rejoicing of all, to think, that at the same Time, such Multitudes of GOD's dear Children, far & near, were sending up their Cries to the same common Father, for the same Mercies. CHRIST speaks of Agreement in asking, as what contributes to the Prevalence of the Prayers of his People. Matth. 18. 19. *Again I say unto you, that if any two of you, shall agree on Earth, as touching any Thing that they shall ask, it shall be done for them of my Father which is in Heaven.* If the Agreement, or united Purpose and Appointment of but two of God's Children, would contribute much to the Prevalence of their Prayers, how much more the Agreement of so many Thousands? CHRIST delights greatly in the Union of his People, as appears by his Prayer in the 17th of *John*: And especially is the Appearance of their Union in Worship, lovely and attractive unto him.

I doubt not but such a Thing as I have now mention'd is practicable, without a great deal of Trouble: Some considerable Number of Ministers might meet together, and draw up the Proposal, wherein a certain Day should be pitch'd upon, at a sufficient Distance, endeavouring therein to avoid any other publick Day, that might interfere with the Design, in any of the Provinces, & the Business of the Day should be particularly mention'd; and these Proposals should be published, and sent abroad, into all Parts, with a Desire, that as many Ministers as are disposed to fall in with 'em, would propose the Matter to their Congregations, and having taken their Consent, would subscribe their Names, together with the Places of which they are Ministers, & send back the Proposals thus subscribed, to the Printer; (the Hands of many Ministers might be to one Paper) & the Printer having receiv'd the Papers, thus subscribed, from all the Provinces, might print the Proposals again, with all the Names; thus they might be sent abroad again, with the Names, that God's People might know who are united with 'em in the Affair:—One of the Ministers of *Boston* might be desir'd to have the Oversight of the printing and dispersing the Proposals.—In such a Way, perhaps, might be fulfilled, in some Measure, such a general Mourning and Supplication of God's People, as is spoken of, *Zech.* 12. at the latter End, with which the Church's glorious Day is to be introduced. And such a Day might be something like the *Day of Attonement* in *Israel*, before the joyful *Feast of Tabernacles.*

One Thing more I would mention concerning Fasting and Prayer, wherein I think there has been a Neglect in Ministers; and that is, that altho' they recommend, and much insist on the Duty of secret Prayer, in their Preaching; so little is said about secret Fasting. It is a Duty recommended by our Saviour to his Followers, just in like Manner as secret Prayer is; as may be seen by comparing the 5. & 6. v. of the 6. Chap. of *Mat.* with v. 16, 17, 18. Tho' I don't suppose that secret Fasting is to be practised in a stated Manner, & steady Course, as secret Prayer, yet it seems to me, 'tis a Duty that all professing Christians should practice, & frequently practice. There are many Occasions, of both a spiritual and temporal Nature, that do properly require it; and there are many particular Mercies, that we desire for our selves or Friends, that it would be proper, in this Manner, to seek of GOD.

Another Thing I would also mention, wherein it appears to me that there has been an Omission, with Respect to the external Worship of GOD. There has been of late, a great Increase of preaching the Word, & a great Increase of social Prayer, and a great Increase of singing Praises: These external Duties of

Religion are attended, much more frequently than they used to be; yet I can't understand that there is any Increase of the Administration of the Lord's Supper, or that God's People do any more frequently commemorate the dying Love of their Redeemer, in this sacred Memorial of it, than they used to do: Tho' I don't see why an Increase of Love to Christ, should not dispose Christians, as much to increase in this, as in those other Duties; or why it is not as proper, that Christ's Disciples should abound in this Duty, in this joyful Season, which is spiritually Supper-Time, a Feast-Day with God's Saints, wherein Christ is so abundantly manifesting his dying Love to Souls, and is dealing forth so liberally of the precious Fruits of his Death. It seems plain by the Scripture, that the primitive Christians were wont to celebrate this Memorial of the Sufferings of their dear Redeemer every Lord's Day: And so I believe it will be again in the Church of Christ, in Days that are approaching. And whether we attend this holy and sweet Ordinance so often now, or no, yet I can't but think it would become us, at such a Time as this, to attend it much oftner than is commonly done in the Land.

But another Thing I would mention, which it is of much greater Importance, that we should attend to; and that is the Duty, that is incumbent upon God's People at this Day, to take Heed, that while they abound in external Duties of Devotion, such as Praying, Hearing, Singing, & attending religious Meetings, there be a proportionable Care to abound in moral Duties, such as Acts of Righteousness, Truth, Meekness, Forgiveness & Love towards our Neighbour; which are of much greater Importance in the Sight of God, than all the Externals of his Worship: Which our Saviour was particularly careful, that Men should be well aware of. Mat. 9. 13. *But go ye, and learn what that meaneth, I will have Mercy, and not Sacrifice.* And Chap. 12. 7. *But if ye had known what this meaneth, I will have Mercy and not Sacrifice, ye would not have condemned the Guiltless.*

The internal Acts & Principles of the Worship of God, or the Worship of the Heart, in the Love and Fear of God, Trust in God, and Resignation to God, *&c.* are the most essential and important of all Duties of Religion whatsoever; for therein consists the Essence of all Religion. But of this inward Religion, there are two Sorts of external Manifestations or Expressions. The one Sort, are outward Acts of Worship, such as meeting in religious Assemblies, attending Sacraments, & other outward Institutions, & honouring God with Gestures, such as bowing, or kneeling before him, or with Words, in speaking honourably of him, in Prayer, Praise, or religious Conference. And the other Sort, are the Expressions of our Love to GOD, by obeying his moral Commands, of Self-denial, Righteousness, Meekness, and Christian Love, in our Behaviour among Men. And the latter are of vastly the greatest Importance in the Christian Life. God makes little Account of the former, in Comparison of them. They are abundantly more insisted on, by the Prophets, in the Old-Testament, and CHRIST & his Apostles, in the New. When these two Kinds of Duties are spoken of together, the latter are evermore greatly preferred. As in *Isa.* 1. 12, to the 18. and *Amos* 5. 21, *&c.*—and *Mic.* 6. 7, 8. and *Isa.* 58. 5, 6, 7. and *Zech.* 7. ten first Verses, and *Jer.* 2. seven first Verses, & *Mat.* 15. 3, *&c.* Often, when the Times were very corrupt in *Israel*, the People abounded in the former Kind of Duties, but were at such Times, always notoriously deficient in the latter; as the Prophets complain, *Isa.* 58. four first Verses, *Jer.* 6. 13, compared with ver. 20. Hypocrites & Self-righteous Persons, do much more commonly abound in the former Kind of Duties, than the latter; as Christ remarks of the Pharisees, *Mat.* 23. 14, 25, & 34. When the Scripture directs us to *shew our Faith by our Works*, it is principally the latter Sort are intended; as appears by *Jam.* 2. from 8 ver. to the End, and 1 *Joh.* 2d Chap. ver. 3, 7, 8, 9, 10, 11. And we are to be judged at the last Day, especially by these latter sort of Works; as is evident by the Account we have of the Day of Judgment, in the 25 of *Matth.* External Acts of Worship, in Words & Gestures, & outward Forms, are of little Use, but as Signs of something else, or as they are a Profession of inward Worship: They are not so properly shewing our Religion by our Deeds; for they are only a shewing our Religion by Words, or an outward Profession. But he that shows Religion in the other Sort of Duties, shews it in something more than a Profession of Words, he shews it in Deeds. And tho' Deeds may be hypocritical, as well as Words; yet in themselves they are of greater Importance, for they are much more profitable to our selves and our Neighbour. We can't express our Love to God, by doing any Thing that is profitable to GOD; GOD would therefore have us do it in those Things that are profitable to our Neighbours, whom he has constituted his Receivers: Our Goodness extends not to God, but to our Fellow Christians. The latter Sort of Duties, put greater Honour upon God, because there is greater Self-denial in them. The external Acts of Worship, consisting in bodily Gestures, Words and Sounds, are the cheapest Part of Religion, and least contrary to our Lusts. The Difficulty of thorough, external Religion, don't lie in them. Let wicked Men enjoy their Covetousness, and their Pride, their Malice, Envy and Revenge, and their Sensuality and Voluptuousness, in their Behaviour amongst Men, & they will be willing to compound the Matter with God, & submit to what Forms of Worship you please, & as many as you please; as is manifest in the *Jews* of old, in the Days of the Prophets, & the Pharisees in Christ's Time, & the Papists & Mahometans at this Day.

At a Time, when there is an Appearance of the Approach of any glorious Revival of God's Church, God does especially call his professing People to the Practice of moral Duties. Isa. 56. 1. *Thus saith the Lord; keep ye Judgment, and do Justice; for my Salvation is near to come, and my Righteousness to be revealed.* So when *John* preached, that *the Kingdom of Heaven was at Hand*, and cried to the People, *Prepare ye the Way of the Lord, make his Paths strait*, as we have an Account, *Luk.* 3. 4. the People ask'd him, *What they should do?* He answers, *He that hath two Coats, let him impart to him that hath none, and he that hath Meat, let him do likewise. The* Publicans *said, What shall we do?* He answers, *Exact no more than that which is appointed you. And the Soldiers asked him,* What shall we do? He replies, *Do Violence to no Man; neither accuse any falsely; and be content with your Wages.* Ver. 10, 11, 12, 13, 14.

God's People, at such a Time as this, ought especially to abound in Deeds of Charity, or Alms-giving. We generally, in these Days, seem to fall far below the true Spirit & Practice of Christianity, with Regard to this Duty, and seem to have but little Notion of it, so far as I can understand the New-Testament.— At a Time when God is so liberal of spiritual Things, we ought not to be strait-handed towards him, & sparing of our temporal

Things.—So far as I can judge by the Scripture, there is no external Duty whatsoever, by which Persons will be so much in the Way, not only of receiving temporal Benefits, but also spiritual Blessings, the Influences of God's Holy Spirit in the Heart, in divine Discoveries, and spiritual Consolations. I think it would be unreasonable to understand those Promises, made to this Duty, in the 58 Chap. of *Isaiah*, in a Sense exclusive of spiritual Discoveries & Comforts. Isa. 58. 7th v. *&c.*—*Is it not to deal thy Bread to the hungry, and that thou bring the Poor that are cast out, to thy House? When thou seest the Naked that thou cover him, & that thou hide not thy self from thine own Flesh? Then shall thy Light break forth as the Morning, and thy Health shall spring forth speedily, and thy Righteousness shall go before thee, & the Glory of the Lord shall be thy Rereward; then shalt thou call, and the Lord shall answer, thou shalt cry, and he shall say, Here I am. If thou take away from the midst of thee, the Yoke, the putting forth of the Finger, and speaking Vanity; and if thou draw out thy Soul to the Hungry, and satisfy the afflicted Soul; then shall thy Light rise in Obscurity, and thy Darkness be as the Noon-day; and the Lord shall guide thee continually, and satisfy thy Soul in Drought, and make fat thy Bones; & thou shalt be like a watered Garden, and like a Spring of Water, whose Waters fail not.* So, that giving to the Poor is the Way to receive spiritual Blessings, is manifest by Psal. 112. 4 Ver. &c. *Unto the Upright, there ariseth Light in the Darkness; he is gracious, and full of Compassion, and righteous: A good Man sheweth Favour and lendeth, he will guide his Affairs with Discretion; surely he shall not be moved for ever; the Righteous shall be in everlasting Remembrance; he shall not be afraid of evil Tidings, his Heart is fixed, trusting in the Lord; his Heart is established, he shall not be afraid, until he see his Desire upon his Enemies: He hath dispersed, he hath given to the Poor; his Horn shall be exalted with Honour.* That this is one likely Means to obtain Assurance, is evident by 1 Joh. 3. 18, 19. *My little Children, let us not love in Word, neither in Tongue, but in Deed, and in Truth; and hereby we know that we are of the Truth, and shall assure our Hearts before him.*

We have a remarkable Instance in *Abraham*, of God's rewarding Deeds of Charity with sweet Discoveries of himself, when he had been remarkably charitable to his Brother *Lot*, and the People that he had redeem'd out of Captivity with him, by exposing his Life to rescue them, & had re-taken not only the Persons, but all the Goods, the Spoil that had been taken by *Chedorlaomer*, and the Kings that were with him, & the King of *Sodom* offer'd him, that if he would give him the Persons, he might take the Goods to himself, *Abraham* refused to take any Thing, even so much as a Thread or Shoe-latchet, but returned all. He might have greatly inrich'd himself, if he had taken the Spoils to himself, for it was the Spoils of five wealthy Kings, and their Kingdoms, yet he coveted it not; the King and People of *Sodom* were now become Objects of Charity, having been stripped of all by their Enemies, therefore *Abraham* generously bestowed all upon them; as we have an Account in *Gen.* 14. and four last Verses. And he was soon rewarded for it, by a blessed Discovery that God made of himself to him; as we have an Account in the next Words, *After these Things, the Word of the Lord came unto* Abram, *in a Vision, saying, Fear not* Abram, *I am thy Shield, and thy exceeding great Reward.* "I am thy Shield, to defend thee in Battle, as I have now done; and tho' thou hast charitably refused to take any Reward, for exposing thy Life, to rescue this People, yet fear not, thou shalt not lose, thou shalt have a Reward, I am thy exceeding great Reward."

When Christ was upon Earth he was poor, and an Object of Charity; and during the Time of his publick Ministry, he was supported by the Charity of some of his Followers, and particularly certain Women, of whom we read *Luk.* 8. 2, 3. And these Women were rewarded, by being peculiarly favoured with gracious Manifestations, which Christ made of himself to them. He discovered himself first to them after his Resurrection, before the twelve Disciples: They first saw a Vision of glorious Angels, who spake comfortably to them; & then Christ appear'd to 'em, & spake Peace to 'em, *saying, All Hail, be not afraid; and they were admitted* to *come, and hold him by the Feet, and worship* him, Mat. 28. And tho' we can't now be charitable in this Way, to Christ in Person, who in his exalted State, is infinitely above the Need of our Charity; yet we may be charitable to Christ now, as well as they then; for tho' Christ is not here, yet he has left others in his Room, to be his Receivers; and they are the Poor. Christ is yet poor in his Members; and he that gives to them, lends to the Lord: And Christ tells us that he shall look on what is done to them, as done to him.

Rebekah, in her Marriage with *Isaac*, was undoubtedly a remarkable Type of the Church, in her Espousals to the Lord Jesus. But she found her Husband, in doing Deeds of Charity, agreeable to the Prayer of *Abraham*'s Servant, who prayed that this might be the Thing that might distinguish & mark out the Virgin, that was to be *Isaac*'s Wife. So *Cornelius* was bro't to the Knowledge of Christ, in this Way. *He was a devout Man, and one that feared God, with all his House; which gave much Alms to the People, and prayed to God alway. And an Angel appeared to him, and said to him, Thy Prayers & thine Alms are come up for a Memorial before God; and now send Men to* Joppa, *and call for one* Simon, *whose Sirname is* Peter, *&c.* Act. 10. at the beginning. And we have an Account in the following Parts of the Chapter, how God, by *Peter*'s Preaching, revealed Christ to *Cornelius* & his Family, & of the Holy Ghost's descending upon them, and filling their Hearts with Joy, and their Mouths with Praises.

Some may possibly object that for Persons to do Deeds of Charity, in Hope of obtaining spiritual Blessings & Comforts in this Way, would seem to shew a Self-righteous Spirit, as tho' they would offer something to God, to purchase these Favours. But if this be a good Objection, it may be made against every Duty whatsoever. All external Duties of the first Table will be excluded by it, as well as those of the second. First-Table-Duties have as direct a Tendency to raise self-righteous Persons Expectations of receiving something from God, on Account of them, as second-Table-Duties; and on some Accounts more, for those Duties are more immediately offer'd *to God*, & therefore Persons are more ready to expect something *from God* for them. But no Duty is to be neglected, for Fear of making a Righteousness of it. And I have always observed, that those Professors that are most partial in their Duty, exact & abundant in external Duties of the first Table, and slack as to those of the second, are the most Self-righteous.

If God's People in this Land, were once brought to abound in such Deeds of Love, as much as in Praying, Hearing, Singing, and religious Meetings and Conference, it would be a most blessed Omen: There is nothing would have a greater

Tendency to bring the GOD of Love down from Heaven to the Earth: So amiable would be the Sight, in the Eyes of our loving and exalted Redeemer, that it would soon as it were fetch him down from his Throne in Heaven, to set up his Tabernacle with Men on the Earth, and dwell with them. I don't remember ever to have read of any remarkable Out-pouring of the Spirit, that continued any long Time, but what was attended with an abounding in this Duty. So we know it was with that great Effusion of the Spirit that began at *Jerusalem* in the Apostle Days: And so in the late remarkable Revival of Religion in *Saxony*, which began by the Labours of the famous Professor *Franck*, & has now been carried on for above thirty Years, and has spread its happy Influences into many Parts of the World; it was begun, and has been carried on, by a wonderful Practice of this Duty. And the remarkable Blessing that God has given Mr. *Whitefield*, & the great Success with which he has crown'd him, may well be thought to be very much owing to his laying out himself so abundantly in charitable Designs. And it is foretold, that God's People shall abound in this Duty, in the Time of the great Out-pouring of the Spirit that shall be in the latter Days. Isai. 32. 5 & 8. *The vile Person shall no more be called liberal, nor the Churl said to be bountiful.—But the Liberal deviseth liberal Things, and by liberal Things shall he stand.*

To promote a Reformation, with Respect to all Sorts of Duties, among a professing People, one proper Means, and that which is recommended by frequent Scripture Examples, is their solemn, publick renewing their Covenant with GOD. And doubtless it would greatly tend to promote this Work in the Land, if the Congregations of GOD's People could generally be brought to this. If a Draught of a Covenant should be made by their Ministers, wherein there should be an express Mention of those particular Duties, that the People of the respective Congregations have been observ'd to be most prone to neglect, and those particular Sins that they have heretofore especially fallen into, or that it may be apprehended they are especially in Danger of, whereby they may prevent or resist the Motions of God's Spirit, and the Matter should be fully proposed and explained to the People, and they have sufficient Opportunity given them for Consideration, and then they should be led, all that are capable of Understanding, particularly to subscribe the Covenant, and also should all appear together, on a Day of Prayer and Fasting, publickly to own it before God in his House, as their Vow to the LORD; hereby Congregations of Christians would do that which would be beautiful, & would put Honour upon GOD, and be very profitable to themselves.

Such a Thing as this, was attended with a very wonderful Blessing in *Scotland*, and followed with a great Increase of the blessed Tokens of the Presence of God, & remarkable Outpourings of his Spirit; as the Author of *the fulfilling of the Scripture* informs, p. 186. 5th Edition.

A People must be taken, when they are in a good Mood, when considerable religious Impressions are prevailing among 'em; otherwise they will hardly be induced to this; but innumerable will be their Objections and Cavils against it.

One Thing more I would mention, which if God should still carry on this Work, would tend much to promote it, and that is, that an History should be publish'd once a Month, or once a Fortnight, of the Progress of it, by one of the Ministers of *Boston*, who are near the Press, & are most conveniently situated, to receive Accounts from all Parts. It has been found by Experience, that the Tidings of remarkable Effects of the Power and Grace of God, in any Place, tend greatly to awaken & engage the Minds of Persons, in other Places. 'Tis great Pity therefore, but that some Means should be used, for the most speedy, most extensive and certain giving Information of such Things, and that the Country ben't left, only to the slow, partial and doubtful Information, and false Representations of common Report.

Thus I have, (I hope, by the Help of GOD,) finished what I proposed. I have taken the more Pains in it, because it appears to me, that now God is giving us the most happy Season to attempt an universal Reformation, that ever was given in *New-England*. And 'tis a thousand Pities, that we should fail of that which would be so glorious, for want of being sensible of our Opportunity, or being aware of those Things that tend to hinder it, or our taking improper Courses to obtain it, or not being sensible in what Way God expects we should seek it. If it should please God to bless any Means, for the convincing the

Country of his Hand in this Work, and bringing them fully and freely to acknowledge his glorious Power and Grace in it, and engage with one Heart and Soul, and by due Methods, to endeavour to promote it, it would be a Dispensation of divine Providence, that would have a most glorious Aspect, happily signifying the Approach of great and glorious Things to the Church of GOD, and justly causing us to hope, that CHRIST would speedily come, to set up his Kingdom of Light, Holiness, Peace and Joy on Earth, as is foretold in his Word. *Amen*; Even so come LORD JESUS!

FINIS.

SERMONS

Justification by Faith Alone

ROMANS IV. 5.
But to him that worketh not, but believeth on him that justifieth the ungodly, his Faith is counted for Righteousness.

THE following Things may be noted in this Verse; 1. That Justification respects a Man as ungodly: This is evident by those Words—*that justifieth the Ungodly.* Which Words can't imply less than that God in the Act of Justification, has no Regard to any Thing in the Person justified, as Godliness, or any Goodness in him; but that nextly, or immediately before this Act, God beholds him only as an ungodly or wicked Creature; so that Godliness in the Person to be justified is not so antecedent to his Justification as to be the Ground of it. When it is said that God justifies the Ungodly, 'tis as absurd to suppose that our Godliness, taken as some Goodness in us, is the Ground of our Justification, as when it is said that Christ gave Sight to the Blind, to suppose that Sight was *Prior to*, and the *Ground of* that Act of Mercy in Christ, or as if it should be said that such an One by his Bounty has made a poor Man rich, to suppose that it was the Wealth of this poor Man that was the Ground of this Bounty towards him, and was the Price by which it was procured.

2. It appears that *by him that worketh not* in this Verse, is not meant only one that don't conform to the ceremonial Law, because *he that worketh not*, and *the Ungodly* are evidently synonimous Expressions, or what signify the same; it appears by the Manner of their Connection; if it ben't so, to what Purpose is the latter Expression *the Ungodly* brought in? The Context gives no other Occasion for it, but only to shew that the Grace of the Gospel appears in that God in Justification has no Regard to any Godliness of ours: The foregoing Verse is, *Now to him that worketh is the Reward not reckon'd of Grace,*

but of Debt: In that Verse 'tis evident, that Gospel Grace consists in the Rewards being given *without Works*; & in this Verse
which nextly follows it & in Sense is connected with it, 'tis evident that Gospel Grace consists in a Man's being justified that
is *ungodly*; by which it is most plain that by *him that worketh
not*, and him that is *ungodly*, are meant the same Thing; and
that therefore not only Works of the ceremonial Law are excluded in this Business of Justification, but Works of Morality
and *Godliness*.

3. 'Tis evident in the Words, that by that Faith that is here
spoken of, by which we are justified, is not meant the same Thing
as a Course of Obedience, or Righteousness, by the Expression,
by which this Faith is here denoted, *viz believing on him that justifies the Ungodly*—They that oppose the *Solifidians*, as they call
them, do greatly insist on it, that we should take the Words of
Scripture concerning this Doctrine, in their most natural and obvious Meaning; and how do they cry out of our clouding this
Doctrine with obscure Metaphors, and unintelligible Figures of
Speech! But is this to interpret Scripture according to it's most
obvious Meaning, when the Scripture speaks of our *believing on
him that justifies the Ungodly*, or the *Breakers of his Law*, to say
that the Meaning of it is performing a Course of *Obedience to his
Law*, and *avoiding the Breaches of it*? Believing on God as a *Justifier*, certainly is a different Thing from submitting to God as a
Lawgiver; especially a believing on him as a Justifier of *the Ungodly*, or Rebels *against the Lawgiver*.

4. 'Tis evident that the Subject of Justification is look'd
upon as destitute of any Righteousness in himself, by that Expression, *it is counted, or imputed to him for Righteousness*; the
Phrase, as the Apostle uses it here, and in the Context, manifestly imports, that God of his sovereign Grace is pleased in his
Dealings with the Sinner, to take and regard, that which indeed
is not Righteousness, and in one that *has no* Righteousness, so
that the Consequence shall be the same as if he *had* Righteousness; (which may be from the Respect that it bears to some
thing that is indeed Righteousness.) 'Tis plain that this is the
force of the Expression in the preceeding Verses: In the last
Verse but one, 'tis manifest that the Apostle lays the Stress of
his Argument for the free Grace of God, from that Text that he
cites out of the old Testament about *Abraham*, on that Word

counted or *imputed*, and that this is the Thing that he supposed God to shew his Grace in, *viz* in his *counting* something
for Righteousness, in his consequential Dealings with *Abraham*, that was no Righteousness in itself. And in the next Verse
which immediately preceeds the Text, *Now to him that worketh
is the Reward not* reckoned *of Grace, but of Debt*; the Word there
translated *reckoned*, is the same that in the other Verses is
render'd *imputed*, and *counted*: And 'tis as much as if the
Apostle had said, "As to *him that works*, there is no need of any
gracious *Reckoning*, or *counting* it for Righteousness, and
causing the Reward to follow *as if it were* a Righteousness; for
if he has Works he has that which *is* a Righteousness *in itself*, to
which the Reward properly belongs." This is further evident
by the Words that follow, Ver. 6. *Even as David also described
the Blessedness of the Man unto whom God imputeth Righteousness without Works*; what can here be meant by imputing
Righteousness without Works, but imputing Righteousness to
him that has none of his own? Ver. 7, 8. *Saying blessed are they
whose Iniquities are forgiven, and whose sins are covered: Blessed
is the Man to whom the Lord will not impute Sin*. How are these
Words of *David* to the Apostle's Purpose? Or how do they
prove any such Thing, as that Righteousness is imputed without Works, unless it be because the Word *imputed* is used, and
the Subject of the Imputation is mentioned, as a Sinner, &
consequently destitute of a moral Righteousness? For *David*
says no such Thing, as that he is forgiven without the Works of
the Ceremonial Law; there is no Hint of the ceremonial Law,
or Reference to it, in the Words. I will therefore venture to
infer this *Doctrine* from the Words, for the Subject of my present Discourse, *viz*.

DOCTRINE,

*We are justified only by Faith in Christ, and not by any
Manner of Vertue or Goodness of our own.*

Such an Assertion as this, I am sensible, many would be
ready to cry out of as absurd, betraying a great deal of Ignorance, and containing much Inconsistence; but I desire every
One's Patience 'till I have done.

In handling this Doctrine I would

I. Explain the *Meaning* of it, and shew how I would be understood by such an Assertion.

II. Proceed to the Consideration of the Evidence of the *Truth* of it.

III. Shew how evangelical Obedience is concern'd in this Affair.

IV. Answer Objections.

V. Consider the Importance of the Doctrine.

I. *I would explain the Meaning of the Doctrine, or shew in what Sense I assert it, and would endeavour to evince the Truth of it*: Which may be done in Answer to these two Enquiries, *viz.* 1. What is meant by *being justified*? 2. What is meant when it is said that this is *by Faith alone, without any Manner of Vertue or Goodness of our own*?

First. I would shew what Justification is, or what I suppose is meant in Scripture by being *justified*. And here I would not at all enlarge, and therefore to answer in short.

A Person is said to be justified when he is approved of God as free from the *Guilt* of Sin, and it's deserved *Punishment*, and as having that *Righteousness* belonging to him that entitles to the *Reward* of Life. That we should take the Word in such a Sense, and understand it as the Judges accepting a Person as having both a negative, and positive Righteousness belonging to him, and looking on him therefore, as not only *quit*, or free from any Obligation to Punishment but also as *just* and *righteous*, and so entitled to a positive Reward, is not only most agreable to the Etimology, and natural Import of the Word, which signifies to make righteous, or to pass One for righteous in Judgment, but also manifestly agreable to the Force of the Word, as used in Scripture.

Some suppose that nothing more is intended in Scripture by *Justification* than barely the *Remission of Sins*: if it be so it is very strange, if we consider the Nature of the Case; for 'tis most evident, and none will deny, that it is with Respect to the Rule, or Law of God that we are under, that we are said in Scripture to be either justified or condemned: Now what is it to justify a Person, as the Subject of a Law or Rule, but to judge him, or look upon him, and approve him as *standing right* with Respect to that Rule? To justify a Person *in a particular Case*, is to approve of him as standing right, as subject to the Law or Rule *in that Case*; and to justify *in general*, is to pass him in Judgment, as standing right, in a State correspondent to the Law or Rule *in general*. But certainly in order to a Person's being looked on as standing right with Respect to the Rule in general, or in a State corresponding with the Law of God, more is needful than what is negative, or a not having the Guilt of Sin; for whatever that Law is, whether a *new* one, or an *old* one, yet doubtless something positive is needed in order to its being answered. We are no more justified by the Voice of the Law, or of him that judges according to it, by a meer Pardon of Sin, than *Adam* our first Surety, was justified by the Law, at the first Point of his Existence, before he had done the Work, or fulfilled the Obedience of the Law, or had had so much as any Trial whether he would fulfil it or no. If *Adam* had finished his Course of perfect Obedience, he would have been *justified*; and certainly his Justification would have implied something more than what is meerly negative; he would have been approved of, as having fulfilled the Righteousness of the Law, and accordingly would have been adjudged to the Reward of it: So Christ our *second Surety*, (in whose Justification all who believe in him, and whose Surety he is, are vertually justified,) was not justified 'till he had done the Work the Father had appointed him, and kept the Father's Commandments, thro' all Trials, and then in his Resurrection he was *justified*: When he that had been put to Death in the Flesh was *quickened* by the Spirit, 1 *Pet.* 3. 18 then he that was manifest in the Flesh was *justified* in the Spirit, 1 *Tim.* 3. 16. But God when he justified him in raising him from the Dead, did not only release him from his Humiliation for Sin, and acquit him from any further Suffering or Abasement for it, but admitted him to that eternal and immortal Life, and to the Beginning of that Exaltation, that was the Reward of what he had done. And indeed the

Justification of a Believer is no other than his being admitted to Communion *in*, or Participation *of* the Justification of this Head and Surety of all Believers; for as Christ suffered the Punishment of Sin, not as a private Person, but as our Surety, so when after this Suffering he was raised from the Dead, he was therein justified, not as a private Person, but as the Surety and Representative of all that should believe in him; so that he was raised again not only for *his own*, but also for *our* Justification, according to the Apostle Rom. 4. 25. *Who was delivered for* our *Offences, and raised again for* our Justification. And therefore it is that the Apostle says as he does in Rom. 8. 34. *Who is he that* condemneth, *it is Christ that died, yea* rather *that is risen again.*

But that a Believer's Justification implies not only Remission of Sins, or Acquittance from the Wrath due to it, but also an Admittance to a Title to that Glory that is the Reward of Righteousness, is more directly taught in the Scripture, as particularly in *Rom.* 5. 1, 2. where the Apostle mentions both these, as joint Benefits implied in Justification, *Therefore being* justified *by Faith, we* have Peace with God *through our Lord Jesus Christ, by whom also we* have Access into this Grace wherein we stand, and rejoice in Hope of the Glory of God. So *Remission of Sins,* and *Inheritance among them that are sanctified,* are mentioned together as what are jointly obtained by Faith in Christ, Acts 26. 18. *That they may receive Forgiveness of Sins, and Inheritance among them that are sanctified,* through Faith *that is in me.* Both these are without Doubt implied in that passing from Death to Life, which Christ speaks of as the Fruit of Faith, and which he opposes to Condemnation, John 5. 24, *Verily I say unto you, he that heareth my Word, and believeth on him that sent me, hath everlasting Life, and shall not come into Condemnation, but is passed from Death to Life.* I proceed now

Secondly. To shew what is meant when it is said that this Justification is by Faith only, and not by any Vertue or Goodness of our own.

This enquiry may be subdivided into two, *viz* 1. How 'tis *by Faith.* 2. How 'tis by Faith *alone, without any Manner of Goodness of ours.*

1. *How Justification is by Faith.* Here the great Difficulty has been about the Import and Force of the Particle BY, or what is

that *Influence* that Faith has in the Affair of Justification that is expressed in Scripture by being *justified BY Faith.*

Here, if I may humbly express what seems evident to me, tho' Faith be indeed the Condition of Justification *so as nothing else is*, yet this Matter is not clearly and sufficiently explained by saying that Faith is the *Condition* of Justification; and that because the Word seems ambiguous, both in common Use, and also as used in Divinity: in one Sense Christ alone performs the Condition of our Justification and Salvation; in another Sense, Faith is the Condition of Justification; in another Sense, other Qualifications and Acts are Conditions of Salvation and Justification too: there seems to be a great deal of ambiguity in such Expressions as are commonly used, (which yet we are forced to use,) such as *Condition of Salvation, what is required in order to Salvation or Justification; the Terms of the Covenant*, and the like; and I believe they are understood in very different Senses by different Persons. And besides as the Word *Condition* is very often understood in the common use of Language, Faith is not the only Thing, in us, that is the Condition of Justification; for by the Word Condition, as 'tis very often, (and perhaps most commonly,) used; we mean any thing that may have the Place of a Condition in a conditional Proposition, and as such is truly connected with the Consequent, especially if the Proposition holds both in the Affirmative and Negative, as the Condition is either affirmed or denied; if it be that *with which*, or *which being supposed*, a thing shall be, and *without which*, or *it being denied*, a Thing shall not be, we in such a Case call it a Condition of that Thing: But in this Sense Faith is not the only Condition of Salvation or Justification, for there are many Things that accompany and flow from Faith, that are Things with which Justification shall be, and without which it will not be, and therefore are found to be put in Scripture in conditional Propositions with Justification and Salvation in Multitudes of Places; such are *Love to God, and Love to our Brethren, forgiving Men their Trespasses*, and many other good Qualifications and Acts. And there are many other Things besides Faith, which are directly proposed to us, to be pursued or performed by us, in order to eternal Life, as those which if they are done, or obtain'd we shall have eternal Life, & if not done or not obtain'd, we shall surely perish. And *if it were so*, that Faith was the only Condition of Justification in this Sense, yet I don't apprehend that to say that Faith was the Condition of Justification, would express the Sense of that Phrase of Scripture of being *Justified BY Faith*: there is a Difference between *being justified by a Thing*, and that Thing *universally, and necessarily, and inseparably attending*, or *going with Justification*; for so do a great many Things that we ben't said to be justified by: it is not the inseparable *connection* with Justification that the Holy Ghost would signify, (or that is naturally signified,) by such a Phrase, but some particular *influence* that Faith has in the Affair, or some certain Dependance that that Effect has on its Influence.

Some that have been aware of this have supposed that the influence or dependance might well be expressed by Faith's being the *Instrument* of our Justification; which has been misunderstood, and injuriously represented, and ridiculed by those that have denied the Doctrine of Justification by Faith alone, as tho' they had supposed that Faith was used as an Instrument in the Hand of God, whereby he performed, and brought to pass that Act of his, *viz.* Approving and Justifying the Believer: Whereas it was not intended that Faith was the Instrument wherewith *God justifies*, but the Instrument wherewith *we receive Justification*; not the Instrument wherewith the justifier acts in Justifying, but wherewith the receiver of Justification acts *in accepting* Justification. But yet it must be own'd that this is an obscure way of Speaking, and there must certainly be some impropriety in calling of it an Instrument wherewith we receive or accept Justification; for the very Persons that thus explain the Matter speak of Faith as being the *Reception* or *Acceptance it self*; and if so how can it be the Instrument *of* Reception or Acceptance? Certainly there is difference between the Act and the Instrument. And besides by their own Descriptions of Faith, Christ the Mediator, *by whom*, and his Righteousness, *by which* we are justified, is more directly the Object of this Acceptance, and Justification which is the Benefit arising therefrom, more indirectly: and therefore if Faith be an Instrument, 'tis more properly the Instrument by which we receive Christ, than the Instrument by which we receive Justification.

But I humbly conceive we have been really to look too far to find out what that Influence of Faith in our Justification is, or what is that Dependance of this Effect on Faith, signified by the Expression of being *justified by Faith*, over looking that which is most obviously pointed forth in the Expression, *viz.* that, the Case being as it is, (there being a Mediator that has purchased Justification,) Faith in this Mediator is that which renders it a *meet* and *suitable Thing*, in the Sight of God, that the Believer rather than others should have this purchased Benefit assigned to him. There is this Benefit purchased, which God sees it to be a more meet and suitable Thing that it should be assigned to some than others, because he sees 'em differently qualified; that qualification wherein the meetness to this Benefit, as the Case stands consists, is that, *in us, by which we are Justified.* If Christ had not come into the World and died, &c. to purchase Justification, no Qualification what ever, *in us*, could render it a meet or fit Thing that we should be justified; but the Case being as it now stands, *viz.* that Christ has actually purchased Justification by his own Blood, for infinitely unworthy Creatures, there may be some certain Qualification found in some Persons, that, either from the Relation it Bears to the Mediator and his Merits, or on some other Account, is the Thing that in the Sight of God renders it a *meet* & *condecent* Thing that they should have an interest in this purchased Benefit, and which if any are destitute of, it renders it an *unfit* & *unsuitable* Thing that they should have it. The Wisdom of God in his Constitutions, doubtless appears much in the Fitness and Beauty of them, so that those Things are *established to be done* that are *fit to be done*, and that these Things are connected in his Constitution, that are agreable one to another: so God justifies a Believer according to his revealed Constitution, without doubt, because he sees something in this Qualification, that as the Case stands, renders it a *fit* Thing that such should be justified; whether it be because Faith is the *Instrument*, or as it were the Hand, by which he that has purchased Justification is apprehended and accepted, or because it is the *Acceptance it self*, or whatever. To be justified is to be *approved* of God as a *proper Subject* of Pardon, and a right to eternal Life; and therefore when it is said that we are Justified *BY* Faith, what else can be understood by it than that Faith is that *BY* which we are render'd *approvable, fitly so*, and indeed, as the Case stands, *proper Subjects* of this Benefit?

This is something different from Faith's being the Condition of Justification, only so as to be inseparably connected with Justification; so are many other Things besides Faith, and yet nothing in us, but Faith, renders it *meet* that we should have Justification assigned to us; as I shall presently shew *how*, in answer to the next Enquiry, *viz.*

2. How this is said to be by Faith *alone, without any manner of Vertue or Goodness of our own.* This may seem to some to be attended with two difficulties, *viz.* How this can be said to be by Faith alone, without any Vertue or Goodness of ours, when Faith it self is a Vertue, and one Part of our Goodness, and is not only *some manner of goodness of ours*, but is a *very excellent* Qualification, and one chief Part of the inherent Holiness of a Christian? And if it be a part of our inherent Goodness or Excellency, (whether it be this Part or any other,) that renders it a condecent or congruous Thing that we should have this Benefit of Christ assigned to us, what this is less than what they mean that talk of a *Merit of Congruity*? And moreover, if this Part of our Christian Holiness qualifies us in the Sight of God, for this Benefit of Christ, and renders it a fit or meet Thing, in his Sight, that we should have it, why should not other Parts of Holiness, and Conformity to God, which are also very excellent, & have as much of the Image of Christ in them, and are no less lovely in God's Eyes, qualify us as much, and have as much Influence to render us meet, in God's Sight, for such a Benefit as this? Therefore I answer,

When it is said that we are not justified by any Righteousness or Goodness of our own, what is meant is that it is not out of Respect to the *Excellency* or *Goodness* of any Qualifications, or Acts, in us, whatsoever, that God judges it *meet* that this Benefit of Christ should be ours; and it is not, in any wise, on Account of any Excellency, or Value that there is *in Faith*, that it appears, in the Sight of God, a meet Thing, that he that believes should have this Benefit of Christ assigned to him, but purely from the Relation Faith has to the Person in whom this Benefit is to be had, or as it *unites* to that Mediator, *in* and *by* whom we are justified. Here for the greater Clearness, I would particularly explain my self under several Propositions.

1. It is certain that there is some Union or Relation that the People *of Christ*, stand in *to him*, that is expressed in Scripture,

from time to time, by being *in Christ*, and is represented frequently by those Metaphors of being *Members of Christ*, or being united to him as *Members to the Head*, and Branches to the Stock,* and is compared to a Marriage Union between *Husband* and *Wife*. I don't now pretend to determine of what Sort this Union is; nor is it necessary to my present Purpose to enter into any Manner of Disputes about it: if any are disgusted at the Word Union, as obscure and unintelligible, the Word *Relation* equally serves my Purpose; I don't now desire to determine any more about it, than all, of all Sorts, will readily allow, *viz.* that there is a peculiar *Relation* between true Christians and Christ, or a certain Relation between him and them, that there is not between him and others; which is signified by those metaphorical Expressions in Scripture, of being *in Christ*, being *Members of Christ*, &c.

2. This Relation or Union to Christ, whereby Christians are said to be *in* Christ, (whatever it be,) is the Ground of their Right to his Benefits. This needs no Proof; the Reason of the Thing, at first Blush, demonstrates it: but yet 'tis exceeding evident also by Scripture, 1 *John* 5. 12. *He that hath the Son hath Life, and he that hath not the Son hath not Life.* 1 Cor. 1. 30. *Of him are ye in Christ Jesus, who of God is made unto us—Righteousness.* First we must be in him, and then he will be made Righteousness, or Justification to us. Eph. 1. 6. *Who hath made us accepted*

---

*"Our Saviour compares his mystical Body, that is his Church, to a Vine, which his Father, whom he compares to a Husbandman, hath planted, *I am the true Vine, and my Father is the Husbandman.* To represent to us the *Union* that is betwixt Christ and all true Christians, and the Influence of Grace and spiritual Life, which all that are *United* to him do derive and receive from him, he sets it forth to us by the Resemblance of a Vine and Branches. As there is a *natural vital Union* between the Vine and the Branches, so there is a *spiritual Union* between Christ and true Christians; and this Union is the Cause of our Fruitfulness, in the Works of Obedience and a good Life. There are some indeed that seem to be *grafted into Christ* by an outward Profession of Christianity, who yet derive no Influence from him, so as to bring forth Fruit, because they are not *vitally united to him.*" Dr. *Tillotson* in his 3d. Vol. of Serm. p. 307.

By this it appears that the vital Union between Christ and true Christians, which is much more of a Mystery than the relative Union, and necessarily implies it, was not thought an unreasonable Doctrine, by one of the greatest Divines, on the other side of the Question in Hand.

in the Beloved. Our being *in him* is the Ground of our being accepted. So it is, in those Unions which the Holy Ghost has thought fit to compare this Union to; the Union of the Members of the Body with the Head is the Ground of their partaking of the Life of the Head; 'tis the Union of the Branches to the Stock, which is the Ground of their partaking of the Sap & Life of the Stock; 'tis the Relation of the Wife to the Husband, that is the Ground of her joynt Interest in his Estate, they are looked upon, in several Respects, as one in Law: so there is a legal Union between Christ and true Christians; so that (as all except *Socinians* allow,) *one*, in some respects, is *accepted for the other*, by the supreme Judge.

3. And thus it is that Faith is that Qualification in any Person, that renders it meet in the Sight of God that he should be looked upon as having Christ's Satisfaction and Righteousness belonging to him, *viz. because it is that in him, which, on his Part, makes up this Union between him and Christ*. By what has been just now observed, 'tis a Person's being, according to Scripture Phrase, *in Christ*, that is the Ground of having his Satisfaction and Merits belonging to him, and a Right to the Benefits procured thereby: and the Reason of it is plain; 'tis easy to see how a having Christ's Merits and Benefits *belonging to us*, follows from our having (if I may so speak) *Christ himself belonging to us*, or a being united to him; and if so it must also be easy to see how, or in what Manner, that, in a Person, that on his Part makes up the Union between his Soul & Christ, should be the Thing on the Account of which God looks on it meet that he should have Christ's Merits belonging to him; and also that it is a very different Thing, for God to assign to a particular Person, a Right to Christ's Merits and Benefits, from Regard to any Qualification in him, in this Respect, from his doing of it for him, out of Respect to the Value or Loveliness of that Qualification, or as a Reward of the Excellency of it.

As there is no Body but what will allow that there is a peculiar Relation between Christ & his true Disciples, by which they are in some sense in Scripture said to be one; so I suppose there is no Body but what will allow, that there may be something that the true Christian does on his Part, whereby he is *active in coming into this Relation* or *Union*, some Act of the Soul of the Christian, that is the Christian's *uniting Act*, or that which is done towards this Union or Relation, (or whatever any please to call it,) on the Christian's Part: Now Faith I suppose to be this Act.

I don't now pretend to define justifying Faith, or to determine precisely how much is contain'd in it, but only to determine thus much concerning it, *viz.* That it is that by which the Soul, that before was seperate, and alienated from Christ, unites it self to him, or ceases to be any longer in that State of Alienation, and comes into that fore mention'd Union or Relation to him, or to use the Scripture Phrase, that 'tis that by which the Soul COMES TO Christ, and RECEIVES him: and this is evident by the Scriptures using these very Expressions to signify Faith. John 6. 35, 36, 37, 38, 39. *He that* cometh *to me shall never hunger, and he that* believeth *on me shall never thirst. But I said unto you that ye also have seen me and* believe *not. All that the Father giveth me shall* come to *me, and him that* cometh to *me I will in no wise cast out; For I came down from Heaven, not to do mine own Will, but the Will of him that sent me.* ver. 40. *And this is the Will of him that sent me, that every one which seeth the Son and* believeth *on him, may have everlasting Life, and I will raise him up at the last Day.* Chap. 5. 38, 39, 40.— *Whom he hath sent, him ye* believe *not. Search the Scriptures for—they are they which testify of me: And ye will not* come unto *me, that ye might have Life.* ver. 43, 44. *I am come in my Fathers name, and ye* receive *me not: if another shall come in his own Name him ye will receive. How can ye* believe *which receive honour one of another*—? Chap. 1. 12. *But as many as* received *him, to them gave he Power to become the Sons of God, even to them that* believe *on his Name.* If it be said that these are obscure figures of Speech, that, however they might be well understood of Old, among those that then commonly used such Metaphors, yet they are difficultly understood now. I allow that the Expressions of *receiving* Christ and *coming* to Christ, are metaphorical Expressions; and if I should allow 'em to be obscure Metaphors; yet so much at least, is certainly *plain* in 'em, *viz.* that Faith is that by which those that before were *seperated*, and *at a distance* from Christ, (that is to say were not so related and united to him as his People are;) do cease to be any longer at such a Distance, and do *come into that Relation* and nearness; unless they are so unintelligible, that nothing at all can be understood by 'em.

God don't give those that believe, an Union *with*, or an interest *in* the Saviour, in *reward* for Faith, but only because Faith is the Soul's active uniting with Christ, or is it self the very act of Unition, on their Part. God sees it fit, that in order to an Union's being established between two intelligent active Beings or Persons, so as that they should be looked upon as one, there should be the mutual Act of both, that each should receive other, as actively joining themselves one to another. God in requiring this in order to an union with Christ as one of his People, treats Men as reasonable Creatures, capable of Act, and Choice; and hence sees it fit that they only, that are *one* with Christ *by their own Act*, should be looked upon as *one in Law*: what is *real* in the Union between Christ and his People, is the Foundation of what is *legal*; that is, it is something that is *really* in them, & between them, uniting them, that is the Ground of the Suitableness of their being *accounted* as one by the Judge: And if there be any Act, or Qualification in Believers, that is of that uniting Nature, that it is meet on that Account that the Judge should look upon 'em, and accept 'em as one, no wonder that upon the Account of the same Act or Qualification, he should accept the Satisfaction and Merits of the one, for the other, as if it were their Satisfaction and Merits: It necessarily follows, or rather is implied.

And thus it is that Faith justifies, or gives an Interest in Christ's Satisfaction and Merits, and a Right to the Benefits procured thereby, *viz.* as it thus makes Christ and the Believer *one* in the Acceptance of the supreme Judge. 'Tis by Faith that we have a Title to eternal Life, because, tis by Faith that we have the Son of God, by whom Life is. The Apostle *John* in those Words, 1 John 5. 12. *He that hath the Son hath Life*, seems evidently to have respect to those Words of Christ that he gives an Account of in his Gospel, Chap. 3. 36. *He that believeth on the Son hath everlasting Life, and he that believeth not the Son shall not see Life*. And in the same Places that the Scripture speaks of Faith as the Soul's *receiving*, or *coming to Christ*, it also speaks of this receiving, or coming *to*, or joyning *with* Christ, as the Ground of an Interest in his Benefits: To as many as received him, *to them gave he Power* to become the Sons of God. Ye will not come unto me *that ye might have Life*. And there is a wide Difference between its being looked on suitable that Christ's Satisfaction and Merits should be theirs that believe, because an Interest in that Satisfaction and Merit is but a fit Reward of Faith, or a suitable Testimony of God's Respect to the Amiableness and Excellency of that Grace, and it's only being looked on suitable that Christ's Satisfaction and Merits should be theirs, because Christ and they are so united, that in the Eyes of the Judge they may suitably be looked upon, and taken, as one.

Altho', on the Account of Faith in the Believer, it is, in the Sight of God, fit and congruous, both that he that believes should be looked upon as in Christ, and also as having an Interest in his Merits, in the way that has been now explain'd, yet it appears that this is very wide from a *merit of Congruity*, or indeed *any moral Congruity at all* to either. There is a twofold Fitness to a State; I know not how to give them distinguishing Names otherwise than by calling the one a *moral*, and the other a *natural* Fitness: A Person has a *moral* Fitness for a State, when his moral Excellency commends him to it, or when his being put into such a good State, is but a *fit* or suitable Testimony of Regard or Love to the *moral Excellency*, or Value, or Amiableness of any of his Qualifications or Acts. A Person has a *natural* Fitness for a State when it appears meet and condecent that he should be in such a State or Circumstances, only from the natural concord or agreableness there is between such Qualifications and such Circumstances; not because the Qualifications are lovely or unlovely, but only because the Qualifications, and the Circumstances are like one another, or do in their nature suit and agree or unite one to another. And 'tis on this latter Account only that God looks on it fit by a *natural Fitness*, that he whose Heart sincerely *unites* it self to Christ as his Saviour, should be looked upon as *united* to that Saviour, and so having an Interest in him; and not from any moral Fitness there is between the excellency of such a Qualification as Faith, and such a glorious Blessedness as the having an Interest in Christ. God's bestowing Christ and his Benefits on a Soul in consequence of Faith, out of Regard only to the natural Concord there is between such a Qualification of a Soul, and such an union with Christ, and Interest in him, makes the Case very widely different from what would be; if he bestowed this from regard to any moral Suitableness; for in the *former* Case, 'tis only from God's Love of *order* that he bestows these Things on the account of Faith. In the *latter* God doth it out of Love to the *Grace of Faith it self*. God will neither look on Christ's Merits as ours, nor adjudge his Benefits to us, till we be *in Christ*: nor will he look upon us as being *in him*, without an active unition of our Hearts and Souls to him; because he is a wise Being, and delights in Order, and not in Confusion, and that Things should be together or asunder according to their nature; and his making such a Constitution is a testimony of his love of Order: whereas if it were out of regard to any moral Fitness or suitableness between Faith and such Blessedness, it would be a Testimony of his Love to the Act or Qualification it self: The one supposes this divine Constitution to be a Manifestation of God's regard to the Beauty of the act of Faith, the other only supposes it to be a Manifestation of his regard to the Beauty of that Order that there is in uniting those Things that have a natural Agreement, and congruity, and unition the one with the other. Indeed a moral Suitableness or Fitness to a State includes a natural; for 'tis never so that if there be a moral Suitableness that a Person should be in such a State, but that there is also a natural Suitableness; but such a natural Suitableness as I have described, by no means necessarily includes a moral.

This is plainly what our Divines intend when they say that Faith don't justify as a *Work*, or a *Righteousness, viz.* That it don't justify as a Part of our moral Goodness or Excellency, or that it don't justify as a Work, in the Sense that Man was to have been justified by his Works by the *Covenant of Works*, which was to have a Title to eternal Life, given him of God in Testimony of his pleasedness with his Works, or his regard to the inherent Excellency and Beauty of his Obedience. And this is certainly what the Apostle *Paul* means, when he so much insists upon it that we are not justified by *works, viz.* that we are not justified by them as *good Works*, or by any *goodness, value*, or *excellency of our Works*. For the proof of this I shall at present mention but one Thing, (being like to have occasion to say what shall make it more abundantly manifest afterwards,) and that is, the Apostles, from Time to Time, speaking of our not being justified by *Works*, as the Thing that excludes all *boasting, Eph.* 2. 9. *Rom.* 3. 27. and Chap. 4. 2. now which way do Works give occasion for boasting, but as *good*? What do

Men use to boast of, but of something they suppose *good* or *excellent*? And on what Account do they boast of any Thing, but for the supposed *Excellency* that is in it?

From these Things we may learn in what manner Faith is the only Condition of Justification and Salvation; for tho' it be not the only Condition, so as alone truly to have the Place of a Condition in an hypothetical Proposition, in which Justification and Salvation are the *Consequent*, yet it is the Condition of Justification in a Manner peculiar to it, and so that nothing else has a parallel Influence with it; because Faith includes the whole Act of Union to Christ as a Saviour: The entire active uniting of the Soul, or the whole of what is called *coming to* Christ, and *receiving* of him, is called Faith in Scripture; and however other Things may be no less excellent than Faith, yet 'tis not the nature of any other Graces or Vertues directly to close with Christ as a Mediator, any further than they enter into the Constitution of justifying Faith, and do belong to its Nature.

Thus I have explained my meaning, in asserting it as a Doctrine of the Gospel, that we are justified by Faith only, without any manner of Goodness of our own.

I now proceed in the

II. Place, *to the Proof of it*, which I shall endeavour to produce in the following Arguments,

First. Such is *our Case*, and the *State of Things*, that neither Faith, nor any other Qualification, or Act, or Course of Acts *does*, or can render it *suitable* or *fit* that a Person should have an Interest in the Saviour, and so a Title to his Benefits, on Account of any excellency therein, or any other way than only as something in him may unite him to the Saviour. It is not *suitable* that God should give fallen Man an Interest in Christ and his Merits, as a Testimony of his respect to any Thing whatsoever as a loveliness in him; and that because 'tis not meet till a Sinner is actually justified, that any Thing in him should be accepted of God, as any excellency or amiableness of his Person; or that God by any Act, should in any manner or degree testify any pleasedness with him, or favour towards him, on the account of any Thing inherent in him; and that for two Reasons, 1. Because the nature of Things will not admit of it. 2. Because an antecedent divine Constitution stands in the way of it.

1. The Nature of Things will not admit of it. And this appears from the infinite Guilt that the Sinner 'till justified is under; which arises from the infinite evil or heinousness of Sin. But because this is what some deny, I would therefore *first* establish that Point, and shew that Sin is a Thing that is indeed properly of infinite Heinousness; and *then* shew the Consequence, and shew that it being so, and so the Sinner under infinite Guilt in God's Sight, it cannot be suitable, 'till the Sinner is actually justified, that God should by any Act testify any pleasedness *with*, or acceptance *of*, any Thing as any excellency or amiableness of his Person, or indeed *have* any acceptance *of* him, or pleasedness *with* him *to testify*.

That the evil and demerit of Sin is infinitely great, is most demonstrably evident, because what the evil or iniquity of Sin consists in, is the violating of an Obligation, the doing contrary to what we are obliged to do, or doing what we should not do; and therefore by how much the greater the Obligation is that is violated, by so much the greater is the Iniquity of the violation. But certainly our Obligation to love or honour any Being is great in proportion to the greatness or excellency of that Being, or his worthiness to be loved and honoured: we are under greater Obligations to love a more lovely Being than a less lovely; and if a Being be *infinitely excellent* and lovely, our Obligations to love him are therein *infinitely great*: The matter is so plain it seems needless to say much about it.

Some have argued exceeding strangely against the infinite evil of Sin, from its being committed against an infinite Object, that if so, then it may as well be argued that there is also an infinite value or worthiness in Holiness and Love to God, because that also has an infinite Object; Whereas the Argument from parity of Reason will carry it in the *reverse*: the Sin of the Creature *against God* is *ill deserving* in proportion to the distance there is between God and the Creature, the *greatness of the Object*, and the *meanness of the Subject* aggravates it; but 'tis the reverse with regard to the *worthiness* of the respect of the Creature to God, 'tis *worthless* (and not *worthy*) in proportion to the *meanness of the Subject*: so much the greater the Distance between God and the Creature, so much the less is the Creature's respect worthy of God's notice or regard. The *unworthiness* of Sin or opposition to God rises, and is great in proportion to the *dignity* of the *Object*, & *inferiority* of the *Subject*; but on the contrary the *worth* or *value* of respect rises in proportion to the *value* of the *Subject*; and that for this plain Reason, *viz.* that the *evil* of *disrespect* is in proportion to the Obligation that lies upon the *Subject* to the *Object*; which Obligation is most evidently encreased by the excellency and superiority of the *Object*; but on the contrary the *worthiness* of *respect* to a Being is in proportion to the Obligation that lies on him who is the *Object*, (or rather the Reason he has) to regard the *Subject*, which certainly is in proportion to the Subject's value or excellency. Sin or *disrespect* is evil or heinous in proportion to the Degree of what it denies in the *Object*, and as it were *takes from it, viz.* its excellency and *worthiness of respect*; On the contrary, respect is valuable in proportion to the value of what is *given to the Object* in that respect, which undoubtedly, (other Things being equal,) is great in proportion to the Subject's value, or worthiness of regard; because the Subject in giving his Respect, can give no more than himself; so far as he gives his respect he gives himself to the Object; and therefore *his gift* is of greater or lesser value in proportion to the value *of himself.*

Hence (by the way,) the Love, Honour, and Obedience of Christ towards God, has infinite Value, from the excellency and dignity of the Person in whom these Qualifications were inherent: and the Reason why we needed a Person of infinite Dignity to obey for us, was because of our infinite comparative Meanness, who had disobeyed, whereby our Disobedience was infinitely aggravated: We needed one, the worthiness of whose Obedience, might be answerable to the unworthiness of our Disobedience; and therefore needed one who was as great and worthy, as we were unworthy.

Another Objection (that perhaps may be thought hardly worth mentioning,) is, that to suppose Sin to be infinitely heinous, is to make all Sins equally heinous; for how can any Sin be more than infinitely heinous? But all that can be argued hence is, that no Sin can be greater with respect *to that aggravation,* the worthiness of the Object against whom it is committed: one Sin can't be more aggravated than another *in that respect,* because in this respect the aggravation of every Sin is infinite; but that don't hinder but that some Sins may be more heinous than others *in other respects*: as if we should suppose a

Cylinder infinitely long, it can't be greater in that respect, *viz.* with respect to the length of it; but yet it may be doubled, and trebled, and made a thousand fold more, by the increase of other Dimensions. Of Sins that are all infinitely heinous, some may be more heinous than others, as well as of divers Punishments that are all infinitely dreadful Calamities, or all of them infinitely exceeding all finite Calamities, so that there is no finite Calamity however great but what is infinitely less dreadful, or more eligible than any of them, yet some of them may be a thousand Times more dreadful than others. A Punishment may be infinitely dreadful by reason of the infinite Duration of it; and therefore can't be greater with respect to that Aggravation of it, *viz.* its length of continuance; but yet may be vastly more terrible on other Accounts.

Having thus, as I imagine, made it clear that all Sin is infinitely heinous, and consequently that the Sinner, before he is justified, is under infinite Guilt in God's Sight, it now remains that I shew the *Consequence*, or how it follows from hence, that it is not suitable that God should give the Sinner an Interest in Christ's Merits, and so a title to his Benefits, from regard to any Qualification, or Act, or course of Acts, in him, on the Account of any Excellency or Goodness whatsoever therein, but only as uniting to Christ; or (which fully implies it) that it is not suitable that God by any Act, should in any Manner or Degree, testify any acceptance *of*, or pleasedness *with* any Thing, as any Vertue, or Excellency, or any part of loveliness, or valuableness, in his Person, until he is actually *already* interested in Christ's Merits; which appears by this, that from the *Premisses* it follows, that before the Sinner is already interested in Christ, & justified, 'tis impossible God should *have* any acceptance of, or pleasedness with the Person of the Sinner, as in any Degree lovely in his Sight, or indeed less the Object of his Displeasure and Wrath: For, by the Supposition, the Sinner still remains infinitely guilty in the Sight of God; for Guilt is not removed but by Pardon; but to suppose the Sinner already pardoned, is to suppose him already justified; which is contrary to the Supposition: But if the Sinner still remains infinitely guilty in God's Sight, that is the same Thing as still to be beheld of God as infinitely the Object of his Displeasure and Wrath, or infinitely hateful in his Eyes; and if so, where is any

room for any Thing in him, to be accepted as some valuableness or acceptableness of him in God's Sight, or for any Act of
Favour, of any Kind towards him, or any Gift whatsoever to
him, in Testimony of God's Respect *to* and Acceptance *of*
something of him lovely and pleasing? If we should suppose
that it could be so, that a Sinner could have Faith, or some
other Grace in his Heart, and yet remain separate from Christ;
and it should continue still to be so, that he is not looked upon
as being in Christ, or having any relation to him, it would not
be meet that that true Grace should be accepted of God as any
loveliness of his Person in the Sight of God: If it should be
accepted as the loveliness of the Person, that would be to accept the Person as in some Degree lovely to God, but this can't
be consistent with his still remaining under infinite Guilt, or
infinite Unworthiness in God's Sight, which that Goodness
has no worthiness to ballance. While God beholds the Man as
separate from Christ, he must behold him *as he is in himself*;
and so his Goodness can't be beheld by God, but as taken with
his Guilt and Hatefulness, and as put in the Scales with it; and
being beheld so, his Goodness is nothing; because there is a
finite on the ballance against an infinite, whose Proportion to
it is nothing: In such a Case, if the Man be looked on as he is
in himself, the excess of the Weight in one Scale above another,
must be looked upon as the quality of the Man: These Con-
traries being beheld together, one takes from another, as one
Number is substracted from another; and the Man must be
looked upon in God's Sight according to the remainder: For
here by the Supposition all Acts of Grace or Favour, in not
imputing the Guilt *as it is*, are excluded, because that supposes
a Degree of Pardon, and that supposes Justification, which is
contrary to what is supposed, *viz.* that the Sinner is not already
justified: and therefore Things must be taken strictly *as they
are*; and so the Man is still infinitely unworthy, and hateful in
God's Sight, as he was before, without diminution, because his
Goodness bears no proportion to his Unworthiness; and
therefore when taken together is nothing.

Hence may be more clearly seen, the Force of that Expression in the Text, of believing on him that *justifieth the ungodly*;
for tho' there is indeed something in Man that is really and
spiritually Good, that is *prior* to Justification, yet there is

nothing that is *accepted* as any godliness or excellency *of the Person*, till after Justification. Goodness or Loveliness of the Person *in the Acceptance of God*, in any Degree, is not to be consider'd as *prior* but *posterior* in the Order and Method of *God's proceeding* in this Affair: Tho' a Respect to the *natural Suitableness* between such a Qualification, and such a State, does go before Justification, yet the Acceptance even of Faith as any Goodness or Loveliness of the Believer, follows Justification: The Goodness is on the forementioned Account justly looked upon as nothing, until the Man is justified: And therefore the Man is respected in Justification, as in himself altogether hateful.—Thus the Nature of Things will not admit of a Man's having an Interest given him in the Merits or Benefits of a Saviour, on the Account of any Thing as a Righteousness, or Vertue, or Excellency in him.

2. A divine Constitution that is antecedent to that which establishes Justification by a Saviour, (and indeed to any need of a Saviour,) stands in the Way of it, *viz.* that original Constitution or Law which Man was put under; by which Constitution or Law the Sinner is condemned, because he is a violater of that Law; and stands condemned, till he has actually an Interest in the Saviour, through whom he is set at liberty from that Condemnation. But to suppose that God gives a Man an Interest in Christ in reward for his Righteousness or Vertue, is inconsistent with his still remaining under Condemnation *'till he has an Interest in Christ*; because it supposes that the Sinner's Vertue is accepted, and he accepted for it, *before he has an Interest in Christ*; inasmuch as an Interest in Christ is given as a Reward of his Vertue; but the Vertue must first be accepted, before it is rewarded, and the Man must first be accepted for his Vertue, before he is rewarded for it, with so great and Glorious a Reward; for the very notion of a Reward is some Good bestowed in testimony of Respect to and Acceptance of Vertue in the Person rewarded. It don't consist with the Honour of the Majesty of the King of Heaven and Earth, to accept of any Thing from a condemned Malefactor, condemned by the Justice of his own holy Law, 'till that Condemnation be removed: and then such acceptance is inconsistent *with*, and contradictory *to* such remaining Condemnation; for the Law condemns him that violates it, to be totally rejected and cast off by God;

but how can a Man continue under this Condemnation, *i. e.* continue utterly rejected and cast off of God, and yet his Righteousness or Vertue be accepted, and he himself accepted on the Account of it, so as to have so glorious Reward as an Interest in Christ bestowed as a testimony of that Acceptance?

I know that the Answer that will be ready for this is, that we now are not subject to that Constitution that Mankind were at first put under; but that God in Mercy to Mankind has abolished that rigorous Constitution or Law that they were under originally, & has put us under a new Law, and introduced a more mild Constitution; And that the Constitution or Law it self not remaining, there is no need of supposing that the Condemnation of it remains, to stand in the Way of the Acceptance of our Vertue. And indeed there is no other way of avoiding this Difficulty; the Condemnation of the Law must stand in force against a Man 'till he is actually interested in the Saviour, that has satisfied and answered the Law, effectually to prevent any Acceptance of his Vertue, before, or in order to such an Interest, unless the Law or Constitution it self be abolished. But the Scheme of those modern Divines by whom this is maintained seems to contain a great deal of Absurdity and Self-Contradiction: they hold that the old Law given to *Adam*, which requires perfect Obedience is entirely repealed, and that instead of it we are put under a new Law, which requires no more than imperfect, sincere Obedience, in compliance with our poor, infirm, impotent Circumstances since the Fall, whereby we are unable to perform that perfect Obedience that was required by the first Law: for they strenuously maintain that it would be unjust in God to require any Thing of us that is beyond our *present* Power and Ability to perform; and yet they hold that Christ died to satisfy for the imperfections of our Obedience, that so our imperfect Obedience might be accepted instead of perfect—Now how can these Things hang together—I would ask what Law these imperfections of our Obedience are a breach of? if they are a breach of no Law, then they ben't Sins; and if they ben't Sins, what need of Christ's dying to satisfy for them? but if they are Sins, and so the breach of some Law, what Law is it? they can't be a breach of their new Law, for that requires no other than imperfect Obedience, or Obedience with imperfections; and they can't be a breach of the old Law, for that they say is entirely abolished, and we never were under it; and we can't break a Law that we never were under.—They say it would not be just in God to exact of us perfect Obedience, because it would not be just in God to require more of us than we can perform in our present State, & to punish us for failing of it; and therefore by their own Scheme the imperfections of our Obedience don't deserve to be punished; What need therefore of Christ's dying to satisfy for them? What need of Christ's Suffering to satisfy for that which is no Fault, and in its own Nature deserves no Suffering? What need of Christ's dying to purchase that our imperfect Obedience should be accepted, when according to their Scheme it would be unjust in it self that any other Obedience than imperfect should be required? What need of Christ's dying to make way for God's accepting such an Obedience, as it would in itself be unjust in him not to accept? Is there any need of Christ's dying to persuade God not to do unjustly?—If it be said that Christ died to satisfy that Law for us, that so we might not be under that Law, but might be delivered from it, that so there might be room for us to be under a more mild Law; still I would inquire what need of Christ's dying that we might not be under a Law, that (according to their Scheme) it would in it self be unjust that we should be under, because in our present State we are not able to keep it? What need of Christ's dying that we might not be under a Law, that it would be unjust that we should be under, whether Christ died or no?

Thus far I have argued principally from *Reason*, and *the Nature of Things*: I proceed now to the

Second *Argument*, which is, That this is a Doctrine that the *holy Scriptures*, the Revelation that God has given us of his Mind and Will, by which alone we can never come to know how those that have offended God can come to be accepted of him, and justified in his Sight, is exceeding full in: Particularly the Apostle *Paul* is abundant in teaching that *we are justified by Faith alone without the Works of the Law*: There is no one Doctrine that he insists so much upon, and is so particular in, and that he handles with so much distinctness, explaining, and giving Reasons, and answering Objections.

Here it is not denied by any, that the Apostle does assert that we are justified by Faith, without the Works of the Law, because the Words are express; but only it is said that we take his Words wrong, and understand that by 'em that never entered into his Heart, in that when he excludes the Works of the Law, we understand him of the whole Law of God, or the Rule which he has given to Mankind to walk by; whereas all that he intends is the *ceremonial* Law.

Some that oppose this Doctrine indeed say, that the Apostle sometimes means that it is by Faith, *i. e.* an hearty embracing the Gospel in its first Act, *only*, or *without any preceeding holy Life*, that Persons are admitted into a justified State; but, say they, 'tis by a persevering Obedience that they are continued in a justified State, and it is by this that they are finally justified. But this is the same Thing as to say that a Man on his first embracing the Gospel is *conditionally* justified and pardon'd.— To pardon Sin, is to free the Sinner from the Punishment of it, or from that eternal Misery that is due to it; And therefore if a Person is pardon'd, or freed from this Misery, on his first embracing the Gospel, and yet not finally freed, but his actual freedom still depends on some Condition yet to be performed, 'tis inconceivable how he can be pardon'd otherwise than conditionally: *that is* he is not properly *actually pardon'd*, and freed from Punishment, but only he has God's Promise that he shall be pardon'd *on future Conditions*; God promises him that now, if he perseveres in Obedience, he shall be finally pardon'd, or actually freed from Hell; which is to make just nothing at all of the Apostle's great Doctrine of Justification by Faith alone: such a conditional Pardon is no Pardon or Justification at all, any more than all Mankind have, whether they embrace the Gospel or no; for they all have a promise of final Justification on Conditions of future sincere Obedience, as much as he that embraces the Gospel.—But not to dispute about this, we will suppose that there may be something or other at the Sinner's *first embracing the Gospel*, that may properly be called Justification or Pardon, and yet that final Justification, or real freedom from the Punishment of Sin, is still suspended on Conditions hitherto unfulfill'd; yet they that hold that Sinners are thus justified on embracing the Gospel, they suppose that they are justified by this, no otherwise than as this is a *leading act of Obedience*, or at least as Virtue and moral Goodness in them, and therefore would be excluded by the Apostle as much as any other Vertue or Obedience; if it be allowed that he means the moral Law, when he excludes *Works of the Law*. And therefore if that Point be yielded that the Apostle means the *moral*, and not only the *ceremonial* Law, their whole Scheme falls to the Ground.

And because the issue of the whole Argument from those Texts in St. *Paul*'s Epistles depends on the determination of this Point, I would be particular in the discussion of it.

Some of our Opponents in this Doctrine of Justification, when they deny that by the Law, the Apostle means the moral Law, or the whole Rule of Life which God has given to Mankind, seem to choose to express themselves thus, that the Apostle only intends the *Mosaic Dispensation*: But this comes to just the same Thing as if they said that the Apostle only means to exclude the Works of the Ceremonial Law; for when they say that 'tis intended only that we ben't justified by the Works of the *Mosaic* Dispensation, if they mean any Thing by it, it must be that we ben't justified by attending, and observing what is *Mosaic in that Dispensation*, or by what was peculiar to it, and wherein it differed from the *Christian Dispensation*; which is the same as that which is ceremonial and positive, and not moral, *in that Administration*—. So that this is what I have to disprove, *viz*. That the Apostle when he speaks of Works of the Law in this Affair, means only Works of the Ceremonial Law, or those Observances that were peculiar to the *Mosaic* Administration.

And here it must be noted, that no Body controverts it with them, whether the Works of the Ceremonial Law ben't included, or whether the Apostle don't particularly argue against Justification by Circumcision, and other ceremonial Observances; but all that is in Question is, whether when he denies Justification by Works of the Law, he is to be understood only of the Ceremonial Law, or whether the moral Law ben't also implied and intended; And therefore those Arguments that are brought to prove that the Apostle meant the Ceremonial Law are nothing to the Purpose, unless they prove more than that, *viz*, that the Apostle meant *those only*.

What is much insisted on is, that it was the *judaising* Christians being so fond of Circumcision, and other Ceremonies of the Law, and depending so much on them, which was the very Occasion of the Apostles writing as he does against Justification by the Works of the Law. But supposing it were so, that their trusting in Works of the Ceremonial Law, were the *sole* Occasion of the Apostle's writing; (which yet there is no reason to allow, as may appear afterwards;) if their trusting in a *particular Work*, as a Work of Righteousness was all that gave *occasion* to the Apostle to write, how does it follow that therefore the Apostle did not upon that *Occasion* write against trusting in *all Works* of Righteousness whatsoever? Where is the absurdity of supposing that the Apostle might take occasion from his observing some to trust in a *certain* Work as a Work of Righteousness, to write to them against Persons trusting in *any* Works of Righteousness *at all*, and that it was a very proper Occasion too? yea it would have been unavoidable for the Apostle to have argued against trusting in a particular Work in that quality of a Work of Righteousness, which quality was general, but he must therein argue against trusting in Works of Righteousness *in general*. Supposing it had been some other particular sort of Works that was the occasion of the Apostle's writing, as for instance, Works of Charity, and the Apostle should hence take occasion to write to them not to trust in their Works, could the Apostle by that be understood of no other Works besides Works of Charity? Would it have been absurd to understand him as writing against trusting in *any Work at all*, because it was their trusting to a *particular Work* that gave occasion to his writing?

Another Thing that is alledged as an Evidence that the Apostle means the ceremonial Law, when he says we can not be justified by the Works of the Law, is that he uses that Argument to prove it, *viz.* that this Law that he speaks of was given so long after the Covenant with *Abraham*, in Gal. 3. 17. *And this I say that the Covenant that was confirmed before of God in Christ, the Law that was four hundred and thirty years after cannot disannul.* But say they, it was only the *Mosaic* Administration, and not the Covenant of Works that was given so long after.—But the Apostle's Argument seems manifestly to be mistaken by them. The Apostle don't speak of a Law that began first *to have being* four hundred and thirty Years after; if he did, there would be some force in their Objection; But he has respect to a certain solemn Transaction, well known among the *Jews*, by the Phrase of *the giving of the Law*, which was that great Transaction at Mount *Sinai*, that we have Account of in the 19, and 20 Chapters of *Exodus*, consisting especially in God's giving the ten Commandments, which is the moral Law, with that terrible Voice, which Law he afterwards gave in Tables of Stone. This Transaction the *Jews* in the Apostles Time misinterpreted, they looked upon it as God's establishing that Law as a Rule of Justification. This conceit of theirs the Apostle brings this invincible Argument against, *viz*. That God would never go about to *disannul* his Covenant with *Abraham*, which was plainly a *Covenant of Grace*, by a Transaction with his Posterity, that was so long after it, and was plainly built upon it: He would not overthrow a *Covenant of Grace* that he had long before established with *Abraham*, for him, and his Seed, (which is often mention'd as the Ground of God's making them his People,) by now establishing a *Covenant of Works* with them at Mount *Sinai*, as the Jews and judaizing Christians supposed.

But that the Apostle don't mean only Works of the ceremonial Law, when he excludes Works of the Law in Justification, but also of the moral Law, and all Works of Obedience, Vertue, and Righteousness whatsoever, may appear by the following Things.

1. The Apostle don't only say, that we are not justified by the Works *of the Law*, but that we are not justified *by Works*, using a general Term; as in our Text it is said, unto him that *worketh not*, but believeth on him that justifieth, &c. and in the 6. v. *God imputeth righteousness* without Works, And Chap 11. 6. *And if by Grace, then it is no more of* Works, *otherwise Grace is no more Grace: But if it be of* Works, *then it is no more Grace; otherwise Work is no more Work. So Eph.* 2. 8, 9. *For by Grace ye are saved, through Faith,—not of* Works. By which, there is no Reason in the World to understand the Apostle of any other than Works in general, as correlates of a Reward, or good Works, or Works of Vertue and Righteousness. When the Apostle says we are justified or saved *not by Works*, without any such Term annexed, as *the Law*, or any other Addition to limit the Expression, what Warrant have any to confine it to Works of a particular Law, or Institution, excluding others? Are not Observances of other Divine Laws Works, as well as of that? It seems to be allowed by the Divines in the *Arminian* Scheme,

in their Interpretation of several of those Texts where the Apostle only mentions *Works*, without any Addition that he means our own good Works in general; but then they say, he only means to exclude any proper merit in those Works. But to say the Apostle means one Thing when he says we ben't justified by *Works*, another when he says we ben't justified by the *Works of the Law*, when we find the Expressions mixed, and used in the same Discourse, and when the Apostle is evidently upon the same Argument, is very unreasonable, it is to dodge, and fly from Scripture, rather than to open and yield our selves to it's teachings.

2. In the third Chapter of *Romans*, our having been guilty of Breaches of the moral Law, is an Argument that the Apostle uses why we cannot be justified *by the Works of the Law*; Beginning with the 9th *v.* There he proves out of the Old Testament, that all are under Sin; *There is none righteous, no not one: Their Throat is an open Sepulchre: With their Tongues they have used deceit: Their Mouth is full of cursing and bitterness; and their Feet swift to shed Blood.* And so he goes on mentioning only those Things that are Breaches of the moral Law, and then when he has done, his Conclusion is, in the 19th, and 20th ver. *Now we know that whatsoever Things the Law saith, it saith to them that are under the Law, that every Mouth may be stopped, and all the World may become guilty before God.* Therefore *by the Deeds of the Law, shall no Flesh be justified in his Sight.* This is most evidently his Argument, because all had sinn'd, (as it was said in the 9th ver.) and been guilty of those Breaches of the moral Law, that he had mentioned, (and it is repeated over again, afterward ver. 23.) *For all have sinn'd and come short of the Glory of God. Therefore* none at all can be justified by the Deeds of the Law: Now if the Apostle meant only that we are not justified by the Deeds of the ceremonial Law, what kind of arguing would that be, *Their Mouth is full of cursing and bitterness, their Feet are swift to shed Blood, therefore,* They can't be justified by the Deeds of the *Mosaic* Administration. They are guilty of the Breaches of the moral Law, and therefore they can't be justified by the Deeds of the ceremonial Law? Doubtless the Apostle's Argument is, that the very same Law that they have broken and sinn'd against, can never justify 'em as Observers of it, because every Law don't justify, but necessarily condemns it's Violaters: And therefore our Breaches of the

moral Law, argue no more, than that we can't be justified by that Law that we have broken.

And it may be noted, that the Apostle's Argument here is the same that I have already used, *viz.* that as we are in our selves, and out of Christ, we are under the Condemnation of that original Law, or Constitution that God established with Mankind; and therefore 'tis no Way fit that any Thing that we do, any Vertue or Obedience of ours, should be accepted, or we accepted on the Account of it.

3. The Apostle, in all the preceeding part of this Epistle, wherever he has the Phrase, *the Law*, evidently intends the moral Law *principally*: As in the 12th ver. of the foregoing Chap. *For as many as have sinn'd without Law, shall also perish without Law.* 'Tis evidently the written moral Law, the Apostle means, by the next ver. but one. *For when the Gentiles, which have not the Law, do by Nature the Things contained in the Law,*—That is, the moral Law that the Gentiles have by Nature: And so the next ver. *Which shew the Work of the Law written in their Hearts.* 'Tis the moral Law, and not the Ceremonial that is written in the Hearts of those that are destitute of Divine Revelation. And so in the 18th ver. *Thou approvest the Things that are more Excellent, being instructed out of the Law.* 'Tis the Moral Law, that shews us the Nature of Things, and teaches us what is Excellent. 20th ver. *Thou hast a form of Knowledge, and truth in the Law.* 'Tis the Moral Law, as is evident by what follows, *ver.* 22, 23. *Thou that sayeth a Man should not commit Adultery, dost thou commit Adultery? Thou that abhorrest Idols, dost thou commit Sacriledge? Thou that makest thy boast of the Law, through breaking the Law dishonourest thou God.* Adultery, Idolatry and Sacriledge, surely are the breaking of the moral, and not the ceremonial Law. So in the 27th *ver. And shall not uncircumcision which is by Nature, if it fulfil the Law, judge thee, who by the letter and circumcision dost transgress the Law.* i.e. The Gentiles, that you despise because uncircumcised, if they live moral and holy Lives, in Obedience to the Moral Law, shall condemn you tho' circumcised. And so there is not one Place in all the preceeding part of the Epistle, where the Apostle speaks of the Law, but that he most apparently intends principally the moral Law: And yet when the Apostle, in continuance of the same Discourse, comes to tell us that we

can't be justified by the Works of the Law, then they will needs have it, that he means only the ceremonial Law; yea tho' all this Discourse about the moral Law, shewing how the Jews as well as Gentiles have violated it, is evidently preparatory, and introductory to that Doctrine, Chap 3. 20. That *no Flesh*, that is none of Mankind, neither Jews nor Gentiles, *can be justified by the Works of the Law*.

4. 'Tis evident that when the Apostle says, we can't be justified by the Works of the Law, he means the Moral as well as ceremonial Law, by his giving this Reason for it, that *by the Law is the Knowledge of Sin*, as *Rom* 3. 20. *By the Deeds of the Law shall no Flesh be justified in his Sight, for by the Law is the knowledge of Sin*. Now that Law by which we come to the knowledge of Sin, is the moral Law chiefly and primarily.—If this Argument of the Apostle be good, *that we can't be justified by the Deeds of the Law, because it is by the Law that we come to the knowledge of Sin*, then it proves that we can't be justified by the Deeds of the Moral Law, nor by the Precepts of Christianity; for by them is the Knowledge of Sin. If the Reason be good, then where the Reason holds, the Truth holds.—'Tis a miserable Shift, and a violent Force put upon the Words, to say that the meaning is, that by the Law of Circumcision is the Knowledge of Sin, because Circumcision signifying the taking away of Sin, puts Men in mind of Sin. The plain meaning of the Apostle is, that as the Law most strictly forbids Sin, it tends to convince us of Sin, and bring our own Consciences to *condemn* us, instead of *justifying* of us; that the Use of it is to declare to us our own Guilt and Unworthiness, which is the reverse of justifying and approving of us as virtuous or worthy. This is the Apostle's meaning, if we will allow him to be his own expositor; for he himself in this very Epistle explains to us how it is that by the Law we have the Knowledge of Sin, and that 'tis by the Law's forbidding Sin *Chap. 7. 7. I had not known Sin, but by the Law, for I had not known Lust, except the Law had said, thou shalt not covet*. There the Apostle determines two Things, *First*, That, the Way in which, *by the Law is the Knowledge of Sin*, is by the Law's forbidding Sin: And *Secondly*, which is more directly still to the Purpose; he determines that 'tis the Moral Law by which we come to the knowledge of Sin; for says he, *I had not known Lust except the Law had said, thou shalt*

not covet: Now 'tis the moral, and not the ceremonial Law, that says thou shalt not covet: Therefore when the Apostle argues that by the Deeds of the Law no Flesh living shall be justifyed, because by the Law is the knowledge of Sin, his Argument proves, (unless he was mistaken as to the force of his Argument,) that we can't be justifyed by the Deeds of the Moral Law.

5. 'Tis evident that the Apostle don't mean only the ceremonial Law, because he gives this Reason why we have Righteousness, and a Title to the Privilege of God's Children, not by the Law, but by Faith, *that the Law worketh Wrath, Rom.* 4. 13, 14, 15, 16. *For the promise that he should be the Heir of the World, was not to* Abraham, *or to his Seed* through the Law, *but through the Righteousness of Faith: For if they which are* of the Law *be Heirs,* Faith *is made void, and the promise made of none effect*: Because the Law worketh Wrath; *for where no Law is there is no Transgression.* Therefore it is of Faith *that it might be by Grace.* Now the way in which the Law works Wrath, by the Apostles own Account, in the Reason he himself annexes, is by forbidding Sin, and aggravating the Guilt of the Transgression; *for*, says he, *where no Law is there is Transgression*: And so, Chap 7. 13. *That Sin by the Commandment might become exceeding sinful.*—If therefore this Reason of the Apostle be good, it is much stronger against Justification by the moral Law, than the ceremonial Law; for 'tis by Transgressions of the moral Law chiefly that there comes Wrath; for they are most strictly forbidden, and most terribly threaten'd.

6. 'Tis evident that when the Apostle says, we ben't justified by the Works of the Law, that he excludes all our own Vertue, Goodness, or Excellency, by that Reason that he gives for it, *viz. That boasting might be excluded.* Rom. 3. 26, 27, 28. *To declare I say at this Time his Righteousness, that he might be just, and the justifier of him that* believes *in Jesus.* Where is boasting then? It is excluded. *By what Law? of* Works? *Nay; but by the Law of* Faith. Therefore, *We conclude that a Man is justified by Faith without the Deeds of the Law.* Eph. 2. 8, 9. *For by Grace are we saved* through Faith; *and that not of your selves, it is the Gift of God*: Not of Works lest any Man should boast.—Now what are Men wont to boast of, but what they esteem their own Goodness, or Excellency?—If we are not justified by

Works of the ceremonial Law, yet how does that exclude boasting, as long as we are justified by our own Excellency, or Vertue and Goodness of our own, or Works of Righteousness which we have done?

But it is said that boasting is excluded, as Circumcision was excluded, which was what the *Jews* especially used to glory in, and value themselves upon, above other Nations.

To this I answer, that the *Jews* were not only used to boast of Circumcision, but were notorious for boasting of their moral Righteousness. The *Jews* of those Days were generally Admirers, and followers of the *Pharisees*, who were full of their Boasts of their moral Righteousness, as we may see by the Example of the Pharisee mention'd in the 18th of *Luke*, which Christ mentions as describing the general Temper of that Sect; *Lord*, says he, *I thank thee, that I am not as other Men, an Extortioner nor Unjust, nor an Adulterer*. The Works that he boasts of were chiefly moral Works: He depended on the Works of the Law for Justification; and therefore Christ tells us that the *Publican*, that renounced all his own Righteousness, *went down to* his House *justified* rather than he. And elsewhere we read of the Pharisees *praying in the corners of the Streets* and *sounding a Trumpet before 'em when they did Alms*: But those Works which they so vainly boasted of were moral Works. And not only so, but what the Apostle, in this very Epistle, is condemning the *Jews* for, is their boasting of the moral Law. *Chap.* 2. 22, 23. *Thou that sayeth a Man should not commit Adultery, dost thou commit Adultery? Thou that abhorrest Idols, dost thou commit Sacriledge. Thou that makest thy* boast of the Law, *through breaking the Law dishonourest thou God*. The Law here mentioned that they made their boast of, was that of which Adultery, Idolatry, and Sacriledge, were the breaches, which is the moral Law: So that this is the boasting which the Apostle condemns them for; and therefore if they were justified by the Works of this Law, then how comes he to say that their boasting is excluded? And besides, when they boasted of the Rites of the *ceremonial* Law, it was under a Notion of it's being a Part of their own Goodness or Excellency, or what made them holier and more lovely in the sight of God than other People; and if they were not justified by this Part of their own supposed Goodness, or Holiness, yet if they were by another, how did that exclude boasting? How was their boasting excluded, unless all Goodness or Excellency of their own was excluded?

7. The Reason given by the Apostle why we can be justified only by Faith, and not by the Works of the Law, in the 3d Chap. of *Gal. viz. That they that are under the Law are under the Curse*, makes it evident that he don't mean only the ceremonial Law. In that Chapter the Apostle had particularly insisted upon it that *Abraham* was justified by Faith, and that it is by Faith only, and not by the Works of the Law, that we can be justified and become the Children of *Abraham*, and be made Partakers of the Blessing of *Abraham*: And he gives this Reason for it, in the 10th *v. For as many as are of the Works of the Law are under the Curse; for it is written cursed is every one that continueth not in all Things which are written in the Book of the Law to do them*. 'Tis manifest that these Words cited from *Deuteronomy*, are spoken not only with Regard to the ceremonial Law, but the whole Law of God to Mankind, and *chiefly* the moral Law; and that all Mankind are therefore as they are in themselves under that Curse, not only while the ceremonial Law lasted, but now since that has ceased: And therefore all that are justified, are redeemed from that curse, by Christ's bearing it for them; as there in the 13. ver. *Christ hath redeemed us from the curse of the Law, being made a curse for us; For it is written, cursed is every one that hangeth on a Tree.*—Now therefore, either it's being said so, that he is cursed that continueth not in all Things which are written in the Book of the Law to do them, is a good Reason why we can't be justified by the Works of *that Law*, of which it is so said, or it is not; if it be, then it is a good Reason why we can't be justified by the Works of the moral Law, and of the whole Rule which God has given to Mankind to walk by; for the Words are spoken of the moral as well as ceremonial Law, and reach every Command, or Precept which God has given to Mankind, and chiefly the moral Precepts, which are most strictly enjoin'd, and the Violations of which in both New Testament and Old, and in the Books of *Moses* themselves, are threatned with the most dreadful *Curse*.

8. The Apostle does in like Manner argue against our being justified by our *own Righteousness*, as he does against being justified by the Works of the Law; and evidently uses the Expressions of our *own Righteousness*, and *Works of the Law*, promiscuously,

and as signifying the same Thing. It is particularly evident by *Rom*. 10. 3. *For they being ignorant of Gods Righteousness, and going about to establish their own Righteousness, have not submitted themselves to the Righteousness of God*. Here 'tis plain that the same Thing is asserted as in the two last Verses but one of the foregoing Chap. *But* Israel *which followed after the Law of* Righteousness, *hath not attained to the Law of* Righteousness: *Wherefore: Because they sought it not* by Faith, *but as it were by* the Works of the Law. And 'tis very unreasonable, upon several Accounts, to suppose that the Apostle by their own Righteousness, intends only their ceremonial Righteousness. For when the Apostle warns us against trusting in our own Righteousness for Justification, doubtless it is fair to interpret the Expression in an Agreement with other Scriptures where we are warned not to think that 'tis for the sake of our *own Righteousness*, that we obtain God's Favour and Blessing; as particularly that in *Deut*. 9. 4, 5, 6. *Speak not thou in thine Heart, after that the Lord thy God hath cast them out from before thee, saying*, for my Righteousness *the Lord hath brought me in, to possess this Land; but for the wickedness of these Nations the Lord doth drive them out from before thee*: Not for thy Righteousness, or for the uprightness of thy Heart, *dost thou go to possess their Land; but for the wickedness of these Nations the Lord thy God doth drive them out from before thee, and that he may perform the word which he sware unto thy Fathers*, Abraham Isaac *and* Jacob. *Understand therefore that the Lord thy God giveth thee not this good Land to possess it*, for thy Righteousness, for thou art a stiff necked People. None will pretend that here the Expression *thy Righteousness*, signifies only a ceremonial Righteousness, but all Vertue or Goodness of *their own*; yea and the inward Goodness of the Heart as well as the outward Goodness of Life; which appears by the beginning of the 5 ver. *Not for thy Righteousness, or for the uprightness of thy Heart*,—and also by the *Antithesis* in the 6. v. *Not for thy Righteousness, for thou art a stiffnecked People*. Their stiffneckedness was their moral Wickedness, Obstinacy, and perverseness of Heart: By Righteousness, therefore, on the contrary, is meant their moral Vertue, and rectitude of Heart, and Life.—This is what I would argue from hence, That the Expression of *our own Righteousness*, when used in Scripture, with Relation to the favour of God, and when we are warned against looking upon it as that by which that Favour, or the Fruits of it are obtained, don't signify only a ceremonial Righteousness, but all manner of Goodness of our own.

The *Jews* also in the New Testament are condemned for trusting in their own Righteousness in this Sense; *Luke* 18. 9. &c.—*And he spake this Parable unto certain that* trusted in themselves that they were Righteous.—This intends chiefly a moral Righteousness, as appears by the *Parable* it self, in which we have an Account of the Prayer of the *Pharisee*, wherein the Things that he mentions, as what he *trusts in*, are chiefly moral Qualifications and Performances, *viz.* That he was *not an Extortioner, unjust*, nor an *Adulterer*, &c.—

But we need not go to the Writings of other Penmen of the Scripture; but if we allow the Apostle *Paul* to be his own Interpreter, he when he speaks of our own Righteousness as that which we are not justified or saved by, don't mean only a ceremonial Righteousness, nor does he only intend a Way of Religion, and serving God, *of our own choosing* and fixing on, without divine Warrant or Prescription; but by our own Righteousness he means the same as a Righteousness *of our own doing*, whether it be a Service or Righteousness of God's prescribing, or our own unwarranted performing: Let it be an Obedience to the ceremonial Law, or a Gospel Obedience, or what it will, if it be *a Righteousness of our own doing*, it is excluded by the Apostle in this Affair, as is evident by *Titus* 3. 5. *Not by Works of Righteousness which we have done.*—But I would more particularly insist on this Text; and therefore this may be the

9. *Argument*, That the Apostle when he denies Justification by Works, and by Works of the Law, and by our own Righteousness, don't only mean Works of the ceremonial Law *viz.* What is said by the Apostle in *Tit* 3. 3, 4, 5, 6, 7. *For we our selves also were sometimes foolish, disobedient, deceived, serving divers Lusts and Pleasures, living in Malice, and Envy, hateful, and hating one another. But after that the Kindness and Love of God our Saviour, toward Man, appeared, not by* Works of Righteousness which we have done, *but according to his Mercy he saved us, by the washing of regeneration, and renewing of the Holy Ghost; which he shed on us abundantly, through Jesus Christ Our Saviour*; that being justified *by his Grace, we should be*

made Heirs, according to the Hope of eternal Life. Works of Righteousness *that we have done*, are here excluded, as what we are neither saved, nor justified by. The Apostle expresly says, we are not saved by 'em; and 'tis evident that when he says this, he has respect to the Affair of *Justification*, and that he means, we are not saved by 'em in not being justified by 'em, by the next verse but one, which is part of the same Sentence, *That being justified by his Grace we should be made Heirs according to the hope of eternal Life*.

'Tis several Ways manifest that the Apostle in this Text, by *Works of Righteousness which we have done*, don't mean only Works of the ceremonial Law. It appears by the 3d v. *For we our selves also were sometimes foolish, disobedient, deceived, serving divers Lusts and Pleasures, living in Malice and Envy, hateful, and hating one another*. These are Breaches of the *moral* Law, that the Apostle observes they lived in before they were justifyed: and 'tis most plain that 'tis this that gives Occasion to the Apostle to observe as he does in the 5 ver. That it was not by Works of Righteousness which they had done, that they were saved or justified.

But we need not go to the Context, 'tis most apparent from the Words themselves, that the Apostle don't mean only Works of the ceremonial Law: If he had only said, it is not by our own Works of Righteousness; what could we understand by *Works of Righteousness*, but only *Righteous Works*, or which is the same Thing, *good Works*? And to say that *it is by our own righteous Works, that we are justified, tho' not by one particular kind of righteous Works*, would certainly be a Contradiction to such an Assertion. But the Words are render'd yet more strong, plain, and determined in their Sense, by those additional Words, *which we have done*; which shews that the Apostle intends to exclude all *our own righteous or vertuous Works* universally. If it should be asserted concerning any Commodity, Treasure, or precious Jewel, that it could not be procured *by Money*, and not only so, but to make the Assertion the more strong, it should be asserted with additional Words, that it could not be procured by Money *that Men possess*; how unreasonable would it be after all to say, that all that was meant was, that it could not be procured *with Brass Money*?

And what renders the interpreting this Text of Works of the ceremonial Law, yet more unreasonable is, that these Works were indeed *no Works of Righteousness at all*, but were only falsly supposed to be so by the *Jews*; and *that* our Opponents in this Doctrine suppose is the very reason why we *ben't justified* by 'em, because they *are not Works of Righteousness*, or because (the ceremonial Law being now abrogated) there is no Obedience in 'em: But how absurd is it to say, that the Apostle when he says we are not justified *by Works of Righteousness that we have done*, meant only Works of the ceremonial Law, and that for that very Reason because they *are not Works of Righteousness*. To illustrate this by the forementioned Comparison; If it should be asserted that such a Thing could not be procured by Money *that Men possess*, how ridiculous would it be to say that the meaning only was, that it could not be procured by counterfeit Money, and that for that Reason, *because it was not Money*,—What Scripture will stand before Men, if they will take liberty to manage Scripture thus? Or what one Text is there in the Bible that mayn't at this rate be explain'd all away, and perverted to any Sense Men please.

But then further, if we should allow that the Apostle intends only to oppose Justification by Works of the ceremonial Law in this Text, yet 'tis evident by the Expression he uses that he means to oppose it under that Notion, or in that quality, of their being *Works of Righteousness of our own doing*. But if the Apostle argues against our being justified by Works of the ceremonial Law under the Notion of their being *of that Nature and Kind*, viz. *Works of our own doing*; then it will follow that the Apostle's Argument is strong against, not only *those*, but *all of that Nature and Kind*, even all that *are of our own doing*.

If there were no other Text in the Bible about Justification but this, this would clearly and invincibly prove that we are not justified by any of our own Goodness, Vertue, or Righteousness or for the Excellency or Righteousness of any Thing *that we have done* in Religion; because 'tis here so fully and strongly asserted: But this Text does abundantly confirm other Texts of the Apostle, where he denies Justification by Works of the Law: There is no doubt can be rationally made but that, when the Apostle here shews that God *saves us according to his Mercy*, in that he don't save us by *Works of Righteousness that we have done*, v. 5, And that so we are *justified by Grace*, v. 7. herein opposing Salvation *by Works*, and Salvation *by Grace*, he means

the same Works as he does in other Places, where he in like
manner opposes *Works* and *Grace*, the same Work as in *Rom* 11. 6.
*And if by Grace then it is no more of Works; otherwise Grace is no
more Grace: But if it be of Works, then it is no more Grace; otherwise Work is no more Work.* And the same Works as in Rom. 4. 4.
*Now to him that worketh, is the reward not reckoned of Grace but
of Debt.* And the same Works that are spoken of in the Context
of the 24. v. of the foregoing Chapter, which the Apostle there
calls *Works of the Law, being justified freely by his Grace*—And of
the 4 Chap. 16. v. *Therefore 'tis of Faith, that it might be by
Grace.* Where in the Context, *the Righteousness of Faith*, is opposed to *the Righteousness of the Law*: For here God's saving us
according to his Mercy, and justifying us by Grace, is opposed
to saving us *by Works of Righteousness that we have done*, in the
same manner as in those Places *justifying us by his Grace*, is
opposed to *justifying us by Works of the Law*.

10. The Apostle could not mean only Works of the ceremonial
Law, when he says we are not justified by the Works of the Law,
*because 'tis asserted of the Saints, under the Old Testament, as well
as new.* If Men are justified by their *sincere Obedience*, it will
then follow that formerly, before the ceremonial Law was abrogated, Men were justified by the Works of the ceremonial Law,
as well as the moral. For if we are justified by our *sincere Obedience* then it alters not the Case, whether the Commands be
moral, or positive, provided they be *God's Commands*, and our
Obedience be *Obedience to God*: And so the Case must be just
the same under the Old Testament, with the Works of the moral
Law, and ceremonial, according to the measure of the *Vertue of
Obedience*, there was in either. 'Tis true their Obedience to the
ceremonial Law would have nothing to do in the Affair of Justification, unless it was *sincere*; and so neither would the Works of
the moral Law: Obedience to the moral Law would have been
concerned in the Affair of Justification, if sincere; and so would
Obedience to the ceremonial. If Obedience was the Thing,
then Obedience to the *ceremonial Law*, while that stood in Force,
and Obedience to the *moral Law*, had just the same sort of
concern, according to the Proportion of Obedience that consists in each. As now under the New-Testament, if Obedience is
what we are justified by, that Obedience must doubtless comprehend Obedience to all God's Commands *now in Force*, to the

positive Precepts of Attendance on Baptism and the Lord's
Supper, as well as moral Precepts. If Obedience be the Thing, it
is not because 'tis Obedience to such a kind of Commands, but
because 'tis Obedience. So that by this Supposition, the Saints
under the Old Testament were justified, at least *in Part*, by their
Obedience to the ceremonial Law.

But 'tis evident that the Saints under the old Testament
were not justified *in any measure*, by the Works of the ceremonial Law. This may be proved proceeding on the Foot of our
Adversaries own Interpretation of the Apostle's Phrase of *the
Works of the Law*; and supposing him to mean by it only the
Works of the ceremonial Law. To Instance in *David*, 'tis evident that he was not justified in any wise, by the Works of the
ceremonial law, by *Rom.* 4. 6, 7, 8. *Even as* David *also described
the blessedness of the Man, unto whom God imputeth Righteousness*
without Works, *saying, blessed are they whose Iniquities are forgiven, and whose Sins are covered; blessed is the Man to whom the
Lord will not impute Sin.* 'Tis plain that the Apostle is here
speaking of Justification, by the preceeding Verse, and by all the
Context; and the Thing spoken of, *viz. forgiving Iniquities*, and
covering Sins, is what our Adversaries themselves suppose to be
Justification, and even the whole of Justification. This *David*,
speaking of himself, says (by the Apostle's Interpretation,) that
he had *without Works.* For 'tis manifest that *David* in the Words
here cited, from the beginning of the 32d *Psalm*, has a special
Respect to himself: He speaks of *his own Sins* being forgiven and
not imputed to him: as appears by the Words that nextly follow,
*When I kept Silence, my Bones waxed old, through my roaring all
the Day long; for Day and Night thy Hand was heavy upon me,
my moisture is turned into the drought of Summer. I acknowledged
my Sin unto thee, and mine Iniquity have I not hid: I said I will
confess my Transgressions unto the Lord*; and thou forgavest the
Iniquity of my Sin. Let us therefore understand the Apostle
which way we will, by *Works*, when he says, *David describes the
blessedness of the Man to whom the Lord imputes Righteousness
without Works*, whether of all manner of Works, or only Works of
the ceremonial Law, yet 'tis evident *at least*, that *David* was not
justified by Works of the *ceremonial Law.* Therefore here is the
Argument; if our own Obedience be that by which Men are
justified, then under the Old Testament, Men were justified

partly by Obedience to the ceremonial Law, (as has been proved;) but the Saints under the Old Testament were not justified partly by the Works of the ceremonial Law; therefore Mens own Obedience is not that by which they are justified.

11. Another Argument that the Apostle when he speaks of the two opposite Ways of Justification, one by the Works of the Law, and the other by Faith, don't mean only the Works of the ceremonial Law, may be taken from that Place, *Rom.* 10. 5, 6. *For* Moses *describeth the Righteousness which is of the Law, that the Man which doth those Things shall live by them; but the Righteousness which is of Faith speaketh on this wise*, &c. Here two Things are evident,

First, That the Apostle here speaks of the same two opposite Ways of Justification, one *by the Righteousness which is of the Law*, the other *by Faith*, that he had treated of in the former Part of the Epistle; and therefore it must be the same Law that is here spoken of: The same Law is here meant as in the last Verses of the foregoing *Chapter*, where he says the *Jews* had *not attained to the Law of Righteousness*: Wherefore, because they sought it not *by Faith*, but as it were *by the Works of the Law*. As is plain, because the Apostle is still speaking of the same Thing, the Words are a Continuation of the same Discourse, as may be seen at first Glance, by any one that looks on the Context.

Secondly, 'Tis manifest that *Moses* when he describes the Righteousness which is of the Law, or the Way of Justification by the Law, in the Words here cited, *He that doth those Things shall live in them*, don't speak only, nor chiefly, of the Works of the ceremonial Law; For none will pretend that God ever made such a Covenant with Man, that he that kept the ceremonial Law should live in it, or that there ever was a Time that it was *chiefly* by the Works of the ceremonial Law, that Men lived and were justified. Yea, 'tis manifest by the forementioned Instance of *David*, mentioned in the 4th of *Romans* that there never was a Time wherein Men were justified *in any Measure*, by the Works of the ceremonial Law, as has been just now shewn. *Moses* therefore in those Words, which the Apostle says, are a Description of *the Righteousness which is of the Law*, can't mean only the ceremonial Law. And therefore it follows that when the Apostle speaks of Justification by *the Works of the*

Law, as opposite to Justification by Faith, he don't mean only the ceremonial Law, but also the Works of the moral Law, which are *the Things* spoken of by *Moses*, when he says he that doth *these Things* shall live in them; and which are *the Things* that the Apostle in this very Place is arguing that we can't be justified by; as is evident by the Context, the last Verses of the preceeding Chapter, *But* Israel *which followed after the Law of Righteousness, hath not attained to the Law of Righteousness: Wherefore? Because they sought it not by* Faith, *but as it were by* the Works of the Law, *&c.* And in the 3d v. of this Chap. *For they being ignorant of God's Righteousness, and going about to establish* their own Righteousness, *have not submitted themselves to the Righteousness of God.*

And further, how can the Apostle's Description that he here gives from *Moses*, of this *exploded* Way of Justification by the Works of the Law, consist with the *Arminian* Scheme of a Way of Justification by the Vertue of a sincere Obedience, that *still remains* as the *true and only Way* of Justification, under the Gospel. 'Tis most apparent that 'tis the design of the Apostle to give a Description of both the legal *rejected*, and the evangelical *valid* Ways of Justification, in that wherein they differ, or are distinguished the one from the other: But how is that, that *he that doth those Things shall live in them*, that wherein the Way of Justification by the Works of the Law, differs, or is distinguished from that in which Christians under the Gospel are justified, according to their Scheme; for still, according to them, it may be said, in the same Manner, of the *Precepts of the Gospel*, he that doth these Things shall live in them: The difference lies only in the Things *to be done*, but not at all, in that that the *doing of them* is not the Condition of living in them, just in the one Case, as in the other. The Words, *He that doth them shall live in them*, will serve just as well for a Description of the latter as the former.—By the Apostle's saying, the Righteousness of the Law is described *thus*, he that doth these Things shall live in them, but the Righteousness of Faith, saith *thus*, plainly intimates that the Righteousness of Faith saith *otherwise*, and in an *opposite manner*.—But besides, if these Words cited from *Moses*, are actually said by him of the moral Law as well as ceremonial, as 'tis most evident they are, it renders it still more absurd to suppose them mentioned by the Apostle,

as the *very Note of Distinction* between Justification by a ceremonial Obedience, and a moral sincere Obedience, as the *Arminians* must suppose.

Thus I have spoken to a second Argument, to prove that we
are not justified by any manner of Virtue or Goodness of our
own, *viz.* That to suppose otherwise is contrary to the Doctrine that is directly urged, and abundantly insisted on by the
Apostle *Paul*, in his Epistles.

   I proceed now to a

Third Argument, *viz.* That to suppose that we are justified
by our own sincere Obedience, or any of our own Virtue or
Goodness, *derogates from Gospel Grace.*

That Scheme of Justification that manifestly takes from, or
diminishes the Grace of God, is undoubtedly to be rejected;
for 'tis the declared Design of God in the Gospel to exalt the
Freedom and Riches of his Grace, in that Method of Justification of Sinners, and Way of admitting them to his Favour, and
the blessed Fruits of it, which it declares. The Scripture teaches
that the Way of Justification that is appointed in the Gospel
Covenant, is appointed, *as it is,* for that end, that free Grace
might be express'd, and glorified; *Rom.* 4. 16. *Therefore it is of
Faith, that it might be by Grace.* The exercising, and magnifying the free Grace of God in the Gospel contrivance for the
Justification and Salvation of Sinners, is evidently the *chief Design of it*: And this Freedom and Riches of the Grace of the
Gospel is every where spoken of in Scripture as the *chief Glory
of it.* Therefore that Doctrine that derogates from the free
Grace of God in justifying Sinners, as it is most opposite to
God's Design, so it must be exceeding offensive to him.

Those that maintain that we are justified by our own sincere
Obedience, do pretend that their Scheme does not diminish
the Grace of the Gospel; for they say that the Grace of God is
wonderfully manifested in appointing such a Way and Method
of Salvation, by sincere Obedience, in assisting us to perform
such an Obedience, and in accepting our imperfect Obedience,
instead of perfect.

Let us therefore examine that Matter, whether their Scheme
of a Man's being justified by his own Vertue, and sincere Obedience, does derogate from the Grace of God or no; or whether
free Grace is not more exalted, in supposing as we do, that we

are justified without any manner of Goodness of our own. In order to this, I will lay down this self evident

Proposition, That *whatsoever that be, by which the abundant Benevolence of the giver is express'd, and Gratitude in the receiver is obliged, that magnifies free Grace.* This I suppose none will ever controvert or dispute.

And it is not much less evident, that it doth both *shew a more abundant Benevolence in the Giver* when he shews kindness without Goodness or Excellency in the Object, to move him to it; and that it *enhances the Obligation to gratitude in the Receiver.*

1. It shews a more abundant goodness in the Giver, when he shews kindness without any Excellency in our Persons or Actions that should move the giver to Love and Beneficence. For it certainly shews the more abundant and overflowing Goodness, or Disposition, to communicate Good, by how much the less Loveliness or Excellency there is to entice Beneficence: The *less* there is in the *receiver* to draw good Will and Kindness, it argues the *more* of the Principle of good Will and Kindness in the *Giver*; For one that has but a little of a principle of Love and Benevolence, may be *drawn* to do Good, and to shew Kindness, when there is a great deal to *draw* him, or when there is much Excellency and Loveliness in the Object to move good Will; when he whose Goodness and Benevolence is more abundant, will shew Kindness, where there is less to draw it forth; for he don't so much need to have it drawn from *without*, he has enough of the principle *within* to move him, of it self. Where there is most of the principle, there it is most sufficient for itself; and stands in least need of something without to excite it: For certainly a more abundant Goodness, more easily flows forth, with less to impell or draw it. Than where there is less; or which is the same Thing, the more any one is disposed of himself, the less he needs. From without himself, to put him upon it, or stir him up to it. And therefore his Kindness and Goodness appears the more exceeding great, when it is bestowed without *any*, Excellency or Loveliness *at all* in the *receiver*, or when the receiver is respected in the Gift, as *wholly* without Excellency: And much more still when the Benevolence of the *Giver* not only finds nothing in the *receiver* to *draw* it, but a great deal of Hatefulness to *repel* it: The

abundance of Goodness is then manifested, not only in flowing forth without any Thing extrinsick to put it forward, but in overcoming great Repulsion in the Object. And then does Kindness and Love appear most Triumphant, and wonderfully Great, when the receiver is respected in the Gift, as not only wholly without all Excellency or Beauty to attract it, but *altogether*, yea *infinitely* vile and hateful.

2. 'Tis apparent also that it enhanses the Obligation to Gratitude in the Receiver. This is agreeable to the common Sense of Mankind, that the less worthy or excellent the Object of Benevolence, or the receiver of Kindness is, the more he is obliged, and the greater Gratitude is due. He therefore is most of all obliged, that receives Kindness without *any* Goodness or Excellency in himself, but with a *total* and *universal* Hatefulness. And as 'tis agreeable to the common Sense of Mankind; so 'tis agreeable to the Word of God: How often does God in the Scripture insist on this Argument with Men, to move them to love him, and to acknowledge his Kindness? How much does he insist on this as an Obligation to Gratitude, that they are so sinful and undeserving, and ill deserving.

Therefore it certainly follows, that that Doctrine that teaches that God, when he justifies a Man, and shews him that great Kindness, as to give him a Right to eternal Life, don't do it for any Obedience, or any manner of Goodness of his; but that Justification respects a Man as ungodly, and wholly without any manner of Vertue, Beauty, or Excellency. I say, this Doctrine does certainly more exalt the free Grace of God in Justificaton, and Man's Obligation to Gratitude to him, for such a Favour, than the contrary Doctrine, *viz.* That God in shewing this Kindness to Man, respects him as sincerely obedient and vertuous, and as having something in him that is truly Excellent, and Lovely, and Acceptable in his Sight, and that this Goodness or Excellency of Man is the very fundamental Condition of the bestowment of that Kindness *on him*, or of the distinguishing him from others by that Benefit. But I hasten to a

Fourth Argument for the Truth of the Doctrine, *That to suppose that a Man is justified by his own Vertue or Obedience, derogates from the Honour of the Mediator, and ascribes that to Man's Vertue, that belongs only to the Righteousness of Christ*: It puts Man in Christs stead, and makes him his own Saviour, in a respect, in which Christ only is his Saviour: And so 'tis a Doctrine contrary to the Nature, and Design of the Gospel which is to abase Man, and to ascribe all the Glory of our Salvation to Christ the Redeemer.—It is inconsistent with the Doctrine of the Imputation of Christ's Righteousness, which is a Gospel Doctrine.

Here I would

1. Explain what we mean by the Imputation of Christ's Righteousness.

2. Prove the Thing intended by it to be true.

3. Shew that this Doctrine is utterly inconsistent with the Doctrine of our being justified by our own Vertue, or sincere Obedience.

First, I would *explain what we mean by the Imputation of Christ's Righteousness.* Sometimes the Expression is taken by our Divines in a larger Sense, for the Imputation of all that Christ did and suffered for our Redemption, whereby we are free from Guilt, and stand Righteous in the sight of God; and so implies the Imputation both of Christ's Satisfaction, and Obedience. But here I intend it in a stricter Sense, for the Imputation of that Righteousness, or moral Goodness, that consists in the Obedience of Christ. And by that Righteousness being *imputed* to us, is meant no other than this, that that Righteousness of Christ *is accepted for us, and admitted instead of that perfect inherent Righteousness that ought to be in our selves*: Christ's perfect Obedience shall be *reckoned to our Account*, so that we shall have *the Benefit of it, as tho' we had performed it our selves*: And so we suppose that a Title to eternal Life is given us as the *reward of this Righteousness.* The Scripture uses the Word *impute* in this Sense, *viz. For reckoning* any Thing belonging to any Person, *to another Person's Account*: As Philem. v. 18. *If he have wronged thee, or oweth thee ought*, put that on mine Account. In the Original it is τοῦτο ἐμοὶ ἐλλόγει: *impute that to me.* 'Tis a Word of the same Root with that which is translated impute, *Rom.* 4. 6. *To whom God* imputeth *Righteousness without Works.* And 'tis the very same Word that is used, *Rom.* 5. 13. that is translated *impute*; sin is not *imputed*, where there is no Law.

The opposers of this Doctrine suppose that there is an absurdity in it: They say that to suppose that God imputes

Christ's Obedience to us, is to suppose that God is mistaken, and thinks that we perform'd that Obedience that Christ performed. But why can't that Righteousness be *reckoned to our Account*, and be *accepted for us*, without any such absurdity? Why is there any more absurdity in it, than in a Merchant's transferring Debt or Credit from one Man's Account to another, when one Man pays a Price for another, so that it shall be accepted as if that other had paid it? Why is there any more absurdity in supposing that Christ's Obedience is imputed to us, than that his Satisfaction is imputed? If Christ has suffered the Penalty of the Law for us, and in our stead, then it will follow, that his suffering that Penalty is imputed to us, *i. e.* That it is accepted *for us*, and in our stead, and is reckon'd to our Account, as tho' *we* had suffered it. But why mayn't his *obeying the Law* of God be as rationally reckon'd to our Account, as his *suffering the Penalty of the Law*? Why may not a Price to *bring into Debt*, be as rationally transferr'd from one Person's Account to another, as a Price to *pay a Debt*—Having thus explain'd what we mean by the Imputation of Christ's Righteousness, I proceed,

Secondly, To prove that the Righteousness of Christ is thus imputed.

1. There is the very same need of Christ's *obeying the Law in our stead, in order to the Reward*, as of his *suffering the Penalty of the Law, in our stead, in order to our escaping the Penalty*; and the same Reason why one should be accepted on our Account, as the other. There is the same need of one as the other, *that the Law of God might be answered*: One was as requisite to *answer the Law* as the other, This is certain, that that was the Reason why there was need that Christ should suffer the Penalty for us, even *that the Law might be answered*; for this the Scripture plainly teaches: This is given as the Reason why Christ was made a *curse for us*, that the Law threatned a *curse to us, Gal.* 3. 10, 13. But the same Law that fixes *the curse* of God, as the *consequent* of *not continuing in all Things written is the Law to do them*, (v. 10.) has as much fixed doing those Things as an *antecedent* of living in them, (as v. 12 the next Verse but one;) There is as much of a Connection established in one Case as in the other. There is therefore exactly the same need *from the Law* of perfect Obedience being *fulfill'd*, in

order to our obtaining the Reward, as there is of Death's being *suffered*, in order to our escaping the Punishment, or the same Necessity *by the Law*, of perfect Obedience *preceeding* Life, as there is of Disobedience being *succeeded* by Death: The Law is without doubt, as much of an established Rule in one Case as in the other.

Christ by suffering the Penalty, and so making Attonement for us, only removes the Guilt of our Sins and so sets us in the same State that *Adam* was in the first Moment of his Creation: And it is no more fit, that we should obtain eternal Life, only on that Account, than that *Adam* should have the Reward of eternal Life, or of a confirmed and unalterable State of Happiness, the first Moment of his existence, without any Obedience at all. *Adam* was not to have the Reward meerly on the Account of his being innocent; if so, he would have had it fixed upon him at once, as soon as ever he was created; for he was as innocent then as he could be: But he was to have the Reward on the Account of his Activeness in Obedience; not on the Account meerly of his not having done ill, but on the Account of his *doing well*.

So on the same Account we han't eternal Life meerly on the Account of being void of Guilt, (as *Adam* was at first existence,) which we have by the *Attonement of Christ*; but on the Account of *Christ's Activeness in Obedience*, and *doing well*. Christ is our second federal Head, and is called the *second Adam*. I *Cor.* 15. 22. because he acted the Part for us, that the first *Adam* should have done: When he had undertaken for us to stand in our stead, he was looked upon, and treated as tho' he were guilty with our Guilt; and by his satisfying, or bearing the Penalty, he did as it were *free himself* from this Guilt. But by this, the *second Adam* did only bring himself into the State that the first *Adam* was in on the first Moment of his Existence, *viz.* a State of meer freedom from Guilt; and hereby indeed was free from any Obligation to suffer Punishment: But this being supposed, there was need of something further, even a positive Obedience, in order to his obtaining, as our second *Adam*, the Reward of eternal Life.

God saw meet to place Man first in a State of Trial, and not to give him a Title to eternal Life, as soon as he had made him:

because it was his will that he should first give Honour to his
Authority, by fully submitting to it, in Will and Act, and perfectly obeying his Law. God insisted upon it that his holy
Majesty and Law should have their due Acknowledgement,
and Honour from Man, such as became the Relation he stood
in to that Being that created him, before he would bestow the
Reward of confirmed and everlasting Happiness upon him;
and therefore God gave him a Law when he created him, that
he might have Opportunity, by giving due Honour to his Authority in obeying it, to obtain this Happiness. It therefore
became Christ, seeing that in assuming Man to himself, he
sought a Title to this eternal Happiness for him, after he had
broken the Law, that he himself should become subject to
God's Authority, and be in the Form of a Servant, that he
might do that honour to God's Authority for him, by his Obedience, which God at first required of Man, as the Condition
of his having a Title to that Reward. Christ came into the
World to that end, to render the Honour of God's Authority
and Law, consistent with the Salvation and eternal Life of Sinners; he came to save them, and yet withal to assert and vindicate the Honour of the Lawgiver, and his holy Law. Now if the
Sinner after his Sin was satisfied for, had eternal Life bestowed
upon him, without active Righteousness, the Honour of his
Law would not be sufficiently vindicated. Supposing this were
possible, that the Sinner himself could by suffering pay the
Debt, and afterwards be in the same State that he was in before
his Probation, that is to say, *negatively righteous*, or meerly
without Guilt; if he now at last should have eternal Life bestowed upon him, without performing that Condition of
Obedience, then God would recede from his Law, and would
give the promised Reward, and his Law never have Respect
and Honour shewn to it, in that Way of being obeyed. But
now Christ by subjecting himself to the Law and obeying of it,
has done great Honour to the Law, and to the Authority of
God who gave it: That so glorious a Person should become
subject to the Law, and fulfil it, has done much more to honour it, than if meer Man had obeyed it: It was a Thing infinitely
honourable to God that a Person of infinite Dignity was not
ashamed to call him *his God*, and to adore and obey him as

such: This was more to God's Honour than if any meer Creature, of any possible Degree of Excellency and Dignity, had so done.

'Tis absolutely necessary that in order to a Sinner's being justified, the Righteousness of some other should be reckoned to his Account; for 'tis declared that the Person justified is looked upon as (in himself) *ungodly*; but God neither *will* nor *can* justify a Person without a Righteousness; for Justification is manifestly a *forensick* Term, as the Word is used in Scripture, and the Thing a judicial Thing, or the act of a Judge: So that if a Person should be justified without a Righteousness, the Judgment would not be according to Truth: The Sentence of Justification would be a false Sentence, unless there be a Righteousness performed that is by the Judge properly looked upon as his. To say, that God don't justify the Sinner without sincere, tho' an imperfect Obedience, don't help the Case; for an imperfect Righteousness *before a Judge* is no Righteousness. To accept of something that falls short of the Rule, instead of something else that answers the Rule, is no judicial Act, or act of a Judge, but a pure Act of sovereignty. An imperfect Righteousness is no Righteousness, before a Judge; For "Righteousness (as one observes) is a relative Thing, and has always Relation to a Law: The formal Nature of Righteousness, properly understood, lies in a conformity of Actions to that which is the Rule and Measure of them." Therefore that only is Righteousness in the Sight of a Judge that answers the Law.*

---

*That it is *perfect Obedience*, that is what is called *Righteousness* in the New-Testament, and that this Righteousness or perfect Obedience is by God's fixed unalterable Rule, the Condition of Justification, is from the plain Evidence of Truth confess'd, by a certain great Man, that no Body will think to be a likely Person to be blinded by a Prejudice in favour of the Doctrine we are maintaining, and one who did not receive this Doctrine, *viz.* Mr. *Locke* in his *Reasonableness of Christianity as delivered in the Scriptures*, Vol. 2d of his Works. p. 474. "To one that thus unbiassed reads the Scripture, what *Adam* fell from is visible, was the State of *perfect Obedience*, which is called *Justice* in the New Testament, though the Word which in the Original signifies *Justice*, be translated *Righteousness*." *Ibid.* p. 476, 477. "For *Righteousness*, or an *exact Obedience* to the Law, seems by the Scripture to have a Claim of Right to eternal Life, *Rom.* 4. 4. *To him that worketh, i. e.* does the Works of the Law, *is the Reward not reckon'd of Grace but of Debt.*—On the other Side it seems the *unalterable* purpose of the divine Justice, that no *unrighteous* Person, no

The Law is the Judges Rule: If he pardons and hides what *really is*, and so don't pass Sentence according to what Things are in themselves, he either don't act the Part of a Judge, or else judges falsly. The very Notion of judging, is to determine *what is*, and *what is not*, in any one's Case. The Judge's Work is two fold, it is to determine first what is *fact*, and then whether what is *in fact* be according to *Rule*, or according to the *Law*. If a Judge has no *Rule* or Law established before Hand, by which he should proceed in judging, he has no Foundation to go upon in judging, he has no Opportunity to be a Judge; nor is it possible that he should do the Part of a Judge. To judge without a Law or Rule by which to judge, is impossible, for the very Notion of judging is to determine whether the Object of Judgment be according to Rule; and therefore God has declared that when he acts as a Judge he will not justifie the

---

one that is *Guilty of any Breach of the Law*, should be in Paradise; but that the Wages of Sin should be to every Man, as it was to *Adam*, an exclusion of him out of that happy State of Immortality, and bring Death upon him. And this is so conformable to the *eternal and established Law of right and wrong*, that it is spoke of too as it could not be otherwise.—Here then we have the *standing and fixed Measures of Life and Death*; Immortality and Bliss belonging to the *Righteous: These who have lived in an exact Conformity to the Law of God* are out of the Reach of Death: But an exclusion from Paradise, and loss of Immortality, is the Portion of *Sinners*, of all those *who have any way broke that Law*, and failed of a *compleat Obedience to it, by the Guilt of any one Transgression*. And thus Mankind by the Law are put upon the Issues of Life or Death, as they are *Righteous* or *Unrighteous, Just or Unjust, i. e. exact Performers, or Transgressors of the Law*." Again in 477. p. "The Law of Works then in short, is that Law which requires *perfect Obedience*, without any Remission or Abatement; so that by that Law a Man cannot be just, or justified, without an *exact Performance of every Title*. Such a *perfect Obedience* in the New Testament is termed δικαιοσύνη, which we translate *Righteousness*." In which last Passage 'tis also to be noted, that Mr. *Locke* by the *Law of Works* don't understand the *Ceremonial Law*, but the *Covenant of Works*: as he more fully expresses himself in the next Paragraph but one. "Where this Law of Works was to be found, the New Testament tells us, *viz*. in the Law delivered by *Moses*. John 1. 17. *The Law was given by Moses, but Grace and Truth came by Jesus Christ*. Chap. 7. 19. *Did not* Moses *give you the Law*, says our Savior, *and yet none of you keep the Law*. And this is the Law which he speaks of, *v*. 28. *This do and thou shalt live*. This is that which St. *Paul* so often stiles *the Law* without any other Distinction. Rom. 2. 13. *Not the Hearers of the Law are just before God, but the doers of the Law are justified*. 'Tis needless to quote any more Places, his Epistles are all full of it, especially this to the Romans."

Wicked, and cannot *clear* the *Guilty*; and by parity of Reason cannot *justify* without *Righteousness*.

And the Scheme of the old Law's being abrogated, and a new Law introduced, won't help at all in this difficulty; for an imperfect Righteousness cannot answer the Law of God that we are under, whither that be an old one or a new one; for every Law requires perfect Obedience to it self: Every Rule whatsoever requires perfect conformity to it self; 'tis a Contradiction to suppose otherwise; for to say, that there is a Law that don't require *perfect* Obedience to it self, is to say that there is a Law that don't require *all* that it requires. That Law that *now* forbids Sin, is certainly the Law that we are *now* under, (let that be an old one, or a new one;) or else it is *not sin*: That which is *not* forbidden, and is the Breach of *no* Law, is *no* Sin: But if we are *now* forbidden to commit Sin, then 'tis by a Law that we are *now* under, for surely we are neither under the forbiddings, nor commandings of a Law that we are not under. Therefore if all Sin is *now* forbidden, then we are now under a Law that requires perfect Obedience; and therefore nothing can be accepted as a Righteousness in the sight of our Judge, but perfect Righteousness. So that our Judge cannot justify us, unless he sees a perfect Righteousness, some way belonging to us, either performed by our selves, or by another, and justly and duly reckon'd to our Account.

God doth in the Sentence of Justification pronounce a Man *perfectly Righteous*, or else he would need a further Justification after he is justified: His Sins being removed by Christ's Atonement, is not sufficient for his Justification; for justifying a Man, as has been already shewn, is not meerly pronouncing him *innocent* or *without Guilt*, but standing Right, with regard to the Rule that he is under, and righteous unto Life; But this according to the established Rule of Nature, Reason, and Divine Appointment, is a positive perfect Righteousness.

As there is the *same need that* Christ's Obedience *should* be reckon'd to our Account, as that his Atonement should; so there is *the same Reason why it should*. As if Adam had persevered, and finished his course of Obedience, we should have received *the Benefit* of his Obedience, as much as now we have the Mischief of his Disobedience; so in like Manner, there is Reason that we should receive the Benefit of the second Adam's

Obedience, as of his *Atonement* of our Disobedience: Believers are represented in Scripture as being so *in* Christ, as that they are legally one, or accepted as one, by the supreme Judge: Christ has assumed our Nature, and has so assumed all, in that Nature, that belong to him, into such an Union with himself, that he is become their Head, and has taken them to be his Members: And therefore what Christ has done in our Nature, whereby he *did honour* to the Law and Authority of God by his *Acts*, as well as the *Reparation to the honour* of the Law, by his *sufferings*, is reckon'd to the believers Account; so as that the believer should be *made happy*, because it was so *well*, and *worthily done* by his Head, as well as *freed from being miserable*, because he has *suffered* for our *ill and unworthy doing*.

When Christ had once undertaken with God, to stand for us, and put himself under our Law, *by that Law* he was obliged to *suffer* and *by the same Law* he was obliged to obey: By the same Law, after he had taken Man's Guilt upon him, he *himself* being our Surety, could not be *acquitted*, 'till he had *suffer'd*, nor *rewarded* 'till he had *obey'd*: But he was not acquitted as a private Person, but as our Head, and Believers are acquitted in his Acquittance; nor was he accepted to a Reward for his Obedience as a private Person, but as our Head, and we are accepted to a Reward in his Acceptance. The Scripture teaches us, that when Christ was raised from the dead, he was justified; which Justification as I have already shewn, implies, both his Acquittance from our Guilt, and his Acceptance to the Exaltation and Glory that was the Reward of his Obedience: But believers, as soon as they Believe are admitted to partake with Christ in this his Justification: Hence we are told that he was *raised again for our Justification*, Rom. 4. 25. Which is true, not only of that Part of his Justification that consists in his Acquittance; but also his Acceptance to his Reward: The Scripture teaches us that he is exalted, and gone to Heaven, to take Possession of Glory *in our Name*, as our forerunner. *Heb.* 6. 20. We are as it were both *raised up together with Christ*, and also *made to set together with Christ, in heavenly Places, and in Him*. Eph. 2. 6.

If it be objected here, that there is *this Reason*, why what Christ suffer'd should be accepted on our Account rather than the Obedience he performed, that *he was obliged to Obedience*

for himself, but was not obliged to suffer but only on our Account.
To this I answer, that Christ was not obliged on his own Account, to *undertake* to obey. Christ in his original Circumstances, was in no subjection to the Father, being altogether equal with him: He was under no Obligation to put himself in Man's stead, and under Man's Law, or to put himself into any State of Subjection to God whatsoever. There was a Transaction between the Father and the Son, that was antecedent to Christ's becoming Man, and being made under the Law, wherein he undertook to put himself under the Law, and both to obey and to suffer; in which Transaction these Things were already virtually done in the sight of God; as is evident by this, that God acted on the Ground of that Transaction, justifying and saving Sinners, as if the Things undertaken had been actually performed long before they were performed indeed. And therefore, without doubt, in order to the estimating the value, and validity of what Christ did and suffered, we must look back to that Transaction, wherein these Things were first undertaken, and vertually done in the sight of God, and see what Capacity and Circumstances Christ acted in then, and then we shall find that Christ was under no manner of Obligation, either to obey the Law, or suffer the Penalty of it. After this he was equally under Obligation to both; for henceforward he stood as our Surety or Representative: And therefore this consequent Obligation, may be as much of an Objection against the validity of his suffering the Penalty, as against his Obedience. But if we look to that original Transaction between the Father and the Son, wherein both these were undertaken and accepted, as vertually done in the sight of the Father, we shall find Christ acting with Regard to both, as one perfectly in his own Right, and under no manner of previous Obligation, to hinder the validity of either.

2. To suppose that all that Christ does is only to make Atonement for us by suffering, is to make him our Saviour but in Part. 'Tis to rob him of half his Glory as a Saviour. For if so, all that he does is to deliver us from Hell, he don't purchase Heaven for us. The adverse Scheme supposes that he purchases Heaven for us, in this Sense, that he satisfies for the imperfections of our Obedience, and so purchases that our sincere imperfect Obedience might be accepted as the Condition

of eternal Life; and so purchases an opportunity for us to obtain Heaven by our own Obedience. But to purchase Heaven for us, only in this Sense, is to purchase it in no Sense at all; for all of it comes to no more than a Satisfaction for our Sins, or removing the Penalty by suffering in our stead: For all the purchasing they speak of, that our imperfect Obedience should be accepted, is only his satisfying for the sinful imperfection of our Obedience, or (which is the same Thing) making Atonement for the Sin that our Obedience is attended with. But that is not purchasing Heaven, meerly to set us at Liberty again, that we may go, and get Heaven by what we do our selves: all that Christ does is only to pay a Debt for us; there is no positive Purchase of any Good.—We are taught in Scripture that Heaven is *purchased* for us, 'tis called the *purchased Possession*, Eph. I. 14. The Gospel proposes the eternal Inheritance, not to be acquired, as the first Covenant did, but as already acquired and purchased: But he that pays a Man's Debt for him, and so delivers him from Slavery, can't be said to purchase an Estate for him, meerly because he sets him at Liberty, so that henceforward he has an opportunity to get an Estate by his own hand Labour. So that according to this Scheme, the Saints in Heaven have no Reason to thank Christ for purchasing Heaven for 'em, or redeeming them *to God*, and making them King's and Priest's, as we have an Account that they do in *Rev.* 5. 9.

3. Justification by the Righteousness and Obedience of Christ, is a Doctrine that the Scripture teaches in very full Terms. *Rom.* 5. 18, 19. *By the* Righteousness of one, *the free Gift came upon all Men unto* Justification *of Life. For as by one Man's Disobedience many were made Sinners, so by the* Obedience of one *shall many be made* Righteous. Here in one verse we are told that we have *Justification* by Christ's *Righteousness*; and that there might be no room to understand the Righteousness spoken of meerly of Christ's Atonement, by his suffering the Penalty, in the next verse, 'tis put in other Terms, and asserted that 'tis by Christ's *Obedience* that we are made *Righteous.* 'Tis scarce possible any Thing should be more full and determined: The Terms, taken singly, are such as do fix their own meaning, and taken together, they fix the meaning of each other: The Words shew that we are justified by that *Righteousness* of Christ, that consists in his *Obedience*, and that we are made

righteous or *justified* by that *Obedience* of his, that is his *Righteousness*, or *moral Goodness* before God.

Here possibly it may be objected, that this Text means only that we are justified by Christ's *passive Obedience*.

To this I answer, whether we call it active or passive, it alters not the Case as to the present Argument, as long as 'tis evident by the Words that 'tis not meerly under the Notion of an *Atonement* for Disobedience, or a *Satisfaction* for Unrighteousness, but under the Notion of a positive *Obedience*, and a *Righteousness*, or moral Goodness, that it *justifies* us, or makes us righteous; because both the Words *Righteousness*, and *Obedience* are used, and used too as the Opposites to *Sin* and *Disobedience*, and an *Offence*. *Therefore, as by the* Offence *of one, Judgment came upon all Men to Condemnation; even so by the* Righteousness *of one, the free Gift came upon all Men to Justification of Life. For as by one Man's* Disobedience, *many were made* Sinners; *so by the* Obedience *of one, shall many be made* Righteous. Now what can be meant by *Righteousness*, when spoken of as the Opposite to Sin, or *moral Evil*, but only *moral* Goodness? What is the Righteousness that is the Opposite of an *Offence*; but only the *Behaviour that is well pleasing*? and what can be meant by Obedience, when spoken of as the Opposite of *Disobedience*, or going *contrary to a Command*, but a positive *obeying* and an actual *complying with the Command*? So that there is no Room for any invented Distinction of *active* and *passive*, to hurt the Argument from this Scripture, as long as 'tis evident by it as any Thing can be, that Believers are justified by the Righteousness and Obedience of Christ under the Notion of his *moral Goodness*, and his *positive obeying*, and *actual complying* with the *Commands* of God, and that *Behaviour* of his, that, because of it's Conformity to his Commands, was *well-pleasing* in his Sight. This is all that ever any need to desire to have granted in this Dispute.

By this it appears, that if Christ's dying be here included in the Words, Righteousness and Obedience, it is not meerly as a Propitiation, or bearing a Penalty of a broken Law in our stead, but as his voluntary submitting and yielding himself to those Sufferings, was an *Act* of Obedience to the Father's Commands, and so was a Part of his *positive Righteousness*, or *moral Goodness*.

Indeed all Obedience considered under the Notion of Obedience or Righteousness, is something *active*, something that is done in active and voluntary Compliance with a Command; whether that which we do in Obedience is something easy, and something that may be done without Suffering, or whether it be something hard and difficult; yet as 'tis Obedience, or Righteousness, or moral Goodness, it must be considered as something voluntary and active. If any one is commanded to go through Difficulties, and Sufferings, and he in Compliance with this command voluntarily does it, he properly obeys in so doing; and as he voluntarily does it, in Compliance with a Command, his Obedience is as *active* as any whatsoever: 'Tis the same sort of Obedience, a Thing of the very same Nature, as when a Man in Compliance with a Command, does a piece of hard Service, or goes through hard Labour; and there is no Room to distinguish between such Obedience and other that is more easy, and to make a different sort of Obedience of it, as if it were a Thing of quite a different Nature, by such opposite Terms as active and passive: all the Distinction that can be pretended, is that which is between obeying an easy Command and a difficult one: But is not the *Obedient it self* of the same Nature, because the *Commands to be obeyed*, are some of 'em more difficult than others? Is there from hence any Foundation to make two Species of Obedience, one active and the other passive?— There is no Appearance of any such Distinction ever entring into the Hearts of any of the Penmen of Scripture.

'Tis true that of late, when a Man refuses to obey the Precept of an human Law, but patiently yields himself up to suffer the Penalty of the Law, it is called *passive Obedience*; but this I suppose is only a modern Use of the Word *Obedience*; be sure it is a Sense of the Word, that the Scripture is a perfect Stranger to; and it is improperly called Obedience, unless there be such a *Precept* in the Law, that he shall yield himself patiently to suffer, to which his so doing shall be an active voluntary Conformity. There may in some Sense be said to be a Conformity to the Law in a Person's Suffering the Penalty of the Law; but no other Conformity to the Law is properly called Obedience to it, but an active voluntary Conformity to the Precepts of it: The Word *obey* is often found in Scripture with Respect to the Law of God to Man, but never in any other Sense.

'Tis true that Christ's willingly undergoing those Sufferings which he endured, is a great Part of that Obedience or Righteousness by which we are justified. The Sufferings of Christ are respected in Scripture under a two-fold Consideration, either meerly as his being substituted for us, or put into our stead, in suffering the *Penalty of the Law*; and so his Sufferings are considered as a *Satisfaction* and *Propitiation for Sin*: Or as he in *Obedience to a Law*, or Command of the Father, voluntarily submitted himself to those Sufferings, and actively yielded himself up to bear them; and so they are considered as his *Righteousness*, and a Part of his *active Obedience*. Christ underwent Death in Obedience to the Command of the Father, Psalm 40. 6, 7, 8. *Sacrifice and Offering thou didst not desire*: mine Ears hast thou bored. *Burnt Offering and Sin Offering thou hast not required: Then said I*, lo I come; *in the Volume of the Book it is written of me: I delight to* do thy Will, *O my God, and thy* Law *is within my Heart.* John 10. 17, 18. I lay down my Life *that I may take it again: No Man taketh it from me; but* I lay it down of my self: *I have Power to lay it down, and I have Power to take it again*: This Commandment have I received of my Father. John 18. 11. *The Cup which my Father hath given me to drink, shall I not drink it?* And this is Part, and indeed the principal Part of that active Obedience that we are justified by.

It can be no just Objection against this, that that Command of the Father to Christ that he should lay down his Life, was no Part of the Law that we had broken, and therefore that his obeying this Command could be no Part of that Obedience that he performed for us, because we needed that he should obey no other Law for us, but only that which we had broken or fail'd of obeying: For altho' it must be the same legislative Authority, whose Honour is repair'd by Christ's Obedience, that we have injured by our Disobedience; yet there is no need that the Law that Christ obeys should be precisely the same that *Adam* was to have obeyed, in that Sense that there should be no *positive* Precepts wanting, nor any added: There was wanting the Precept about the forbidden Fruit, and there was added the ceremonial Law. The Thing required was perfect Obedience: It is no Matter whether the *positive* Precepts were the same, if they were equivalent. The positive Precepts that

Christ was to obey, were much more than equivalent to what was wanting, because infinitely more difficult, particularly the Command that he had received to lay down his Life, which was his principal Act of Obedience, and which above all others, is concern'd in our Justification. As that *Act of Disobedience* by which we *fell*, was Disobedience to a positive Precept that Christ never was under, *viz.* that of abstaining from the Tree of Knowlege of Good and Evil, so that *Act of Obedience* by which principally we are *redeemed*, is Obedience to a positive Precept that *Adam* never was under, *viz.* the Precept of laying down his Life. It was sutable that it should be a positive Precept that should try both *Adam*'s and *Christ*'s Obedience: Such Precepts are the greatest and most proper Trial of Obedience, because in them, the meer Authority and Will of the Legislator is the sole Ground of the Obligation, (and nothing in the nature of the Things themselves;) and therefore they are the greatest Trial of any Person's Respect to that Authority and Will.

The Law that Christ was subject to, and obeyed, was in some Sense the same that was given to *Adam*: There are innumerable particular Duties that are required by the Law only conditionally; and in such Circumstances, are comprehended in some great and general Rule of that Law. Thus for Instance, there are innumerable Acts of *Respect* and *Obedience to Men*, which are required by the Law of Nature, (which was a Law given to *Adam*,) which yet ben't required absolutely, but upon many prerequisite Conditions; as that there be Men standing in such Relations to us, and that they give forth such Commands, and the like: So many Acts of *Respect* and *Obedience to God*, are included, in like manner, in the moral Law conditionally, or such and such Things being supposed, as *Abraham*'s going about to sacrifice his Son, the *Jews* circumcising their Children when eight Days old, and *Adam*'s not eating the forbidden Fruit; they are virtually comprehended in that great general Rule of the moral Law, that we should obey God, and be subject to him in whatsoever he pleases to command us. Certainly the moral Law does as much require us to obey God's *positive* Commands, as it requires us to obey the *positive* Commands of our Parents. And thus all that *Adam*, and all that Christ was commanded, even his observing the Rites and

Ceremonies of the Jewish Worship, and his laying down his Life, was virtually included in this same great Law.*

'Tis no Objection against the last mention'd Thing, even Christ's laying down his Life, its being included in the moral Law given to *Adam*, because that Law it self allowed of no Occasion for any such Thing; for the moral Law virtually includes all right Acts, on all *possible Occasions*, even Occasions that the Law it self allows not: Thus we are obliged by the moral Law to mortify our Lusts, and repent of our Sins, tho' that Law allows of no Lust to mortify, or Sin to repent of.

There is indeed but one great Law of God, and that is the same Law that says, *if thou sinnest thou shalt die*, and *cursed is every one that continues not in all Things contained in this Law to do them*: All Duties of positive Institution, are virtually comprehended in this Law: and therefore if the *Jews* broke the ceremonial Law, it exposed 'em to the Penalty of the Law, or Covenant of Works, which threaten'd, *thou shalt surely die*. The Law is the eternal and unalterable *Rule of Righteousness*, between God and Man, and therefore is the Rule of *Judgment*, by which all that a Man does shall be either justified or condemn'd; and no Sin exposes to Damnation, but by the Law: So now he that refuses to obey the Precepts that require an Attendance on the Sacraments of the New-Testament, is exposed to Damnation, by Virtue of the Law or Covenant of Works.—It may moreover be argued, that all Sins whatsoever, are Breaches of the Law or Covenant of Works, because all

---

*Thus Mr. *Locke* in his *Reasonableness of Christianity, as deliver'd in the Scriptures*, Vol. 2d. of his Works, p. 478. "Nay *whatever God requires any where to be done*, without making any Allowance for Faith, that is a Part of the Law of Works. So that forbidding *Adam* to eat of the Tree of Knowlege, was Part of the Law of Works: Only we must take notice here, that some of God's positive Commands being for peculiar Ends, and suted to particular Circumstances of Times, Places and Persons, have a limited, and only temporary Obligation, by Virtue of God's positive Injunction: Such as was that Part of *Moses*'s Law, which concerned the outward Worship, or political Constitution of the *Jews*, and is called the ceremonial and *judaical* Law". Again, p. 479. "Thus then, as to the Law in short, the civil and ritual Part of the Law delivered by *Moses* obliges not Christians, though to the *Jews it were a Part of the Law of Works; it being a Part of the Law of Nature*, that Men ought to obey every positive Law of God, whenever he shall please to make any such Addition to the Law of his Nature".

Sins, even Breaches of the positive Precepts, as well as others, have Atonement by the Death of Christ: But what Christ died for, was to satisfy the Law, or to bear the Curse of the Law; as appears by *Gal.* 3. 10, 11, 12, 15. and *Rom.* 8. 3, 4.

So that Christ's laying down his Life might be Part of that Obedience by which we are justified, tho' it was a positive Precept, not given to *Adam*. It was doubtless Christ's main Act of Obedience, because it was Obedience to a Command that was attended with immensely the greatest Difficulty, and so to a Command that was the greatest Trial of his Obedience; his Respect shown to God in it, and his Honour to God's Authority, was proportionably great: It is spoken of in Scripture as Christ's principal Act of Obedience. Philip. 2. 7, 8. *But made himself of no Reputation, and took upon him* the Form of a Servant, *and was made in the Likeness of Man, and being found in Fashion as a Man, he humbled himself and* became obedient unto Death, even the Death of the Cross. Heb. 5. 8. *Though he were a Son, yet learned he Obedience by the Things that he suffered.* It was mainly by this Act of Obedience, that Christ purchased so glorious a Reward *for himself*; as in that Place in Philippians 2. 8, 9. *He became obedient unto Death, even the Death of the Cross*; wherefore *God also hath highly exalted him, and given him a Name, which is above every Name.* And it therefore follows from what has been already said, that it's mainly by this Act of Obedience, that Believers in Christ also, have the Reward of Glory, or come to partake with Christ in his Glory. We are as much saved by the Death of Christ, as his yielding himself to die *was an Act of Obedience*, as we are, as it was *a Propitiation for our Sins*: For as it was not the only Act of Obedience that merited, he having performed meritorious Acts of Obedience through the whole Course of his Life; so neither was it the only Suffering that was propitiatory; all his Sufferings through the whole Course of his Life being propitiatory, as well as every Act of Obedience meritorious: Indeed this was his *principal Suffering*; and it was as much his *principal Act of Obedience.*

Hence we may see how that the Death of Christ did not only make Atonement, but also merited eternal Life; and hence we may see how by the Blood of Christ we are not only redeemed from Sin, but *redeemed unto God*; and therefore the

Scripture seems every where to attribute the whole of Salvation to the Blood of Christ: This precious Blood is as much the main Price by which *Heaven is purchased*, as 'tis the main Price by which we are *redeemed from Hell*. The positive Righteousness of Christ, or *that Price* by which he merited, was of equal Value with *that* by which he satisfied; for indeed it was the same Price: *He spill'd his Blood* to satisfy, and by Reason of the infinite Dignity of his Person, his Sufferings were looked upon as of infinite Value, and equivalent to the eternal Sufferings of a finite Creature: And *he spill'd his Blood* out of Respect to the Honour of God's Majesty, and in Submission to his Authority, who had commanded him so to do, and his Obedience therein was of infinite Value; both because of the Dignity of the Person that performed it, and because he put himself to infinite Expence to perform it, whereby the infinite Degree of his Regard to God's Authority appear'd.

One would wonder what *Arminians* mean by Christ's *Merits*: They talk of Christ's *Merits* as much as any Body, and yet deny the Imputation of Christ's positive Righteousness: What should there be that any one should merit or deserve any Thing by, besides Righteousness or Goodness? If any Thing that Christ did or suffered, merited or deserved any Thing, it was by Virtue of the Goodness, or Righteousness, or Holiness of it: If Christ's Sufferings and Death merited Heaven, it must be because there was an excellent Righteousness, and transcendent moral Goodness in that Act of laying down his Life: And if by that excellent Righteousness he merited Heaven *for us*, then surely that Righteousness is *reckon'd to our Account*, that we have the Benefit of it, or which is the same Thing, *it is imputed to us*.

Thus I hope I have made it evident, that the Righteousness of Christ is indeed imputed to us. I proceed now to the

Third, and last Thing under this Argument, That this Doctrine of the Imputation of Christ's Righteousness is utterly inconsistent with the Doctrine of our being justified by *our own* Virtue, or sincere Obedience. If Acceptance to God's Favour, and a Title to Life, be given to Believers, as the Reward of *Christ's Obedience*, then it is not given as the Reward of *our own Obedience*. *In what respect soever*, Christ is our Saviour, that doubtless excludes our being our own Saviours, *in that same respect*. If we can be our own Saviours *in the same respect* that Christ is, it will thence follow that the Salvation of Christ is needless, *in that respect*; according to the Apostle's reasoning, *Gal.* 5. 4. *Christ is render'd of no effect unto you, whosoever of you are justified by the Law.* Doubtless 'tis Christ's Prerogative *to be our Saviour*, in that Sense wherein *he is our Saviour*: And therefore if it be by his Obedience that we are justified, then it is not by our own Obedience.

Here perhaps it may be said, that a Title to Salvation is not directly given as the Reward of our Obedience; for that is not by any Thing of ours; but only by Christ's Satisfaction and Righteousness; but yet an *Interest in* that Satisfaction and Righteousness is given as a Reward of our Obedience.

But this don't at all help the Case; for this is to ascribe as much to our Obedience, as if we ascribed Salvation to it *directly*, without the Intervention of Christ's Righteousness: For it would be as great a Thing for God to give us Christ, and his Satisfaction and Righteousness, in Reward for our Obedience, as to give us Heaven *immediately*; it would be as great a Reward, and as great a Testimony of respect to our Obedience. And if God gives as great a Thing as Salvation, for our Obedience, why could he not as well give Salvation it self directly? And then there would have been no need of Christ's Righteousness. And indeed if God gives us *Christ*, or an Interest in him, properly in reward of our Obedience, he does really give us *Salvation* in reward for our Obedience; for the former implies the latter; yea it implies it as the greater implies the less. So that indeed it exalts our Vertue and Obedience more, to suppose that God gives us Christ in reward of that Vertue and Obedience, than if he should give Salvation without Christ.

The Thing that the Scripture guards, and militates against, is our imagining that 'tis our own Goodness, Vertue, or Excellency, that instates us in God's Acceptance and Favour. But to suppose that God gives us an Interest in Christ in Reward for our Vertue, is as great an Argument that it instates us in God's Favour, as if he bestowed a title to eternal Life, as it's *direct reward*. If God gives us an Interest in Christ, as a reward *of our Obedience*, it will then follow, that we are instated in God's Acceptance and Favour by our own Obedience, antecedent to our having an Interest in Christ. For a rewarding any one's Excellency, evermore supposes Favour and Acceptance on the Account of that Excellency: It is the very Notion of a reward, that it is a good Thing, bestowed in Testimony of respect and Favour for the Vertue or Excellency rewarded. So that it is not by Vertue of our Interest in Christ and his Merits, that we first come into Favour with God, according to this Scheme; for we are in God's Favour before we have any Interest in those Merits; in that we have an Interest in those Merits given as a Fruit of God's Favour for our own Vertue. If our Interest in Christ be the Fruit of God's Favour, then it can't be the Ground of it. If God did not accept us, and had no Favour for us, for our own Excellency, he never would bestow so great a Reward upon us, as a Right in Christ's Satisfaction and Righteousness. So that such a Scheme destroys it self, for it supposes that Christ's Satisfaction and Righteousness are necessary for us to recommend us to the Favour of God; and yet supposes that we have God's Favour and Acceptance, before we have Christ's Satisfaction and Righteousness, and have these given as *a Fruit of God's Favour*.

Indeed, neither Salvation it self, nor Christ the Saviour, are given as a Reward of any Thing in Man: They are not given as a Reward of Faith, nor any Thing else of ours: We are not united to Christ as a Reward of our Faith, but have Union with him *by Faith*, only as Faith is the very *Act of uniting*, or *closing* on our Part. As when a Man offers himself to a Woman in Marriage, he don't give himself to her as a Reward of her receiving him in Marriage: Her receiving him is not consider'd as a worthy Deed in her, for which he rewards her, by giving himself to her; but 'tis by her receiving him, that *the Union is made*, by which she hath him for her Husband: 'Tis on her Part the Unition it self.—By these Things it appears how contrary to the Scheme of the Gospel of Christ, their Scheme is, who say that Faith justifies *as a Principle of Obedience*, or as a *leading Act of Obedience*; or (as others) *the Sum*, and *Comprehension* of all evangelical Obedience: For by this 'tis the Obedience or Virtue that is in Faith, that is the Thing, that gives it its justifying Influence; and that is the same thing as to say, that we are justified by our own Obedience, Virtue or Goodness.

Having thus considered the Evidence of the Truth of the Doctrine, I proceed now to the

IIId Thing proposed, viz. *To shew in what Sense the Acts of a christian Life, or of evangelical Obedience, may be looked upon to be concern'd in this Affair.*

From what has been said already, it is manifest that they cannot have any Concern in this Affair as *good Works*, or by Virtue of any moral Goodness in them; not as Works of the Law, or as that moral Excellency, or any Part of it, that is the answering or Fulfilment of that great, and universal, and everlasting Law or Covenant of Works, that the great Lawgiver has established, as the highest and unalterable Rule of Judgment; which Christ alone answers, or does any Thing towards it.

And it having been shown, out of the Scripture, that 'tis only by Faith, or the Soul's receiving, and uniting to the Saviour, that has wrought out Righteousness, that we are justified; it therefore remains that the Acts of a christian Life can't be concerned in this Affair any otherwise, than as they imply, and are the Expressions of Faith, and may be looked upon as so many Acts of Reception of Christ the Saviour.

But the determining what concern Acts of christian Obedience can have in Justification in this Respect, will depend on the resolving of another Point, *viz.* Whether any other Act of Faith besides the first Act, has any Concern in our Justification, or how far Perseverance in Faith, or the continued and renewed Acts of Faith, have Influence in this Affair.

And it seems manifest that Justification is *by* the first Act of Faith, in some Respects, in a Peculiar Manner, because a Sinner is actually and finally justified as soon as he has performed one Act of Faith; and Faith in its first Act does, virtually at least, depend on God for Perseverance, and intitles to this among other Benefits. But yet the Perseverance of Faith is not excluded in this Affair; it is not only certainly connected with Justification, but it is not to be excluded from that on which the Justification of a Sinner has a *Dependance*, or that *by which* he is justified.

I have shown that the Way in which Justification has a Dependance on Faith, is that it is the Qualification on which the

Congruity of an Interest in the Righteousness of Christ depends, or wherein such a Fitness consists. But the Consideration of the Perseverance of Faith, can't be excluded out of this Congruity or Fitness, for it is congruous that he that believes in Christ should have an Interest in Christ's Righteousness, and so in the eternal Benefits purchased by it, because Faith is that by which the Soul hath Union or Oneness with Christ, and there is a natural Congruity in it, that they that are one with Christ, should have a joint Interest with him in his eternal Benefits; but yet this Congruity depends on its being an *abiding Union*. As it is needful that the Branch should abide in the Vine, in order to its receiving the lasting Benefits of the Root, so it is necessary that the Soul should abide in Christ, in order to its receiving those lasting Benefits of God's final Acceptance and Favour. John 15. 6, 7. *If a Man abide not in me, he is cast forth as a Branch. If ye abide in me, and my Words abide you, ye shall ask what ye will, and it shall be done unto you.* Verses 9, 10. *Continue ye in my Love: If ye keep* (or abide in) *my Commandments, ye shall abide in my Love, even as I have kept my Father's Commandments, and abide in his Love.* There is the same Reason why it is necessary that the Union with Christ should remain, as why it should be begun, why it should continue to be, as why it should once be: If it should be begun without remaining, the beginning would be in vain. In order to the Soul's being *now* in a justified State, and *now* free from Condemnation, 'tis necessary that it should *now* be in Christ, and not only that it should once have been in him. Rom. 8. 1. *There is no Condemnation to them* are in *Christ Jesus.* The Soul is saved *in* Christ, as being now in him, when the Salvation is bestowed, and not meerly as remembering that it *once was* in him. Philip. 3. 9. *That I may be FOUND IN HIM, not having mine own Righteousness, which is of the Law, but that which is through the Faith of Christ, the Righteousness which is of God by Faith.* 1 John 2. 28. *And now little Children abide in him; that when he shall appear, we may have Confidence, and not be ashamed before him at his Coming.* In order to Persons being blessed after Death, 'tis necessary not only that they should once be in him, but that they should *die in him.* Rev. 14. 13. *Blessed are the Dead that die in the Lord.*

And there is the same Reason why Faith, the uniting Qualification, should remain, in order to the Union's remaining, as why it should once be, in order to the Union's once being.

So that altho' the Sinner is actually, and finally justified on the first Act of Faith, yet the Perseverance of Faith, even then, comes into Consideration, as one Thing on which the Fitness of Acceptance to Life depends. God in the Act of Justification, which is passed on a Sinner's first believing, has Respect to Perseverance, as being virtually contain'd in that first Act of Faith; and 'tis looked upon and taken by him that justifies, as being as it were a Property in that Faith that then is: God has Respect to the Believer's Continuance in Faith, and he is justified by that, as tho' it already were, because by divine Establishment it shall follow; and it being by divine Constitution connected with that first Faith, as much as if it were a Property in it, it is then consider'd as such, and so Justification is not suspended; but were it not for this it would be needful that it should be suspended, till the Sinner had actually persevered in Faith.

And that it is so, that God in that Act of final Justification that he passes at the Sinner's Conversion, has Respect to Perseverance in Faith, and future Acts of Faith, as being virtually implied in that first Act, is further manifest by this, *viz*. That in a Sinner's Justification at his Conversion, there is virtually contained a Forgiveness as to eternal, and deserved Punishment, not only of all past Sins, but also of all future Infirmities and Acts of Sin, that they shall be guilty of; because that first Justification is decisive and final. And yet Pardon, in the Order of Nature, properly follows the Crime, and also follows those Acts of Repentance and Faith that respect the Crime pardoned, as is manifest both from Reason and Scripture. *David* in the beginning of *Psalm* 32. speaks of the Forgiveness of Sins of his, that were doubtless committed long after he was first godly, as being consequent on those Sins, and on his Repentance and Faith with Respect to them; and yet this Forgiveness is spoken of by the Apostle in the 4th of *Romans*, as an Instance of Justification by Faith. Probably the Sin *David* there speaks of is the same that he committed in the Matter of *Uriah*, and so the Pardon the same with that Release from Death, or eternal Punishment, that the Prophet *Nathan* speaks of, 2 Sam. 12. 13. *The Lord also hath put away thy Sin; thou shalt not die.* Not only does the Manifestation of this Pardon follow the Sin in the

Order of Time, but the Pardon it self, in the Order of Nature, follows *David*'s Repentance and Faith with Respect to this Sin; for it is spoken of in the 32nd *Psalm* as depending on it.

But in as much as a Sinner, in his first Justification, is forever justified and freed from all Obligation to eternal Punishment, it hence of necessity follows, that future Faith and Repentance are beheld in that Justification, as virtually contained in that first Faith and Repentance; because Repentance of those future Sins, and Faith in a Redeemer, with Respect to them, or, at least, the Continuance of that Habit and Principle in the Heart, that has such an actual Repentance and Faith, in it's Nature and Tendency, is now made sure by God's Promise.

If Remission of Sins, committed after Conversion, in the order of Nature, follows that Faith and Repentance that is after them, then it follows that future *Sins* are respected in the first Justification, no otherwise than as future *Faith* and *Repentance* are respected in it. And future Repentance and Faith are looked upon by him that justifies, as virtually implied in the first Repentance and Faith, in the same Manner as Justification from future Sins, is virtually implied in the first Justification; which is the Thing that was to be proved.

And besides, if no other Act of Faith could be concerned in Justification but the first Act, it will then follow that Christians ought never to seek Justification by any other Act of Faith. For if Justification is not to be obtain'd by after Acts of Faith, then surely it is not a Duty to seek it by such Acts: And so it can never be a Duty for Persons after they are once converted, by Faith to seek to God; or believingly to look to him for the Remission of Sin, or Deliverance from the Guilt of it, because Deliverance from the Guilt of Sin is Part of what belongs to Justification. And if it ben't proper for Converts by Faith to look to God through Christ for it, then it will follow that it is not proper for them to pray for it, for christian Prayer to God for a Blessing is but an Expression of Faith in God for that Blessing; Prayer is only the Voice of Faith. But if these Things are so, it will follow that that Petition of the Lord's Prayer, *forgive us our Debts*, is not proper to be put up by Disciples of Christ, or to be used in christian Assemblies, and that Christ improperly directed his Disciples to use that Petition, when they were all of them, except *Judas*, converted before. The

Debt that Christ directs his Disciples to pray for the Forgiveness of, can mean nothing else, but the Punishment that Sin deserves, or the Debt that we owe to divine Justice, the ten thousand Talents we owe our Lord. To pray that God would forgive our *Debts*, is undoubtedly the same Thing as to pray that God would release us from Obligation to *due Punishment*; but releasing from Obligation to the Punishment due to Sin, and forgiving the Debt that we owe to divine Justice, is what appertains to Justification.

And then to suppose that no after Acts of Faith are concerned in the Business of Justification, and so that it is not proper for any ever to seek Justification by such Acts, would be forever to cut off those Christians, that are doubtful concerning their first Act of Faith, from the Joy and Peace of Believing. As the Business of a justifying Faith is to obtain Pardon and Peace with God, by looking to God and trusting in him for these Blessings, so the Joy and Peace of that Faith, is in the Apprehension of Pardon and Peace obtain'd by such a Trust. This a Christian that is doubtful of his first Act of Faith, can't have from that Act, because, by the Supposition, he is doubtful whether it be an Act of Faith, and so whether he did obtain Pardon and Peace by that Act: The proper Remedy, in such a Case, is now by Faith to look to God in Christ for these Blessings; but he is cut off from this Remedy, because he is uncertain whether he has Warrant so to do, for he don't know but that he has believed already; and if so, then he has no Warrant to look to God by Faith for these Blessings now, because by the Supposition no new Act of Faith is a proper Means of obtaining these Blessings. And so he can never properly obtain the Joy of Faith; for there are Acts of true Faith, that are very weak Acts, and the first Act may be so as well as others; it may be like the first Motion of the Infant in the Womb, it may be so weak an Act that the Christian by examining of it, may never be able to determine whether it was a true Act of Faith or no; and it is evident from Fact, and abundant Experience, that many Christians are forever at a Loss to determine which was their first Act of Faith. And those Saints that have had a good Degree of Satisfaction concerning their Faith, may be subject to great Declensions and Falls, in which Case they are liable to great Fears of eternal Punishment; and the proper Way of Deliverance is to forsake their Sin by Repentance, and by Faith now to come to Christ for Deliverance from the deserved eternal Punishment; but this it would not be, if Deliverance from that Punishment, was not this Way to be obtain'd.

But what is a still more plain and direct Evidence of what I am now arguing for, is that that Act of Faith that *Abraham* exercised in the great Promise of the Covenant of Grace that God made to him, of which it is espresly said, Gen. 15. 6. *It was accounted to him for Righteousness*; which is the grand Instance and Proof, that the Apostle so much insists upon throughout the 4th Chapter of *Romans*, and 3d. Chapter of *Galatians*, to confirm his Doctrine of Justification by Faith alone, was not *Abraham*'s first Act of Faith, but was excited long after he had by Faith forsaken his own Country, *Heb.* 11. 8. and had been treated as an eminent Friend of God.

Moreover, The Apostle *Paul* in the third Chapter of *Philippians*, tells us how earnestly he sought Justification by Faith, or to win Christ and obtain that Righteousness which was by the Faith of him, in what he did after his Conversion, Verses 8, 9. *For whom I have suffered the loss of all Things, and do count them but Dung that I may win Christ, and be found in him, not having on mine own Righteousness, which is of the Law, but that which is through the Faith of Christ, the Righteousness which is of God by Faith.* And in the two next Verses he expresses the same Thing in other Words, and tells us how he went through Sufferings, and became conformable to Christ's Death, that he might be a Partaker with Christ in the Benefit of his Resurrection; which the same Apostle elsewhere teaches us, is especially Justification: Christ's Resurrection was his Justification; in this, he that was put to Death in the Flesh, was justified by the Spirit, and he that was delivered for our Offences, rose again for our Justification. And the Apostle tells us in the Verses that follow, in that third Chapter of *Philippians*, that he thus sought to attain the Righteousness which is through the Faith of Christ, and so to partake of the Benefit of his Resurrection, still, as tho' he had not already attain'd, but that he continued to follow after it.

On the whole, it appears that the Perseverance of Faith is necessary, even to the Congruity of Justification, and that not the less, because a Sinner is justified, and Perseverance promised on the first Act of Faith, but God in that Justification has

Respect not only to the past Act of Faith, but to his own Promise of future Acts, and to the fitness of a Qualification beheld as yet only in his own Promise.

And, that Perseverance in Faith is thus necessary to Salvation, not meerly as a *sine qua non*, or as an universal Concomitant of it, but by Reason of such an Influence and Dependance, seems manifest by many Scriptures; I would mention two or three; Heb. 3. 6. *Whose House are we, if we hold fast the Confidence, and the Rejoycing of the Hope, firm unto the End.* Verse 14. *For we are made Partakers of Christ, if we hold the beginning of our Confidence, stedfast unto the End.* Chap. 6. 12. *Be ye followers of them, who through Faith and Patience inherit the Promises.* Rom 11. 20. *Well, because of Unbelief they were broken off, but thou standest by Faith: Be not high-minded, but fear.*

And as the Congruity to a final Justification depends on Perseverance in Faith, as well as the first Act, so oftentimes the Manifestation of Justification in the Conscience, arises a great deal more from after Acts, than the first Act. And all the difference whereby the first Act of Faith has a Concern in this Affair that is peculiar, seems to be as it were only an accidental Difference, arising from the Circumstance of Time, or its being first in Order of Time; and not from any peculiar Respect that God has to it, or any Influence it has of a peculiar Nature, in the Affair of our Salvation.

And thus it is that a truly christian Walk, and the Acts of an evangelical, child-like, believing Obedience, are concerned in the Affair of our Justification, and seem to be sometimes so spoken of in Scripture, *viz.* as an Expression of a persevering Faith in the Son of God, the only Saviour. Faith unites to Christ, and so gives a Congruity to Justification, not meerly as remaining a dormant Principle in the Heart, but as being, and appearing in its active Expressions.

The Obedience of a Christian, so far as it is truly evangelical, and performed with the Spirit of the Son sent forth into the Heart, has all relation to Christ the Mediator, and is but an Expression of the Soul's believing Unition to Christ: All evangelical Works are Works of that Faith that worketh by Love; and every such Act of Obedience, wherein it is inward, and the Act of the Soul, is only a new effective Act of Reception of Christ, and Adherence to the glorious Saviour. Hence that of the

Apostle, Gal. 2. 20. *I live, yet not I; but Christ liveth in me; and the Life that I now live in the Flesh, is by the Faith of the Son of God.* And hence we are directed, in whatever we do, whether in Word or Deed, to do all in the Name of the Lord Jesus Christ. *Col.* 3. 17.

And that God in Justification has respect, not only to the first Act of Faith, but also to future persevering Acts, in this Sense, *viz.* as expressed in Life, seems manifest by *Rom.* 1. 17. *For therein is the Righteousness of God revealed, from Faith to Faith: As it is written, the Just shall live by Faith.* And Heb. 10. 38, 39. *Now the Just shall live by Faith; but if any Man draw back, my Soul shall have no Pleasure in him. But we are not of them that draw back unto Perdition, but of them that believe to the saving of the Soul.*

So that as was before said of Faith, so may it be said of a child-like, believing Obedience, it has no concern in Justification by any Vertue, or Excellency in it; but only as there is a Reception of Christ in it. And this is no more contrary to the Apostle's frequent Assertion of our being justified without the Works of the Law, than to say that we are justified by Faith; for Faith is as much a Work or act of christian Obedience, as the Expressions of Faith, in spiritual Life and Walk. And therefore as we say that Faith don't justify as a Work, so we say of all these effective Expressions of Faith.

This is the reverse of the Scheme of our modern Divines, who hold that Faith justifies only as an Act, or Expression of Obedience; whereas in Truth, Obedience has no concern in Justification, any otherwise than as an Expression of Faith.

I now proceed to the

IV. Thing proposed, *viz. To answer Objections.*

Object 1. We frequently find Promises of eternal Life and Salvation, and sometimes of Justification itself, made to our own Vertue and Obedience. Eternal Life is promised to Obedience, in Rom. 2. 7. *To them who by patient Continuance in well doing, seek for Glory, Honour and Immortality, eternal Life.* And the like in innumerable other Places. And Justification it self is promised to that Vertue of a forgiving Spirit or Temper in us, Mat. 6. 14. *For if ye forgive Men their Trespasses, your heavenly Father will also forgive you; but if ye forgive not Men their Trespasses, neither will your Father forgive your Tres-*

passes. All allow that Justification in great Part consists in the *forgiveness of Sins.*

To this I answer,

1. These Things being promised to our Vertue and Obedience, argues no more, than that there is a Connection between them and evangelical Obedience; which I have already observed is not the Thing in dispute. All that can be proved by Obedience and Salvation being connected *in the Promise,* is that Obedience and Salvation are *connected in fact*; which no body denies, and whether it be own'd or denied, is as has been shewn, nothing to the Purpose. There is no need that an Admission to a Title to Salvation, should be given *on the Account* of our Obedience, in order to the Promises being true. If we find such a Promise, that *he that obeys shall be saved,* or *he that is holy shall be justified,* all that is needful in order to such Promises being true, is that it *be really so,* that he that obeys *shall* be saved, and that Holiness and Justification *shall indeed* go together: That Proposition may be a Truth, that *he that obeys shall be saved,* because Obedience and Salvation are connected together *in fact*; and yet an Acceptance to a Title to Salvation not be granted upon the Account of any of our own Vertue or Obedience. What is a Promise, but only a Declaration of future Truth, for the Comfort and Encouragement of the Person to whom it is declared? Promises are conditional Propositions; and as has been already observed, it is not the Thing in Dispute, whether other Things besides Faith mayn't have the Place of the Condition in such Propositions wherein Pardon and Salvation are the *consequent.*

2. *Promises* may rationally be made to *Signs* and Evidences of Faith, and yet the *Thing promised* not be upon the Account of the *Sign,* but the *Thing signified.* Thus for Instance, human Government may rationally make Promises of such and such Priviledges, to those that can shew such *Evidences* of their being free of such a City, or Members of such a Corporation, or descended of such a Family; when it is not at all for the sake of that which is the *Evidence* or *Sign,* in it self consider'd, that they are admitted to such a Priviledge, but only, and purely, for the sake of that which it is an evidence of.

And tho' God don't stand in need of Signs to know whether we have true Faith or not, yet our own Consciences *do*; so that 'tis much for our Comfort that Promises are made to Signs of Faith. A finding in our selves a forgiving Temper and Disposition, may be a most proper and natural Evidence to our Consciences that our Hearts have, in a Sense of our own utter unworthiness, truly closed, and fallen in, with the way of free, and infinitely gracious forgiveness of *our* Sins, by Jesus Christ; whence we may be enabled, with the greater Comfort to apply to our selves the Promises of forgiveness by Christ.

3. It has been just now shown, how that Acts of evangelical Obedience are indeed concern'd in our Justification it self, and are not excluded from that Condition that Justification depends upon, without the least Prejudice to that Doctrine of Justification by Faith, without any Goodness of our own, that has been maintain'd, and therefore it can be no Objection against this Doctrine, that we have sometimes in Scripture, Promises of Pardon and Acceptance, made to such Acts of Obedience.

4. Promises of particular Benefits implied in Justification and Salvation, may especially be fitly made to such Expressions and Evidences of Faith, as they have a peculiar natural Likeness and Suitableness to: As *forgiveness* is promised to a *forgiving Spirit* in us; *obtaining Mercy* is fitly promised to *mercifulness* in us, and the like: And that upon several Accounts; they are the most natural Evidences of our Heart's closing with those Benefits by Faith; for they do especially shew the sweet Accord and Consent that there is between the Heart and these Benefits; and by Reason of the natural Likeness that there is between the *Vertue* and the *Benefit*, the one has the greater Tendency to bring the other to mind; the Practice of the Vertue tends the more to renew the Sense, and refresh the Hope of the Blessing promised; and also to convince the Conscience of the justice of being denied the Benefit, if the Duty be neglected.

And besides the Sense and Manifestation of divine Forgiveness in our own Consciences; yea and many Exercises of God's forgiving Mercy, as it respects God's fatherly Displeasure, that are granted *after Justification*, thro' the course of a christian's Life, may be given as the proper *Rewards* of the Vertue of a forgiving Spirit, and yet this not be at all to the prejudice of the Doctrine we have maintain'd; as will more fully appear, when we come to answer another Objection hereafter to be mention'd.

Object. 2. Our own Obedience, and inherent Holiness, is necessary to prepare Men *for Heaven*; and therefore is doubtless what recommends Persons to God's Acceptance, as the Heirs *of Heaven*.

To this I answer,

1. Our own Obedience being necessary, in order to a Preparation for an actual bestowment of Glory, is no Argument that 'tis the Thing, upon the Account of which we are accepted to a Right to it. God *may*, and *does*, do many Things to prepare the Saints for Glory, after he has accepted them as the Heirs of Glory. A Parent may do much to prepare a Child for an Inheritance in it's Education, after the Child is an Heir: yea there are many Things necessary to fit a Child for the actual Possession of the Inheritance, that ben't necessary in order to it's having a Right to the Inheritance.

2. If every Thing, that is necessary to prepare Men for Glory, must be the proper Condition of Justification, then perfect Holiness is the Condition of Justification. Men must be made perfectly Holy, before they are admitted to the Enjoyment of the blessedness of Heaven; for there must *in no wise* enter in there any spiritual Defilement: And therefore when a Saint dies he leaves all his Sin and Corruption, when he leaves the Body.

Object. 3. Our Obedience is not only indissolubly connected with Salvation, and Preparatory to it, but the Scripture expresly speaks of bestowing eternal Blessings as *Rewards* for the good Deeds of the Saints. Math. 10. 42. *Whosoever shall give to drink, unto one of these little ones, a Cup of cold Water, only in the Name of a Disciple, he shall in no wise lose his Reward.* 1 Cor. 3. 8. *Every Man shall receive his own Reward, according to his own Labour.* And in many other Places. This seems to militate against the Doctrine that has been maintain'd, two Ways, 1. The bestowing a Reward carries in it a Respect to a *moral Fitness*, in the Thing rewarded, to the Reward: The very Notion of a Reward being a Benefit bestowed in Testimony of Acceptance *of*, and respect *to*, the goodness or amiableness of some Qualification or Work, in the Person rewarded. And besides the Scripture seems to explain it self in this Matter, in *Rev.* 3. 4. *Thou hast a few Names, even in* Sardis, *which have not defiled their Garments; and they shall walk with me in White*; for they are Worthy. This is here given as the Reason why they should have such a Reward, *because they were Worthy*: Which, tho' we suppose it to imply no proper *Merit*, yet it at least implies a moral fitness, or that the excellency of their Vertue in God's Sight, *recommends* them to such a Reward; which seems directly repugnant to what has been supposed, *viz.* That we are accepted, and approved of God, as the Heirs of Salvation, not out of Regard to the Excellency of our own Vertue or Goodness, or any *moral fitness* therein to such a Reward, but only on the Account of the Dignity, and *moral fitness* of Christ's Righteousness. 2. Our being eternally rewarded for our own Holiness, and good Works, necessarily supposes that our future Happiness will be greater or smaller, in some Proportion, as our own Holiness and Obedience is more or less; and that there are different Degrees of Glory, according to different Degrees of Vertue and good Works, is a Doctrine very expresly, and frequently taught us in Scripture. But this seems quite inconsistent with the Saints all having their future blessedness as a Reward of Christ's Righteousness: For if Christ's Righteousness be imputed to all, and this be what entitles each one to Glory, then 'tis the same Righteousness that entitles one to Glory, which entitles another: But if all have Glory as the Reward of the *same Righteousness*, why han't all the *same Glory*? Don't the same Righteousness merit as much Glory, when imputed to one, as when imputed to another.

In *Answer* to the *first* Part of this Objection, I would observe, that it don't argue that we are justified by our good Deeds, that we shall have eternal Blessings in Reward for them; for 'tis in *Consequence of our Justification*, that our good Deeds become *rewardable*, with spiritual and eternal Rewards. The acceptableness, and so the rewardableness of our Vertue is not antecedent to Justification, but follows it, and is built entirely upon it; which is the reverse of what those in the adverse Scheme of Justification suppose, *viz.* That Justification is built on the Acceptableness and Rewardableness of our Vertue. They suppose that a saving Interest in Christ is given as a Reward of our Vertue, or (which is the same Thing,) as a Testimony of God's Acceptance of our Excellency, in our Vertue. But the contrary is true; that God's respect to our Vertue, as our amiableness in his Sight, and his Acceptance of it as rewardable, is entirely built on our Interest in Christ already established. So that that Relation to Christ, whereby Believers in Scripture Language, are said to be *in* Christ, is the very Foundation of our Vertues, and good Deeds, being accepted of God, and so of their being rewarded; for a Reward is a Testimony of Acceptance. For we, and all that we do, are accepted only *in the beloved*, Eph. 1. 6. Our Sacrifices are acceptable, only through our Interest in him, and through his Worthiness, and Preciousness, being as it were made ours. 1 Pet. 2. 4, 5. To whom coming *as unto a living Stone, disallowed indeed of Men, but chosen of God and* precious; *ye also as lively Stones*, are built *up a spiritual House, an holy Priesthood, to offer up spiritual Sacrifices*, acceptable to God by Jesus Christ. Here a being actually built on this Stone, *precious to God*, is mentioned as all the Ground of the *Acceptableness* of our good Works to God, and their becoming, *also precious* in his Eyes. So Heb. 13. 21. *Make you perfect in every good Work, to do his Will, working in you that which is* well pleasing in his Sight, through Jesus Christ. And hence we are directed, whatever we offer to God, to offer it in Christ's Name, as expecting to have it accepted no other Way, than from the Value that God has to that Name. Col. 3. 17. *And whatsoever ye do, in Word or Deed, do all in the Name of the Lord Jesus, giving Thanks to God, and the Father by him.* To act in Christ's Name, is to act under him, as our Head, and as having him to stand for us, and represent us to God ward.

The Reason of this may be seen, from what has been already said, to shew that it is not meet that any Thing in us, should be accepted of God, as any Excellency of our Persons, until we are actually in Christ, and justified through him. The Loveliness of the Vertue of fallen Creatures, is nothing in the Sight of God, till he beholds them in Christ, and clothed with his Righteousness. 1. Because till then we stand condemned before God, by his own holy Law, to his utter Rejection, and Abhorrence, And, 2. Because we are infinitely Guilty before him, and the Loveliness of our Vertue bears no Proportion to our Guilt; and must therefore pass for nothing before a strict Judge. And, 3. Because our good Deeds, and vertuous Acts themselves, are in a Sense corrupt, and the hatefulness of the Corruption of them, if we are beheld as we are in our selves, or seperate from Christ, infinitely outweighs the Loveliness of the Good that is in them: So that if no other Sin was considered, but only that which attends the Act of Vertue itself, the Loveliness vanishes into nothing in Comparison of it: And therefore the Virtue must pass for nothing, out of Christ. Not only are our best Duties defiled, in being attended with the Exercises of Sin and Corruption, that precede them and follow them, and are *intermingled with holy Acts*; but even the *holy Acts themselves*, and the gracious Exercises of the godly, tho' the Act most simply considered is good, yet take the Acts in their Measure, and Dimensions, and the manner in which they are exerted, and they are *corrupt Acts*; that is, they are defectively corrupt, or sinfully defective; there is that defect in them, that may well be called the Corruption of them; that defect is properly Sin, an Expression of a vile Sinfulness of Heart, and what tends to provoke the just anger of God; not because the Exercise of Love and other Grace, is not equal to God's loveliness; for 'tis impossible the Love of Creatures (Men or Angels) should be so; but because the Act is so very disproportionate to the Occasion given for Love or other Grace, considering God's loveliness, and the Manifestation that is made of it, and the exercises of Kindness, and the capacity of human Nature, and our Advantages, (and the like) together. A negative Expression of Corruption may be as truly Sin, and as just Cause of Provocation, as a positive. Thus if a Man, a worthy & excellent Person, should from meer Generosity and Goodness, exceedingly lay out himself, and should with great Expence and Suffering, save another's Life, or redeem him from some extream Calamity; and when he had done all, that other Person should never thank him for it, or express the least Gratitude any way; this would be a negative Expression of his Ingratitude and Baseness; but is Equivalent to an *Act* of Ingratitude, or *positive* exercise of a base unworthy Spirit; and is truly an Expression of it, and brings as much Blame, as if he by some positive Act, had much injured another Person. And so it would be, (only in a lesser Degree,) if the Gratitude was but very small, bearing no Proportion to the Benefit and Obligation; as if for so great and extraordinary a Kindness, he should express no more Gratitude than would have been becoming towards a Person that had only given him a cup of Water when thirsty, or shewn him the Way in a Journey, when at a loss, or had done him some such small Kindness: If he should come to his Benefactor to express his Gratitude, and should do after this manner, he might truly be said to act unworthily and odiously; he would shew a most ungrateful Spirit: And his doing after such a Manner might justly be abhorr'd by all: And yet the Gratitude, that little there is of it, most simply considered, and so far as it goes, is good. And so it is with respect to our exercise of Love, and Gratitude, and other Graces towards God, they are defectively corrupt and sinful, and take 'em as they are, in their Manner, and Measure, might justly be odious, and provoking to God, and would necessarily be so, were we beheld out of Christ: For in that this Defect is Sin, it is *infinitely hateful*; and so the hatefulness of the very Act, infinitely outweighs the Loveliness of it; because all Sin has infinite hatefulness and heinousness; but our Holiness has but little Value and Loveliness, as has been elsewhere demonstrated.

Hence, tho' it be true that the Saints are rewarded for their good Works, yet it is for Christ's sake only, and not for the Excellency of their Works in themselves considered, or beheld seperately from Christ; for so they have no excellency in God's sight, or acceptableness to him, as has now been shewn. 'Tis acknowledged that God in rewarding the Holiness and good Works of Believers, does in some respect give them Happiness as a Testimony of his Respect to the Loveliness of their Holiness and good Works in his Sight; for that is the very Notion of a Reward: But in a very different Sense from what would have been, if Man had not fallen; which would have been to bestow eternal Life on Man, as a Testimony of God's Respect to the Loveliness of what Man did, considered as in it self, and as in Man, seperately by himself, and not beheld as a Member of Christ: In which Sense also, the Scheme of Justification we are opposing, necessarily supposes, the Excellency of our Virtue to be respected and rewarded; for it supposes a saving Interest in Christ *it self* to be given as a Reward of it.

Two Things come to pass, relating to the Saints Reward for their inherent Righteousness, by Virtue of their Relation to Christ. 1. The Guilt of their Persons is all done away, and the Pollution and Hatefulness that attends, and *is in*, their good

Works, is hid. 2. Their Relation to Christ adds a *positive* Value and Dignity to their good Works, in God's Sight. That little Holiness, and those faint and feeble Acts of Love, and other Grace, receive an exceeding Value in the Sight of God, by Virtue of God's beholding them as in Christ, and as it were Members of one so infinitely Worthy in his Eyes; and that because God looks upon the *Persons*, as Persons of greater Dignity on this Account. Isai 43. 4. *Since thou wast precious in my Sight, thou hast been honourable.* God, for Christ's Sake, and because they are Members of his own righteous and dear Son, sets an exceeding Value upon their Persons; and hence it follows, that he also sets a great Value upon their good Acts and Offerings. The same Love and Obedience, in a Person of greater Dignity and Value in God's Sight, is more valuable in his Eyes, than in one of less Dignity. Love and Respect (as has been before observed,) is valuable, in Proportion to the Dignity of the Person, whose Love it is; because, so far as any one gives his Love to another, he gives *himself*, in that he gives his Heart: But this is a more excellent Offering, in Proportion as the Person whose *self* is offered, is more worthy. Believers are become immensely more honourable in God's Esteem, by Virtue of their Relation to Christ, than Man would have been, considered as by himself, tho' he had been free from Sin; as a mean Person becomes more honourable when married to a King. Hence God will probably reward the little weak Love, and poor and exceeding imperfect Obedience of Believers in Christ, with a more glorious Reward, than he would have done *Adam*'s perfect Obedience. According to the Tenour of the first Covenant, the Person was to be accepted and rewarded, only for the Work's Sake; but by the Covenant of Grace, the Work is accepted and rewarded, only for the Person's Sake; the Person being beheld antecedently, as a Member of Christ, and clothed with his Righteousness. So that tho' the Saints inherent Holiness is rewarded, yet this very Reward is indeed, not the less founded on the Worthiness and Righteousness of Christ: None of the Value that their Works have in his Sight, nor any of the Acceptance they have with him, is out of Christ, and out of his Righteousness; but his Worthiness as Mediator, is the prime and only Foundation on which all is built, and the universal Source whence all arises. God indeed doth great

Things out of Regard to the Saints Loveliness, but 'tis only as a secondary and derivative Loveliness, as it were.—When I speak of a derivative Loveliness, I don't mean only, that the *Qualifications themselves*, that are accepted as lovely, are derived from Christ, and are from his Power and Purchase; but that the *Acceptance of them* as a Loveliness, and all the Value that is set upon them, and all their Connection with the Reward, is founded *in*, and derived *from* Christ's Righteousness and Worthiness.

If we suppose that not only higher Degrees of Glory in Heaven, but Heaven it self, is in some Respect given in Reward for the Holiness, and good Works of the Saints, in this secondary and derivative Sense, it won't prejudice the Doctrine we have maintain'd. 'Tis no Way impossible that God may bestow Heaven's Glory wholly out of Respect to Christ's Righteousness, and yet in Reward for Man's inherent Holiness, in different Respects, and different Ways. It may be only Christ's Righteousness, that God has respect to, for its own Sake, the independent Acceptableness, and Dignity of it being sufficient of it self, to recommend all that believe in Christ, to a Title to this Glory; and so it may be only by this that Persons *enter* into a Title to Heaven, or have their prime Right to it: And yet God may also have Respect to the Saints own Holiness, *for Christ's Sake*, and as deriving a Value from Christ's Merit, which he may testify in bestowing Heaven upon them. The Saints being beheld as Members of Christ, their Obedience is looked upon by God, as something of Christ's, it being the Obedience of the Members of Christ; as the *Sufferings* of the Members of Christ, are looked upon, in some Respect, as the *Sufferings* of Christ. Hence the Apostle speaking of his Sufferings, says Col. 1. 24. *Who now rejoyce in my Sufferings for you*, and fill up that which is behind of the Afflictions of Christ in my Flesh. To the same Purpose is Matth. 25. 35, &c. *I was an hungred, naked, sick, and in Prison*, &c. And so that in Rev. 11. 8. *And their dead Bodies shall lie in the Street of the great City, which spiritually is called Sodom, and Egypt*, where also our Lord was crucified.

By the Merit and Righteousness of Christ, such Favour of God towards the Believer may be obtained, as that God may hereby, be already, as it were disposed to make them perfectly and eternally happy: But yet this don't hinder, but that God in his Wisdom, may choose to bestow this perfect and eternal Happiness, in this Way, *viz.* in some Respect, as a Reward of their Holiness, and Obedience: 'Tis not impossible but that the Blessedness may be bestowed as a Reward for that which is done after that an Interest is already obtain'd in that Favour, which (to speak of God after the Manner of Men) disposes God to bestow the Blessedness. Our heavenly Father may already have that Favour for a Child, whereby he may be thoroughly ready to give the Child an Inheritance, *because he is his Child*; which he is by the Purchase of Christ's Righteousness; and yet that don't hinder but that it should be possible, that the Father may choose to bestow the Inheritance on the Child, in a Way of Reward for his Dutifulness, and behaving becoming a Child. And so great, and exceeding a Reward, may not be judged more than a meet Reward for his Dutifulness; but that so great a Reward *is judged meet*, don't arise from the Excellency of the Obedience, absolutely considered, but from his standing in so near, and honourable a Relation to God, as that of a Child, *which is obtained only by the Righteousness of Christ*. And thus the Reward, and the Greatness of it, arises properly from the Righteousness of Christ; tho' it be indeed in some sort the Reward of their Obedience. As a Father might justly esteem the Inheritance, no more than a meet Reward for the Obedience of his Child, and yet esteem it more than a meet Reward for the Obedience of a Servant. The Favour whence a Believer's heavenly Father bestows the eternal Inheritance, and his Title as an Heir, is founded in that Relation he stands in to him as a Child, purchased by Christ's Righteousness; tho' he in Wisdom, chooses to bestow it in such a Way, as therein to testify his Acceptance of the Amiableness of his Obedience in Christ.

Believers having a Title to Heaven by Faith antecedent to their Obedience, or it's being absolutely promised to them before, don't hinder but that the actual Bestowment of Heaven may also be a Testimony of God's Regard to their Obedience, tho' performed afterwards. Thus it was with *Abraham*, the Father and Pattern of all Believers: God bestowed upon him that Blessing of multiplying his Seed as the Stars of Heaven, and causing that in his Seed all the Families of the Earth should be blessed, in Reward for his Obedience, in Offering up his

Son *Isaac*, Gen. 22. 16, 17, 18. *And said, by my self have I sworn, saith the Lord*; for because thou hast done this Thing, and hast not withheld thy Son, thine only Son, *that in blessing I will bless thee; and in multiplying I will multiply thy Seed, as the Stars of Heaven, and as the Sand which is upon the Sea Shore, and thy Seed shall possess the Gate of his Enemies, and in thy Seed shall all the Nations of the Earth be blessed*; because thou hast obeyed my Voice. And yet the very same Blessings had been from time to time promised to *Abraham*, in the most positive Terms, and the Promise with great Solemnity, confirmed and sealed to him; as *Chap.* 12. 2, 3. *Chap.* 13. 16. *Chap.* 15. 1, 4, 5, 6, 7, *&c. Chap.* 17. *throughout. Chap.* 18. 10, 18.

From what has been said we may easily solve the Difficulty arising from that Text, in Rev. 3. 4. *They shall walk with me in white, for they are worthy.* Which is parallel with that Text in Luke 20. 35. *But they which shall be accounted worthy to obtain that World, and the Resurrection from the Dead*—. I allow (as in the Objection) that this *Worthiness* does doubtless denote a moral Fitness to the Reward, or that God looks on these glorious Benefits a meet Testimony of his Regard to the Value which their Persons and Performances have in his Sight.

1. God looks on these glorious Benefits as a meet Testimony of his Regard to the Value which their Persons have in his Sight. But he sets this Value upon their Persons purely for Christ's Sake: They are such Jewels, and have such Preciousness in his Eyes, only because they are beheld in Christ, and by Reason of the Worthiness of the Head, they are the Members of, and the Stock they are grafted into. And this Value that God sets upon them on this Account is so great, that God thinks meet from Regard to it to admit them to such exceeding Glory. The Saints on the Account of their Relation to Christ are such precious Jewels in God's Sight, that they are thought *worthy* of a Place in his own Crown. *Mal.* 3. 17. *Zech.* 9. 16. So far as the Saints are said to be *valuable* in God's Sight, upon whatever Account they are so, so far may they properly be said to be *worthy*, or meet for that Honour that is answerable to that Value or Price which God sets upon them. A Child, or Wife of a Prince, is worthy to be treated with great Honour, and therefore if a mean Person should be adopted to be a Child of a Prince, or should be espoused to a Prince, it would

be proper to say that she was worthy of such and such Honour and Respect, and there would be no Force upon the Words in saying that she ought to have such Respect paid her, *for she is worthy*, tho' it be only on the Account of her Relation to the Prince that she is so.

2. From the Value God sets upon their Persons, for the Sake of Christ's Worthiness, he also sets a high Value on their Virtues and Performances. Their *meek and quiet Spirit is of great Price in his Sight*. Their Fruits are *pleasant Fruits*, their Offerings are *an Odour of sweet Smell* to him: And that because of the Value he sets on their Persons, as has been already observed and explained. This Preciousness, or high Valuableness of Believers is a moral Fitness to a Reward, and yet this Valuableness is all *in* the Righteousness of Christ, that is the Foundation of it. The Thing that Respect is had to, is not the Excellency that is in them, *seperately by themselves*, or in their Virtue *by it self*, but to the Value that *in God's Account* arises thereto on other Considerations; which is the natural import of the Manner of Expression in Luke 20. 35. *They which shall be* accounted worthy, *to obtain that World*, &c. And Luke 21. 36. *That ye may be* accounted worthy *to escape all these Things that shall come to pass, and to stand before the Son of Man*. 2 Thess. 1. 5. *That ye may be* accounted worthy *of the Kingdom of God, for which ye also suffer*.

There is a vast Difference between this Scheme, and what is supposed in the Scheme of those that oppose the Doctrine of Justification by Faith alone. This lays the Foundation of *first Acceptance* with God, and all *actual Salvation* consequent upon it, wholly in Christ and his Righteousness. On the contrary, in their Scheme, a Regard to Man's own Excellency or Virtue is supposed to be *first*, and to have the Place of the first Foundation in *actual Salvation*, tho' not in that *ineffectual Redemption*, which they suppose common to all: They lay the Foundation of all *discriminating Salvation* in Man's own Virtue and moral Excellency: This is the very bottom Stone in this Affair; for they suppose that it is from Regard to our Virtue, that even a *special* Interest in Christ it self is given. The Foundation being thus contrary, the whole Scheme becomes exceeding diverse and contrary; the one Scheme is an *evangelical* Scheme, the other a *legal* one; the one is utterly inconsistent with our being justified by Christ's Righteousness, the other not at all.

From what has been said we may understand what has been before mention'd, *viz.* How that not only is that Forgiveness of Sin that is granted in Justification indissolubly connected with a forgiving Spirit in us, but there may be many Exercises of forgiving Mercy that may properly be granted in Reward for our forgiving those that trespass against us: For none will deny but that there are many Acts of divine Forgiveness towards the Saints, that don't presuppose an unjustified State immediately preceeding that Forgiveness; none will deny that Saints, that never fell from Grace or a justified State, do yet commit many Sins which God forgives afterwards, by laying aside his fatherly Displeasure. This Forgiveness may be in Reward for our Forgiveness, without any Prejudice to the Doctrine that has been maintained, as well as other Mercies and Blessings *consequent on Justification.*

With Respect to the *second* Part of the Objection, that relates to the different Degrees of Glory, and the seeming Inconsistence there is in it, that the Degrees of Glory in different Saints should be greater or lesser according to their inherent Holiness and good Works, and yet that every ones Glory should be purchased with the Price of the very same imputed Righteousness.

I *answer*, That Christ by his Righteousness purchased for every one, compleat and perfect Happiness, *according to his Capacity*: But this don't hinder but that the Saints being of *various Capacities*, may have *various Degrees of Happiness*, and yet all their Happiness be the Fruit of Christ's Purchase. Indeed it can't be properly said that Christ purchased any particular Degree of Happiness, so that the Value of Christ's Righteousness in the Sight of God, is sufficient to raise a Believer *so high*, in Happiness, and *no higher*; and so that if the Believer were made happier, it would exceed the Value of Christ's Righteousness: But in general, Christ purchased eternal Life, or perfect Happiness for all, according to their several Capacities. The Saints are as so many Vessels, of different Sizes, cast into a Sea of Happiness, where every Vessel is full; this Christ purchased for all: But after all 'tis left to God's sovereign Pleasure to determine the Largeness of the Vessel; Christ's

Righteousness meddles not with this Matter. Eph. 4. 4, 5, 6, 7. *There is one Body, and one Spirit; even as ye are called in one Hope of your Calling; one Lord, one Faith, one Baptism*, &c.— *But unto every one of us, is given Grace according to the Measure of the Gift of Christ.* God may dispense in this Matter according to what Rule he pleases, not the less for what Christ has done: He may dispense either without Condition, or upon what Condition he pleases to fix. 'Tis evident that Christ's Righteousness meddles not with this Matter; for what Christ did, was to fulfil the Covenant of Works; but the Covenant of Works did not meddle at all with this: if *Adam* had persever'd in perfect Obedience, he and his Posterity would have had perfect and full Happiness; every ones Happiness would have so answer'd his Capacity, that he would have been compleatly blessed; but God would have been at Liberty to have made some of one Capacity, and others of another as he pleased. The Angels have obtained eternal Life, or a State of confirmed Glory by a Covenant of Works, whose Condition was perfect Obedience; but yet some are higher in Glory than others, according to the several Capacity that God, according to his sovereign Pleasure, hath given them. So that it being still left with God, notwithstanding the perfect Obedience of the second *Adam*, to fix the Degree of each ones Capacity, by what Rule he pleases, he hath been pleased to fix the Degree of Capacity, and so of Glory, by the Proportion of the Saints Grace and Fruitfulness here: He gives higher Degrees of Glory, in Reward for higher Degrees of Holiness and good Works, *because it pleases him*; and yet all the Happiness of each Saint is indeed the Fruit of the Purchase of Christ's Obedience. If it had been but one Man, that Christ had obeyed and died for, and it had pleased God to make him of a very large Capacity, Christ's perfect Obedience would have purchased that his Capacity should be fill'd, and then *all* his Happiness might properly be said to be the Fruit of Christ's perfect Obedience; though if he had been of a less Capacity, he would not have had *so much* Happiness, by the *same* Obedience; and yet would have had as much as Christ merited for him. Christ's Righteousness meddles not with the Degree of Happiness, any otherwise than as he merits that it should be full, and perfect, according to the Capacity: And so it may be said to be concern'd in the Degree of Happiness, as *perfect* is a Degree, with Respect to *imperfect*; but it meddles not with Degrees of perfect Happiness.

This Matter may be yet better understood, if we consider that Christ and the whole Church of Saints, are as it were, one Body, of which he is the Head and they Members, of different Place and Capacity: Now the whole Body, Head and Members, have Communion in Christ's Righteousness, they are all Partakers of the Benefit of it; Christ himself the Head is rewarded for it, and every Member is Partaker of the Benefit and Reward: But it does by no Means follow, that every Part should equally partake of the Benefit; but every Part in Proportion to its Place and Capacity; the Head partakes of far more than other Parts, because it is of a far greater Capacity; and the more noble Members partake of more than the Inferiour. As it is in a natural Body that enjoys perfect Health, the Head, and the Heart, and Lungs have a greater Share of this Health, they have it more seated in them, than the Hands and Feet, because they are Parts of greater Capacity; tho' the Hands and Feet are as much in perfect Health as those nobler Parts of the Body: So it is in the mystical Body of Christ, all the Members are Partakers of the Benefit of the Righteousness of the Head; but 'tis according to the different Capacity and Place they have in the Body; and God determines that Place & Capacity as he pleases; he makes whom he pleases the Foot, and whom he pleases the Hand, and whom he pleases the Lungs, &c. 1 Cor. 12. 18. *God hath set the Members, every one of them, in the Body, as it hath pleased him.* And God *efficaciously* determines the Place, and Capacity of every Member, by the different Degrees of Grace, and Assistance in the Improvement of it, here in this World: Those that he intends for the highest Place in the Body, he gives them most of his Spirit, the greatest Share of the divine Nature, the Spirit and Nature of Christ Jesus *the Head*, and that Assistance whereby they perform the most excellent Works, and do most abound in them.

Object. 4. It may be objected against what has been supposed, *viz.* That Rewards are given to our good Works only in Consequence of an Interest in Christ, or in Testimony of God's Respect to the Excellency or Value of them in his Sight, as built on an Interest in Christ's Righteousness already obtain'd, *that the Scripture speaks of an Interest in Christ it self, as being given out of Respect to our moral Fitness.* Matth. 10. 37, 38, 39. *He that loveth Father or Mother more than me, is not* worthy of me: *He that loveth Son or Daughter more than me, is not* worthy of me: *He that taketh not up his Cross, and followeth after me, is not* worthy of me. *He that findeth his Life shall lose it,* &c. *Worthiness* here, at least signifies a moral Fitness, or an Excellency or Virtue that recommends: And this Place seems to intimate as tho' it were from Respect to a moral Fitness that Men are admitted, even to an Union with Christ, and Interest in him: And therefore this Worthiness cannot be consequent on a being in Christ, and by the Imputation of his Worthiness, or from any Value that is in us, or in our Actions in God's Sight, *as beheld in Christ.*

To this I *answer*, That tho' Persons when they are accepted, are not accepted as *worthy*, yet when they are rejected, they are rejected as *unworthy*. He that don't love Christ above other Things, that treats him with such Indignity, as to set him below earthly Things, shall be treated as *unworthy* of Christ; his Unworthiness of Christ, especially in that Particular, shall be marked against him, and imputed to him: And tho' he be a professing Christian, and live in the Enjoyment of the Gospel, and has been visibly ingrafted into Christ, and admitted as one of his Disciples, as *Judas* was, yet he shall be thrust out *in Wrath, as a Punishment* of his vile Treatment of Christ. The foremention'd Words don't imply that if a Man does love Christ above Father and Mother, &c. that he would be worthy; the most they imply is, that such a visible Christian shall be treated, and thrust out, as unworthy. He that believes is not received for the Worthiness, or moral Fitness of Faith; but yet the *visible Christian* is cast out by God, for the Unworthiness and moral Unfitness of Unbelief. A being accepted as one of Christ's, is not the *Reward* of Believing; but being thrust out from being one of Christ's Disciples, after a visible Admission as such, is properly a *Punishment* of Unbelief. John 3. 18, 19. *He that believeth on him is not condemned; but he that believeth not is condemned already, because he hath not believed on the Name of the only begotten Son of God: And this is the Condemnation, that Light is come into the World, and Men loved Darkness rather than Light, because their Deeds were Evil.* Salvation is promised to Faith as a free Gift, but Damnation is threaten'd to Unbelief as a Debt, or Punishment due to Unbelief. They that believed in the Wilderness, did not enter into *Canaan*, because of the Worthiness of their Faith; but God sware *in his Wrath* that they that believed not should not enter in, because of the Unworthiness of their Unbelief. The admitting a Soul to an Union with Christ is an *Act of free and sovereign Grace*; but an excluding at Death, and at the Day of Judgment, those Professors of Christianity that have had the Offers of a Saviour, and enjoyed great Privileges as God's People, is a *judicial Proceeding*, and a just Punishment of their unworthy Treatment of Christ. The Design of this Saying of Christ is to make sensible of the Unworthiness of their Treatment of Christ, that profess'd him to be their Lord and Saviour, and set him below Father and Mother, &c. and not to perswade of the Unworthiness of loving him above Father and Mother. If a Beggar should be offer'd any great and precious Gift, but as soon as offer'd, should trample it under his Feet, it might be taken from him, as unworthy to have it: Or if a Malefactor should have his Pardon offered him, that he might be freed from Execution, and should only scoff at it, his Pardon might be refused him, as unworthy of it; tho' if he had received it, he would not have had it for his Worthiness, or as being recommended to it by his Virtue; for his being a Malefactor supposes him unworthy, and its being offered him to have it only on accepting, supposes that the King looks for no Worthiness, nothing in him for which he should bestow Pardon as a Reward.—This may teach us how to understand Acts 13. 46. *It was necessary that the Word of God should first be spoken to you; but seeing ye put it from you, and judge your selves* unworthy of everlasting Life, *lo we turn to the Gentiles.*

Object. 5. 'Tis objected against the Doctrine of Justification by Faith alone, That *Repentance* is evidently spoken of in Scripture as that which is in a special Manner the Condition of *Remission of Sins*: But Remission of Sins is by all allowed to be that wherein Justification does, (at least) in great Part consist.

But it must certainly arise from a Misunderstanding of what the Scripture says about Repentance, to suppose that Faith and Repentance are two distinct Things, that in like manner are the Conditions of Justification. For 'tis most plain from the

Scripture that the Condition of Justification, or that in us by which we are justified, is but one, and that is Faith. Faith and Repentance are not *two distinct Conditions* of Justification, nor are they *two distinct Things, that together make one Condition* of Justification; but Faith comprehends the whole of that by which we are justified, or by which we come to have an Interest in Christ, and there is nothing else has a parallel Concern with it, in the Affair of our Salvation. And this the Divines on the other Side themselves are sensible of, and therefore they suppose that that Faith that the Apostle *Paul* speaks of, which he says we are justified by *alone*, comprehends in it Repentance.

And therefore, in Answer to the Objection, I would say, That when Repentance is spoken of in Scripture as the Condition of Pardon, thereby is not intended any particular Grace, or Act, properly distinct from Faith, that has a parallel Influence with it, in the Affair of our Pardon or Justification; but by Repentance is intended nothing distinct from active Conversion, (or Conversion actively considered,) as it respects the *Term from which*. Active Conversion is a Motion or Exercise of the Mind, that respects two *Terms, viz.* Sin and God: And by Repentance is meant this Conversion, or active Change of the Mind, so far as it is conversant about the *Term from which*, or about *Sin*. This is what the Word *Repentance* properly signifies; which in the Original of the New-Testament is *Metanoia* which signifies *a Change of the Mind*, or which is the same Thing, the turning or the *Conversion* of the Mind. Repentance is this turning, as it respects what is turned from. Acts 26. 20. *Whereupon, O King* Agrippa, *I shewed unto them of* Damascus, *and at* Jerusalem, *and throughout all the Coasts of* Judea, *and then to the Gentiles, that they should* repent and turn to God. Both these are the same turning, but only with Respect to opposite *Terms*; in the former is express'd the Exercise of Mind that there is about Sin in this Turning, in the other the Exercise of Mind towards God.

If we look over the Scriptures that speak of evangelical Repentance, we shall presently see that Repentance is to be understood in this Sense; as Matth. 9. 13. *I am not come to call the Righteous, but Sinners to Repentance.* Luke 13. 3. *Except ye repent, ye shall all likewise perish*; And Chap. 15. 7, 10. *There is Joy in Heaven over one Sinner that repenteth*, i. e. over one Sinner that is converted. Acts 11. 18. *Then hath God, also to the Gentiles, granted Repentance unto Life.* This is said by the Christians of the Circumcision at *Jerusalem*, upon *Peter*'s giving an Account of the Conversion of *Cornelius* and his Family, and their embracing the Gospel, tho' *Peter* had said nothing expresly about their Sorrow for Sin. And again, Acts 17. 30. *But now commandeth all Men, every where, to repent.* And Luke 16. 30. *Nay Father Abraham, but if one went to them from the Dead, they would repent.* 2 Pet. 3. 9. *The Lord is not slack concerning his Promise, as some Men count Slackness, but is Long-suffering to us ward not willing that any should perish, but that all should come to Repentance.* 'Tis plain that in these and other Places, by Repentance is meant Conversion.

Now, 'tis true, that *Conversion* is the Condition of Pardon and Justification: But if it be so, how absurd is it to say that Conversion is one Condition of Justification, and Faith another; as though they were two distributively distinct and parallel Conditions? Conversion is the Condition of Justification, because it is that great Change by which we are brought from Sin to Christ, and by which we become Believers in him: Agreeable to Matth. 21. 32. *And ye when ye had seen it*, repented *not afterwards* that ye might believe him. When we are directed to repent that our Sins may be blotted out, 'tis as much as to say, Let your Minds and Hearts be changed that your Sins may be blotted out: But if it be said, *Let your Hearts be changed* that you may be justified; and also said, *Believe* that you may be justified; does it therefore follow that the Heart's being changed is one Condition of Justification, and Believing another? But our Minds must be changed, that we may believe, and so may be justified.

And besides, evangelical Repentance, being active Conversion, is not to be treated of as a particular Grace, properly and entirely distinct from Faith, as by some it seems to have been. What is Conversion, but the sinful, alienated Soul's closing with Christ, or the Sinner's being brought to believe in Christ? That Exercise of Soul that there is in Conversion, that respects Sin, cannot be excluded out of the Nature of Faith in Christ: There is something in Faith, or closing with Christ that respects Sin, and that is evangelical Repentance: That Repentance which in Scripture is called *Repentance for the Remission of Sins*, is that very Principle or Operation of the Mind it self, that is called Faith, so far as it is conversant about Sin. Justifying Faith in a Mediator, is conversant about two Things: It is conversant about Sin or *Evil*, to be rejected and to be delivered from by the Mediator, and about *positive Good* to be accepted and obtained by the Mediator; as conversant about the former of these, it is *evangelical Repentance* or *Repentance for Remission of Sins*. Surely they must be very *ignorant*, or at least very *inconsiderate*, of the whole Tenour of the Gospel, that think that that Repentance by which Remission of Sins is obtained, can be compleated, as to all that is essential to it, without any Respect to Christ, or Application of the Mind to the Mediator, who alone has made *Atonement for Sin*: Surely so great a Part of *Salvation* as Remission of Sins, is not to be obtained, without looking, or coming, to the great and only *Saviour*. 'Tis true Repentance in its more general abstracted Nature, is only a Sorrow for Sin, and forsaking of it, which is a Duty of *natural Religion*; but *evangelical Repentance*, or Repentance for Remission of Sins, hath more than this essential to it; a Dependance of Soul on the Mediator for Deliverance from Sin is of the Essence of it.

That justifying Repentance has the Nature of Faith seems evident by Acts 19. 4. *Then said Paul, John verily baptised with the Baptism of Repentance, saying unto the People, that they should believe on him that should come after him, that is on Christ Jesus.* The latter Words, *Saying unto the People, that they should believe on him*, &c. are evidently exegetical of the former, and explain how he *preached Repentance for the Remission of Sins*: When it is said that he preached Repentance for the Remission of Sin, saying that they should believe on Christ, it can't be supposed but that 'tis intended, that his saying that they should believe on Christ, was as directing them what to do that they might obtain the Remission of Sins. So 2 Tim. 2. 25. *In Meekness instructing those that oppose themselves, if God peradventure will give them* Repentance, to the acknowleging of the Truth. That acknowleging of the Truth which there is in Believing, is here spoken of as what is attained in Repentance. And on the other Hand, that Faith includes Repentance in its Nature, is evident by the Apostle's speaking of Sin as *destroyed in Faith*, Gal. 2. 18. In the preceeding Verses, the Apostle mentions an Objection against the Doctrine of Justification by Faith alone, *viz.* that it tends to encourage Men in Sin, and so to make Christ the Minister of Sin: This Objection he rejects and refutes with this, *If I build again the Things that I destroyed, I make my self a Transgressor.* If Sin be destroyed by Faith, it must be by Repentance of Sin included in it; for we know that it is our Repentance of Sin, or the *Metanoia*, or turning of the Mind from Sin, that is our destroying our Sin.

That in justifying Faith, that directly respects *Sin*, or *the Evil to be delivered from* by the Mediator, is as follows, *A Sense of our own Sinfulness, and the Hatefulness of it, and an hearty Acknowlegement of its Defeat of the threaten'd Punishment, looking to the free Mercy of God in a Redeemer, for Deliverance from it and its Punishment.*

Concerning this, here described, three Things may be noted, 1. That 'tis the very same with that evangelical Repentance to which Remission of Sins is promised in Scripture. 2. That 'tis all of it of the Essence of justifying Faith, and is the same with that Faith, so far as it is conversant about *the Evil to be delivered from* by the Mediator. 3. That this is indeed the proper and peculiar Condition of Remission of Sins.

1. *All of it is essential to evangelical Repentance, and is indeed the very Thing meant by that Repentance, to which Remission of Sins is promised in the Gospel.* As to the former Part of the Description, *viz. A Sense of our own Sinfulness, and the Hatefulness of it, and an hearty Acknowlegement of its Desert of Wrath*, none will deny it to be included in Repentance: But this don't comprehend the whole Essence of evangelical Repentance; but what follows does also properly and essentially belong to its Nature, *looking to the free Mercy of God in a Redeemer, for Deliverance from it, and the Punishment of it.* That Repentance to which Remission is promised not only always has this *with* it, but it is contained *in* it, as what is of the proper Nature and Essence of it: And Respect is ever had to *this* in the Nature of Repentance, whenever Remission is promised to it; and it is especially from Respect to this in the Nature of Repentance, that it has that Promise made to it: If this latter Part be missing, it fails of the Nature of that evangelical Repentance to which Remission of Sins is promised: If Repentance remains in Sorrow for Sin, and don't reach to a looking to the free Mercy

of God in Christ for Pardon, 'tis not that which is the Condition of Pardon, neither shall Pardon be obtained by it. Evangelical Repentance is an Humiliation for Sin *before God*; but the Sinner never comes and humbles himself before God, in any other Repentance, but that which includes an hoping in his Mercy for Remission: If his Sorrow be not accompanied with that, there will be no coming to God in it, but a flying further from him. There is some Worship of God in justifying Repentance; but that there is not in any other Repentance, but that which has a Sense *of*, and Faith *in* the divine Mercy to forgive Sin. Psalm 130. 4. *There is Forgiveness with thee, that thou mayst be feared.* The Promise of Mercy to a true Penitent, in Prov. 28. 13. is expressed in these Terms, *Whoso confesseth, and forsaketh his Sins, shall have Mercy.* But there is Faith in God's Mercy in that *confessing.* The Psalmist in Psalm 32, speaking of the *Blessedness of the Man whose Transgression is forgiven, and whose Sin is covered, to whom the Lord imputes not Sin,* says, that *while he kept Silence, his Bones waxed old, but then he acknowleged his Sin unto God, his Iniquity he did not hide, he said he would confess his Transgression to the Lord, and then God forgave the Iniquity of his Sin.* The Manner of Expression plainly holds forth that then he began to encourage himself in the Mercy of God, when before his Bones waxed old, while he kept Silence; and therefore the Apostle *Paul*, in the 4 of *Romans* brings this Instance, to confirm the Doctrine of Justification *by Faith* alone, that he had been insisting on. When Sin is aright confess'd to God, there is always Faith in that Act: That confessing of Sin that is join'd with Despair, such as was in *Judas*, is not the Confession to which the Promise is made. In Acts 2. 38. the Direction that was given to those that were pricked in their Heart, with a Sense of the Guilt of Sin, was to *repent & be baptised in the Name of Jesus Christ, for the Remission of their Sins.* A being *baptised in the Name of Christ* for the Remission of Sins, implied *Faith in Christ* for the Remission of Sins. Repentance for the Remission of Sins, was typified of old by the Priests confessing the Sins of the People over the Scape Goat, laying his Hands on him, *Lev.* 16. 21. denoting that 'tis that Repentance and Confession of Sin only that obtains Remission, that is made over the Scape-Goat, over Christ the great Sacrifice, and with Dependance on him. Many other

Things might be produced from the Scripture, that do in like manner confirm this Point, but these may be sufficient.

2. *All the foremention'd Description is of the Essence of justifying Faith, and not different from it, so far as it is conversant about Sin, or the Evil to be deliver'd from, by the Mediator.* For it is doubtless of the Essence of justifying Faith, to *embrace Christ as a Saviour from Sin and its Punishment,* and all that is contain'd in *that Act* is contain'd in *the Nature of Faith it self*: But in *the Act* of embracing Christ as a Saviour from *our Sin* and its *Punishment,* is implied a Sense of *our Sinfulness,* and a Hatred of *our Sins,* or a rejecting them with Abhorrence, and a Sense of our Desert of their *Punishment.* An *embracing* Christ as a Saviour from Sin implies the contrary Act towards Sin, *viz rejecting* of Sin: If we fly to the Light to be delivered from Darkness, the same Act is contrary towards Darkness, *viz.* a rejecting of it. In Proportion to the Earnestness or Appetite with which we embrace Christ as a Saviour from Sin, in the same Proportion is the Abhorrence with which we reject Sin, in the same Act. Yea if we suppose there to be in the Nature of Faith as conversant about Sin, no more than the hearty embracing Christ as a Saviour from the *Punishment* of Sin, this Act will imply in it the whole of the abovemention'd Description. It implies *a Sense of our own Sinfulness*: Certainly in the hearty embracing a Saviour from the Punishment of our Sinfulness, there is the Exercise of a *Sense of our Sinfulness,* or that we be sinful: We can't heartily embrace Christ as a Saviour from the Punishment of that which we are not sensible we are guilty of. There is also in the same Act, *a Sense of our Desert of the threaten'd Punishment*: We can't heartily embrace Christ as a Saviour from that, which we be not sensible that we have deserved: For if we are not sensible that we have deserved the Punishment, we shall not be sensible that we have any Need of a Saviour from it, or at least, shall not be convinced but that the God that offers the Saviour, unjustly makes him needful; and we can't heartily embrace such an Offer. And further, there is implied in a hearty embracing Christ as a Saviour from Punishment, not only a Conviction of Conscience, that we have deserved the Punishment, such as the Devils and Damned have; but there is a hearty Acknowlegement of it, with the Submission of the Soul, so as with the Accord of the Heart, to

own that God might be *just*, and *worthy* in the Punishment. If the Heart rises against the Act or Judgment of God, in holding us obliged to the Punishment, when he offers us his Son as a Saviour from the Punishment, we cannot with the Consent of the Heart receive him in that Character: But if Persons thus submit to the Righteousness of so dreadful a Punishment of Sin, this carries in it an Hatred of Sin.

That such a Sense of our Sinfulness, and utter Unworthiness, and Desert of Punishment, belongs to the Nature of saving Faith, is what the Scripture from time to time seems to hold forth; as particularly in Matth. 15. 26, 27, 28. *But he answered and said, it is not meet to take the Children's Bread, and to cast it to Dogs. And she said, truth Lord: yet the Dogs eat of the Crumbs which fall from their Master's Table. Then Jesus answered, and said unto her, O Woman*, great is thy Faith. And Luke 7. 6, 7, 8, 9. *The Centurion sent Friends to him, saying unto him, Lord trouble not thy self, for I am not worthy that thou shouldst enter under my Roof: wherefore neither thought I my self worthy to come unto thee, but say in a Word, and my Servant shall be healed: for I am a Man set under Authority*, &c.— *When Jesus heard these Things, he marvelled at him, and turned him about and said unto the People that followed him, I say unto you*, I have not found so great Faith, *no not in Israel*. And also Verses 37, 38. *And behold a Woman in the City, which was a Sinner, when she knew that Jesus sat at Meat in the Pharisees House, brought an Alabaster Box of Ointment, and stood at his Feet behind him weeping, and began to wash his Feet with Tears, and did wipe them with the Hairs of her Head, and kissed his Feet, and anointed them with the Ointment.* Together with Verse 50. *He said unto the Woman, thy Faith hath saved thee; go in Peace.*

These Things don't necessarily suppose that *Repentance* and *Faith* are Words of just the same Signification; for 'tis only so much in justifying Faith, as respects the Evil to be delivered from, by the Saviour, that is called Repentance: And besides, both Repentance and Faith, take them only in their general Nature, and they are entirely distinct; Repentance is a Sorrow for Sin, and forsaking of it; and Faith is a trusting in God's Sufficiency and Truth: But Faith and Repentance, as evangelical Duties, or justifying Faith, and Repentance for Remission of Sins, contain more in them, and imply a Respect to a Mediator, & involve each others Nature;* though it be true, that they still bear the Name of Faith and Repentance, from those general moral Virtues, that Repentance which is a Duty of natural Religion, and that Faith that was a Duty required under the first Covenant, that are contained in this evangelical Act; which severally appear, when this Act is consider'd with Respect to its different Terms and Objects, that it is conversant about.

It may be objected here, that the Scripture sometimes mentions Faith and Repentance together, as if they were entirely distinct Things; as in Mark 1. 15. *Repent ye, and believe the Gospel.* But there is no need of understanding these as two distinct Conditions of Salvation, but the Words are exegetical one of another: It is to teach us after what Manner we must repent, *viz.* as believing the Gospel, and after what Manner we must believe the Gospel, *viz.* as repenting: These Words no more prove Faith and Repentance to be entirely distinct, than those forementioned. Matth. 21. 32. *And ye when ye had seen it, repented not afterwards, that ye might believe him.* Or those 2 Tim. 2. 25. *If per adventure God will give them Repentance, to the acknowleging of the Truth.* The Apostle in *Acts* 19. 4. seems to have Reference to these Words of *John the Baptist, John baptised with the Baptism of Repentance, saying unto the People, that they should believe,* &c. where the latter Words, as we have already observed, are to explain how he preached Repentance.

Another Scripture, where Faith and Repentance are mentioned together, is Acts 20. 21. *Testifying both to the* Jews, *and also to the* Greeks, Repentance *towards God, and* Faith *towards the Lord Jesus Christ.* It may be objected, that in this Place, Faith and Repentance are not only spoken of as distinct Things, but having distinct Objects.

To this I answer, That 'tis true that Faith and Repentance in

---

*Agreeable to this, is what Mr. *Locke* says in his second *Vindication of the Reasonableness of Christianity,* &c. Vol. 2. of his Works, p. 630, 631. "The believing him therefore, to be the Messiah, is very often, with great Reason put both for Faith and Repentance too, which are sometimes set down singly, where one is put for both, as implying the other."

their general Nature, are distinct Things: And Repentance for
the Remission of Sins, or that in justifying Faith that respects the
Evil to be delivered *from*, so far as it regards that Term, which
is what especially denominates it Repentance, has Respect to
God as the Object, because he is the Being offended by Sin,
and to be reconciled, but that in this justifying Act, whence it
is denominated Faith, does more especially respect Christ.—
But let us interpret it how we will, the Objection of Faith
being here so distinguished from Repentance, is as much of an
Objection against the Scheme of those that oppose Justification by Faith alone, as against this Scheme; for they hold that
the justifying Faith that the Apostle *Paul* speaks of, includes
Repentance, as has been already observed.

   3. *This Repentance that has been described, is indeed the special
Condition of Remission of Sin.* This seems very evident by the
Scripture, as particularly, Mark 1. 4. John *did baptise in the
Wilderness, and preach the Baptism of* Repentance, for the Remission of Sins. So, Luke 3. 3. *And he came into all the Country
about Jordan, preaching the Baptism of* Repentance for the Remission of Sins. Luke 24. 47. *And that* Repentance, and Remission of Sins, *should be preached in his Name among all Nations.*
Acts 5. 31. *Him hath God exalted with his own Right Hand to be
a Prince and a Saviour, for to give* Repentance unto Israel, and
Forgiveness of Sins. Chap. 2. 38. Repent, *and be baptised every
one of you, in the Name of Jesus Christ*, for the Remission of
Sins. And, Chap. 3. 19. Repent, *ye therefore and be converted*,
that your Sins may be blotted out. The like is evident by *Lev.*
26. 40, 41, 42. *Job* 33. 27, 28. *Psalm* 32. 5. *Prov.* 28. 13. *Jer.* 3. 13.
and 1 *John* 1. 9. and other places.

   And the Reason may be plain from what has been said. We
need not wonder that that in Faith, that especially respects Sin,
should be especially the Condition of Remission of Sins; or
that this Motion, or Exercise of the Soul, as it rejects and flies
from *Evil*, and embraces Christ as a Saviour from it, should
especially be the Condition of being free from *that Evil*; in like
manner as the same Principle or Motion, as it seeks *good*, and
cleaves to Christ as the Procurer of *that Good*, should be the
Condition of obtaining that Good. Faith with Respect to *Good*
is accepting, and with Respect to Evil it is rejecting. Yea this
rejecting Evil, is it self an Act of Acceptance; 'tis accepting

Freedom or Seperation from that Evil; and this Freedom or Seperation is the Benefit bestowed in Remission. No Wonder that that in Faith which immediately respects this Benefit, and is our Acceptance of this Benefit, should be the special Condition of our having it: 'Tis so with Respect to all the Benefits that Christ has purchased. Trusting in God through Christ for such a particular Benefit that we need, is the special Condition of obtaining that Benefit. When we need Protection from Enemies, the Exercise of Faith with Respect to such a Benefit, or trusting in Christ for Protection from Enemies, is especially the Way to obtain that particular Benefit, rather than trusting in Christ for something else; and so of any other Benefit that might be mentioned. So Prayer, (which is the Expression of Faith) for a particular Mercy needed, is especially the Way to obtain that Mercy.*

So that we see that no Argument can be drawn from hence against the Doctrine of Justification by Faith alone. And there is that in the Nature of Repentance, which peculiarly tends to establish the Contrary of Justification by Works: for nothing so much renounces our own Worthiness and Excellency, as Repentance; the very Nature of it is to acknowlege our own utter Sinfulness and Unworthiness, and to renounce our own Goodness, and all Confidence in self; and so to trust in the Propitiation of the Mediator, and ascribe all the Glory of Forgiveness to him.

Object. 6. The last Objection I shall mention, is that Paragraph in the second Chapter of *James*, where Persons are said expresly to be justified by Works; Verse 21. *Was not Abraham our Father justified by Works?* Verse 24. *Ye see then how that by Works a Man is justified, and not by Faith only.* Verse 25. *Was not Rahab the Harlot justified by Works?*

In *Answer* to this Objection, I would

1. Take notice of the great Unfairness of the Divines that oppose us, in the Improvement they make of this Passage against us. All will allow that in that Proposition of St. *James,*

---

*If Repentance justifies, or be that by which we obtain Pardon of Sin any other Way than this, it must be either as a Virtue or Righteousness, or something amiable in us; or else it must be, that our Sorrow and condemning what is past, is accepted as some Atonement for it; both which are equally contrary to the Gospel Doctrine of Justification by Christ.

By Works a Man is justified, and not by Faith only, one of the Terms, either the Word *Faith*, or else the Word *justify*, is not to be understood precisely in the same Sense, as the same Terms when used by St. *Paul*; because they suppose, as well as we, that it was not the Intent of the Apostle *James* to contradict St. *Paul*, in that Doctrine of Justification by Faith alone, that he had instructed the Churches in: But if we understand both the Terms, as used by each Apostle, in *precisely* the same Sense, then what one asserts is a *precise*, direct, and full Contradiction of the other, the one affirming and the other denying the very same Thing. So that all the Controversy from this Text comes to this, *viz.* Which of these two Terms, shall be understood in a Diversity from St. *Paul*. *They* say that it is the Word *Faith*; for they suppose, that when the Apostle *Paul* uses the Word, and makes Faith that by which alone we are justified, that then by it is understood a Compliance with, and Practice of Christianity in general; so as to include all saving christian Virtue and Obedience. But as the Apostle *James* uses the Word Faith in this Place, they suppose thereby is to be understood only an Assent of the Understanding to the Truth of Gospel Doctrines, as distinguished from good Works, and that may exist seperate from them, and from all saving Grace. We on the other hand suppose that the Word *Justify* is to be understood in a different Sense from the Apostle *Paul*. So that they are forced to go as far, in their Scheme, in altering the Sense of Terms from *Paul*'s Use of them, as we. But yet at the same Time, that they freely vary the Sense of the *former* of them, *viz. Faith*, yet when we understand the *latter, viz. Justify*, in a different Sense from St. *Paul*, they cry out of us, *What Necessity of framing this Distinction, but only to serve an Opinion? At this Rate a Man may maintain any Thing, tho' never so contrary to Scripture, and elude the clearest Text in the Bible!* Tho' they don't shew us why we have not as good Warrant to understand the Word *Justify* in a Diversity from St. *Paul*, as they the Word *Faith*. If the Sense of one of the Words must be varied on either Scheme, to make the Apostle *James*'s Doctrine consistent with the Apostle *Paul*'s, and the varying the Sense of one Term or the other, be all that stands in the Way of their agreeing with either Scheme, & the varying the Sense of the latter be in it self *as fair* as of the former, then the Text lies *as fair* for one Scheme as the other, and can no more fairly be an Objection against our Scheme than theirs. And if so, what becomes of all this great Objection from this Passage in *James*?

2. If there be no more Difficulty in varying the Sense of one of these Terms than another, from any Thing in the Text it self, so as to make the Words sute with either Scheme, then certainly that is to be chosen, that is most agreable to the Current of Scripture, and other Places where the same Matter is more particularly and fully treated of; and therefore that we should understand the Word *Justify*, in this Passage of *James*, in a Sense in some Respect diverse from that in which St. *Paul* uses it. For by what has been already said it may appear, that there is no one Doctrine in the whole Bible is more fully asserted, explained, and urged than the Doctrine of Justification by Faith alone, without any of our own Righteousness.

3. There is a very fair Interpretation of this Passage of St. *James*, that is no Way inconsistent with this Doctrine of Justification, which I have shown that other Scriptures do so abundantly teach, which Interpretation the Words themselves will as well allow of, as that which the Objectors put upon them, and much better agrees with the Context; and that is, that Works are here spoken of as justifying as *Evidences*. A Man may be said to be justified by that which *clears* him, or *vindicates* him, or *makes the Goodness of his Cause manifest*. When a Person has a Cause tried in a civil Court, & is *justified* or *clear'd*, he may be said in different Senses to be justified or cleared, by the *Goodness* of his Cause, & by the Goodness of the Evidences of it. He may be said to be cleared by what *evidences* his Cause to be good; but not in the same Sense as he is by that which *makes* his Cause to be good. That which renders his Cause good, is the proper Ground of his Justification; 'tis by that that he is himself a proper Subject of it; but Evidences justify, only as they manifest that his Cause is good in Fact, whether they are of such a Nature as to have any Influence to render it so or no. 'Tis by Works that our Cause *appears* to be good; but by Faith our Cause not only *appears* to be good, but *becomes* good; because thereby we are united to Christ. That the Word *Justify* should be sometimes understood to signify the former of these, as well as the latter, is agreable to the Use of the Word in common Speech; as we say such an one *stood up to justify*

another, i. e. he endeavour'd to *shew* or *manifest* his Cause to be good. And 'tis certain that the Word is sometimes used in this Sense in Scripture, when speaking of our being *justified before God*: as where it is said we shall be justified by our Words; Matth. 12. 37. *For by thy Words thou shalt be justified, and by thy Words thou shalt be condemned.* It can't be meant that Men are accepted before God, *on the Account* of their *Words*; for God has told us nothing more plainly, than that 'tis the *Heart* that he looks at, and that when he acts as Judge towards Men, in order to justifying or condemning, *he tries the Heart*, Jer. 11. 20. *But, O Lord of Hosts, that* judgest righteously, *that* triest the Reins and the Heart, *let me see* thy Vengeance *on them; for* unto thee have I revealed my Cause. Psalm 7. 8, 9. *The Lord shall judge the People: judge me, O Lord, according to my Righteousness, and according to mine Integrity that is in me. O let the Wickedness of the Wicked come to an End; but establish the Just; for the righteous God* trieth the Hearts and Reins. Verse 11. *God judgeth the Righteous.* And many other Places to the like Purpose. And therefore Men can be justified by their Words, no otherwise than as *Evidences* or Manifestations of what is in the Heart. And 'tis thus that Christ speaks of *Words* in this very Place, as is evident by the Context. Verse 34, 35. *Out of the Abundance of the Heart the Mouth speaketh. A good Man out of the good Treasure of the Heart*, &c. The Words, or Sounds themselves, are neither Parts of Godliness, nor Evidences of Godliness, but as Signs of what is inward.

God himself when he acts towards Men as Judge, in Order to a *declarative Judgment*, makes use of Evidences, and so judges Men by their Works. And therefore at the Day of Judgment, God will judge Men according to their Works: For tho' God will stand in no Need of Evidence to inform him what is right, yet 'tis to be considered that he will then sit in Judgment; not as earthly Judges do, to *find out* what is right in a Cause, but to *declare* and *manifest* what is right; and therefore that Day is called by the Apostle, *the Day of the Revelation of the righteous Judgment of God*, Rom. 2. 5.

To be justified is to be approved and accepted: But a Man may be said to be approved and accepted in two Respects; the one is to be approved *really*, and the other to be approved and accepted *declaratively*. Justification is twofold; 'tis either the Acceptance and Approbation of the Judge it self, or the Manifestation of that Approbation, by a Sentence or Judgment declared by the Judge, either to our own Consciences, or to the World. If Justification be understood in the former Sense, for the Approbation it self, that is *only that by which we become fit to be approved*: But if it be understood in the latter Sense, for the Manifestation of this Approbation, it is *by whatever is a proper Evidence of that Fitness*. In the former, *only Faith is concerned*; because 'tis by that only *in us*, that we become fit to be accepted and approved: In the latter, *whatever is an Evidence of our Fitness, is alike concerned*. And therefore take Justification in this Sense, and then Faith, and all other Graces, and good Works, have a common and equal Concern in it: For any other Grace, or holy Act, is equally an Evidence of a Qualification for Acceptance or Approbation, as Faith.

To *justify* has always, in common Speech, signified indifferently, either simply *Approbation*, or *testifying that Approbation*; sometimes one, and sometimes the other: And that because they are both the same, only as one is *outwardly*, what the other is *inwardly*. So we, and it may be all Nations, are wont to give the same Names to two Things, when one is only declarative of the other. Thus sometimes *judging*, intends only judging in our Thoughts; at other Times, testifying & declaring Judgment. So such Words as *justify, condemn, accept, reject, prize, slight, approve, renounce*, are sometimes put for *mental Acts*, at other Times for an *outward Treatment*. So in the Sense in which the Apostle *James* seems to use the Word *justify*, for *manifestative Justification*, a Man is justified not only by Faith, but also by Works; as a Tree is *manifested* to be good, not only by immediately examining the Tree, but also by the Fruit. Prov. 20. 11. *Even a Child* is known *by his Doings, whether his Work be pure, and whether it be right.*

The Drift of the Apostle don't require that he should be understood in any other Sense: For all that he aims at, as appears by a View of the Context, is to prove that good Works *are necessary*. The Error of those that he opposed was this, That good Works were not necessary to Salvation; that if they did but believe that there was but one God, and that Christ was the Son of God, and the like; and were baptised; they were safe, let them live how they would: which Doctrine greatly tended to Licentiousness. The evincing the contrary of this, is evidently the Apostle's Scope.

And that we should understand the Apostle of Works justifying as an *Evidence*, and in a *declarative Judgment*, is what a due Consideration of the Context will naturally lead us to. For 'tis plain that the Apostle is here insisting on Works in the Quality of a necessary *Manifestation* and *Evidence* of Faith, or as what the Truth of Faith is *shewed* or *made to appear* by: As Verse 18. Shew *me* thy Faith *without thy Works, and I will* shew thee my Faith by my Works. And when he says, Verse 26. *As the Body without the Spirit is dead, so Faith without Works is dead also*. 'Tis much more rational and natural, to understand him as speaking of Works as the proper *Signs* and *Evidences* of the Reality, *Life* and Goodness of Faith. Not that the very Works or Actions done are properly the Life of Faith, as the Spirit in the Body; but 'tis the *active, working Nature* of Faith, of which the Actions or Works done are the Signs, that is it self the Life and Spirit of Faith. The Sign of a Thing is often in Scripture Language said to be that Thing. As it is in that Comparison by which the Apostle illustrates it. 'Tis not the Actions themselves of a Body, that is properly the Life or Spirit of the Body; but 'tis the *active Nature*, of which those Actions or Motions are the Signs, that are the Life of the Body. That which makes Men call any Thing alive, is that they observe that it has an active operative Nature in it; which they observe no otherwise than by the Actions or Motions that are the Signs of it. 'Tis plainly the Apostle's Aim to prove that Works are necessary from that, That if Faith hath not Works, 'tis a *Sign* that 'tis not a good Sort of Faith; which would not have been to his Purpose, if it was his Design to shew that it is not by Faith alone, *tho' of a right Sort*, that we have Acceptance with God, but that we are accepted on the Account of Obedience *as well as* Faith. 'Tis evident by the Apostle's Reasoning, that the Necessity of Works that he speaks of, is not as having a *parallel* Concern in our Salvation with Faith; but he speaks of Works only as *related to Faith*, and *expressive of it*; which after all leaves Faith the *alone fundamental* Condition, without any Thing else having a parallel Concern with it in this Affair, and other Things Conditions, only as several Expressions, and Evidences of it.

That the Apostle speaks of Works justifying only as a *Sign*, or *Evidence*, and in God's *declarative Judgment*, is further confirmed by Verse 21. *Was not Abraham our Father justified by Works, when he had offered up Isaac his Son upon the Altar?* Here the Apostle seems plainly to refer to that *declarative Judgment* of God, concerning *Abraham*'s Sincerity, manifested to him, for the Peace and Assurance of his own Conscience, after his offering up *Isaac* his Son on the Altar, that we have Account of, Gen. 22. 12. *Now I know that thou fearest God; seeing thou hast not withheld thy Son, thine only Son from me.* But here it is plain, and expressed in the very Words of Justification or Approbation, that this Work of *Abraham*'s, his offering up his Son on the Altar, justified him *as an Evidence.* When the Apostle *James* says we are justified by Works, he may, and ought to be understood in a Sense agreeable to the Instance he brings for the Proof of it: But Justification in that Instance appears by the *Words of Justification* themselves refer'd to, to be by Works as an *Evidence.* And where this Instance of *Abraham*'s Obedience is elsewhere mention'd, in the *New Testament,* 'tis mention'd as a Fruit and Evidence of his Faith. Heb. 11. 17. *By Faith* Abraham, *when he was tried, offered up* Isaac, *and he that had received the Promises, offered up his only begotten Son.*

And in the other Instance which the Apostle mentions, Verse 25. *Likewise also was not Rahab the Harlot justified by Works, when she had received the Messengers, and had sent them out another Way?* The Apostle refers to a *declarative Judgment,* in that particular Testimony which was given of God's Approbation of her as a Believer, in directing *Joshua* to save her, when the Rest of *Jericho* was destroyed, Josh. 6. 25. *And Joshua saved Rahab the Harlot alive, and her Father's Houshold, and all that she had; and she dwelleth in Israel even unto this Day; because she hid the Messengers which Joshua sent to spy out Jericho.* This was accepted as an *Evidence* and Expression of her Faith. Heb. 11. 31. *By Faith the Harlot Rahab perished not with them that believed not, when she had received the Spies with Peace.* The Apostle in saying, *Was not Rahab the Harlot justified by Works?* by the Manner of his Speaking has Reference to something in her History; but we have no Account in her History of any other Justification of her but this.

4. If notwithstanding, any choose to take Justification in St. *James*, precisely as we do in *Paul*'s Epistles, for God's Acceptance or Approbation it self, and not any Expression of that Approbation, what has been already said concerning the Manner in which Acts of evangelical Obedience are concerned in the Affair of our Justification, affords a very easy, clear, and full Answer: For if we take Works as Acts or Expressions of Faith, they are not excluded; so a Man is not justified by Faith only, but also by Works; i. e. he is not justified only by Faith as a Principle in the Heart, or in its first and more immanent Acts, but also by the effective Acts of it in Life, which are the Expressions of the Life of Faith, as the Operations and Actions of the Body are of the Life of that; agreable to *Verse* 26.

What has been said in Answer to these Objections, may also, I hope, abundantly serve for an Answer to that Objection, that is often made against this Doctrine, *viz.* That it encourages Licentiousness in Life. For, from what has been said, we may see, that the Scripture Doctrine of Justification by Faith alone, without any Manner of Goodness or Excellency of ours, does in no wise diminish, either the Necessity, or Benefit of a sincere evangelical universal Obedience: In that Man's Salvation is not only indissolubly connected with it, and Damnation with the Want of it, in those that have Opportunity for it, but that it depends upon it in many Respects; as 'tis the Way to it, and the necessary Preparation for it, and also as eternal Blessings are bestowed in Reward for it, and as our Justification in our own Consciences, and at the Day of Judgment, depends on it, as the proper Evidence of our acceptable State, and that, even in accepting of us as intitled to Life in our Justification, God has Respect to this, as that on which the Fitness of such an Act of Justification depends: So that our Salvation does as truly depend upon it, as if we were justified for the moral Excellency of it. And besides all this, the Degree of our Happiness to all Eternity is suspended on, and determined by the Degree of this. So that this Gospel-Scheme of Justification is as far from encouraging Licentiousness, and contains as much to encourage and excite to strict and universal Obedience, and the utmost possible

Eminency of Holiness, as any Scheme that can be devised, and indeed unspeakably more.

I come now to the

V. and last Thing proposed, which is to consider the *Importance of this Doctrine.*

I know there are many that make as tho' this Controversy was of no great Importance; that it is chiefly a Matter of nice Speculation, depending on certain subtil Distinctions, which many that make use of them don't understand themselves; and that the Difference is not of such Consequence, as to be worth the being zealous about; and that more Hurt is done by raising Disputes about it, than good.

Indeed I am far from thinking that it is of absolute Necessity that Persons should understand, and be agreed upon, all the Distinctions needful particularly to explain and defend this Doctrine, against all Cavils and Objections; (tho' all Christians should strive after an Increase of Knowlege; and none should content themselves without some clear and distinct Understanding in this Point:) But that we should believe in the General, according to the clear and abundant Revelations of God's Word, that 'tis none of our own Excellency, Virtue, or Righteousness, that is the Ground of our being received from a State of Condemnation into a State of Acceptance in God's Sight, but only Jesus Christ, and his Righteousness, and Worthiness, received by Faith. This I think to be of great Importance, at least in Application to our selves; and that for the following Reasons.

1. The Scripture treats of this Doctrine, as a Doctrine of very great Importance. That *there is* a certain Doctrine of Justification by Faith, in Opposition to Justification by the Works of the Law, that the Apostle *Paul* insists upon as of the greatest Importance, none will deny; because there is nothing in the Bible more apparent. The Apostle under the infallible Conduct of the Spirit of God, thought it worth his most strenuous and *zealous* disputing about and defending. He speaks of the contrary Doctrine as fatal and ruinous to the Souls of Men, in the latter End of the ninth Chapter of *Romans*, and beginning of the tenth. He speaks of it as *subversive of the Gospel of Christ*, and calls it *another Gospel*, and says concerning it, if any one, *though an Angel from Heaven*

preach it, let him be accursed. Gal 1. 6, 7, 8, 9. compared with the following Part of the Epistle. Certainly we must allow the Apostles to be good Judges of the Importance and Tendency of Doctrines; at least the Holy Ghost in them. And doubtless we are safe, and in no Danger of Harshness and Censoriousness, if we only follow him, and keep close to his express Teachings, in what we believe and say of the hurtful and pernicious Tendency of any Error.—Why are we to blame, or to be cried out of, for saying what the Bible has taught us to say, or for believing what the Holy Ghost has taught us to that End that we might believe it?

2. The adverse Scheme lays another Foundation of Man's Salvation than God hath laid. I don't now speak of that ineffectual *Redemption* that they suppose to be universal, and what all Mankind are equally the Subjects of; but, I say, it lays intirely another Foundation of Man's *actual, discriminating* Salvation, or that Salvation wherein true Christians differ from wicked Men. We suppose the Foundation of this to be Christ's Worthiness and Righteousness: On the contrary, that Scheme supposes it to be Men's own Virtue; even so, that this is the Ground of a saving Interest in Christ it self. It takes away Christ out of the Place of the bottom Stone, and puts in Men's own Virtue in the Room of him: So that Christ himself in the Affair of distinguishing actual Salvation, is *laid upon* this Foundation. And the Foundation being so different, I leave it to every one to judge whether the Difference between the two Schemes consists only in *Punctilios* of small Consequence. The Foundations being contrary makes the whole Scheme exceeding Diverse and Opposite; the one is a *Gospel* Scheme, the other a *legal* one.

3. 'Tis in this Doctrine, that the most essential Difference lies, between the Covenant of Grace, and the first Covenant. The adverse Scheme of Justification supposes that we are justified by our Works, in the very same Sense wherein Man was to have been justified by his Works under the first Covenant. By that Covenant our first Parents were not to have had eternal Life given them, for any *proper Merit* in their Obedience; because their perfect Obedience was a Debt that they owed God: Nor was it to be bestowed for any *Proportion* between the Dignity of their Obedience, and the Value of the

Reward; but only it was to be bestowed from a Regard to a moral Fitness in the Virtue of their Obedience, to the Reward of God's Favour; and a Title to eternal Life was to be given them, as a Testimony of God's Pleasedness with their Works, or his Regard to the inherent Beauty of their Virtue. And so it is the very same Way that those in the adverse Scheme suppose that we are received into God's special Favour now, and to those saving Benefits that are the Testimonies of it. I am sensible the Divines of that Side, intirely disclaim the popish Doctrine of Merit; and are free to speak of our utter Unworthiness, and the great Imperfection of all our Services: But after all, 'tis our Virtue as imperfect as it is, that recommends Men to God, by which good Men come to have a saving Interest in Christ, and God's Favour, rather than others; and these Things are bestowed in Testimony of God's Respect to their Goodness. So that whether they will allow the Term *Merit* or no, yet they hold that we are accepted by our own *Merit*, in the same Sense, tho' not in the same Degree, as under the first Covenant.

But the great and most distinguishing Difference between that Covenant, and the Covenant of Grace is, that by the Covenant of Grace we are not thus justified by our own Works, but only by Faith in Jesus Christ. 'Tis on this Account chiefly that the new Covenant deserves the Name of a *Covenant of Grace*, as is evident by Rom. 4. 16. *Therefore it is of Faith, that it might be by Grace.* And, Chap. 3. 20, 24. *Therefore by the Deeds of the Law there shall no Flesh be justified in his Sight;—Being justified freely, by his Grace, through the Redemption that is in Jesus Christ.* And, Chap. 11. 6. *And if by Grace, then it is no more of Works, otherwise Grace is no more Grace: But if it be of Works, then it is no more Grace, otherwise Work is no more Work.* Gal. 5. 4. *Whosoever of you are justified by the Law, ye are fallen from Grace.* And therefore the Apostle when he in the same Epistle to the *Galatians*, speaks of the Doctrine of Justification by Works as another Gospel, he adds, *which is not another*, Chap. 1. Verse 6, 7. 'Tis *no Gospel at all*; 'tis Law: 'Tis no Covenant of *Grace*, but of *Works*: 'Tis not an *evangelical*, but a *legal* Doctrine. Certainly that Doctrine wherein consists the greatest and most essential Difference between the Covenant of Grace and the first Covenant, must be a Doctrine of great

Importance. That Doctrine of the Gospel by which above all others it is worthy of the Name of *Gospel*, is doubtless a very important Doctrine *of the Gospel*.

4. This is the main Thing that fallen Men stood in Need of divine Revelation for, to teach us how we that have sinn'd, may come to be again accepted of God; or which is the same Thing, *How the Sinner may be justified*. Something beyond the Light of Nature is necessary to Salvation, chiefly on this Account. Meer natural Reason afforded no Means by which we could come to the Knowlege of this, it depending on the sovereign Pleasure of the Being that we had offended by Sin. This seems to be the great Drift of that Revelation that God has given, & of all those Mysteries it reveals, all those great Doctrines that are peculiarly Doctrines of Revelation, and above the Light of Nature. It seems to have been very much on this Account that it was requisite that the Doctrine of the *Trinity* it self should be revealed to us; that by a Discovery of the Concern of the several divine Persons, in the great Affair of our Salvation, we might the better understand and see how all our Dependence in this Affair is on God, and our Sufficiency all in him, and not in our selves; that he is all in all in this Business, agreable to that in I Cor. I. 29, 30, 31. *That no Flesh should glory in his Presence: But of him, are ye in Christ Jesus, who of God, is made unto us, Wisdom, & Righteousness, and Sanctification, and Redemption. That according as it is written, he that glorieth let him glory in the Lord.* What is *the Gospel*, but only the glad Tidings of a new Way of Acceptance with God, unto Life, a Way wherein Sinners may come to be free from the Guilt of Sin, and obtain a Title to eternal Life? And if when this Way is revealed, it is rejected, and another of Man's devising, be put in the Room of it, without Doubt, it must be an Error of great Importance, and the Apostle might well say it was *another Gospel*.

5. The contrary Scheme of Justification derogates much from the Honour of God, and the Mediator. I have already shewn how it diminishes the Glory of the Mediator, in ascribing that to Man's Virtue and Goodness, which belongs alone to his Worthiness and Righteousness. By the Apostle's Sense of the Matter it renders Christ needless. Gal. 5. 4. *Christ is become of no Effect to you, whosoever of you are justified by the Law.* If

that Scheme of Justification be followed in it's Consequences, it utterly overthrows the Glory of all the great Things that have been contrived, and done, and suffered in the Work of Redemption. Gal. 2. 21. *If Righteousness come by the Law, Christ is dead in vain.* It has also been already shewn, how it diminishes the Glory of divine Grace; (which is the Attribute God hath especially set himself to glorify in the Work of Redemption;) and so that it greatly diminishes the Obligation to Gratitude in the Sinner that is saved: Yea that, in the Sense of the Apostle, it makes void the distinguishing Grace of the Gospel. Gal. 5. 4. *Whosoever of you are justified by the Law, are fallen from Grace.* It diminishes the Glory of the Grace of God and the Redeemer, and proportionably magnifies Man: It makes him *something* before God, when indeed he is *nothing*: It makes the Goodness and Excellency of fallen Man to be something, which I have shewn are nothing. I have also already shewn that 'tis contrary to the Truth of God in the Threatning of his holy Law, to justify the Sinner for *his* Virtue. And whether it were contrary to God's Truth or no, it is a Scheme of Things very unworthy of God, that supposes that God, when about to lift up a poor forlorn Malefactor, condemned to eternal *Misery*, for sinning against *his Majesty*, out of his Misery, and to make him unspeakably and eternally happy, by bestowing his Son and himself upon him, as it were sets all this to Sale, for the Price of *his* Virtue and Excellency. I know that those that we oppose do acknowlege that the Price is very disproportionate to the Benefit bestowed; and say that God's Grace is wonderfully manifested in accepting so little Virtue, and bestowing so glorious a Reward, for such imperfect Righteousness. But seeing we are such infinitely sinful and abominable Creatures in God's Sight, and by our infinite Guilt have brought our selves into such wretched and deplorable Circumstances, and all our Righteousnesses are nothing, and ten thousand times worse than nothing, (if God looks upon them as they be in themselves) is it not immensely more worthy of the infinite Majesty and Glory of God, to deliver and make happy such poor filthy Worms, such wretched Vagabonds and Captives, without any Money or Price of theirs, or any Manner of Expectation of any Excellency or Virtue in them, in any wise to recommend them? Will it not betray a foolish exalting

Opinion of our selves, and a mean one of God, to have a Thought of offering any thing of ours, to recommend us, to the Favour of being brought from wallowing like filthy Swine in the Mire of our Sins, and from the Enmity and Misery of Devils in the lowest Hell, to the State of God's dear Children, in the everlasting Arms of his Love, in heavenly Glory; or to imagine that that is the Constitution of God, that we should bring our filthy Rags, and offer them to him as the Price of this?

6. The opposite Scheme does most directly tend to lead Men to trust in their own Righteousness for Justification, which is a Thing fatal to the Soul. This is what Men are of themselves exceeding prone to do, (and that tho' they are never so much taught the contrary) through the exceeding partial and high Thoughts they have of themselves, and their exceeding Dulness of apprehending any such Mystery, as our being accepted for the Righteousness of another. But this Scheme does *directly teach Men* to trust in their own Righteousness for Justification; in that it teaches them that this is indeed what they must be justified by, being the Way of Justification that God himself has appointed. So that if a Man had naturally no Disposition to trust in his own Righteousness, yet if he embraced this Scheme, and acted consistent with it, it would lead him to it. But that trusting in our own Righteousness, is a Thing fatal to the Soul, is what the Scripture plainly teaches us: It tells us that it will cause that Christ shall profit us no thing, and be of no Effect to us, *Gal.* 5. 2, 3, 4. For tho' the Apostle speaks there particularly of Circumcision, yet (I have shown already, that) it is not meerly being circumcised, but trusting in Circumcision as a Righteousness, that the Apostle has Respect to. He could not mean that meerly being circumcised would render Christ of no Profit or Effect to a Person; for we read that he himself for certain Reasons, took *Timothy* and circumcised him, *Acts* 16. 3. And the same is evident by the Context, and by the Rest of the Epistle. And the Apostle speaks of trusting in their own Righteousness, as fatal to the *Jews*, Rom. 9. 31, 32. *But Israel, which followed after the Law of Righteousness, hath not attained to the Law of Righteousness: Wherefore? Because they sought it not by Faith, but as it were by the Works of the Law; for*

they stumbled at that stumbling Stone. Together with Chap. 10. Verse 3. *For they being ignorant of God's Righteousness, and going about to establish their own Righteousness, have not submitted themselves unto the Righteousness of God.* And this is spoken of as fatal to the *Pharisees*, in the Parable of the *Pharisee* and the *Publican*, that Christ spake to them, to reprove them for *trusting in themselves, that they were Righteous.* The Design of the Parable is to shew them that the very Publicans shall be justified, *rather than they*; as appears by the Reflection Christ makes upon it, Luke 18. 14. *I tell you this Man went down to his House justified, rather than the other.* That is, this and not the other.—The fatal Tendency of it might also be proved from its Inconsistence with the Nature of justifying Faith, and also its Inconsistence with the Nature of that Humiliation that the Scripture often speaks of, as absolutely necessary to Salvation; but these Scriptures are so express, that it is needless to bring any further Arguments.

How far a wonderful and mysterious Agency of God's Spirit, may so influence some Men's Hearts, that their Practice in this Regard may be contrary to their own Principles, so that they shall not trust in their own Righteousness, tho' they profess that Men are justified by their own Righteousness; or how far they may believe the Doctrine of Justification by Men's own Righteousness in *general*, and yet not believe it in a particular Application of it to themselves; or how far that Error, which they may have been led into by Education, or cunning Sophistry of others, may yet be indeed contrary to the prevailing Disposition of their Hearts, and contrary to their Practice: Or how far some may *seem* to maintain a Doctrine contrary to this Gospel Doctrine of Justification, that *really* do not, but only express themselves differently from others; or seem to oppose it through their Misunderstanding of our Expressions, or we of theirs, when indeed our real Sentiments are the same in the Main; or may seem to differ more than they do, by using Terms that are without a precisely fix'd and determinate Meaning; or to be wide in their Sentiments from this Doctrine, for Want of a distinct Understanding of it; whose Hearts at the same Time intirely agree with it, and if once it was clearly explain'd to their Understandings, would immediately close with it, and embrace it: How far these things may be I won't determine, but am fully perswaded that great Allowances are to be made, on these, and such like Accounts, in innumerable Instances; tho' it is manifest from what has been said, that the teaching & propagating contrary Doctrines and Schemes is of a pernicious and fatal Tendency.

1734

Pressing Into the Kingdom of God

LUKE XVI. 16.
THE Law and the Prophets were until John: *Since that Time the Kingdom of GOD is preached, and every Man presseth into it.*

I<small>N</small> these Words two Things may be observed; *First*, Wherein the Work and Office of *John the Baptist* consisted, *viz. preaching the Kingdom of God*, to prepare the Way for it's Introduction to succeed the *Law and the Prophets.* By the Law & the Prophets, in the Text, seems to be intended the ancient *Dispensation* under the Old Testament, which was received from *Moses* and the Prophets. These are said to be *until John*; not that the Revelations given by them are out of Use since that Time, but that the State of the Church founded and regulated, under God, by them, the Dispensation of which they were the Ministers, and wherein the Church depended mainly on Light received from them, fully continued till *John*; who first began to introduce the New Testament Dispensation, or Gospel-State of the Church; which with its glorious spiritual and eternal Privileges and Blessings, is often called the *Kingdom of Heaven*, or *Kingdom of God. John the Baptist* preached that the Kingdom of God was at Hand. That is the Account that we have of his Preaching, by the Evangelists, *Repent*, says he, *for the Kingdom of Heaven is at Hand: Since that Time*, says Christ, *the Kingdom of God is preached. John the Baptist* first began to preach it; and then after him, Christ, and his Disciples, preached the same. Thus Christ preached, Matth. 4. 17. *From that Time Jesus began to preach, and to say, Repent, for the Kingdom of Heaven is at Hand*. So the Disciples were directed to preach, Matth. 10. 7. *And as ye go preach, saying, the Kingdom of Heaven is at Hand*. It was not *John the Baptist*, but Christ that fully brought in, and actually established this Kingdom of God; but he as Christ's Forerunner, to prepare his Way before him, did the first Thing that was done towards introducing it. The old Dispensation was abolished, and the new brought in by Degrees; as the Night gradually ceases, and gives Place to the increasing Day, which succeeds in it's Room: First the Day Star rises; next follows the Light of the Sun it self, but dimly reflected, in the dawning of the Day; but this Light increases, and shines more and more, and the Stars that served for Light during the foregoing Night, gradually go out, and their Light ceases, as being now needless, till at length the Sun rises, and enlightens the World by his own direct light, which increases as he ascends higher above the *Horizon*, till the Day Star it self is gradually put out, and disappears; agreeable to what *John* says of himself, John 3. 30. *He must increase; but I must decrease.* *John* was the Forerunner of Christ and Harbinger of the Gospel-Day; much as the Morning-Star is the Forerunner of the Sun. He had the most honourable Office of any of the Prophets; when as the other Prophets foretold Christ to come, he revealed him as already come, & had the Honour to be that Servant that should come immediately before him and actually introduce him, & even to be the Instrument concern'd in his solemn Inauguration, as he was in Baptizing him. He was the greatest of the Prophets that came before Christ, as the Morning-Star is the brightest of all the Stars, *Matth.* 11. 11. He came to prepare Men's Hearts to receive that Kingdom of God, that Christ was about more fully to reveal and erect. Luke 1. 17. *To make ready a People prepared for the Lord.*

Secondly, We may observe wherein his Success appeared, *viz.* in that since he began his Ministry, *every Man pressed* into that Kingdom of God that he preached. The Greatness of his Success appeared in two Things;

1. In the Generalness of it, with Regard to the Subject, or the Persons in whom the Success appeared; *every Man*: Here is a Term of Universality; but 'tis not to be taken as universal with Regard to Individuals, but Kinds; as such universal Terms are often used in Scripture. When *John* preached there was an extraordinary pouring out of the Spirit of God, that attended his preaching; and an uncommon Awakening, and Concern for Salvation, appeared on the Minds of all sorts of Persons; and even in the most unlikely Persons, and those from whom such a Thing might least be expected; as the *Pharisees*, who were exceeding proud, and self-sufficient, and conceited of

their own Wisdom and Righteousness, and looked on them-selves fit to be Teachers of others, and used to scorn to be taught; and the *Sadducees*, who were a kind of Infidels, that denied any Resurrection, Angel, or Spirit, or any future State: So that *John* himself seems to be surprized to see them come to him, under such Concern for their Salvation; as in Mat. 3. 7. *But when he saw many of the* Pharisees *and* Sadducees *come to his Baptism, he said unto them, O Generation of Vipers, Who hath warned you to flee from the Wrath to come?* And besides these, the *Publicans* who were some of the most infamous sort of Men, came to him, inquiring what they should do to be saved. And the *Soldiers*, that were doubtless a very profane, loose, and profligate sort of Persons; they made the same In-quiry. Luke 3. 12 & 14. *Then came also Publicans to be baptised, and said unto him, Master, What shall we do? And the Soldiers likewise demanded of him, saying, And what shall we do?*

2. His Success appear'd in the Manner in which his Hearers sought the Kingdom of God, they *pressed into it*: It is else-where set forth by their being *violent* for the Kingdom of Heaven, and *taking it by Force*. Matth. 11. 12. *From the Days of* John the Baptist *until now, the Kingdom of Heaven suffers Vio-lence, and the Violent take it by Force.*

The DOCTRINE that I observe from the Words is this.

IT concerns every one that would obtain the Kingdom of God, to be pressing into it.

In discoursing on this Subject, I would
First, Shew what is that Way of seeking Salvation that seems to be pointed forth, in the Expression of *pressing into the Kingdom of God.*
Secondly, Give the Reasons why it concerns every one that would *obtain* the Kingdom of God, to seek it in this Way.
And *then* make Application.

I. I would shew what Manner of seeking Salvation seems to be denoted by pressing into the Kingdom of God.
1. This Expression denotes *Strength of Desire*. Men in general,

that live under the Light of the Gospel, and be not Atheists, do desire the Kingdom of God; that is, they desire to go to Heaven rather than to Hell; but most of them are not much concerned about it; but on the contrary live a secure and careless Life. And there are those that are many Degrees above these, that are under some Degrees of the Awakenings of God's Spirit, that yet are not *pressing into the Kingdom of God*. But they that may be said to be truly so have *strong Desires* to get out of a natural Condition, and to get an Interest in Christ: They have such a Conviction of the Misery of their *present* State, and of the extreme Necessity of obtaining a *better*, that their Minds are as it were possessed *with*, and wrapt up *in* Concern about it: To obtain Salvation is desired by them above all Things in the World: This Concern is so great that it very much shuts out other Concerns: They used before to have the Stream of their Desires after other Things, or it may be had their Concern divided between this and them; but when they come to answer the Expression in the Text, of *pressing into the Kingdom of God*, this Concern prevails above all others; it lays other Things low, and does in a Manner engross the Care of the Mind.—This seeking eternal Life should not only be *one* Concern that our Souls are taken up about, *with other Things*; but Salvation should be sought as the *one Thing* needful, *Luke* 10. 42. And as the *one Thing* that is *desired*, *Psalm* 27. 4.

2. Pressing into the Kingdom of Heaven denotes *Earnestness and Firmness of Resolution*. There should be Strength of *Resolution*, accompanying Strength of *Desire*, as it was in the Psalmist in the Place just now refer'd to; *One Thing have I desired, and that will I seek after*. In order to a thorough Engagedness of the Mind in this Affair, both these must meet together; besides Desires after Salvation, there should be an earnest Resolution in Persons to pursue this Good as much as lies in their Power; to do all that in the Use of their utmost Strength they are able to do, in an Attendance on every Duty, and resisting and militating against all Manner of Sin, and to continue in such a Pursuit.

There are two Things needful in a Person in order to these strong Resolutions in him: there must be a Sense of the great Importance & *Necessity* of the Mercy sought, and there must also be a Sense of *Opportunity* to obtain it, or the Encouragement there is to seek it. The Strength of Resolution depends on the Sense which God gives the Heart of these Things. Persons without such a Sense may seem to themselves to take up Resolutions; they may as it were force a Promise to themselves, and say with in themselves, *I will seek as long as I live, I will not give out till I obtain*, when they do but deceive themselves, their Hearts are not in it; neither do they indeed take up any such Resolution as they seem to themselves to do; 'tis the Resolution of the Mouth more than of the Heart; their Hearts ben't strongly bent to fulfil what their Mouth says. The Firmness of Resolution lies in the Fulness of the Disposition of the Heart to do what is resolved to be done. Those that are *pressing into the Kingdom of God* have a Disposition of Heart to do every Thing that is required, and that lies in their Power to do, and to continue in it: They have not only Earnestness, but Steadiness of Resolution: They don't seek with a wavering unsteady Heart, by Turns, or Fits, being off and on; but 'tis the constant Bent of the Soul, if possible, to obtain the Kingdom of God.

3. By pressing into the Kingdom of God is signified *Greatness of Endeavour*. 'Tis expressed in Eccles. 9. 10. by *doing what our Hand finds to do with our Might*. And this is the natural and necessary Consequence of the two foremention'd Things; where there is *Strength of Desire*, and *Firmness of Resolution*, there will be answerable *Endeavours*: Persons thus engaged in their Hearts will *strive to enter in at the strait Gate*, and will be *violent for Heaven*; their Practice will be agreable to the Counsel of the wise Man, in Prov. 2. at the beginning, *My Son, if thou wilt receive my Words, and hide my Commandments with thee; so that thou incline thine Ear unto Wisdom, and apply thine Heart to Understanding: Yea, if thou criest after Knowlege, and liftest up thy Voice for Understanding; if thou seekest her as Silver, and searchest for her as for hid Treasures; then shalt thou understand the Fear of the Lord, and find the Knowlege of God*. Here the Earnestness of *Desire* and Strength of *Resolution* is signified by inclining the Ear to Wisdom, and applying the Heart to Understanding; and the Greatness of *Endeavour* is denoted by crying after Knowlege, and lifting up the Voice for Understanding, seeking her as Silver, and searching for her as for hid Treasures: Such Desires and Resolutions, and such Endeavours go together.

4. Pressing into the Kingdom of God denotes *an Engaged-ness and Earnestness, that is directly about that Business of get-ting into the Kingdom of God*. Persons may be in very great Exercise and Distress of Mind, and that about the Condition of their Souls; their Thoughts and Cares may be greatly en-gaged and taken up about Things of a spiritual Nature, and yet not be pressing *into* the Kingdom of God, nor *towards* it; be-cause the Exercise of their Minds is not directly about the Work of seeking Salvation, in a diligent Attendance on the Means that God hath appointed in order to it; but something else that is beside their Business; it may be about God's Decrees, and secret Purposes, prying into them, searching for Signs whereby they may determine, or at least conjecture, what they be, before God makes them known by the Accomplishment of them; and dis-tressing their Minds with Fears that they be not elected, or that they have committed the unpardonable Sin, or that their Day is past, and that God has given them up to judicial and final Hard-ness, and never intends to shew them Mercy, and therefore that 'tis in vain for them to seek Salvation; or intangling themselves about the Doctrine of original Sin, and other mysterious Doc-trines of Religion, that are above their Comprehension. Many Persons that seem to be in great Distress about a future eternal State, get much into a Way of perplexing themselves with such Things as these. When it is so, let them be never so much con-cerned and engaged in their Minds, they can't be said to be press-ing towards the Kingdom of God; because their Exercise is *not in their Work*, but rather in that which tends to *hinder them in their Work*: If they are violent, they are only working violently to in-tangle themselves, and lay Blocks in their own Way: Their Pres-sure is not forwards: Instead of getting along, they do but loose their Time, and worse than meerly loose it; instead of fighting with the Giants that stand in the Way to keep them out of *Ca-naan*, they spend away their Time and Strength in conflicting with Shadows, that appear by the Way side.

Hence we are not to judge of the Hopefulness of the Way that Persons are in, or of the Probability of their Success in seeking Salvation, only by the Greatness of the Concern and Distress that they are in; for many Persons have needless Dis-tresses that they had much better be without. 'Tis thus very often with Persons that are over run with the Distemper of

Melancholly; whence the Adversary of Souls is won't to take great Advantage. But then are Persons in the most likely Way to obtain the Kingdom of Heaven, when the Intent of their Minds, and the Engagedness of their Spirits, is about their proper Work and Business, and all the Bent of their Souls is to attend on God's Means, and to do what he commands and directs them to. The Apostle tells us, 1 Cor. 9. 26. that he did *not fight as those that beat the Air*. Our Time is short enough; we had not need to spend it in that which is nothing to the Purpose. There are real Difficulties and Enemies enough for Persons to encounter, to employ all their Strength; they had not need to waste it in fighting with any Phantoms.

5. By pressing into the Kingdom of God is denoted *a breaking through Opposition and Difficulties*. There is in the Expression a plain Intimation of Difficulty. If there were no Opposition, but the Way was all clear and open, there would be no Need of pressing to get along. They therefore that are pressing into the Kingdom of God, go on with such Engagedness, that they break through the Difficulties that are in their Way: They are so set for Salvation that those Things by which others are discouraged, and stop'd, and turn'd back, don't stop *them*, but they press through them. Persons ought to be so resolved for Heaven, that if by any Means they can use they *can* obtain, they *will* obtain. Whether those *Means* be *difficult* or *easy, cross* or *agreable*, if they are requisite *Means of Salvation*, they should be complied with. When any Thing is presented to be done, the Question should not be, Is it easy, or hard? Is it agreable to my carnal Inclinations or Interest, or against them? But is it a required Means of my obtaining an Interest in Jesus Christ, and eternal Salvation? Thus the Apostle, Philip 3. 11. *If by any Means I might obtain the Resurrection of the Dead*. He tells us there in the Context, what Difficulties he broke through, that *he suffered the Loss of all Things*, and was willingly *made conformable* even *to* Christ's *Death*, tho' that was attended with such extreme Torment and Ignominy.

He that is pressing into the Kingdom of God, commonly finds many Things in the Way that are against the Grain; but he is not stop'd by the Cross that lies before him, but takes it up and carries it: If there be something that it is incumbent on him to do as he is one that seeks Salvation, that is cross to his

natural Temper, and is irksome to him on that Account, or
something that he can't do without Suffering in his Estate, or
that he apprehends will look odd and strange in the Eyes of
others, and expose him to Ridicule and Reproach, or any
Thing that will offend a Neighbour, and get his ill Will, or
something that will be very cross to his own carnal Appetite,
he'll press through such Difficulties: Every Thing that is found
to be a Weight that hinders him in running this Race, he casts
from him, though it be a Weight of Gold or Pearls; yea, if it be
a Right Hand or Foot that offends him, he'll cut them off; and
won't stick at plucking out a Right Eye *with his own Hands.*
These Things are insuperable Difficulties to those that are not
thoroughly engaged in seeking their Salvation; they boggle
exceedingly at them; they are stumbling Blocks that they never
get over. But it is not so with him that presses into the Kingdom of God: those Things that, before he was thoroughly
roused from his Security, he used to stick at, and was wont to
have long Parlyings and Disputings with his own Conscience
about, and set carnal Reason to work to invent Arguments and
Pleas to excuse himself from, he now sticks at no longer; he
has done with this endless Disputing and Reasoning, and
presses violently through all Difficulties; let what will be in the
Way, Heaven is what he must, and will obtain, not *if he can
without Difficulty,* but *if it be possible.* He meets with Temptation; the Devil is often whispering him in his Ear, setting Al-
lurements before him, magnifying the Difficulties of the Work
he is engaged in, telling him that they are insuperable, and that
he can never conquer them, and trying all Ways in the World
to discourage him; but still he presses forward: God has given
and maintains such an earnest Spirit for Heaven, that the Devil
can't stop him in his Course; he is not at Leisure to lend an Ear
to what he has to say.

   I come now,
  II. To shew *why* the Kingdom of Heaven should be sought
in this Manner.
   It should be thus sought
  1. On Account of the extreme *Necessity* we are in of getting
into the Kingdom of Heaven. We are in a *perishing Necessity* of
it: Without it we are utterly and eternally lost. Out of the

Kingdom of God is no Safety; there is no other hiding Place; this is the only City of Refuge, in which we can be secure from the Avenger that pursues all the Ungodly. The Vengeance of God will pursue, overtake, and eternally destroy, them that are not in this Kingdom. All that are without this Inclosure will be swallowed up in an overflowing fiery Deluge of Wrath: They may stand at the Door and knock, and cry Lord, Lord, open to us, in vain; they will be thrust back; and God will have no Mercy on them; they shall be eternally left of him; his fearful Vengeance will seize them; the Devils will lay hold on them; and all Evil will come upon them; and there will be none to pity or help; their Case will be utterly desperate, and infinitely doleful: It will be a gone Case with them; all Offers of Mercy, and Expressions of divine Goodness will be finally withdrawn, and all Hope will be lost: God will have no Kind of Regard to their Well-Being; will take no Care of them to save them from any Enemy, or any Evil; but himself will be their dreadful Enemy, and will execute Wrath with Fury, and will take Vengeance in an inexpressibly dreadful Manner. Such as shall be in this Case will be lost and undone indeed! They will be sunk down into Perdition, infinitely below all that we can think: For who knows the Power of God's Anger? And who knows the Misery of that poor Worm, on whom that Anger is executed without Mercy?

2. On Account of the *Shortness* and *Uncertainty of the Opportunity* for getting into this Kingdom. When a few Days are past, all our Opportunity for it will be gone. Our Day is limited; God has set our Bounds, and we know not where. While Persons are out of this Kingdom, they are in Danger every Hour of being overtaken with Wrath. We know not how soon we shall get past that Line, beyond which there is no Work, Device, Knowlege, nor Wisdom; and therefore we should do what we have to do with our Might. *Eccles.* 9. 10.

3. On Account of the *Difficulty* of getting into the Kingdom of God. There are innumerable Difficulties in the Way; such as few conquer; most of them that try have not Resolution, Courage, Earnestness, and Constancy enough; but they fail, give out, and perish. The Difficulties are too many, and too great for them that don't violently press forward, to grapple with; they never get along, but stick by the Way, or are turn'd

aside, and turned back, and ruin'd. Matth. 7. 14. *Strait is the Gate, and narrow is the Way which leadeth unto Life, and few there be that find it.* Luke 13. 24. *Strive to enter in at the strait Gate; for many, I say unto you, will seek to enter in, and shall not be able.*

4. The *Possibility* of obtaining. Tho' it be a Thing attended with so much Difficulty, yet 'tis not a Thing impossible. Acts 8. 22. *If perhaps the Thought of thine Heart may be forgiven thee.* 2 Tim. 2. 25. *If peradventure God will give them Repentance, to the acknowleging of the Truth.* However sinful a Person is, and whatever his Circumstances are, there is notwithstanding a Possibility of his Salvation; he himself is capable of it; and God is able to accomplish it, and has Mercy sufficient for it; and there is sufficient Provision made through Christ, that God may do it consistent with the Honour of his Majesty, Justice, and Truth: So that there is no Want either of Sufficiency in God, or Capacity in the Sinner, in order to this: The greatest and vilest, most blind, dead, hard hearted Sinner living, is a Subject capable of saving Light and Grace. Seeing therefore there is such Necessity of obtaining the Kingdom of God, and so short a Time, and such Difficulty, and yet such a Possibility, it may well induce us to press into it. *Jonah* 3. 8, 9.

5. 'Tis meet that the Kingdom of Heaven should be thus sought, because of the great *Excellency* of it. We are willing to seek earthly Things, of trifling Value, with great Diligence, and through much Difficulty; it therefore certainly becomes us to seek that with great Earnestness, which is of infinitely greater Worth and Excellence: And how well may God expect and require it of us, that we should seek it in such a Manner, in order to our obtaining it!

6. Such a Manner of seeking is needful to *prepare* Persons for the Kingdom of God. Such Earnestness and Thoroughness of Endeavours, is the ordinary Means that God makes Use of, to bring Persons to an Acquaintance with themselves, to a Sight of their own Hearts, to a Sense of their own Helplesness, and to a Despair in their own Strength and Righteousness. And such Engagedness and Constancy in seeking the Kingdom of Heaven prepare the Soul to receive it the more joyfully and thankfully, and the more highly to prize and value it when obtained. So that 'tis in Mercy to us, as well as for the Glory of

his own Name, that God has appointed such earnest Seeking, to be the Way in which he will bestow the Kingdom of Heaven.

APPLICATION.

The USE I would make of this Doctrine, is of *Exhortation* to all Christless Persons to press into the Kingdom of God. Some of you are inquiring what you shall do. You seem to desire to know what is the Way wherein Salvation is to be sought, and how you may be likely to obtain it: You have now heard the Way that the holy Word of God directs to.—Some are seeking, but it can't be said of them that they are *pressing* into the Kingdom of Heaven. There are many that in Time past have sought Salvation, but not in this Manner, and so they never obtain'd, but are now gone to Hell: Some of them sought it Year after Year, but fail'd of it, and perished at last: They were overtaken with divine Wrath, and are now suffering the fearful Misery of Damnation, and have no Rest Day nor Night, having no more Opportunity to seek, but must suffer and be miserable throughout the never ending Ages of Eternity. Be exhorted therefore not to seek Salvation as they did, but let the Kingdom of Heaven suffer Violence from you.

Here I would *first* answer an *Objection* or two, and *then* proceed to give some *Directions* how to press into the Kingdom of God.

Object. 1. *Some may be ready to say, We can't do this of our selves, that Strength of Desire, and Firmness of Resolution, that have been spoken of, is out of our Reach: If I endeavour to resolve and to seek with Engagedness of Spirit, I find I fail: my Thoughts are presently off from the Business, and I feel my self dull, and my Engagedness relax'd in Spite of all I can do.*

Ans. 1. Tho' Earnestness of Mind be not immediately in your Power, yet the Consideration of what has been now said of the Need of it, may be a Means of stirring you up to it. 'Tis true, Persons never will be thoroughly engaged in this Business, unless it be by God's Influence; but God influences Persons by Means: Persons are not stirr'd up to a thorough Earnestness without some Considerations that move them to it: And if Persons can but be made sensible of the Necessity of

Salvation, and also do duly consider the exceeding Difficulty of it, and the Greatness of the Opposition, and how short and uncertain the Time is, but yet are sensible that they have an Opportunity, and that there is a Possibility of their obtaining, they will need no more in order to their being thoroughly engaged & resolved in this Matter. If we see Persons slack, and unresolved, and unsteady, it is because they don't enough consider these Things.

2. Though strong Desires and Resolutions of Mind be not in your Power, yet Painfulness of Endeavours is in your Power. 'Tis in your Power to take Pains in the Use of Means, yea very great Pains. You can be very painful and diligent in watching your own Heart, and striving against Sin; though there is all Manner of Corruption in the Heart, that is continually ready to work, yet you can very laboriously watch and strive against these Corruptions; and 'tis in your Power, with great Diligence to attend the Matter of your Duty towards God, and towards your Neighbour. 'Tis in your Power to attend all Ordinances, and all publick and private Duties of Religion, and to do it with your Might. It would be a Contradiction to suppose that a Man can't do these Things with *all the Might* he has, tho' he can't do them with *more might* than he has. The Dulness and Deadness of the Heart, and Slothfulness of Disposition, don't hinder Men's being *able* to take Pains; tho' it hinders their being willing: That is one Thing wherein your Laboriousness may appear, even striving against your own Dulness. That Men have a dead and sluggish Heart, don't argue that they be not able to take Pains; it is so far from that, that it gives Occasion for Pains: It is one of the Difficulties in the Way of Duty, that Persons have to strive with, and that gives Occasion for Struggling and Labour. If there were no Difficulties attended seeking Salvation there would be no Occasion for Striving; a Man would have nothing to strive about. There is indeed a great Deal of Difficulty attending all Duties required of those that would obtain Heaven. 'Tis an exceeding difficult Thing for them to keep their Thoughts; 'tis a difficult Thing seriously, or to any good Purpose, to consider of Matters of the greatest Importance; 'tis a difficult Thing to hear, or read, or pray attentively: But it don't argue that a Man can't strive in these Things because they are difficult; nay, he could not strive in them if there were not Difficulty in them: For what is there

excepting Difficulties that any can have to strive or struggle with, in any Affair or Business?—Earnestness of Mind, and Diligence of Endeavour, tend to promote each other. He that has an Heart earnestly *engaged*, will *take Pains*; and he that is diligent and *painful* in all Duty, probably won't be *so* long, before he finds the *Sensibleness* of his Heart, and *Earnestness* of his Spirit greatly increased.

Object. 2. *Some may object that if they are earnest, and take a great Deal of Pains, they shall be in Danger of trusting to what they do; they are afraid of doing their Duty for Fear of making a Righteousness of it.*

Ans. There is ordinarily no Kind of Seekers that trust so much to what they do, as slack and dull Seekers. Though all that are seeking Salvation, that have never been the Subjects of a thorough Humiliation, do trust in their own Righteousness; yet some do it much more fully than others. Some tho' they trust in their own Righteousness, yet be not quiet in it. And those that are most disturbed *in* their Self-Confidence, and are therefore in the likeliest Way to be wholly brought off from it, are not those that go on in a remiss Way of Seeking, but those that are most earnest and thoroughly engaged; partly because in such a Way Conscience is kept more sensible. A more awaken'd Conscience won't rest so quietly in moral and religious Duties, as one that is less awaken'd. A dull Seeker's Conscience will be in a great Measure satisfied and quieted with his own Works and Performances; but one that is thoroughly awaken'd can't be still'd or pacified with such Things as these. And, *partly*, because in this Way Persons gain much more Knowlege of themselves, and Acquaintance with their own Hearts, than in a negligent flighty Way of Seeking; for they have a great Deal *more Experience* of themselves. 'Tis Experience *of our selves*, and finding what we are, that God commonly makes Use of as the Means of bringing us off from all Dependence *on our selves*: But Men never get Acquaintance with themselves so fast, as in the most earnest Way of Seeking. They that are in this Way, have more to engage them to think of their Sins, and strictly to observe themselves, and have much more to do with their own Hearts than others. Such an one has much more Experience of his own *Weakness*, than another that don't put forth, and try his *Strength*; and will therefore sooner see himself dead in Sin: Such an one, though he hath a Disposition continually to be flying to his own Righteousness, yet finds Rest *in nothing*; he wanders about from one Thing to another, seeking something to ease his disquieted Conscience; he is driven from one Refuge to another, goes from Mountain to Hill, seeking Rest and finding none; and therefore will the sooner prove that there is no Rest to be found, nor Trust to be put, in any Creature Confidence whatsoever.

'Tis therefore quite a wrong Notion that some entertain, that the more they do, the more they shall depend on it: Whereas the Reverse is true; the more they *do*, or the more thorough they are in *seeking*, the less will they be likely to rest *in their Doings*, and the sooner will they see the Vanity of *all that they do*. So that Persons will exceedingly miss it, if ever they neglect to do any Duty either to God or Man, whether it be any Duty of Religion, Justice, or Charity, under a Notion of its exposing them to trust in their own Righteousness. 'Tis very true, that 'tis a common Thing for Persons, when they earnestly seek Salvation, to trust in the Pains that they take: But yet commonly those that go on in a more flighty Way, trust a great Deal more securely to their dull Services, than he that is pressing into the Kingdom of God does to his Earnestness. Men's Slackness in Religion, and their Trust in their own Righteousness, do strengthen and establish one another. Their Trust in what they have done, and what they now do, settles them in a slothful Rest and Ease, and hinders their being sensible of their Need of rousing up themselves and pressing forward. And on the other Hand, their Negligence tends so to benumb them, and keep them in such Ignorance of themselves, that the most miserable Refuges are stupidly rested in as sufficient. Therefore we see that when Persons have been going on for a long Time in such a Way, and God afterwards comes more thoroughly to awaken them, and to stir them up to be in good Earnest, he shakes all their old Foundation, and rouses them out of their old Resting Places; so that they cannot quiet themselves with those Things that formerly kept them secure.

I would now proceed to give some *Directions* how you should press into the Kingdom of God.

1. Be directed as it were to sacrifice every Thing to your Souls eternal Interest. Let seeking this be so much your Bent, and what you are so resolved in, that you will make every Thing give Place to it. Let nothing stand before your Resolution of Seeking the Kingdom of God. Whatever it be that you used to look upon as a Convenience, or Comfort, or Ease, or Thing desirable on any Account, if it stands in the Way of this great Concern, let it be dismiss'd without Hesitation; and if it be of that Nature that it is like always to be an Hindrance, then wholly have done with it, and never entertain any Expectation from it more. If in Time past, you have, for the sake of worldly Gain, involved your self in more Care and Business than you find to be consistent with your being so thorough in the Business of Religion as you ought to be, then get into some other Way, tho' you suffer in your worldly Interest by it. Or if you have heretofore been conversant with Company that you have Reason to think have been, and will be a Snare to you, and a Hindrance to this great Design, in any wise break off from their Society, however it may expose you to Reproach from your old Companions, or let what will be the Effect of it. Or whatever it be that stands in the Way of your most advantagiously seeking Salvation, if it be some dear sinful Pleasure, or strong carnal Appetite, or if it be Credit and Honour, or if it be the Good-Will of some Person whose Friendship you Desire, or a being accounted of by those whose Esteem and Liking you have highly valued, and there be Danger if you do as you ought, you shall be looked upon by them as odd, and ridiculous, and become contemptible in their Eyes; or if it be your Ease and Indolence, and Aversion to continual Labour; or if it be your outward Convenience in any Respect, whereby you might avoid Difficulties of one Kind or another; LET ALL GO; offer up *all* such Things together, as it were in one Sacrifice to the Interest of your Soul: Let nothing stand in Competition with this, but make every Thing to fall before it. If the Flesh must be cross'd, then cross it, spare it not, crucify it, and don't be afraid of being too cruel to it. Gal. 5. 24. *They that are Christ's, have crucified the Flesh with the Affections and Lusts.* Have no Dependence on any worldly Enjoyment whatsoever. Let Salvation be the one Thing with you. This is what is certainly required of you: and this is what many stick at; this

giving up other Things for Salvation, is a stumbling Block that few get over. While others press'd into the Kingdom of God, at the preaching of *John the Baptist*, there was *Herod*, one of his Hearers, that was pretty much stirr'd up by his Preaching; it is said, *he heard him, and observed him, and did many Things*; but when he came to tell him that he must part with his beloved *Herodias*, here he stuck; this he never would yield to, *Mark* 6. 18, 19, 20. The rich young Man was considerably concern'd for Salvation; and accordingly was a very strict Liver in many Things; but when Christ came to direct him to go and sell all that he had, and give to the Poor, and come and follow him, he could not find in his Heart to comply with it, but went away sorrowful; he had great Possessions, and set his Heart much on his Estate, & could not bear to part with it. It may be if Christ had directed him only to give away a considerable *Part* of his Estate, he would have done it; yea, perhaps, if he had bid him part with *half* of it, he would have complied with it; but when he directed him to throw up *all*, he could not grapple with such a Proposal. Herein the Straitness of the Gate very much consists, and 'tis on this Account that so many seek to enter in, and are not able. There are many that have a great Mind to have Salvation, and spend great Part of their Time in wishing that they had it, but they will not comply with the necessary Means of it.

2. Be directed to forget the Things that are behind; that is, not to keep thinking and making much of what you have done, but let your Mind be wholly intent on what you have to do. In some Sense you ought to look back; you should look back on your Sins. Jer. 2. 23. *See thy Way in the Valley, know what thou hast done.* You should look back on the Wretchedness of your religious Performances, and consider how you have fallen short in them, and how exceedingly polluted all your Duties have been, and how justly God might reject and loath them, and you for them: But you ought not to spend your Time in looking back, as many Persons do, thinking how much they have done for their Salvation, what great Pains they have taken and how that they have done what they can, and don't see how they can do more, how long a Time they have been seeking, and how much more they have done than others, and even than such and such who have obtained Mercy; and so think

with themselves how hardly God deals with them, that he don't extend Mercy to them, but turns a deaf Ear to their Cries; and hence discourage themselves, and complain of God. Don't thus spend your Time in looking on what is past, but look forward, and consider what is before you, consider what it is that you *can do*, and what 'tis necessary that you *should do*, and what God calls you still *to do*, in order to your own Salvation. The Apostle in the third Chapter to the *Philippians*, tells us what Things he did while a *Jew*, how much he had to boast of, if any could have any Thing of their own to boast of; but he tells us that he forgot those Things, and all others that were behind, and reached forth towards the Things that were before, pressing forwards, towards the Mark, for the Prize of the high Calling of God in Christ Jesus.

3. Labour to get your Heart thoroughly disposed to go on and hold out to the End. Many that seem to be earnest have not a Heart thus disposed. 'Tis a common Thing for Persons to appear greatly affected for a little while; but all is soon past away, and there is no more to be seen of it. Labour therefore to obtain a thorough Willingness, and Preparation of Spirit, to continue Seeking, in the Use of your utmost Endeavours, without Limitation; and don't think your whole Life too long. And in order to this be advised to two Things.

1. Remember that if ever God bestows Mercy upon you, he will use his sovereign Pleasure about the Time when. He will bestow it on some in a little Time, and on others not till they have sought it long. If other Persons are soon enlighten'd and comforted, while you remain long in Darkness, there is no other Way but for you to wait. God *will* act arbitrarily in this Matter, and you can't help it. You *must* e'en be content to wait, in a Way of laborious and earnest Striving, till his Time comes. If you refuse, you will but undo your self; and when you shall hereafter find your self undone, and see that your Case is past Remedy, how will you condemn your self for foregoing a great Probability of Salvation, only because you had not Patience to hold out, and was not willing to be at the Trouble of a persevering Labour? And what will it avail before God, or your own Conscience, to say that you could not bear to be obliged to seek Salvation so long, when God bestowed it on others that

sought it but for a very short Time? Though God may have bestowed the Testimonies of his Favour on others in a few Days, or Hours after they have begun earnestly to seek it, how does that alter the Case as to you, if there proves to be a Necessity of your laboriously seeking many Years before you obtain them? Is Salvation the less Worth the taking a *great Deal* of Pains for, because, through the sovereign Pleasure of God, others have obtained with comparatively but *little* Pains? If there are two Persons, the one of which has obtain'd converting Grace with comparative Ease, and another that has obtained it after continuing for many Years in the greatest and most earnest Labours after it, how little Difference does it make at last, when once Salvation is obtain'd! Put all the Labour, and Pains, and long continued Difficulties and Strugglings of the one, in the Scale *against* Salvation, and how little does it subtract; and put the Ease with which the other has obtain'd, in the Scale *with* Salvation, and how little does it add? What is either added or subtracted, is lighter than Vanity, and a Thing worthy of no Consideration, when compar'd with that *infinite* Benefit that is obtain'd. Indeed if you were to live ten thousand Years, and all that Time should strive and press forward with as great Earnestness as ever a Person did for one Day, all this would bear no Proportion to the Importance of the Benefit, and would doubtless appear little to you, when once you come to be in actual Possession of eternal Glory, and to see what that eternal Misery is that you have escaped.—You must not think much of your Pains, and of the length of Time; you must press towards the Kingdom of God, and do your utmost, and hold out to the End, and learn to make no Account of it when you have done. You must undertake the Business of seeking Salvation upon these Terms, and with no other Expectation than this, that if ever God bestows Mercy it *will be* in his own Time, and not only so, but also that when you have done all, God will not hold himself obliged to show you Mercy at last.

2. Endeavour now thoroughly to weigh in your Mind the *Difficulty*, and to count the *Cost* of Perseverance in seeking Salvation. You that are now setting out in this Business, (as there are many here that have very lately set about it;—Praised be the Name of God that he has stirr'd you up to it!) be exhorted to attend this Direction. Don't undertake in this Affair,

with any other Thought, but of giving your self wholly to it for the remaining Part of your Life, and going through many and great Difficulties in it. Take heed that you don't engage secretly upon this Condition, that you shall obtain in a little Time, promising your self that it shall be within this present Season of the pouring out of God's Spirit, or with any other Limitation of Time whatsoever. Many when they begin, seeming to set out very earnestly, don't expect that they shall need to seek very long; and so don't prepare themselves for it: And therefore when they come to find it otherwise, and meet with unexpected Difficulty, they are found unguarded, and easily overthrown. But let me advise all that are now seeking their Salvation, not to entertain any self flattering Thoughts; but weigh the utmost Difficulties of Perseverance, and be provided for them, having your Mind fix'd in it to go through them, let them be what they will. Consider now beforehand, how tedious it would be, with utmost Earnestness and Labour, to strive after Salvation, for many Years, in the mean time receiving no joyful or comfortable Evidence of your having obtain'd. Consider what a great Temptation to Discouragement there probably would be in it; how apt you would be to yield the Case; how ready to think that 'tis in vain for you to seek any longer, and that God never intends to shew you Mercy, in that he has not yet done it; how apt you would be to think with your self, "What an uncomfortable Life do I live! how much more unpleasantly do I spend my Time than others, that don't perplex their Minds about the Things of another World, but are at Ease, and take the Comfort of their worldly Enjoyments!" Consider what a Temptation there would probably be in it, if you saw others brought in, that began to seek the Kingdom of Heaven long after you, rejoycing in a Hope and Sense of God's Favour, after but little Pains, and a short Time of Awakening; while you from Day to Day, and from Year to Year, seem'd to labour in Vain. Prepare for such Temptations now: Lay in beforehand for such Trials and Difficulties, that you may not think any strange Thing has happen'd when they come.

I hope that those that have given Attention to what has been said, have by this Time conceived in some Measure what is signified by the Expression in the Text, and after what Manner they ought to *press into the Kingdom of God*. Here is this to induce you to a Compliance with what you have been directed to; if you sit still you die, if you go backward behold you shall surely die, if you go forward you may live. And though God has not bound himself to any Thing that a Person does, while destitute of Faith, & out of Christ, yet there is great Probability, that in a Way of hearkening to this Counsel you *will live*, & that by pressing onward, & persevering, you will at last as it were by Violence take the Kingdom of Heaven. Those of you that have now heard me, that have not only *heard* the Directions that have been given, but shall, through God's merciful Assistance, *practice* according to them, are those that probably will overcome, that we may well hope at last to see *standing with the Lamb on Mount* Sion, *cloathed in white Robes, with Palms in their Hands*; when all your Labour and Toil will be abundantly compensated, and you will not repent that you have taken so much Pains, and denied your self so much, and waited so long: This Pains, this Self-Denial, this Waiting, will then look little, and vanish into nothing in your Eyes, being all swallowed up in the first Minutes Enjoyment of that Glory, that you will then be in Possession of, and will uninterruptedly possess and enjoy to all Eternity.

4th Direction. Improve the present Season of the pouring out of the Spirit of God on this Town. Prudence in any Affair whatsoever consists very much in minding and improving our Opportunities. If you would have spiritual Prosperity, you must exercise Prudence in the Concerns of your Souls, as well as in outward Concerns, when you seek outward Prosperity. The prudent Husbandman will observe his Opportunities; he will improve Seed-time and Harvest; he will make his Advantage of the Showers and Shines of Heaven. The prudent Merchant will discern *his* Opportunities; he won't be idle in a Market Day; he is careful not to let slip his Seasons for inriching himself: So will those that prudently seek the Fruits of Righteousness, and the Merchandize of Wisdom, improve their Opportunities for their eternal Wealth and Happiness.

God is pleased at this Time, in a very remarkable Manner, to be pouring out his Spirit amongst us; (Glory be to his Name therefor!) You that have a Mind to obtain converting Grace, and to go to Heaven when you die, now is your Season! *Now*, if you have any Sort of Prudence for your own Salvation, and have not a Mind to go to Hell, improve this Time! Now is the accepted Time! Now is the Day of Salvation! You that in Time past have been called upon, and have turn'd a deaf Ear to God's Voice, and long stood out and resisted his Commands and Counsels, hear God's Voice to Day, while it is called to Day! Don't harden your Hearts at such a Day as this is! Now you have a special and remarkable Price put into your Hands to get Wisdom, if you have but a Heart to improve it.

God hath his certain Days, or appointed Seasons of the Exercise both of Mercy and Judgment. There are some Seasons that are remarkable Times of Wrath, that are laid out by God for that Purpose, *viz.* for his awful Visitation, and the Executions of his Anger; which Times are called Days of Vengeance, *Prov.* 6. 34. And Days wherein God will visit for Sin, *Exod.* 32. 34. And so on the contrary, there are some other Times, that God has laid out in his sovereign Counsels, for Seasons of remarkable Mercy, wherein he will appear, and manifest himself, in the Exercises of his Grace and Lovingkindness, more than at other Times: Such Times, in Scripture are called by Way of Eminency, accepted Times, and Days of Salvation, and also Days of God's Visitation; because they are Days wherein God will visit in a Way of Mercy; as Luke 19. 44. *And shall lay thee even with the Ground, and thy Children within thee, and they shall not leave in thee one Stone upon another, because* thou knewest not *the Time of thy Visitation.* 'Tis such a Time now in this Town; 'tis with us a Day of God's gracious *Visitation.* It is indeed a *Day of Grace* with us as long as we live in this World, in the Enjoyment of the *Means of Grace*; but such a Time as this, is especially, and in a distinguishing Manner, a Day of Grace. There is a Door of Mercy always standing open for Sinners; but at such a Day as this God opens an extraordinary Door.

We are directed to seek the Lord while he may be found, and to call upon him while he is near, *Isai.* 55. 6. If you that are hitherto Christless, be not strangely besotted and infatuated, you will by all Means improve such an Opportunity as this to get Heaven, when Heaven is brought so near, when the Fountain is open'd in the midst of us in so extraordinary a Manner. Now is the Time to obtain a Supply of the Necessities of your poor perishing Souls! This is the Day for Sinners that have a Mind to be converted before they die, when God is dealing forth so liberally and bountifully amongst us, when *Conversion* and *Salvation* Work is going on amongst us from Sabbath to Sabbath, and many are pressing into the Kingdom of God! Now don't stay behind, but press in among the Rest! Others have been stirred up to be in good Earnest, and have taken Heaven by Violence; be intreated to follow their Example, if you would have a Part of the Inheritance with them, and would not be *left* at the great Day, when they are taken!

How should it move you to consider, that you have this Opportunity *now in your Hands*! You are in the actual Possession of it! If it were past, it would not be in your Power to recover it, or in the Power of any Creature to bring it back for you; but 'tis not past; 'tis NOW, at this Day; NOW is the accepted Time, even while it is called to Day! Will you sit still at such a Time? Will you sleep in such a Harvest? Will you deal with a slack Hand, and stay behind out of meer Sloth, or Love to some Lust, or Lothness to grapple with some small Difficulty, or to put your self a little out of your Way, when so many are flowing to the Goodness of the Lord? You are behind still! and so you will be in Danger of being left behind, when the whole Number is compleated that are to enter in, if you don't earnestly bestir your self! To be left behind, at the close of such a Season as this, will be awful, next to the being left behind on that Day when God's Saints shall mount up as with Wings to meet the Lord in the Air, and will be what will appear very threatning of it.

God is now calling you in an extraordinary Manner, and 'tis agreable to the Will and Word of Christ that I should now, in his Name call you, as one set over you, and sent to you to that End; so 'tis his Will that you should hearken to what I say, as his Voice: I therefore beseech you in Christ's Stead now to press into the Kingdom of God! Whoever you are, whether young or old, small or great; whatever you be; if you are a great Sinner, if you have been a Backslider, if you have quenched the Spirit, let you be who you will, and whatever you have done, don't stand making Objections, but arise, apply your self to your Work! Do, what you have to do, with your Might. Christ is calling you *before*, and holding forth his Grace and everlasting Benefits, and Wrath is pursuing you *behind*; wherefore fly for your Life, and look not behind you!

But here I would particularly direct my self to several Sorts of Persons.

I. To those Sinners that are in a Measure awaken'd, and are concern'd for their Salvation. You have Reason to be glad that you have such an Opportunity, and to prize it above Gold. To induce you to prize and improve it, consider several Things.

1. God has doubtless a Design now to deal forth saving Blessings to a Number. God *has done it* to some already, as we have Reason to think; and 'tis not probable that he has yet finished his Work, that he at this Time is come forth to do amongst us: We may well hope still to see others brought out of Darkness into marvellous Light. And therefore,

2. God comes this Day and knocks at many Persons Doors, and at your Door among the Rest. God seems to be come in a very unusual Manner amongst us, upon a gracious and merciful Design, a Design of saving a Number of poor miserable Souls out of a lost and perishing Condition, and bringing them into a happy State, in Safety from Misery, and a Title to eternal Glory! This is offered to you, not only as it has always been in the Word and Ordinances, but by the particular Influences of the Spirit of Christ awakening of you! This special Offer is made to many amongst us; and *you* be not pass'd over: Christ has not forgot or over looked you; but has come to *your* Door; and there as it were stands waiting for you to open to him. If you have Wisdom & Discretion to discern your own Advantage, you will know that now is your Opportunity.

3. How much more easily converting Grace is obtained at such a Time, than at other Times. The Work is equally easy with GOD at all Times; but there is far less Difficulty in the Way, as to *Men*, at such a Time, than at other Times. It is, as I said before, a Day of God's gracious Visitation, a Day that he has as it were set apart for the more liberally and bountifully dispensing his Grace; a Day wherein God's Hand is opened wide: Experience shews it. God seems to be more ready to help, to give proper Convictions, to help against Temptations, and let in divine Light: He seems to carry on his Work, with a more glorious Discovery of his Power, and Satan is more chain'd up, than at other Times: Those Difficulties & Temptations that Persons before stuck at, from Year to Year, they are soon

helped over: The Work of God is carried on with greater Speed and Swiftness, and there are often Instances of sudden Conversion at such a Time. So it was in the Apostle's Days, when there was a Time of the most extraordinary pouring out of the Spirit that ever was: How quick and sudden were Conversions in those Days! Such Instances as that of the Jayler abounded then, in Fulfilment of that Prophecy, Isai. 66. 7, 8. *Before she travailed she brought forth; before her Pain came she was delivered of a Man child. Who hath heard such a Thing? Who hath seen such Things? For as soon as* Zion *travailed, she brought forth her Children.* So it is in some Degree, whenever there is an extraordinary pouring out of the Spirit of God; more or less so, in Proportion to the Greatness of that Effusion. There is seldom such quick Work made of it at other Times: Persons are not so soon delivered from their various Temptations, and Intanglements; but are much longer wandring in a Wilderness, and groping in Darkness.   And yet,

4. There are probably some here present, that are now concerned about their Salvation, that never will obtain. 'Tis not to be supposed that all that are now *moved* and *awaken'd*, will ever be savingly *converted*: Doubtless there are many now seeking that will not be able to enter. When has it been so in Times past, when there have been Times of great Out pourings of God's Spirit, but that many that for a while, have inquired with others, what they should do to be saved, have failed, and afterwards grown hard and secure? All of you that are now awaken'd, have a Mind to obtain Salvation, and probably hope to get a Title to Heaven, in the Time of this present moving of God's Spirit: But yet, (though it be awful to be spoken, and awful to be thought) we have no Reason to think any other, than some of you will burn in Hell to all Eternity. You all are afraid of Hell, and seem at present disposed to take Pains to be delivered from it; and yet it would be unreasonable to think any other, than that some of you will have your Portion in the Lake that burns with Fire and Brimstone. Tho' there are so many that seem to obtain *so easily*, having been but a little while under Convictions, yet, for all that, some *never* will obtain. Some will soon loose the Sense of Things they now have; tho' their Awakenings seem to be very considerable for the present, they wont hold; they have not Hearts

disposed to hold on through very many Difficulties. Some that
have set out for Heaven, and hope as much as others to obtain,
are indeed but flighty and slack, even *now*, in the midst of such
a Time as this: And others, that for the present seem to be
more in Earnest, will probably before long decline, and fail,
and gradually return to be as they were before. The Convictions of some seem to be great, while that which is the Occasion
of their Convictions is new; which when that begins to grow
old, will gradually decay, and wear off. Thus, it may be, the
Occasion of your Awakening has been the Hearing of the Conversion of some Person, or your seeing so extraordinary a
Dispensation of Providence as this is, in which God now appears
amongst us; but by and by the Newness and Freshness of these
Things *will be gone*, and so won't affect your Mind as now they
do; and it may be your Convictions will go away with it.

Tho' such a Time as this, be a Time wherein God doth more
liberally bestow his Grace than at other Times, and so a Time
of greater Advantage for obtaining it, yet there seems to be,
upon some Accounts, greater Danger of Backsliding, than
when Persons are awaken'd at other Times. For commonly
such extraordinary Times don't last long; and then when they
cease there are Multitudes that loose their Convictions as it
were together: As the Spirit of God departs, awakenings ease
off from the Minds of Persons all over a Town.

We speak of it as an happy Thing, that God is pleased to be
causing of it to be such a Time amongst us; and so it is indeed:
but there are some that it will be no Benefit to; it will but be an
Occasion of their greater Misery; they will wish they had never
seen this Time; it will be more tolerable for those that never saw
it, or any Thing like it, in the Day of Judgment than for them.
'Tis an awful Consideration, that there are probably those here,
that the great Judge will hereafter call to a strict Account about
this very Thing, why they no better improved this Opportunity,
when he did *so* set open the Fountain of his Grace, and did so
loudly call upon them, and came and strove *with them in particular*, by the Awakening Influences of his Spirit; and they will
have no good Account to give to the Judge, but their Mouths
will be stop'd, and they will stand Speechless before him.

You had need therefore to be earnest, and very thorough
and resolved in this Affair, that you may not be one of those

that shall thus fail, that you may so fight, as not uncertainly, and so run, as that you may win the Prize.

5. Consider what sad Circumstances Times of extraordinary Effusion of God's Spirit commonly leave Persons in, when they leave them unconverted. They find them in a *doleful* Condition, because in a *natural* Condition, but commonly leave them in a much *more doleful* Condition. They are left dreadfully harden'd, and with a great Increase of Guilt, and their Souls under a more strong Dominion and Possession of Satan. And frequently, Seasons of extraordinary Advantage for Salvation, when they pass over Persons, and they don't improve them, nor receive any Good in them, seal their Damnation. As such Seasons leave them, God for ever leaves them, and gives them up to judicial Hardness. Luke 19. 41, 42. *And when he was come near, he beheld the City, and wept over it, saying, If thou hadst known, even thou, the Things which belong to thy Peace!—But now they are hid from thine Eyes.*

6. Consider, that 'tis very uncertain whether you will ever see such another Time as this is. If there should be such another Time, 'tis very uncertain whether you will live to *see* it. Many that are now concerned for their Salvation amongst us, will probably be in their Graves, and it may be in Hell before that Time; and if you should miss this Opportunity, it may be so with you. And what Good will that do you, to have the Spirit of God poured out upon Earth, in the Place where you once lived, while you are tormented in Hell? What will it avail you, that others are crying, *What shall I do to be saved*? while you are shut up for ever in the bottomless Pit, and are wailing and gnashing your Teeth in everlasting Burnings?

Wherefore improve this Opportunity, while God is pouring out his Spirit on Earth, & you are on Earth, & while you dwell in that Place where the Spirit of God is thus poured out, & you your self have the awakening Influences of it, that you may never wail and gnash your Teeth in Hell, but may sing in Heaven for ever, with others that are redeemed from amongst *Men*, and redeemed amongst *us*.

7. If you should see another such Time, it will be under far greater Disadvantages than you now see this Time. You will probably then be much older, and will have more harden'd your Heart; and so will be under less Probability of receiving

Good. Some Persons are so harden'd in Sin, and so left of God, that they can live through such a Time as this, and not be much awaken'd or affected by it; they can stand their Ground, and be but little moved. And so may it be with you, by another such Time, if there should be another amongst us, and you should live to see it. The Case in all Probability will be greatly altered with you by that Time. If you should continue Christless and Graceless till then, you will be much further from the Kingdom of God, and much deeper involved in Snares and Misery; and the Devil will probably have a vastly greater Advantage against you, to tempt and confound you.

8. We don't know but that God is now gathering in his Elect, before some great and sore Judgment. It has been God's Manner before he casts off a visible People, or brings some great and destroying Judgments upon them, first to gather in his Elect, that *they* may be secure. So it was before the casting off of the *Jews* from being God's People: There was first a very remarkable pouring out of the Spirit, and gathering in of the Elect, by the Preaching of the Apostles and Evangelists, as we read in the beginning of the *Acts*: But after this Harvest, and it's Gleanings were over, *the Rest were blinded*, and harden'd; the Gospel had little Success amongst them, and the Nation was given up, and cast off from being God's People, and their City and Land was destroyed by the *Romans*, in a terrible Manner; and they have been cast off by God now for a great many Ages, and still remain a harden'd and rejected People. So we read in the beginning of the 7th Chapter of the *Revelations*, that God, when about to bring destroying Judgments on the Earth, first sealed his Servants in the Forehead: He set his Seal upon the Hearts of the Elect, gave them the saving Influences and Indwelling of his Spirit, by which they were *sealed to the Day of Redemption*. Rev. 7. 1, 2, 3. *And after these Things, I saw four Angels, standing on the four Corners of the Earth, holding the four Winds of the Earth, that the Wind should not blow on the Earth, nor on the Sea, nor on any Tree. And I saw another Angel ascending from the East, having the Seal of the living God: And he cried with a loud Voice, to the four Angels, to whom it was given to hurt the Earth, and the Sea, saying, Hurt not the Earth, neither the Sea, nor the Trees, till we have sealed the Servants of our God in their Foreheads.*

And we don't know but that this may be the Case now, that God is about, in a great Measure, to forsake this land, and give up this People, and to bring most awful and overwhelming Judgments upon it, and that he is now gathering in his Elect, to secure them from the Calamity. The State of the Nation, and of this Land, never looked so threatning of such a Thing as it does at this Day. The present Aspect of Things exceedingly threatens the dying of vital Religion, and even of those Truths that are especially the Foundation of it, out of this Land, and so God's departing from us. If it should be so, how awful will the Case be with those that shall be left, and not brought in, while God continues the Influences of his Spirit, to gather in those that are to be redeemed from amongst us!

9. If you neglect the present Opportunity, and be finally unbelieving, those that are converted in this Time of the pouring out of God's Spirit, will rise up in Judgment against you. Your Neighbours, your Relations, Acquaintance, or Companions that are converted, will that Day appear against you: They won't only be taken while you are left, mounting up with Joy to meet the Lord in the Air, while you are left below with those that are to be destroyed, and will stand at the *Right Hand* with glorious Saints and Angels, while you are at the *left* with Devils, but they will rise up in Judgment against you. However friendly you have been together, and have taken Pleasure in one anothers Company, and have often familiarly conversed together, they will then surely appear against you. They will rise up against you as *Witnesses*, and will declare what a precious Opportunity you had, and did not improve; how you continued unbelieving, and rejecting the Offers of a Saviour, when those Offers were made in so extraordinary a Manner, and when so many others were prevailed upon to accept of Christ; how you was negligent and slack, and did not know the Things that belonged to your Peace, in that your Day. And not only so, but they shall be your *Judges*, as Assessors with the great Judge; and as such will appear against you; they will be with the Judge in passing Sentence upon you. 1 Cor. 6. 2 *Know ye not that the Saints shall judge the World*. Christ will admit them to the Honour of judging the World with him: They shall *sit with him in his Throne*, Rev. 3. 21. They shall sit with Christ in his Throne of *Government*, and they shall sit with

him in his Throne of *Judgment*, and shall be Judges with him when you are judged, and as such shall condemn you.

10. and lastly. You don't know that you shall live through the present Time of the pouring out of God's Spirit. You may be taken away in the midst of it, or you may be taken away in the beginning of it; as God in his Providence is putting you in mind by the late Instance of Death, in a young Person in the Town.* God has of late been very awful in his Dealings with us, in the repeated Deaths of young Persons that have happen'd amongst us. This should stir every one up to be in the more haste to press into the Kingdom of God, that so you may be safe whenever Death comes. This is a blessed Season and Opportunity; but you don't know how little of it you may have: You may have much less of it than others: You may by Death be suddenly snatched away from all Advantages that are here enjoyed for the Good of Souls. Therefore make haste and escape for thy Life: One Moment's Delay is dangerous; for Wrath is pursuing, and divine Vengeance hanging over every unconverted Person.

Let these Considerations move every one to be improving this Opportunity, that while others receive saving Good, and are made Heirs of eternal Glory, you may not be left behind, in the same miserable doleful Circumstances in which you came into the World, a poor Captive to Sin and Satan, a lost Sheep, a perishing undone Creature, sinking down into everlasting Perdition; that you may not be one of them spoken of, Jer. 17. 6. that shall be *like the Heath in the Desert, and shall not see Good when Good comes.*—If you don't improve this Opportunity, *remember* I have told you, you will hereafter lament it; and if you don't lament it in this World, then I will leave it with you for you to *remember* throughout a miserable Eternity.

II. I would address my self to such as yet remain unawaken'd. 'Tis an awful Thing that there should be any one Person remaining secure amongst us, at such a Time as this; but yet it is to be feared that there are some of this Sort. I would here a little expostulate with such Persons.

* *Joseph Clark*'s Wife, a young Woman that had been lately married, that died suddenly the Week before this was delivered.

I would put it to you,

1. When you expect that it will be more likely that you should be awaken'd, and wrought upon than now? You are in a Christless Condition; but yet without Doubt intend to go to Heaven; and therefore intend to be converted some Time before you die; which is not to be expected till you are first awaken'd, and deeply concerned about the Welfare of your Soul, and brought earnestly to seek God's converting Grace. And when do you intend that this shall be? How do you lay Things out in your own Mind, or what Projection have you about this Matter? Is it ever so likely that a Person will be awaken'd, as at such a Time as this? How do we see that many that before were secure are now roused out of their Sleep, and are crying, What shall I do to be saved? But you are yet secure!— Do you flatter your self that it will be more likely that you should be awaken'd, when it is a dull and dead Time? Do you lay Matters out thus in your own Mind, that tho' you are Senseless when others are generally awaken'd, that yet you shall be awaken'd when others are generally Senseless? Or do you hope to see another such Time of the pouring out of God's Spirit hereafter? And do you think that it will be more likely that you should be wrought upon then, than now? And why do ye think so? Is it because then you shall be so much older than you are now, and so that your Heart will be grown softer and more tender with Age? Or because you will then have stood out so much longer against the Calls of the Gospel, and all Means of Grace? Do you think it more likely, that God will give you needed Influences of his Spirit then, than now, because then you will have provoked him so much more, and your Sin and Guilt will be so much greater? And do you think it will be any Benefit to you, to stand it out thro' the present Season of Grace, as Proof against the extraordinary Means of Awakening that now there are? Do you think that this will be a good Preparation for a saving Work of the Spirit hereafter?

2. What Means do you expect to be awaken'd by? As to the awakening awful Things of the Word of God, those you have had set before you Times without Number, in the most moving Manner that the Dispensers of the Word have been capable of. As to particular solemn Warnings, directed to those that are in your Circumstances, those you have frequently had, and have

them now from Time to Time. Do you expect to be awaken'd by awful Providences? Those also you have lately had, of the most awakening Nature, one after another. Do you expect to be moved by the Deaths of others? We have lately had repeated Instances of these: There have been Deaths of old and young: The Year has been remarkable for the Deaths of young Persons, in the Bloom of Life, and some of them very sudden Deaths. Will the Conversion of others move you?—There is indeed scarce any Thing that is found to have so great a Tendency to stir Persons up as this: But this you have been tried with of late in frequent Instances; but are hitherto Proof against it. Will a general pouring out of the Spirit, and seeing a Concern about Salvation amongst all Sorts of People do it? This Means you now have, but without Effect. Yea you have all these Things together; you have the solemn Warnings of God's Word, and awful Instances of Death, and the Conversion of others, and see a general Concern about Salvation: But all together don't move you to any great Concern, about your own precious, immortal, and miserable Soul. Therefore consider by what Means it is that you expect ever to be awakened.

You have heard that 'tis probable that some that are now *awaken'd*, will never obtain Salvation; how dark then does it look upon you that remain stupidly *unawaken'd*!—Those that be not moved at such a Time as this, that are come to adult Age, have Reason to fear whether or no they be not given up to judicial Hardness. I don't say they have Reason to conclude it, but they have Reason to fear it—How dark doth it look upon you, that God comes and knocks at so many Persons Doors, and misses yours! that God is giving the Strivings of his Spirit so generally amongst us, while you are left Senseless!

3. Do you expect to obtain Salvation without ever seeking of it? If you are sensible that there is a Necessity of your seeking in order to obtaining, and ever intend to seek, one would think you could not avoid it at such a Time as this. Inquire therefore whether you intend to go to Heaven, living all your Days a secure, negligent, careless Life.   Or,

4. Do you think you can bear the Damnation of Hell? Do you imagine that you can tolerably endure the devouring Fire, and everlasting Burnings? Do you hope that you shall be able to grapple with the Vengeance of God *Almighty*, when he

girds himself with Strength, and cloaths himself with Wrath? Do you think to strengthen your self against God, and to be able to make your Part good with him? 1 Cor. 10. 22. *Do we provoke the Lord to Jealousy? Are we stronger than he?* Do you flatter your self that you shall find out Ways for your Ease and Support, and to make it out tolerable well, to bear up your Spirit in those everlasting Burnings, that are prepared for the Devil and his Angels? Ezek. 22. 14. *Can thine Heart endure, or can thine Hands be strong, in the Days that I shall deal with thee?*—'Tis a difficult Thing to conceive what such Christless Persons think, that are unconcerned at such a Time as this is.

III. I would direct my self to them that are grown considerably into Years, and are yet in a natural Condition. I would now take Occasion earnestly to exhort you, to improve this extraordinary Opportunity, and press into the Kingdom of God. You have lost many Advantages that once you had, and now have not the same Advantages that others have: The Case is very different with you from what it is with many of your Neighbours. You above all had need to improve such an Opportunity. Now is the Time for you to bestir your self, and take the Kingdom of Heaven!

Consider,

1. Now there seems to be a Door opened for old Sinners. Now God is dealing forth freely to all Sorts: His hand is opened wide, and he don't pass by old ones so much as he used to do. You are not under such Advantages as others are that are younger; but yet, so wonderfully has God ordered it, that now you are not destitute of great Advantage: Tho' old in Sin, God has put a new and extraordinary Advantage into your Hands. O, improve this Price that you have to get Wisdom! You that have been long seeking to enter in at the strait Gate, and yet remain without, now take your Opportunity and press in! You that have been long in the Wilderness, fighting with various Temptations, and have been labouring under Discouragements, and have been ready to give up the Case, have been often tempted to Despair, now, behold the Door that God opens for you! Don't give Way to Discouragements now; this is not a Time for it: Don't spend Time in thinking that you

have done what you can already, and that you see Signs that
you be not elected, and in giving Way to other perplexing,
weakening, disheartening Temptations: Don't waste away this
precious Opportunity in such a Manner: You have no Time to
spare for such Things as these: God calls you now to something
else: Improve this Time in seeking and striving for Salvation,
and not in that which tends to hinder it. 'Tis no Time now for
you to stand talking with the Devil; but hearken to God, and
apply your self to that, which he does now so loudly call you to.

Some of you have often lamented the Loss of past Opportunities: As particularly the Loss of the Time of Youth, and have
been wishing that you had so good an Opportunity again;
have been ready to say, *O! if I was young again, how would I
improve such an Advantage!* That Opportunity that you have
had in Time past, is irrecoverable; you can never have it again:
but God can give you other Advantages of another Sort, that
are very great, and he is so doing at this Day. He is now putting
a new Opportunity into your Hands; tho' not of the *same Kind*
with that which you once had, and have lost, yet in some Respects as great of *another Kind*. If you lament, and are ready to
cry out of your Folly in neglecting and loosing past Opportunities, then don't be guilty of the Folly of neglecting the Opportunity which God now gives you. This Opportunity you could not
have *purchased*, if you would have given all that you had in the
World for it: But God is putting of it into your Hands, of himself, of his own free and sovereign Mercy, *without your purchasing* of it. Therefore when you have it, don't neglect it.

2. It is a great deal more likely with Respect to such Persons
than others, that this is their last Time. There will be a last
Time of any special Offer of Salvation to impenitent Sinners.
God's Spirit shall not always strive with Man, Gen. 6. 3. God
sometimes continues long knocking at the Doors of wicked
Men's Hearts; but these are the last Knocks, and the last Calls,
that ever they shall have. And sometimes God's last Calls are
the loudest, and then if Sinners don't hearken, God finally
leaves them. How long has God been knocking at many of
your Doors, that are old in Sin! 'Tis a great deal more likely
that these are his last Knocks. You have resisted God's Spirit in
Times past, and have harden'd your Heart once and again; but
God will not be thus dealt with always: There is Danger, that if

now, after so long a Time, you won't hearken, he will utterly desert you, and leave you to walk in your own Counsels.

It seems, by God's Providence, as tho' God had yet an elect Number amongst old Sinners in this Place, that perhaps he is now about to bring in. It looks as tho' there were some that long lived under Mr. *Stoddard*'s Ministry, that God has not utterly cast off, tho' they so stood it out under such great Means as they then enjoyed. 'Tis to be hoped that God will now bring in a Remnant from among them. But 'tis the more likely that God is now about finishing with them, one Way or the other, for their having been so long the Subjects of such extraordinary Means. You have seen former Times of the pouring out of God's Spirit upon the Town, when others were taken and you left, others were called out of Darkness into marvellous Light, and were brought into a glorious and happy State, and you was one that saw not Good when Good came. How dark will your Circumstances appear, if you shall also stand it out through this Opportunity, and still be left behind! Take heed that you be not one of those spoken of, Heb. 6. 7, 8. that are like *the Earth that has Rain coming oft upon it, and only bears Briars and Thorns.* As we see there are some Pieces of Ground, the more Showers of Rain fall upon them, the more fruitful Seasons there are, the more do the Briars, and other useless and hurtful Plants, that are rooted in them, grow and flourish. Of such Ground the Apostle says, *It is rejected, and is nigh unto cursing, whose End is to be burned.* The Way that the Husbandman takes with such Ground, is to set Fire to it, to burn up the Growth of it.—If you miss this Opportunity, there is Danger that you will be utterly *rejected*, and that your *End* will be *to be burned*. And if this is to be, it is to be feared, that you are not *far from*, but *nigh unto Cursing*.

Those of you that are already grown old in Sin, and are now under Awakenings, when you feel your Convictions begin to go off, if ever that should be, *then* remember what you have now been told: It may well *then* strike you to the Heart!

IV. I would direct the Advice to those that are Young, and now under their first special Convictions. I would earnestly urge such to improve this Opportunity, and press into the Kingdom of God.

Consider two Things,

1. You have all Manner of Advantages now centring upon you. It is a Time of great Advantage for all; but your Advantages are above others. There is no other Sort of Persons, that have now so great and happy an Opportunity as you have. You have that great Advantage that is common to all that live in this Place, *viz.* That now it is a Time of the extraordinary pouring out of the Spirit of God; and also have that great Advantage, that you have the awakening Influences of the Spirit of God on you in particular; and besides that, you have this peculiar Advantage, that you are now in your Youth: And added to this, you have another unspeakable Advantage, that you now are under your first Convictions. Happy is he that never has hardened his Heart, and blocked up his own Way to Heaven by *backsliding*, and has now the awakening Influences of God's Spirit, if God does but enable him thoroughly to improve them! Such above all in the World bid fair for the Kingdom of God. God is wont, on such, above any Kind of Persons, as it were easily and readily to bestow the saving Grace and Comforts of his Spirit. Instances of speedy and sudden Conversion are most commonly found among such.—Happy are they that have the Spirit of God with them, and never have quenched it, if they did but know the Price they have in their Hands!

If you have a Sense of your Necessity of Salvation, and the great Worth and Value of it, you will be willing to take the surest Way to it, or that which has the greatest Probability of Success; and that certainly is, thoroughly to improve your first Convictions: If you do so, it is not likely that you will fail; there is the greatest Probability that you will succeed. What is it not worth to have such an Advantage in ones Hands, for obtaining *eternal Life?*—The present Season of the pouring out of God's Spirit, is the first such Season that many of you that are now under Awakenings have ever seen, since you came to Years of Understanding: On which Account, and because it is the first Time that you have ever been stirr'd up by the Spirit of God your self, 'tis the greatest Opportunity that ever you have had, and probably by far the greatest that ever you will have. There are many here present that wish they had such an Opportunity, but they never can obtain it; they can't buy it for

Money; but you have it in your Possession, and can improve it if you will.

But yet,

2. There is on some Accounts greater Danger that such as are in your Circumstances will fail of thoroughly improving their Convictions, with Respect to Stedfastness and Perseverance, than others. Those that are young are more unstable than elder Persons: They that never had Convictions before, have less Experience of the Difficulty of the Work they have engaged in; they are more ready to think that they shall obtain Salvation easily, and are more easily discouraged by Disappointments; and young Persons have less Reason and Consideration to fortify them against Temptations to Backsliding: You should therefore labour now the more to guard against such Temptations—By all Means be thorough now! Make but one Work of seeking Salvation! Make thorough Work of it the first Time!—There are vast Disadvantages that they bring themselves under, that have several Turns of Seeking with great Intermissions: By such a Course Persons exceedingly wound their own Souls, and intangle themselves in many Snares.—Who are those that commonly meet with so many Difficulties, and are so long labouring in Darkness and Perplexity, but those that have had several Turns at seeking Salvation, who have one while had Convictions, and then have quenched them, and then have set about the Work again, and have backslidden again, and have gone on after that Manner? The Children of *Israel* would not have been forty Years in the Wilderness, if they had held their Courage, and had gone on as they set out; but they were of an unstable Mind, and were for going back again into *Egypt*. Otherwise if they had gone right forward, without Discouragement, as God would have led them, they would have soon entred, and taken Possession of *Canaan*: They had got to the very Borders of it, when they turned back, but then were thirty-eight Years after that, before they got through the Wilderness. Therefore as you regard the Interest of your Soul, don't run your self into a like Difficulty, by Unsteadiness, Intermission, and Backsliding; but press right forward, from henceforth, and make but one Work of seeking converting and pardoning Grace, however great, and difficult, and long a Work that may be.

February 1735

God Amongst His People

Nov. 1735   Thanksgiv.

Isai 12. 6.
*Cry out & shout thou Inhabitant of Zion for Great is
the Holy one of Israel in the midst of thee.*

In the foregoing Chapter is a Prophecy of the Glor. Kingd. of
the messiah, how that there should come a Rod out of the
stem of——— & how that the wolf should dwell——— &
how that the Gentiles should seek to that Root of Jesse & after
due time the Jews also should be called & they and the Gentiles should be joined together in the worship of the true God
& in a trust on the same Saviour.

They are very Glorious Times of the Chh that are there
prophesied of by Reason of an Extraordinary flourishing of
religion & the Glorious Kingd. of Jesus X.

This Chap. is a song of the Church on this Joyfull occasion
& suited to such a Glo. dispensation as is here Prophesied
of. & there being but 6 verses of it I will Read the whole of it
to you.———

In this last verse which I have taken for my text 1. Who is
here Called upon & that is the Inhabitant of Zion. by which is
Intended the Chh. She is here Called the Inhabitant of Zion &
is often in Scripture called the daughter of Zion. Zion was a
particular part of the City of Jerusalem that was strong by nature being built upon a steep Rocky mountain which mount
was called mount Zion. The same was called the City of David
because David took it from the Jebusites & dwelt there. 2 Samuel 5. 7. Nevertheless David took the stronghold of Zion the
same is the City of David.

This City of Zion or this part of the city of Jerusalem Called
Zion was one of the principal types of the Chh of X & was fitly
so made use of upon several accounts. It was part of that City
that G. had Chosen to place his name there part of the Holy
City as it was called. It was as it were a City within a City.—&
then it was built exceeding strong upon a high Rock or mountain. & thereof suitably Represents the Chh. of X that is Built

upon the everlasting Rock and is like Mt. Zion that Cannot be Removed but abideth forever—& then it was the City of David that King that was the most Remarkable type of X—& it was a City that David took out of the hands of his Enemies by his own valour as X Redeemed the Chh out of the hands of his Enemies.— there was Davids palace as X hath as it were his House & dwelling place in the Chh.—The ÷ thereof that is here called the inhabitant of Zion is the church the spouse of the King of Zion.

2. what she is called upon to do viz to Cry out & shout as a Company or host are wont to do on any occasion of Extra-ordinary Joy as the People shouted with a great shout when they brought the ark into the camp so that the Earth Rang again 1 Sam 4. 5. & as the people shouted at the Proclamation of the King 1 Sam. 10. 24. The Inhabitant of Zion is here called upon to shout with the voice of Joy & Praise.

3. The Reason why she should shout viz. that the G. of Israel was in the midst of her. He was in the midst of her as her King as Balaam observes of Israel in his parable. Numb. 23. 21, The L. his G. is with him & the shout of a King is among them.

4. why this should be such Cause of Shouting that the G. of Israel was the midst of her viz because he was so Great & holy a G. Great is the Holy one of Is. in———

Doc. When G. is in the midst of a People tis Just Cause of exceeding Joy & Praise in them that so Great & holy an one is amongst them.

I. Briefly shew what is intended by Gods being in the midst — 2. when God is amongst———

First. what is Intended by God.

1. Tis not Intended merely that G. is with them by his omni-presence. for so he fills Heaven & Earth. & is Present Every where. In him Live & move——— Present in all Places & with all People & all Persons Equally. nor,

2. Tis not merely that he appears to be there Present by very Great & Extraordinary Providences for so he may be said to be Present with a People in a way of Judgment. He may visit a People with awfull manifestations of his Power & wrath. & so may be said to be in the midst of them. So he was said to Come into Egypt. Isai 19.1——— But

3. G. is said to be amongst a People in the sense of the doc-trine when he is with them in the Exercises of his Grace &

mercy towards them as their God. In this sense most Commonly it is that G. is said in the Sc. to be with a People & in the midst of a People & to Dwell amongst them & the Like.

We observe that when persons are Great Friends one to another they delight to be together to be with one another. They Choose to dwell together. Thus Parents & Children are wont to dwell together. Whereas Enemies are wont to stand at a distance. & theref. Gs manifesting himself in works of mercy amongst a people as their God he is said to be with them.

Tis sometimes so with Respect to a people that G. may be said to be their G. Deut 10. 21. He is thy Praise he is thy G. that hath done for thee these Great things which thine Eyes have seen & Levit 26. 12. I will be your G. & ye shall be my People.—So G. becomes the Covenant G. of a people. He is their King Isai 33. 22 The L.—Judge—Lawgiver—is our King Deut 32. 6. He is thy Father that hath bought thee.

& when he manifests hims to be such by the Exercises of his mercy & Grace amongst them then is G. said to be with a People. Thus tis said Isai 41. 10. Fear not for I am with thee be not dismayed for I am thy G. This Great Privilege is Promised to Gods People in Gospel times Ezek 37. 26, 27 moreover I will make a Cov. of Peace with them. It shall be an Everlast. Cov. with them & I will place them & multiply, & set my sanct. in the midst of them forevermore. My Tabernacle also shall be with them. Yea I will be their G. & they———

SECONDLY when G. is thus in the midst tis Just Cause of——— that so great———. Tis the Greatest Cause that a People can have to Rejoice & to Praise tho they may be Low in the ☉ they have Greater Cause of Joy & thankfulln. than if they abounded never so much in the wealth & good things of the ☉ more than if the Earth should bring forth by handfulls or the abundance & wealth of the seas should be gathered together to them & the Heavens should shower down Silver & Gold & pearls on them & the Rock should Pour out Rivers of oil to them—They have Greater Cause to Rejoice & Praise than they that find Great Spoils.

1. Because of his Being so great & holy a G. he is worthy to be Exceedingly Rejoiced in & Praised. The sum of the divine Glory consists in his greatn. & in his Holiness & his goodn. & Each of these are Expressed as signified in the text. His Greatn.

& Holiness are Expressed & his Goodn. & Grace are Signified
by his Condescending to be in the midst of poor sinf fallen
men.

& hereby he is a most Glorious being, Infinitely the most
Excellent object that can Entertain our understandings affections & Praises. His name alone is Excell. in all the E. & his
Glo. is above———— among the Gods there is none Like
unto———— There is none in H can be compared————

So great is he that the nations before are as the drop————.
he is worthy to be Exceedingly Praised for his Greatn. Ps. 95. 1.
2. 3.———— & he is Glo. in holin. fearful in———— Glo. in
Holin. fearf. in Praises doing wonders. There is none Holy as
the L.—Ps. 77. 13. who is so Great a G. as our G. is.

G. is not only omniscient so that he Knows every thing &
almighty whereby he can do Every thing so is an Infinitely
Great G. but he is also infinitely Holy which Renders his Great
Power & Knowl. Infinitely Beautiful & Lovely. Gods People
are called upon to Praise him upon this account. Ps. 99. 2, 3.
The L. is Great in Zion & he is high above all People. Let
them Praise thy Great & Terrible name for it is Holy. & v. 5.
Exalt ye the L. our G. & worship at his footstool for he is holy
& again 9 v. Exalt ye the L. our G. and worship at his Holy
Hill for the L. our G. is Holy. With what Rapture of Joy do the
Angels of Heaven praise G. on the account of his Holiness.
Rev. 4. 8. Cry Holy————

& G. is also most worthy to be Rejoiced in & Praised that
he is so Infinitely Good that tho he be so great & holy yet he
will be Pleased to be in the midst of such poor unworthy Crea.
as we are. 1 King. 8. 27. Will G. indeed dwell on the E. behold
the H. & the H. of Hs.————

There is glory sufficient in these things Exceedingly to delight our souls & Raise them to the highest Possible Pitch of
Joy & Praise.

2. By Gods being amongst a People they have opportun. to
behold this Exceeding Glo. & Excellency of G. If G. were far
off from them then they would not behold him he would be
out of sight to them. But by his being in the midst of them
they have opportunity to Entertain the Eye of their souls with
the views of his Glo.—for this is one of those Exercises of his
Grace & mercy whereby he is said to be amongst them as their

G. They that G. thus dwells with he will manifest hims. to Joh. 14. 21.

If G. dwells with a Peop. they thereby have opp. of acquaint with him & seeing his Greatn. & his beauty. They have opportun. to see his Glo. in those Great works of mercy in which he manifests hims. amongst them.

G. dwells amongst them and as it were walks amongst them & they have oppor. as it were to see his footsteps Ps 68. 24. They have seen thy Goings O G. Even the Goings of my G. my King in his sanctuary.

G. Reveals hims. to such as he dwells with by his Sp. Such a People know G. God Reveals hims. to them tho not unto the ⊙ They are like the Chil. of Is. in Egypt who when all the Rest of the Land was Covered with thick darkn. they had Light in their Dwellings. G. Reveals his Greatn. & majesty. he discovers his Beauty. 2. Cor. 3. 18. we all with open Face beholding as in a Glass———

If G. were never so Glorious a being yet if his Glory were not seen, there would not be that cause for Joy & Praise. But a People with whom G. dwells they have thereby opportun. to see his Glo.

3. When so Great & Holy an one is in the midst of a People they have Cause of Exceeding Joy & Praise for Gods Kindness to them & that because,

1. Hereby they have a most sufficient & sure defence from Evil. Such as have G. with them have Cause Exceedingly to Rejoice in their safety. They are not Exposed as others are for they dwell on high & their Place of defence is the munitions of Rocks. For so Great is G. that none can Reach him none can overcome him or controul him—they that have him for their King they are safe. They need not fear their Enemies. He is the L. strong & mighty the L. mighty in Battle. He is above all the Enemies of his People. They are all before him as the Chaff before the wind. They that set thems. against them the moth shall Eat them up they shall consume & vanish away. If at any time they are afraid they may safely put their trust on him. If at any time they are assaulted they may Resort to him & he is a strong Rock & high Tower. The name of the L. is a strong Tow. the Righ. runneth——— Prov. 18. 10—G. is one that is able to help. There is none Like the G. of Jeshurun who Rideth

on the Heaven in their help & in his Excellency on the sky. The Etern. G. is their Refuge & underneath are not mortal but Everlasting arms.

How is it possible that any one should be more safe than he that dwells in the secret Place of the most high & abides under the Shadow of the almigh. Truly they need not be afraid of the terrour by night nor of the arrow that flieth by day of the Pestilence that walks.

No Society are so defended as the Chh is. Ps 48 11 &c— Let Mt Zion Rejoice & the daughters of Judah be Glad because of thy Judgments walk about Zion & go round about her tell the Towers thereof mark well her Bulwarks & Consid her Palaces that ye may tell it to the Gen. following for this G. is our G. forever & Ever. He will be our Guide Even unto death.

The Reason why Zion is so strong & safe is because G. is Known in her Palaces for a Refuge. There is his Tabernacle & dwelling Place & there he baffles the designs of the Enemies of his People there he breaks the arrows of the Bow the shield & the sword & the Battle.—as the mountains are Round about Jerus——— There therefore God's People need not be afraid of ten thous of their Enem. that set thems. against them round about, for no weap that is formed against them shall Prosp.

This Holy G. has firmly Promised his People that he will help them & Protect them. Isai 43 first five verses———

Hence that People that have so great & Holy an one dwelling with them they dwell in a Peaceable Habitation & in sure dwellings & in Quiet Resting Places. They may therefor justly Glory in G. & say The L. is our defense & the Holy one of Is. is our King. G. is our Refuge & Str. Therefor will we not fear tho the Earth were Removed & the m——— tho the waters——— The L. of Hosts is with us & the G. of Jacob is our Refuge as in Ps 46. Such a People have Reason to Shout with the voice of triumph as triumphing over their Enemies. Ps 47. 1. Shout with the voice of triumph.

2. Tis the Greatest Glory & honour of a People to have so Great & Holy a G. in the midst of them. G. hereby puts the Greatest possible honour upon a People. How can a People be more highly dignified than by having so Glorious a being dwelling with them—tis spoken of as the Greatest honour. Deut 4. 7. what nation is there so Great who hath G. so nigh

unto them as the L. our G. is in all things that they call upon him for.— This Renders a People Excellent above all other things. That people that have this Great & Holy one midst of them they partake of his Glory. His Glory is in a measure Reflected from them. They shine with somewhat of the Glory of G. upon them & theref tis said to the Chh. in the 60 of Isaiah 1 v. arise shine.

When G. Comes to dwell amongst a People he makes of those that were a Company of poor naked destitute polluted helpless Creatures, an Eternal Excellency a Holy & blessed People. He Clothes them with Change of Raiment & adorns them with the most Excellent ornam.—He in Infinite Grace says to them as Isai 52. 1. awake awake put on thy Strength O Zion. Put on thy Beautif. Garm. O Jerus. the Holy City. & as in the 54 of Isai 11. 12. Oh thou afflicted tossed with Tempest & not Comforted Behold I will Lay thy stones with fair Colours & Lay thy foundations with Sapphires & I will make thy windows of agates & Gates of Carbuncles & all thy borders of Pleasant stones.

3. A People that have such an one Dwelling in the midst of them have the best comforter. He is the G. that Comforts those that are cast down. Yea, he is the G. of all Consolation he is a fount. of Peace & Comfort to such a People.

He affords the best Relief to poor sad & burdened souls. In him they may find Rest. Those that have wandered & have been tossed to & fro & have found no Rest, in him they have Rest—They that have been afraid & terrified in him they may have quietness & assurance forever. He is to a People that he dwells with as an hiding place from the wind——— The Comforts he bestows are not sensual & fleshly but spiritual & holy all Joy & Peace in believing. He Gives Peace not as the ☉ Giveth. That Comfort & Quietn. that he bestows on his People is vastly more valuable than all that they can have from their ☉ly Enjoyments. He puts Joy & Gladn. into the H. better than when Corn & wine & oil are Increased.—G. is a tender Father to his People Ready to Pity them under all their affliction & takes care of them. In all their affliction he is afflicted & the angel of his Pres. saves them in his Love & in his Pity he Redeems them he bears them & carries them Continually—he has a most Constant Love to them & care for them than as a tender mother to her sucking Child. Isai 49. 15, 16 Can a woman forget her sucking child that she should not have Compassion on the son of her womb. yea she may forget yet will not I——— behold I have graven thee on the palms of my hands thy walls are continually before me.—Gods Comforting his People is Compared to a mothers tenderly Comforting a Child that is hurt. Isai 66. 13. As one whom his mother Comforteth so will I Comfort you.—X Comes to such a People on that Errand to Preach Good Tidings to the meek & to bind up the broken hearted to Proclaim Lib.——— and the opening of the prison——— to Comfort all that mourn. To appoint to them that mourn amongst them beauty for ashes the oil of Joy——— that so Everlasting Joy may be to them so that they may Greatly Rejoice in the L. & their soul be Joyf. in their G. who Clothes them with the Garments of Salva. & Covers them with the Robe of Righteousness.— Whatever afflictions & sorrows such a People might Labour under before yet if G. be amongst them, they shall no more be termed forsaken. G. will be amongst them as their shepherd who will Gather his Lambs with his arm & gently Lead those that are with young.

Such a People are an happy People they partake of the sweetest Joys. G. deals bountifully with them he Leads them as in green Pastures by the side of still——— they partake of that River the streams whereof make Glad the City of G.

4. a People that has so Great & holy a G. in the midst of them are sure of a supply of all their wants in that he is so Great he is able to supply them & in that he is so holy & dwelling in the midst of them they may be sure that he will supply them for he dwells amongst them as their Covenant G. he has bound hims. to supply them. & in that he is so holy tis Impossible that he should fail of his Promise—G. has often Promised that he will take care for the supply of his People. Isai 33. 15. 16. he that walketh Righteously & speaketh uprightly bread shall be Given him & his waters shall be sure & Ps 34. 10. The young Lions do Lack & suffer Hunger but they that seek the L. shall not want any Good Thing.

The River that supplies the City of G. is a full & never failing stream there is Enough & it never is Dry & they that trust in G. & whose hope the L. is they shall be Like trees planted by the waters that spreadeth forth her Roots & shall not see when heat Comes but her Leaf shall be Green & shall not be caref. in the year of drought nor shall Cease from yielding fruit. G. has Promised that he will never fail them nor forsake them.

The People that has G. amongst them they have the fount of all good in the midst of them. There is a full fount. indeed an Inexhaustible & Infinite fount. Enough for the supply of every one under all their Circumstances & necessities whatever any one wants he may go to this fount. & there he may have a supply.—Such a People that have this G. amongst them may Glory in him & say the L. is our sheph. we shall not want. & may say as in Hab. 3. 17. 18. altho the Fig tree shall not bl. neither shall fr be in the v. the Lab. of the olive shall f. & the fields shall y. no m. the flock shall be cut off from the fold & there be no herd in the st. yet will we Rejoice in the L. & Joy in the G. of our Salv. They shall have a supply of all Good for the body that they need. & they shall have in G. all that they need for their souls. Ps. 84. 11. for the L. G. is a sun & shield the L. will give Grace & Glory & no Good thing———

5. They that have G. such an one dwelling with them are not only sure of supplies for the Present but to all Eternity. They not only have such mercies as other People have temporal blessings & favours but they have Everlasting Good bestowed upon them. For G. will forever be with his People as their G. Ps. 48. 14. for this God is our G. forever & Ever. When all those Earthly things fail yea when their bodies fail G. wont fail. Ps. 73. 26. my flesh & my H. faileth but G. is the strength of my H & my Portion forever. G. will save & defend them from Evil forever Isai 45. 17. But Isr. shall be saved in the L. with an Everlasting salva. ye shall not be ashamed nor Confounded ⊙ without End. X has Promised that his sheep shall never Perish. Joh 10. 27, 28. & I give unto them Etern. Life & they shall never Perish & none is able to Pluck them out of my hand.—& G. will not only defend them from Evil forever but they shall be supplied with Everlasting Good. He will feed them & Lift them up forever. They have an Everlasting Inheritance that they shall be Eternally Rich in the Possession of. 1 Pet. 1. 3, 4. Blessed be the G. & F. of our L. J. X which according to his abund. mercy has begotten us again ——— to an Inherit. Incorruptible & undefiled that———

& they shall have Everlasting Comforts & Joys. He hath given us Everlasting Consolation. 2. Thess. 2. 16. They shall

dwell in Gods Pres. where there is fulln. of———— That People
amongst whom G. dwells there he Commands the bless. Even
Life for————

This Renders such a People happy above all. It adds an Infi-
niteness to their happiness & Gives them Cause of Joy & Praise
unspeakable.

6. when so Great & Holy a G. dwells among a People he not
only is able to supply them with all Good but he hims. is the
Sum of all Good. G. is theirs & theref. they are happy if they
have nothing Else. If all other things fail the Enjoym. of G. is
suffic. to make them Completely Happy. They that have G. for
their portion they have a sufficient portion. Such a People may
well Glory in their Portion & make their boast in the L. & say
the L. is the Portion of our Inherit. & our Cup thou maintain-
est our Lot. The lines are fallen———— whom have we in H
but thee————

7. & Lastly when so Glorious a G. is in the midst this Renders temporal mercies to be mercies indeed to them. This is
the blessing of blessings a blessing that makes all Enjoyments
to be blessings.

If G. bent amongst a People tis in vain to them tho they
have never so many other things if they have never so great
outw. Prosperity their Prosperity is in vain to them it cant
Profit them. But if G. be with a People this will Render outw.
Good things Profitable to them. They have much more to
Rejoice in & Praise G. for the fruits of the Earth. The Earth
yields her Increase to such a People in mercy & in fulfillm. of
Gods Covenant Promises. All things are then Covenant Blessings. Ps. 67. 6. Then shall the Earth yield her Increase & G.
Even our own G. shall bless us. This Renders Publick mercies
to be blessings to such a People. They have the more Reason
to Rejoice in & Praise G. for all their Enjoyments whether
Publick or Private for they may be assured that all is in mercy
unto them for all things shall work together for their Good.

& this dont only render other mercies Profitable but when
G. is with a People it sweetens all other Enjoyments it adds a
sweetness & Relish to all that they have for they may take it as
the fruit of Gods Love & Partake of in Peace & Joy in the
Lord. Thus it was with the primitive Xtians when G. was so
Remarkably amongst them Acts 2. 46. and they, continuing

daily with one accord in the Temple & breaking bread from House to House did eat their———

Application:

I. Hence we in this Town have Cause Exceedingly to Rejoice in G. & Praise his name at this time. We have that Cause to Rejoice & praise that is spoken of in the doc. for G. has most Evidently & wonderfully manifested hims amongst us of Late. He hath appeared amongst us in his Glory. He hath manifested hims. in his Greatness he hath made bare his Glorious arm & Proceeded to do mighty works & works of wonder amongst us.

He hath appeared amongst as one that is far above all the Enemies of our Souls as stronger than Satan & all the Powers of darkness. He hath Conquered Principalities & Powers & made a show of them openly. It hath appeared that stronger is he that has been with us than he that is in the ☉. G. has in the midst of us Punished Leviathan that Piercing Serpent—There has been a Great Battle between X & his angels & the dragon & his angels & the dragon has been in a Great measure cast out. That old Serpent who is the Devil & Satan. & G. Has Rid in triumph amongst in the Chariots of Salvation.

He hath appeared amongst in the Exercises of Infinite & Sovereign Grace. In the abundant bestowm. of the Greatest blessing that tis Possible should be bestowed on any People—The manner in which G. has appeared has been very Extra-ordinary & Calls for Extraordinary notice from us. We should take heed to our selves that we never forget these signs & Great wonders that we have seen—when we consid how Great the work how Extraordinarily it was Carried on & what a Great & what an happy Change & alteration has been made in this Town within this twelvemonth past I say when we Consid this we have Reason to say as Balaam Prophesied it should be said of Jacob & of Isr. what hath G. wrought. How Great are Gods works there are no works Like his. Gods alsufficient Gr. & mighty Power has appeared in many Respects in a very Extraordinary manner in that the awakening Influences of his Sp. were so General & almost universal. & in that there has Been so much of the saving Influences of his Sp. For tho none Can tell the Exact number & none can certainly distinguish the Particular Persons that have Experienced, yet tis beyond all

Question that there have been a very Great number that have
been savingly Converted to G. None Can doubt of it that
have had opportunity to observe what has been to be observed.

& also in that so Great things have been done in so little
time, in some measure agreeable to the Prophecy Isai 66. 8.
who hath heard such a thing who hath seen such things. Shall
the Earth be made to bring forth in one day. Shall a nation be
born at once for as soon as Zion travailed she brought forth
her Childr.

& the sovereignty & alsufficiency of divine Power & Grace
has Glo. appeared in being Extended so to so many of all sorts
young & old Great & small old men & little child. We have
multitudes of Influences of this nature any one of which before
would have been accounted very Extraordinary & worthy to
be Greatly noted.

& in the Extraordinary degrees of Light & Comf which G.
has afforded to many Persons. But I need not Insist on a description of the work of G. amongst us for G. hath not wrought
those things long ago in the Days of your fathers so that you
need to be told of them but your Eyes have seen Gods Greatn.
& his mighty Hand & his stretched out arm.

& tho there be not that Progress made now in this work
that there was & there be a Great alteration as to that yet G. is
still in the midst of us. There are so many amongst that G. has
made his own People that he will never Leave nor forsake but
always dwell with that tho the work of Conversion should
Wholly Cease yet G. would be in the midst of us. There would
be very much of the Presence of G. amongst.—G. is surely
Here in this Place & amongst this People. We have theref this
day Cause of Exceeding Joy & Praise.

We are a People blessed of the L. of his free & sovereign &
undeserved Grace. He hath made us an Happy People By
Granting his own Presence amongst us. It may well be said to
this Town this day Cry out & Shout O Northampton for Great
is the H.——— Praise the L. Call on his name declare his doings among the People make mention that his name is Exalted.
Sing unto the L. for he hath done Excellent things.

How many Poor sinf. Creatures, poor miserable distressed
souls amongst us have of Late been brought together to Mt
Zion to a Glo. feast Prepared there to sing & Rejoice in G.

God hath sent a Plentif. Rain amongst us whereby he has Refreshed his Inherit. when it was weary. We have seen the Goings Even the Goings of G. our King in his Sanctuary here. Mercy & Truth have here met together Righteousness & Peace have Kissed Each other. Truth has Sprung out of the Earth & Righ. has Looked down from H. Gods work is Honourable & Glorious & his Righ. Endureth forever. He hath made his wonderf. works to be Remembered because he is Gracious & full of Compassion. He hath Given meat to them that fear him. He hath shewed his People the Power of his works. The works of his hands are verity & Judgm. They stand fast forever & ever & are done in Truth & uprightness. He hath sent Redemption to his People. He hath Commanded his Covenant forever. Holy & Revd is his name.

Mot. 1. Let it be Considered That this is Evidently Gods work & not mans. None of us Can attribute any of it to our selves or to any of our own Strength. There has been most Evidently the finger of G. to be seen an Immediate Invisible living hand that he wrought on the minds of multitudes amongst us. Things most apparently beyond the Powers of nature have been wrought. Many of the subjects of this work have in the Time of it Known that it was not owing to them nor to any m. Their own sense has been witness Enough that they were under the Influence of a Superiour Power.—And as to the means that have been used how Long have the same means been used in vain—all has been dead. Why should there be such a diff. that there should be as much done in a week yea Probably in some particular days as used at some times before to be done in a year.

This work has appeared to be only of G. in that it has been in so many Instances wrought on those that we should have thought to be most unlikely to be the Subjects of such a work.

& This Particularly manifested it to be of G. & not from any natural Cause or human Endeavors that tho it has been of Late times before now so very Rare that any Remarkable work of this nature has appeared in any Towns at all in the Country, that yet now such a work began in several other Places of the Country about the same time that it did here, without being Influenced at all One by another for it was begun in them before they had opportunity to hear one of another. So it began

here and at Winsor and at York at the Eastward part of the
country.

If it were owing to any particular conjuncture of Circumstances in a Town tis strange that there should happen such a
Conjuncture at several distant Places that have no Communication one with another at the same time, when otherwise it is
so Rare that there Ever happens to be such a Conjuncture of
Circumstances at all in any place.

This shews that tis unreasonable to ascribe it to any other
than an Immediate divine Power that works arbitrarily where
& when God will. We have Reason theref to give all the Praise
to G. & say as Ps. 72. 18, 19. Blessed be the L. G. the G. of Israel who only doth wondrous things & blessed be his Glo.
name forever & Ever.

Mot. 2. What Reason have we to acknowl. that this is not
owing to any worthiness in us but to free & sovereign Gr.
alone that we have such a Privilege bestowed upon us.—Let
none say it was because we were better than other People for if
it were so that then there were more Godly People in the
Town before the begin. of this——— yet that is part of the
mercy that I speak of that was owing to free & sovereign
Grace. We are by nature no better than others.—Let none say
that it was because this Town have been better trained up &
Instructed from their beginning than other People for if it has
been so who must we thank for that that is wholly owing to G.
if in that Respect this Place has been made to differ from
others—and if we have had Greater Privileges in this Respect
our Guilt has been Greater than other People that we were so
sinf. & unprofitable under such Priv.

Let none say that it was because there was more of a Sp. of
Prayer, in this Place than other Towns for if there was more of
a Sp. of Prayer God did not bestow this mercy on us because
we had a Sp. of Prayer for it but on the contrary he stirred up
a Sp. of Prayer because he had a design of bestowing this
mercy. The Sp. of Prayer is the fruit of this Gr of G. to us &
not the Cause.

No it is not for any thing in us we have been Exceeding
undeserving of such a mercy. What dulln. & dead. was there
amongst. How much unbelief. How was the Glo. Redeemer
treated amongst. How did he Knock & call in vain. How was

he made Light of & how few was there that seemed to be so much as seriously Concerned for the Good of their Souls.

There is this to shew that tis only Sovereign Grace that all this is to be attributed to that. Many of those that have had the Experience of the saving Gr. of G. were our most vain Light Irreligious Persons. So that tis Sov. Grace has made us to differ from any other People. If any one ask how Comes this People to have so much more of the Pres. of G. than some other People the Reason to be Given is that this was according to the Good Pleasure of Gods will.—If it be asked why he should shew such Favour to this People the Right answ. is he Loved us because he loved us & to G. we ought to say not to us not to us O L. but thy name be the Glo.

3. Consid that this mercy that G. has bestowed upon us is spoken of in Sc. as the Greatest Cause of Joy & Praise to a People. So it is in Isai 54. 1. Sing O Barren & thou that didst not bear break forth into singing & Cry aloud thou that didst not travail with Child. & 5 v. Thy maker is thy Husb. the L. of hosts is his name & thy Redeemer the Holy one of Is. the G. of the whole Earth shall he be Called.

So in the 55 of Isai 11, 12, 13. v. so shall my word be that goeth——— not Return unto me void——— for ye shall Go forth with Joy & be Led forth with Peace. The mountains & the hills shall Break forth before you into singing and all the trees of the field shall clap their hands. Instead of the thorn——— instead of Brier——— and it shall be to the L. of hosts for a name for an Everlasting Sign that shall not be cut off. & Isai 29. 18, 19. and in that day shall the deaf hear the words of this Book & the Eyes of the Blind shall see out of obscurity & out of darkn. The meek also shall Increase their Joy in the L. & the Poor among men shall Rejoice in the Holy one of Israel.

We have had such an occasion of Joy & Praise amongst us as that described in the 35 Chap. of Isai. The wilderness & the solitary Place——— 7v——— 10v——— That which G. the F says to X in the 49 of Isa 8 & 9 v. is applicable in our Case. Thus saith the L. In an acceptab. Time have I Heard thee in a day of salva have I helped thee & I will Preserve thee & Give thee for a Cov. of the People, to Establish the Earth to Cause to Inherit the desolate heritages that thou mayst say to the Prisoners Go forth to them that are in darkn Shew your selves which is spoken of in the 13 v. as occasion of Joy & Praise to Heaven & Earth Sing O Heavens & be Joyf O Earth & break forth into Singing O mountains: for the L. hath Comforted his People.

4. we have not only the bestow. of so Great mercy on our selves to Praise G. for but also on other People. Herein the dispensation of G. is very Extraordinary as well as on other accounts that this Blessing should be so Extensive that so many Towns should be Partakers of it at once not only those near but many far off.—This Renders the work more Glo. so that we should Rejoice and Praise as we Love our fellow Crea. and have a Concern for the Kingd of our G.—Such a thing is new to us & unknown in our day & in being so Extraordinary Gives us Cause to hope for yet more Glorious things Concerning the City of our G.

5. our obliga. to Praise is added to in that G. has not only bestowed this Great mercy but Even Given many Temporal blessings with it. It has been a time of Remarkable Health amongst us Especially the Last winter & spring in the time when the work of G. did most Remarkably Prevail. There has not been such a time of Remarkable Health for many years.— & G. has also made the Earth to yield her Increase to us. He has bestowed a plenty of outw. Good things. Gods Paths have dropped fatness to us.—& he has Continued Peace to us when we have been afraid of war.

Let us theref this day & from day to day with the Greatest ardency & in yet the most Exalted manner we are Capable of Rejoice in Gods Goodness & Praise his Holy name. 1. we ought to Praise G. singly & separately. 2. & Let Every Family Praise G. There is now Great Cause for the voice of Joy & Praise to be heard in our Houses. Salva has this year Past as we have Reason to hope Come to most of the Houses of this Town & to many in many of our Houses.

There never was so much Cause why our Houses should be filled with Holy Rejoicings & Praises as now. How many Parents have Reason to Rejoice & praise G. with their Children & Children with their Parents & Brothers & Sisters together.

How many Parents can say this my son this my daughter was dead & is alive was Lost & is found. How many Can Come Joyfully to G. & say here am I & the Chil. which thou hast Graciously Given.

3. & Let all Private Societies be filled with Praises. When Private Companies used in time past to be filled up much with unprofitable discourse now they should be filled with Praises.— Let G. be Praised in your private meetings for Relig. & Let your tongues Praise the L. in your occasional meetings with your Companions & neighbors.—Societies of young People that were wont to be filled with vain talk & Lewd songs should now be filled with Praise.

4. Let us with the Greatest Joy & Exaltation of Soul Praise G. in our Publick Solemn assemblies. We never had so much Cause to Rejoice & Praise G. in Publick for when we meet together G. is now more Remarkably amongst & Great is the H. one of Is. in the midst of us. There never was a time wherein all sorts young men & maids old men & little Chil. had so much Cause to Praise the name of the L. together for there never was a time in the Town wherein there were so many of Each of these Sorts that had a new Song put into their mouths.

How Beautiful & becoming is it for a Congregation a multitude, to Join together in sincerely Praising & magnifying the most high G. Ps. 111. 1. Praise ye the L. I will Praise the L. with my whole Heart, in the assembly of the upright & in the Congrega. & Ps. 149. 1. Praise ye the L. Sing unto the L. a new song & his Praise in the Congregation of the Saints.

Object 1 Some may Object & say they hant Partook of the Benefit of this Great mercy & why should they Praise G.

Answ. You are not Excused from the Duty of Praising G. for so Glo an opportuni. because you hant made a Good Improvement of it. Tis true so much the more Cause to Lament your own sin & folly.

Tis because you would not. You had the offer of the same Blessings—But—no Relish for them no Real desire of them.

Your duty is to Bless G. & humble & abase your self.

If you are not thankf it shews a Continuance in the same obstinacy.

Object 2 I have met with Great & sore afflict. G. has dealt awfully with me.

Ans. You bent Excused from Praising G. for undeserved mercy because you have had deserved affliction.—all afflictions are deserved.—Less than deserved—mercies not the less undeserved. The mercies spoken of are in thems nevertheless Great & meriting your Praises.

Praise G. for mercies & humble your self under affliction at the same time.

There is such a thing as Praising G. in a humble Broken Hearted manner & yet in a very Joyfull manner at the same time.

This shews the blamableness of that which I understand is too much a Custom here that after some Great afflict. they wont Join their voices in that part of divine worship saying Praise to G. It would be more becoming to shew thems. more of Jobs Sp. who when under Exceeding Great affliction yet said blessed be the name of the L.

II. Use is to stir up those that Remain yet in a Xless Condition that they may be partakers of the Benefit of this Great mercy of having G. in the midst of us.

This may well make you sensible of your mis. who are as aliens from the Common——— have not G. dwelling with you tho he dwells in the Town——— are a Poor Destitute miserable Creature, having no G. for your Covenant G. to help you & bless you.—Your Case is Exceeding Doleful, but yet this blessed. is what you also may obtain. Its being Granted so abundantly all around you should stir you up with utmost & Indefatigable Earnestness & to seek the same.—Earnestly & frequently make that Prayer in the 106 Ps. 4 & 5 v. Rememb. me O L. with the Favour that thou bearest to thy People. O visit me with thy Salva. that I may see the Good of thy Chosen that I may Rejoice in the Gladn. of thy nation that I may Glory with thine Inheritance.

III. use is to Exhort those amongst us Especially to Praise G. that have Good Grounds to think that they have Experienced the Saving Effects of Gods Presence. Others have Reason to Praise G. but these above all others. One such has Received more mercy than all the natural m. in the ⊙—Consid you are no more worthy than any other. Tis G. has made you to differ.

Praise is a thing Especially becoming of the Saints. Ps. 33. 1. Rejoice in the L. O ye Righ. for Praise is Comely for the upright.

The work of Xtians should be Praise. They are Called Converted & made new Creatures that they might be to the Praise of Gods Glory. Every Xtian should be a Priest. G. has called

them that they might be a Holy Priesthood to offer up Sp.
Sacrifices 1 Pet 2. 5.

& the Sacrifices that they should offer should be the calves
of their Lips.—The saints are especially Called to the work of
Praise in the H. Sc. as Ps 97. 12. Rejoice in the L. ye Righ. Give
thanks at the Rem. of his Holiness. Ps 22. 23. Ye that fear the
L. Praise him. Ps 30. 4 Sing unto the L. O ye Saints of his &
132. 9. Let thy Saints shout for Joy. 145. 10, 11, 12. all thy works
shall Praise thee O L. & thy Saints shall bless thee. They shall
speak of the Glory of thy Kingd. & talk of thy Power to make
Known to the sons of m. his migh. acts & the Glo. majesty of
his Kingd.

Rememb theref the Great things that G. has done for you.
Tho you have as it were Lien among the Pots yet G. has made
you as the wings of a dove Covered with Silver & her feathers
with yellow Gold.—when you was Poor & in a forlorn Case
and as it were beggars on the dung hill G. hath Exalted you to
Glo dignity he has set you among Princes & made you to Inherit the throne of his Glory.

Rememb. the misery of your Case. Rememb. the sorrow
you was in your fears & darkness & misgivings of H. & how
G. delivered. You have Reason to say as in the 18. Ps. at the
Begin.———

Rememb. how helpless you was & how G. helped you. For
tis G. that gives Strength & Power to his People.

Rememb. what tempta. you had & how much too strong
your Enemies were for you. If it had not been the L. that was
on my side then had your Enemies swallowed me up quick.

Rememb. how you cried to the L. & he unsnared & delivered you. You have cried to G. with your mouth & let him be
Extolled with your tongue for verily G. hath heard you & attended to the voice of your Prayer. Let that theref be the
Language of your Heart. Ps. 116. at begin——— I love the L.
because he hath heard the voice of my Supplications. Because
he hath Inclined his Ear unto me therefor will I Call upon him
as Long as I Live. G. hath brought you up out of an horrible
Pit & out of the miry Clay & set——— Let a new song theref
be Ever in your mouth even Praise unto your G.

Consid that all the Trib. that you can Render for those great
things is Praise. You can make no other Return for X Laying

down his Life. Can't be Profitable—G. Expects no other Tribute. & how meet & suitable is it that you should Render this
with all your heart & soul.

You have Reason to be Glad & Rejoice for your selves &
one for another. This is the disposition of the Saints & tis beautiful in them. Ps. 142. 7. The Righ. shall Compass me about for
thou shalt deal bountifully with me & Ps. 34 at begin———

A City on a Hill

July 1736

MATT 5. 14.
—A City that is set on an Hill Cannot be Hid

Here in this 5, 6, & 7. Verses of Math which is Commonly Called Xs Sermon on the mount there is a Summary of the Practical Part of Xtianity.—It is to be Observed that as of old, the Law of Moses was delivered on a mountain. The voice which G. spoke in which he gave the ten Commandments was from Mt Sinai. And Moses went up to G. on the Top of the mountain, & there G. gave him the two Tables of stone on which were written the same Commandments & there also it was that G. gave the Judicial & Ceremonial Laws & so also now X delivers the mind and will of G. on a mountain.

In the first and second verses it is said & seeing the multitudes he went up into a mountain and when he was set his disciples Came to him and he opened his mouth & taught them.

So that it appears that those that X did more Especially direct hims. to in this discourse were his disciples. & in what follows in this & the two next Chapters we have an account what he taught them.

& first he tells them in many Instances who they are that are truly Happy & blessed Persons or what is the way to true blessedness, viz that they should be Poor in Sp. that they should be Spiritual mourners that they should be meek that they should Hunger & Thirst after R.—merciful—pure in H.—peacemakers—that they should willingly & Patiently Endure Persecution for Righteousness sake.

Thus X Enforces these things by the blessedness that attends them. & then in the 13 & following verses he adds some further Enforcements or motives to Influence his disciples to be of such a Sp & Practice as he had spoken of.

As Particularly he tells 'em they are the Salt of the Earth. They are persons Chosen & Called out from the Rest of the world that they might Purifie others & keep the ☉ from

Corruption. & therefore they had need to be pure & holy and of an Excellent disposition & practice thems. other wise they would be worse than others & their Guilt much Greater in the sight of G. If the Salt have Lost its savour it is thenceforth Good for nothing———

& in the 14. v. of the Text he tells them that they are the Light of the ☉ & Compares them to a City that is set on an hill that Can't be hid.

This was verified of the disciples in a degree before X's death. They by Reason of their being the Professed followers of such an Extraordinary Person as X was who was so Remarkable for his doctrine & miracles were greatly observed & taken notice of.

But this was more Especially verified of them after his Resurrection when the Sp. of G. Came to be so wonderfully Poured out upon them & so Remarkably accompanied their Preaching. It was so Remarkable a thing that they were upon that account extraordinarily observed & taken notice of in Judea & not only so but all over the ☉.

What X here says to his disciples is not to be understood only of those that were then his disciples but of his Chh. & People then and afterwards for they were all his disciples.

& we have an account of the Remarkable fulfilling of it in the book of the acts, of the Great noise that was made in all parts of the ☉ from the Remarkable flourishing of Religion that there was & Great Increase of the Xtian Chh. The Chh. then was in a Remarkable manner as a City set on an Hill.

Doc. When any professing society is as a City set on an Hill tis a very Great obligation upon them to Honour Religion in their Practice.

I would speak to this doc. first by briefly shewing How a Xtian society may be as a City set on an Hill. 2. Give the Reasons why when they are so tis a very Great obligation on them.

I—How any Professing People may be said to be as a City set on an hill.

And in the General a Professing society may be said to be as a City set on an hill when they as to what Pertains to their Profession are Remarkably set forth to Publick notice & observation.—when there is that in them or in their Circumstances or any thing belonging to them that is very Remarkable & is of great fame far & near any thing that does very much draw the observation of others & causes them much to be taken notice of.

When others have a Great Deal of Opportunity & Great occasion to observe them when they are very much heard of & talked of & much observed, then may they be said to be as a City set on an hill. The occasion of this must be something very Remarkable & distinguishing.

As a City set on an hill stands on distinguished Ground above the Level of the Common Surface of the Earth the place is Eminent & Lifted up, & this sets it forth to view. It can be seen a Great way off & its Prospect Invites & Draws the observation of all that Pass by.—It Cant be hid & no other can be Expected than that all should observe it. No other can be expected than that those that are around it or that come near it should see what a Sort of City it is. If it be a magnificent City full of Stately Buildings that will be taken notice of. If it be meanly built and the houses or walls broken down that will be observed & what a Kind of City it is as to the beauty & magnificence of it will be known.

So when a Professing People have something appertaining to them whereby they are very much distinguished from others that will draw the notice and observa. of the ☉ upon them.— because mankind are wont to take Great notice of things that are strange & singular & by which either a Person or People are Distinguished from others. Any thing that is new or very unusual it makes the stronger Impression on Peoples minds & more Powerfully Influences their Curiosity & draws their attention.

Thus when X made his Last Entrance into Jerusalem, & Came in in a very unusual manner Riding on a Colt—the People spreading their Garments & Branches of Trees in the way & the multitude Crying Hosanna to the Son of David we Read Matt. 21. 10. that the whole City was moved saying who is this?

There are three Distinguishing things Especially that make a Professing People or society as a City set on an hill.

1. When their Profession is distinguishing. The Profession of a People may be distinguishing in two Respects.

1. When they Profess that which is different in its Kind & nature from what the Generality of others do Profess, if they Profess doctrines that differ from those that others do, Profess

a different Kind of Religion. Thus it was with the disciples then whom X says are as a City———— They Differed from all the ⊙ in their Profession they Professed faith in J. of Nazareth as the True Messiah & Saviour of mankind & the doctrines of Redemption that he taught.—herein their Profession Distinguished them from the Jews who did not believe that X was the messiah. & It also distinguished them from the Heathen who Professed other Gods & other mediators. X Crucified this was to the Jews a stumbling block & to the Greeks fool.———— 1 Cor. 1. 23.—This made them as a City set on an hill they were much the more observed & taken notice of for their differing so from all the ⊙ in Professing a Crucified Saviour.

& Sometimes a People tho they dont differ from other People in the doctrines they Profess yet they differ from them as to those things that they mainly Insist on as the most Essential things & differ from many others as to what they think it most to be Looked at in order to Eternal Salvation which may Cause 'em to be much taken notice of.—The disciples in their Profession were distinguished from the Jews in this Respect. The Jews they Professed that we ought to obey all Gods Comm. now, that we should observe the Ceremonial Law even in the minutest Parts of it even to the Paying tithe of mint———— & also they Professed that men ought to seek judgmt mercy & faith.—& so did the Disciples Profess the same things but herein they differed that the Jews Laid the Greatest weight on those Ceremonial observances but the disciples Laid the Greatest weight on judgmt mercy & faith Matt. 23. 23. Such a difference as this in the Profession of a People from other People will tend to make em the Objects of distinguishing notice.

2. When they make an higher Profession than other People, or when they are Distinguished as to the Degree of what they Profess when they Profess Greater Degrees of Holiness than others or that Greater numbers of them are holy. When they make a Profession of having Greater Degrees of the Presence of G. with them of God having done more for them & of Greater mercies that G. has bestowed upon them than on other People.—When there is a far Greater number among them that do make Profession of Special Experiences & of Extraordinary Light that they have had.—When they make

Profession of Greater acquaintance with G. & more Communion with him & of Greater hopes of what G. will do for them
hereafter & of the Happiness that they Expect to be admitted
to.—When there is a Greater manifestation and Show of Relig.
in their talk & discourse.—Hereby a People are set forth to the
notice of others. Such a People will be much observed.—Some
will observe & watch them out of a Sp. of Pride. There is such
a disposition in the Hearts of men that if others Profess to be
better than they that it is Cross to them. They naturally dislike
it & are averse to it that others should Count them so better
than they & there is a secret Resentment of it when others
make such a Profession. & this Resentmt will stir them up to
Observe them diligently & watch for their halting.

&such a Profession docs also excite the observation of
those that are of a Good Spirit that would be Glad if their
Profession were true they will observe em to see whether it
be True or no.

2. another thing that makes a Professing society as a City set
on an Hill is their being Distinguished by any Remarkable
works that G. has wrought among them. Thus the Childr. of
Israel in Egypt & in the wildern. were Distinguished. G. did
wonderfull things for them in Egypt & at the Red Sea & in the
wild. & this was heard of by the nations of Canaan & in all the
nations Round about & drew their observation & notice.

& so it was with Respect to the Xtians or disciples of X after
his Resurrection. G. wrought wonderfull & marvellous things
among them he Remarkably Poured out his Sp. at Pentecost
& filled them with extraordinary & miraculous Gifts. So did
G. Continue in a wonderfull manner to set in with the Preaching of the apostles & Evangelists at Samaria, at Antioch, at
Iconium, Ephesus & Corinth & many other Places which drew
the observa. of all the world on this Sort of People. They were
all intent upon them to observe what sort of People this was of
whom they heard such wonderfull things.

& so it is still when G. appears in any very Remarkable &
wonderfull works amongst a People. It Draws the attention &
observa. of Good & bad. For those that Know not what it is yet
it appears Something Strange & this excites their observation.
—The Godly will observe them as Rejoicing in the Great
works of G. towards them & desiring to see the Good fruits of

it.—others will observe 'em some out of Curiosity & some from Envy as hoping to find something amiss in them. The

3. & Last thing I shall mention that makes a professing People to be as a City set on an Hill is a Remarkable Influence that they or any thing in them has had upon others when either their Extraordinary Profession or any Extraordinary work of G. among them has had a Great & Remarkable Influence on others Round about to make a Great alteration among them to awaken them & Reform them & to Cause Religion to flourish among them. This does Remarkably tend to draw the Eyes of the world on such a People or Society.

So it was with Respect to the disciples and Primitive Xtians. G. wonderfully Poured out his Sp. on them which was of Great Influence on others through all parts of the then known ☉. They were made the means of others in vast multitudes being awakened & Converted.

The Pouring out of the Sp. began at Jerusalem & from thence it spread into other Cities in that Land & in all Parts of the ☉. The Law went forth out of Zion & the W. of G. from Jerusalem agreeable to Isai. 2. 3.—The Sp. of G. seems at first to have Been Poured out on those that had been the discip. of X while he Lived here on Earth & they thereby had Great Influence on others to the Conversion of many thousands. Thus fixed the Eyes of the ☉ upon them & they were Greatly taken notice of & observed every where.

And so Paul & those that were with him became noted & Renowned from the Great Influence they had had on others. Thus they say of them Acts 17. 6. These that have turned the ☉ upside down are Come hither also.—& so sometimes it is with Respect to others. A Professing society is some times as a City set on an hill on this account by Reason of the Great & Extensive Influence that they have or what is Seen in them or heard of them has on others. I Proceed now to the

II. thing Proposed, viz to Give the Reasons why when a People are thus as a City set on an Hill tis a very Great obligation on them to Honour Religion by an Holy an Amiable Practice. For this End was it that X told his discip. that they were as a City set on a hill, viz to convince em of their obligation of being such and Living as such as he had been speaking of: viz. poor—

Sp. Mourners—meek.—Hunger—merciful—pure—peace makers
—Enduring Persecutions—

& it Lays a Great Obligation on any Professing Society on
the following accounts

1. If such a People dont Honour Relig. by———— they will
above all People appear Inconsistent with thems. For this their
Great & Extraordinary Profession of Relig. is one thing,
whereby they are thus set up to the view of the ☉ & if they
thus set thems. up to view and when they have Done Dont
hold forth the Proper Tokens & fruits of that which they Profess, they will, above all People act Contrary to their own
Profession, & Contrary to what G. & all mankind might Justly
Expect from their Profession Expect & Look for. Their Profession is Eminent & higher than others & therefore if they are
Consistent with thems. they will be Eminent in their Practice.

2. When G. sets up a Professing Society as a City on an Hill
he does it so that they may honour Relig. by— If G. distinguishes them from other People by what he does for them or
among them & so sets em up to the view of the ☉ tis a Call of
G. to them that way to honour him before the ☉. This we are
taught in the next v. to the text neither do men Light and Put
it under a Bushel, but on a Candlestick and it giveth Light
unto all that are in the House. To what End does a man Light
a Candle & set it up in fair sight not under a Bushel but on a
Candlestick but that it may Give Light to all that are in an
house. So to what End does G. distinguish a professing People
with Extraordinary mercy & set em up to the view of the ☉
but that they may be the Light of the ☉—that they may shew
forth Gods Praise in the sight of those in whose view they are
set as in the first Clause of the v. of the text ye are the Light of
the ☉—but how can such a People be a Light to the ☉ but
only by causing their Light so to shine before men that others
seeing their good W.———— as it follows in the 16. v.————

3. a Professing People or Society that is thus set up, if they
do thus may do more Good & by the Contrary may do more
hurt than any other People. As they are thus set up on an hill
so they are under advantage to do either more Good or
more hurt, than any People in the ☉ that are not set on an
hill as they are—If they carry thems. unsuitably & unXtianly &

Contrary to their Profession their Carriage will do vastly more hurt than the Like Ill Carriages of other People. It will be abundantly more to Gods dishonour & to the dishonour of Relig. because they being distinguished to the Eye of the ☉ by the Profession & shews of Relig. that are amongst them the ☉ Looks to them to form a Judgmt of that Relig. which they Profess by the fruits they see in them & will have either Honourable or dishonourable thoughts of Relig. by what they see.—& if such a People shew forth the Praises of G. the amiableness of True Relig. by their walk & Conversa. so that Xtianity appears in them untainted & not marred & defiled but in its native Beauty & Excellency, they may thereby do more towards giving Credit & Reputa. to Relig. & promoting of it amongst others than any People in the ☉ that are not so set up & distinguished—because they being set on high, what is to be seen in them that is honourable to Relig. is seen further & much more notice is taken of it.

This will tend to Cause that the works that G. has wrought among them shall have their due Effect in others' minds to stir them to such after a Like blessing.—It will tend to Convince the ☉ that G. is in em of a Truth & that the work they behold is Indeed the work of G. & so Cause them to fall down on their face & worship G.—We have seen Lately what a Great Influence the beholding of the Great & wonderfull works of G. in a People have on other People when once they are Convinced of the Reality of it but nothing has so Great a tendency to Convince Persons as this.

4. Such a People are under obligations thus to do as they would Regard their own Honour & Reputation. A People ought to have a Regard to their own Honour, otherwise G. never would have Encouraged his People that he would Put honour upon them in the sight of others as Josh. 3. 7. & Deut 4. 6. & many other places & threatened the wicked with bringing them to Reproach & disgrace.

When G. thus exalts a People & makes them as a City that is set on an hill G. exercises distinguishing Grace & favour unto them by the Honour he put upon them & he Gives them advantage of appearing with Peculiar & distinguished Honour in the sight of all that do behold them if they will but shew forth fruits answerable to what G. has done for them—this is the

way to obtain the high Esteem & Great Respect of all wise &
solemn persons & Even to be Reverenced in the Hearts of the
wicked whose Consciences will necessarily bear a Testimony to
the Honourableness of such things as they see in them.—The
more Persons are set up to the view of the ☉ the more does it
Concern them to appear so as may be to their Honour because
what is either to their Honour or disgrace is more publickly
Known & Generally observed.—They do the more extensively
obtain Credit by what is Honourable in them, & are more
Extensively dishonoured when that appears in them which is
disagreeable to their Profession & dishonourable.

X seems Plainly to have Respect to this in the Text. A City
that is set on an hill Cannot be hid, as much as to say if you
dont behave your selves well you Cant hide it for you are as a
City that is set on an Hill, & it will be observed by all about
you to your Shame & Reproach.

& such a People that make such an high Profession if they dont
walk Answerable are exposed to Greater Reproach than others
because of their high Pretences. A man or People that dont
Pretend to much is not had in that Contempt as he that Pre-
tends to much and appears indeed to have but little.—Tis so in
Every thing if a Person makes a Great Pretence to wisd. &
Knowledge but appears upon acquaint. to be a fool is more
exposed abundantly to be despised & Ridiculed than a man of
but mean ability, & never Pretended to anything Great.—& so
tis with Respect to Goodness he that makes Profession of
being Eminently Good & better than others if to observation
of by standers he appears no better but to be a very ill man he
Lies much more Liable to disgrace & Contempt than he that
makes no Pretences beyond what he is.

Application.

FIRST Use is of Instruction. in three Inferences

1. Hence we need not wonder if such a People if they fail of
suitably Honouring Relig. in their Practices should be Exercised with temporal Judgmts & frowns as much or more than
other People. Because if their obligations are Exceeding Great
as has been observed then their Guilt will also be Peculiarly
Great if they notably fail of doing as they are obliged.

The Honour of Gods holy name suffers more from such a
People than others if they carry it unsuitably & therefore it will

not be to be wondered at if G should Cause them to suffer in their Temporal Interest more than others—their sins are Attended with more than ordinary Ingratitude for mercies & theref it will be no wonder if G. withholds & Cuts em short of temporal mercies that they need to Correct them for their Ingratitude.

& that the many of them may be truly Converted & may be Gods Children. Gods own People Do by their unsuitable & ungratefull Carriage expose thems. as much to Temporal Calamities as any persons whatsoever. What Great & sure Calamities did David meet with for his—. Yea G. oftentimes Lets others alone in their Sins & Lets em go on & Prosper when he will Correct his own Childr.—& a People that have been Remarkably distinguished & set on high as a City set on an hill are more Exposed to temporal Chastisemts if they dishonour Gods name by unworthy Carriages than any People whatsoever. Amos 3. 2. You only have I Known of all the Families that are on the Earth theref will I Punish you for all your Iniq.

& if we in this Town whom G. has of Late Remarkably set up as a City on an hill should carry our selves so as Remarkably to dishonour that Profession we make, there seems to be no People that will be more Exposed to temporal Chastisemts. To whom much is Given. If a man has been abundantly Kind to a Child or servant.

2. Hence we may Learn that if such a People or Society Do Remarkably dishonour Relig. by their behaviour what danger there will be that G. will for the future withhold such mercies, as he has bestowed. God has indeed mercy sufficient to overlook & forgive this & all sins however aggravated but yet Persons may Greatly expose thems. by abuse of Past mercies to the Judgmt of being Denied future mercies.—& if the obligation be so Great then the Provocation will be answerably Great & if G. has set a People high in the sight of the world but they dont Improve their Exalted State to his Honour it will be no wonder if G. should thrust them down Low into the dirt & make them an hissing & Perpetual Reproach.

3. if there be any Particular Persons in such a Society that do in an Especial manner bring Great & Publick dishonour on the Profession of that Society, this doc. may teach how Great their Guilt must needs be. When there has been a Great & very

Remarkable work of G. amongst a People the notable miscarriages & unsuitable & wicked behaviour of a few Particular
Professors, may very very much wrong the Credit & Reputation of the whole work, & all the profession that is made—
these Inferences are Known abroad and the ⊙ is Ready to pass
their Judgmt of all the Rest what they see in them. & this is
one way wherein that is verified in Eccles. 9. 18. One Sinner
destroys much Good.—But when it is so the Guilt of such
Persons must needs be exceeding Great because it Robs G. in
a Great measure of the Honour of so Great a work & darkens
the Light of the whole Society & brings a Great discredit on
Relig. in General.

One such Professor that Carries hims. thus unsuitably in
such a Society may do as much hurt to the Interest of Religion
as an hundred other wicked men & how much Greater then
must we Conclude his Guilt will be than the Guilt of others.
Here that place may well be applied in Matt. 18. 7. It must
needs be that offences Come but wo to that man by whom the
offence Cometh.

I Come now Particularly to apply this doc. to the case of this
Town. This Town is in a Remarkable degree such a Society as
is spoken of in the Text & doctrine.—It has been so in a Considerable degree formerly. It has in time past been a Town of
an higher Profession & more noted for the works which G.
had wrought in it than most Towns if not than any Town in
the Land. But it is become more Remarkably so of Late by
means of the Late wonderfull Pouring out of the Sp. of G.
upon us. G. has hereby set us up on high to the view & observa. of the ⊙.—We are as a City set upon an hill in all those
ways that have been mentioned. We are so by the distinguishing Profession that we make & we have been made so by the
distinguishing & Remarkable works that G. hath wrought
amongst us & we have been made so by the Great & Remarkable Influence that what has been seen & heard of amongst us
and the Profession we make has had on many other places.—
tho the whole work was the work of G. & we have nothing to
attribute of it to our selves yet G. was pleased Evidently to
make use of his own Great & wonderf. work here as a means to
stir up & awaken others all around us & it has been Improved

by G. as the occasion & means whereby he has begun a Great & wonderfull work in many other Places far & near.—It has been with us very much as it was of old with the Chh of Thessalonica. 1 Thes. 1. 7, 8. So that ye were Ensamples to all that believe in macedonia & achaia for from you sounded out the word of the Lord not only in macedonia & achaia, but also in Every Place your faith to Godward is Spread abroad.

The Country in General was Probably never so filled with talk of any work of such a nature. The fame of it spread abroad Every where and all sorts were earnestly Enquiring about it. Some have Enquired from Real hearty Concern for the Kingd of G. & have heartily Rejoiced to hear of Such a work & others have Enquired from Curiosity because it was so strange & unusual a thing—others have Enquired from Something of Concern in their own minds they have been a Little Startled & their hearts something touched by hearing the news of such a wonderf. work of G. and others have Enquired out of Enmity against such a work—but the whole Country has been filled from one End of it to the other with the fame of what has been here done and what is here Professed & the Eyes of all the Land have been drawn upon us to observe us & Every one has been Enquiring how the affair went on here & after what manner the work was carried on & what Effect it has upon those that are the Subjects of it & how they behave thems. & the Like—so that there probably never was any Town in this Land under so Great obligations of that Kind mentioned in the Text & Doc. to Honour their Profession by their Practice as this Town.

Here I would mention Several things in Particular Respecting our being set as a City on an hill which shew our extraordinary obligation to adorn our Profession by our Practice.

1. we may Consider the Great & violent Endeavours that Satan has used to hinder the Credit of the work that has been wrought amongst us. The devil has seemed extraordinarily to bestir hims. to this Purpose for he Knew that the bringing a Reproach on this work of G. would be the Likeliest way to hinder the Progress of it.—Hell seems to be alarmed by the Extraordinary breaking forth of the work of G. here & the sudden & swift Propagation of it from Town to Town. The devils seem to have been all up in arms if Possible to Put a stop to it & the way they have seemed Chiefly to betake thems. to has been to

destroy the Credit of the work, to hinder People abroad from believing that it was a Good work, & to Possess them with ill thoughts of it.

Thus you may Remember that when the work was first begun in this Town that the neighbouring Towns seemed to be filled almost with talk against it many would speak Contemptibly of it some made a mean scoff & Ridicule of it & others that did not do so yet seemed to suspect it.—& when G. notwithstanding Carried on his work & in a little Time carried it into the neighbouring Towns in spite of Satans Endeavours to Prejudice them against it then the devil seemed to be yet more alarmed & to be more violent & Labour to bring a Reproach on this work of G. by the violent onsets that he made on some particular Persons, by Extraordinary Temptation to mischief & destroy themselves. In which G. in his Sov. Provid. was Pleased to suffer him to Prevail especially in one Instance viz in that very awfull disaster the death of Mr Hawley by which Satan did seem in a Great measure for the Present to Gain his End viz to bring a blot upon the work of G. amongst us.

& another device of Satan to hurt the Credit of this work by which he has been no Less succcssfull has been to Lead away & deceive some particular Professors by Enthusiastical Impressions & Imaginations which they have Conceited were divine Revelations such as were wont to be Given to the Prophets of old.—& the noise of this has been swiftly spread abroad in the Country to the Great wounding of the Credit of the work of G. in this part of the Land.—And another device of Satan to hinder the Credit of this work has been to fill the Country with Innumerable false & Groundless Reports. It has been astonishing to see how many Strange & Ridiculous stories have been Carried abroad that have no founda.—& how that those things that have been in part true that have been a blemish to Relig. amongst us have been magnified & added to.

And another thing wherein the spite & violence of Satan against the work of G. here has been manifest is the Extraordinary means that have Lately been used to Cast an Odium upon this County & Raise a Kind of a mobbish Rage & fury against the ministry of the County & to Prejudice the minds of the Country against them. Especially those of them that have

Chiefly stood in the defence of those Truths of the Gospel in which the Late work of G. amongst us has mainly depended.

In this also G. in his Holy Provid has suffered Satan to be in a Great measure successful as we have been well Informed to Lessen the Credit of the work of G. amongst us.

& in all it has been very Evident that Satans spite has been Chiefly against Northampton if Possible to beget a Prejudice in the minds of the Country against this Town which has been the original & Principal seat of this W. of G.—If Satan therefore be so Great in his Endeavours to bring a discredit on this work of G. Certainly we that have been so Peculiarly favoured of G. ought to be Great in our Endeavours to uphold & Promote the Credit of it.

We may Conclude that Satan Knows that if this work be in Credit it will Greatly tend to Promote the Glory of G. & the Interest of Relig. other wise he would never so Exert hims. to hinder its being in Credit.—This should make us the more Carefull that we do nothing to discredit it & that we do our utmost to Promote the Reputation of it.

& there is no way in the world that we Can do so much as by adorning our Profession by our Practice & holding forth to the ⊙ the Good & Lovely fruits of this work of G.

2. Let it be Considered that the Truth of this work has been from the beginning & is to this very day very much Suspected in the Country. There never was a work of this nature in the Country so much taken notice of & that there has been so much talked of.

But it has not been Generally & fully Received as true. At the first beginning when it was first heard of in the Country it was Suspected from the Extraordinariness of the thing—and afterwards People had their Suspicions Increased by the stories they heard Partly by those Stories that were true & partly by those that were false & Groundless.

But to this very day the Country is not Convinced. & there seem to have been two Principal Reasons of it. One is those devices & attempts of Satan that have already been mentioned. —and another is that there seems to be a Strong Prejudice in a Great Part of the Country against any work of such a nature. They are Strangers to it they dont Know what it means it has been a degenerate dead time so long in the Country that vital

Religion & the Power of Godliness seems to be Grown a Shy Stranger in many Places.—In the first times of the Country such things were Common & such a work as this then would not have met with such Prejudices in mens minds against it. But there has been so Great a decay of the Power of Relig. so Long in the Country that the Country has in a Great measure forgot the Language. It is strange Kind of talk to them the very notion of such Powerfull works of Gods Sp. seems to be Raced out of their minds.—& the Country seems, in Great Part of it to be got into another way of thinking of things of Relig. Looking Chiefly at morality & a sober Life.—and then another Great Prejudice in the Country has been the Late Extraordinary Growth of Arminianism or doctrines that savour of it, Especially amongst those that are set to teach others.

But the natural tendency of those doctrines is to make men have such things as have Lately been Experienced and talked of amongst us in the Greatest Contempt. Persons of such Principles do Commonly make a scoff & derision of them.

But it being so that there is so Great a Suspicion of the Truth of this work it behoves this Town that has been Especially the subject of this work to do their utmost to Give Evidences of the Truth of it.

& there is no other way that we Can do it but by Honouring our Profession & shewing the Truth of it by our Practice. There is no other way that we Can be Likely to Convince such Persons.

There are multitudes in the Country that have already concluded that the work is nothing & they stand Ready to hear of our miscarriages & declensions to Confirm their opinion & would Gladly Catch at any thing of that nature.—And others that hant Concluded yet have Greatly suspected who would be Confirmed & settled down in it that it is nothing by only hearing a few Reports of this nature when a Person has already a suspicion, the mind stands Ready to catch & Receive Impressions from Every thing that seems to Confirm it. A few things of this nature will turn a Strong Suspicion into down Right Conclusions.

3. Consid what a Good Effect the Report of work of G. has already had in places where it has been Credited. The Effect has been very Extraordinary & wonderfull & the main thing

that has seemed to hinder the yet Greater Progress of this work has been that the Truth of it has not been believed.—Where it has been drunk in that this work was the work of G. we have seen that it has had a Powerfull Influence to awaken many & has Issued in the saving Conversion of multitudes.—& the ill thought or the suspicion that the Country have had of it seems to have been the main Impediment to its having the Like Effect more Extensively.

It concerns us therefore to do our utmost to Remove that Impediment which can be done no way so Effectually as by its being apparent in the Eyes of the Country that there is a Good & Lasting Effect & fruit of the work appearing in our Lives & Conversations.

4. Many of the more Prudent sort of People have suspended their Judgmts of this work till they could see what the effect would be on our Lives & Conversation. This has been the Case without doubt with many natural men, who tho they were stranger to any such work in their own hearts yet from their moral Prudence have at once Concluded against it that it was not of G. Like Gamaliel Acts 5. 38.—& this also doubtless has been the Case of some Godly People that dwell in dist parts that hant had opportunity to see what the work was & did not Know what to make of it from what they heard & have suspended their Judgmts Concluding that they should be better able to pass a Judgmt afterward when it should be seen & Known what the effect of it would be in their Lives & Conversations, have Concluded within thems. that if the work was not of G. it would Come to nothing & would appear to be nothing by the fruits that should be brought forth. This seems to have been the Case with many in the Country.

Certainly theref it stands it in hand, not to fail of Giving of them that Evidence of the Truth of the work which they have waited for, & to Let em see those signs of the Reality of our Profession by our holy & Xtian & amiable Practice so that they need neither to suspend their Judgmts any Longer nor think that they have any cause to determine against us.

5. If we dont adorn our Profession by our Practice we shall disappoint them that have believed this work to be a work of G. Tho there have been multitudes in the Country that have doubted of the Truth of this work & many that have spake

against it yet there has been a number that have believed it. There have been some such in all parts of the Country by what they have heard they have Concluded it was a Real & wonderfull work of G. & they have stood up in defence of it against those that have opposed it.

But if they hear that our Carriage is notably unsuitable to our Profession, if they hear that Persons seem to Return again in a Considerable measure to their old ways & the young People Grow disorderly again & there seems to be Prevailing of a very Unchristian Sp. in the Town a Sp. of Contention & strife, a very niggardly narrow & Private Sp., or the Like we shall dreadfully disappoint them we shall doubtless stumble them they wont Know what in the ⊙ to make of it they'll begin to fear whether they were not too sudden & hasty in their Charity for us—They have Pleaded for us hitherto & stood up for us against our adversaries but if such things be Reported of us & we Give occasion for it we shall stop their mouths they wont know what to say nor what to think.

Wise & Prudent & Godly People will doubtless be Greatly Stumbled by it & we shall wound the Charity even of the best People in the Land, & those whose Charity & Good opinion is most to be valued. They will think they have warrant to doubt from Xs own Rule. Matt. 7. 16. Ye shall Know them by their fruits.

6. People in the Country are now often Enquiring how those that were Looked upon to be Lately Converted Behave thems. Tis a Question that I am very often asked where I Go, by ministers & others. The Country in General have been waiting to see & they are very Inquisitive about it & I expect still to be asked the same Question. Let me Intreat of you that I may always have a Good account to Give. You may be sure that I am Disposed to Give the best when I am thus Enquired of. I Should be Glad to be able to say that such Persons as make a Profession of Special Experiences amongst us do adorn their Profession by a very Excellent walk. They seem to be truly of a very Amiable & Xtian Sp. & behaviour. & to tell them that the Glo. Effects of the work of G. are to be seen in the Town in that we dwell all in peace & Love that there is nothing of any disorder amongst young People nor nothing of any party Sp. or Sp. of Contention but that all Publick affairs

seem to be managed with Love & meekness & that there is an harmonious Sweet agreemt amongst all Sorts of People. & that People in generally are most evidently altered in being abundantly of a more free Sp. to do for G. & to part with the ⊙ for pious & Charitable uses & the Like—such a Report as this would wonderfully Confirm Peoples minds In the Goodn. of that Late work amongst us & the Goodness of our Profession.—Let me Therefore Intreat you all that there may be such a Report truly Carried & such an answer truly Given to all that Enquire. Here I may apply the words of the apostle. 2. Cor. 9. 3. 4———

7. People abroad have Heard of those things that have happened amongst us that have been any blemish to our Profession & take Great notice of them. What has fallen out that has been matter of Scandal People abroad have heard of it to the Great wounding of the Credit of the Glo. W. of G. amongst us.

I have heard such things mentioned abroad & have been Enquired of about them & have Perceived that they have been spoken of to our disparagement.

& those Circumstances have been all Rehearsed now that were most aggravating & that Rendered them Peculiarly dishonourable to this work. & no wonder for we are a City that is set on an hill & such a City Cant be hid. We must not Expect to hide our blemishes & those things that might be matter of Reproach to us or our Profession they will be Known we cant hide them.—what there has been of this nature already is Known & is Improved to our dishonour as well as the dishonour of Relig.

& if there should be any thing hereafter if some of our young People that Pretend to be Converted should be found in any notable wickedness, or any other Pretenders to Special Experience should be Guilty of Scandal or there should be any Publick disorder or Contention or any such thing, it will be Known. The Birds of the air will Carry it & that which hath wings shall tell the Matter. It will spread about swiftly—there are many that watch to hear of such things among us & if they once get hold of it they will Improve it to the utmost.

Let what has happened in time Past be a warning to us, that the Enemy may have nothing from us for an occasion to Reproach us & Reproach Relig. for time to come. Again,

8. What has been wrought amongst us & the Profession we make has been much taken notice of even beyond the bounds of this Country. I have had Special opportunity to Know in the Journey that I took the Last fall. They had heard much of it in New York & there were many People there that were Inquisitive about it.

I there met with some that belonged to the Jerseys & particularly a minister that lives in those Parts & they Informed me that they had heard much of it in those Parts & that many People took Great notice of it there. Ministers there mentioned in their Pulpits as I saw in a Printed Sermon that was Preached in the Jerseys, & those that I saw that belonged there were very Inquisitive about it.—& so upon Long Island from one End of it to the other they talked much of it & asked me particularly about it—& since I came home I have had a Letter from a minister in the Jerseys Informing me how much they had heard there about it & desiring me to send him a particular account.—and another from the Highlands on Hudsons River signifying that they had heard of it there. & Every where this Town is principally mentioned & Enquired of.

& not only so but this wonderfull work has been heard of & taken much notice of in England. One of the ministers of London some time since wrote over to the Rev'd Dr Colman of Boston signifying to him his Rejoicing to hear the tydings of such a wonderfull work of G. in this Land.

& since that very Lately he & another minister of London both Doctors of Divinity & very Eminent Divines have written over again desiring to be Informed how it is now amongst us—& how much to be Lamented is it that they cant be Informed that the work of G. still continues Gloriously to be carried on amongst us & that there still Remains & Extraordinary Lively & Earnest Sp. for Relig. in the midst of us.

Tis to be Expected that we shall yet further be Inquired of. The ⊙ seems to be Inquisitive about the Progress & Issue of the work. Tis probable these London Divines will yet further Enquire about us & what a thousand Pities is it that they should hear any thing of us but what tends to Confirm their Good opinion of the work & to Increase their Joy in it.— Certainly tis our duty to take notice of these things. G. & all mankind will Condemn us if we dont.—What a pity is it but that the news of this Glo. work of G. should be carried abroad into distant parts of the ☉ without any bad Report Joined with it to be a blemish to it.—O what pity is it but that they should hear that our fruits are answerable, that there is a Lasting wonderfull alteration in our practice, that the wolf now Dwells with the Lamb.

Isai. 11. 6.————

How much would this be to our Honour as well as to the Honour of Relig. & tis very Likely if there be no Reports Carried to wound the Credit of this work but on the Contrary that it will have a tendency to Give some Revival of Relig. Even in other Countrys & I believe has had that Effect some measure already.

Who can Conceive what Obligations Lie upon us to be carefull of our walk, & how shall we Provoke G. & bring Guilt on our selves if we are not. & how might Justly hereafter set us forth to be an Example of his Judgmts as he has to be an Instance of his wonderfull mercy.

9. & Lastly Consid. How much it will be not only to the discredit of this particular work of G. but of all that Kind of Relig. that we Profess if we dont walk according to our Profession. It wont only make other People that behold us & hear of us Question the truth of this work but it will Prejudice all Talk or pretences of such a work of Conversion as we Profess the necessity of it and against All such Special Experiences of the Operations of the Sp.

The Land & the ☉ are Grown of Late very much into Prejudice against such sort of things. It is Quite Contrary to that divinity that is Lately Every where fashionable.

& now in this work, there has been a notable Instance Given to the ☉ of that which they are thus Prejudiced against & their Eyes are very much drawn to see what this will come to & if they see that there bent answerable fruits, it will Exceedingly Confirm em in their Rejecting all such things as being nothing but meer whimsy & Enthusiasm.—they have Cried it down before but then they will Cry it down a Great deal more they will think they have Demonstration against It. They will say there is the People at Northampton that Experienced so much of such sorts of things. See what it comes to.—& so all vital Religion will suffer & come into discredit by our miscarriages.—

it seems so to be ordered in Providence at Present that not only our own Credit and the Credit of the Late work of G. amongst us but the Credit of all vital Relig. & the Power of Godliness in this Land, depends very much on the behaviour of the People in this Town. For the Interest of Relig. depends on outward means.

Let me hence take occasion Earnestly to address my self to all sorts amongst us, to Consid. these things & to Lay that weight on them that is due to them—& O that it may be the Earnest Care of Every one to his utmost to watch over hims.— Let us Consider that the ☉ has heard so much of a wonderfull work of G. amongst us that they dont meerly Expect to hear of things that are negative amongst us & that we are a Preferred People but they will expect to hear something positive. What a Good Sp. there is appears amongst us how Ready we are to Good works how Ready to deny our selves how forward to Promote any Good design how Charitable & how Publick Spirited we be how Ready to Lay out our Substance for the Poor or for the worship of G. & the Like.

I would Intreat that there may be such a Sp. as this manifest in the managemt of our Publick affairs, & not a backward Loth fearfull Sp in that that is Good an over fearfullness Lest we should spend too much —a disposition & aptness to Quarrel for our money Lest too much of it should be Laid out for Publick designs & Especially for the Honour of Gods Publick worship, & an Aptness to have our Spirits something on an Edge in opposition to them that differ from us in opinion or are Endeavoring to carry a Contrary design. These things dont become a People that are as a City set on an hill in the manner that we are.

& Let me Intreat that G. may be honoured & Xtianity adorned in families. Let Family orders & family Religion be strictly Kept up & attended & dont let us have any Custom of breaking of it by being unseasonably absent from our home a-nights or any thing of that nature.—& dont Let us Return to those disorders that we have forsaken to frequenting the tavern to night walking & frolicking & Rioting & Licentious Company Keeping to Contending & Quarreling. Dont let us as the dog Return to this vomit or as the sow that was washed to wallowing in this filthy mire.

& here I would particularly direct my self to our young People. You are a Generation that I hope are blessed of the Lord. I cannot but hope that many of you are beloved of G. are the objects of the dear Love of G. & the dying Love of the L. Jesus.—This Great blessing that G. has Lately Poured out on our Town tho it has descended on all sorts yet has fell more Remarkably on your Generation.—Let me beseech you to hold fast that which you have Received whereunto you have attained in Escaping the Pollutions of the ⊙ therein abide. Dont Return to any disorders & Licentious Practices or any thing that is not of Good Report. Shew your selves Ready to hearken to Come & set as you have done that you may be a Generation to Gods Praise.—Dont Esteem the Service of G. your burden. Serve the Lord & you will find that you serve a Good master. Walk in wisdoms ways & you will find you Loose no Pleasure by it.

When you are together Let your Company be beautified & sweetened with Religion & virtue and in no wise tainted or sullied with any thing vicious or Extravagant.

I hope that many of you are the Children of G. O Let me pray you to walk as becomes such walk not as the Childr. of darkness but as the Children of the Light & of the day. 1 Thes. 5. 5. ye are all the Chil. Eph. 5. 8.—Love the Lord with all your Hearts. Let him be the object of your highest Love & whatever Love or friendship there be amongst you in any one towards another. Let all be sanctified with the Love of G.

& whatever Company you Keep one with another Let it not be marred & defiled by any manner of thing in word or deed that is Lewd or unchaste or unseemly.

Let virtue & Xtianity Rule in your Company Keeping & Let your society be Improved for Relig. discourse. This will make your Company & Conversa. together sweet to you in the time of it & not only so but sweet in your Reflections on it & sweet in the fruits of.—& you will find that nothing Makes Earthly Love & Company so sweet as the Love of G. and the Exercise of virtue & Piety.

Zeal an Essential Virtue of a Christian

April 1740.

Tit. 2. 14.
*Who Gave hims. for us that he might Redeem us from
all Iniq. & purify unto hims. a peculiar People
zealous of Good works.*

I have already in discerning from these words observed several
things in them which I have no need of my repeating. What I
now Intend from these words Leads me especially to observe
three things in em.

1. A Certain virtue or Good Quality, here mention, viz. a
being zealous of Good works. &

2. We may take notice that this virtue is mentioned as part of
the description of those that belong to Xs Invisible Chh. The
People that are Redeemed by X from all Iniq. and that X puri-
fies to hims. & that are his peculiar People are deciphered by
this that they are Zealous of Good works—This is here mentioned as a main part of their Character, & that by which they
are distinguished from others.

3. I would observe how much X has done that his People
might be endowed with this virtue. He gave hims. for them to
this End. So Great a Regard had he to such a qualification in
his Chosen People so much did he seek to have a people of
such a Character that he gave hims. offered up hims. a sacrif.
to div. Justice to make way for their being Possessed of it.

Theref. the doc. that I would now observe from the words is
this.

Doc. Zeal is an Essential virtue of a Xtian.—

This is evident from the Text because in the Text it is men-
tnd as what belongs to description of a true Xtian & part of his
distinguishing Character. & also because tis mentioned as a
virtue that X purchased for all his Elect & not only so but one
Great & main thing that he aimed at in that sacrifice which he
made of hims. whereby they were purchased. Zeal is a word
often used & persons are often spoken of as being Zealous
persons & very Commonly tis understood in an ill sense.

& such an Idea is very commonly annexed to the word as

carries in it weakness & pride, superstition & anger & probably most Persons have no distinct notion of what is meant by it & the notion that they have is a disadvantageous one. The word is so often used to signify some weak & improper Heat & vehemence of mind, that it scarcely adds any thing to the Goodness of any persons Character in the Eyes of most to hear it said of him that he is a Zealous man but rather detracts from it.—But yet we from time to time find Zeal Recommended in Sc. and spoken of as a Xtian Qualification & whatever disadvantageous notions persons may have of Zeal through the abuse of words yet that Zeal which the Sc. recommends is indeed a noble & Excellent Qualification. To be zealous in this sense is to be one of an amiable & divine Character, & tis one thing wherein the Excellency of pure Xtian virtue does very much appear. To be a Zealous man in the Sc. Sense of the word is an Excellent Character of any one. It has nothing unlovely or unsuitable in it & is not only very Commendable but Essential in a true Xtian.

To Clear up this point I would 1. Describe this virtue or shew what it is. 2. would give the Reasons why it is to be Looked upon as an Essential Qualification of a Xtian.

I. I would shew what is True Xtian Zeal. Christian Zeal is a fervent disposition an affection of mind in prosecuting that which is for Gods Glory & in opposing those things that are against it.

This affection or disposition of mind is called Zeal principally from its fervour or ardency whereby tis like an Inward heat or flame in the Soul.—It might have defined more briefly a fervent disposition or affection of mind in pursuing the Glory of G. For Gods pleasure & Glory are the principal object of the Exercises of this virtue, and next to that the means of pleasing & Glorifying G. either the prosecution of those things that leads to or the Removal of the hindrances of it.

But to give a more Clear & distinct notion of this Excellent Quality of mind, I would more particularly describe it by shewing what affections are Exercised in it & the manner of their Exercise & the acts in which this virtue Exerts it self.

As to the first viz the Affections in which true Xtian Zeal has its seat or which are Exercised in it

1. That affection that is principal in this virtue is Love. Zeal is an Inward heat or fervency of Sp. & Love is the flame

whence that heat comes.—This is the fire that fills the soul with that holy fervour that is called Zeal.

Love to G. & X Divine Love is the founda. of all those other affections that are exercised in Xtian Zeal.—Divine Love is an active principle. It is fire from heaven may be compared to an holy flame Kindled in the soul by a beam from thence.—No man is truly Zealous without it. It is the Sp. that animates & actuates the truly Zealous man.—He that is Zealous from any other principle than Love, his Zeal is no Xtian Zeal it is of a spurious Kind. It is nothing amiable it is a vice & not a virtue —The Psalmist Expressed a Great Love to G. when he said, Ps. 119. 139. My Zeal hath Consumed me because mine Enemies have forgotten thy words & so did Phinehas in that act of which G. speaks in Numb. 25. 11, 12, 13.————

2. From Love to G. arises a desire that he may be Glorified. One way in which love is exercised in Zeal is desire that this G. that is so beloved may be pleased that his will may be done that his Commands may be obeyed, that his name may be Glorifi. that he may be feared that he may be Loved that men may be holy & he is holy & that his Kingd. may be advanced & that Every thing that is against these things may be Removed.— The Apostle Joins vehement Desire & Zeal to gether in 2. Cor. 7. 11. yea what vehement desire yea what zeal.

3. There is in Zeal an aversion to what is Contrary to Gods Command & glory. From that Love which is the principal thing in Xtian Zeal & the founda. of all the Rest that is in it arises Hatred. There is both Love & Hatred exercised in Zeal. The Love of G. & Hatred of Sin, Hatred of those things that G. hates a hatred of what is against the Interest & reputation of Relig. & opposes the flourishing of Xs Kingd.

4. Another affection that is Exercised in Xtian Zeal is a Sp. of Jealousy for G. Zeal & Jealousy in the original of the N. T. are the same word—He that has a Sp. of True Xtian Zeal is Jealous for the Cause of X. If it at any time be injured a Sp. of Jealousy is excited in him. & when the Interest of Relig. is touched his heart is touched & he is rocked & alarmed.

5. Another affection that is exercised in true Zeal is courage a Sp. of fortitude in Enervating the difficulties that are in the way of doing Gods will & the Enemies that oppose his Glory.

2. As to the manner wherein these affections are Exercised in

True Zeal it is with ardor or fervency of Sp. That divine Love which is the main Thing in Xtian Zeal is a Powerfull principle. Tis a fire Kindled in the soul by the active sun beams of the Sun of Righ.

That desire that there is that God would his will should be done & his name Glorified is no faint but an ardent desire.

That hatred there is to sin in Xtian Zeal & the aversion there is to whatever is against Gods Glory has a vehemence to it— that Jealousy by which they are Jealous for the L. of Hosts is also an ardent affection that alarms the Soul & awakens its active principles—there is also a fervour of and in those, a holy fortitude & courage that is exercised in the Heart of him that is Zealous with a truly Xtian Zeal.

3. as to the acts in which this virtue Exerts it self, in one word it is in persuing the Glory of G. Tis not all holy fervency of Sp. that is properly intended by Zeal but it is a holy fervour of mind as it Relates to practice only, or the pursuit of the Glory of G. as those things that are well pleasing to him. & Therefore tis a being Zealous of Good works as the expression is in the Text.—There are many Examples of True Love to G. & fervent Love to G. that dont properly come within the signification of this Term as for instance Love to G. as exercised in delight & Complacence & Contentmt in him in Rejoicing in a View of Glory of his Glory or communion with him & tasting the sweetness of his Love. These things are not properly called Zeal.—But tis Love with Respect to that Exercise of it that is called Zeal that there is in pursuing his Glory that is called Zeal.

So tis not all truly Gracious & ardent desires after G.—after the Enjoymt of G.—but tis an ardent desire to do something whereby G. may be Pleased & honoured.

So the hatred of sin & the Jealousy for Gods Honour that is properly comprehended in Zeal is Exercised in opposing sin & that which is opposite to Gods Glory.—So the courage & fortitude that is in Zeal Relates to action that action that is in pursuing Gods Glory.

& these acts that Zeal is exercised in are of two Kinds. They are either

1. a Prosecuting that which tends to promote Gods Glory, as when a Person exercises a fervency of Sp. in doing Gods works

in loving & Glorifying G. our selves or to promote such things in others—which appears in an ardent disposition of mind in promoting not only the worship of G. but also the good of men so the Zeal of the Corinthians argued in their Deeds of Charity 2 Cor. 9. 2. Good of mens souls so here Epaphras. Col. 4. 12, 13. In one word a fervency of Sp. that Good may be done for Gods & Xs sake either to do it our selves or to promote others doing of it whether this Good be what Immediately Respects the Honour of G. or nextly concerns the Good.

2. It appears in a fervency of Sp. in opposing those things that are against Gods Honour. So it was that Phinehas manifested his Zeal when he took the Javelin, for which G. did so Greatly Rewd him. So also Xs Zeal was Exercised when he drove the buyers & sellers. Matt. 21. 12, 13.——— & also when he Looked round about em with anger.

Having thus shown what true Zeal is I Proceed now in the

II. Place. That is an Essential virtue of a Xtian, insomuch that not only is true Zeal a noble attainmt of a Xtian but he that is not a Zealous Xtian is not allowed in Sc. to be any true Xtian for,

1. This is the Qualification principally by which true Xtians are distinguished from those that are Lukewarm. The Sc. distinguishes mankd into three Sorts those that are Cold who are those that have no appearance or Shew of Relig. and are not to be Looked upon as visible Xtians.—& those that are hot i.e. those that are true Xtians that are fervent in Sp. serving the L. that have within them that holy ardour & Engagedness of mind in Relig. that has been Spoken of—& those that are Lukewarm that is those that make a profession of Relig. & have some shew of Relig. but are not thrgh in it are cold dull & lifeless are an Indifferent sort of Professor have no Great Concern about the Honour of G. & Interest of Relig. who are not true Xtians and never will be accepted of X as some of his if they continue. For we may observe that of those three those that are most abominable to X are those that are Lukewarm that bent Zealous Xtians. Rev. 3. 15, 16.———

The Lukewarm Xtians are more hatefull to X than the openly profane than the very Heathen that make no pretenses to Relig. X declares expressly that he had rather men should be quite Cold than only Lukewarm.

I would Says he that thou were cold or hot. As the Stomach nauseates Lukewarm water more than either cold or hot so doth X abominate Lukewarm Xtians that are destitute of Xtian Zeal in Relig.

2. This is one thing wherein the Power of Godliness appears & wherein it differs from the form of it. These two are spoken of by the apostle in 2. Tim. 3. 5. The one as being Peculiar to true Xtians the other Common to Hypocrites with them.

Sincere Grace is a Powerfull principle in the soul, and the Power of it appears partly in the nature of its actings. It is no dull inactive ineffectual thing. There is an Holy ardency & vigour in the actings of Grace. It is a Kind of inw. Sp. fire in the Soul & theref. when a man is Converted & G. pours out his H. Sp. upon him he is said in Sc. Language to be baptized with the H. Gho. & with fire.—There is an inexpressible ardour of soul when True Grace is in exercise so that the hearts of the saints do as it were burn within them. Luke 24. 32. did not our Hearts burn within us while he talked to us by the way &———

And this Holy ardour that is in the Exercises of True Grace rises not in men by Contemplation & Enjoymt but has Respect to practice. It seeks the Glory of G. it struggles after those means that tend to promote it & against those things that do oppose. & so it has the nature of Zeal.

He that experiences the Power of Godliness at times finds within hims. breathings & Longings of soul not only after more of a Sight of G. & more of an Enjoyment of him but also holiness & Conformity to G. such as have a strength & such a peculiar sort of Inward vigour as other desires have not.—They sometimes cause the Soul to pant after G. and occasion a vehement struggle against sin.

& Even in them that have Comparatively small degrees of Grace yet G. is wont sometimes so far to quicken the principle as to Let the Powerfull nature of it appear in some measure.

There is something in the vigour of the actings of true Grace that is inimitable & inexpressible that does properly shew that there is an omnipotent agent at work in the soul of a Godly man.

This makes true Xtians Zealous in prosecuting those things that tend to Gods Glory & opposing what is against whereas others that have only the form of Godliness without the Power of it are indifferent Lifeless & Lukewarm with Respect to these things.

3. An Indifferent & Lukewarm Sp. in divine Laws in no wise become the nature of divine objects. Divine objects are infinitely great immensely surpassing all temporal things in their Importance & Excellency.—When G. gives men True Grace & Rightly disposes their hearts with Respect to divine things he will give em such Kind of dispositions & affections towards them as do in some measure become their nature & Importance.

Hence X says he that Loves F & mother more than him is not worthy—he that Loves son or daughter—He that takes up—that is he that has no other affection towds him than such an one as falls below or at Least is not above his affection to any temporal objects or Enjoyments, his affection & Respect is in no wise becoming its object & so will never be accepted. & theref. he says elsewhere that he that comes to him & hates not his F. Luke. 14. 26.———

But here a Question or Objection may arise which I will now take occasion to speak some thing to. The

OBJECTION is this viz. How can it be ncsry that men in order to a being true Xtians should Love G. above all things else in the ⊙ when we are so often taught that true Xtians have so little Grace & so much corruption.—We are often taught that Grace in this Life is but in an Infant state that Grace is but as a Spark faith but as a Grain of mustard seed—but that men carry about with them a Load of sin a body of sin & death—his corruption which is so great inclines him to Love the ⊙ & make that his happiness & if there be so much of it & so little Grace how can it be that all truly Godly men should Love G. more than the ⊙.

I ANSW 1. Tis from the nature of the Object Loved rather than the degree of the principle in the Lover. The Object beloved is of supreme Excellency of a Loveliness Immensely above all worthy he is to be chosen pursued & Cleaved to & delighted in far above all—& he that truly Loves him Loves him as seeing this superlative seeing of it as superlative & as being Convinced that it is far above all. Tho a man has but a faint discovery of the Glo. of G. yet if he has any true discovery of him so far as he is discovered he sees this he is sensible that he is worthy to be Loved far above all—The Sp. of G. is a Sp. of truth & if he makes any true discovery of G. it must be a discovery of him as Lovely above all—if such an Excellency is not discovered there is no divine Excellency discovered for the notion of divine Excellency is superlative supreme Excellency.

Now that wherein a Godly m. may be said to Love G. above all seems to be no more than what Immediately & necessarily follows from a sight of this Supreme Excellency. Tho it may be a comparatively faint discovery yet tis a Convincing discovery —Hence G. must be above all in his Esteem: for to be Convinced that he is more Excellent than all is in fact to Esteem him above all.

& so He must be above all in his Choice for the Choice follows the Esteem—& hence also it will follow that G. is above all in his purposes & Resolutions he Cleaves to the Lord with purpose of Heart & so in the sense of the Sc. with his whole Heart.

Tho there may be but Little of the Principle of Love yet the principle that there is being built on such a Conviction will be of this nature viz to prize G. above all.—There may be an Endless variety of degrees of the principle but the nature of the Object is unalterable theref if there be a discovery of the object whether in a Greater or Lesser degree if that discovery be true & agreeable to the nature of the Object the nature of the principle that is the Effect of the discovery will answer the nature of the object & so it will ever more be the nature of it to prize G. above all tho there may be but little of such a principle.

2. another way whereby Grace is predominant in the Soul of a Saint is by virtue of that Cov. of Grace & the promises of G. on which Xtian Grace Relies & which Engages Gods Strength & assistance to be on its Side & to help it against its Enemy which would otherwise be overpowered.

Where G. infuses Grace he will give it a predominancy by his upholding of it & time after time giving it the victory when it seemed for a time to be overborne & ready to be swallowed. This is not owing to our Strength but the Strength of G. who wont forsake the w. of his hands & will carry on his w. when he has begun it & alwaies causeth us to triumph in X Jesus who is the author & has undertaken to be the finisher of our faith.

I conclude with a

4. & Last Reason why Zeal is an Essential virtue of a Xtian. Viz that that affection that is short of this dont agree with the work that a Xtian has to do. The work that a Xtian is called to is the work of a Soldier. Tis a warfare. He is not called to sleep but to Conflict with principalities & powers & the Rulers of the darkn of this ⊙ Sp. wickedness in high places: he is called to take heaven by violence & to obtain the prize by Conquest.

And theref tis absolutely necessary that he should want the Sp. of a Soldier. A Lukewarm Soldier is never Like to obtain the victory he wont take Strong Cities & win Crowns & Kingdoms.

The Sc. tells us of no other way of getting to heaven but by running & fighting & obtaining of it as it were by Conquest.

& theref there is no other disposition or Sp. that will carry us there but a Sp. of zeal an inward ardency of mind to excite us to acquit our selves like men in the Race & in the Battle.— Tho' G. will assist those that trust in him & overcome difficulties for them yet he wont assist the Lukewarm & indifferent but the fervent the vigorous & active nor will he assist any so but that they shall have occasion & exercise for their vigour & Zeal.—he by his assistance will carry men to heaven though all opposing but he wont carry em so that they shall have no occasion to run nor will he so fight for them but that their Faith & Zeal shall be tried in the battle.

I. Use of Examin. If it be thus this should put Persons on Examining thems. whether or no they are possessed of this virtue. Have you a fervency of Sp. Gods being served & honoured. Have you a holy ardour of Soul to prosecute those things that tend to advance the Interest of Relig. & in opposing those things that are against it.—Do you find within you ardent desires that true holiness may be promoted in your own soul that sin may be weaken'd & mortified there & that Grace may flourish that you may be a more Holy humble heavenly Xtian may be of a more Excellent Sp. & may walk more Closely with G.—and do you also Experience fervent desires that true Relig. Real Xtian piety of heart & Conversation may flourish among others in the place where you live in the Land & in the ⊙.

And are you one that is Jealous for the Lord of Hosts. Does

that which wounds the Interest of Relig. touch the apple of Your Eye are you Grieved for the men that sin against G.

Have you an aversion of Sp. against such things that wound the Chh of G. & detract from the honour of Xs name in the ☉ and have you a Sp of courage & fortitude to bear & Go through difficulties for G.

Or does not the Epithet of Lukewarm properly belong to you are you not of a very indifferent Sp. about the Interest of Relig. not much Concerned whether it flourishes or not not much moved at the sight of its wounds nor much pleased when you see or hear anything of its prosperity.

Not much Concerned at Religions being at a Low ebb in your own Heart any otherwise than only as it makes you Something afraid whether your hope be right and so whether your Soul wont miscarry at Last but otherwise feel no fervent desires after any increase of Holiness in your Heart or Conversation.

When any thing is proposed that has a tendency to advance Religion dont you find a Cold & backward or at Least a very indifferent Sp. on such occasions.

Are you not one in Whom there Commonly prevails a Sp. of objecting against those things that tend to the Good of Xs Chh by any expense or difficulty with them.

And particularly Enquire whether or no you are a man that is of a Sp. to prefer the Interests of Religion above your own private Interest—how often & how plainly has X told us that this is necessary. That we should Love him above F or mother—yea should hate—should sell—These sayings of X signify something. They are neither false nor meer Insignificant sentences words without a meaning, or carrying no such thing in them as they seem to signify.—One would wonder how it is possible for men that have a vastly Greater Regard for their private Temporal Interest for the flourishing of their Efforts for the upholding & advancing their Reputation for mainting their Interest among men and Gaining these & those ☉ly designs than they have for the flourishing of the Kingd. of X or the Credit & Interest of Relig. I say one would wonder how such make it out to maintain their hope & opinion of thems. as true Xtians with such Sc. as these Just now mentioned staring of em in the face.

But men will do any thing with the Sc. to uphold a false hope they will twist and use it as if it were a nose of wax turn it any way that suits em put the most violent Glosses upon it rather than Let Go a false hope.—This is the manner of Luke-warm Xtians & those Professors that are destitute of a true Zeal for Good works.

It may be many will be ready to say that they are not Luke-warm but are Zealous persons & so be ready to conclude that the Character of that peculiar people which X has purchased to hims. belongs to thems.

But it is not sufficient that you can determine that you are a Zealous person but you must Enquire whether your Zeal be a truly Xtian Zeal.

Tis not all Zealous persons that are truly Xtians nor is it all those that are Zealous with a Religious Zeal.—The Jews that were the Enemies of X & the apostles as the apostle Paul bears record of them had a Zeal of G. i.e. a relig. Zeal. Rom. 10. 2. And the apostle hims. while he was a persecuter had such a Zeal as he says of hims. Acts 22. 3. I am verily a m. which am a Jew born in Tarsus a City of Cilicia yet brought up in this city at the feet of Gamaliel and taught according to the Perfect manner of the Law of the Fathers and was Zealous towards G. as ye all are this Day.

So Saul of old tho he was a wicked man yet in some things was very Zealous. He manifested a Great Zeal against witch-craft.

& so it is said of him 2. Sam. 21. 2. that Saul sought to slay the Gibeonites in his Zeal for the Chil. of Is. & Judah—so Jehu Boasted of his Zeal 2. Kings 10. 16. He says to Jehonadab, the son of Rechab, Come with me & see my Zeal for the Lord.

There is a Zeal that is no virtue at all but rather a vice tho it puts on a Religious mask. There is a Zeal that does no good but is a mischievous principle it renders men very uncomfort-able to those about them & greatly wounds the Interest of Relig. instead of promoting it & makes persons Sometimes even ridiculous in their behaviour.

Therefore I would mention some things by which a true Xtian zeal may be Known & whereby it is distinguished from a false Zeal.

1. A True Xtian Zeal is a Zeal according to Knowl. Every

true Grace has its foundation in Light. What is Counterfeit has its foundation in darkness.—In false Zeal there is heat but without Light which a Certain author says is Like hell fire. But Xtian Zeal is fire from Heaven tis a holy flame in which Light & heat burning & shining go together.—Tis first Kindled in the soul by a Ray of Light shining down from Heaven into the Heart.

The false Zeal of the Jews is said not to be according to Knowl. False Zeal is without Light in several Respects. It is without any Sp. Knowl. of G. & oftentimes is founded on mistakes & delusions & is directed without discretion.—A false Zeal is often for those things that bent worthy to be the objects or matter of Zeal. Tis often for those things that are evil being Falsely Supposed to be good. So is the Zeal of the papists & of Mohametans & so was the Zeal of the Jews of old. They were Exceeding Zealous of the traditions of their Fathers.

Sometimes mens Zeal is Spent on trifles, things of such little Importance that they are not worthy of their Zeal. So was the Zeal of the Pharisees who were so Zealous about their Philactering & tithing mint anise & Cummin & the mere Circumstantials of Relig. while they neglected the weightier matters of the Law.

A true Zeal is about those things that are in thems. Good. Gal. 4. 18. tis Good to be Zealously affected alwaies in a good thing.

Tis the truth & not Errors that are falsely supposed to be truths. Tis a Zeal for Good works & not superstitious Practice. It is guided by the doctrines & precepts of the W. of G.—& it is Chiefly exercised about those things that are of the Greatest Importance & proportionably Less about things of Lesser Importance.

A true Zeal is no Rash Inconsiderate Zeal. It seeks an End that is Good & worthy to be Pursued & it is employed in pursuing that End by suitable & proper means Prov. 8. 12. I wisd dwell with prud.

Ps. 112. 5. a good m. will guide his affairs with discretion.

Not but that a Godly man that has really a Xtian Zeal may in the Exercise of his Zeal be subject to some mistakes. But yet this Evermore is predicable of True Zeal that it has its founda. in Light & is guided by Spiritual wisdom making the Instructions & directions of the W. of God its rule.

2. A man rightly Zealous Exercises his Zeal in the First Place against his own sins. He is Zealous to oppose sin in others to oppose what is against the Kingd. of G. in the ☉ but his Zeal dont begin there it begins at home & has Employed against the Enemies of G. & the opposers of the Interest of Relig. in his own heart—he is one that has seen hims. to be an Enemy to G. & has treated hims. as such an one.—he is Zealous to suppress & mortify those vile & abominable dispositions which he sees in him.—He sees Great occasion for Zeal in what he sees of his own wickedness which very much employs it & makes a Great deal of work for his Zeal.

This is that Zeal that X directs the Chh. of Laodicea to Rev. 3. 19. Be Zealous theref. & repent. That Zeal that is exercised in repentance of Sin is exercised against mens own sins in opposing & renouncing them.—So it was such a Zeal that the Apostle commends the Xtian Corinthians for 2 Cor. 7. 10, 11.———

When men are full of Zeal & Indignation against the Sins of others and at the same time have but little to do at home find little to employ their zealous opposition against them, & while they seem strenuous in speech & behaviour to oppose others Iniquities & all the while Indulge thems. in the same things as others as bad & are careless & quiet in their own wickedness their Zeal will serve to no other purpose but their Condemnation their Great Judge Shall Condemn them as those that are self condemned. Rom. 2. at begin.——— & 21. v.

3. A truly Xtian Zeal is such as is attended with Humility. This naturally Follows from what was but now mentioned of Zeals being Exercised in the first place against our own sins.

A true Zeal is not a proud or an Ostentatious Zeal. They that are possessed of it dont fiercely oppose those things that they account evil in others from a disposition to Exalt thems. & depreciate others and set thems. off as much better than they.—They dont Zealously oppose them out of a proud conceit of their own Judgmt & fondness for their own ways as tho' it were a Great Crime for any one to presume to differ from them or to take any Liberties that they are denied.

There is a sort of Zeal that is the fount of Pride and is most hot & fierce in the Proudest men such a Zeal there was of old in the Proud Pharisees & such a Zeal there is in the Proud Persecuting Romish Clergy.

But a true Xtian Zeal even when most warm & most Engaged is attended with Humility, & is in no wise inconsistent with it. It is attended with no Self Exaltation but on the Contrary a Low Self depression.

4. A true Zeal is not inconsistent with a Sp. of Love & meekness. A false Zeal is Commonly a Spitefull Zeal attended with Prejudice against mens Persons & a fierceness & wrathfull heat of Sp.

But it is far otherwise with a true Zeal as was said before Love to G. is the main thing in it the principall affection that is in Exercise. Tis the very flame whence that Kind of Heat that is in Zeal arises. & from Love to G. naturally arises a Xtian Love to men & theref. there is nothing in true Zeal inconsistent with a Sp. of Love no bitterness or heat of Sp. of a Contrary nature to a fervent hearty Xtian Charity.—True Zeal is not against men but against sin. Their sin Earnestly opposed but their Persons fervently Loved.

Herein it Greatly differs from a persecuting Zeal such as the apostle Paul had while a Pharisee. Philip. 3. 6. Concrng Zeal Persecuting the Chh. of G.

A true Zeal is attended with meekness, not with high un-Xtian Resentmts. No it stirs not up persons to a fierce way of Pursuing its End—the weapons of its warfare are not carnal but Sp. They are not Reproachfull Reflections & angry Speeches but fervent prayers & Earnest but yet meek endeavours to suppress Iniq. & to promote holiness.

Men may be thus Zealous & yet not the Less like Lambs in meekness not the Less like the blessed Jesus the Lamb of G. who tho' he was meek & Lowly of Heart yet manifested a fervent Zeal against the sins of men.

II. Use may be of Exhorta. To Exhort Persons to be Zealous in Religion dont content your self with a dead form of Religion when your heart is but little Engaged in it under a notion that your first work is right—A right first work alwaies has this Effect it Leaves in Persons an abiding principle of holy Zeal in Relig. The first work is only Kindling up the fire in the soul which fire is Like the fire in the altar that came from Heaven that never Goes out and not only never Goes out but increases.

He that is Converted is said to be baptized with the H. Gh. & with fire. That principle of Grace that is then Imparted to him is of the nature of fire in this Respect that as when you put a little fire into the midst of much fuel the fire will increase it will Kindle more & more till the whole be in a flame.

Tis with Sp. Heat as tis with Sp. Light it increases more & more—X hims. has taught us that the K. of H. is like a Leaven which a woman took & hid in three measures of meal—————Matt. 13. 33. Tis so not only with the Kingd. of G. in the ☉ but also the K. of G. in the H. tho Grace may at first be but as a little Leaven yet by degrees it will Leaven the whole Lump.

As tis said of him that is born of G. that his seed abideth in him so may it be said of that holy fire from Heaven put into his soul in Conv. that it abides in him & doubtless will be felt in the effects of it in the Heart from time to time.

A dead form of Godliness without the Power of it a lifeless attendance on the Externals without Zeal will be wholly un-profitable & vain. It can serve to no other purpose but only to nourish a false comfort & Establish the soul in carnal security. —The Comfort that such Lukewarm Xtians have is like to Last them but a little while it wont avail 'em on a death bed when the soul shall go naked out of the ☉ to appear before its Great Judge.

But further to stir you up to seek this virtue Consider particularly,

1. How dishonourable to G. is a Cold & indiff. Sp. in his Service how unbecomg is it of Gods Infinite Greatness & Glorious Perfections & that absolute right which G. hath to us & to the utm. that our nature is capable of in his service—how unsuitable is such a Sp. in those that have been the subjects of so much of Gods goodness as we have been & that hope to be saved by the dying Love of X.—How dishonourably do they behave thems. towards a being of Infin. Glory & mercy, who are commonly backw. to do much to put thems. to much dif-ficulty in his service & whose manner it is to give way to an objecting Sp. having their Hearts more Earnestly & Zealous going out after their farms & merchandise than after X & his

Benefits, being much more Concerned what they shall eat
———— than that Xs Kingd. may be advanced in the ☉.

2. How men are wont to Resent coldness & Indifference in
those that profess Friendship to them that Lukewarm Xtians
manifest towards G. If there be any that have professed an
high Esteem of us and have Gone so far as to profess a preference of us in their affections to all others in the ☉—But when
it comes to a trial & we stand in particular need of their help
we commonly find em very dull & backward, Loth to put
thems. any thing out of their way to help us more Regarding
their own Slothfull Ease a Great deal than our Good.—& we
find that when our name suffers they seem too Easy to see it
reproached & trampled on. Can stand by & behold it & be
very little moved—& find that they fail us time after time when
we stand in special need of them by reason of our suff. Circumstances in one Respect or another.

& when we Earnestly desire their good offices find that they
are difficultly persuaded are from time to time full of their excuses & objections—will men much value such friends & have
any Great Regard to their high professions of Love & friendship yea wont common prudence teach them to have no dependence at all on them.

Men abhor such false friends as these & nauseate their flattering pretenses. Men Love warm & hearty friends that will
stand by them & not fail them in time of need that will be
ready to Exert thems. for their sakes, but detest those of a
Contrary character. Such friends as these men are wont to
value but those of a contrary Character they are wont to abhor.

How much more cause is there that G. should abhor Dull
backwards Lukewarm professors of friendship to him who is
infinitely more worthy that we should love him with all our
hearts & all our souls & all our strength than men can be of
the Love one of another. No wonder that G. is ready to Spue
such Kind of Lukewarm friends out of his mouth.

3. Let us Consid. what a shame it will be if we are Lukewarm
in Gods service Considering how Zealous men Commonly are
in serving thems. & in the Pursuit of the ☉. The way in which
men commonly serve mammon is not to serve it with backwardness & Indifferency with Great warmth & Zeal. In this
affair the ☉ in General acts as tho it was greatly engaged. Such

is the Zeal of mankind in pursuing their ☉ly good that the ☉ is Kept exceedg Busy by it by sea & Land.

Men bent only willing to do some small things have their ☉ly interest but they are so Zealous that Great things are done. Great things are done by particular persons. Mens Zeal for the ☉ prompts em to many Great Enterprises and one after another.

& Great things are done by states & Kingdoms bloody wars are Engaged in multitudes venture their lives & Run upon the points of the swords of their Enemies and Go up before the mouths of their Cannon & much blood is spilt. The ☉ is Kept in as it were in a Continual tumult with this sort of Zeal yea & often has been turned upside down by it. & tho it has often cost men dear yet they are not weary But still continue their pursuit.

They dont only shew their Zeal for the ☉ by their activity & Labour in the pursuit of it but by Exercising their wit & Invention. How many ways are devised by men to get the ☉ how many schemes are Laid.

How are projects multiplied. They Labour hard in the day time & the night is much of it spent in Contriving—this is the Subject of mans study alone & this is what they Consult about & Enter in plots & Combinations about one with another. How do men unite their strength & wit to this End that they may Get much of the ☉.

Men are not wont to seek the ☉ only by fits & starts but they are Constant & Continual in it they dont Esteem their whole lives too long to be spent in Labouring & striving after it.

They dont do it only during some Remarkable Seasons but at all times.

Times of Great concerng & striving about the things of Relig. Commonly are of short continuance & then they die away but the ☉ always continues in a Great stir about the things of the ☉. This is Constant. There is no need of ministers Earnestly preaching crying aloud Labouring & spending their strength to bring it to pass. Men need nothg to stir em up: they fall onto it of thems. by the strong propensity of their own natures. Times of Remarkable stirring about the things of Religion are not to be found at all but in a few places. Tis but here and there a people in whom any such thing is ever to be found but—

& in those places where there sometimes are such stirrings they are but Rare. They come once in a Great while & then Quickly Cease. But—

Men Shew their Zeal for the ☉ by their hearts being so tender with Respect to things—so quick to feel,—so Easily moved—so Jealous—apt to be alarmed.

& By Pressg forwd without discouragemt never give out whatever difficulties & disappointmts.—

Now what a shame will be if the servants of mammon, & you.

Yea Let the Consideration of your Lives Engagedness after the ☉ stir you.

Consid how Earnest you are.

Seeing it is thus how can you expect to be owned as a true disciple a faithfull servant of J. X if you are Lukewarm, dull & backward, full of Excuses & objections in Xs service.

Sinners in the Hands
of an Angry God

DEUT. XXXII. 35.
—Their Foot shall slide in due Time.—

In this Verse is threatned the Vengeance of God on the wicked unbelieving Israelites, that were God's visible People, and lived under Means of Grace; and that, notwithstanding all God's wonderful Works that he had wrought towards that People, yet remained, as is expressed, *ver.* 28. void of Counsel, having no Understanding in them; and that, under all the Cultivations of Heaven, brought forth bitter and poisonous Fruit; as in the two Verses next preceeding the Text.

The Expression that I have chosen for my Text, *Their Foot shall slide in due Time*; seems to imply the following Things, relating to the Punishment and Destruction that these wicked Israelites were exposed to.

1. That they were *always* exposed to Destruction, as one that stands or walks in slippery Places is always exposed to fall. This is implied in the Manner of their Destruction's coming upon them, being represented by their Foot's sliding. The same is express'd, Psal. 73. 18. *Surely thou didst set them in slippery Places; thou castedst them down into Destruction.*

2. It implies that they were always exposed to *sudden* unexpected Destruction. As he that walks in slippery Places is every Moment liable to fall; he can't foresee one Moment whether he shall stand or fall the next; and when he does fall, he falls at once, without Warning. Which is also expressed in that, Psal. 73. 18, 19. *Surely thou didst set them in slippery Places; thou castedst them down into Destruction. How are they brought into Desolation as in a Moment?*

3. Another Thing implied is that they are liable to fall *of themselves*, without being thrown down by the Hand of another. As he that stands or walks on slippery Ground, needs nothing but his own Weight to throw him down.

4. That the Reason why they are not fallen already, and don't fall now, is only that God's appointed Time is not come.

For it is said, that when that due Time, or appointed Time comes, *their Foot shall slide*. Then they shall be left to fall as they are inclined by their own Weight. God won't hold them up in these slippery Places any longer, but will let them go; and then, at that very Instant, they shall fall into Destruction; as he that stands in such slippery declining Ground on the Edge of a Pit that he can't stand alone, when he is let go he immediately falls and is lost.

The Observation from the Words that I would now insist upon is this,

> *There is nothing that keeps wicked Men, at any one*
> *Moment, out of Hell, but the meer Pleasure of GOD.*

By the meer Pleasure of God, I mean his sovereign Pleasure, his arbitrary Will, restrained by no Obligation, hinder'd by no manner of Difficulty, any more than if nothing else but God's meer Will had in the least Degree, or in any Respect whatsoever, any Hand in the Preservation of wicked Men one Moment.

The Truth of this Observation may appear by the following Considerations.

1. There is no Want of *Power* in God to cast wicked Men into Hell at any Moment. Mens Hands can't be strong when God rises up: The strongest have no Power to resist him, nor can any deliver out of his Hands.

He is not only able to cast wicked Men into Hell, but he can most *easily* do it. Sometimes an earthly Prince meets with a great deal of Difficulty to subdue a Rebel, that has found Means to fortify himself, and has made himself strong by the Numbers of his Followers. But it is not so with God. There is no Fortress that is any Defence from the Power of God. Tho' Hand join in Hand, and vast Multitudes of God's Enemies combine and associate themselves, they are easily broken in Pieces: They are as great Heaps of light Chaff before the Whirlwind; or large Quantities of dry Stubble before devouring Flames. We find it easy to tread on and crush a Worm that we see crawling on the Earth; so 'tis easy for us to cut or singe a slender Thread that any Thing hangs by; thus easy is it for God when he pleases to cast his Enemies down to Hell. What are we, that we should think to stand before him, at whose

Rebuke the Earth trembles, and before whom the Rocks are thrown down?

2. They *deserve* to be cast into Hell, so that divine Justice never stands in the Way, it makes no Objection against God's using his Power at any Moment to destroy them. Yea, on the contrary, Justice calls aloud for an infinite Punishment of their Sins. Divine Justice says of the Tree that brings forth such Grapes of Sodom, *Cut it down, why cumbreth it the Ground*, Luk. 13. 7. The Sword of divine Justice is every Moment brandished over their Heads, and 'tis nothing but the Hand of arbitrary Mercy, and God's meer Will, that holds it back.

3. They are *already* under a Sentence of Condemnation to Hell. They don't only justly deserve to be cast down thither; but the Sentence of the Law of God, that eternal and immutable Rule of Righteousness that God has fixed between him and Mankind, is gone out against them, and stands against them; so that they are bound over already to Hell. Joh. 3. 18. *He that believeth not is condemned already.* So that every unconverted Man properly belongs to Hell; that is his Place; from thence he is. Joh. 8. 23. *Ye are from beneath.* And thither he is bound; 'tis the Place that Justice, and God's Word, and the Sentence of his unchangeable Law assigns to him.

4. They are now the Objects of that very *same* Anger & Wrath of God that is expressed in the Torments of Hell: and the Reason why they don't go down to Hell at each Moment, is not because God, in whose Power they are, is not then very angry with them; as angry as he is with many of those miserable Creatures that he is now tormenting in Hell, and do there feel and bear the fierceness of his Wrath. Yea God is a great deal more angry with great Numbers that are now on Earth, yea doubtless with many that are now in this Congregation, that it may be are at Ease and Quiet, than he is with many of those that are now in the Flames of Hell.

So that it is not because God is unmindful of their Wickedness, and don't resent it, that he don't let loose his Hand and cut them off. God is not altogether such an one as themselves, tho' they may imagine him to be so. The Wrath of God burns against them, their Damnation don't slumber, the Pit is prepared, the Fire is made ready, the Furnace is now hot, ready to receive them, the Flames do now rage and glow. The glittering

Sword is whet, and held over them, and the Pit hath opened her Mouth under them.

5. The *Devil* stands ready to fall upon them and seize them as his own, at what Moment God shall permit him. They belong to him; he has their Souls in his Possession, and under his Dominion. The Scripture represents them as his *Goods*, Luk. 11. 21. The Devils watch them; they are ever by them, at their right Hand; they stand waiting for them, like greedy hungry Lions that see their Prey, and expect to have it, but are for the present kept back; if God should withdraw his Hand, by which they are restrained, they would in one Moment fly upon their poor Souls. The old Serpent is gaping for them; Hell opens its Mouth wide to receive them; and if God should permit it, they would be hastily swallowed up and lost.

6. There are in the Souls of wicked Men those hellish *Principles* reigning, that would presently kindle and flame out into Hell Fire, if it were not for God's Restraints. There is laid in the very Nature of carnal Men a Foundation for the Torments of Hell: There are those corrupt Principles, in reigning Power in them, and in full Possession of them, that are Seeds of Hell Fire. These Principles are active and powerful, and exceeding violent in their Nature, and if it were not for the restraining Hand of God upon them, they would soon break out, they would flame out after the same Manner as the same Corruptions, the same Enmity does in the Hearts of damned Souls, and would beget the same Torments in 'em as they do in them. The Souls of the Wicked are in Scripture compared to the troubled Sea, *Isai.* 57. 20. For the present God restrains their Wickedness by his mighty Power, as he does the raging Waves of the troubled Sea, saying, *Hitherto shalt thou come, and no further*; but if God should withdraw that restraining Power, it would soon carry all afore it. Sin is the Ruin and Misery of the Soul; it is destructive in it's Nature; and if God should leave it without Restraint, there would need nothing else to make the Soul perfectly miserable. The Corruption of the Heart of Man is a Thing that is immoderate and boundless in its Fury; and while wicked Men live here, it is like Fire pent up by God's Restraints, when as if it were let loose it would set on Fire the Course of Nature; and as the Heart is now a Sink of Sin, so, if

Sin was not restrain'd, it would immediately turn the Soul into a fiery Oven, or a Furnace of Fire and Brimstone.

7. It is no Security to wicked Men for one Moment, that there are no *visible Means* of *Death* at Hand. 'Tis no Security to a natural Man, that he is now in Health, and that he don't see which Way he should now immediately go out of the World by any Accident, and that there is no visible Danger in any Respect in his Circumstances. The manifold and continual Experience of the World in all Ages, shews that this is no Evidence that a Man is not on the very Brink of Eternity, and that the next Step won't be into another World. The unseen, unthought of Ways and Means of Persons going suddenly out of the World are innumerable and inconceivable. Unconverted Men walk over the Pit of Hell on a rotten Covering, and there are innumerable Places in this Covering so weak that they won't bear their Weight, and these Places are not seen. The Arrows of Death fly unseen at Noon-Day; the sharpest Sight can't discern them. God has so many different unsearchable Ways of taking wicked Men out of the World and sending 'em to Hell, that there is nothing to make it appear that God had need to be at the Expence of a Miracle, or go out of the ordinary Course of his Providence, to destroy any wicked Man, at any Moment. All the Means that there are of Sinners going out of the World, are so in God's Hands, and so universally absolutely subject to his Power and Determination, that it don't depend at all less on the meer Will of God, whether Sinners shall at any Moment go to Hell, than if Means were never made use of, or at all concerned in the Case.

8. Natural Men's *Prudence* and *Care* to preserve their own *Lives*, or the Care of others to preserve them, don't secure 'em a Moment. This divine Providence and universal Experience does also bear Testimony to. There is this clear Evidence that Men's own Wisdom is no Security to them from Death; That if it were otherwise we should see some Difference between the wise and politick Men of the World, and others, with Regard to their Liableness to early and unexpected Death; but how is it in Fact? Eccles. 2. 16. *How dieth the wise Man? as the Fool.*

9. All wicked Men's *Pains* and *Contrivance* they use to escape *Hell*, while they continue to reject Christ, and so remain

wicked Men, don't secure 'em from Hell one Moment. Almost every natural Man that hears of Hell, flatters himself that he shall escape it; he depends upon himself for his own Security; he flatters himself in what he has done, in what he is now doing, or what he intends to do; every one lays out Matters in his own Mind how he shall avoid Damnation, and flatters himself that he contrives well for himself, and that his Schemes won't fail. They hear indeed that there are but few saved, and that the bigger Part of Men that have died heretofore are gone to Hell; but each one imagines that he lays out Matters better for his own escape than others have done: He don't intend to come to that Place of Torment; he says within himself, that he intends to take Care that shall be effectual, and to order Matters so for himself as not to fail.

But the foolish Children of Men do miserably delude themselves in their own Schemes, and in their Confidence in their own Strength and Wisdom; they trust to nothing but a Shadow. The bigger Part of those that heretofore have lived under the same Means of Grace, and are now dead, are undoubtedly gone to Hell: and it was not because they were not as wise as those that are now alive: it was not because they did not lay out Matters as well for themselves to secure their own escape. If it were so, that we could come to speak with them, and could inquire of them, one by one, whether they expected when alive, and when they used to hear about Hell, ever to be the Subjects of that Misery, we doubtless should hear one and another reply, 'No, I never intended to come here; I had laid out Matters otherwise in my Mind; I thought I should contrive well for my self; I thought my Scheme good; I intended to take effectual Care; but it came upon me unexpected; I did not not look for it at that Time, and in that Manner; it came as a Thief; Death outwitted me; God's Wrath was too quick for me; O my cursed Foolishness! I was flattering my self, and pleasing my self with vain Dreams of what I would do hereafter, and when I was saying Peace and Safety, then sudden Destruction came upon me.'

10. God has laid himself under *no Obligation* by any Promise to keep any natural Man out of Hell one Moment. God certainly has made no Promises either of eternal Life, or of any Deliverance or Preservation from eternal Death, but what are

contained in the Covenant of Grace, the Promises that are given in Christ, in whom all the Promises are Yea and Amen. But surely they have no Interest in the Promises of the Covenant of Grace that are not the Children of the Covenant, and that don't believe in any of the Promises of the Covenant, and have no Interest in the *Mediator* of the Covenant.

So that whatever some have imagined and pretended about Promises made to natural Men's earnest seeking and knocking, 'tis plain and manifest that whatever Pains a natural Man takes in Religion, whatever Prayers he makes, till he believes in Christ, God is under no manner of Obligation to keep him a *Moment* from eternal Destruction.

So that thus it is, that natural Men are held in the Hand of God over the Pit of Hell; they have deserved the fiery Pit, and are already sentenced to it; and God is dreadfully provoked, his Anger is as great towards them as to those that are actually suffering the Executions of the fierceness of his Wrath in Hell, and they have done nothing in the least to appease or abate that Anger, neither is God in the least bound by any Promise to hold 'em up one moment; the Devil is waiting for them, Hell is gaping for them, the Flames gather and flash about them, and would fain lay hold on them, and swallow them up; the Fire pent up in their own Hearts in struggling to break out; and they have no Interest in any Mediator, there are no Means within Reach that can be any Security to them. In short, they have no Refuge, nothing to take hold of, all that preserves them every Moment is the meer arbitrary Will, and uncovenanted unobliged Forbearance of an incensed God.

APPLICATION.

The USE may be of *Awakening* to unconverted Persons in this Congregation. This that you have heard is the Case of every one of you that are out of Christ. That World of Misery, that Lake of burning Brimstone is extended abroad under you. *There* is the dreadful Pit of the glowing Flames of the Wrath of God; there is Hell's wide gaping Mouth open; and you have nothing to stand upon, nor any Thing to take hold of: there is nothing between you and Hell but the Air; 'tis only the Power and meer Pleasure of God that holds you up.

You probably are not sensible of this; you find you are kept out of Hell, but don't see the Hand of God in it, but look at other Things, as the good State of your bodily Constitution, your Care of your own Life, and the Means you use for your own Preservation. But indeed these Things are nothing; if God should withdraw his Hand, they would avail no more to keep you from falling, than the thin Air to hold up a Person that is suspended in it.

Your Wickedness makes you as it were heavy as Lead, and to tend downwards with great Weight and Pressure towards Hell; and if God should let you go, you would immediately sink and swiftly descend & plunge into the bottomless Gulf, and your healthy Constitution, and your own Care and Prudence, and best Contrivance, and all your Righteousness, would have no more Influence to uphold you and keep you out of Hell, than a Spider's Web would have to stop a falling Rock. Were it not that so is the sovereign Pleasure of God, the Earth would not bear you one Moment; for you are a Burden to it; the Creation groans with you; the Creature is made Subject to the Bondage of your Corruption, not willingly; the Sun don't willingly shine upon you to give you Light to serve Sin and Satan; the Earth don't willingly yield her Increase to satisfy your Lusts; nor is it willingly a Stage for your Wickedness to be acted upon; the Air don't willingly serve you for Breath to maintain the Flame of Life in your Vitals, while you spend your Life in the Service of God's Enemies. God's Creatures are Good, and were made for Men to serve God with, and don't willingly subserve to any other Purpose, and groan when they are abused to Purposes so directly contrary to their Nature and End. And the World would spue you out, were it not for the sovereign Hand of him who hath subjected it in Hope. There are the black Clouds of God's Wrath now hanging directly over your Heads, full of the dreadful Storm, and big with Thunder; and were it not for the restraining Hand of God it would immediately burst forth upon you. The sovereign Pleasure of God for the present stays his rough Wind; otherwise it would come with Fury, and your Destruction would come like a Whirlwind, and you would be like the Chaff of the Summer threshing Floor.

The Wrath of God is like great Waters that are dammed for the present; they increase more and more, & rise higher and higher, till an Outlet is given, and the longer the Stream is stop'd, the more rapid and mighty is it's Course, when once it is let loose. 'Tis true, that Judgment against your evil Works has not been executed hitherto; the Floods of God's Vengeance have been with-held; but your Guilt in the mean Time is constantly increasing, and you are every Day treasuring up more Wrath; the Waters are continually rising and waxing more and more mighty; and there is nothing but the meer Pleasure of God that holds the Waters back that are unwilling to be stopped, and press hard to go forward; if God should only withdraw his Hand from the Flood-Gate, it would immediately fly open, and the fiery Floods of the Fierceness and Wrath of God would rush forth with inconceivable Fury, and would come upon you with omnipotent Power; and if your Strength were ten thousand Times greater than it is, yea ten thousand Times greater than the Strength of the stoutest, sturdiest Devil in Hell, it would be nothing to withstand or endure it.

The Bow of God's Wrath is bent, and the Arrow made ready on the String, and Justice bends the Arrow at your Heart, and strains the Bow, and it is nothing but the meer Pleasure of God, and that of an angry God, without any Promise or Obligation at all, that keeps the Arrow one Moment from being made drunk with your Blood.

Thus are all you that never passed under a great Change of Heart, by the mighty Power of the SPIRIT of GOD upon your Souls; all that were never born again, and made new Creatures, and raised from being dead in Sin, to a State of new, and before altogether unexperienced Light and Life, (however you may have reformed your Life in many Things, and may have had religious Affections, and may keep up a Form of Religion in your Families and Closets, and in the House of God, and may be strict in it,) you are thus in the Hands of an angry God; 'tis nothing but his meer Pleasure that keeps you from being this Moment swallowed up in everlasting Destruction.

However unconvinced you may now be of the Truth of what you hear, by & by you will be fully convinced of it. Those that are gone from being in the like Circumstances with you, see that it was so with them; for Destruction came suddenly upon most of them, when they expected nothing of it, and while they were saying, *Peace and Safety*: Now they see, that

those Things that they depended on for Peace and Safety, were
nothing but thin Air and empty Shadows.

The God that holds you over the Pit of Hell, much as one
holds a Spider, or some loathsome Insect, over the Fire, abhors
you, and is dreadfully provoked; his Wrath towards you burns
like Fire; he looks upon you as worthy of nothing else, but to
be cast into the Fire; he is of purer Eyes than to bear to have
you in his Sight; you are ten thousand Times so abominable in
his Eyes as the most hateful venomous Serpent is in ours. You
have offended him infinitely more than ever a stubborn Rebel
did his Prince: and yet 'tis nothing but his Hand that holds
you from falling into the Fire every Moment: 'Tis to be ascribed to nothing else, that you did not go to Hell the last
Night; that you was suffer'd to awake again in this World, after
you closed your Eyes to sleep: and there is no other Reason to
be given why you have not dropped into Hell since you arose
in the Morning, but that God's Hand has held you up: There
is no other Reason to be given why you han't gone to Hell
since you have sat here in the House of God, provoking his
pure Eyes by your sinful wicked Manner of attending his solemn Worship: Yea, there is nothing else that is to be given as a
Reason why you don't this very Moment drop down into Hell.

O Sinner! Consider the fearful Danger you are in: 'Tis a
great Furnace of Wrath, a wide and bottomless Pit, full of the
Fire of Wrath, that you are held over in the Hand of that God,
whose Wrath is provoked and incensed as much against you as
against many of the Damned in Hell: You hang by a slender
Thread, with the Flames of divine Wrath flashing about it, and
ready every Moment to singe it, and burn it asunder; and you
have no Interest in any Mediator, and nothing to lay hold of to
save yourself, nothing to keep off the Flames of Wrath, nothing of your own, nothing that you ever have done, nothing
that you can do, to induce God to spare you one Moment.

And consider here more particularly several Things concerning that Wrath that you are in such Danger of.

1. *Whose* Wrath it is: It is the Wrath of the infinite GOD. If it
were only the Wrath of Man, tho' it were of the most potent
Prince, it would be comparatively little to be regarded. The
Wrath of Kings is very much dreaded, especially of absolute
Monarchs, that have the Possessions and Lives of their Subjects

wholly in their Power, to be disposed of at their meer Will. Prov. 20. 2. *The Fear of a King is as the Roaring of a Lion: whoso provoketh him to Anger, sinneth against his own Soul.* The Subject that very much enrages an arbitrary Prince, is liable to suffer the most extream Torments, that human Art can invent or human Power can inflict. But the greatest earthly Potentates, in their greatest Majesty and Strength, and when cloathed in their greatest Terrors, are but feeble despicable Worms of the Dust, in Comparison of the great and almighty Creator and King of Heaven and Earth: It is but little that they can do, when most enraged, and when they have exerted the utmost of their Fury. All the Kings of the Earth before GOD are as Grashoppers, they are nothing and less than nothing: Both their Love and their Hatred is to be despised. The Wrath of the great King of Kings is as much more terrible than their's, as his Majesty is greater. Luke 12. 4, 5. *And I say unto you my Friends, be not afraid of them that kill the Body, and after that have no more that they can do: But I will forewarn you whom ye shall fear; fear him, which after he hath killed, hath Power to cast into Hell; yea I say unto you, fear him.*

2. 'Tis the *Fierceness* of his Wrath that you are exposed to. We often read of the *Fury* of God; as in Isai. 59. 18. *According to their Deeds, accordingly he will repay Fury to his Adversaries.* So Isai. 66. 15. *For behold, the Lord will come with Fire, and with Chariots like a Whirlwind, to render his Anger with Fury, and his Rebukes with Flames of Fire.* And so in many other Places. So we read of God's *Fierceness.* Rev. 19. 15. There we read of *the Winepress of the Fierceness and Wrath of Almighty God.* The Words are exceeding terrible: if it had only been said, *the Wrath of God*, the Words would have implied that which is infinitely dreadful: But 'tis not only said so, but *the Fierceness and Wrath of God*: the Fury of God! the Fierceness of Jehovah! Oh how dreadful must that be! Who can utter or conceive what such Expressions carry in them! But it is not only said so, but *the Fierceness and Wrath of ALMIGHTY GOD.* As tho' there would be a very great Manifestation of his almighty Power, in what the fierceness of his Wrath should inflict, as tho' Omnipotence should be as it were enraged, and exerted, as Men are wont to exert their Strength in the fierceness of their Wrath. Oh! then what will be the Consequence! What will become of

the poor Worm that shall suffer it! Whose Hands can be strong? and whose Heart endure? To what a dreadful, inexpressible, inconceivable Depth of Misery must the poor Creature be sunk, who shall be the Subject of this!

Consider this, you that are here present, that yet remain in an unregenerate State. That God will execute the fierceness of his Anger, implies that he will inflict Wrath without any Pity: when God beholds the ineffable Extremity of your Case, and sees your Torment to be so vastly disproportion'd to your Strength, and sees how your poor Soul is crushed and sinks down, as it were into an infinite Gloom, he will have no Compassion upon you, he will not forbear the Executions of his Wrath, or in the least lighten his Hand; there shall be no Moderation or Mercy, nor will God then at all stay his rough Wind; he will have no Regard to your Welfare, nor be at all careful lest you should suffer too much, in any other Sense than only that you shall not suffer beyond what strict Justice requires: nothing shall be with-held, because it's so hard for you to bear. Ezek. 8. 18. *Therefore will I also deal in Fury; mine Eye shall not spare, neither will I have Pity; and tho' they cry in mine Ears with a loud Voice, yet I will not hear them.* Now God stands ready to pity you; this is a Day of Mercy; you may cry now with some Encouragement of obtaining Mercy: but when once the Day of Mercy is past, your most lamentable and dolorous Cries and Shrieks will be in vain; you will be wholly lost and thrown away of God as to any Regard to your Welfare; God will have no other Use to put you to but only to suffer Misery; you shall be continued in Being to no other End; for you will be a Vessel of Wrath fitted to Destruction; and there will be no other Use of this Vessel but only to be filled full of Wrath: God will be so far from pitying you when you cry to him, that 'tis said he will only *Laugh and Mock*, Prov. 1. 25, 26, &c.

How awful are those Words, Isai. 63. 3. which are the Words of the great God, *I will tread them in mine Anger, and will trample them in my Fury, and their Blood shall be sprinkled upon my Garments, and I will stain all my Raiment.* 'Tis perhaps impossible to conceive of Words that carry in them greater Manifestations of these three Things, *viz.* Contempt, and Hatred, and fierceness of Indignation. If you cry to God to pity you, he will be so far from pitying you in your doleful

Case, or shewing you the least Regard or Favour, that instead of that he'll only tread you under Foot: And tho' he will know that you can't bear the Weight of Omnipotence treading upon you, yet he won't regard that, but he will crush you under his Feet without Mercy; he'll crush out your Blood, and make it fly, and it shall be sprinkled on his Garments, so as to stain all his Raiment. He will not only hate you, but he will have you in the utmost Contempt; no Place shall be thought fit for you, but under his Feet, to be trodden down as the Mire of the Streets.

3. The Misery you are exposed to is that which God will inflict to that End, that he might *shew* what that *Wrath* of JEHOVAH is. God hath had it on his Heart to shew to Angels and Men, both how excellent his Love is, and also how terrible his Wrath is. Sometimes earthly Kings have a Mind to shew how terrible *their* Wrath is, by the extream Punishments they would execute on those that provoke 'em. *Nebuchadnezzar*, that mighty and haughty Monarch of the *Chaldean* Empire, was willing to shew *his* Wrath, when enraged with *Shadrach, Meshach*, and *Abednego*; and accordingly gave Order that the burning fiery Furnace should be het seven Times hotter than it was before; doubtless it was raised to the utmost Degree of Fierceness that humane Art could raise it: But the great GOD is also willing to shew *his Wrath*, and magnify his awful Majesty and mighty Power in the extream Sufferings of his Enemies. Rom. 9. 22. *What if God willing to shew HIS Wrath, and to make his Power known, endured with much Long-suffering the Vessels of Wrath fitted to Destruction?* And seeing this is his Design, and what he has determined, to shew how terrible the unmixed, unrestrained Wrath, the Fury and Fierceness of JEHOVAH is, he will do it to Effect. There will be something accomplished and brought to pass, that will be dreadful with a Witness. When the great and angry God hath risen up and executed his awful Vengeance on the poor Sinner; and the Wretch is actually suffering the infinite Weight and Power of his Indignation, then will God call upon the whole Universe to behold that awful Majesty, and mighty Power that is to be seen in it. Isai. 33. 12, 13, 14. *And the People shall be as the burning of Lime, as Thorns cut up shall they be burnt in the Fire. Hear ye that are far off what I have done; and ye that are near*

acknowledge my Might. The Sinners in Zion are afraid, fearful-
ness hath surprized the Hypocrites &c.

Thus it will be with you that are in an unconverted State, if
you continue in it; the infinite Might, and Majesty and Terribleness of the OMNIPOTENT GOD shall be magnified upon
you, in the ineffable Strength of your Torments: You shall be
tormented in the Presence of the holy Angels, and in the Presence of the Lamb; and when you shall be in this State of Suffering, the glorious Inhabitants of Heaven shall go forth and
look on the awful Spectacle, that they may see what the Wrath
and Fierceness of the Almighty is, and when they have seen it,
they will fall down and adore that great Power and Majesty.
Isai. 66. 23, 24. *And it shall come to pass, that from one new*
Moon to another, and from one Sabbath to another, shall all Flesh
come to Worship before me, saith the Lord; and they shall go forth
and look upon the Carcasses of the Men that have transgressed
against me; for their Worm shall not die, neither shall their Fire
be quenched, and they shall be an abhorring unto all Flesh.

4. 'Tis *everlasting* Wrath. It would be dreadful to suffer this
Fierceness and Wrath of Almighty God one Moment; but you
must suffer it to all Eternity: there will be no End to this exquisite horrible Misery: When you look forward, you shall see
a long Forever, a boundless Duration before you, which will
swallow up your Thoughts, and amaze your Soul; and you will
absolutely despair of ever having any Deliverance, any End,
any Mitigation, any Rest at all; you will know certainly that
you must wear out long Ages, Millions of Millions of Ages, in
wrestling and conflicting with this almighty merciless Vengeance; and then when you have so done, when so many Ages
have actually been spent by you in this Manner, you will know
that all is but a Point to what remains. So that your Punishment will indeed be infinite. Oh who can express what the
State of a Soul in such Circumstances is! All that we can possibly say about it, gives but a very feeble faint Representation
of it; 'tis inexpressible and inconceivable: for *who knows the*
Power of God's Anger?

How dreadful is the State of those that are daily and hourly
in Danger of this great Wrath, and infinite Misery! But this is
the dismal Case of every Soul in this Congregation, that has
not been born again, however moral and strict, sober and

religious they may otherwise be. Oh that you would consider it, whether you be Young or Old. There is Reason to think, that there are many in this Congregation now hearing this Discourse, that will actually be the Subjects of this very Misery to all Eternity. We know not who they are, or in what Seats they fit, or what Thoughts they now have: it may be they are now at Ease, and hear all these Things without much Disturbance, and are now flattering themselves that they are not the Persons, promising themselves that they shall escape. If we knew that there was one Person, and but one, in the whole Congregation that was to be the Subject of this Misery, what an awful Thing would it be to think of! If we knew who it was, what an awful Sight would it be to see such a Person! How might all the rest of the Congregation lift up a lamentable and bitter Cry over him! But alass! instead of one, how many is it likely will remember this Discourse in Hell? And it would be a Wonder if some that are now present, should not be in Hell in a very short Time, before this Year is out. And it would be no Wonder if some Person that now sits here in some Seat of this Meeting-House in Health, and quiet & secure, should be there before to morrow Morning. Those of you that finally continue in a natural Condition, that shall keep out of Hell longest, will be there in a little Time! your Damnation don't slumber; it will come swiftly, and in all probability very suddenly upon many of you. You have Reason to wonder, that you are not already in Hell. 'Tis doubtless the Case of some that heretofore you have seen and known, that never deserved Hell more than you, and that heretofore appeared as likely to have been now alive as you: Their Case is past all Hope; they are crying in extream Misery and perfect Despair; but here you are in the Land of the Living, and in the House of God, and have an Opportunity to obtain Salvation. What would not those poor damned, hopeless Souls give for one Day's such Opportunity as you now enjoy!

And now you have an extraordinary Opportunity, a Day wherein CHRIST has flung the Door of Mercy wide open, and stands in the Door calling and crying with a loud Voice to poor Sinners; a Day wherein many are flocking to him, and pressing into the Kingdom of God; many are daily coming from the East, West, North and South; many that were very lately in the same miserable Condition that you are in, are in now an happy State, with their Hearts filled with Love to Him that has loved them and washed them from their Sins in his own Blood, and rejoycing in Hope of the Glory of God. How awful is it to be left behind at such a Day! To see so many others feasting, while you are pining and perishing! To see so many rejoycing and singing for Joy of Heart, while you have Cause to mourn for Sorrow of Heart, and howl for Vexation of Spirit! How can you rest one Moment in such a Condition? Are not your Souls as precious as the Souls of the People at *Suffield*,* where they are flocking from Day to Day to Christ?

Are there not many here that have lived *long* in the World, that are not to this Day born again, and so are Aliens from the Common-wealth of Israel, and have done nothing ever since they have lived, but treasure up Wrath against the Day of Wrath? Oh Sirs, your Case in an especial Manner is extreamly dangerous; your Guilt and Hardness of Heart is extreamly great. Don't you see how generally Persons of your Years are pass'd over and left, in the present remarkable & wonderful Dispensation of God's Mercy? You had need to consider your selves, and wake thoroughly out of Sleep; you cannot bear the Fierceness and Wrath of the infinite GOD.

And you that are *young Men*, and *young Women*, will you neglect this precious Season that you now enjoy, when so many others of your Age are renouncing all youthful Vanities, and flocking to CHRIST? You especially have now an extraordinary Opportunity; but if you neglect it, it will soon be with you as it is with those Persons that spent away all the precious Days of Youth in Sin, and are now come to such a dreadful pass in blindness and hardness.

And you *Children* that are unconverted, don't you know that you are going down to Hell, to bear the dreadful Wrath of that God that is now angry with you every Day, and every Night? Will you be content to be the Children of the Devil, when so many other Children in the Land are converted, and are become the holy and happy Children of the King of Kings?

And let every one that is yet out of Christ, and hanging over the Pit of Hell, whether they be old Men and Women, or

*The next neighbour Town.

middle Aged, or young People, or little Children, now hearken to the loud Calls of God's Word and Providence. This acceptable Year of the LORD, that is a Day of such great Favour to some, will doubtless be a Day of as remarkable Vengeance to others. Men's Hearts harden, and their Guilt increases apace at such a Day as this, if they neglect their Souls: and never was there so great Danger of such Persons being given up to hardness of Heart, and blindness of Mind. God seems now to be hastily gathering in his Elect in all Parts of the Land; and probably the bigger Part of adult Persons that ever shall be saved, will be brought in now in a little Time, and that it will be as it was on that great out-pouring of the SPIRIT upon the *Jews* in the Apostles Days, the Election will obtain, and the rest will be blinded. If this should be the Case with you, you will eternally curse this Day, and will curse the Day that ever you was born, to see such a Season of the pouring out of God's Spirit; and will wish that you had died and gone to Hell before you had seen it. Now undoubtedly it is, as it was in the Days of *John the Baptist*, the Ax is in an extraordinary Manner laid at the Root of the Trees, that every Tree that brings not forth good Fruit, may be hewen down, and cast into the Fire.

Therefore let every one that is out of CHRIST, now awake and fly from the Wrath to come. The Wrath of almighty GOD is now undoubtedly hanging over great Part of this Congregation: Let every one fly out of *Sodom: Haste and escape for your Lives, look not behind you, escape to the Mountain, least you be consumed.*

FINIS.

The Curse of Meroz

Decem. 1741.

JUDG. 5. 23.

Curse ye Meroz: Said the angel of the L: Curse ye bit-
terly The inhabitants thereof because they came not
to the Help of the L. to the Help of the L. against
the mighty.

THIS is part of the Song of Deborah & Barak which they sung
on occasion of the Glo. Victory—

The Land before this victory were in distressing Circumstances. They were Greatly oppressed by the Canaanites were
brought into miserable Bondage & slavery by them & were
cruelly used, & their Enemies were Exceeding strong & powerfull. Chap. 4. 2, 3.——— This distress is Represented v.
6. 7. —11.—

They were Delivered by a Glo. W. of G. that he wrought for
his People Israel by the hands of Deborah & Barak, with
whom a Great part of the People Israel Join'd thems. & willingly offered thems. to assist in this war without either being
pressed or hired. It was a Common cause that nearly concerned them all & theref. they voluntarily when called thereto
by Deborah & Barak went forth to the war in Great multitudes. Being animated to it by the Sp. that same Sp. that
moved Deborah & Barak to undertake in this Glo. Cause. See
v. 2.——— v. 9.———

But yet there were some particular parts of the Land the
Inhabitants of which did not offer to promote this Glorious
work. They were not animated as others were were not willing
to follow Deborah & B. to the war without wages & theref.
Let their brethren fight the Lords Battles & Jeopard their lives
while they Indolently staid at home. They chose not to put
thems. to the toils & Difficulties of the war, but had Rather
indulge their Sloth & Sleep in a whole skin at home & more of
the Same Sp. that the Chil. of Is. were in Egypt who said to
Moses, when——— Let us alone Let——— So these did
practically say, Let us———

Thus it was particularly with the Tribe of Reuben,—The

Inhabitants of Gilead, & The Tribes of Dan & Asher. v. 15, 16, 17.——— And also the Town of Meroz, who thereby brought that Heavy Curse upon thems. that we have in the Text. Wherein I would obs.

1. By whom it is that this curse is denounced.

Capt of the Lords Hosts in Josh. 5. 13, 14, 15.———

2. The Greatness of the Curse.———

3. Who they were that were thus Bitterly Cursed

Supposed to be a city near Kedesh the place whence Barak.

4. The sin that brought this bitter Curse, viz. not putting to their hand to assist & forward the victory that was obtained—.

Two aggravations are mentioned:

1. That it was the work of G.—That victory—& deliverance that was thereby procured for the Chil. of Is. was a Glo. work of G. that he wrought for his People & against his Enemies.— It is all along Represented as a work of G.—cried to the L. —a prophetess.—By those that were very feeble in Comparison of their Enemies. Enemies Exceeding Strong.—poor Slaves—under Great Disadvantages—unarmed—v. 8.—This song Represents it as the Glo. work of G. It was not by the strength of the People but a Remarkable & most visible hand of G. v. 20.———

The Inhabitants of Meroz are Blamed that they came not to the Help of the L. The expression is Remarkable f. tho G. stands in no need of mans help, yet he is pleased to make use the Endeavors of men in carrying on his work, & as it were makes use of their help, as a King that goes forth to war is helped by his soldiers—

2. Another aggravation of their sin mentioned is the power of their Enemies & the Great need there was upon that account for all to Join & assist one another to their utmost in this Great work. The Case was more extreme, the distress of Israel the Greater, & more badly calling for help, & there was the more need of the help of all.

Doc. when G. Remarkably appears in a Great work for his Chh. & against his Enemies, it is a most dangerous thing for any of his Professing people to lie still & not to put to an helping hand.

It is a thing that Exposes to the Curse of the angel of the L. i.e. of Jesus X and to his bitter Curse.

Here I would 1. briefly mention some Reasons of the doc. and then proceed to the application. 2. Observe what Evils they will expose thems. to.

REASONS

1. Xs People are his army & he may well highly Resent it if when he in a Remarkable manner leads the way they won't follow him to the battle.

X is often spoken of in Sc. as the L. of Hosts or armies the Lord mighty in Battle & the Capt of the Salvation of his People. Thus when he appeared to Joshua. And his People are his soldiers his Chh is his army. So the Chh is Represented in Cantic. 6. 13.——— company of two armies.

And all Gods visible People do professedly belong to this Army by their Profession they have listed under this Captain. —& therefore it may well be highly Resented if they dont Resort to him when he in a remarkable manner orders his honour to be displayed & if they Refuse to follow him when he in an extraordinary manner orders his trumpet to be blown and Gloriously appears Going forth against his Enemies.—Amongst men martial Laws are exceeding severe & if any soldier in such a Case should Refuse to follow his General he would Immed. be shot down or thrust through with a Sword.

When X appears Remarkably going forth against his Enemies he as it were blows the Trumpet as Ehud did when he had slain Eglon King of Moab & Gods Israel should be gathered after X as they were after him. Judges 3. 27, 28.

2. God at such a time appears in peculiar manifestations of his Glory, & therefore not to follow him at such a time is to cast Great contempt on him. Tis very heinous at any Time not to be much affected with the divine Glory & argues a mean & Low thought of G. but especially not to be animated at a time when G. does in a very unusual & Extraordinary manner display his Glory.

A subject that stood in the way & should not appear to bow before his King when he appeared Riding in triumph or in a magnificent procession in all his majesty & magnificence, would be Looked upon as Casting Great Contempt on his prince & would be thought unworthy to live he would perish from the way.—So if a Person should stand by on a Kings Coronation Day & Should be a Spectator of the Solemnity of his Coronation & should appear silent & mute when all the multitude were Crying God save the King, he would soon be taken notice of and would not be suffered to stand Long on his feet but would be smitten down for his open Contempt.

At a time when G. Remarkably appears Going forth—he gives peculiar manifestations of Glory—majesty—& therefore according as the displays of Gods Glory before our Eyes are greater a proportionably Greater Curse do we expose our selves to if we are not affected & animated by it.

3. G. at such a time appears in a remarkable Exercise of Kindness to his People, whereby all such as are his People are laid under high obligations to Join with him. He dont only appear in a Glo. manifestation of his majesty, but also of his Love to his People.—When God remarkably appears in a Great work for his Chh, & against his & their Enemies if those that are of it his Chh will sit still & wont come and Join with their Lord & Savior in such a work of Goodness & Grace to them they will make themss Guilty of the most Extreme & intolerable ingratitude. They will sin against their own mercies & their own happiness—as if the Citizens of a City that is besieged by an Enemy should sit still & Refuse to arise & open their Gates to a Glorious deliverer that appears in mighty Power & fervent Love to fight for them & save their Lives to Raise the siege of their Enemies & to set em at Liberty.

4. At such a Time as that wherein G.——— There is no such thing as being neuters. There is a necessity of being either for or against the King that then Glo. appears.—as it would be if a King should come into one of his Provinces that had been opposed by an Enemy, where some of the People had fallen off to the Enemy & Joined with them against their Lawfull Sovereign & against his Loyal Subjects & the Lawfull Sovereign hims should come into the Province & should Ride forth there against his Enemies & should call upon all that were on his Side to Come to gather themss to him. There would be no such thing in such a Case as standing neuter. They that Lay Still & Did not Come to the King might Justly be looked upon as his Enemies & treated as some that were undoubtedly Rebels.—& in the day of battle when the two armies Join there is no such thing as being of neither party all must be of one side or the other.

So when a King is Crowned & there are publick manifestations of Joy on that account there is no such thing as standing by an indifferent spectator all must appear as Loyal Subjects & express their Joy on that occasion or be accounted Enemies.—So it alwaies is when G. in any Great dispensa. of his Provid. does Remarkably set his King on his Holy Hill of Zion, & when X does in an extraordinary manner Come down from Heaven to the Earth and appears in his visible Chh. in a work of Salvation for his People.—So it was when X came down from Heaven in his incarnation & appeared on Earth in his Human Pres. There was no such Thing as being neuters neither of his Side nor against him. Those that Sat still & did nothing & did not declare for him & come & Join with him were Justly looked upon as his Enemies. As X says Matt 12. 30. He that is not with us———

So it is in a time when X is Remarkably spiritually Present as well as when he was bodily present, & when he comes to carry on the W. of R. in the application of it as well as in the Imputation.

& therefore

5. They that dont Join with X in such a work must Expect to be sharers with his Enemies. For the time that we speak of is a time when G. Remarkably appears going forth against his Enemies, that as supposed in the doctrine, X then Remarkably Goes forth to Execute vengeance on his Enemies, & therefore all such as at that time dont appear on his Side but rather against him must expect to share in that Remarkable vengeance he Executes on his Enemies at that time.

But as has been now observed all that bent with him are against him all that on such an occasion dont arise & follow the Capt must be looked upon as on the Enemies side & accordingly must expect to have the weapons of the Glorious Conqueror turned against them & to fall amongst the Rest of his Enemies that at that time he destroys.—Thus when X appears to destroy the Sp. Babilon tis Loudly proclaimed to Xs People to come out of her that——— Rev. 18. 4. and another voice from H. saying Come out of her my People that ye be not partakers of her Sins & that ye Receive not of her Plagues i.e. come out of the City of my Enemies come And Join with me & dont Join with mine Enemies Lest ye partake of their Plagues.

6. At such a time G. appears especially determined to put honour upon his Son & therefore they that wont Glorify him actively must Expect that he will be Glorified upon them in their suffering. G. had much in his heart to Glorify his dear & only begotten Son. He has sworn that Every Knee, & there are some Special Seasons that appoint that End, wherein he comes forth to fulfill that promise & oath.

There are some special seasons when G. did in a more Re-markable manner Set his King on his H. Hill of Z.—Such a time is spoken of in the second Psalm when G. should be about to Give him the Heathen for his Inherit.————

When such a time it will be every ones wisd whether they be great or small to Kiss the Son to Come & Join with him & those that Refuse must expect that he will be angry & that as he rides forth in the Chariots of his Power they shall be smit-ten & shall perish from the way, & that he will dash 'em in pieces with his rod of Iron. Ps. 2. 7. &c———— as much as to say I am determined upon it that my Son shall be Honoured— it is my declared decree———— There seems to be an allusion to a Kings Riding forth in triumph in a solemn Procession.

7. Such a Time is alwaies spoken of as a Resemblance of a Day of Judgmt. There are often in Sc. predictions of times when X shall come & Remarkably appear in the ☉ to destroy the King-dom of his Enemies & to———— & such seasons are almost al-waies spoken of in Language adapted to the day of Judgmt as tho they were all types of the Great day of Xs Coming, so that Great Great Gathering in of the Elect that accompanied the Destruction of Jerusalem———— so the pouring out of the Sp. at the destruction of antiX———— so the Glorious Gospel times in Psalms. Ps. 9. 6. Latter End.———— 9. 7. Ps———— 9. 8.———— Such a time is like a day of Judgmt on this account.———— Thus it is foretold Ps. 110.————

8. At such a time the Enemies of X do greatly exert thems. to hinder his work, & therefore surely his professing Friends are Loudly called upon to exert thems. to promote it.—Surely it will be provoking to G. if his pretended friends will stand by & see his Enemies Greatly & vigorously exerting thems. against his Cause & Kingd. & they sit still & not put to their hand to promote it.

If they have any true friendship to X in them to see the

violent opposition of Enemies would have a Great tendency to animate them & Excite their Zeal. That is the nature of true friendship———

This is mentioned as a Great aggravation of the sin of the Inhabit. of Meroz, that the Enemies of the L. were mighty against his work.———

9. At such a time there are Glorious Examples to animate the Friends of X of those that do Greatly Exert thems.——— there alwaies is a Sp. Poured out on a number. Some Jeopard their lives——— this will be a Great aggravation to stand by & see their brethren. This was a Great aggravation of the sin of the Inhabit. of Meroz. 14. 15——— 18 v——— Angels & men were Jointly Engaged.——— It is alwaies so.

II. What curse they will Expose thems. to.

1. To have no part in the blessing.

2. To be sealed up in hardness & lewdness.

3. To be set forth as visible monuments of Gods displeasure in this ⊙.

4. To an aggravated Punishmt hereafter.

APPLICATION.

1. Use may be of warning to warn all to take heed to thems. that they dont make thems. Guilty by that which is spoken of in the doc. at this day when G. remarkably appears in a Great work for his Chh. & against his Enemies.

Cant lie still at such a time as this. Now G. is Going forth— We are his professing People—Let all take heed to thems. that they dont expose thems. to the Curse of the Inhabit. of Meroz by lying still & not putting to an helping hand.

There are a Great many here present that do make an explicit profession of an Experience—profess to find in thems. Evidences of being true & sincere Friends of G.—in them it will be especially aggravated & Especially dangerous—You that call your selves true saints if your practice is such as not to help forward this Great W. you hinder vastly more than others. Dull sleepy carnal saints are especial Clogs to the work.

Let such Enq. how it has been whether they when they take a view of the State of Relig. & the things which G. has been doing since this Great work began here seven years ago— & view their own practice & the Consequences of it whether this work has been promoted its Reputation & purpose advanced——— & how it has been this year.

If it has been so hitherto it must not be any Longer. You must rouse up your self. It grows more & more Intolerable. The Trumpet Sounds Louder & Louder to call you to battle. ——— It is insufferable for those that call thems. true saints to continue still, loitring at home—slumbring & sleeping.

2. Particularly Let all take heed to thems. that they dont do those things that have a direct tendency to hinder this work Rather than to help it forward. Indeed only dullness & inactivity has a tendency.—He that is not with me——— But there are other things that are positive that have a more direct tendency & these may be either in a persons talk or behaviour. Talk may be such as has a Considerable tendency to—create suspicions. What wounds the Reputation of a work wounds the work it self.

& so a Persons Practice may be such as exceedingly tends ——— To move those things that tend to youth full vanity. To do any thing that tends to Contention—to Enter into any broil.

MOTIVE.

1. The work of G. in Israel Spoken of in the text was a type of that very work of G. that is to be wrought for his Chh in the Latter days that we are expecting & which seems to be now beginning.

There is a Great work of G. often foretold wherein———

This Great Battle of Deborah & Barak with the Canaanites that the Inhabit's of Meroz are Cursed for not joining was designed for a type of this very thing I prove it thus, when that Great Battle between X & his Enemies wherein——— is foretold——— Rev. 16. 16.——— 19 v. of the Context———

Canaanites Types of the Sp Enemies of the Chh. Deborah a type of the Chh. Barak a type of the ministry.

2. The Circumstances of the Inhabitants of Meroz, more Especially Parallel with the Circumstances of the Inhabit. of this Town.

That is supposed to be the Reason why the Inhabit. of Meroz brought a Greater curse——— There were others that did not Join——— v. 15, 16, 17———

3. Consid that Curse denounced against the Ammonites &

Moabites & Amalekites because they did not Join & Lend an helping hand in the Time of that Great work of G.——— but opposed. Deut 23. 3, 4.——— Amalekites, Exodus 17 at the Latter End. They were Related to the Israelites which made their crime the more aggravated.

4. Let the Instance of Reuben & Gad & the Half tribe of Manasseh, when G. was bringing the Chil. of Israel into Canaan.

5. Let it be considered what befell those who were unbelieving & would not Join with Gideon at a time when G. wrought a Great work for Israel & against their Enemies by him. It is observed how multitudes in Israel Came to the help of the Lord on that occasion, Judg. 7. 23. &c——— But the men of Succoth & Penuel Chp. 8. 6—17. v.

6. How it was Resented in Israel when the men of Jabesh Gilead did not come to their Help against the open Enemies of G.— Judg. 21. 10———

7. How X Represents the Hard-heartedness manifested by silence at the Time when he made his solemn Entry into Jerusalem. Luke 19. 37 &c.——— This solemn Publick joyfull Entry—was a designed Representation of the Glorious time prophesied of in Zech. 9. 9.——— Matt. 21. 5.———

8. Consid what we are told of Xs going forth against his Enemies at the time of the Introduction of the Glo. Times of the Chh. in the 19. Chp. of Rev.

9. What a mark of Infamy is set on the Elder brother that would not Join in the Rejoicings on occasion of the Return of the Prodigal Son. So if you stand abroad dumb & finding fault you will be guilty of the very same thg.

10. Consid how when G. wrought a Great work for his Chh. in bringing em out of Babilon & Restoring & Rebuilding Jerus. How all were Required to assist in Rebuilding Jerusalem. Neh. 2:20. we his servants will arise & build. See Nehemi. Chp. 3. In Jerusalem not only Publick persons but Private Persons were to put to their Hand, & act in their Spheres. v. 10.——— v. 23, 28———. 30——— Those that did not dwell at Jerusalem yet were to Help in the Building.—They were exceeding diligent & Laborious put not off their Clothing, Chap. 4. 21 &c——— weapon in one hand 4 Chap. 17 ——— A Mark of Infamy set on those that did not assist. Nehem. 3. 5.———

11. Consid the dreadfull Curses denounced against them
that should not Join with Gods People in the Glo. times of the
Xtian Chh. in 14 Chp. Of Zech. Against those that should not
Join v. 16. &c——— Against those that should oppose at that
time 12. v——— Thus abundant has G. been in warning us of
the Great Danger of———

12. Let it be considered how much Persons will be in the
way of Gods favour & blessing by cheerfully & vigorously Exerting thems. to promote so Great a work. What a mark of
Honour does God put upon those that cheerfully came to the
help of the L. against the mighty when Deborah & Barak went
forth. v. 14, 15——— What great notice is taken of those that
cheerfully put thems. to Great hardship & expense trouble &
Hazard to promote this work v. 9.——— v. 18.——— Here is
a blessing upon the Great m. Rulers Judg. 5. 9, 10———
15——— Scribes. 14——— & not only so but the Common
People. & what a Great blessing is pronounced even on a
woman for the hand she had in promoting this affair. next v. of
the text 24 &c———

What Particular notice is taken in Sc. of Davids Helpers
when he came to the throne after a Long continued Low and
afflicted State. & what marks of Honour are put upon them in
the 12. Chap. 1 Chron 23. v. &c———

And particular notice is taken of those that had understanding of the times. v. 32. There are some that in the time of a
Glo. Outpouring—are like the Pharisees they dont understand
these times—alwaies at a loss, stumbling & so do nothing to
help forward.

& so a mark of Honour is set upon those that were hearty &
Engaged in coming & Joining in the affair of turning about
the K. to David. v. 33.——— & v. 38.———

Now these are the times when is turning about the K. to the
Sp. David.

Let these things effectually warn & Excite us of.

Now the Armies which are in Heaven are Going forth the
stars in their Courses.

Here I would mention some particular things that Persons
should avoid & do as they would not expose thems. to the
Curse of the Inhabitants of Meroz.

1. If at any time you are of a doubtfull md concerning the

work that is carried on in any parts of the Land, avoid a being forward to express your Doubts—or to talk after such a manner that others may plainly shew your doubts. Very foolish thing. It may be of very ill Consequences. Ill consequences to your self. Keep you from any share—Keep you miserably back. After you have expressed it you will be prejudiced that way. Loth to own the Contrary. Hard to come back.

Tends to beget doubts in the minds of others to cause em to doubt of the whole work instead of comg to the help of the Lo. you will hinder.

They that throw out hints that tend to bring the present Great W. of G. under some suspicion dont consider what they do. Tis a wonder they cant have so much Prudence as Gamaliel—If they are under doubt it would be a much more proper Course for them to Go & discourse with those that may probably enlighten them—tis Inconceivable what such Persons aim at.

They had need to be well satisfied that these & those things are not of G. before they Give any Hint against them. If X was now upon Earth as he once was men had better not throw out hints & suspicions against him.

Those that talk doubtfully of the work because of extraordinary Terrors & Exceeding Joys that in some Respects carry Persons beyond thems. talk in the Dark, object against they Know not what.

I dare appeal to the Consciences of Every one that has done so whether they were not at that time when they did so in Cold & dead frames—or had had for a Long time any Remarkable income of the Sp. of G. into their souls.

Tis no wonder at all that some are carried something beyond thems.—cup over flows. Those that are ready to object against Extraordinary Comforts, would do well to Consider the Instance of Michal.———

There is a strange Restlessness in an opposing Sp. When men give way to a disposition to speak against the work that is carried on in the Land or to speak suspiciously—they seem to be urged on. They cant be at Rest unless they vent thems. tho it be at such times & places as tends to no Good in the ☉.

2. Persons insisting much on the blemishes that attend this work. Looks as if they were disposed to find what Very faults

they can & Glad to find blemishes to obs.—Looks as tho they were out of Humour with the work it self & theref. would object what they could. If they Greatly Rejoiced—they would not Love to speak of the blemishes. Who loves in a day of Great Joy & Gladness to insist on those things that are uncomfortable that attend the affair the Bridegroom on the wedding day.

& would it not be very improper on a Coronation day.—To Insist on the blemishes of the Kings Family.

If the substance of that work that is carried on in the Land be a work of G. Tis a Joyfull day indeed. We if we are the Friends of X ought to be swallowed up with Joy. This is a Day of Rejoicing with X hims. & shall not we Rejoice with him— He calls together his Friends & neighbours.

Joy in Heaven over one sinner—

So Great an Event as the Conversion of so many souls is worthy to deserve attention far beyond—

We have an account how that in Nehemiahs time many of the People wept at the faults that were found amongst the People. Nehem. 8. 9, 10.——— Much insisting on the blemishes of the work greatly tends to hinder it, for whatsoever tends to wound the Reputation of the work tends to hinder it. Tis Principally in these two ways that the work of G. has been opposed in the Land, talking suspiciously & doubtfully of a Great part of the work, insisting much on the blemishes.

They will own there is a work of G. but if one were to Judge by their actions they are more displeased than they were before. The Jews in X time owned his miracles to be the works of G.

There are undoubtedly imprudences & Errors that attend the work of G. & alwaies will be no other are to be expected. But must we theref. alwaies harp upon them.

Tis true proper Endeavors should be used to Correct the Errors they are & if you think you can do any thing towards it then take a proper Course in order to it.—

But your speaking against & finding fault with many things that attend this work tends to make others stumble at the whole for persons of weak Capacities dont Know how to distinguish. Besides you'll shut Relig. out of your own Heart.

Tis to be feared some Persons find fault & object—to shew their Knowl. that others may take notice how discerning they are—& think them wiser than others that are imprudent—tis difficult to conceive of any other End they should have in it. While they talk so much of Imprudences they thems. are guilty of the Greatest Imprudence.

3. Take heed you dont Retain the accursed thing,—old Rancour. This wont help but hinder. The whole Congregation were hindered.

4. You must freely & voluntarily Go through Great difficulties & self denial. So did the Children of. Willingly offered thems. Jeoparded their lives.

5. Let every soul avoid stirring up any Contention. Take heed in the managemt of Publick affairs.

6. Let Every one promote it in his own sphere.

7. Let all Gods People Cry Earnestly to G.

Conclude with a word of awakening to Xless Sinners. You are all Enemies especially foolish sinners.

LETTERS

To Benjamin Colman

Northampton May 19. 1737

Rev & Honoured Sir,

I humbly thank you for such respect put upon me by you in so large a letter, and those kind and acceptable presents you sent me; which is much more than I deserve or could expect. It is refreshing to hear of the notice that Gods Servants abroad take of the great things God has done for us; it as it were renews the joy of those mercies; but yet at the same time it is a great damp to that joy to consider how we decline and what decays that lively Spirit in religion suffers amongst us, while others are rejoicing & praising God for us. The work that went on so swiftly & wonderfully while God appear'd in mighty & irresistible power to carry it on, has seemed to be very much at a stop in these Towns for a long Time, and we are sensibly by little and little, more and more declining: And tho' some that were wrought upon in the time of this great work of God have lately been favoured with blessed tokens of Gods presence in their Souls; enlivening and comforting them, yet there is an evident appearance of a general languishing of persons lively affections and engagedness of heart in religion, which appears not so much by a return to ways of lewdness & sensuality, among young or old, as by an over-carefullness about, & eagerness after the possessions of this life, and undue heats of spirit among persons of different judgments in publick affairs. Contention and a party Spirit has been the old iniquity of this Town; and as Gods Spirit has been more and more with drawn, so this Spirit has of late manifestly revived: not that the generality of the people have been affected with it, there are many that seem sincerely to lament such an appearance of declension; and contention has not been in any wise at the height that it has sometimes formerly been; But yet I am ashamed, and am ready to blush, to Speak or think of such an appearance of Strife, and division of the People into parties as there has been, after such great and wonderful things as God has wrought for us, which others far off are rejoicing in, and praising God for, & expecting, (as justly they may) to hear better things of us: But I would by no means represent us better than we are. Many in the Town seemed to be greatly affected with the Late marvelous preservation of so many of us, when so exceedingly exposed to immediate death, (and no life is yet lost, and all are restored to health and soundness but one very pious young woman, who has been held down ever since with exceeding inward bruises and ulcers, but seems very slowly to mend,) & some seem to be affected still; but yet it has had in no wise the effect that ten times less things were wont to have two or three years ago. God is pleased to let us see how entirely & immediately the great work lately wrought was his, by withdrawing, & letting us see how little we can do, and how little effect great things have without him. I would pray honored Sir, if the hearing such things dont dishearten you, that you would earnestly pray for us, that God would not leave us, but as it has been his good pleasure to do such great things for us, notwithstanding our unworthiness, for his own names sake so that he would not forsake the work of his own hands, but magnify the same infinite grace, by returning to us, and re-newing of us after our ingratitude. If God leaves us to our selves we shall greatly dishonour religion, and sadly wound and dis-honour our selves. I am sensible I have reason to lie down in the dust in my own infirmities & unworthiness: God Shows me that whatever he has done here among the people under my minis-try, that yet I am nothing, and can do nothing: I desire your prayers that I may be more sensible of it, & that God would grant me his presence and assistance, & *again* grant me success. There seems to be a Spirit of Strife prevailing in most of the neighbouring towns, at the same time that God is frowning upon us in our temporal interests: We in this town indeed have been remarkably preserved from the *throat distemper*, which has been so terrible in multitudes of towns in the land; but we have been distress'd by the backwardness of the Spring; tho not as they have been in many other places in the country, where multitudes of cattle have died of hunger and cold. The severity of the past winter has (I suppose) kill'd more than half of the winter grain that was sown in this county, and by what I can hear, no less in other parts of the country: And it now begins to be a time of drought with us. A dark cloud seems to hang over the Land in general, by our being pursued by one judgment after another, &, which is darkest of all, by our being Left, at the same time, to such a degree, to the vile corruptions of our own hearts, and particularly a Spirit of contention, disorder, & tumult, in our capital town, & many other places. What seems to be for us to do, is to *wait upon God in our Straits and difficulties*, according to one of the sermons you kindly sent me, which seems to be very seasonable not only for the present circumstances of *Boston*, and of the country in general.

You mention, Sir, my being displeased of the liberty taken in the extract at the end of my Uncle *Williams's* sermons: certainly some body has misrepresented the matter to you: I alwaies looked upon it an honour too great for me for you to be at the trouble to draw an extract of my letter to publish to the world, and that it should be annexed to my Honoured Uncle *Williams's* sermons: And my main objection against it was that my uncle *Williams* himself never approved of its being put into his book. With regard to the *letter* it self that I wrote, which you have sent to Dr. *Watts*, & Dr. *Guise* I willingly submit it to their correction, if they think fit to publish it after they come to see it. I am sensible there are some things in it that it would not be best to publish in *England*. I humbly thank you for the honour you have done me in the notice you have taken of that *letter* in one respect or another. I desire Honoured Sir, that among the many that you have to bear on your mind, and to bring before the mercy seat in your prayers, you would not forget

> your most humble, &
>
> most obliged Son & Servt
>
> Jonathan Edwards.

To the Rev. Dr Colman of Boston

To George Whitefield

Northampton in New-England, Feb. 12, 1739/40.

Rev. Sir,

My Request to you is, that in your intended Journey through New-England the next Summer, you would be pleased to visit

Northampton. I hope it is not wholly from Curiosity that I desire to see and hear you in this Place; But I apprehend, from what I have heard, that you are one that has the Blessing of Heaven attending you wherever you go: and I have a Great desire, if it may be the will of God, that Such a Blessing as attends your Person & Labours may descend on this Town, and may enter mine own House, and that I may receive it in my own Soul. Indeed I am fearfull whether you will not be disappointed in New-England, and will have less Success here than in other Places: we who have dwelt in a Land that has been distinguished with Light, and have long enjoyed the Gospel, and have been glutted with it, and have despised it, are I fear more hardend than most of those places where you have preached hitherto. But yet I hope in that Power and mercy of God that has appeared so triumphant in the Success of your Labours in other places, that he will send a Blessing with you even to us, tho' we are unworthy of it. I hope, if God preserves my Life, to see something of that Salvation of God in New-England which he has now begun, in a benighted, wicked and miserable world and age & in the most guilty of all nations. It has been with refreshment of soul that I have heard of one raised up in the Church of England to revive the mysterious, Spiritual, despised and exploded Doctrines of the Gospel, and full of a Spirit of Zeal for the promotion of real vital piety, whose Labours have been attended with such Success. Blessed be God that hath done it! who is with you, and helps you, and makes the weapons of your warfare mighty. We see that God is faithfull, and never will forget the promises that he has made to his Church; and that he will not Suffer the smoking flax to be quenched, even when the floods seem to be overwhelming it; but will revive the flame again, even in the darkest times. I hope this is the dawning of a day of Gods mighty Power & glorious grace to the world of mankind. May you go on Rev. Sir! and may God be with you more and more abundantly, that the work of God may be carried on by a Blessing on your Labours still, with that Swift Progress that it has been hitherto, and rise to a greater height, and extend further and further, with an irresistable Power bearing down all opposition! and may the Gates of Hell never be able to prevail against you! and may God send forth more Labourers into his Harvest of a Like

Spirit, until the Kingdom of Satan shall shake, and his proud Empire fall throughout the Earth and the Kingdom of Christ, that glorious Kingdom of Light, holiness, Peace and Love, shall be Established from one end of the Earth unto the other!

Give my Love to Mr Seward: I hope to see him here with you. I believe I may venture to say that what has been heard of your Labours & Success has not been taken notice of more in any place in New-England than here, or recieved with fuller credit. I hope therefore if we have opportunity, we shall hear you with greater attention. The way from New-York to Boston through Northampton is but little further than the nearest that is; and I think leads through as populous a part of the Country as any. I desire that you and Mr Seward would come directly to my house. I shall account it a Great favour & Smile of Providence to have opportunity to Entertain such Guests under my Roof, & to have some Acquaintance with such Persons.

I fear it is too much for me to desire a particular Remembrance in your prayers, when I consider how many thousands do doubtless desire it, who can't all be particularly mention'd; and I am far from thinking my self worthy to be distinguished. But pray Sir Let your heart be lifted up to God for me among others, that God would bestow much of that blessed Spirit on me that he has bestowed on you, and make me also an instrument of his Glory. I am Rev. Sir

> unworthy to be called your
>
> fellow Labourer,
>
> Jonathan Edwards.

To the Rev. Mr George Whitefield.

To Deborah Hatheway

> Northampton June ye 3
> A. D. 1741.

Dear Child

As you desired me to send to you in writing Some directions how to conduct your Self in your Christian course: I would now answer your request; the Sweet remembrance of the great things I have lately Seen at Suffield, & the dear affections I have for those persons I have there conversed with that give good evidences of a Saving work of God upon their hearts inclines me to do any thing that lies in my power to contribute to the Spiritual Joy & prosperity of Gods people there. And what I write to you I would also Say to other young women there that are your friends & Companions & the Children of God; & therefore desire you would communicate it to them as you have oppertunity.

I. I would advise you to keep up as great a Strife & earnestness in religion in all parts of it, as you would do if you knew your Self to be in a State of nature & were Seeking Conversion. We advise persons under Convictions to be earnest & violent for the kingdom of heaven: but when they have attained to Conversion they ought not to be the less watchfull, laborious & earnest in the whole work of religion but the more: for they are under infinitely greater obligations: for want of this many persons in a few months after their Conversion have begun to loose the Sweet & lively Sense of things & to grow cold & flat & dark & have pierced themselves through with many Sorrows: Whereas if they had done as the Apostle did Philip. 3. 12, 13, 14: their path would have been as the Shining light that shines more & more to the perfect day.

II. Dont leave off Seeking Striving & praying for the very Same things that we exhort unconverted persons to Strive for & a degree of which you have had already in Conversion: thus pray that your eyes may be opened that you may receive your Sight that you may know your Self & be brought to Gods foot, & that you may See the glory of God & Christ, & may be raised from the dead: & have the love of Christ Shed abroad in your heart: for those that have most of these things had need Still to pray for them: for there is so much blindness & hardness & pride & death remaining that they Still need to have the work of God wrought upon them further to enlighten and enliven them that Shall be a bringing out of darkness into Gods marvellous light, & a kind of new Conversion & Resurrection from the dead there are very few requests that are proper for a natural person, but that in some Sense are proper also for the godly.

III. When you hear Sermons hear 'em for your Self: though

what is Spoken in them may be more especially directed to the
unconverted, or to those that in other respects are in different
Circumstances from your Self: yet let the chief intent of your
mind be to consider with your Self, in what respects is this that
I hear Spoken applicable to me, & what improvement ought I
to make of this for my own Souls good.

4. Though God hath forgiven & forgotten your past Sins
yet dont forget 'em your Self: often remember what a wretched
bond Slave you was in the land of Egypt: often bring to mind
your particular acts of Sin before Conversion: as the blessed
Apostle Paul is often mentioning his old blaspheming persecuting & injuriousness to the renewed humbling of his heart,
& acknowledging that he was the least of the apostles, & not
worthy to be called an Apostle. & the least of all Saints, & the
chief of Sinners. And be often in confessing your old Sins to
God, & let that text be often in your mind Ezek. 16. 63. That
thou mayest remember & be confounded, & never open thy
mouth any more because of thy Shame when I am pacified
towards thee for all that thou hast done Saith the Lord God.

5. Remember that you have more cause on Some accounts a
thousand times to lament & humble your Self for Sins that
have been Since Conversion than before; because of the infinitely greater obligations that are upon you to live to God. &
look upon the faithfulness of Christ in unchangeably continuing his loving favour & the unspeakable & Saving fruits of his
everlasting love notwithstanding all your great unworthyness
Since your Conversion to be as wonderfull as his grace in
converting you.

6. Be always greatly abased for your remaining Sin, & never
think you lie low enough for it, but yet dont be at all discouraged or disheartened by it: for tho' we are exceeding Sinfull,
yet we have an advocate with the Father Jesus Christ the righteous, the preciousness of whose blood & the merit of whose
righteousness & the greatness of whose love & faithfulness
does infinitely overtop the highest mountains of our sins.

7. When you engage in the duty of prayer, or come to the
Sacrament of the Lords Supper, or attend any other duty of
divine worship come to Christ as Mary Magdalene did Luke
7. 37, 38. come & cast your Self down at his feet & kiss 'em, &
pour forth upon him the Sweet perfumed ointment of divine

love out of a pure & broken heart, as She poured out her precious ointment out of her pure Alabaster broken box.

8. Remember that pride is the worst yt is in the heart, the greatest disturber of the Souls peace & Sweet communion with Christ; was the first Sin yt ever was, & lies lowest in the foundation of Satans whole building, & is most difficultly rooted out, & is the most hiden Secret & deceitfull of all lusts, & often creeps in insensably into the midst of religion, & Sometimes under the disguise of humility.

9. That you may pass a good Judgement of the frames you are in always look upon those the best discoveries, & the best comforts that have most of these two effects viz those that make you least & lowest & most like a little Child. & Secondly those that do most engage & fix your heart in a full & firm disposition to deny your Self for God & to Spend & be Spent for him.

10. If at any time you fall into doubts about the State of your Soul under dark & dull frames of mind, tis proper to look over past experiences: but yet dont consume too much of your time & Strength in poring & puzling thoughts about old experiences that in dull frames appear dimm & are very much out of Sight, at least as to that which is the cream and life & Sweetness of them, but rather apply your Self with all your might to an earnest pursuit after renewed experience new light & new lively acts of faith & love: one new discovery of the glory of Christs face, & the fountain of his Sweet grace & love, will do more towards Scattering clouds of darkness & doubting in one minute than examining old experiences by the best marks that can be given a whole year.

11. When the exercise of Grace is at a low ebb, & Corruption prevails, & by that means fear prevails, dont desire to have fear cast out any other way than by the reviving & prevailing of love, for tis not agreable to the method of Gods wise dispensations that it Should be cast out any other way; for when love is asleep the saints need fear to restrain 'em from Sin, & therefore it is so ordered that at Such times fear comes upon them, & that more or less as love Sinks, but when love is in lively exercise persons dont need fear: & the prevailing of love in the heart naturaly tends to cast out fear; as darkness in a room vanishes away as you let more & more of the pleasant beams of the Sun into it. 1 John. 4. 18.

12. You ought to be much in exhorting counseling & warning others, especially at such a day as this Heb. 10. 25: & I would advise you especially to be much in exhorting Children & young women your equals: & when you exhort others that are men, I would advise that you take oppertunities for it chiefly when you are alone with them or when only young persons are present. See 1 Tim. 2. 9, 11, 12.

13. When you counsel & warn others do it earnestly & effectionately & thoroughly: & when you are Speaking to your equals let your warnings be intermixed with expressions of your Sense of your own unworthiness & of the Sovereign Grace that makes you differ: & if you can with a good Conscience say how that you in your Self are more unworthy than they.

14. If you would Set up religious meetings of young women by your Selves to be attended once in a while besides the other meetings that you attend; I should think it would be very proper & profitable.

15. Under Special difficulties, or when in great need of, or great longings after any particular mercy for your Self or others; Set apart a day of Secret fasting & prayer by your Self alone: & let the day be Spent not only in petitions for the mercies you desire, but in Searching your heart & looking over your past life & confessing your Sins before God; not as is wont to be done in publick prayer, but by a very particular rehersal before God of the Sins of your past life from your childhood hitherto, before & after Conversion with particular Circumstances & aggravations, also very particularly & fully as possible spreading all the abominations of your heart before him.

16. Dont let the Adversaries of Religion have it to say, that these Converts dont carry themselves any better than others Mat. 5. 47. what do ye more than others. how holy should the Children of God & the redeemed & beloved of the Son of God behave themselves. therefore walk as a Child of the light & of the day, and adorn the doctrin of God your Saviour: And particularly be much in those things that may especially be called Christian vertues, & make you like the Lamb of God be meek & lowly of heart & full of a pure heavenly & humble love to all, & abound in deeds of love to others, & Self denial

for others, & let there be in you a disposition to account others better than your Self.

17. Dont talk of things of Religion and matters of experience with an air of lightness & laughter which is too much the manner in many places.

18. In all your Course walk with God & follow Christ as a little poor helpless Child, taking hold of Christs hand, keeping your eye on the marks of the wounds on his hands & Side whence came the blood that cleanses you from Sin & hideing your [nakedness under the Skirt] of the white [Shining Robe of his Righteous]ness.

19. Pray much for the Church of God and especially that he would carry on this glorious work that he has now begun: & be much in prayer for the Ministers of Christ, & particularly I would beg a Special interest in your prayers & the prayers of your Christian Companions, both when you are alone & when you are together, for your affectionate friend that rejoyces over you & desires to be your Servant In Jesus Christ

Jonathan
Edwards

To Deborah
Hatheway in
Suffield.—

To Thomas Prince

NEW-ENGLAND.

Continuation *of the State of Religion at* NORTHAMPTON *in the County of* HAMPSHIRE *about a* hundred *Miles* westward *of* BOSTON; *By the Rev. Mr.* EDWARDS, *in a Letter to the Rev. Mr.* PRINCE, *dated* Dec. 12. 1743.

Ever since the great Work of GOD that was wrought here about *nine Years ago*, there has been a great abiding Alteration in *this Town* in many Respects. There has been vastly more Religion kept up in the Town, among all Sorts of Persons, in religious Exercises, and in common Conversation, than used to be before: There has remain'd a more general Seriousness and

Decency in attending the publick Worship: There has been a very great Alteration among the *Youth* of the Town, with Respect to revelling, frolicking, profane and unclean Conversation, and lewd Songs: Instances of Fornication have been very rare: There has also been a great Alteration amongst both *old* and *young* with Respect to Tavern-haunting. I suppose the Town has been in no Measure so free of Vice in these Respects, for any long Time together, for *this sixty Years*, as it has been *this nine Years* past. There has also been an evident Alteration with Respect to a charitable Spirit to the Poor: (tho' I think with Regard to this, we in this Town, as the Land in general, come far short of Gospel Rules.) And tho' after that great Work *nine Years ago* there has been a very lamentable Decay of religious Affections, and the Engagedness of People's Spirit, in Religion; yet many Societies for Prayer and social Religion were all along kept up; and there were some few Instances of Awakening and deep Concern about the Things of another World, even in the most dead Time.

In the Year 1740 in the *Spring*, before Mr. WHITEFIELD came to this Town, there was a visible Alteration: There was more Seriousness, and religious Conversation, especially among *young* People: Those Things that were of ill Tendency among them were more foreborn: and it was a more frequent Thing for Persons to visit their Minister upon Soul Accounts: and in some particular Persons there appeared a great Alteration, about that Time. And thus it continued till Mr. *Whitefield* came to Town, which was about the middle of *October* following: he preached here *four Sermons* in the Meeting-House, (besides a *private Lecture* at my House) one on *Friday*, another on *Saturday*, and two upon the *Sabbath*. The Congregation was extraordinarily melted by every Sermon; almost the whole Assembly being in Tears for a great Part of Sermon Time. Mr. *Whitefield*'s Sermons were suitable to the Circumstances of the Town; containing just Reproofs of our Backslidings, and in a most moving and affecting Manner, making Use of our great Profession and great Mercies as Arguments with us to return to GOD, from whom we had departed. Immediately after this the Minds of the People in general appear'd more engaged in Religion, shewing a greater Forwardness to make Religion the Subject of their Conversation, and to meet frequently together for religious Purposes, and to embrace all Opportunities to hear the Word preached. The *Revival* at *first* appear'd chiefly among *Professors*, and those that had entertained the Hope that they were in a State of Grace, to whom Mr. *Whitefield* chiefly address'd himself; but in a very short Time there appeared an *Awakening* and deep Concern among some *young Persons* that looked upon themselves as in a Christless State; and there were some hopeful Appearances of *Conversion*; and some Professors were greatly revived. In about a *Month* or *six Weeks* there was a great Alteration in the Town, both as to the Revivals of Professors, and Awakenings of others. By the *middle* of *December* a very considerable Work of GOD appeared among those that were *very young*; and the Revival of Religion continued to increase; so that in the *Spring*, an Engagedness of Spirit about Things of Religion was become very general amongst *young People* and *Children*, and religious Subjects almost wholly took up their Conversation when they were together.

IN the Month of *May* 1741, a *Sermon* was preached to a Company at a *private House*: Near the Conclusion of the Exercise *one* or *two* Persons that were *Professors*, were so greatly affected with a Sense of the Greatness and Glory of divine Things, and the infinite Importance of the Things of Eternity, that they were not able to conceal it; the Affection of their Minds overcoming their Strength, and having a very visible Effect on their Bodies. When the Exercise was over, the *young People* that were present removed into the other Room for religious Conference; and particularly that they might have Opportunity to inquire of those that were thus affected what Apprehensions they had; and what Things they were that thus deeply impressed their Minds: and there soon appeared a very great Effect of their Conversation; the Affection was quickly propagated through the Room: many of the *young People* and *Children* that were *Professors* appeared to be overcome with a Sense of the Greatness and Glory of divine Things, and with Admiration, Love, Joy and Praise, and Compassion to others, that looked upon themselves as in a State of Nature; and many others at the same Time were overcome with Distress about their sinful and miserable State and Condition; so that the whole Room was full of nothing but *Out-cries Faintings* and such like. *Others* soon heard of it, in several Parts of the Town, and came to them; and what they saw and heard there was greatly affecting to them; so that many of them were over-power'd in like Manner: and it continued thus for *some Hours*; the Time being spent in *Prayer, Singing, Counselling* and *Conferring*. There seemed to be a consequent *happy Effect* of *that Meeting* to several particular Persons, and in the State of Religion in the Town in general. After this were *Meetings* from Time to Time attended with *like Appearances*. But a little after it, at the Conclusion of the publick Exercise on the *Sabbath*, I appointed the *Children* that were *under sixteen Years of Age* to go from the Meeting-House to a *neighbour House*; that I there might further inforce what they had heard in publick, and might give in some Counsels proper for their Age. The *Children* were there very generally and greatly affected with the Warnings and Counsels that were given them, and many exceedingly overcome; and the Room was filled with *Cries*: and when they were dismissed, they, almost all of them, *went home crying aloud through the Streets*, to all Parts of the Town. The *like Appearances* attended several such Meetings of *Children* that were appointed. But their Affections appeared by what followed to be of a very different Nature: in many they appeared to be indeed but childish Affections; and in a Day or two would leave 'em as they were before: others were deeply impressed; their Convictions took fast hold of them, and abode by them: and there were some that from one Meeting to another seem'd extraordinarily affected for some Time, to but little Purpose, their Affections presently vanishing, from Time to Time; but yet afterwards were seized with abiding Convictions, and their Affections became durable.

About the *middle* of the *Summer*, I call'd together the *young People* that were *Communicants*, from *sixteen* to *twenty six Years of Age* to *my House*; which proved to be a most happy Meeting: many seemed to be very greatly and most agreably affected with those Views which excited Humility, Self-Condemnation, Self-Abhorrence, Love and Joy: many fainted under these Affections. We had *several Meetings* that *Summer* of *young People* attended with like Appearances. It was *about that Time* that there first began to be *cryings out* in the *Meeting-House*; which several Times occasion'd many of the Congregation to stay in the House, after the publick Exercise was over, to confer with those who seemed to be overcome with religious Convictions and Affections; which was found to tend much to the Propagation of their Impressions, with lasting Effect upon many; *Conference* being at these Times commonly joined with *Prayer* and *Singing*. In the *Summer* and *Fall* the *Children* in various Parts of the Town had religious Meetings by themselves for *Prayer*, sometimes joined with *Fasting*; wherein many of them seemed to be greatly and properly affected, and I hope some of them savingly wrought upon.

The Months of *August* and *September* were the most remarkable of any *this Year*, for *Appearances* of *Conviction* and *Conversion* of *Sinners*, and great *Revivings, Quickenings*, and *Comforts* of *Professors*, and for extraordinary external Effects of these Things. It was a *very frequent* Thing to see an *House full* of *Out-cries, Faintings, Convulsions* and such like, both with *Distress*, and also with Admiration and *Joy*. It was not the Manner here to hold Meetings all Night, as in some Places, nor was it common to continue 'em 'till very late in the Night: but it was pretty often so that there were some that were so affected, and their Bodies so overcome, that they could not go home, but were obliged to stay all Night at the House where they were. There was no *Difference* that I know of here, with Regard to these extraordinary Effects, in Meetings in the *Night*, and in the *Day* Time: the Meetings in which these Effects appeared in the Evening, being commonly begun, and their extraordinary Effects, in the Day, and continued in the Evening; and some Meetings have been very remarkable for such extraordinary Effects that were both begun and finished in the *Day* Time.

There was an *Appearance* of a glorious Progress of the Work of *God* upon the Hearts of Sinners in *Conviction* and *Conversion* this *Summer* and *Fall*; and great Numbers, I think we have Reason to hope, were brought savingly home to CHRIST. But this was remarkable, the Work of GOD in his Influences of this Nature, seem'd to be almost wholly upon a *new Generation*; those that were not come to Years of Discretion in that wonderful Season *nine Years* ago, *Children*, or those that were *then Children*: Others that had enjoyed that former glorious Opportunity without any Appearance of saving Benefit, seem'd now to be almost wholly pass'd over and let alone. But *now* we had the most wonderful Work among *Children* that ever was in NORTHAMPTON. The former great Out-pouring of the SPIRIT was remarkable for Influences upon the Minds of *Children*, beyond all that had ever been before; but *this* far exceeded *that*. Indeed as to Influences on the Minds of *Professors*, this Work was by no Means confined to a new Generation: many of all Ages partook of it: but yet, in this Respect it was *more general* on those that were of the *younger Sort*. Many that had formerly been wrought upon, that in the Times of our Declension had fallen into Decays, and had in a great Measure left GOD, and gone after the World, now pass'd under a very remarkable *new Work* of the SPIRIT of GOD, *as if* they had been the Subjects of a *second Conversion*. They were first led into the Wilderness, and had a Work of *Conviction*, having much greater Convictions of the Sin of both Nature and Practice than ever before, (tho' with some new Circumstances, and something new in the Kind of Conviction) in some with great Distress, beyond what they had felt before their *first Conversion*: under *these Convictions* they were excited to strive for Salvation, and the Kingdom of Heaven suffer'd Violence from some of them in a far more remarkable Manner than before: and after great Convictions and Humblings, and Agonizings with GOD, they had CHRIST discovered to them anew, as an All-sufficient Saviour, and in the Glories of his Grace, and in a far more clear Manner than before; and with greater Humility, Self-Emptiness and Brokenness of Heart, and a purer and higher Joy, and greater Desires after Holiness of Life, but with greater Self-Diffidence, and distrust of their treacherous Hearts.

One Circumstance wherein this Work differed from that which had been in the Town *five* or *six Years* before, was that Conversions were frequently wrought *more sensibly and visibly*; the Impressions stronger, and more manifest by external Effects of them; and the Progress of the SPIRIT of GOD in Conviction, from Step to Step, more apparent; and the Transition from one State to another more sensible and plain; so that it might, in many Instances, be as it were seen by By-standers. The *preceeding Season* had been very remarkable on this Account beyond what had been before; but *this* more remarkable than *that*. And in this Season these apparent or visible Conversions (if I may so call them) were more frequently in the Presence of others, at religious Meetings, where the Appearances of what was wrought on the Heart fell under publick Observation.

After *September* 1741, there seem'd to be some Abatement of the extraordinary Appearances that had been; but yet they did not wholly cease, but there was something of them from Time to Time *all Winter*.

About the *Beginning* of *February* 1741, 2. Mr. BUEL came to this Town; I being then absent from Home, and continued so 'till about a *Fortnight* after. Mr. BUEL preach'd from Day to Day, almost every Day, in the *Meeting-House*, (I having left to him the free Liberty of my Pulpit, hearing of his designed Visit before I went from Home) and spent almost the whole Time in religious Exercises with the People, either in publick or private, the People continually thronging him. When he first came, there came with him a Number of the zealous People from SUFFIELD, who continued here for some Time. There were *very extraordinary Effects* of Mr. BUEL's Labours; the People were exceedingly moved, *crying out in great Numbers* in the *Meeting-House*, and great Part of the Congregation commonly staying in the House of GOD for Hours after the publick Service, many of them in uncommon Circumstances. Many also were exceedingly moved in *private Meetings*, where Mr. BUEL was: and almost the *whole Town* seemed to be in a great and continual Commotion, Day and Night; and there was indeed a *very great Revival* of Religion. But it was principally among *Professors*; the Appearances of a Work of *Conversion* were in no Measure equal to what had been the *Summer before*. When I came home I found the Town in very extraordinary Circumstances, such in some Respects as I never saw it in before. Mr. BUEL continued here a *Fortnight* or *three Weeks* after I returned: there being still great Appearances attending his Labours; many in their religious Affections being raised far beyond what they ever had been before: and there were *some Instances* of Persons lying in a *Sort of Trance*, remaining for perhaps a whole *twenty-four Hours* motionless, and with their Senses locked up; but in the mean Time under strong Imaginations, as tho' they went to Heaven, and had there a Vision of glorious and delightful Objects. But when the People were raised to this Height, *Satan* took the Advantage, and his Interposition in many Instances soon became very apparent: and a great deal of Caution and Pains were found necessary to keep the People, many of them, from running wild.

In the Month of *March* I led the People into a *solemn publick* RENEWAL *of their* COVENANT *with* GOD. To that End I made a Draught of a COVENANT: and first proposed it to some of the principal Men in the Church; then proposed it to the People in their several religious Societies, in various Parts of the Town; and then proposed it to the whole Congregation in publick; and then deposited a Copy of it in the Hands of each of *our four Deacons*, that all that desired it might resort to them, and have Opportunity to view and consider it. Then the *People in general* that were *above fourteen Years of Age* first subscribed the *Covenant* with their Hands, and then on a *Day of Fasting and Prayer*, all together presented themselves before the LORD in his House, and stood up, and solemnly manifested their Consent to it, as *their Vow to GOD.* The COVENANT was as follows:

A Copy of a Covenant *enter'd into and subscribed, by the People of GOD at* Northampton, *and own'd before GOD in his House, as their Vow to the* LORD, *and made a solemn Act of publick Worship, by the* Congregation in general, *that were* above fourteen Years of Age, *on a* Day of Fasting and Prayer *for the Continuance and Increase of the gracious Presence of GOD in that Place.* March 16. 1741, 2.

"Acknowledging GOD's great Goodness to us, a sinful unworthy People, in the blessed *Manifestations*, and *Fruits* of his *gracious Presence* in this Town, both *formerly* and *lately*, and particularly in the *very late* spiritual *Revival*; and adoring the glorious Majesty, Power, and Grace of GOD, manifested in the *present* wonderful *Out-pouring* of his SPIRIT, in many Parts of this Land, and in this Place; and lamenting our past Backslidings and ungrateful Departings from GOD; and humbly begging of GOD, that he would not mark our Iniquities, but for CHRIST's Sake, come over the Mountains of our Sins, and visit us with his Salvation, and continue the Tokens of his Presence with us, and yet more gloriously pour out his blessed SPIRIT upon us, and make us all Partakers of the divine Blessings, he is, at this Day, bestowing here, and in many Parts of this Land;

We do *this Day* present our Selves before the LORD, to renounce our evil Ways, and put away our Abominations from before GOD's Eyes, and with one Accord, to *Renew our Engagements* to seek and serve GOD: And particularly do now solemnly promise and vow to the LORD as follows.—

"In all our Conversation, Concerns, and Dealings with our *Neighbour*, we will have a strict Regard to Rules of Honesty, Justice, and Uprightness; that we don't overreach or defraud our Neighbour, in any Matter, and either wilfully, or thro' Want of Care, injure him in any of his honest Possessions, or Rights; and in all our Communication, will have a tender Respect, not only to our own Interest, but also to the Interest of our Neighbour; and will carefully endeavour, in every Thing, to do to others, as we should expect, or think reasonable, that they should do to us, if we were in their Case, and they in ours.

"And particularly we will endeavour to *render to every one his Due*; & will take Heed to our selves, that we don't wrong our Neighbour, and give them a just Cause of Offence, by wilfully, or negligently forbearing to pay our honest Debts.

"And wherein any of us, upon strict Examination of our past Behaviour, may be conscious to our selves, that we have by any Means, wrong'd any of our Neighbours in their outward Estate; we will not rest, 'till we have made *that Restitution*, or given *that Satisfaction*, which the Rules of moral Equity require: or if we are, on a strict and impartial Search, conscious to our selves, that we have in any other Respect, considerably injured our Neighbour; we will truly endeavour to do that, which we, in our Consciences, suppose Christian Rules require, in Order to a *Reparation* of the *Injury*, and *removing* the *Offence* given thereby.

"And furthermore we promise, that we will not allow our selves in *Backbiting*; and that we will take great Heed to our selves to avoid all Violations of those Christian Rules, Tit. 3. 2. *Speak Evil of no Man.* Jam. 4. 11. *Speak not Evil one of another, Brethren.* And 2 Cor. 12. 20. *Lest there be Strifes, Backbitings, Whisperings.* And that we will not only, *not slander* our Neighbour, but also will not, to feed a Spirit of Bitterness, Ill-Will, or secret Grudge against our Neighbour, insist on *his real Faults*, needlessly, and when not called to it; or from such a Spirit, speak of his Failings and Blemishes with *Ridicule*, or an *Air of Contempt.*

"And we promise that we will be very careful to avoid doing

any Thing to our Neighbour from a Spirit of *Revenge*. And
that we will take great Care that we do not, for private Interest, or our own Honour, or to maintain our selves against
those of a contrary Party, or to get our Wills, or to promote
any Design in Opposition to others, do those Things which
we, on the most impartial Consideration we are capable of, can
think in our Consciences, will *tend to wound Religion*, and the
Interest of CHRIST's *Kingdom*.

"And particularly, that so far as any of us, by divine Providence, have any special Influence upon others, to lead them, in
the Management of publick Affairs; we will not make our own
worldly Gain, or Honour, or Interest in the Affections of
others, or getting the better of any of a contrary Party, that are
in any Respect our Competitors, or the bringing, or keeping
them down, our governing Aim, to the Prejudice of the Interest of Religion, and the Honour of CHRIST.

"And in the Management of any *publick Affair*, wherein there
is a Difference of Opinions, concerning any outward Possessions, Priviledges, Rights or Properties; we will not *wittingly vio-
late Justice*, for private Interest: and with the greatest Strictness
and Watchfulness, will avoid all unchristian *Bitterness, Vehemence*,
and *Heat* of Spirit; yea tho' we should think our selves injured
by a contrary Party: and in the Time of the Management of such
Affairs, will especially watch over our selves, our Spirits, and our
Tongues, to avoid all unchristian *Inveighings, Reproachings, bitter Reflectings, judging* and *ridiculing* others, either in publick
Meetings, or in private Conversation, either to Men's Faces, or
behind their Backs; but will greatly endeavour, so far as we are
concerned, that all should be managed with Christian *Humility,
Gentleness, Quietness* and *Love*.

"And furthermore we promise that we will not tolerate the
Exercise of *Enmity* and *Ill-Will*, or *Revenge* in our *Hearts*,
against any of our Neighbors; and we will *often be strictly
searching and examining our Hearts* with Respect to that
Matter.

"AND if any of us find that we have an *old secret Grudge* against
any of our Neighbours, we will not gratify it, but cross it, &
endeavour, to our utmost, to root it out, crying to GOD for his

Help; and that we will make it our true & faithful Endeavour, in our Places, that a Party Spirit may not be kept up amongst us, but that it may utterly cease; that for the future we may all be one, united in undisturbed Peace, and unfeigned Love.

"And those of us that are *in Youth*, do promise never to allow our selves in any *youthful Diversions* and *Pastimes*, in Meetings, or Companies of young People, that we *in our Consciences*, upon *sober Consideration, judge not well to consist with*, or would *sinfully tend to hinder* the devoutest, and most engaged Spirit in Religion; or *indispose the Mind* for that devout, and profitable Attendance on the Duties of the *Closet*, which is most agreable to GOD's Will; or that we in our most impartial Judgment, can think *tends* to rob GOD of that Honour which he expects, by our orderly, serious Attendance on *Family-Worship*.

"And furthermore we promise that we will strictly avoid all *Freedoms* and *Familiarities* in *Company*, so tending, either to stir up, or gratify a Lust of Lasciviousness, that we cannot in our Consciences think will be approved by the infinitely pure and holy Eye of GOD; or that we can think on serious and impartial Consideration, we should be afraid to practise, if we expected in a few Hours to appear before that holy God, to give an Account of our selves to him, as fearing they would be condemned by him as unlawful and impure.

"We also promise, with great Watchfulness, to perform *Relative Duties*, required by Christian Rules, in the Families we belong to; as we stand related respectively, towards *Parents* and *Children, Husbands* and *Wives, Brothers* and *Sisters, Masters* or *Mistresses* and *Servants*.

"And we now appear before GOD, *depending on divine Grace and Assistance*, solemnly to devote our whole Lives, to be laboriously spent in the Business of Religion: ever making it our greatest Business, without backsliding from such a Way of living; not hearkening to the Solicitations of our Sloth, and other corrupt Inclinations, or the Temptations of the World, that tend to draw us off from it; and particularly, that we will not abuse an Hope, or Opinion that any of us may have of our being interested in CHRIST, to indulge our selves in Sloth, or the more easily to yield to the Solicitations of any sinful Inclinations; but will run with Perseverance, the Race that is set before us, and work out our own Salvation with Fear and Trembling.

"And because we are sensible that the keeping these solemn Vows may hereafter, in many Cases, be very contrary to our corrupt Inclinations, and carnal Interests; we do now therefore appear before GOD, to make a Surrender of all to him, and to make a Sacrifice of every carnal Inclination, and Interest to the great Business of Religion, and the Interest of our Souls.

"And being sensible of our own Weakness, and the Deceitfulness of our own Hearts, and our Proneness to forget our most solemn Vows, and loose our Resolutions; we promise to be *often strictly examining our selves by these Promises, especially before the Sacrament of the* LORD's *Supper*; and beg of GOD that he would, for CHRIST's Sake, keep us from wickedly dissembling in these our solemn Vows; and that he who searches our Hearts, and ponders the Path of our Feet, would from Time to Time help us in trying our selves by THIS COVENANT, and help us to keep Covenant with him, and not leave us to our own foolish wicked and treacherous Hearts."

In the *Beginning* of the *Summer* 1742, there seem'd to be *some Abatement* of the Liveliness of People's Affections in Religion: But yet many were often in a great Height of them. And in the *Fall* and *Winter* following there were at Times extraordinary Appearances. But in the *General* People's Engagedness in Religion and the Liveliness of their Affections have been on the Decline: and *some* of the *young People* especially, have shamefully lost their Liveliness and Vigour in Religion, and much of the Seriousness & Solemnity of their Spirits. But there are *many* that walk as becometh Saints; and to this Day, there are a considerable Number in the Town that seem to be near to GOD, and maintain much of the Life of Religion, and enjoy many of the sensible Tokens and Fruits of his gracious Presence.

With Respect to the *late Season* of Revival of Religion amongst us, for *three* or *four Years* past; it has been observable, that in the former Part of it, in the Years 1740, and 1741, the Work seem'd to be much *more pure*, having less of a corrupt Mixture, than in the former great Out-pouring of the Spirit in 1735, and 1736. Persons seem'd to be sensible of their former

Errors, and had learnt more of their own Hearts, and Experience had taught them more of the Tendency and Consequences of Things: They were now better guarded, and their Affections were not only greater, but attended with greater *Solemnity*, and greater *Humility* and *Self-Distrust*, and greater *Engagedness* after *holy Living* and *Perseverance*; and there were fewer Errors in Conduct. But in the latter Part of it, in the Year 1742, it was otherwise: The Work continued more pure 'till we were infected from abroad: our People hearing, and some of them seeing the Work in other Places, where there was a greater visible Commotion than here, and the outward Appearances were more extraordinary; were ready to think that the Work in those Places far excell'd what was amongst us; and their Eyes were dazled with the high Profession and great Shew that some made who came hither from other Places.

That those People went so far beyond them in Raptures and violent Emotions of the Affections, and a vehement Zeal, and what they called Boldness for CHRIST; our People were ready to think was owing to their far greater Attainments in Grace, and Intimacy with Heaven: They look'd little in their own Eyes in Comparison of them, and were ready to submit themselves to 'em, and yield themselves up to their Conduct, taking it for granted that every Thing was right that they said and did. These Things had a strange Influence on the People, and gave many of them a deep and unhappy Tincture, that it was a hard and long Labour to deliver 'em from, and which some of them are not fully delivered from to this Day.

The *Effects* and *Consequences* of Things amongst us plainly shews the following Things, *viz.* That the Degree of *Grace* is by no Means to be judged of by the Degree of *Joy*, or the Degree of *Zeal*; and that indeed we can't at all determine by these Things, who are gracious and who are not; and that it is not the *Degree* of religious Affections, but the *Nature* of them that is chiefly to be looked at. *Some* that have had very great Raptures of Joy, and have been extraordinarily fill'd, (as the vulgar Phrase is) and have had their Bodies overcome, and that very often, have manifested far less of the Temper of Christians, in their Conduct since, than some others that have been still, and have made no great outward Show. But then again there are *many others*, that have had extraordinary Joys and Emotions of

Mind, with frequent great Effects on their Bodies, that behave themselves stedfastly, as humble, amiable, eminent Christians.

'Tis evident that there may be great religious Affections, that may in Shew and Appearance imitate gracious Affections, and have the same Effects on their *Bodies*, but are far from having the same Effect in the *Temper* of their *Minds*, and *Course* of their *Lives*. And likewise there is nothing more manifest by what appears amongst us, than that the Goodness of Persons *State* is not chiefly to be judged of by any exactness of Steps, and Method of Experiences, in what is supposed to be the first Conversion; but that we must judge more by the *Spirit* that *breathes*, the *Effect* wrought on the *Temper* of the *Soul*, in the Time of the Work, and *remaining afterwards*. Tho' there have been very few Instances among Professors amongst us, of what is ordinarily called scandalous Sin, known to me; yet the Temper that some of them shew, and the Behaviour they have been of, together with some Things in the Kind and Circumstances of their Experiences, make me much afraid least there be a considerable Number that have wofully deceived themselves. Tho' on the other Hand, there is a great Number whose Temper and Conversation is such as justly confirms the Charity of others towards them; and not a few in whose Disposition and Walk, there are amiable Appearances of eminent Grace. And notwithstanding all the corrupt Mixtures that have been in the late Work here; there are not only many blessed Fruits of it in *particular Persons*, that yet remain, but some good Effects of it upon the *Town in general*. A *Party-Spirit* has *more ceased*: I suppose there has been less Appearance these *three* or *four Years past*, of that Division of the Town into two Parties, that has long been our Bane, than has been these *thirty Years*; and the People have apparently had much *more Caution*, and a *greater Guard* on their *Spirit*, and their *Tongues*, to avoid Contention and unchristian Heats, in Town-Meetings and on other Occasions. And 'tis a Thing greatly to be rejoyced in, that the People very lately have come to an *Agreement* and *final Issue*, with Respect to their grand Controversy, relating to their Common Lands; which has been above any other particular Thing, a Source of mutual Prejudices, Jealousies, and Debates, for *fifteen* or *sixteen Years past*. The People are also generally of late in some Respects considerably alter'd and meliorated in their Notions of Religion: particularly they seem to be much more sensible of the *Danger* of *resting* in *old Experiences*, or what they were Subjects of at their supposed first Conversion; and to be more fully convinced of the *Necessity* of forgetting the Things that are behind, and *pressing forward*, and *maintaining earnest Labour, Watchfulness* and *Prayerfulness as long as they live*.

NORTHAMPTON, Decemb.
12. 1743.

The Christian History i, 1743

PERSONAL NARRATIVE

An Account of his Conversion, Experiences, and
Religious Exercices, given by himself.

I had a variety of Concerns and Exercises about my Soul from
my Childhood; but had two more remarkable Seasons of
Awakening, before I met with that Change, by which I was
brought to those new Dispositions, and that new Sense of
Things, that I have since had. The first Time was when I was a
Boy, some Years before I went to College, at a Time of remarkable Awakening in my Father's Congregation. I was then very
much affected for many Months, and concerned about the
Things of Religion, and my Soul's Salvation; and was abundant
in Duties. I used to pray five times a Day in secret, and to
spend much Time in religious Talk with other Boys; and used
to meet with them to pray together. I experienced I know not
what Kind of Delight in Religion. My Mind was much engaged
in it, and had much self-righteous Pleasure; and it was my Delight to abound in religious Duties. I, with some of my School-
mates joined together, and built a Booth in a Swamp, in a very
secret and retired Place, for a place of Prayer. And besides, I
had particular secret Places of my own in the Woods, where I
used to retire by my self; and used to be from time to time
much affected. My Affections seemed to be lively and easily
moved, and I seemed to be in my Element, when engaged in
religious Duties. And I am ready to think, many are deceived
with such Affections, and such a kind of Delight, as I then had
in Religion, and mistake it for Grace.

But in process of Time, my Convictions and Affections wore
off; and I entirely lost all those Affections and Delights, and
left off secret Prayer, at least as to any constant Performance of
it; and returned like a Dog to his Vomit, and went on in Ways
of Sin.

Indeed, I was at some Times very uneasy, especially towards
the latter Part of the Time of my being at College. 'Till it

pleas'd GOD, in my last Year at College, at a Time when I was in the midst of many uneasy Thoughts about the State of my Soul, to seize me with a Pleurisy; in which he brought me nigh to the Grave, and shook me over the Pit of Hell.

But yet, it was not long after my Recovery, before I fell again into my old Ways of Sin. But God would not suffer me to go on with any Quietness; but I had great and violent inward Struggles: 'till after many Conflicts with wicked Inclinations, and repeated Resolutions, and Bonds that I laid my self under by a kind of Vows to God, I was brought wholly to break off all former wicked Ways, and all Ways of known outward Sin; and to apply my self to seek my Salvation, and practise the Duties of Religion: But without that kind of Affection and Delight, that I had formerly experienced. My Concern now wrought more by inward Struggles and Conflicts, and Self-reflections. I made seeking my Salvation the main Business of my Life. But yet it seems to me, I sought after a miserable manner: Which has made me some times since to question, whether ever it issued in that which was saving; being ready to doubt, whether such miserable seeking was ever succeeded. But yet I was brought to seek Salvation, in a manner that I never was before. I felt a Spirit to part with all Things in the World, for an Interest in Christ. My Concern continued and prevailed, with many exercising Things and inward Struggles; but yet it never seemed to be proper to express my Concern that I had, by the Name of Terror.

From my Childhood up, my Mind had been wont to be full of Objections against the Doctrine of GOD's Sovereignty, in choosing whom he would to eternal Life, and rejecting whom he pleased; leaving them eternally to perish, and be everlast-ingly tormented in Hell. It used to appear like a horrible Doctrine to me. But I remember the Time very well, when I seemed to be convinced, and fully satisfied, as to this Sover-eignty of God, and his Justice in thus eternally disposing of Men, according to his sovereign Pleasure. But never could give an Account, how, or by what Means, I was thus convinced; not in the least imagining, in the Time of it, nor a long Time after, that there was any extraordinary Influence of God's Spirit in it: but only that now I saw further, and my Reason apprehended the Justice and Reasonableness of it. However, my Mind rested in it; and it put an end to all those Cavils and Objections, that had 'till then abode with me, all the preceeding part of my Life. And there has been a wonderful Alteration in my Mind, with respect to the Doctrine of God's Sovereignty, from that Day to this; so that I scarce ever have found so much as the rising of an Objection against God's Sovereignty, in the most absolute Sense, in shewing Mercy on whom he will shew Mercy, and hardening and eternally damning whom he will. God's absolute Sovereignty, and Justice, with respect to Salvation and Damnation, is what my Mind seems to rest assured of, as much as of any Thing that I see with my Eyes; at least it is so at Times. But I have often times since that first Conviction, had quite another Kind of Sense of God's Sovereignty, than I had then. I have often since, not only had a Conviction, but a *delightful* Conviction. The Doctrine of God's Sovereignty has very often appeared, an exceeding pleasant, bright and sweet Doctrine to me: and absolute Sovereignty is what I love to ascribe to God. But my first Conviction was not with this.

The first that I remember that ever I found any thing of that Sort of inward, sweet Delight in GOD and divine Things, that I have lived much in since, was on reading those Words, I *Tim.* i. 17. "Now unto the King eternal, immortal, invisible, the only wise GOD, be Honor and Glory for ever and ever, Amen." As I read the Words, there came into my Soul, and was as it were diffused thro' it, a Sense of the Glory of the Divine Being; a new Sense, quite different from any Thing I ever experienced before. Never any Words of Scripture seemed to me as these Words did. I thought with my self, how excellent a Being that was; and how happy I should be, if I might enjoy that GOD, and be wrapt up to GOD in Heaven, and be as it were swallowed up in Him. I kept saying, and as it were singing over these Words of Scripture to my self; and went to Prayer, to pray to GOD that I might enjoy him; and prayed in a manner quite different from what I used to do; with a new sort of Affection. But it never came into my Thought, that there was any thing spiritual, or of a saving Nature in this.

From about that Time, I began to have a new Kind of Apprehensions and Ideas of Christ, and the Work of Redemption, and the glorious Way of Salvation by him. I had an inward, sweet Sense of these Things, that at times came into my

Heart; and my Soul was led away in pleasant Views and Con-
templations of them. And my Mind was greatly engaged, to
spend my Time in reading and meditating on Christ; and the
Beauty and Excellency of his Person, and the lovely Way of
Salvation, by free Grace in him. I found no Books so delightful
to me, as those that treated of these Subjects. Those Words
Cant. ii. 1. used to be abundantly with me: *I am the Rose of
Sharon, the Lilly of the Valleys.* The Words seemed to me,
sweetly to represent, the Loveliness and Beauty of Jesus Christ.
And the whole Book of Canticles used to be pleasant to me;
and I used to be much in reading it, about that time. And
found, from Time to Time, an inward Sweetness, that used, as
it were, to carry me away in my Contemplations; in what I
know not how to express otherwise, than by a calm, sweet
Abstraction of Soul from all the Concerns of this World; and a
kind of Vision, or fix'd Ideas and Imaginations, of being alone
in the Mountains, or some solitary Wilderness, far from all
Mankind, sweetly conversing with Christ, and wrapt and swallowed up in GOD. The Sense I had of divine Things, would
often of a sudden as it were, kindle up a sweet burning in my
Heart; an ardor of my Soul, that I know not how to express.

Not long after I first began to experience these Things, I
gave an Account to my Father, of some Things that had pass'd
in my Mind. I was pretty much affected by the Discourse we
had together. And when the Discourse was ended, I walked
abroad alone, in a solitary Place in my Father's Pasture, for
Contemplation. And as I was walking there, and looked up on
the Sky and Clouds; there came into my Mind, a sweet Sense
of the glorious Majesty and Grace of GOD, that I know not
how to express. I seemed to see them both in a sweet Con-
junction: Majesty and Meekness join'd together: it was a sweet
and gentle, and holy Majesty; and also a majestick Meekness;
an awful Sweetness; a high, and great, and holy Gentleness.

After this my Sense of divine Things gradually increased,
and became more and more lively, and had more of that inward
Sweetness. The Appearance of every thing was altered: there
seem'd to be, as it were, a calm, sweet Cast, or Appearance of
divine Glory, in almost every Thing. God's Excellency, his
Wisdom, his Purity and Love, seemed to appear in every
Thing; in the Sun, Moon and Stars; in the Clouds, and blue

Sky; in the Grass, Flowers, Trees; in the Water, and all Nature; which used greatly to fix my Mind. I often used to sit & view the Moon, for a long time; and so in the Day time, spent much time in viewing the Clouds & Sky, to behold the sweet Glory of GOD in these Things: in the mean Time, singing forth with a low Voice, my Contemplations of the Creator & Redeemer. And scarce any Thing, among all the Works of Nature, was so sweet to me as Thunder and Lightning. Formerly, nothing had been so terrible to me. I used to be a Person uncommonly terrified with Thunder: and it used to strike me with Terror, when I saw a Thunder-storm rising. But now, on the contrary, it re-joyced me. I felt GOD at the first Appearance of a Thunder-storm. And used to take the Opportunity at such Times, to fix my self to view the Clouds, and see the Lightnings play, and hear the majestick & awful Voice of God's Thunder: which often times was exceeding entertaining, leading me to sweet Contemplations of my great and glorious GOD. And while I viewed, used to spend my time, as it always seem'd natural to me, to sing or chant forth my Meditations; to speak my Thoughts in Soliloquies, and speak with a singing Voice.

I felt then a great Satisfaction as to my good Estate. But that did not content me. I had vehement Longings of Soul after GOD and CHRIST, and after more Holiness; wherewith my Heart seemed to be full, and ready to break: which often brought to my Mind, the Words of the Psalmist, Psal. cxix. 20. *My Soul breaketh for the Longing it hath.* I often felt a mourning and lamenting in my Heart, that I had not turned to GOD sooner, that I might have had more time to grow in Grace. My Mind was greatly fix'd on divine Things; I was almost perpetually in the Contemplation of them. Spent most of my Time in thinking of divine Things, Year after Year. And used to spend abundance of my Time, in walking alone in the Woods, and solitary Places, for Meditation, Soliloquy and Prayer, and Converse with GOD. And it was always my Manner, at such times, to sing forth my Contemplations. And was almost constantly in ejaculatory Prayer, wherever I was. Prayer seem'd to be natural to me; as the Breath, by which the inward Burnings of my Heart had vent.

The Delights which I now felt in Things of Religion, were of an exceeding different Kind, from those forementioned, that I had when I was a Boy. They were totally of another

Kind; and what I then had no more Notion or Idea of, than one born blind has of pleasant and beautiful Colours. They were of a more inward, pure, Soul-animating and refreshing Nature. Those former Delights, never reached the Heart; and did not arise from any Sight of the divine Excellency of the Things of GOD; or any Taste of the Soul-satisfying, and Life-giving Good, there is in them.

My sense of divine Things seem'd gradually to increase, 'till I went to preach at *New-York*; which was about a Year and a half after they began. While I was there, I felt them, very sensibly, in a much higher Degree, than I had done before. My Longings after GOD & Holiness, were much increased. Pure and humble, holy and heavenly Christianity, appeared exceeding amiable to me. I felt in me a burning Desire to be in every Thing a compleat Christian; and conformed to the blessed Image of Christ: and that I might live in all Things, according to the pure, sweet and blessed Rules of the Gospel. I had an eager thirsting after Progress in these Things. My Longings after it, put me upon pursuing and pressing after them. It was my continual Strife Day and Night, and constant Inquiry, How I should be more holy, and live more holily, and more becoming a Child of God, and Disciple of Christ. I sought an encrease of Grace and Holiness, and that I might live an holy Life, with vastly more Earnestness, than ever I sought Grace, before I had it. I used to be continually examining my self, and studying and contriving for likely Ways and Means, how I should live holily, with far greater diligence and earnestness, than ever I pursued any thing in my Life: But with too great a Dependence on my own Strength; which afterwards proved a great Damage to me. My Experience had not then taught me, as it has done since, my extream Feebleness and Impotence, every manner of Way; and the innumerable and bottomless Depths of secret Corruption and Deceit, that there was in my Heart. However, I went on with my eager pursuit after more Holiness; and sweet conformity to Christ.

The Heaven I desired was a Heaven of Holiness; to be with GOD, and to spend my Eternity in divine Love, and holy Communion with Christ. My Mind was very much taken up with Contemplations on Heaven, and the Enjoyments of those there; and living there in perfect Holiness, Humility and Love. And it used at that Time to appear a great Part of the Happiness of Heaven, that there the Saints could express their Love to Christ. It appear'd to me a great Clog and Hindrance and Burden to me, that what I felt within, I could not express to GOD, and give vent to, as I desired. The inward ardor of my Soul, seem'd to be hinder'd and pent up, and could not freely flame out as it would. I used often to think, how in Heaven, this sweet Principle should freely and fully vent and express it self. Heaven appeared to me exceeding delightful as a World of Love. It appear'd to me, that all Happiness consisted in living in pure, humble, heavenly, divine Love.

I remember the Thoughts I used then to have of Holiness. I remember I then said sometimes to my self, I do certainly know that I love Holiness, such as the Gospel prescribes. It appeared to me, there was nothing in it but what was ravishingly lovely. It appeared to me, to be the highest Beauty and Amiableness, above all other Beauties: that it was a *divine* Beauty; far purer than any thing here upon Earth; and that every thing else, was like Mire, Filth and Defilement, in Comparison of it.

Holiness, as I then wrote down some of my Contemplations on it, appeared to me to be of a sweet, pleasant, charming, serene, calm Nature. It seem'd to me, it brought an inexpressible Purity, Brightness, Peacefulness & Ravishment to the Soul: and that it made the Soul like a Field or Garden of GOD, with all manner of pleasant Flowers; that is all pleasant, delightful & undisturbed; enjoying a sweet Calm, and the gently vivifying Beams of the Sun. The Soul of a true Christian, as I then wrote my Meditations, appear'd like such a little white Flower, as we see in the Spring of the Year; low and humble on the Ground, opening it's Bosom, to receive the pleasant Beams of the Sun's Glory; rejoycing as it were, in a calm Rapture; diffusing around a sweet Fragrance; standing peacefully and lovingly, in the midst of other Flowers round about; all in like Manner opening their Bosoms, to drink in the Light of the Sun.

There was no Part of Creature-Holiness, that I then, and at other Times, had so great a Sense of the Loveliness of, as Humility, Brokenness of Heart and Poverty of Spirit: and there was nothing that I had such a Spirit to long for. My Heart as it were panted after this, to lie low before GOD, and in the Dust; that I might be nothing, and that GOD might be all; that I might become as a little Child.

While I was there at *New-York*, I sometimes was much affected with Reflections on my past Life, considering how late it was, before I began to be truly religious; and how wickedly I had lived till then: and once so as to weep abundantly, and for a considerable time together.

On *January* 12. 1722, 3. I made a solemn Dedication of my self to GOD, and wrote it down; giving up my self, and all that I had to GOD; to be for the future in no Respect my own; to act as one that had no right to himself, in any Respect. And solemnly vowed to take GOD for my whole Portion and Felicity; looking on nothing else as any Part of my Happiness, nor acting as if it were: and his Law for the constant Rule of my Obedience: engaging to fight with all my Might, against the World, the Flesh and the Devil, to the End of my Life. But have Reason to be infinitely humbled, when I consider, how much I have fail'd of answering my Obligation.

I had then abundance of sweet religious Conversation in the Family where I lived, with Mr. *John Smith*, and his pious Mother. My Heart was knit in Affection to those, in whom were Appearances of true Piety; and I could bear the Thoughts of no other Companions, but such as were holy, and the Disciples of the blessed JESUS.

I had great Longings for the Advancement of Christ's Kingdom in the World. My secret Prayer used to be in great Part taken up in praying for it. If I heard the least hint of any thing that happened in any Part of the World, that appear'd to me, in some Respect or other, to have a favourable Aspect on the Interest of Christ's Kingdom, my Soul eagerly catch'd at it; and it would much animate and refresh me. I used to be earnest to read publick News-Letters, mainly for that End; to see if I could not find some News favourable to the Interest of Religion in the World.

I very frequently used to retire into a solitary Place, on the Banks of *Hudson*'s River, at some Distance from the City, for Contemplation on Divine Things, and secret Converse with GOD; and had many sweet Hours there. Sometimes Mr. *Smith* and I walked there together, to converse of the Things of GOD; and our Conversation used much to turn on the Advancement of Christ's Kingdom in the World, and the glorious Things that GOD would accomplish for his Church in the latter Days.

I had then, and at other Times, the greatest Delight in the holy Scriptures, of any Book whatsoever. Oftentimes in reading it, every Word seemed to touch my Heart. I felt an Harmony between something in my Heart, and those sweet and powerful Words. I seem'd often to see so much Light, exhibited by every Sentence, and such a refreshing ravishing Food communicated, that I could not get along in reading. Used often-times to dwell long on one Sentence, to see the Wonders contained in it; and yet almost every Sentence seemed to be full of Wonders.

I came away from *New-York* in the Month of *April*, 1723, and had a most bitter parting with Madam *Smith* and her Son. My Heart seemed to sink within me, at leaving the Family and City, where I had enjoyed so many sweet and pleasant Days. I went from *New-York* to *Weathersfield* by Water. As I sail'd away, I kept Sight of the City as long as I could; and when I was out of Sight of it, it would affect me much to look that Way, with a kind of Melancholly mixed with Sweetness. However, that Night after this sorrowful parting, I was greatly comforted in GOD at *Westchester*, where we went ashore to lodge: and had a pleasant Time of it all the Voyage to *Saybrook*. It was sweet to me to think of meeting dear Christians in Heaven, where we should never part more. At *Saybrook* we went ashore to lodge on Saturday, and there kept Sabbath; where I had a sweet and refreshing Season, walking alone in the Fields.

After I came home to *Windsor*, remained much in a like Frame of my Mind, as I had been in at *New-York*; But only some times felt my Heart ready to sink, with the Thoughts of my Friends at *New-York*. And my Refuge and Support was in Contemplations on the heavenly State; as I find in my Diary of *May* 1. 1723. It was my Comfort to think of that State, where there is fulness of Joy; where reigns heavenly, sweet, calm and delightful Love, without Alloy; where there are continually the dearest Expressions of this Love; where is the Enjoyment of the Persons loved, without ever parting; where these Persons that appear so lovely in this World, will really be inexpressibly more lovely, and full of love to us. And how sweetly will the mutual Lovers join together to sing the Praises of GOD and the LAMB! How full will it fill us with Joy, to think, that this Enjoyment, these sweet Exercises will never cease or come to an End; but will last to all Eternity!

Continued much in the same Frame in the general, that I had been in at *New-York*, till I went to *New-Haven*, to live there as Tutor of the College; having one special Season of uncommon Sweetness: particularly once at *Bolton*, in a Journey from *Boston*, walking out alone in the Fields. After I went to *New-Haven*, I sunk in Religion; my Mind being diverted from my eager and violent Pursuits after Holiness, by some Affairs that greatly perplexed and distracted my Mind.

In *September*, 1725, was taken ill at *New-Haven*; and endeavouring to go home to *Windsor*, was so ill at the North Village, that I could go no further: where I lay sick for about a Quarter of a Year. And in this Sickness, GOD was pleased to visit me again with the sweet Influences of his Spirit. My Mind was greatly engaged there on divine, pleasant Contemplations, and Longings of Soul. I observed that those who watched with me, would often be looking out for the Morning, and seemed to wish for it. Which brought to my Mind those Words of the Psalmist, which my Soul with Sweetness made it's own Language. *My Soul waiteth for the Lord, more than they that watch for the Morning, I say, more than they that watch for the Morning.* And when the Light of the Morning came, and the Beams of the Sun came in at the Windows, it refreshed my Soul from one Morning to another. It seemed to me to be some Image of the sweet Light of GOD's Glory.

I remember, about that Time, I used greatly to long for the Conversion of some that I was concerned with. It seem'd to me, I could gladly honor them, and with Delight be a Servant to them, and lie at their Feet, if they were but truly holy.

But some Time after this, I was again greatly diverted in my Mind, with some temporal Concerns, that exceedingly took up my Thoughts, greatly to the wounding of my Soul: and went on through various Exercises, that it would be tedious to relate, that gave me much more Experience of my own Heart, than ever I had before.

Since I came to this Town,* I have often had sweet Compla-

*Northampton.

cency in GOD, in Views of his glorious Perfections, and the Excellency of Jesus Christ. GOD has appeared to me, a glorious and lovely Being, chiefly on the account of his Holiness. The Holiness of GOD has always appeared to me the most lovely of all his Attributes. The Doctrines of God's absolute Sovereignty, and free Grace, in shewing Mercy to whom he would shew Mercy; and Man's absolute Dependance on the Operations of God's Holy Spirit, have very often appeared to me as sweet and glorious Doctrines. These Doctrines have been much my Delight. GOD's Sovereignty has ever appeared to me, as great Part of his Glory. It has often been sweet to me to go to GOD, and adore Him as a sovereign GOD, and ask sovereign Mercy of Him.

I have loved the Doctrines of the Gospel: They have been to my Soul like green Pastures. The Gospel has seem'd to me to be the richest Treasure; the Treasure that I have most desired, and longed that it might dwell richly in me. The Way of Salvation by Christ, has appeared in a general Way, glorious and excellent, and most pleasant and beautiful. It has often seem'd to me, that it would in a great Measure spoil Heaven, to receive it in any other Way. That Text has often been affecting and delightful to me, Isai. xxxii. 2. *A Man shall be an hiding Place from the Wind, and a Covert from the Tempest &c.*

It has often appear'd sweet to me, to be united to CHRIST; to have Him for my Head, and to be a Member of his Body: and also to have CHRIST for my Teacher and Prophet. I very often think with Sweetness and Longings and Pantings of Soul, of being a little Child, taking hold of CHRIST, to be led by Him through the Wilderness of this World. That Text, *Matth.* xviii. at the Beginning, has often been sweet to me, *Except ye be converted, and become as little Children &c.* I love to think of coming to CHRIST, to receive Salvation of him, poor in Spirit, and quite empty of Self; humbly exalting Him alone; cut entirely off from my own Root, and to grow into, and out of CHRIST: to have GOD in CHRIST to be all in all; and to live by Faith on the Son of GOD, a Life of humble, unfeigned Confidence in Him. That Scripture has often been sweet to me, Psal. cxv. 1. *Not unto us, O LORD, not unto us, but unto thy Name give Glory, for thy Mercy, and for thy Truth's sake.* And those Words of Christ, *Luk.* x. 21. *In that Hour Jesus rejoyced in Spirit, and said, I thank thee, O Father, Lord of Heaven and Earth, that thou hast hid these Things from the wise and prudent, and hast revealed them unto Babes: Even so Father, for so it seemed good in thy Sight.* That Sovereignty of GOD that Christ rejoyced in, seemed to me to be worthy to be rejoyced in; and that rejoycing of CHRIST, seemed to me to shew the Excellency of CHRIST, and the Spirit that he was of.

Sometimes only mentioning a single Word, causes my Heart to burn within me: or only seeing the Name of CHRIST, or the Name of some Attribute of GOD. And GOD has appeared glorious to me, on account of the TRINITY. It has made me have exalting Thoughts of GOD, that he subsists in three Persons; FATHER, SON, and HOLY GHOST.

The sweetest Joys and Delights I have experienced, have not been those that have arisen from a Hope of my own good Estate; but in a direct View of the glorious Things of the Gospel. When I enjoy this Sweetness, it seems to carry me above the Thoughts of my own safe Estate. It seems at such Times a Loss that I cannot bear, to take off my Eye from the glorious, pleasant Object I behold without me, to turn my Eye in upon my self, and my own good Estate.

My Heart has been much on the Advancement of Christ's Kingdom in the World. The Histories of the past Advancement of Christ's Kingdom, have been sweet to me. When I have read Histories of past Ages, the pleasantest Thing in all my reading has been, to read of the Kingdom of Christ being promoted. And when I have expected in my reading, to come to any such thing, I have lotted upon it all the Way as I read. And my Mind has been much entertained and delighted, with the Scripture Promises and Prophecies, of the future glorious Advancement of Christ's Kingdom on Earth.

I have sometimes had a Sense of the excellent Fulness of Christ, and his Meetness and Suitableness as a Saviour; whereby he has appeared to me, far above all, the chief of ten Thousands. And his Blood and Atonement has appeared sweet, and his Righteousness sweet; which is always accompanied with an Ardency of Spirit, and inward Strugglings and Breathings and Groanings, that cannot be uttered, to be emptied of my self, and swallowed up in CHRIST.

Once, as I rid out into the Woods for my Health, *Anno* 1737;

and having lit from my Horse in a retired Place, as my Manner commonly has been, to walk for divine Contemplation and Prayer; I had a View, that for me was extraordinary, of the Glory of the Son of GOD; as Mediator between GOD and Man; and his wonderful, great, full, pure and sweet Grace and Love, and meek and gentle Condescention. This Grace, that appear'd to me so calm and sweet, appear'd great above the Heavens. The Person of Christ appear'd ineffably excellent, with an Excellency great enough to swallow up all Thought and Conception. Which continued, as near as I can judge, about an Hour; which kept me, the bigger Part of the Time, in a Flood of Tears, and weeping aloud. I felt withal, an Ardency of Soul to be, what I know not otherwise how to express, than to be emptied and annihilated; to lie in the Dust, and to be full of Christ alone; to love him with a holy and pure Love; to trust in him; to live upon him; to serve and follow him, and to be totally wrapt up in the Fullness of Christ; and to be perfectly sanctified and made pure, with a divine and heavenly Purity. I have several other Times, had Views very much of the same Nature, and that have had the same Effects.

I have many Times had a Sense of the Glory of the third Person in the Trinity, in his Office of Sanctifier; in his holy Operations communicating divine Light and Life to the Soul. GOD in the Communications of his Holy Spirit, has appear'd as an infinite Fountain of Divine Glory and Sweetness; being full and sufficient to fill and satisfy the Soul: pouring forth it self in sweet Communications, like the Sun in its Glory, sweetly and pleasantly diffusing Light and Life.

I have sometimes had an affecting Sense of the Excellency of the Word of GOD, as a Word of Life; as the Light of Life; a sweet, excellent, Life-giving Word: accompanied with a thirsting after that Word, that it might dwell richly in my Heart.

I have often since I lived in this Town, had very affecting Views of my own Sinfulness and Vileness; very frequently so as to hold me in a kind of loud Weeping, sometimes for a considerable time together: so that I have often been forced to shut my self up. I have had a vastly greater Sense of my own Wickedness, and the Badness of my Heart, since my Conversion, than ever I had before. It has often appeared to me, that if GOD should mark Iniquity against me, I should appear the very worst of all Mankind; of all that have been since the beginning of the World to this time: and that I should have by far the lowest Place in Hell. When others that have come to talk with me about their Soul Concerns, have expressed the Sense they have had of their own Wickedness, by saying that it seem'd to them, that they were as bad as the Devil himself; I thought their Expressions seemed exceeding faint and feeble, to represent my Wickedness. I thought I should wonder, that they should content themselves with such Expressions as these, if I had any Reason to imagine, that their Sin bore any Proportion to mine. It seemed to me, I should wonder at my self, if I should express *my* Wickedness in such feeble Terms as they did.

My Wickedness, as I am in my self, has long appear'd to me perfectly ineffable, and infinitely swallowing up all Thought and Imagination; like an infinite Deluge, or infinite Mountains over my Head. I know not how to express better, what my Sins appear to me to be, than by heaping Infinite upon Infinite, and multiplying Infinite by Infinite. I go about very often, for this many Years, with these Expressions in my Mind, and in my Mouth, "Infinite upon Infinite. Infinite upon Infinite!" When I look into my Heart, and take a view of my Wickedness, it looks like an Abyss infinitely deeper than Hell. And it appears to me, that were it not for free Grace, exalted and raised up to the infinite Height of all the fulness and glory of the great JE-HOVAH, and the Arm of his Power and Grace stretched forth, in all the Majesty of his Power, and in all the Glory of his Sovereignty; I should appear sunk down in my Sins infinitely below Hell it self, far beyond Sight of every Thing, but the piercing Eye of God's Grace, that can pierce even down to such a Depth, and to the bottom of such an Abyss.

And yet, I ben't in the least inclined to think, that I have a greater Conviction of Sin than ordinary. It seems to me, my Conviction of Sin is exceeding small, and faint. It appears to me enough to amaze me, that I have no more Sense of my Sin. I know certainly, that I have very little Sense of my sinfulness. That my Sins appear to me so great, don't seem to me to be, because I have so much more Conviction of Sin than other Christians, but because I am so much worse, and have so much more Wickedness to be convinced of. When I have had these Turns of weeping and crying for my Sins, I thought I knew in the Time of it, that my Repentance was nothing to my Sin.

I have greatly longed of late, for a broken Heart, and to lie low before GOD. And when I ask for Humility of GOD, I can't bear the Thoughts of being no more humble, than other Christians. It seems to me, that tho' their Degrees of Humility may be suitable for them; yet it would be a vile Self-exaltation in me, not to be the lowest in Humility of all Mankind. Others speak of their longing to be humbled to the Dust. Tho' that may be a proper Expression for them, I always think for my self, that I ought to be humbled down below Hell. 'Tis an Expression that it has long been natural for me to use in Prayer to God. I ought to lie infinitely low before GOD.

It is affecting to me to think, how ignorant I was, when I was a young Christian, of the bottomless, infinite Depths of Wickedness, Pride, Hypocrisy and Deceit left in my Heart.

I Have vastly a greater Sense, of my universal, exceeding Dependence on God's Grace and Strength, and meer good Pleasure, of late, than I used formerly to have; and have experienced more of an Abhorrence of my own Righteousness. The Thought of my Comfort or Joy, arising in me, on any Consideration, or Reflection on my own Amiableness, or any of my Performances or Experiences, or any Goodness of Heart or Life, is nauscous and detestable to me. And yet I am greatly afflicted with a proud and self-righteous Spirit; much more sensibly, than I used to be formerly. I see that Serpent rising and putting forth it's Head, continually, every where, all around me.

Tho' it seems to me, that in some Respects I was a far better Christian, for two or three Years after my first Conversion, than I am now; and lived in a more constant Delight and Pleasure: yet of late Years, I have had a more full and constant Sense of the absolute Sovereignty of GOD, and a delight in that Sovereignty; and have had more of a Sense of the Glory of CHRIST, as a Mediator, as revealed in the Gospel. On one Saturday Night in particular, had a particular Discovery of the Excellency of the Gospel of CHRIST, above all other Doctrines; so that I could not but say to my self; "This is my chosen Light, my chosen Doctrine": and of Christ, "This is my chosen

Prophet." It appear'd to me to be sweet beyond all Expression, to follow Christ, and to be taught and enlighten'd and instructed by him; to learn of him, and live to him.

Another Saturday Night, *January* 1738, 9. had such a Sense, how sweet and blessed a Thing it was, to walk in the Way of Duty, to do that which was right and meet to be done, and agreeable to the holy Mind of GOD; that it caused me to break forth into a kind of a loud weeping, which held me some Time; so that I was forced to shut my self up, and fasten the Doors. I could not but as it were cry out, "How happy are they which do that which is right in the Sight of GOD! They are blessed indeed, they are the happy ones!" I had at the same time, a very affecting Sense, how meet and suitable it was that GOD should govern the World, and order all Things according to his own Pleasure; and I rejoyced in it, that GOD reigned, and that his Will was done.

Chronology

held captive for two and a half years before being ran-
somed. Daughter Eunice Williams, however, who was
seven when kidnapped, will remain with her adopted Mohawk family and later marry into the tribe. Her case will
become a cause célèbre across New England, and the
subject of many family prayers in East Windsor.

1711   Jonathan is raised in a household steeped in the Calvinist
religion of his Puritan forebears, which emphasizes five
key points of doctrine: the inherent sinfulness of human
beings, which causes an inability to repent and believe
without the prompting of God; the mystery of God's
foreordained redemption of only a portion of humanity
(predestination); the limited scope of Christ's atonement
(that is, that Christ's sacrifice on the cross effects the salvation only of those foreordained to be saved); the irresistible and unmerited nature of this saving grace; and the
durability of salvation in the face of all earthly trials. Un-
dergirding all of this is the core Protestant principle of
"justification by faith alone," the idea that it is only faith—
itself a divinely imparted gift of grace—and not good
behavior (works), that renders the believer worthy of salvation. Earmarked for the ministry from a young age, Jonathan is schooled at home by his father, who also tutors
other young men in preparation for Harvard and Connecticut's Collegiate School (founded 1701, later renamed Yale
College), the two principal seminaries in New England.
(With the exception of ministers to the region's Anglican
and Baptist minorities, the great majority of clergy in New
England, that is, those of the established Congregational
churches, are trained at these two small institutions. They
are conceived as bulwarks of orthodoxy, though the varied
clerical response to the revivals will reveal significant theological differences among their graduates.) In summer, father departs East Windsor to serve as chaplain for a military
expedition against New France, but soon falls ill and pro-
gresses only as far as Albany, New York, before being forced
to return home. While away he writes numerous letters to
his wife full of detailed instructions and admonitions, often
about Jonathan's training, as for instance: "I desire you to
take care that Jonathan don't lose what he has learned but
that as he has got the accidence [inflection], and above two
sides of *propria Quae moribus* [a Latin grammar] by heart
so that he keep what he has got."

1712   In the fall, East Windsor experiences a surge in the numbers of individuals willing to come forward and testify to their experience of saving grace. Like his father-in-law in Northampton, Timothy Edwards will oversee several such awakenings, and his son will later recall that "my honored *Father*'s Parish . . . has *in times past*, been a Place favored with Mercies of this nature, *above any* on this western side of *New-England*, excepting *Northampton*." Fired by the religious enthusiasm about them, Jonathan and his father's other pupils construct a booth "in a Swamp, in a very secret and retired Place," for prayer and meditation. He will later lament the passage of these seasons of renewal, after which he "returned like a Dog to his Vomit, and went on in Ways of Sin."

1716   Writes a letter to his favorite sister, Mary—the earliest of his writings known to have survived—in which he recounts the latest awakening in East Windsor. In the fall, begins study at Connecticut's Collegiate School, which is divided into three sites. Edwards attends the school at Wethersfield, Connecticut, only ten miles downriver from East Windsor, where he is instructed by the Reverend Elisha Williams, a half cousin of the Williams-Stoddard clan.

1718   New Haven emerges as the principal site for the Collegiate School, which is renamed Yale College after a gift from English merchant Elihu Yale. In the fall the Connecticut General Assembly orders the Wethersfield students to move to the newly constructed campus in New Haven. Dissatisfied with Samuel Johnson, his new tutor at Yale, Edwards returns to Wethersfield.

1719   After Johnson's dismissal, Edwards returns to New Haven, where he becomes seriously ill with pleurisy, a respiratory inflammation. As he will later recall, he feels spiritually unprepared to die and is terrified, as though God "shook me over the Pit of Hell." Once recovered and continuing with his studies, he explores Yale's new library, where he is exposed to the revolutionary works of Locke, Newton, and others, which will inform his theological and philosophical vision.

1720   Completes his course of study for the baccalaureate degree under the college's new rector, Timothy Cutler, in May, and in September graduates as valedictorian, delivering his commencement oration in Latin, as is customary. Remains at New Haven to continue his theological studies, and begins to record occasional thoughts on God, the natural world, and the human faculties, the first fruits of what will be a lifelong project.

1721   In the spring, experiences what he will later identify as his conversion, when "I was brought to seek Salvation, in a manner that I never was before" and "there came into my Soul, and was as it were diffused thro' it, a Sense of the Glory of the Divine Being; a new Sense, quite different from any Thing I ever experienced before." After a conversation with his father during a visit home to East Windsor, he retires to nearby fields for reflection: "And as I was walking there, and looked up on the Sky and Clouds; there came into my Mind, a sweet Sense of the glorious Majesty and Grace of GOD, that I know not how to express." In New Jersey, a recently arrived Dutch Reformed clergyman named Theodore Frelinghuysen engenders a strong response to his preaching, manifested in both conversions and controversy. This marks the beginning of a long wave of revivalism in the Middle Colonies, a precursor of the movement that will later be called the Great Awakening. (The term "Great Awakening" will be first employed by Protestant clergyman Joseph Tracy in his 1842 work *The Great Awakening: A History of the Revival of Religion in the Time of Edwards and Whitefield.*)

1722   Edwards completes his graduate studies in May and in August travels to New York City, where he serves as an unordained minister to a small Presbyterian church, and boards with an ardently Calvinist family, the Smiths, recently immigrated from England. During this summer, hostilities once again flare between New England and its Indian neighbors to the north (and their French allies), a conflict that will become known as Father Râle's War. Back at Yale, in September, Rector Cutler and two other tutors question the validity of their Congregational ordinations and the following spring sail to England to seek ordination by an Anglican bishop, an episode soon known as "the Connecticut Apostacie." The Yale trustees remove Cutler from office and will eventually replace him in 1726, after a long and difficult search, with Elisha Williams. On December 18, Edwards begins his diary. This same year he begins to frame his occasional writings as "Miscellanies."

1723   Edwards's ministry in New York ends in April, and he returns to East Windsor. In September, in New Haven, he successfully defends his "Quaestio" (master's thesis) on the proposition that a sinner is fully dependent on God for salvation. On November 11, he somewhat reluctantly agrees to undertake the pastorate in Bolton, Connecticut, approximately fifteen miles south of East Windsor. In this year he is thought to have composed the "Apostrophe to Sarah Pierpont," an ardently devout tribute to the young sister of a tutor at Yale. Born January 9, 1710, Sarah Pierpont (or Pierrepont, as Edwards spells her name in the family Bible) is the daughter of James Pierpont, a founder of the College, and Mary Hooker Pierpont, granddaughter of the Reverend Thomas Hooker, founder of the Connecticut colony.

1724   Elected in May to serve as a tutor at Yale, Edwards promptly resigns from his pastorate in Bolton. With two others, he is responsible for the education of about forty students at the College, which is still without a rector.

1725   Falls gravely ill in September from overwork and recuperates at East Windsor. Begins to organize his "Miscellanies," which by year's end number close to two hundred. Father Râle's War, which has been fought across northern New England and in Nova Scotia, ends in December.

1726   In August, Edwards is called to Northampton to assist his grandfather Stoddard, now eighty-three, and begins preaching there on October 26, responsible thereafter for one of the two Sabbath sermons. The town approves a salary of £100 for him, plus £300 to build a house and a grant of 50 acres. Over the course of his long career at Northampton, Stoddard has overseen five evangelical "harvests," in 1679, 1683, 1696, 1712, and 1718, setting up an expectation that such periodic revivals will continue.

1727   Edwards is ordained at Northampton on February 15 and on July 28 marries Sarah Pierpont. On October 29, a major earthquake strikes New England, sparking widespread anxiety that spawns several localized revivals, including in Northampton, where some twenty new converts join the church (in what will be the last "harvest" of Stoddard's career). New Jersey Presbyterian minister William Tennent Sr. establishes his "Log College" in Neshaminy, Pennsylvania, to train revivalists. Along with his sons Gilbert and William Jr., he will emerge as a leader of the Awakening in the Middle Colonies.

1728   Settled into his new life in Northampton, Edwards begins each day at four or five in the morning, so that he can spend a dozen or more hours in his study. "I think Christ has recommended rising early in the morning," he observes in his diary, "by his rising from the grave very early." Daughter Sarah born, August 25.

1729   Solomon Stoddard dies on February 11 and is widely eulogized, including at his funeral service by his son-in-law, the Reverend William Williams of nearby Hatfield, now the de facto intellectual leader among Valley clergy. "The death of a prophet," Williams laments, is "like the falling of a mighty spreading tree in a forest, which . . . makes all the trees about it to shake, [and] leaves a wide Breech where it stood which may be long ere it be filled again." Edwards succeeds Stoddard as senior pastor of the Northampton congregation and becomes spiritual leader of a large community prone to political tensions. "The people of Northampton," he will later observe, "are not the most happy in their natural temper. They have, ever since I can remember, been famed for a high-spirited people, and close, and of a difficult, turbulent temper." His health soon begins to fail under the stress, and in late April and May he retreats with his wife and daughter to East Windsor and to New Haven. In June, back in Northampton, he relapses and cannot preach for a month. Finally recovered in July, he returns to the pulpit where he delivers cycles of sermons treating such subjects as the glory of the Trinity, the means of grace and the benefits of salvation, and the perennial danger of hypocrisy. In his notebooks, he gives vent to a mounting concern about the number of unconverted communicants in his church, a legacy of his grandfather's liberal admission policy. In December, sister Jerusha (born 1710) dies amid an epidemic of diphtheria, or "the throat distemper."

1730   Daughter Jerusha born, April 26.

1731   In May, purchases a "Negro girl named Venus" for £80 from Richard Perkins of Newport, Rhode Island. (At his death Edwards's estate will include two slaves, who will be sold for £23.) Travels to Boston to deliver the public lecture on Thursday, July 8, before the annual clerical assembly gathered for the Harvard commencement. His sermon, "God Glorified in Man's Dependence," is a thoroughly orthodox repudiation of the anti-Calvinist theology called "Arminianism" (after Dutch divine Jacobus Arminius, 1560–1609), which allows that though sinners are saved by faith alone, their faith is the result of a free will decision, not the irresistible prompting of God: "Schemes of divinity [that deny] an absolute and universal dependence on God," he warns, "derogate his glory, and thwart the design of our redemption." It is well received and will become his first publication, *God Glorified in the Work of Redemption*. Travels in October to Westfield, Massachusetts, for a meeting of the Hampshire Association, a twice-yearly gathering of regional clergy that he will thereafter faithfully attend.

1732   In Northampton, as he will later recall, Edwards begins to detect a change in a segment of his congregation: "In *two* or *three* Years after Mr. *Stoddard*'s Death . . . the *young People* shew'd more of a Disposition to hearken to Counsel, and by degrees left off their *Frolicking*, and grew observably more *Decent* in their Attendance on the publick Worship, and there were more that manifested a *Religious Concern* than there used to be." Daughter Esther born, February 13.

1734   Daughter Mary born, April 7. In August, Edwards preaches "A Divine and Supernatural Light," which powerfully describes the experiential dimension of grace and which is soon published in Boston. In December, a five-month sequence of revivals in Northampton and the surrounding Connecticut River towns (later called "the Little Awakening") begins. Edwards attributes the revivals to his emphasis on orthodox Calvinist doctrine and notes that although the increased interest in religion starts among the younger parishioners, it soon spreads to people of all ages.

1735   On May 30, he drafts a letter describing the revivals to Benjamin Colman (1673–1747, Harvard 1692), who with the passing of Cotton Mather in 1728 is now the leading minister in Boston. Before sealing the letter he adds a grim postscript describing the suicide, on June 1, of his uncle Joseph Hawley, who had slit his throat amidst the spiritual intensity of the revival, an event that for Edwards seems to mark the beginning of the end of the Little Awakening. In August, Edwards and other ministers in the Hampshire Association hear the case against Robert Breck (1713–1784, Harvard 1730), a candidate for the pulpit in Springfield, Massachusetts, for his purportedly Arminian views. The Springfield church decides to exercise its congregational prerogative and proceed with his ordination, even though the Association questions the wisdom of so doing. Edwards believes that ministers are responsible to their peers, and the controversy confirms his fears about the rising threat of Arminianism. It also casts a light on emerging doctrinal divisions among the Massachusetts clergy. Edwards travels in the fall to New York City to restore his health, and there learns about the revivals in New Jersey.

1736   Grandmother Esther Warham Mather Stoddard dies, February 10. Sister Lucy dies of "throat distemper," August 21. Daughter Lucy born, August 31. In September, construction begins on a new, larger meetinghouse in Northampton. Responding to Benjamin Colman's entreaty, in November Edwards drafts a more detailed account of the previous year's revivals, which Colman then abridges and appends to a collection of sermons by Edwards's uncle William Williams then at press entitled *The Duty and Interest of a People*, which is published in Boston in December. Joseph Bellamy (1719–1790, Yale 1735) travels to Northampton to begin two years of theological studies with Edwards.

1737   On March 12, the crowded gallery of the old meetinghouse in Northampton collapses with no loss of life, an outcome that Edwards regards as a remarkable providence. Colman forwards his abridgement of Edwards's narrative to the English Dissenting clergymen John Guyse and Isaac Watts, who request to see the whole manuscript, which Colman sends. After some edits of their own, Guyse and Watts facilitate its publication in London as *A Faithful Narrative of the Surprising Work of God in the Conversion of Many Hundred Souls in Northampton, and the Neighboring Towns and Villages*. An edition is also published in Edinburgh, and within a year it will appear in a German translation. On December 25, the new meetinghouse is dedicated.

1738   In May, English evangelist George Whitefield, who will
        figure prominently in the Great Awakening, makes his first
        journey to America. An associate of Charles and John
        Wesley, founders of the Methodist movement within the
        Church of England, Whitefield travels to Georgia where
        he joins the Wesleys in founding a mission and orphanage
        in Savannah. Reflecting the influence of his colleagues,
        Whitefield's preaching emphasizes the necessity for con-
        verts to experience a "New Birth." Disappointed that the
        revivals have ended, Edwards tries to reignite them by
        publishing *Discourses on Various Important Subjects*, five
        sermons (selected from among the roughly four hundred
        he has preached from 1734 to 1738) that he believes greatly
        contributed to the conversions in his parish during the
        Little Awakening; it is the only collection of pastoral ser-
        mons he ever publishes. Son Timothy born, July 25. Upset
        by the editorial changes made to his manuscript in the
        London edition of the *Faithful Narrative*, Edwards super-
        vises a complete, corrected edition, which is published in
        Boston. Joseph Bellamy is settled as minister at Bethlehem,
        Connecticut.

1739   From March to August Edwards preaches a sermon series
        that will be published posthumously in 1774 as *A History
        of the Work of Redemption*. In it, he looks for signs of a
        coming revival by surveying the work of evangelical re-
        formers in Europe, including George Whitefield, whom he
        elsewhere describes as "one raised up in the Church of
        England to revive the mysterious, Spiritual, despised and
        exploded Doctrines of the Gospel, and full of a Spirit of
        zeal for the promotion of real vital piety." Whitefield
        makes his second journey to the North American colonies,
        landing at Lewes, Delaware, on October 30. Soon thereaf-
        ter he preaches in Philadelphia to an enormous outdoor
        crowd of six thousand (which includes Benjamin Franklin)
        and then travels to New York City (where he ignites a
        newspaper controversy) before returning to Philadelphia
        by way of Neshaminy, home of the Tennents' evangelical
        "Log College," where he preaches to three thousand.
        Newspapers (Franklin's among them) spread word of
        Whitefield's appearances, and he becomes a traveling sen-
        sation. Though he draws large audiences, especially among
        Presbyterians, Pietist immigrants from Germany, and
        others of strong Calvinist bent, his reception among the

colonial elite, who are mostly of the established Anglican Church, is considerably cooler. In Philadelphia, Whitefield reads Edwards's *Faithful Narrative*, and in Northampton, Edwards eagerly follows news of Whitefield's progress in the Boston papers.

1740   Whitefield's journey continues throughout the year, with stops in Charleston, South Carolina, Savannah, Georgia, and other sites along the seaboard. In February, Edwards writes to invite him to visit Northampton. Daughter Susannah born, June 20. In a July letter to Benjamin Colman, Whitefield announces his intention to visit New England, where he hopes a combination of a vibrant newspaper market and a sympathetic reception from the region's Congregational establishment will ensure his greatest success yet. "Surely," he exults, "our Lord intends to put the whole world in a flame." Edwards travels on September 3 to Longmeadow, Massachusetts, to see his cousin Eunice Williams, the famous "unredeemed captive" of the 1704 raid on Deerfield. With her Mohawk husband, François-Xavier Arosen, and an interpreter (as the couple speaks only Mohawk and French), Williams—whose Mohawk name is Kanenstenhawi, and who is also known as Marguerite Arosen—is making her first tentative visit to a family she little remembers. On September 14, Whitefield lands in Newport, Rhode Island, and anticipation builds for his arrival in Boston, where in one week he attracts crowds of four, six, and eight thousand; these are comparable in size to the audiences he has drawn in London, though Boston, with a population of just seventeen thousand, is a small fraction of the size of the English metropolis. Having accepted Edwards's invitation, Whitefield preaches in Northampton and surrounding villages, October 17–19, and stays in the Edwards household. The celebrated itinerant makes many references to the awakening of 1735 during his visit, and after preaching at Edwards's church on the morning of the Sabbath (October 19), he observes that "good Mr. Edwards wept during the whole time of exercises. The people were equally affected; and, in the afternoon, the power increased yet more." Edwards follows Whitefield to nearby Suffield, Connecticut, where the latter preaches to another large crowd on October 21; there Whitefield engages with the question that will roil the colonies, especially New England, in the wake of his visit—whether or not it is "absolutely necessary for a Gospel minister [to] be converted." In answering in the affirmative, Whitefield announces his agreement with Gilbert Tennent, whose inflammatory sermon "The Danger of an Unconverted Ministry" (preached at Nottingham, Pennsylvania, on March 8 and soon published by Franklin in Philadelphia) urges church members to bar from the pulpit any clergy who cannot or will not testify to having themselves experienced conversion. Mother-in-law Mary Hooker Pierpont dies, November 1, and Edwards travels to New Haven to execute her will. It is believed that this is the year he writes what becomes known as his "Personal Narrative," perhaps in reply to a request from one of his divinity students, Aaron Burr (born 1716, Yale 1735).

1741   In the afterglow of Whitefield's visit, Edwards travels to preach at several churches throughout the Valley. On July 8, in Enfield, Connecticut, he delivers to great effect his sermon "Sinners in the Hands of an Angry God" on Deuteronomy 32:35: "Their foot shall slide in due time." In it he expounds on the utter fragility of Christians' lives in the face of God's omnipotence, and on the justness of God's damnation of sinners. The service is often interrupted by the great "moans & crying" of the parishioners. Although its stress on hellfire and damnation is not typical of his preaching, the sermon will become Edwards's best-known work. Back in Northampton, Edwards holds numerous prayer meetings in addition to his regular services, and spiritual fervor, especially among the young, grows. He notes that the "Months of *August* and *September* were the most remarkable of any *this year*, for *Appearances* of *Conviction* [awareness of personal sin] and *Conversion* of *Sinners*, and great *Revivings*, *Quickenings*, and *Comforts* of *Professors*, and for extraordinary external Effects of these Things." Uncle William Williams of Hatfield dies on August 29 and Edwards preaches his funeral sermon on September 2, soon published in Boston as *The Resort and Remedy of Those that are Bereaved by the Death of an Eminent Minister*. Edwards now becomes the leading minister in the Connecticut River Valley. At Yale commencement (September 10), he preaches a sermon, later published as *The Distinguishing Marks of a Work of the Spirit of God*, that refines his philosophy of religious revival and counters charges by some in the Hampshire Association that the revivals have gotten out of hand, with many too easily accepting any emotional display as a sign of genuine religious experience. Edwards urges moderation and toleration. Charles Chauncy (1705–1787, Harvard 1721), who is co-minister of Boston's First Church and an outspoken critic of the revivals (which he regards as self-indulgent "enthusiasm"—long a term of opprobrium in Puritan New England), almost simultaneously delivers a sermon entitled "Enthusiasm Described and Cautioned Against" (published under the same title early in 1742) at Harvard's commencement. These sermons ignite a "pamphlet war" between Edwards and Chauncy over the revival and its effects, and sharp divisions begin to form among the New England clergy, with supporters of the revivals coming to be identified as "New Lights" and opponents as "Old Lights." ("Such distinguishing Names of Reproach," Edwards will observe, "do as it were divide us into two Armies, separated, and drawn up in Battle-Array, ready to fight one with another, which greatly hinders the Work of GOD.") In December, recent Yale graduate Samuel Hopkins (1721–1803) begins his first stay in Northampton to study with Edwards.

1742   Much in demand as a guest preacher, in late January and February Edwards embarks on second tour, this time to eastern Massachusetts. While he is away, his wife experiences a two-week period of spiritual ecstasy so intense that her neighbors fear for her life. Edwards incorporates her account of this episode into a long work he is writing in defense of the revivals and the necessary role of emotional experience in the process of conversion. Over the course of this year and into the next, he delivers a cycle of sermons about the latter topic that will be the genesis of a second major work, on religious affections. Divisions among the clergy begin to be replicated among the people, as splinter groups form within congregations in opposition to whichever side the minister favors. In May, the Massachusetts General Court (legislature) forbids itinerant preaching in any of the province's parishes unless the resident minister consents.

1743   In March, Edwards publishes the book-length *Some Thoughts Concerning the Present Revival of Religion in New-England*, his major attempt to address the criticism of the Awakening. Shortly after it is released, Charles Chauncy writes to his brother: "Mr. Edwards' book of 378 pages upon the good work [the revivals] is at last come forth; and I believe will do much hurt; . . . I am preparing an antidote, and if the world should see cause to encourage it, it may in time come to light." Chauncy's equally lengthy rejoinder, *Seasonable Thoughts on the State of Religion in New England*, is published later in the year. Chauncy had written ministers throughout New England to obtain examples of the revivalists' excesses, thus making his book a comprehensive compendium of anti-revivalist views. "The plain truth is," Chauncy concludes, "an *enlightened mind*, and not *raised affections*, ought always be the guide of those who call themselves men; and this, in the affairs of religion, as well as other things." In May, a narrow plurality of the Massachusetts annual ministerial convention publishes a pamphlet against "several errors in doctrine and disorders in practice which have of late obtained in various parts of the land," a clear repudiation of the revivals. New Light ministers are angered and convene in a rump session of their own in July in protest. While condemning some of the same excesses singled out by the Old Light convention—overreliance on emotional evidence, unwelcome itinerancy, lay preaching, censoriousness, and especially separatism—the pro-Awakening clergy nonetheless conclude, like Edwards (who does not attend but offers his support by letter), that these abuses do not negate the real and essential work of the Spirit in the revivals. Elsewhere on the New Light side, the Reverend Thomas Prince Sr. of Boston begins *The Christian History*, edited by his son Thomas Jr. and devoted to news of the revivals. Published from March 1743 to February 1745, it is the first religious periodical in the British colonies and consists of letters from pro-revival clergy throughout New England as well as correspondence and reports of revival activity from the British Isles. Edwards contributes an account of Northampton's experiences in the December 1743 issue. At the same time, radical New Light itinerant preacher James Davenport (1716–1757, Yale 1732) stages in New London, Connecticut, a large bonfire of "worldly" books (construed so broadly as to include works by Increase Mather and Benjamin Colman) and luxurious clothing including, by some accounts, the very pants he is

wearing. This unseemly behavior provides new fuel for
Old Lights who see such extremism as the logical outcome
of the forces unleashed by the revivalists. Daughter Eunice
born, May 9.

1744   Great Britain's American colonies are once again at war
with the French and their Indian allies as King George's
War, the North American phase of the War of the Austrian
Succession (1740–48), breaks out. Colonel John Stoddard, Solomon Stoddard's eldest son and Northampton's
leading resident, is the chief military commander in western Massachusetts. (Preoccupied with the spiritual contest
made evident by the revivals, Edwards had written somewhat dismissively about these recurring imperial conflicts
in the preface to *Some Thoughts*: "We in *New-England* are
at this Day engaged in a more important War.") Tensions
between Old Lights and New Lights increase with news
that Whitefield will return to New England in the fall.
Edwards will later recall that "many ministers were more
alarmed at his coming, than they would have been by the
arrival of a fleet from France, and they began soon to
preach and write against him, to warn people to beware of
him, as a most dangerous person." For his part, Edwards is
consumed with the "bad books" case in his church. He
asks the parish to appoint a committee to look into complaints against some young men (converts in the recent
awakenings) who have gained access to and are circulating
Aristotle's Masterpiece; or, The Secrets of Nature Displayed
and a book for midwives, both of which treat matters of
reproduction and pregnancy. The young men are accused
of teasing and harassing young women in town with the
knowledge they have gleaned from these books. The
charges are found to be true and the guilty are disciplined
for public lewdness and contemptuous behavior toward
the church. Some of those involved in the book's circula-
tion come from the town's leading families, who think that
Edwards does not show enough circumspection and discretion in handling the matter. This disciplinary procedure
marks the beginning of serious opposition to his ministry.

1745   Son Jonathan Jr. born, May 26. On June 17, after a six-week
siege, British forces (mostly New England men) capture the
vital fortress at Louisburg, on Cape Breton. In retaliation,
French and Indian forces launch attacks against English

outposts in northern New England and New York, forcing the abandonment of many frontier settlements.

1746   In the spring, Northampton erects defensive watchtowers, and troops are quartered in the Edwards parsonage. In August, Indians attack nearby Southampton. Edwards publishes *A Treatise Concerning Religious Affections*, the work that had had its genesis in a series of sermons delivered 1742–43. In it he distills his understanding of religious experience during the Awakening, offering twelve signs by which genuine affections or emotions can be recognized. After his death it becomes one of his most frequently republished works. In Elizabeth, New Jersey, the College of New Jersey (renamed Princeton in 1896) is founded by New Light Presbyterians as a pro-revival institution. Edwards's former student Aaron Burr is one of the founders, and becomes the institution's second president.

1747   Daughter Elizabeth born, May 6. Later the same month, David Brainerd (born 1718) arrives in Northampton and stays at the Edwards parsonage. Tuberculous from an early age, Brainerd had studied at Yale, 1739–42, until he was expelled for observing of one of his instructors that he had "no more grace than a chair." Edwards and others attempted to have him reinstated, without success. Thereafter he had served as a missionary for the Society in Scotland for the Propagation of Christian Knowledge among Indian tribes in New York and New Jersey, until his failing health induced him to return to his native New England. He is nursed by Edwards's daughter Jerusha and in June the two travel together to Boston (encouraging later speculation by historians that they may have been engaged), returning to Northampton on July 25. In August, Indians again strike nearby Southampton. David Brainerd dies of consumption at the Edwards home on October 9, and Edwards preaches his funeral sermon three days later. Exploring Brainerd's journals, and finding in them a powerful example of the kind of piety he believes the awakenings inspire, Edwards contemplates writing an account of the young man's life. Also in October publishes *An Humble Attempt to Promote Explicit Agreement and Visible Union of God's People*, an ecumenical call for prayer to forward the coming of Christ's kingdom and his first formal exploration of the theme of millennialism. As it has been periodically since his arrival as Stoddard's assistant, Edwards's salary, which is variable from year to year, is once again a source of dispute between minister and congregation. "These things," daughter Sally (Sarah) notes, "I am sensible have done much toward making my father willing to leave . . . if convenient opportunity present."

1748   Daughter Jerusha, age seventeen, dies in the predawn hours on February 14. "Generally esteemed the flower of the family," as Edwards had once written of his second oldest daughter, she is likely a victim of tuberculosis contracted from Brainerd. In an attempt to address his grievances, in March the Northampton church awards Edwards a permanent salary of £700. As Indian raids continue to unsettle the countryside, Colonel John Stoddard, Edwards's uncle and the chief military man in the Valley, dies on June 19 in Boston, where he has been nursed by Edwards's wife. Stoddard has long been his nephew's staunchest supporter among the Northampton magistracy, and Edwards uses Stoddard's funeral sermon to give vent, through an attack on wartime profiteering, to his mounting frustration with the townsfolk: "persons of a narrow, private spirit, that may be found in little tricks and intrigues to promote their private interest. Such will shamefully defile their hands to gain a few pounds, are not ashamed to grind the faces of the poor, and screw their neighbors." In December, completes his life of Brainerd. When a young man comes forward to seek admission to the church, Edwards reveals that he has decided to require a profession of conversion, in contravention of his grandfather's policy of open membership. The young man declines to join under these terms, and the ensuing controversy alienates much of the congregation from its minister. Critics question why Edwards has waited until after Colonel Stoddard's death, and until he has at last received a long-sought-after fixed salary, to announce so momentous a deviation from the church's traditional practice.

1749   *An Account of The Life of the Late Reverend Mr. David Brainerd* is published in Boston and will become another of his most frequently reprinted works. It is his final engagement with the revivals and their legacy. Edwards also publishes, in August, *An Humble Inquiry into the Rules of the Word of God, Concerning Full Communion in the Visible Church*, in which he defends the need for prospective church members to offer narratives of their religious experiences, believing that during the recent revivals even he had been too lenient in evaluating converts' suitability for church membership. In the book's preface, he asserts that "it may possibly be a fault to depart from the ways of our fathers: but it may also be a virtue, and an eminent act of obedience, to depart from them in *some* things." In December, writes to Joseph Bellamy that "the tumult is vastly greater than when you were here, and is rising higher and higher continually."

1750   Son Pierpont born, April 8. Daughter Sarah marries Elihu Parsons, of Northampton, June 11. With the new year the rift between Edwards and his congregation reaches a final crisis. Under the platforms of New England Congregationalism, a church needs the approval of a committee of representatives from neighboring churches to sever its relationship with its minister; in the spring both Edwards and the church's lay leaders seek to shape to their benefit the membership of the committee that will hear their case, which finally meets June 19–22. By a vote of 10–9, the committee urges immediate separation and the congregation votes to dismiss Edwards shortly thereafter. On July 1 Edwards delivers his farewell sermon to the Northampton congregation, reminding them that there will come a day, the Judgment Day, when all disputations of the sort that have divided them will end and a determination made of who has held the correct views. Then, he tells them, he will be vindicated in his views of church membership. Four days later he writes to his Scottish correspondent, the Reverend John Erskine: "I am now thrown upon the wide ocean of the world, and know not what will become of me, and my numerous and chargeable family." Edwards remains in the Northampton pulpit, now as a supply minister, until November. His opponents enlist his cousin, Solomon Williams, a minister in Lebanon, Connecticut, to answer the *Humble Inquiry*, which Williams does in *The True State of the Question Concerning the Qualifications Necessary to Lawful Communion in the Christian Sacraments*, published the following year. In September, Joseph Bellamy publishes *True Religion Delineated*, a lengthy exposition of the dangers of both formalism and enthusiasm. In a commendatory preface Edwards observes that "the Remarkable Things that have come to pass in late Times, respecting the State of Religion, I think, will give every Wise Observer great Reason to determine that the Counterfeits of the Grace of God's Spirit, are many more than have been generally taken Notice of heretofore; and that therefore we stand in great Need of having the certain and distinguishing Nature and Marks of genuine Religion more clearly and distinctly set forth . . . [for] Satan transforming himself into an Angel of Light, has shewn himself in many of his Artifices more plainly than ordinary; and given us Opportunity to see more clearly and exactly the difference between his Operations, and the saving Operations and Fruits of the Spirit of Christ." Travels in October to preach at the small frontier settlement and Indian mission at Stockbridge, Massachusetts, fifty miles west of Northampton. Daughter Mary marries Timothy Dwight (1726–1777, Yale 1744), a Northampton merchant, on November 8.

1751   In February, despite the opposition of members of the Williams clan, who have been used to exercising a controlling interest over the Stockbridge mission, Edwards is offered the pastorate there and in August is formally installed as minister to Stockbridge's two congregations. One is a resident community of Housatonic Indians, a remnant of the once powerful Mahican confederacy, now reduced to a meager existence under the custodianship of provincial authorities. The other is a cluster of white settlers gathered in and around the Indian mission. A small church salary is supplemented by support from the provincial legislature and the London Society for the Propagation of the Gospel in New England, which jointly fund the Indian school and mission. Begins work on his great theological treatises.

1752   Grandson Timothy Dwight, future president of Yale College, born May 14. Granddaughter Esther Parsons born, May 29. On June 29, daughter Esther marries Aaron Burr, now settled at the College of New Jersey's new home in Newark. That same summer, Edwards responds to Solomon Williams's pamphlet with *Misrepresentations Corrected, and Truth Vindicated*, his final word on the controversy that ended his twenty-five-year ministry in

Northampton. Travels in September to Newark, where he preaches a sermon entitled "True Grace, Distinguished From the Experience of Devils" (published the following year), and attends the Presbyterian Synod of New York.

1753   In April, completes the manuscript of *A Careful and Strict Enquiry into the Modern Prevailing Notions of the Freedom of the Will*, which he will publish the following year. This substantial work is a systematic assault on Arminianism as manifested in the works of three English clergymen: Thomas Chubb, whose *The Supremacy of the Father Asserted* (1714) revives the ancient Christian heresy known as Arianism by arguing that Christ was fully human and therefore not of the same substance as the Father; Daniel Whitby, whose *Discourse on the Five Points* (1710) argues against man's inherent depravity; and Isaac Watts, whose *Essay on the Freedom of the Will in God and in Creatures* (1732) argues that man's will is self-determining. Son Timothy travels in the spring to Newark to study at the College of New Jersey. Grandson Elihu Parsons born, December 9.

1754   In February, the French and Indian War, as the Seven Years' War (1754–63) is known in the colonies, commences. Edwards has finally wrested control of the Indian school from agents of the Williams clan, only to learn that a large contingent of the mission's Mohawk residents have announced their intention to leave. Within a little more than a month the mission is largely depopulated. Granddaughter Sarah Burr born, May 3. In July, Edwards enters into what will be a nearly yearlong period of illness, with periodic fevers weakening him until, as he later recalls, he "became like a skeleton." Heightened tensions that have led to the fortification of the Edwards parsonage during the summer erupt in September when a raiding party of Abenaki Indians kills four, including an infant, in Stockbridge. Retaliations by white settlers against the remnant of resident Indians include, in December, the desecration of the grave of a recently deceased member of the community. Grandson Sereno Edwards Dwight born, December 10.

1755   Edwards completes drafts of *The Nature of True Virtue* and *The End for Which God Created the World*, published posthumously as *Two Dissertations* (1765). In the former, he addresses the arguments of Francis Hutcheson's *Inquiry into the Original of Our Ideas of Beauty and Virtue* (1725), which posits a universal moral sense that allows an individual to judge virtue and vice; Edwards finds this merely another apology for self-interest. In the latter, his most mystical work, Edwards argues that God's purpose in creation is best described as the self-projection of divine emanation throughout the universe, including to his creatures, and the entire universe exists as testament to God's glory. In the spring, son Jonathan travels on a mission to Onaquaga, New York. In the fall, Edwards travels to Newark to attend college commencement and the Presbyterian Synod of New York.

1756   Grandson Aaron Burr Jr., future vice president of the United States, born in Newark, February 6; the Burr family soon moves to Princeton, the new, and permanent, home of the College of New Jersey. Edwards continues to record his "Miscellanies" in his notebooks; they now total more than thirteen hundred in number. Grandson Erastus Dwight born, September 13.

1757   Granddaughter Lydia Parsons born, June 17. Edwards is called to the presidency of the College of New Jersey after the death on September 24 of son-in-law Aaron Burr, who had worked tirelessly and successfully to put the school on a solid footing. Edwards does not make his decision easily, citing his need to continue writing his theological works— he has completed a draft of a lengthy exposition of the doctrine of original sin and has begun to refashion his 1739 sermons into what will become the *History of the Work of Redemption*—and a desire not to uproot his family again. He also considers himself more a scholar than an administrator or teacher, but the school's trustees prevail.

1758   Early in January, Edwards is released from his duties at Stockbridge and leaves, without most of his family, for Princeton. According to daughter Susannah, he departs "as affectionately, as if he should not come again." Shortly after arriving in Princeton, he learns of his father's death on January 27. Initiated as president of the College of New Jersey on February 16, and the following week is inoculated for smallpox, a process he has championed to others. Though at first he responds well, he soon contracts the disease in his mouth, and is unable to swallow. During this final illness, daughter Lucy records the following testament: "It seems to me to be the will of God that I must shortly leave you; therefore give my kindest love to my dear wife, and tell her, that the uncommon union, which has so long subsisted between us, has been of such a nature, as I trust is spiritual, and therefore will continue forever; and I hope she will be supported under so great a trial, and submit cheerfully to the will of God. And as to my children, you are now like to be left fatherless, which I hope will be an inducement to you all to seek a Father, who will never fail you. And as to my funeral, I would have it be [unostentatious] like Mr. Burr's; and any additional sum of money that might be expected to be laid out that way, I would have it disposed of to charitable uses." Edwards dies on the afternoon of March 22. Daughter Esther Burr dies, also of smallpox, April 7. Grandson Eliphalet Parsons born, June 18. On October 2, Sarah Pierpont Edwards dies from complications of dysentery. Grandson Maurice William Dwight born, December 15. *The Great Christian Doctrine of Original Sin Defended*, Edwards's answer to English clergyman John Taylor's *Scripture-Doctrine of Original Sin, Proposed to Free and Candid Examination* (1740), to which his Scottish correspondent John Erskine had alerted him, is published. In this work Edwards posits the inherent unity of mankind from Adam on and argues that the strongest proof of original sin comes from experience, citing the general tendency of mankind toward evil through all history. He concludes that God did not create something positive called "sin," but that man's sinfulness consists of God's grace being withheld; that is, sin is privative, not positive. After his death Edwards's legacy is carried on and his theology is further developed by former students Joseph Bellamy and Samuel Hopkins. In 1765, Hopkins will publish his *Life and Character of the Late Reverend Mr. Jonathan Edwards*, which includes Edwards's "Personal Narrative." In 1829, great-grandson Sereno Edwards Dwight will publish a ten-volume collection, *Works of President Edwards, with a Memoir of His Life*, that includes much hitherto unpublished primary material.

Note on the Texts

This volume gathers the narratives, books, sermons, and letters through which Jonathan Edwards sought to inspire, describe, and defend the series of religious revivals in New England in the 1730s and '40s that collectively became known as the Great Awakening: *A Faithful Narrative of the Surprising Work of God in the Conversion of Many Hundred Souls*; *The Distinguishing Marks of a Work of the Spirit of God*; and *Some Thoughts Concerning the Present Revival of Religion in New-England*, along with seven sermons and four letters from the period and Edwards's "Personal Narrative" of his own religious experience.

A Faithful Narrative of the Surprising Work of God in the Conversion of Many Hundred Souls had its genesis in an eight-page letter, dated May 30, 1735, that Edwards sent to Benjamin Colman, the leading minister in Boston, describing the recent surge of conversions in his church in Northampton, Massachusetts, and in surrounding villages in the Connecticut River Valley. Colman included much of Edwards's report in a letter he sent to John Guyse, a Dissenting minister in London. Guyse incorporated the news about the New England revivals into a sermon, which his congregation requested be printed. Guyse agreed and wrote to Colman asking him to grant permission to quote from the report in print. Colman instead wrote to Edwards's uncle, William Williams, the minister in Hatfield, Massachusetts, and the leading minister in the Valley, to suggest that Edwards write a more detailed account. Edwards did so in a lengthy letter to Colman, which Colman abridged and attached as an appendix to a volume he was then seeing through the press, two sermons by Williams entitled *The Duty and Interest of a People*, which was published in Boston in December 1736. Colman then forwarded the appendix to Guyse and his fellow London minister, Isaac Watts. Guyse and Watts replied, asking Colman to publish the full version of Edwards's account. Instead Colman sent them the entire manuscript, which they had printed at the London press of John Oswald in 1737, although they note in a letter to Colman of October 13, 1736, that they "omitted many things in it." A presentation copy of this first edition was given to Yale College, where it was inspected by Edwards, who marked his corrections into that copy, writing on the flyleaf that "the Rev. publishers of the ensuing narrative, by much abridging of it, and altering the phrase and manner of expression, and not strictly observing the words of the original, have through mistake, published some things diverse from fact." All of those corrections were incorporated into the first American edition (called "the Third Edition"), published in Boston by Samuel Kneeland and Thomas Green in 1738, which Edwards presumably oversaw, and which the present volume takes as its source. Edwards's original manuscript is not known to have survived.

The Distinguishing Marks of a Work of the Spirit of God began as a sermon on 1 John 4:1 ("Beloved, believe not every spirit, but try the spirits whether they are of God; because many false prophets are gone out into the world"), which Edwards delivered at Yale College's commencement on September 10, 1741. It was published in Boston by Kneeland and Green in 1741 and was reprinted within a year in Philadelphia, London, Glasgow, and Edinburgh. The first edition is the source for the text in this volume.

As the revivals grew and became increasingly controversial, Edwards undertook his most substantial defense of the Awakening in *Some Thoughts Concerning the Present Revival of Religion in New-England*, published in Boston by Kneeland and Green in 1742 and reprinted in Edinburgh in 1743. The first edition is the source for the text in this volume.

Of the seven sermons chosen for inclusion in this volume, three were printed during Edwards's lifetime. "Justification by Faith Alone" and "Pressing into the Kingdom of God" were included in *Discourses on Various Important Subjects, Nearly Concerning the Great Affair of the Soul's Eternal Salvation*, a collection of five of Edwards's sermons published in Boston by Kneeland and Green in 1738. "Sinners in the Hands of an Angry God" was published as a pamphlet by Kneeland and Green in 1741. Those editions are the sources for the texts included here.

The other four sermons, "God Amongst His People," "A City on a Hill," "Zeal an Essential Virtue of a Christian," and "The Curse of Meroz," were never published by Edwards. The manuscripts of these four sermons are housed in the Jonathan Edwards Collection at the Beinecke Rare Book & Manuscript Library at Yale University. Because Edwards never prepared the sermons for publication, these manuscripts are rough copies used when delivering the sermons to his congregation and were not altered or cleaned up by Edwards or any other hand afterward. The texts of these four sermons are newly transcribed from these manuscripts. Some emendations have been necessary in the preparation of clear texts, due to the unfinished nature of Edwards's manuscripts. Where a sentence clearly ends, but Edwards did not punctuate it, a period has been added. In a few places the sense of a passage demanded that a mark of punctuation be added, altered, or omitted for the sake of intelligibility. In some places, redundancies indicate that Edwards was considering alternative phrasings but neglected to cancel one of them; the present text emends accordingly (choosing in most cases his second alteration as the more likely), and records the emendation. Edwards's abbreviations and shorthand have been preserved: for example, where Edwards would have read a verse of Scripture in full during a sermon, he often in his manuscript only wrote the citation followed by a long dash (represented in this volume by a three-em dash). Words ending "ment" are often written ending "mt" (for example, "judgmt" for "judgment" and "chastisemts" for "chastisements") or "m" (for example, "Enjoym." for "enjoyment"). Words ending "ness" are often written ending "n" (for example, "goodn." for "goodness" and "thankfulln." for "thankfulness"). Words ending "full" are often written ending "f" (for example, "wonderf." for "wonderfull" and "sinf" for "sinful"). And words ending in "tion" are often written with the ending omitted (for example, "founda." for "foundation").

Some of the more frequent of Edwards's abbreviations are:

÷	division	Glo., Glor.	Glorious
☉	World	Gr.	Grace
☉ly	Worldly	H.	Holy, Holiness,
almigh.	almighty		Heaven, Heart
altho	although	hims.	Himself
Answ.	Answer	Inhabit.	Inhabitants
Beautif.	Beautiful	Inherit.	Inheritance
begin.	beginning	Iniq.	Iniquity
Chh.	Church	Is., Isr.	Israel
Childr.,	Children	J.	Jesus
Chil.		Jerus.	Jerusalem
Comf.	Comfort	K., Kingd.	Kingdom
comg	coming	Knowl.	Knowledge
Comm.	Commandments	L.	Lord
Consid.	Consider	Lab.	Labour
Cov.	Covenant	m.	man, men
Crea.	Creatures	mis.	misery
discip.	disciples	Mot.	Motive
Doc.	Doctrine	Objec	Objection
E.	Earth	obs	observe
Etern.	Eternal	opp.,	opportunity
Everlast.	Everlasting	oppor.,	
Excell.	Excellent	opportun.	
F.	Father	outw.	outward
G., Gs	God, God's	Peop.	People
Gh., Gho.	Ghost	Pres.	Presence

Provid.	Providence	tempta.	Temptations
R., Righ.	Righteous,	thems.	themselves
	Righteousness	theref	therefore
Relig.	Religion	tho	though
Rememb.	Remember	v.	verse
Rev'd	Reverend	W.	Word, Work
sanct.	sanctuary	wild.,	wilderness
Sc.	Scripture	wildern.	
sheph.	shepherd	wisd.	wisdom
Sov.	Sovereign	X, Xs,	Christ, Christ's,
Sp.	Spirit, Spiritual	Xtian,	Christian,
Str.	Strength	Xtianity	Christianity
suffic.	Sufficient		

Of the four letters included in this volume, three have been newly transcribed. The letter to Benjamin Colman, May 19, 1737, comes from a manuscript in the Benjamin Colman Papers in the Massachusetts Historical Society. It is not known to have been printed during Edwards's lifetime. The manuscript of the letter to George Whitefield, February 12, 1740, is housed in the John Rylands Library at the University of Manchester. It is also not known to have been printed during Edwards's lifetime. The letter to Deborah Hatheway, June 3, 1741, was reprinted often in the nineteenth century with significant changes and under the title "Advice to Young Converts." The original manuscript of this letter appears not to have survived; the text for the current edition is an eighteenth-century copy in an unknown hand from the Jonathan Edwards Collection at the Beinecke Rare Book & Manuscript Library at Yale University, thought to have been made by one of Edwards's former students. The penultimate page of the manuscript is torn. The bracketed words on page 665 were drawn from a manuscript copy of the letter, also in the Beinecke collection.

The original manuscript of the letter to Thomas Prince is not known to be extant. It was included in *The Christian History, Containing Accounts of the Revival and Propagation of Religion in Great-Britain & America, for the Year 1743* (Boston: S. Kneeland and T. Green, 1744), 367–81, which is the source for the text in this volume. (See Chronology for 1743.)

Edwards's "Personal Narrative" may have been written at the request of his former student and future son-in-law Aaron Burr, who wrote to Edwards in March 1741 thanking him for a letter of December 14, 1740, saying, "I desire to bless God that he inclined you to write and especially to write so freely of your own experiences." Edwards's letter has not been found, but when Samuel Hopkins, another former student of Edwards, first published the "Personal Narrative" in 1765 as part of *Life and Character of the Late Reverend Mr. Jonathan Edwards* (Boston: S. Kneeland), he dated it to about that time. This volume uses Hopkins's text as its source.

This volume presents the texts of the printings and manuscripts chosen as sources here but does not attempt to reproduce features of their physical presentation. The texts are printed without alteration except for the correction of typographical errors and the modernization of the use of quotation marks (only beginning and ending quotation marks are provided here, instead of placing a quotation mark at the beginning of every line of a quoted passage). The prefaces in *Faithful Narrative, Distinguishing Marks,* and *Some Thoughts,* printed in italics in the originals to distinguish them from the text of Edwards's books, are printed in roman type here (with styling accordingly reversed). This volume does not attempt to reproduce features of eighteenth-century typography, such as the long "s" (with three exceptions for the decorative title pages for *Faithful Narrative, Distinguishing Marks,* and *Some Thoughts* on pages 1, 85, and 165). Spelling, punctuation, and capitalization are often expressive features, and they are not otherwise altered, even when inconsistent or irregular. Edwards included lists of errata in the first editions of *The Distinguishing Marks of a Work of the Spirit of God, Some Thoughts Concerning the Present Revival of Religion in New-England,* and *Discourses on Various Important Subjects.* Those corrections have been silently incorporated into the texts in this volume. The following is a list of typographical errors corrected, cited by page and line number: 4.34, amougst; 8.8, *not as*; 8.32, dangrous; 9.16, so every; 16.16, is general; 16.30, 1728·9; 19.20, accordingly; 19.30–31, themselve; 22.19, Persence; 23.30, rmongst; 30.39, others; 31.6, themseves; 32.4, Conditon; 34.8, dreard; 36.17, prehaps; 50.1, so such; 51.31, prefectly; 54.9, conrtary; 56.23, at at peace; 56.27, particulary; 65.20, *Adam*'s, Sin,; 65.30, their.; 66.15, with a; 73.16, catrchism; 76.6, *because BECAUSE;* 76.40, where; 81.39, hemself; 83.14, *seeeing*; 90.20, *Thus He.*; 100.30, Necesiity; 109.3, sitting; 120.38, I. the; 126.13, Vicegerent; 128.33, bafflle; 132.22, *God's Loove*; 134.37–38, 18.21; 143.32, God,; 148.26, be-believe; 150.1, hardned; 150.29, ventered; 154.28, maraculous; 155.23, 11,; 160.3, *Job.*; 163.32, 2 Tim. 24. 25,; 183.7, entred; 187.27, benummb'd,; 193.5, Chureh; 194.22, 2 *Tim.*; 201.4, Tendercess; 217.22, Mattets; 232.25, Chap. 18.; 232.40, Isai. 24. 19.; 234.23, so so so.; 236.24, Tahernacle; 239.15, Deut. 32.; 241.28, Hundren; 243.3, Mamagements;; 244.25, then; 244.39, Streets.; 245.12, setled; 257.25, Tabernable; 261.9, Partions; 266.3, Isai,; 266.7, *Abomination*; 270.30, abundanly; 282.9, (*Ver.* 20.); 294.10, *be guide*; 298.20, Languge.; 299.6, CHIRST!; 302.33, Gofpel; 305.11, reproches; 310.5, succeded,; 321.3, agreable; 323.6, seen; 327.39, Eph.; 330.40, 3. 11. 2.; 381.34, Matth.

5. 9.; 383.16, In his; 406.28, ver. 3.; 425.4, betwen; 425.21, I. Cor. 1. 3.; 427.26, Chap. 5.; 428.13, betwen; 434.9, eligable; 441.13, anu- avoidable; 442.30, *otherwise Grace is no more Grace.*; 444.24, 20th,; 445.20 and *passim*, 'Tis; 454.30, Summer I; 459.40, Christ stead; 461.5, then in; 461.27, other, There; 462.25, fedeal; 464.26, Law*; 465.31, *Tittle.*; 469.31, *Rightoousness*;; 471.22, too Species; 474.1, jew- ish; 484.7, Gen. 15. 16.; 485.11, Chap. 5. 12.; 486.28, *Trespasse,*; 488.35, thro'; 489.37, Mattter,; 491.32, condemnned; 493.24, Belivers; 500.23, gree of each . . . pleases; [line repeated]; 500.36–37, would had; 510.12, *not not*; 516.13, Psalm 7. 8. 9.; 529.31, *is an*; 532.38, and their; 533.9, says,.; 533.29, *inclin*; 543.31, or ather; 544.7–8, *Mark* 7.; 552.31, than than; 558.8, Grace,; 565.27–28, 2 Samuel 10. 5. 7.; 566.39, said in; 569.7, an as; 573.19, that G.; 573.30, he his; 576.27, midst us; 576.29–30, theref Reason this; 581.25, Objec; 582.17, are an; 582.20, your your; 583.26, to; 586.22, Remarkably; 587.40, do Profess; 589.36, wonderfull very; 590.26, were became; 591.23, House to; 595.14–15, Religion an; 596.4, I Thes. 7. 8.; 598.5, Carry the Lessen; 598.12, to Great; 598.15, will be Greatly; 598.21–22, forth the; 599.27, multitude; 601.10, of an a; 602.11, 2. 9. 3. 4———; 602.12, 6. People; 603.1, 7. What; 604.15, &&; 604.19, 8. &; 605.6, outwards; 605.7, Ear- nestly address; 605.9, may the; 605.13, amonst &; 609.8, actuates & animates; 609.31, Exercise; 610.5, Gods; 610.8, vehemence it; 610.11, those holy; 610.14, in which in which; 610.39, a a; 610.40, has exer- cises; 611.10, thing; 611.18, is is; 611.18–19, Xtian be a Zealous Xtian but; 611.34, of of; 612.35–36, show the that; 613.30, a all; 614.7, to be built seems to be no more; 615.5–6, but & to; 615.23, shall no; 616.4, are detract; 616.37, of Relig. of Relig.; 617.3, Glosses & upon; 619.13, Rev. 3. 10.; 619.33, to to; 622.23, Are not men; 624.14, to owned; 628.38, whenas; 630.36, me.; 637.19–20, Meshech; 640.21, throughly; 643.18, whom Great; 644.25, in need; 646.1, save me King; 646.4, when Remarkably; 646.28, em Liberty; 647.11, did declare; 648.6, ap- points; 649.27, take expose; 650.5, you battle.; 651.31, Required were Req.; 652.23, Chap. 2 Chron; 652.24, were had; 653.20, better throw; 654.22, tends hinder; 654.24–25, of Great; 658.22, thnk; 660.7, more more; 661.4, contrabute; 661.32, there is so; 661.36, knew conver- sion; 662.21, humble your for; 664.38, Christians vertues; 670.3, Out- powering; 672.1, become; 677.11, then; 682.36, Acccount,; 684.15, o this; 685.25, Psal. cxix. 28.; 687.23, inexpressile; 695.17, Hppocrisy; 695.23–24, Perfomances.

Notes

In the notes below, the reference numbers denote page and line of this volume (the line count includes headings, but not rule lines). No note is made for material included in the eleventh edition of *Merriam-Webster's Collegiate Dictionary*, except for certain cases where common words and terms have variant historical or religious meanings. Notes are provided for scriptural references and allusions that Edwards does not identify in the text. These are keyed to the King James version, the version Edwards himself used. For further historical and biographical background, and references to other studies, see Philip F. Gura, *Jonathan Edwards: America's Evangelical* (New York: Hill and Wang, 2005); George M. Marsden, *Jonathan Edwards: A Life* (New Haven, CT: Yale University Press, 2003); Patricia J. Tracy, *Jonathan Edwards, Pastor: Religion and Society in Eighteenth-Century Northampton* (New York: Hill and Wang, 1979); and *The Works of Jonathan Edwards*, Kenneth P. Minkema, Executive Editor (26 vols., 1957–2008, New Haven, CT: Yale University Press), especially volume 4, *The Great Awakening* (1979), edited by C. C. Goen.

A FAITHFUL NARRATIVE

3.9 Dr. *Colman* of *Boston*] Founding pastor of Boston's Brattle Street Church (established 1699), Benjamin Colman (1673–1747) was the city's leading minister, and therefore one of the principal voices among the Massachusetts (Congregational) clergy. Having traveled and preached in England as a young man, he maintained extensive contacts with Dissenting clergy there.

3.26 *for this Thing was not done in a Corner.*] Cf. Acts 26:26.

3.36 Miracle of *Gideon's* Fleece] Cf. Judges 6:36–40.

4.5 the late Earthquake there] A severe earthquake struck eastern New England on October 29, 1727, occasioning much soul-searching among those who viewed the tremors as evidence of divine wrath.

4.16–20 *The Wilderness . . . Excellency of our God*] Isaiah 35:1–2.

4.20–21 *seen the Out goings . . . Sanctuary.*] Psalm 68:24.

4.27–28 *The Hand of God . . . save*] Isaiah 59:1.

4.35–36 "Return, O Lord, . . . midst of us."] Cf. Habakkuk 3:2.

5.16–17 the *Antinomians . . .* the *Arminians*] Orthodox Reformed theology was often characterized as a middle path between two dangerous extremes: antinomianism (at root: "against or opposed to the law"), which posited that Christians suffused with free grace were no longer subject to moral law; and Arminianism (after Dutch theologian Jacobus Arminius, 1560–1609), which held that though sinners are saved by faith alone, their faith is the result of a free will decision, not the irresistible prompting of God. The former "heresy" was seen by the defenders of orthodoxy as an invitation to anarchic enthusiasm and licentiousness, the latter to cold formalism and hypocrisy.

5.29–30   *What shall we do . . . Wrath to come?*] Cf. Acts 16:30 and Isaiah 20:6.

5.37   *a Nation shall be born in a Day*] Cf. Isaiah 66:8.

6.14   the formal Professor] That is, one given to unfeeling, perfunctory religious observance. Alert to its troubling presence even in his own congregation, Edwards primarily identified formalism with the Catholic and Anglican churches, and with the Pharisees, who functioned as a biblical "type" of those churches (see note 87.16–19).

6.16   *Who shall dwell with everlasting Burnings?*] Isaiah 33:14.

6.39   like *Paul's* . . . from his Hand] Cf. Acts 28:3–6.

7.4–5   Letter . . . publish'd] Edwards's letter first appeared in the March 28–April 4, 1737, issue of *The Boston Gazette.*

7.13   *Cells*] Supporting frames.

8.13   *imminently*] "Eminently" in the account that appeared in *The Boston Gazette.*

8.22   *Alley*] Aisle.

9.26–27   hold fast what they have received] Cf. Revelation 3:3.

9.36–37   *Come Lord Jesus, come quickly*] Cf. Revelation 22:20.

9.39–40   *ISAAC WATTS. JOHN GUYSE.*] Isaac Watts (1674–1748), the famous hymn writer, and John Guyse (1680–1761) were ministers to Dissenting congregations in London, and regular correspondents with Benjamin Colman. See the Note on the Texts in this volume for their role in the London publication of Edwards's *Faithful Narrative.*

10.10–11   *Apostles went forth . . . with them*] Mark 16:20.

10.12–13   *Not by Might, . . . Lord of Hosts.*] Zechariah 4:6.

10.17–19   *that wicked One . . . Spirit of his Mouth*] 2 Thessalonians 2:8.

10.31   When God . . . shook the Earth] See note 4.5.

10.33   *still Voice*] Cf. 1 Kings 19:12.

10.34–35   *What must we do to be saved?*] Acts 16:30.

11.12   a *very mortal Distemper*] Massachusetts experienced a widespread outbreak of smallpox in 1721–22.

11.18–19   *Why should ye . . . more and more.*] Isaiah 1:5.

11.34   *Dew falls in the Night*] Cf. Numbers 11:9.

11.35   *Light which goeth forth*] Cf. Hosea 6:5.

11.36   *What has God wrought!*] Numbers 23:23.

11.37   publish'd] Made known, announced.

12.1–2   Psalmist observes . . . *remembred.*] Psalm 111:4.

12.8   Impressions] Printings.

12.18–19   *He that hath an ear . . . Churches.*] Repeated four times in the second chapter of Revelation.

13.18   all the Ends . . . Salvation!] Isaiah 52:10.

13.19–22   Joseph Sewall . . . William Cooper] Four Boston clergymen: Joseph Sewall (1688–1769), pastor of the Old South Church, 1713–69; Thomas Prince (1687–1758), Sewall's co-pastor, 1718–58; John Webb (1687–1750), pastor of the New North Church, 1714–50; and William Cooper (1694–1743), junior colleague of Benjamin Colman at the Brattle Street Church, 1716–43.

15.8   Uncle *Williams*] William Williams (1665–1741) was pastor at Hatfield, Massachusetts, from 1685 until his death. His second wife, Christian Stoddard, was Edwards's maternal aunt.

15.30   Grandfather *Stoddard*] Edwards's maternal grandfather, Solomon Stoddard (1643–1729), was minister at Northampton (seat of Hampshire County) from 1672 until his death and the intellectual leader of the Connecticut River Valley clergy. Edwards joined his grandfather as co-pastor at Northampton for the last two years of Stoddard's life. See Chronology.

16.1–2   late lamentable *Springfield Contention.*] Controversy over Robert Breck (1713–1784), whom the Springfield, Massachusetts, church wished to ordain despite the reservations of some in the Hampshire Ministers Association, including Edwards, who were troubled by his purportedly Arminian principles. See Chronology for 1735.

16.21   *Heart* religion] A favorite expression of Edwards's Puritan forebears, used to distinguish the inward experience of grace from outward observance of religious forms.

16.30   *Feb.* 11. 1728/9.] February 11, 1729, in the modern Gregorian calendar.

17.39   Contention between *two Parties*] In a July 1, 1751, letter to the Reverend Thomas Gillespie of Carnock, Scotland, Edwards elaborates on this contention, writing that for the past half century there had been a "sort of settled division of the people into two parties, somewhat like the Court and Country party in England." He suggests that the conflict was rooted in envy, with the latter party ("which has commonly been the greatest") suspicious of the wealth and influence of the former. This letter is published in C. C. Goen, ed., *The Great Awakening* (New Haven, CT: Yale University Press, 1979), 561–66.

18.15   our publick *Lecture*] New England's ministers generally offered three sermons each week, two on the Sabbath (Sunday) and a third, typically on Thursday, known as the lecture or the public lecture. The latter was often used to explore more topical concerns (as on fast or thanksgiving days) or to delve more deeply into complex concepts of systematic theology than was considered appropriate for regular Sabbath sermons.

19.25–26   the great *Noise* . . . about *Arminianism*] An allusion to the Springfield controversy (see note 16.1–2) and to accusations recently leveled against William Rand, pastor in nearby Sunderland, Massachusetts. According to another minister, Stephen Williams of Longmeadow, Massachusetts, Rand had preached "some new notions as to the doctrines of justification" that if left unchallenged would render the "people's spirit exasperated and religion deeply wounded." There was enough consternation generated for the Hampshire Association to get involved, and Rand was quickly convinced to retract his errors.

20.1–3   There were then . . . *Justification by Faith alone.*] A reference to a cycle of sermons (pp. 415–528 in this volume) on Romans 4:5 ("But to him that worketh not, but believeth on him that justifieth the ungodly, his faith is counted for righteousness") that Edwards delivered in late 1734 in an effort to counteract the perceived Arminian threat. These sermons are typical of the orthodox Calvinist response to Arminianism in that they attempt to clarify the relationship between two key theological concepts: justification and sanctification. The former refers to the imputation through grace of Christ's righteousness to the sinner, the latter to the manifestation of the indwelling of that grace through the long, difficult, and in this life incomplete process of turning away from sin (repentance). Edwards reinforced the core Calvinist contention that justification (apprehended only by and through faith) produced sanctification (righteousness), and not vice versa, as Arminianism was said to imply. Edwards credited these sermons with sparking the revival in Northampton.

21.10   Noise amongst the *Dry Bones*] Cf. Ezekiel 37:1–14.

21.32–33   Kingdom of Heaven . . . pressing into it] Cf. Luke 16:16. For Edwards's 1735 sermon on this verse, see pp. 529–64 in this volume.

21.38   *fly from the Wrath to come.*] Luke 3:7.

22.7   experimental Religion] Associated today with scientific investigations of the material world, "experimental" in the Reformed tradition referred to the ability of the regenerate to test and verify the truth of Scripture through personal experience.

22.12–13   *out of Darkness into marvellous Light*] 1 Peter 2:9.

22.13–15   *out of an horrible Pit . . . their mouths.*] Psalm 40:2–3.

22.17   true Saints] The regenerate or the elect in the language of Reformed Protestantism. Saints in this sense could be ordinary people from every walk of life, and were therefore thicker on the ground than the extraordinary and miraculous figures of the Catholic tradition.

22.25–26   *The goings of God . . . Sanctuary*] Cf. Psalm 68:24.

22.26   God's *Day* was *a delight*] Cf. Isaiah 58:13.

22.27   his *Tabernacles* were *amiable*] Psalm 84:1.

22.28   *alive* in God's Service] Cf. Romans 6:11.

22.30   the *Minister*] Edwards frequently refers to himself in the third person in his account.

22.36–37   *Beauty of Holiness.*] Cf. Psalm 29:2, Psalm 96:9, 1 Chronicles 16:29, 2 Chronicles 20:21.

22.39   Hearts *so lifted up*] Cf. Lamentations 3:41.

23.21   *according to the measure of the Gift of Christ*] Ephesians 4:7.

23.37   on occasion of the *Court*] Northampton was the shire town of Hampshire County, which in the eighteenth century comprised all of western Massachusetts, and as such it was the site of the county court, which met seasonally. Until the first courthouse was built in 1737, the court's sessions were conducted in the meetinghouse or in one of the town's taverns.

23.39   Neighbourhood] That is, the towns and villages near Northampton.

24.34   Rev. Mr. *Bull* of *Westfield*] Nehemiah Bull (1701–1740) was minister at Westfield, Massachusetts, from 1726 until his death.

25.5–6   *his* Word . . . return'd *not void.*] Cf. Isaiah 55:11.

25.7–8   *Who are these . . . their Windows?*] Isaiah 60:8.

25.18   *pouring out of the Spirit of God*] Cf. Acts 2:17.

25.22   Rev. Mr. *Marsh*] Jonathan Marsh (1685–1747) was pastor at Windsor, Connecticut, from 1710 until his death.

25.27   my honoured *Father*'s Parish] Timothy Edwards (1669–1758) was pastor at East Windsor, Connecticut, from 1694 until 1758. See Chronology.

25.35   Rev. Mr. *Meacham*] Joseph Meacham (1686–1752) was pastor at South Coventry, Connecticut, from 1714 until his death.

25.39–40   Rev. Mr. *Wheelock*] Eleazer Wheelock (1711–1779) was minister to the north parish of Lebanon, Connecticut (today the town of Columbia), from 1735 until 1770, when he founded and became the first president of Dartmouth College.

26.2   Rev. Mr. *Chauncy*] Nathaniel Chauncy (1681–1756) was pastor at Durham, Connecticut, from 1711 until his death.

26.4–5   Rev. Mr. *Gould*] Hezekiah Gold (1695–1761) was pastor at Stratford, Connecticut, from 1722 until 1752, when he was dismissed.

26.12   Rev. Mr. *Mills*] Jedediah Mills (1697–1776) was minister to Ripton, the second parish of Stratford, Connecticut (today the town of Huntington), from 1724 until his death.

26.12   Rev. Mr. *Noyes*] Joseph Noyes (1688–1761) was pastor of the First Church in New Haven, Connecticut, from 1715 until his death.

26.24   Rev. Mr. *Eleazer Williams*] Williams (1688–1742) was pastor at Mansfield, Connecticut, from 1710 until his death.

26.30–31   Rev. Mr. *Lord* . . . Rev. Mr. *Owen*] Hezekiah Lord (1698–1761) was pastor at North Preston, Connecticut, from 1720 until his death. John Owen (1699–1753) was pastor at Groton, Connecticut, from 1727 until his death.

27.4   *Woodbury*] Edwards's uncle Anthony Stoddard (1678–1760) was pastor at Woodbury, Connecticut, from 1700 until his death.

27.8   at that time of the Year] Edwards traveled to New York City in September and October of 1735.

27.10   Mr. *William Tennent*] Presbyterian clergyman William Tennent Jr. (1705–1777) was pastor at Freehold, New Jersey, from 1733 until his death. Like his brothers John (who died in 1732 and whom he succeeded in the Freehold pulpit) and Gilbert, he was a graduate of the "Log College," an evangelical seminary founded by his father in eastern Pennsylvania (in present-day Warminster) in 1727.

27.12–13   the *Mountains* . . . Mr. *Cross*] Presbyterian clergyman John Cross (d. 1748) was pastor at Basking Ridge, New Jersey, 1732–41, as well as a fervent revivalist and an active itinerant preacher. It was likely in 1735 that his preaching sparked a revival among "The Mountain Society," a daughter church of Newark, New Jersey, established in the Orange Mountains west of the town.

27.15   *Gilbert Tennent*] The younger Tennent (1703–1764) was pastor of a Presbyterian church at New Brunswick, New Jersey, from 1727 until 1743, when he became active as a traveling evangelist. After a period of itinerancy, he founded the Second Presbyterian Church of Philadelphia.

27.17   *Freelinghousa*] German-born clergyman Theodorus Jacobus Frelinghuysen (1691–1748) was minister to five Dutch Reformed congregations in New Jersey's Raritan Valley, where his Pietist preaching inspired revivals in the 1720s.

27.38–39   Our *Sacraments*] That is, celebrations of the Lord's Supper.

28.5 it is not the Custom here] As Edwards notes, many of New England's Congregational churches required applicants for full membership (that is, as communicants) to present a conversion narrative testifying to their personal experience of grace, while reserving non-communicant member status for those who felt unable to offer such an account. Solomon Stoddard had deviated from this approach at Northampton, where he admitted all upstanding town residents to the Lord's Supper, and Edwards inherited this policy when he succeeded to the Northampton pulpit.

29.5 a particular Account] See pp. 71–78 in this volume.

29.24–25 old Things have . . . become new] 2 Corinthians 5:17.

31.30 *What shall we do to be saved?*] Acts 16:30.

33.1 Stumbling Blocks] Scripturally resonant imagery: cf. Jeremiah 6:21, Romans 14:13.

33.30 legal Awakenings] Called "legal Terrors," "legal Troubles," and "legal Humblings" elsewhere in the *Faithful Narrative*, these constitute the first stage of conversion in the Reformed tradition, when the individual is made painfully aware of the depths of personal sin and of the resulting inability to obey the Law of God as handed down at Sinai (Exodus 20). This awareness or "sight of sin," as it was commonly described by Puritan preachers, triggers a mournful sense of the justness of one's condemnation in God's eyes (conviction), which is itself a necessary preliminary to the new frame of mind (humiliation) that opens the soul, through faith, to an apprehension of God's mercy (grace). For a key scriptural source of this understanding of the relationship between the Law and faith, see Galatians 3:22–25.

36.14–15 the unpardonable Sin] The willful repudiation or obstruction of grace in oneself or—especially heinous—in others, commonly called "sinning against the Spirit." Cf. Matthew 12:31–32 and Hebrews 10:26.

36.34–35 Thus they wander . . . Hill] Cf. Jeremiah 50:6.

37.9 wash away their own . . . clean] Cf. Psalm 51:2.

37.35 his Footsteps can't be traced] Cf. Psalm 77:19.

37.36 his Ways are past finding out] Romans 11:33.

37.37 what is preparatory to Grace] Even as they consistently emphasized the unmerited nature of grace, New England Calvinists had by Edwards's time been theorizing for more than a century about the "means" by which Christians must prepare themselves for experiencing it. These included daily prayer, meditation on Scripture, diary-keeping and other forms of self-examination, and observance of the Sabbath.

38.12 Songs of Deliverance] Cf. Psalm 32:7.

39.1 to succeed] Archaic: to give success to.

42.28   *the Son of the living God*] Cf. Matthew 16:16.

46.4   crying out with a loud Voice] Cf. Matthew 27:50, Luke 4:33, Acts 7:57.

47.21–22   those that were dead . . . are found.] Cf. Luke 15:24.

48.17   *Fruits brought forth*] Cf. Luke 8:15.

49.13–14   *out of Darkness into marvellous Light.*] 1 Peter 2:9.

49.25–26   *old Things are . . . become new*] 2 Corinthians 5:17.

49.39   immediate Revelation] A loaded phrase for defenders of orthodoxy in New England, one associated with lawless excesses of antinomianism. When Anne Hutchinson (1591–1643) was asked during her 1637 trial to explain her alleged accusation that certain ministers were crypto-Arminians preaching a "covenant of works," she had notoriously asserted that she had received the insight directly from God "by an immediate revelation." This claim, self-incriminating in the eyes of her interrogators, led to Hutchinson's banishment from the Massachusetts Bay Colony as "a woman not fit for our society."

54.8   Enthusiasts] Though they were themselves branded as enthusiasts by critics on both sides of the Atlantic, New England Puritans had long assigned this label to radical dissenters—Antinomians, Quakers, Baptists—who challenged the ecclesiastical order they had established. As the revivals of the 1730s and 1740s spread, their detractors suggested that they were driven not by the Spirit, as Edwards thought, but by rampant enthusiasm.

54.37–38   *Meat to eat that* others *knew not of.*] Cf. John 4:32.

57.23   unsearchableness of the Wisdom of God] Cf. Romans 11:33.

58.3   Hypocrite] Generally associated with insincerity or willful deception to-day, hypocrisy was understood by Edwards and his Puritan forebears to refer as well to the capacity of the unregenerate, those who have not been justified and have therefore not experienced the infusion of the Holy Spirit, to nonetheless genuinely seem—both to themselves and to others—to pass through the emotional stages commonly associated with conversion. The presence of such hidden hypocrites within their congregations ("Wolves in Sheep's cloathing," as Edwards calls them at 82.3–4) was a constant concern for many New England ministers and the subject of much sermonizing.

60.16   distinguishing *Wheat* from *Chaff.*] Cf. Matthew 3:12.

61.10   Rev. Messi *Lord* and *Owen*] I.e., Messrs. See note 26.30–31.

64.7–8   the young Woman before mention'd] See p. 20 in this volume.

64.30   *Blackness of Darkness*] Jude 1:13.

64.35   her Original Sin] That is, her inheritance of the legacy of sin resulting from Adam's fall.

65.4–5   *as the Heathen . . . much speaking*] Matthew 6:7.

65.34   *The Words of the Lord are pure Words*] Psalm 12:6.

65.34–35   *Health to* the Soul, *and Marrow to the Bones*] Cf. Proverbs 3:8.

65.36   *the Blood of Christ cleanses from all Sin*] 1 John 1:7.

65.39–40   *'Tis a pleasant . . . Sun*] Ecclesiastes 11:7.

67.12–13   *Worthy is the Lamb that was slain.*] Revelation 5:12.

67.17   *MEEK AND LOWLY IN HEART*] Matthew 11:29.

68.17–18   *lying in the Dust all the Days of her Life*] Cf. Job 21:26.

68.26   *pull them all* to her] Cf. Matthew 23:27.

68.26–27   she could *not hear to have one lost.*] Cf. John 17:12.

68.37–39   *I am quite willing . . . upon me!*] Cf. Romans 14:8.

69.8   *suffer for Christ's sake*] Cf. Philippians 1:29.

69.9   *spend and be spent*] Cf. 2 Corinthians 12:15.

69.13–14   reading in *Job* . . . dead Body] Either Job 21:26 or Job 24:20.

69.30–31   the worst bit . . . sweet to her] Cf. Luke 15:16.

73.8   *the Kingdom of Heaven is come to me!*] Cf. Matthew 4:17, 19:14.

73.13   *Thy will be done*] Matthew 6:10.

73.14   *Enjoy him for ever*] See the first question in the Westminster Shorter Catechism: "Q. What is the chief end of man? A. Man's chief end is to glorify God, and to enjoy him forever." Written by English and Scottish divines in 1647, the Westminster Shorter Catechism was widely used in the New England colonies, including in the Edwards household.

73.23–25   Her Mother asked . . . *Father and Mother*] Cf. Matthew 10:37.

75.19   wistly] Wistfully.

75.22–23   the Fear of God . . . her Eyes] Cf. Psalm 36:1.

77.33   Bowels of Compassion] Cf. 1 John 3:17.

77.36   my long Journey] See note 27.8.

78.23   Bills] Notices given to the minister before a service requesting special prayers.

78.32   God's Countenance] Cf. Numbers 6:26.

79.4   a Gentleman] Edwards's uncle Joseph Hawley (1682–1735), a Northampton merchant.

80.34–36   the Governour's coming . . . the *Indians*] Jonathan Belcher (1682–1757), governor of Massachusetts, 1730–41, and the Governor's Council, the upper house of the provincial legislature (the General Court), traveled to nearby Deerfield, Massachusetts, in late August 1735 to treat with representatives of Caughnawaga, Housatonic, Scatacook, and Mohawk tribes. These negotiations led to the establishment of an Indian mission at Stockbridge, near the province's western border, where Edwards would later settle.

80.36   *Springfield* Controversy] See note 16.1–2.

80.38   new Meetting-house] Northampton's new, larger meetinghouse was dedicated in December 1737. Pews were assigned to families in New England churches, and the lay committee charged with devising a seating plan for the new building elected to determine priority based on the rank (i.e., wealth) of the families' patriarchs, rather than their seniority, as had been customary. This decision provoked considerable controversy, and much grieved Edwards.

81.17–18   *Groanings that cannot be uttered.*] Romans 8:26.

82.3–5   Wolves in Sheep's cloathing . . . Fruit.] Cf. Matthew 7:15–16. See note 58.3.

82.7   watch for our Halting] Cf. Jeremiah 20:10.

82.18   the Instrument] Edwards here refers to himself.

83.11   Throne of Grace] Cf. Hebrews 4:16.

83.12   enable us to bring forth Fruit] Cf. John 15:16.

83.13–15   our *Light may shine . . . Heaven*] Cf. Matthew 5:16.

83.19   *A City that is set upon an Hill cannot be hid.*] Matthew 5:14. For Edwards's 1736 sermon on this verse, see pp. 585–606 in this volume.

THE DISTINGUISHING MARKS

85.17   Mr. COOPER of *Boston*] See note 13.28–31.

87.16–19   The *Mosaic . . .* the Sun ariseth] An expression of the commonly held Christian belief that the New Testament supersedes the Old along a continuum of progressively clearer divine revelation. According to this idea, the Gospels make plain a divine plan that is foreshadowed, often only obscurely, through allegorical motifs ("Types and Figures") in the Hebrew Bible. Thus, to take one example of this typology, Jonah's three days in the belly of a great fish prefigure Jesus Christ's three days in the tomb.

87.20–22   the chief Thing . . . *the Ministration of the SPIRIT*] 2 Corinthians 3:8.

88.34–35   *the Days of the Son of Man*] Cf. Luke 17:22–30.

88.36–89.1   the *white horse . . .* in his Hand] Cf. Revelation 6:2.

89.1–2   like that of *Jonathan's, returned not empty.*] Cf. 2 Samuel 1:22.

89.18–19   *pour out his Spirit upon us*] Cf. Joel 2:28–29.

89.19 *revive his Work in the midst of the Years.*] Cf. Habakkuk 3:2.

89.22–23 *come and rain down Righteousness upon us.*] Cf. Isaiah 45:8.

89.25 *suddenly come to his Temple.*] Malachi 3:1.

89.28–29 the extraordinary pouring . . . Lord's Ascension.] See Acts 2.

89.35 Mr. *How*] John Howe (1630–1705), an English Dissenting minister much admired in New England. His collected works, including the 1678 sermon cycle *The Prosperous State of the Christian Interest Before the End of Time*, were published in two volumes in London in 1724.

91.1–2 made these *his Ministers* . . . Service] Cf. Hebrews 1:7.

91.2–3 his *Word* in their Mouths . . . *Rock in Pieces.*] Cf. Jeremiah 23:29.

91.5 *confirm'd the Word by Signs following.*] Cf. Mark 16:20.

91.8 *glorified the House of his Glory.*] Cf. Isaiah 60:7.

91.11–12 *He sendeth forth . . . very swiftly.*] Psalm 147:15.

91.15 the *Seats of Learning*] The Great Awakening roiled both Harvard and Yale, where students were generally more enthusiastic about the revivals than were their teachers.

91.17–18 *polish'd Shafts*] Cf. Isaiah 49:2.

91.23 *What must I do to be saved?*] Acts 16:30.

91.24 this our *Metropolis*] Boston, with some 16,400 residents, was the largest city in British North America in 1740.

91.34–35 out of the Mouths of *Babes* . . . Praise] Cf. Matthew 21:16.

91.38 *Ethiopia* has stretched out her Hand] Cf. Psalm 68:31.

92.3–4 the foolish Things of the World] Cf. 1 Corinthians 1:27.

92.4–6 Babes in Knowledge . . . wise & prudent.] Cf. Matthew 11:25.

92.7–8 Things revealed to them . . . do not teach] Cf. Matthew 16:17.

92.13–15 their Faith no longer . . . *God.*] Cf. 1 Corinthians 2:5.

92.22–23 seek first . . . Righteousness.] Matthew 6:33.

94.1–2 strait Gate.] Cf. Matthew 7:14.

94.4–5 cleave to the Lord with full Purpose of Heart.] Cf. Acts 11:23.

94.24 *sincere Milk of the Word.*] 1 Peter 2:2.

94.30–31 An Evening in God's Courts . . . many elsewhere.] Cf. Psalm 84:10.

95.8–9 *the Spirit of this World . . . God*] Cf. 1 Corinthians 2:12.

95.25   *Arminian Ground*] See note 5.17–18.

95.28   see *Him increase, tho' we* should *decrease.*] Cf. John 3:30.

95.36   unpardonable Sin] See note 36.14–15.

95.37   *the sin which is unto Death.*] Cf. Romans 5:21.

96.9   Conviction] See note 33.30.

96.11   *whether it be of God*] Cf. John 7:17 and 1 John 4:1.

96.22   *Scribe instructed unto the Kingdom of Heaven*] Matthew 13:52.

97.2–3   *haply . . . fight against God—*] Acts 5:39.

97.29   Golden Candlestick] Cf. Revelation 1:20.

99.1–2   *The Marks of a Work of the True SPIRIT*] Edwards delivered this sermon on September 10, 1741, at the Yale College commencement and later enlarged it for publication.

100.1–2 the last Verse of the foregoing Chapter] 1 John 3:24.

105.24–25 no Man can see God and live] Cf. Exodus 33:20.

105.31–33 the Queen of *Sheba* fainted . . . *Solomon*] Cf. 1 Kings 10:4–5.

107.5   *Auxesis*] Rhetorical term, obsolete: a gradual increase in intensity of meaning.

107.17–18 The Spouse . . . the Love of Christ] Edwards writes in the typological tradition that holds the Song of Solomon (also known as the Song of Songs or simply Canticles) to be a celebration of the mystical union of Christ and the church.

107.24   the Saints] See note 22.17.

107.28   *Quakers* used to tremble] The Religious Society of Friends was one of the few radical sects born amid the English Revolution (1640–60) to survive that tumultuous era. According to some accounts, the sect's members were called "Quakers" because they were moved to tremble and quake while preaching and praying. As with the label "Puritan," the sobriquet was in time co-opted by those it had been intended to insult.

108.3   *Pharisees . . . ostentatious*] As for example in the parable that Jesus tells in Luke 18:11. Cf. Matthew 6:5.

109.2   *in the Deserts, and in the secret Chambers*] Cf. Matthew 24:26.

110.6   Faculty] Though Edwards continued to use traditional language when speaking of the "faculties" of the mind, he had absorbed the integrative insights of John Locke's *An Essay Concerning Human Understanding* (1689), which argued that the faculties—the will, the reason, the passions, the imagination, the conscience, etc.—were all attributes of the unitary mind, not self-contained entities that operated independently of one another.

110.33–34   St. *Paul*'s Rapture into Paradise.] 2 Corinthians 12:2.

113.19   stony Ground Hearers] Cf. Matthew 13:5.

114.10–13   she *would not leave . . . her God.*] Cf. Ruth 1:16.

114.13–14   *Ruth* who was the Mother of *David* and of Christ] Cf. Matthew 1:5–16.

116.37   the Marks of Hypocrisy] See note 58.3.

117.17   the Apostle] Paul.

117.18–20   *He that eats . . . giveth God Thanks.*] Romans 14:6.

117.21–22   extolling some Ministers, and censuring others] Cf. 1 Corinthians 3:4–5.

117.25–31   And after this . . . humble and penitent.] Cf. 2 Corinthians 2:5–11.

117.32   *Constantine the Great*] While Constantine I (272–337), the first Roman emperor to embrace Christianity, did initiate some measures against pagans—prohibiting certain sacrifices, raiding temple treasuries—large-scale persecution of the Empire's traditional religion began later in the fourth century during the reign of Theodosius (347–395).

117.37   the great *Calvin*] During John Calvin's (1509–1564) tenure as the ecclesiastical leader of the city-state of Geneva, several individuals were executed for heresy, most notoriously the Spanish physician Michael Servetus, who was burnt alive in 1553 for challenging the scriptural basis for infant baptism and the Trinity.

118.13–14   *Jannes* and *Jambres* wrought false Miracles] Cf. Exodus 7:10–12 and 2 Timothy 3:8.

119.17   the visible Church of God] That is, the visible church as it exists in this world—with its inevitable mix of regenerate and unregenerate—as opposed to the true and eternal church of the saints, which becomes visible only in heaven.

119.33   Set of vile Hereticks] Edwards follows an interpretation dating to the second-century Church Father Irenaeus, whose treatise *Adversus Haereses* (*Against Heresies*) associates the Nicolas mentioned in Acts with the deviant sect decried in Revelation. This tradition attributes the Nicolaitans' sexual immorality and scandalous attitude toward ritual foods to antinomianism.

120.2   gross Enthusiasm] See note 54.8.

120.5   *Gnosticks*] A centrifugal force in the development of Christianity during the second century, Gnosticism was a diverse and complex belief system that eschewed doctrinal conformity and emphasized intuitive knowledge (*gnosis* in Greek) as the key to salvation.

120.6 *Anabaptists*] Originating in Zurich in the 1520s and spreading quickly throughout the Holy Roman Empire (Germany), Anabaptism took the Protestant dictum *sola scriptura* ("by scripture alone") to radical new lengths. The movement's signature reform—Anabaptist literally means "rebaptizer"—was the rejection of infant baptism as unscriptural.

120.6–7 *Anthony Burgess*] An English Puritan nonconformist (1600–1663). Edwards quotes from Burgess's sermon collection *Spiritual Refining: Or, A Treatise of Grace and Assurance*, first issued in London in 1652.

120.18–19 like Tares . . . good Wheat] Cf. Matthew 13:26.

120.23–24 *Luther* . . . carnal Gospel."] The Anabaptist leader Thomas Müntzer (c. 1489–1525) accused Martin Luther (1483–1546) of being worse than the Pope because he preached only a halfway reformation.

120.27–31 So in *England* . . . broke out.] Viewing themselves as hewing to the straight and narrow way of God as they understood it, Puritans in England and New England often felt themselves beset by persecution and derision from formalists and crypto-papists—as they would call them—on their right (e.g., the royal authorities under Charles I and later the Anglican establishment after the Restoration) and by outrageous provocation from enthusiasts and biblical literalists on their left (Familists, Fifth Monarchists, Quakers, Baptists, etc.) who flourished in the upheaval of the English Revolution. For the theological dimension of this perception, see note 5.17–18.

122.22 *Christ is the End of the Law for Righteousness*] Romans 10:4.

123.12–13 Chapter wherein is my Text] 1 John 4.

123.19–20 crucified without the Gates] Cf. Hebrews 13:12.

124.33 *Light within*] In Quaker doctrine, a divine presence in the soul that can enlighten and guide the believer.

125.8–9 *Michael* . . . *Dragon* that is at War with him.] Cf. Revelation 12:7.

125.23–24 *My Kingdom is not of this World.*] John 18:36.

125.25 *the God of this World.*] 2 Corinthians 4:4.

126.12–14 Candle of the Lord . . . Viceregent of God in the Soul] Imagery (see Proverbs 20:27) commonly used to describe the conscience, that faculty which, once activated by the Spirit, functions as an inward prosecutor and judge of the self and its actions. It was, in this sense, the first locus of grace in the regenerate soul.

126.34 Gall of Bitterness] Cf. Acts 8:23.

128.21–22 as *Abraham* . . . *hear them*] Luke 16:29.

128.22–23 Voice from Heaven . . . *Hear ye him.*] Cf. Matthew 17:5.

128.34–35 the main Weapon . . . War with him] Cf. Revelation 12:7–9.

128.35   the Sword of the Spirit] Ephesians 6:17.

128.36–38   *great, and sore . . . crooked Serpent*] Cf. Isaiah 27:1.

128.39   *him that sat on the Horse*] Cf. Revelation 19:11.

129.32   in the Margin] The King James Bible Edwards used included variant translations and cross-references to other Bible passages in the margins.

129.36   *a Liar, and the Father of Lies*] Cf. John 8:44.

129.40–130.1   *the Rulers of the Darkness of this World.*] Ephesians 6:12.

131.32   *Gnosticks*] See note 120.5.

131.35   the *Family of Love.*] A movement in Holland and England inspired by the example of a Dutch religious community founded *c.* 1540 by a German mystic named Hendrik Niclaes (1502–1580). More commonly known as Familists in England, they valued the indwelling of the Holy Spirit above obedience to the Law and were therefore called antinomians by their orthodox critics.

132.28   *Learn of me . . . lowly in Heart.*] Matthew 11:29.

133.22–23   the Finger of God] Cf. Luke 11:20.

133.27   *Object.*] Objection.

134.28–29   miraculous Gifts of the Holy Spirit] Cf. 1 Corinthians 12: the gifts of the Spirit listed there are wisdom, knowledge, faith, healing, miracles, prophecy, discerning of spirits, and tongues.

135.8   common Influences of the Spirit] Edwards here reminds his readers of a fearsome mystery: the Spirit can trigger in the unregenerate certain experiences, as for instance a genuine-seeming conviction of sin brought on by an active conscience, that mimic the process of conversion among the truly regenerate. Such unfortunate individuals were often called hypocrites. See note 58.3.

136.7–8   Improvement . . . Grace] Improvement is used here in the now-archaic sense of "taking advantage of." For the means of grace, see note 37.37.

136.24–25   these Things ben't done in a Corner] Cf. Acts 26:26.

137.19   Deism] Given expression in the writings of Thomas Hobbes, David Hume, and John Locke among others, and often called the religion of the "Age of Reason," Deism was a rationalist worldview that emphasized God's role as creator while denying any ongoing divine engagement with creation (providence). As a record of such engagement, the Bible was consequently devalued by Deists. In his autobiography, Edwards's contemporary Benjamin Franklin (1706–1790) recalls that he was "scarce 15" when he became "a thorough Deist."

143.17   the venerable STODDARD] See note 15.30.

143.25–26   six or seven Years ago] That is, the "Little Awakening" of 1735 that Edwards describes in the *Faithful Narrative*.

144.3   *Let there be Light*] Genesis 1:3.

144.6   false Wonders mix'd with true] Cf. Exodus 7:11–12.

144.12–13   At the Time when the Sons of God . . . *among them.*] Cf. Job 1:6.

144.13–15   *Solomon's* Ships . . . brought *Apes and Peacocks.*] Cf. 1 Kings 10:22. In medieval iconography apes sometimes represented the devil, lust, or irreverence, while peacocks symbolized pride.

145.27   Princes of the Earth] Cf. Ezekiel 39:18.

145.38–39   *Jacob* . . . when he saw the Ladder] Cf. Genesis 28.

145.40   *How dreadful is this Place*] Genesis 28:17.

146.1   when God shewed him his Glory] Cf. Exodus 34:5–7.

146.2   *he made haste . . . Earth.*] Cf. Exodus 34:8.

146.13–15   Christ then *was in the World . . . received him not.*] Cf. John 1:10–11.

146.20   counted him a Madman] Cf. John 10:20.

146.21   Spirit that he wrought by the Spirit of the Devil.] Cf. Matthew 12:24.

146.23–24   stumbling Blocks] See note 33.1.

147.2   the unpardonable Sin against the Holy Ghost.] See note 36.14–15.

147.29–30   Christ and his Work were . . . a stumbling Block] Cf. 1 Peter 2:8.

147.30–31   *But blessed is he . . . stumbled) in me.*] Matthew 11:6.

147.36–39   *they could discern . . . what is right?*] Cf. Luke 12:56–57.

148.2   bowed the Heavens . . . into this Land] Cf. 2 Samuel 22:10 and Psalm 18:9.

148.17–18   *He that is not with us is against us.*] Cf. Luke 9:50.

148.29–32   *Behold, if the Lord . . . eat thereof.*] 2 Kings 7:2.

148.32–33   this Work is a Cloud . . . to the *Egyptians.*] Cf. Exodus 14:20.

149.7–8   *It must needs be that Offences come.*] Matthew 18:7.

149.14–15   Stone of Stumbling . . . Snare to many.] Cf. Isaiah 8:14.

149.17–19   God *would be as the Dew . . . spread, &c.*] Hosea 14:5–6.

149.33–34   *seeing might see and not understand.*] Cf. Mark 4:12, Matthew 13:14.

149.38   they wanted a Sign from Heaven] Cf. Mark 8:11.

150.12–13   Fountain is set open] Cf. Joel 3:18, Zechariah 13:1, Revelation 7:17.

150.38–39   *Gamaliel*] The "unbelieving Jew" mentioned at lines 30–31. He is introduced as a Pharisee and "a doctor of the law" in Acts 5:34 and is revealed in Acts 22:3 to have been mentor to Saul of Tarsus (Paul).

151.12   the unpardonable Sin] See note 36.14–15.

151.27   Judg. 5. 23. *Curse ye Meroz*] For Edwards's sermon on this verse, see pp. 643–55 in this volume.

151.39–40   When God sends forth . . . void;] Cf. Isaiah 55:11.

152.6–8   *that whether . . . Prophet among them.*] Ezekiel 2:5.

152.19   *to cut off Occasion from those that desired Occasion.*] 2 Corinthians 11:12.

152.24–25   wise as Serpents and harmless as Doves.] Matthew 10:16.

152.32   we are but little Children] Cf. John 13:33.

152.32   this roaring Lion] Cf. 1 Peter 5:8.

152.33   this old Serpent] Cf. Genesis 3:1, Revelation 12:9.

153.14–15   *he wist not that his Face shone.*] Cf. Exodus 34:29.

153.19   the third Heaven] Synonymous with Paradise, the highest realm in the traditional tripartite division of the heavens derived from readings of Genesis 1:6–8 and 2 Corinthians 12:2.

153.29–30   The Devil has come in at this Door] Cf. Genesis 4:7.

154.4–5   *extraordinary Gifts* of the Spirit] See note 134.28–29.

154.31–32   a Root . . . excellent Fruit] Cf. Romans 15:12.

154.40–155.1   *Balaam, Saul,* and *Judas*] Cf., respectively, 2 Peter 2:15 and Revelation 2:14; 1 Samuel 16:14; John 13:2.

155.3–5   *Have we not prophesied . . . wonderful Works.*] Matthew 7:22.

155.10–13   *David* comforting . . . Light, Love & Joy.] See, for example, Psalm 27.

155.15–16   all Things but Loss . . . Knowledge of Christ.] Cf. Philippians 3:8.

155.17–19   names being written . . . subject to them.] Cf. Luke 10:20.

156.5–8   Prophecy and Tongues . . . which never faileth.] Cf. 1 Corinthians 13:8.

156.17   childish Things] 1 Corinthians 13:11.

157.38   *a more excellent Way*] Cf. 1 Corinthians 12:31.

158.13–14   *a Jack with a Lanthorn.*] A will-o'-the-wisp or ignis fatuus.

159.6–9   cast our selves down . . . against a Stone] Cf. Matthew 4:5–6.

159.19   Scripture very often . . . forbids.] As in Matthew 7:1 and Luke 6:37.

160.20   seperate the Sheep from Goats] Cf. Matthew 25:32.

160.39–40   Lord of the Harvest . . . Labourers in his Harvest] Cf. Luke 10:2.

161.35   *hidden Manna*] Cf. Revelation 2:17.

161.35–36   they *have Meat to eat that others know not of*] Cf. John 4:32.

161.36–37   *a Stranger intermeddles not with their Joys*] Cf. Proverbs 14:10.

162.15   *Achitophel*] Cf. 2 Samuel 15:12, 31–37, 17:1–23.

162.18–19   *knew more than all . . . the Ancients*] Cf. Psalm 119:99–100.

163.27–30   We should not . . . their Villages.] Cf. Luke 9:52–54.

164.18–19   *to swerve . . . vain Jangling.*] Cf. 1 Timothy 1:6.

SOME THOUGHTS

167.23–24   War with *Spain*] Later called the War of Jenkins' Ear, a part of the larger European conflict known as the War of the Austrian Succession (1740–48).

170.11–12   *Clay . . . Potter.*] Cf. Jeremiah 18:6, Romans 9:21.

170.12   *GOD gives not Account of his Matters:*] Job 33:13.

170.12–13   *His Judgments are a great Deep:*] Psalm 36:6.

170.13–14   *He hath his Way . . . not known;*] Psalm 77:19.

170.14–15   *and who shall teach GOD Knowledge,*] Job 21:22.

170.15   *or enjoin him his Way,*] Job 36:23.

170.15–16   *or say unto him what doest thou?*] Job 9:12.

170.16–18   *We know not . . . who maketh all.*] Ecclesiastes 11:5.

170.22–23   the Calamity . . . Ark of GOD] Cf. 1 Samuel 6:19.

170.32   pour Contempt] Cf. Job 12:21.

170.39   Stumbling-blocks] See note 33.1.

171.14   Levites] Cf. Numbers 18.

175.4–6   Charity, or divine Love . . . Heart] Cf. Matthew 22:37–40 and 1 Corinthians 13.

175.12   when Knowledge, and Tongues, and Prophesyings shall cease] Cf. 1 Corinthians 13:8.

175.20–21   the Peace . . . all Understanding] Philippians 4:7.

175.21–22   Joy in the Holy Ghost] Cf. Romans 14:17 and 1 Thessalonians 1:6.

175.22   Joy unspeakable and full of Glory] 1 Peter 1:8.

176.5–6   So the Spirit is represented . . . Fire,] Cf. Acts 2:2–3.

177.25–35   *Jacob* . . . prevailed.] Cf. Genesis 32:24–28.

177.34   as a Prince . . . prevailed.] Genesis 32:28.

178.1   sick of Love] Cf. Song of Solomon 2:5 and 5:8.

178.23–24   human Nature, . . . withering Flower] Cf. 1 Peter 1:24.

178.26   Dust and Ashes] Cf. Job 30:19 and Genesis 18:27.

178.28   *No Man can see me and live*] Exodus 33:20.

178.28–29   *Flesh . . . Kingdom of GOD.*] 1 Corinthians 15:50.

178.32–33   Apostle *John* . . . as dead;] Revelation 1:17.

179.38   *Children have ye any Meat?*] John 21:5.

180.7–8   *Moses*'s Life was taken away after this Manner] Cf. Deuteronomy 34:5–6.

180.33   whose Judgments are a great Deep] Psalm 36:6.

180.33–34   his Ways past finding out] Romans 11:33.

182.4–5   strong Crying and Tears] Hebrews 5:7.

182.7–8   he is said to see of the *Travail* of his Soul.] Cf. Isaiah 53:11.

182.12–13   a *Woman crying . . . delivered.*] Revelation 12:2.

182.16   *wish himself accursed from CHRIST*] Cf. Romans 9:3.

183.7–8   Eye had not seen, . . . Heart of Man] Cf. 1 Corinthians 2:9.

183.32   *Who hath heard . . . such Things?*] Isaiah 66:8.

184.1–9   Mr. *Bolton* . . . p. 103, 104.] *The Fulfilling of the Scripture* (Rotterdam, 1669; 5th ed., London, 1726) by Scottish dissenter Robert Fleming (1630–1694), includes an account of the conversion of Robert Bolton (1572–1631), an "eminently prophane" Oxford classicist who later became a clergyman. Edwards suggests that Bolton's conversion had been prompted by the preaching of the famous Puritan divine William Perkins (1558–1602), whom Bolton had previously demeaned as "a barren empty fellow, and a passing meane scholar." But he appears to have misread the passage in question, for in fact Fleming does not say that it was Perkins's preaching that had been responsible for Bolton's conversion. Edwards's adversary Charles Chauncy seized on this error in *Seasonable Thoughts on the State of Religion in New England*, his 1743 rebuttal to *Some Thoughts* (see Chronology).

184.9   An Account of another] To show the great compass of God's grace to better effect, Fleming, immediately after relating the conversion of the eminent scholar Bolton, tells the story of the redemption of "a most stupid and brutish person," an anonymous "poor buggerer who not many years ago was put to death . . . for that horrid wickedness." Before his execution, this individual had purportedly made the following exemplary statement: "*O he is a great forgiver, he is a great forgiver.* . . . I know God hath nothing to lay against me, for Jesus Christ hath payed all, and those are free whom the Son makes free."

184.14   Life of Mr. *George Trosse*] *The Life of the Reverend Mr. George Trosse* (London, 1714) contained the autobiography and sermons of Trosse (1631–1713), along with an account of his death by fellow minister Isaac Gilling.

184.34   *Farel* and *Viret*] For a time a colleague of Calvin in Geneva, Guillaume Farel (1489–1565) trained and inspired a number of evangelists, Pierre Viret (1511–1571) among them, to spread the principles of reformed Christianity throughout western Europe.

185.1   Mrs. *Catherine Brettergh*] The subject of two widely reprinted funeral sermons, Catherine Bruen Brettergh (1579–1601) was considered a paragon of godly piety.

185.22   Mr. *Harrison*] William Harrison (d. 1625), Puritan clergyman from Huyton, Lancashire, who preached one of Brettergh's funeral sermons.

185.36   Mr. *Alexander Allyn*] Scottish-born wine merchant Allyn (c. 1659–1708) arrived in Windsor, Connecticut, sometime prior to 1693.

186.5   *John Rogers* of *Dedham*] A dramatic preaching style earned this Puritan divine (c. 1570–1636) the nickname "Roaring Rogers."

186.12   Mr. *Flavel*] John Flavel (or Flavell) (1627–1691) was an English Dissenting minister known on both sides of the Atlantic for his works of practical piety. This excerpt is from *Pneumatologia: A Treatise of the Soul of Man* (London, 1685).

186.14–15   the Apostle *Paul* . . . Third Heaven.] See note 153.19.

186.18–19   swell higher . . . *Ezekiel*'s vision.] Cf. Ezekiel 47:1–5.

187.5–6   Capt. *Clap*'s Memoirs . . . Mr. *Prince*.] The memoirs of Captain Roger Clap, an early settler in Dorchester, Massachusetts, in 1630, were published in Boston in 1731, with a preface by Thomas Prince, pastor of Boston's Old South Church.

187.8–10   GOD's holy Spirit . . . Child of GOD.] Cf. Romans 8:16.

187.20   Mr. *Williams* of *Deerfield*] John Williams (1664–1729) was pastor at Deerfield, Massachusetts, from 1686 until his death. His wife was the stepdaughter of Edwards's grandfather Solomon Stoddard. See Chronology for 1704.

188.4 *French Prophets*] Also known as Camisards, Protestants (Huguenots) in mountainous southern France who were driven underground and radicalized by the revocation of the Edict of Nantes in 1685. In 1706, a small group of these prophets traveled to England, where they gained notoriety for their strange bodily fits and chiliastic pronouncements, which they attributed to the workings of the Holy Spirit.

190.1 a People or Society] A minister often spoke of his congregation as "my people" or simply "the people." The covenanted, pew-holding members of the congregation constituted its society, or ecclesiastical society, empowered to administer the church's legal and business matters.

191.12 *Causa sine quâ non*] Latin: indispensable cause. Edwards is trying to draw a distinction between the essential and accidental aspects of the revivals. The generative force behind the revivals, as behind all things, was God. However, when the workings of the Holy Spirit are manifested in a given historical context—the corrupted realm of human behavior—they are inevitably experienced "through a glass, darkly," as the Apostle Paul says (1 Corinthians 13:12). Thus, Edwards cautions, the essential work of the Spirit in the revivals should not be discredited by the occasional untoward conduct (excessive emotions, censoriousness, etc.) or mistaken beliefs "that are accidental to it."

191.16–17 they would have Fire . . . *Samaritans*] Cf. Luke 9:53–54.

191.21–22 he *was very meek . . . Earth*] Numbers 12:3.

192.15–16 *Luther . . .* Bitterness with his Zeal.] As the Reformation he initiated grew from a small ideologically coherent movement of like-minded individuals into a major political force within the fractured institutions of the Holy Roman Empire, Martin Luther experienced many frustrations and disappointments, his hopes for the spread of a simpler Christianity confounded by intransigent traditionalism and proliferating sectarianism. Even as he raged at his congregation in Wittenberg for their failure to fully cast off their old Catholic practices and to live to the Gospel ideals he preached, he was incensed by those who sought to extend the reforming impulse beyond the bounds of what he thought acceptable, and could be vituperative in his condemnation of radical reformers (see note 289.18–19). Even Luther's notorious anti-Semitism was rooted in thwarted evangelical zeal. In his 1523 work *That Jesus Christ was Born a Jew* he had advocated for kindness toward Jews with the aim of converting them to Christianity. Twenty years later, his dreams for the conversion of the Jews having coming to naught, he pronounced in *On the Jews and Their Lies* that the once chosen people had become "the devil's people."

193.11–12 the Spirit of GOD . . . Waters] Genesis 1:2.

193.15–16 GOD saw every Thing . . . very good.] Genesis 1:31.

193.21–22 he *shook the Heavens . . . all Nations*] Cf. Haggai 2:6–7.

194.15–16 I am of *Paul . . .* I of *Cephas*] 1 Corinthians 1:12.

199.22–23   As when *David* . . . bring back the Ark] Cf. 1 Chronicles 13, 15.

200.40–201.1   *What shall I do to be saved?*] Acts 16:30.

204.34   solemn Covenant with GOD.] As exemplified in Northampton, where on March 16, 1742, Edwards led his church through a covenant renewal ceremony in an effort to consolidate the spirit of the revivals. For Edwards's description of this process, and the text of the covenant he wrote, see his letter to Thomas Prince, pp. 672–76 in this volume.

205.11   the poor *Indians*] Confronted by the dismal record of their missionary efforts among the region's native inhabitants, New Englanders often sounded the dismissive, contemptuous tone that Edwards employs here. What few could acknowledge was that their austere, text-based religion was unlikely to strike much of a chord with the Indians, animists who enjoyed a rich, dream-centered spiritual life. The Catholic French, who employed a more syncretic approach in New France, on the whole enjoyed greater success.

206.5   the Valley of the Shadow of Death.] Psalm 23:4.

206.14   the *Montanists*] Second-century followers of Montanus of Phrygia, who identified himself with the Comforter (*Paraclete* in Greek) promised in John 14:16. Montanists were given to ecstatic prophecies of the second coming of Christ (chiliasm).

206.15   the *French Prophets*] See note 188.4.

207.12   I have been particularly acquainted . . .] Edwards here begins a lengthy description of his wife Sarah's religious experiences. See Chronology for 1742.

208.32–33   Mr. *Whitefield*, or Mr. *Tennent*] Old Light critics of the revivals placed much of the responsibility for their spread at the well-traveled feet of itinerant preachers like George Whitefield (1714–1770) and Gilbert Tennent (see note 27.14–15). Whitefield was an evangelically minded Anglican who made sensational tours throughout the colonies, preaching to enormous crowds (see Chronology, 1738–44). Tennent also toured, most controversially in New England, having gained much celebrity with the publication in 1740 of his confrontational sermon *The Danger of an Unconverted Ministry.*

213.1–2   I AM THAT I AM] Exodus 3:14.

214.13   bearing the Cross for CHRIST] Cf. Matthew 16:24, Luke 9:23, Mark 8:34 and 10:21.

215.35   *The Riches of full Assurance*] Colossians 2:2.

217.11   the Notion of the *Wesleys*] John (1703–1791) and Charles Wesley (1707–1788), founders of Methodism, an evangelical movement emerging within the Church of England. Edwards here attributes to them the belief that in this world one can become perfectly free from sin, and implies that they have been tainted with the antinomian heresy. In fact, the Wesleys rejected antinomianism, and their advocacy of "Christian perfection" is better viewed as a kind of evangelical Arminianism (see note 5.17–18).

218.7   *The Peace . . . all Understanding*;] Philippians 4:7.

218.8–9   *Rejoicing . . . unseen Saviour*;] Cf. 1 Peter 1:8.

218.9   *All Joy & Peace in believing*;] Romans 15:13.

218.10–11   *GOD's shining . . . Jesus Christ*;] 2 Corinthians 4:6.

218.11–14   *with open Face . . . the Lord*;] 2 Corinthians 3:18.

218.14–15   *Having the Love . . . given to us*;] Romans 5:5.

218.15–16   *Having the Spirit . . . rest upon us*;] Cf. 1 Peter 4:14.

218.16–17   *A being called . . . Light*;] 1 Peter 2:9.

218.17–18   *and having the Day-Star arise in our Hearts*] 2 Peter 1:19.

218.21   Fruits of the true Spirit] Cf. Galatians 5:22.

221.1   *exceeding Greatness of GOD's Power*] Cf. Ephesians 1:19.

221.1–2   *the Glory and Riches of divine Grace*] Cf. Ephesians 1:7.

221.37   a new Thing] Cf. Isaiah 43:19.

223.5–6:   The *New-Jerusalem . . .* has begun] Cf. Revelation 21:2. Edwards was hopeful that the Awakening heralded the opening of the millennium, the thousand-year Golden Age that precedes the Second Coming of Christ.

223.6–7   *New-Jerusalem . . .* down from Heaven,] Cf. Revelation 21:2.

224.7–8   Captain of his People's Salvation] Cf. Hebrews 2:10.

226.5–7   kiss the Son . . . *perish from the Way*] Cf. Psalm 2:12.

226.8   *dash'd in Pieces with a Rod of Iron.*] Cf. Psalm 2:9.

226.9–10   *sets his King on his holy Hill of* Zion] Cf. Psalm 2:6.

226.36   *Stone that the Builders . . . Corner.*] Psalm 118:22.

228.18–19   *rejoicing . . . loud Voices*?] Cf. Luke 19:37.

230.12–13   when he creates . . . *Earth.*] Cf. Isaiah 65:17.

230.19–26   As the elder Sister . . . Famine] Cf. Genesis 29–30. Jacob worked seven years for his father-in-law, Laban, in order to marry Rachel, but was tricked into marrying Rachel's elder sister Leah first, and then to work another seven years for Rachel.

230.30–31   as by the Horns of a Unicorn . . . Earth] Cf. Deuteronomy 33:17.

232.39   the First shall be last, and the Last first;] Cf. Matthew 19:30.

233.4   Sun of Righteousness] Malachi 4:2.

233.4–5   Sun of the new Heavens and new Earth] Cf. Revelation 21:23.

235.1–2   Feast of the first Fruits] Cf. Exodus 23:16.

235.29   Feast of the *Passover*] Cf. Exodus 12:1–20.

235.30–31   Feast of *Ingathering*] Cf. Exodus 23:16.

236.10–12   Angel of the Covenant . . . gathered.] Cf. Revelation 14:16–18.

236.28–30   The World . . . appointed] Clerics James Ussher (1581–1656) and John Lightfoot (1602–1675) both published chronologies which claimed that creation occurred near the autumnal equinox.

237.20–23   stood in *Jerusalem* . . . *living Waters.*] John 7:37–38.

237.31–32   *upon them shall be no Rain*] Zechariah 14:17.

237.38–238.3   *And this shall be the Plague . . . Mouth.*] Zechariah 14:12.

239.24–25   he deliver'd them . . . *Deborah & Barak*] Cf. Judges 4.

239.35–36   without *a Shield . . . of 'em*] Cf. Judges 5:8.

239.37   nine Hundred Chariots of Iron.] Cf. Judges 4:3.

241.8–9   the Victory . . . *Amalekites*] Cf. Judges 6, 7.

241.9–11   they came up . . . numbered.] Cf. Judges 6:5.

241.15–16   not by human Sword . . . earthen Vessels.] Cf. Judges 7:16–22.

241.39–242.2   *took them, . . . Men of the City*] Judges 8:16–17.

243.6–7   barren to the Day of her Death.] Cf. 2 Samuel 6:23.

244.18–20   these Sons . . . Free-Woman.] Cf. Galatians 4:30.

244.21–23   if we have run . . . Horses?] Jeremiah 12:5.

245.22–27   *What do these feeble . . . Wall.*] Nehemiah 4:2–3.

248.30–32   *girds his Sword . . . terrible Things.*] Cf. Psalm 45:3–4.

248.33–38   Princes of . . . Men of *Succoth.*] Cf. Judges 8:15–16.

250.37–39   *Be wise now . . . the Way.*] Cf. Psalm 2:10, 12.

251.17–18   Co-workers with Christ] Cf. 1 Corinthians 3:9.

251.18   his Ambassadors] Cf. 2 Corinthians 5:20.

251.31–32   he must give an Account] Cf. Luke 16:2.

251.33   Understanding . . . ought to do] Cf. 1 Chronicles 12:32.

251.38   Watchmen over the City . . . *Zion*] Cf. Isaiah 62:6, 10–11.

252.1–2   we refuse to open . . . Wrath?] Cf. 2 Kings 15:16.

252.3   Captains of the Host] Cf. 1 Chronicles 12:21.

254.17   *Michal*, without any Child] Cf. 2 Samuel 6:23.

255.3   The Example of the unbelieving Lord in *Samaria*] Cf. 2 Kings 7:1–2, 20.

256.3–6   the elder Brother . . . Joy of the Feast] Cf. Luke 15:25–32.

256.6–7   like *Michal* . . . offended at the Musick and Dancing] Cf. 2 Samuel 6:16.

258.33   Those therefore that publish Pamphlets] The division in the New England clergy over the revivals was mirrored among the printers in Boston, the region's publication hub. Edwards's publisher, the Queen Street firm of Samuel Kneeland and Timothy Green Jr.—both of whom were members of Thomas Prince's Old South Church—was staunchly supportive, while Anglican Thomas Fleet, over on Cornhill, devoted much press time to anti-revival tracts, in addition to the publication of the aggressively Old Light *Boston Evening-Post*.

259.6–11   *Gadarenes* . . . their Coasts] Cf. Mark 5:8–17.

260.16–19   when he finds his Sheep . . . rejoyce with me] Cf. Luke 5:5–6.

260.27–29   great Rejoicing . . . Sinners that have repented] Cf. Luke 15:10.

261.4   Tirshatha] A term of Persian origin, referring to a governor, or "one who takes the place of the king."

263.10–16   I would . . . Work of GOD.] Edwards here sketches an outline for the remainder of *Some Thoughts*, with I referring to Part III, just begun, II to Part IV, and III to Part V.

269.4–5   heal the Hurt slightly . . . no Peace.] Cf. Jeremiah 6:14.

270.25–26   Co-workers with him] Cf. 1 Corinthians 3:9.

272.28   *born as the wild Asses Colt*] Job 11:12.

273.13   first Table] The first four of the Ten Commandments, those that pertain to the proper reverence of God.

273.17   second Table] The remaining commandments, which prescribe right conduct toward others.

274.6   *six Days shalt thou Labour*] Exodus 20:9.

274.11–12   attend a Lecture] See note 18.13.

276.29   Destruction of the City of *Jericho*] Cf. Joshua 6.

277.2–4   Sounding of Trumpets . . . Jubilee] Cf. Leviticus 25:8–10.

277.4–5   reading of the Law . . . Tabernacles.] Cf. Deuteronomy 31:10–11.

277.6–7   Crowing of the Cock . . . Repentance] Cf. Matthew 26:74–75.

279.21–22   *the Marks of . . . true Spirit*] Published as *The Distinguishing Marks of a Work of the Spirit of God*, pp. 85–164 in this volume.

283.22–24   *Blessed be the King . . . Disciples.*] Luke 19:38–39.

283.28–30   *I tell you . . . cry out.*] Luke 19:40.

284.37–39   singing Praises . . . Day or Night] Cf. Revelation 4:8.

285.29–30   found Fault with . . . Hymns of humane Composure.] There still was controversy in New England churches over the singing of hymns not found in Scripture—as Edwards puts it, those of human composition—in addition to or instead of the traditional Psalms. As he recalled in a May 22, 1744, letter to Benjamin Colman, Edwards's church began using Isaac Watts's *Hymns and Spiritual Songs* (1707) sometime in 1742: "I introduced it principally because I saw in the people a very general inclination to it. Indeed, I was not properly he that introduced it: they began it in my absence on a journey; and seemed to be greatly pleased with it; and sang nothing else, and neglected the Psalms wholly. When I came home I disliked not their making some use of the hymns, but did not like their setting aside the Psalms; and therefore used them principally."

287.5–6   perfect Praise . . . Sucklings] Cf. Matthew 21:16.

289.18–19   *Luther* . . . many Excesses] Martin Luther's zealous and uncompromising nature was well documented. To take one of many examples, in the midst of a controversy with Swiss Protestants led by fellow reformer Ulrich Zwingli (1484–1531) over the precise nature of the sacrament of communion, Luther famously declared: "In a word, either they or we must be ministers of Satan! There is not room here for negotiation or mediation." Tired of being "treated like an ass" by the great German reformer during the debate, an exasperated Zwingli likened Luther to two Catholic controversialists of the day: "May I die if he does not surpass [Johannes] Eck in impurity, [Johannes] Cochlaeus in audacity, and, in brief, all the vices of men!"

292.4–5   out of their Bellies flowed Rivers of living Water] Cf. John 7:38.

292.9–10   put on the whole Armour . . . evil Day] Cf. Ephesians 6:11, 13.

292.19–20   CHRIST . . . carried into the Wilderness] Cf. Matthew 4:1, Mark 1:12, Luke 4:1, all of which suggest that Jesus was led into the desert by the Spirit, not the Devil.

292.24   *This is my beloved . . . pleased.*] Cf. Matthew 3:17.

293.31   Smoke from the bottomless Pit] Cf. Revelation 9:2.

294.13–14   pull the Beam out of our Eye] Cf. Matthew 7:3–5.

295.5–6   *Dagon*'s Temple] Cf. 1 Samuel 5:1–7, Judges 16:23.

295.21   When he was exalted] For scriptural allusions to Satan's former place in heaven, and to his pride-induced fall, see Job 1:6, Revelation 12:9, 1 Timothy 3:6, Jude 1:6.

296.24   He that trusts his own Heart is a Fool.] Proverbs 28:26.

297.36   esteem others better than himself] Cf. Philippians 2:3.

300.13–14   worse Language than *Michael* . . . Devil himself.] Cf. Jude 1:9.

300.28–29   *What, could ye not . . . weak.*] Cf. Matthew 26:40–41.

300.31–32   he looked upon him with a Look of Love] Cf. Luke 22:61.

300.33–34   *turned and said . . . get thee behind me* Satan] Matthew 16:23.

301.21   to become all Things to all Men] Cf. 1 Corinthians 9:22.

302.36–37   the Sword of the SPIRIT] Cf. Ephesians 6:17.

302.40   Sons of Thunder] Cf. Mark 3:17.

302.40–303.4   sharper than . . . Joints and Marrow] Cf. Hebrews 4:12.

304.18   the Seed of the Serpent.] Cf. Genesis 3:15.

305.34   *Peter* wounds] Cf. John 18:10. The synoptic Gospels do not identify the swordsman: cf. Matthew 26:51, Mark 14:47, and Luke 22:38.

306.9–10   I will be yet more . . . own Sight.] 2 Samuel 6:22.

308.15–16   *vaunteth not . . . it self unseemly*] Cf. 1 Corinthians 13:4–5.

308.16–17   *prefer others in Honour.*] Cf. Romans 12:10.

309.22–23   *Hear now ye Rebels . . . this Rock?*] Numbers 20:10.

310.8–9   offer Sacrifice to him . . . at *Lystra*] Cf. Acts 14:11–13.

310.18–23   *Gideon* . . . Ruin of his Family.] Cf. Judges 8:24–27.

310.26   *Uzza* the Son of Abinadab.] Cf. 1 Chronicles 13:9–10.

312.3–4   Come let us reason together] Isaiah 1:18.

312.20   διδακτικος] In the Greek New Testament, διδακτικόν. Edwards changed the case from accusative to nominative to fit the grammar of his English sentence. In the Greek verse, "δοῦλον δὲ κυρίου οὐ δεῖ μάχεσθαι, ἀλλὰ ἤπιον εἶναι πρὸς πάντας, διδακτικόν, ἀνεξίκακον," the construction "δεῖ" calls for an accusative.

314.28   one sows and another reaps] Cf. John 4:37.

317.8–9   what *Balaam* had from GOD] Cf. Numbers 22, 23.

317.12–13   *a more excellent Way*] 1 Corinthians 12:31.

317.26–27   making their Eye single . . . Light.] Cf. Luke 11:34.

318.6–7   Eyes to see . . . Hearts to understand] Cf. Deuteronomy 29:4.

318.7–8   understand the Fear of the Lord] Proverbs 2:5.

318.8–11   brings the Blind . . . strait.] Cf. Isaiah 42:16.

326.19   a wise Steward] Cf. Luke 12:42.

326.29–30   the Work of the Ministry . . . Architect] Cf. Luke 14:28–30.

326.35–36   compar'd to the Business . . . Merchant] Cf. Matthew 25:14–30.

326.39–40   represented by the Business of a Fisherman] Cf. Matthew 4:19.

327.1–2   compar'd to the Business . . . War] Cf. 2 Timothy 2:3–4.

328.33–34   the Doctrine . . . Seed of the Serpent] Cf. Genesis 3:15.

329.4–5   *I came not . . . Division*] Cf. Matthew 10:34.

329.21   a Stone of Stumbling and Rock of Offence] 1 Peter 2:8.

331.2   new Wine into old Bottles] Cf. Luke 5:37.

331.29   taking] Captivating, alluring.

332.13   rectifying all Disorders by Force] Perhaps the most famous example of the excesses of the radical Reformation was the short-lived (1534–35) Anabaptist commune at Münster, in Westphalia. Under the leadership of the charismatic Dutch "prophet" Jan Matthys and his disciple John of Leiden, the German city was transformed into a volatile "New Jerusalem" where ecstatic visions abounded—one of John of Leiden's led to the institution of polygamy—and Catholics and Lutherans who refused to be rebaptized were driven into exile or forced to undergo the procedure in the public marketplace. Acutely sensitive to anything that might serve to discredit the larger Reformation, Luther heaped scorn on the Anabaptists, proclaiming that in Münster "the devils sit upon each other like toads."

332.14–15   *Sleiden*'s Hist. of the Reformation] *The General History of the Reformation of the Church from the Errors and Corruptions of the Church of Rome* (London, 1689), Edmund Bohun's translation of *Commentariorum de statu religionis et reipublicae, Carolo Quinto Casesare* (*Commentary on the state of religion and commonwealth during the reign of Emperor Charles the Fifth*), a 1555 work by humanist historian Johannes Sleidanus (1506–1556). The book's narrative is supplemented by a large collection of important primary documents.

333.12–14   GOD was pleased . . . Proceeding of his] Cf. Genesis 25:29–34.

333.25–27   *God has his Way . . . not known*] Cf. Psalm 77:19.

333.27   *he gives us no Account of any of his Matters*] Cf. Job 33:13.

339.1–2   *taught to keep . . . their Youth*] Cf. Zechariah 13:5.

339.31   *Ye Serpents, ye Generation of Vipers*] Matthew 23:33.

343.6   as I have observ'd elsewhere] In *The Distinguishing Marks*, pp. 109–11 in this volume.

343.33   take all for Gold that glisters] Cf. *The Merchant of Venice* II.vii.65.

347.5   *Causa sine qua non*] See note 191.12.

347.9   suffering] Permitting.

349.2–3   *all that sat . . . Face of an Angel.*] Cf. Acts 6:15.

349.26   distinguishing the Wheat from the Chaff] Cf. Matthew 3:12.

351.10   the abominable Notions . . . Community of Women.] A reference to radical sects like the Familialists (see note 131.35), the French Prophets (see note 188.4), and the Anabaptists in Münster (see note 332.13), that practiced, or were alleged to have practiced, plural marriage.

352.5–6   jealous over our selves . . . *Corinthians*] Cf. 2 Corinthians 11:2.

352.7–8   as the Serpent beguiled *Eve* thro' his Subtilty] Cf. Genesis 3:1–7.

354.1–2   the Woman of *Canaan* . . . the Widow of *Nain*] Cf. Matthew 15:22–28; Mark 5:22–24, 35–42; John 11:1–45; Matthew 8:5–13; and Luke 7:11–15.

354.6–7   *Brethren and Kinsmen according to the Flesh;*] Romans 9:3.

354.16   wise Man] The author of Ecclesiastes, sometimes identified as Solomon but probably living in the third century B.C.E., after the Babylonian exile.

354.16   *a being righteous over-much*] Ecclesiastes 7:16.

356.27   what I have elsewhere said] In *The Distinguishing Marks*, pp. 159–63 in this volume.

358.19   CHRIST's scourging . . . Temple;] Cf. Matthew 21:12–13.

358.34   Wolves in Sheep's Clothing] Cf. Matthew 7:15.

359.3–4   that Disposition . . . *Samaria.*] Cf. Luke 9:51–56.

360.3   Ministers . . . flaming Fire] Cf. Psalm 104.4.

360.32   Judge and Searcher of Hearts] Cf. Jeremiah 17:10.

360.39–361.2   two-edged Sword . . . Joints and Marrow] Cf. Hebrews 4:12.

363.30–32   divide between Sheep and Goats . . . left.] Cf. Matthew 25:32–33.

363.34   prepare the Way of the Lord.] Cf. Mark 1:3.

364.20   *Bless and curse not.*] Romans 12:14.

364.22   *Elisha* cursed the Children . . . *Bethel.*] Cf. 2 Kings 2:23–24.

366.15–16   GOD has appointed . . . *Teachers*] Cf. Ephesians 4:11.

371.15–16   Lord made a Breach . . . in his Anger.] Cf. 1 Chronicles 13:5–14.

373.3   the third Commandment.] "Thou shalt not take the name of the LORD thy God in vain" (Exodus 20:7).

373.16–17   *putting new Wine into old Bottles.*] Cf. Matthew 9:17.

376.3–4   *Come, let us go* . . . said to him,] Cf. Psalm 122:1.

376.17   the governing Part of the worshipping Societies] See note 190.1.

377.17–19   *those that rule over them* . . . *give Account.*] Cf. Hebrews 13:17.

380.18   worse than that] Another reference to the unpardonable sin. See note 36.14–15.

380.36–37   Mr. *Whitefield* . . . Retractions] Much criticized for injudicious remarks made on his preaching tours, George Whitefield issued public apologies through pamphlets like *A Letter from the Rev. Mr Whitefield to Some Church Members of the Presbyterian Persuasion* (Philadelphia, 1740) and through newspapers like *The Boston Gazette*, which on March 16, 1742, published his July 25, 1741, letter "To the Students, etc. under Convictions at the Colleges of Cambridge and New Haven."

381.34–35   *But with the froward* . . . *unsavoury.*] Cf. 2 Samuel 22:27.

383.25   *He that believeth shall not make haste*;] Isaiah 28:16.

383.33–34   *I charge you,* . . . *he please*] Song of Solomon 8:4.

384.7–8   CHRIST was asleep . . . Storm] Cf. Mark 4:37–38.

387.18–19   *their little ones* . . . *a Prey*] Cf. Numbers 14:31.

387.35–36   *he swore in his Wrath* . . . *Wilderness*] Cf. Hebrews 3:11, 17–18.

387.39   90 Psalm.] This psalm is traditionally attributed to Moses.

388.4–5   a Land flowing with Milk and Honey] Cf. Exodus 3:17.

390.5–6   the Angels, that are a Flame of Fire.] Cf. Exodus 3:2.

391.38   *Alexander*] Alexander III of Macedon, known as Alexander the Great (356–323 B.C.E.)

392.2   *Mr. Whitefield*] See note 208.32–33.

392.38   turn'd the World upside down.] Cf. Acts 17:6.

393.12–13   *that Hands be laid suddenly on no Man*] Cf. 1 Timothy 5:22.

393.13   they should *first be tried*] Cf. 1 Timothy 3:10.

393.39–40   I have heretofore had some Acquaintance . . . College] As an undergraduate, 1716–20, divinity student, 1720–22, and tutor, 1724–26, at Yale College.

394.39   Dr. *Doddridge*] Philip Doddridge (1702–1751), an English educator and prolific author of hymns, treatises, and devotional writings.

395.2   Mr. *Wadsworth*] Daniel Wadsworth (1704–1747) was pastor of Hartford's First Church from 1732 until his death.

397.7–10   Sons of *Zion* . . . Israel] Cf. Isaiah 60:9.

397.11–14   *their Merchandize* . . . *Clothing*] Cf. Isaiah 23:18.

397.16–17   *to the Place* . . . *Feet glorious*] Cf. Isaiah 60:13.

397.17–18   *the abundance of the Sea* . . . *God's Church*] Cf. Isaiah 60:5.

397.18–19   *she shall suck* . . . *Breasts of Kings.*] Cf. Isaiah 60:16.

397.22–23   spread their Garments . . . *Jerusalem*] Cf. Matthew 21:8.

397.24–25   their Silver & Gold . . . Moth-eaten] Cf. James 5:1–3.

398.23–24   blessed Fruits of the Effusions of his Spirit] Cf. Galatians 5:22–23.

401.2–3   *as Princes, they* . . . *prevail*] Cf. Genesis 32:28.

406.16   *Amos* 5. 21, *&c.*] Here and in a few additional scriptural identifications in the following pages, Edwards uses "et cetera" to mean "et sequens," "and the following."

406.25–26   *shew our Faith by our Works*] Cf. James 2:18.

409.16–19   *After these Things* . . . *Reward.*] Genesis 15:1.

410.4–9   *Rebekah* . . . *Isaac*'s Wife.] Cf. Genesis 24.

410.25–26   first Table . . . second.] See notes 273.13 and 273.17.

411.11–12   Professor *Franck*] August Hermann Francke (1663–1727), German Lutheran minister, professor at the University of Halle, and a leader of the Pietist movement.

411.18   charitable Designs.] Whitefield's chief charitable cause in America was Bethesda ("House of Mercy" in Hebrew), an orphanage he founded in Savannah, Georgia, in 1740. He collected offerings for the project throughout his evangelical tours.

412.8–12   Such a Thing . . . 5th Edition.] See note 184.1–9. The passage Edwards cites refers to Scotland's National Covenant of 1638.

413.9–10   *Amen*; Even so come LORD JESUS!] Revelation 22:20.

SERMONS

416.14   *Solifidians*] From *sola fide*, Latin for "by faith alone," a taunt directed at proponents of the doctrine of justification by faith alone.

416.21   *Breakers of his Law*] Cf. Romans 2:25.

416.22–23 *Obedience to his Law*] Cf. Isaiah 42:24.

416.29 *it is counted . . . for Righteousness*] Cf. Romans 4:22.

416.37–38 In the last Verse but one] Romans 4:24.

421.34 *Love to God*] Cf. 1 John 2:5.

421.34 *Love to our Brethren*] Cf. 1 John 4:21.

421.34–35 *forgiving Men their Trespasses*] Cf. Matthew 6:14.

425.26–27 *I am the true Vine . . . Husbandman.*] John 15:1.

425.34 *grafted into Christ*] Cf. Romans 11:19.

425.36 Dr. *Tillotson*] Though he was Archbishop of Canterbury, John Tillot-son (1630–1694) was much admired by English Dissenting ministers and their New England brethren for his conciliatory attitude toward nonconformists, for his efforts to reform abuses within the Anglican establishment, and for his many works of practical theology.

426.11 *Socinians*] Like Arminianism and Deism, Socinianism was a dire rationalist heresy in Edwards's eyes. Named for Fausto Sozzini (1539–1604), it rejected the doctrines of the divinity of Christ, the Trinity, original sin, the complete omniscience of God, and the propitiatory atonement of Christ. Edwards was well acquainted with the literature associated with the Socinian controversy that upset the Church of England in the wake of the 1689 Act of Toleration.

444.13–14 *For as many as have sinn'd . . . without Law.*] Romans 2:12.

447.21 *praying in the corners of the Streets*] Cf. Matthew 6:5.

447.21–22 *sounding a Trumpet . . . Alms*] Cf. Matthew 6:2.

450.6–7 *Luke* 18. 9. &c.] See note 406.16.

460.33 τοῦτο ἐμοὶ ἐλλόγει] Edwards followed eighteenth-century editions of the New Testament in correcting the grammatical mistake in Paul's Greek from ἐλλόγα to ἐλλόγει.

462.25 Christ is our second federal Head] John Calvin was trained as a lawyer and the theological tradition that bears his name, with its strong emphasis on covenants, carries an unmistakable legalistic strain. In Calvinist covenant theology, God established a covenant of works with Adam, who represented all humanity as its federal head. Thus when Adam violated that covenant, his failure—his sin—became the legacy of all humankind. However, a second covenant, the covenant of redemption, forged between God and Christ, transforms and partially supersedes the covenant of works. In this covenant, Christ becomes a second federal head, representing not all humankind but only the elect, on whose behalf he fulfills the terms of the covenant of works through his perfect life and expiatory death. This justifying work is imparted to the elect through yet a third covenant, the covenant of grace. For a key scriptural source of this theology, see Romans 5:12–21.

463.14   in the Form of a Servant] Cf. Philippians 2:7.

464.32   Mr. *Locke*] Better known today for his writings on psychology and political science, John Locke (1632–1704) was the author of several rationalist works on religion, including *The Reasonableness of Christianity, as Delivered in the Scriptures* (1695), which Edwards dissects in this footnote.

465.39   *v. 28. This do and thou shalt live.*] Luke 10:28.

469.16   the first Covenant] The covenant of works. See note 462.25.

474.12   *if thou sinnest thou shalt die*] Cf. Augustine, *City of God* Bk. XIII, Ch. 4.

474.12–14   *cursed is every one . . . do them:*] Galatians 3:10.

474.27–28   Mr. *Locke . . . p. 478.*] See note 464.32.

475.29   *Propitiation for our Sins*] Cf. 1 John 2:2, 4:10; Romans 3:25.

482.36–37   that Petition . . . *forgive us our Debts*] Cf. Matthew 6:12.

498.8–9   *meek and quiet . . . his Sight.*] Cf. 1 Peter 3:4.

498.9   *pleasant Fruits*] Cf. Song of Solomon 4:16.

498.10   *an Odour of sweet Smell*] Cf. Philippians 4:18.

503.4–5   God sware *in his Wrath . . .* enter in] Cf. Hebrews 3:11.

505.40   *Repentance for the Remission of Sins*] Cf. Mark 1:4.

511.35–36   Mr. *Locke . . .* 631.] See note 464.32.

529.24–25   *Repent . . . at Hand.*] Matthew 3:2.

529.33–34   to prepare his Way before him] Cf. Matthew 3:3.

533.25   *strive to enter in at the strait Gate*] Luke 13:24.

536.9–11   if it be a Right Hand . . . *Hands.*] Cf. Matthew 5:30.

537.2   City of Refuge] Cf. Numbers 35:11.

544.8–14   The rich young Man . . . part with it.] Cf. Matthew 19:21–22.

548.12–13   *standing with the Lamb . . . Hands*] Cf. Revelation 7:9.

549.1–2   accepted Time! . . . Day of Salvation!] Cf. Isaiah 49:8.

550.24–25   that Day when God's Saints . . . Air] Cf. 1 Thessalonians 4:17.

554.27   *What shall I do to be saved?*] Acts 16:30.

554.28   bottomless Pit] Cf. Revelation 9:1–2.

554.28–29   wailing . . . Burnings?] Cf. Matthew 13:41–42.

555.21   *the Rest were blinded*] Cf. Romans 11:7.

556.20   to meet the Lord in the Air] 1 Thessalonians 4:17.

556.21–22   stand at the *Right Hand* . . . Angels] Cf. 2 Chronicles 18:18.

556.22–23   at the *left Hand* with Devils] Cf. Matthew 25:41.

557.37   *Joseph Clark*'s Wife] Mary Wright Clark died on February 13, 1735.

560.33–34   in the Wilderness . . . Temptations] Cf. Matthew 4:1.

562.2   leave you to walk in your own Counsels.] Cf. Psalm 81:12.

562.6   Mr. *Stoddard*'s Ministry] See note 15.30.

565.7–8   there should come a Rod out of the stem of———] Isaiah 11:1.

565.8   the wolf should dwell———] Isaiah 11:6.

565.9   the Gentiles should seek to that Root of Jesse] Cf. Isaiah 11:10.

565.18–19   I will Read the whole of it to you.———] Isaiah 12.

566.31   In him Live & move———] Cf. Acts 17:28.

568.6–7   His name alone . . . above———] Psalm 148:13.

568.7–8   among the Gods there is none Like unto———] Cf. Exodus 15:11.

568.8   There is none in H can be compared———] Cf. Psalm 89:6.

568.9   the nations before are as the drop———] Isaiah 40:15.

568.11   Glo. in holin. fearful in———] Exodus 15:11.

568.12–13   There is none Holy as the L.—] 1 Samuel 2:2.

569.12–13   God Reveals . . . the ☉] Cf. John 14:22.

569.13–15   when all . . . Light in their Dwellings.] Cf. Exodus 10:22–23.

569.28–29   they dwell on high . . . munitions of Rocks.] Cf. Isaiah 33:16.

569.32   L. strong & mighty the L. mighty in Battle.] Psalm 24:8.

569.33–34   as the Chaff before the wind.] Cf. Psalm 35:5.

569.34–35   the moth shall Eat them up] Cf. Isaiah 51:8.

569.38   strong Rock] Cf. Psalm 31:2.

569.38   high Tower] Cf. Psalm 18:2.

569.40–570.3   There is none . . . arms.] Deuteronomy 33:26–27.

570.5–8   he that dwells . . . walks.] Cf. Psalm 91:1, 5–6.

570.18–19   there he breaks . . . Battle.—] Psalm 76:3.

570.19–20 as the mountains are Round about Jerus———] Psalm 125:2.

570.22 no weap . . . shall Prosp.] Isaiah 54:17.

570.26–27 they dwell in Peaceable . . . Resting Places.] Cf. Isaiah 32:18.

570.28–29 The L. is our defense . . . our King.] Psalm 89:18.

570.29–30 G. is our Refuge . . . the m———] Psalm 46:1–2.

571.11 with Change of Raiment] Cf. Zechariah 3:4.

571.12 Excellent ornam.] Cf. Ezekiel 16:7.

571.21–22 G. that Comforts those that are cast down.] 2 Corinthians 7:6.

571.22 G. of all Consolation] Cf. Romans 15:5.

571.24–25 In him they may find Rest.] Cf. Matthew 11:29.

571.28 quietness & assurance forever] Cf. Isaiah 32:17.

571.29 as an hiding place from the wind———] Isaiah 32:2.

571.31 all Joy & Peace in believing.] Cf. Romans 15:13.

571.35 Corn & wine & oil] Cf. Hosea 2:8 and Joel 2:19.

571.37–39 In all their affliction . . . carries them] Cf. Isaiah 63:9.

572.9–12 to Preach Good Tidings . . . Joy———] Cf. Isaiah 61:1–3.

572.14–16 their soul be Joyf. . . . Righteousness.—] Cf. Isaiah 61:10.

572.18 they shall no more be termed forsaken.] Cf. Isaiah 62:4.

572.19–20 their shepherd . . . young.] Cf. Isaiah 40:11.

572.22–23 he Leads them . . . still———] Cf. Psalm 23:2.

572.24 River the streams . . . City of G.] Cf. Psalm 46:4.

572.39–573.2 Like trees . . . yielding fruit.] Jeremiah 17:8.

573.10 the L. is our sheph. we shall not want.] Cf. Psalm 23:1.

573.34 He will feed them . . . forever.] Cf. Psalm 28:9.

573.40–574.1 They shall dwell . . . fulln. of———] Cf. Psalm 16:11.

574.2–3 there he Commands the bless. Even Life for———] Cf. Psalm 133:3.

574.14–15 the L. is the Portion . . . fallen———] Cf. Psalm 16:5–6.

574.15–16 whom have we in H. but thee———] Cf. Psalm 73:25.

574.34 all things shall work together for their Good.] Cf. Romans 8:28.

575.15–16 stronger is he that . . . the ☉] Cf. 1 John 4:4.

575.17 Punished Leviathan that Piercing Serpent—] Cf. Isaiah 27:1.

575.19–20   the dragon has been . . . cast out.] Cf. Revelation 12:9.

575.21   Chariots of Salvation.] Cf. Habakkuk 3:8.

575.32–33   as Balaam Prophesied . . . G. wrought.] Cf. Numbers 23:23.

576.18–21   G. hath not wrought . . . stretched out arm.] Cf. Deuteronomy 11:2, 7.

576.25   he will never Leave nor forsake] Cf. Hebrews 13:5.

577.1–2   God hath sent . . . weary.] Cf. Psalm 68:9.

577.2–3   We have seen the Goings . . . Sanctuary here.] Cf. Psalm 68:24.

577.4–6   Mercy & Truth . . . from H.] Cf. Psalm 85:10–11.

577.6–14   Gods work is . . . his name.] Cf. Psalm 111:3–9.

579.12–13   not to us . . . be the Glo.] Cf. Psalm 115:1.

580.37–38   this my son . . . is found.] Cf. Luke 15:24.

580.39–40   I & the Chil. which thou hast Graciously Given.] Cf. Isaiah 8:18.

581.17–18   a new Song put into their mouths.] Cf. Psalm 40:3.

582.13   blessed be the name of the L.] Cf. Job 1:21.

582.18   aliens from the Common———] Cf. Ephesians 2:12.

583.3–4   the calves of their Lips.—] Cf. Hosea 14:2.

583.14–16   Tho you have . . . yellow Gold.—] Cf. Psalm 68:13.

583.17–19   beggars on the dung hill . . . Glory.] Cf. 1 Samuel 2:8.

583.27–28   If it had not been . . . up quick.] Cf. Psalm 124:2–3.

583.30–32   You have cried . . . your Prayer.] Cf. Psalm 66:17, 19.

583.36–38   G. hath brought you . . . your G.] Cf. Psalm 40:2–3.

594.22–23   To whom much is Given.] Cf. Luke 12:48.

594.35–36   make them an hissing & Perpetual Reproach.] Cf. Jeremiah 29:18.

597.17–18   the death of Mr. Hawley] See note 79.4.

599.13   Arminianism] See note 5.17–18.

602.17–19   I have heard such . . . disparagement.] Possibly an allusion to an incident that took place some months before this sermon was preached, when Northampton farmer Bernard Bartlett was publicly whipped for slandering Edwards, whom he had called "as Great an Instrument as the Devil Had on this Side [of] Hell to bring Souls to Hell."

602.34–35   The Birds of the air . . . Matter.] Cf. Ecclesiastes 10:20.

603.22–23 One of the ministers of London] See note 10.4–5.

605.38–40 as the dog . . . filthy mire.] Cf. 2 Peter 2:22.

606.8 hold fast that which you have Received] Cf. Revelation 2:25.

606.23–24 Love the Lord with all your Hearts.] Cf. Matthew 22:37.

607.10 I have already . . . observed] This sermon is a continuation of an earlier one on the same text, preached in March 1740, with the doctrine, "One main thing that Christ aimed at in what he did and suffered in the work of redemption, was to save men from sin."

612.14–15 baptized with the H. Gho. & with fire.—] Cf. Matthew 3:11.

612.29 the Soul to pant after G.] Cf. Psalm 42:1.

613.11–13 he that Loves F . . . takes up—] Cf. Matthew 10:37–38.

613.26 faith but as a Grain of mustard seed] Cf. Matthew 13:31.

614.40 the author & . . . finisher of our faith.] Cf. Hebrews 12:2.

615.6–7 Conflict with principalities . . . high places] Cf. Ephesians 6:12.

615.7–8 take heaven by violence] Cf. Matthew 11:12.

616.1–2 the apple of Your Eye] Cf. Proverbs 7:2.

616.27–28 should Love him above F or mother—] Cf. Matthew 10:37.

616.28 yea should hate—] Cf. Luke 14:26.

616.28 should sell—] Cf. Matthew 19:21.

618.3 a Certain author says is Like hell fire] Possibly a reference to John Milton, *Paradise Lost* I.61–64: "A Dungeon horrible, on all sides round / As one great Furnace flam'd, yet from those flames / No light, but rather darkness visible / Serv'd only to discover sights of woe."

618.18–19 Philactering] Philacteries, pairs of small black leather boxes containing scrolls inscribed with verses from the Torah, worn on the head and arm. Cf. Deuteronomy 6:8.

618.19 tithing mint anise & Cummin] Cf. Matthew 23:23.

620.40–621.1 fire in the altar . . . never Goes out] Cf. Leviticus 6:12–13.

621.14–15 him that is born of G. that his seed abideth in him] Cf. 1 John 3:9.

622.1–2 what they shall eat———] Cf. Matthew 6:25.

622.31–32 love him with all our . . . strength] Cf. Mark 12:30.

626.33–35 light Chaff . . . devouring Flames.] Cf. Job 21:18 and Isaiah 5:24.

628.30–31 *Hitherto shalt thou come, and no further*;] Job 38:11.

630.31–32   as a Thief] Cf. 2 Peter 3:10.

630.35–36   when I was saying Peace . . . upon me.'] Cf. 1 Thessalonians 5:3.

631.2   Christ . . . Yea and Amen.] Cf. 2 Corinthians 1:20.

632.38   like the Chaff of the Summer threshing Floor.] Cf. Daniel 2:35.

633.40   while they were saying, *Peace and Safety*] Cf. 1 Thessalonians 5:3.

635.12–13   All the Kings . . . Grashoppers] Cf. Numbers 13:33.

637.17–23   *Nebuchadnezzar* . . . raise it:] Cf. Daniel 3.

638.35–36   *who knows the Power of God's Anger*?] Cf. Psalm 90:11.

639.39   pressing into the Kingdom of God] Cf. Luke 16:16.

641.12–14   that great out-pouring . . . blinded.] Cf. Romans 11:25.

641.19–21   the Ax is . . . Fire.] Cf. Matthew 3:10.

641.23   fly from the Wrath to come.] Cf. Luke 3:7.

641.25–27   *Haste and escape* . . . *consumed*.] Cf. Genesis 19:17, 22.

643.38   Let us alone . . . Let us————] Cf. Exodus 14:12.

645.8–9   the Lord mighty in Battle] Psalm 24:8.

645.9   Capt of the Salvation of his People.] Cf. Hebrews 2:10.

648.5   He has sworn that Every Knee] Cf. Isaiah 45:23.

648.11   Give him the Heathen for his Inherit.————] Cf. Psalm 2:8.

648.13   Kiss the Son] Cf. Psalm 2:12.

648.27–28   Great Great Gathering . . . Jerusalem————] Cf. Mark 13:27.

648.29   destruction of antiX————] Cf. 2 Thessalonians 2:8.

650.11   He that is not with me————] Matthew 12:30.

651.6–7   the Instance . . . Canaan.] Cf. Numbers 32.

651.25–27   the Elder brother . . . Prodigal Son.] Cf. Luke 15:25–32.

652.35–36   the stars in their Courses.] Judges 5:20.

653.13–14   so much Prudence as Gamaliel—] Cf. Acts 5:34.

653.31   cup over flows.] Cf. Psalm 23:5.

653.33   Michal] Cf. 2 Samuel 6:16–23.

654.15   Joy in Heaven over one sinner—] Cf. Luke 15:7.

654.28   The Jews in X . . . works of G.] Cf. John 3:2.

LETTERS

656.26–27   Contention and a party Spirit] See note 17.30.

657.4   Late marvelous preservation] For Edwards's account of the collapse of the Northampton church gallery, see pp. 7–8 in this volume.

657.32   throat distemper] Diphtheria.

658.5   our capital town] Northampton was the shire town, or county seat, of Hampshire County, which then comprised all of western Massachusetts.

658.6–7   *wait upon God in our Straits and difficulties*] Cf. Hosea 12:6. Edwards refers to Colman's sermon *The Great Duty of Waiting on God in Our Straits & Difficulties* (Boston: J. Draper, 1737).

658.11   extract . . . Uncle *Williams's* sermons] See the Note on the Texts in this volume for Colman's role in the publication of Edwards's *Faithful Narrative*.

658.19   Dr. *Watts*, & Dr. *Guise*] See note 10.4–5.

659.27   weapons of your warfare mighty.] Cf. 2 Corinthians 10:4.

659.29–30   smoking flax to be quenched] Cf. Isaiah 42:3.

659.39   may the Gates of Hell never be able to prevail against you!] Cf. Matthew 16:18.

659.40   more Labourers into his Harvest] Cf. Matthew 9:38.

660.5   Mr. Seward] Wealthy Methodist William Seward (1702–1740) had been Whitefield's associate since early 1739, functioning as both underwriter and advance man, traveling ahead of Whitefield's tours in England and the American colonies to arrange for the evangelist's itinerary and publicize his preaching in local newspapers. He did not make it to Northampton, however, having died on October 22, 1740, from injuries suffered when he was attacked while preaching before an anti-Methodist crowd on a mission to Wales.

660.33   *Deborah Hatheway*] In October 1740 Edwards had traveled with George Whitefield from Northampton to Suffield, a border town claimed by both Massachusetts and Connecticut, where Whitefield preached to a large crowd at the invitation of Suffield's minister Ebenezer Devotion, an ardent promoter of the revivals. Edwards may have met eighteen-year-old Suffield resident Deborah Hatheway then or later, in the spring of 1741, when he made a return visit to the village to fill the pulpit after Devotion's death in April. Edwards's preaching prompted a surge in converts to the Suffield church, and Hatheway, temporarily bereft of a minister of her own, appealed to Edwards for spiritual direction. Often republished in the nineteenth century as *Advice to Young Converts*, this letter became Edwards's second most printed work, after *Sinners in the Hands of an Angry God*.

661.13   persons under Convictions] See note 33.30.

661.20–21   pierced . . . with many Sorrows] Cf. 1 Timothy 6:10.

661.22–23   the Shining light . . . perfect day.] Proverbs 4:18.

661.30–31   love of Christ Shed abroad in your heart] Cf. Romans 5:5.

661.35–36   a bringing out . . . marvelous light] Cf. 1 Peter 2:9.

661.38   a natural person] That is, an unconverted sinner. In *Advice to Young Converts* this phrase is commonly replaced with "an impenitent man."

662.5   improvement] See note 136.7–8.

662.14   least of all Saints] Cf. Ephesians 3:8.

662.15   chief of Sinners.] Cf. 1 Timothy 1:15.

663.3   yt] That.

664.35   Child of the light] Cf. Ephesians 5:8.

664.39   meek & lowly of heart] Cf. Matthew 11:29.

665.9–11   hideing . . . Rightousness] Cf. Ezekiel 16:8, Matthew 28:3.

665.24   *Thomas Prince*] See note 13.28–31.

665.30–31   the great Work . . . *nine Years ago*] The "Little Awakening" of 1735 that Edwards describes in the *Faithful Narrative*.

666.14   religious Affections] Edwards delivered in 1742 and 1743 a cycle of sermons that became the basis of one of his most important works, *A Treatise Concerning Religious Affections* (1746).

666.19–20   Mr. WHITEFIELD came to this Town] See Chronology for 1740.

666.35–36   our great Profession] That is, the Northampton church's avowal of the Spirit as experienced in the revivals, especially in the "Little Awakening" of 1735, which Edwards's *Faithful Narrative* had made famous on both sides of the Atlantic, and to which Whitefield many times referred during his visit.

667.3–4   *Professors* . . . State of Grace] Edwards distinguishes the converted, those who had professed to an experience of "saving" faith, from those church members who possessed only what was traditionally called a "general" or "historical" faith in the tenets of Christianity. See note 28.5.

670.14   led into the Wilderness] Cf. Matthew 4:1.

670.21   Heaven suffer'd Violence] Cf. Matthew 11:12.

671.8   Mr. BUEL] A recent graduate of Yale College, Samuel Buell (1716–1798) had intended to study with Edwards at Northampton but instead became a licensed itinerant. He filled the Northampton pulpit while Edwards undertook a two-week preaching tour throughout the Connecticut River Valley (see Chronology for 1741). In 1746 Buell was ordained as minister in East Hampton, Connecticut, where he remained for the rest of his life.

672.24   March 16. 1741, 2.] March 16, 1742, in the modern Gregorian cal-endar.

675.11   the Duties of the *Closet*] That is, private prayer.

675.40–676.1   run with Perseverance . . . before us] Cf. Hebrews 12:1.

676.1–2   work out . . . Trembling.] Cf. Philippians 2:12.

676.15–16   he who searches our Hearts] Cf. Romans 8:27.

676.16   ponders the Path of our Feet] Cf. Proverbs 4:26.

676.29   Saints] See note 22.17.

678.19   wofully deceived themselves] See note 135.8.

678.29   Division of the Town into two Parties] See note 17.30.

PERSONAL NARRATIVE

681.10   my Father's Congregation.] See note 25.27.

681.31   returned like a Dog to his Vomit] Cf. Proverbs 26:11.

682.20   succeeded.] See note 39.1.

683.7   shewing Mercy on whom he will shew Mercy] Cf. Exodus 33:19.

683.18   my first Conviction] See note 33.30.

684.10   the whole Book of Canticles] See note 107.17–18.

686.9   I went to preach at *New-York*] See Chronology for 1722.

690.13   North Village] The northeast parish of New Haven, today North Haven, Connecticut.

690.22–24   *My Soul waiteth . . . Morning.*] Psalm 130:6.

691.15   green Pastures.] Cf. Psalm 23:2.

691.25   to have Him for my Head] Cf. 1 Corinthians 11:3.

691.25   a Member of his Body] Cf. Romans 12:5.

692.28   lotted] To lot upon, to count or reckon upon; rest one's hopes on; depend or rely on; look for, hope for, expect.

692.34–35   the chief of ten Thousands.] Cf. Song of Solomon 5:10.

692.38   Groanings, that cannot be uttered] Cf. Romans 8:26.

696.10–12   "How happy . . . the happy ones!"] Cf. Psalm 106:3.

Scriptural Index

(For a General Index see page 785.)

The Old Testament

General Index

(For a Scriptural Index see Page 769.)

Aaron, 153, 304, 371
Abednego, 637
Abiathar, 252
Abinadab, 310
Abraham, 128, 243–44, 408–10, 416–17, 441–42, 446, 448–49, 473, 484, 496–97, 505, 513, 519
Achaia, 113–14
Achitophel, 162
Actions versus words, 112, 122
Adam, 65, 231, 244, 419, 437, 462, 464–66, 472–75, 494, 500, 522
Adultery, 444, 447, 450
Affections, 47, 58, 70, 102, 124, 129, 131, 188, 220, 243, 280, 325, 344, 369, 371–72, 378; and convictions, 668–69, 681; and error, 335, and love, 350–53; of the mind, 109, 111–12, 176, 263–65, 667; and ministers, 263–66, 278, 391; natural, 319, 341–43, 347–49; religious, 35, 113, 127, 172–75, 192, 199, 202, 207–8, 210–11, 216–19, 279, 283, 318, 342, 354–56, 365, 633, 656, 666, 669, 676–78, 681–83; of the soul, 172–73, 356; of women, 351; and zeal, 199, 219, 347, 350–51
Agrippa, 504
Alexander the Great, 391
Allyn, Alexander, 185
Amalek/Amalekites, 238–39, 241, 651
Amasai, 246
America, 229, 231, 234, 402
American colonies, 3, 9, 221, 223, 234
Aminadab, 252
Ammonites, 239, 650
Anabaptists, 120
Angels, 52, 101, 125, 134, 159, 172, 174, 178, 183, 189, 222–23, 233, 236, 240, 242, 246, 251, 260, 284, 296, 300, 315, 349, 386, 390, 409–10, 492, 531, 556, 568, 575, 638, 644
Antichrist, 10, 232, 238, 289
Antinomianism, 5
Antioch, 109, 116, 589

Apollos, 194
Apostasy, 4, 10, 93, 119, 149, 219, 232, 289
Apostles, 4, 10, 89, 96, 99–100, 103, 109, 113, 115, 117–20, 127–28, 133–34, 146, 154–55, 175, 183, 194–95, 219, 243, 252, 292, 305, 315, 323, 330–31, 340, 370, 385–86, 393, 396, 406, 411, 430, 522, 552, 589, 641. *See also individual apostles*; Disciples; Evangelists
Armageddon, 240
Arminianism, 5, 19, 95, 385–86, 442, 456–57, 476, 599
Asaiah, 252
Ascension, 4, 89, 147, 227, 242, 273, 331
Asher, 644
Asia, 229, 274
Assyria/Assyrians, 233
Atheists, 532
Atonement, 35, 39, 42, 237, 399, 404, 462, 467–70, 475, 506, 692
Awakenings, 48, 94, 259, 547, 554, 590, 595, 600, 631, 655, 681; in Britain, 184–86; and children, 27, 29, 205, 272; degrees of, 38, 222, 270, 532, 552–53; and elderly persons, 27–28; general, 17, 24–27, 389; and John the Baptist, 530; need for encouragement, 38–39; in New England, 20–29, 187, 666–67; persons not thoroughly awakened, 38, 552–53; persons most awakened, 270; physical effects of, 31–32; process of, 30–35, 37–40, 562–63; role of ministers, 267–70, 303, 360; skepticism about, 558–59; and Whitefield, 666–67; and women, 63–78; and young persons, 20–21, 23, 27–28, 205. *See also* Revival of religion

Babylon/Babylonians, 245–46, 388, 647, 651

Death, 6, 9, 11, 19, 38, 43, 63, 68–71, 78,
    95, 196, 204–6, 210, 215–16, 272, 294,
    420, 475, 480–81, 557, 559, 629–30
Deborah, 239–41, 249, 643, 650, 652
Dedham, England, 186
Deerfield, Mass., 24, 187
Deism, 137, 385
Demoniacs, 141
Devil. *See* Satan
Devils, 509, 526, 537, 556, 560, 596,
    628, 633
Devotion, Ebenezer, 14
Dionysius the Areopagite, 92
Disciples, 10, 87, 107, 119, 146, 159,
    162, 179–80, 191, 228, 274, 283, 285,
    291–92, 300, 308, 326, 359–60, 382,
    384, 390, 405, 409, 426, 482–83,
    502, 529, 585–86, 588–90. *See also*
    Apostles; Evangelists
Doddridge, Philip, 394–95
Doubt, 23, 58–59, 79, 96, 150, 164,
    175–76
Durham, Conn., 26
Duties, 399, 402, 404–8, 410–11
Duty to God, 21, 41, 100, 366–67, 376,
    482, 540–42, 544, 681, 696

Earnestness, 13, 48, 143, 210, 214, 264,
    266–67, 275, 280, 344, 400, 534,
    537–39, 541–42, 546–47, 550, 553,
    582, 605, 621–22, 655, 657, 661, 664,
    686
East Windsor, Conn., 25
Edinburgh, Scotland, 185
Education, 158–59, 314, 338, 366–70,
    393–95, 398, 489, 521, 527
Edwards, Timothy, 25, 185–86, 681,
    684
Effects of experiences, 340, 354–56
Eglon, 224, 645
Egypt/Egyptians, 118, 144, 148, 191,
    235, 238–39, 242, 309, 387, 495, 564,
    566, 569, 589, 643, 662
Ehud, 224, 645
Elderly persons, 19, 27–28, 91, 140, 351,
    387, 402
Elect, 555–56, 607, 641, 648. *See also*
    Saints
Eliel, 252
Elisha, 148, 244, 364
End of the world, 183, 258, 406

Enfield, Mass. (now Conn.), 14, 24
England, 4, 9, 10, 12, 83, 120, 184–86,
    223, 229, 392–93, 395, 603, 658
Enos, 316
Enthusiasm, 30, 53, 63, 79, 96, 107,
    120, 129, 131, 145, 187–88, 193–94,
    196, 206, 209, 211, 217, 289, 322,
    349–50, 389, 597, 604
Epaphras, 611
Ephesus, 109, 113, 273, 589
Error, 161, 199, 223, 296, 310, 400,
    522; and affections, 335; censuring
    others, 197, 207; in conduct, 133, 152,
    198, 323, 334; heresy, 118–20; in
    judgment, 118, 190, 200; in
    ministers, 144, 288–89, 303, 307,
    332; from misunderstood principles,
    169, 172, 190, 192, 195–96, 270, 291–
    93, 306, 312–13, 323, 325, 332, 336; in
    otherwise good persons, 116–17,
    290, 320; in religious revivals, 293,
    303, 356; with respect to duty, 192;
    spirit of, 128–29; seeking/correcting,
    378, 381–82, 654; in understanding,
    169; from zeal, 207, 260, 340, 402
Esau, 333
Europe, 229
Evangelical humility, 41
Evangelicalism, 5, 42, 87, 243, 485,
    498, 510–11
Evangelical obedience, 478–79, 488,
    520
Evangelical repentance, 504–8
Evangelists, 529, 555, 589. *See also*
    Apostles; Disciples
Eve, 231, 244, 352, 522
Evil, 34, 127, 132, 143, 196, 203, 265,
    297, 299, 381, 432–33, 470, 473, 502,
    506–7, 509, 512–13, 537, 569, 619,
    633, 645
Excellency. *See* Goodness
Exhorting, 307, 366–72, 539, 620, 661,
    664
Experiences of Christians, 340–56, 359,
    378; defect of, 344–49, 351;
    degeneracy of, 349–54
Ezekiel, 152, 186
Ezra, 261

Faith, 9, 13, 96, 128, 156–57, 213, 320–
    22, 343, 383, 401, 436, 588, 615; act

This book is set in 10 point ITC Galliard Pro, a
face designed for digital composition by Matthew Carter
and based on the sixteenth-century face Granjon. The paper
is acid-free lightweight opaque and meets the requirements
for permanence of the American National Standards Institute.
The binding material is Brillianta, a woven rayon cloth made
by Van Heek–Scholco Textielfabrieken, Holland.
Composition by Dedicated Book Services. Printing and
binding by Edwards Brothers Malloy, Ann Arbor.
Designed by Bruce Campbell.

THE LIBRARY OF AMERICA SERIES

The Library of America fosters appreciation and pride in America's literary heritage by publishing, and keeping permanently in print, authoritative editions of America's best and most significant writing. An independent nonprofit organization, it was founded in 1979 with seed funding from the National Endowment for the Humanities and the Ford Foundation.

To subscribe to the series or to order individual copies, please visit www.loa.org or call (800) 964.5778.